The Reign of Mary Tudor
Politics, Government, and Religion in England
1553–1558

D. M. Loades

Reader in History, University of Durham

The Reign of Mary Tudor

Politics, government, and religion
in England, 1553–1558

St. Martin's Press
New York

ISBN 0-312-67029-X

Library of Congress Cataloging in Publication Data

Loades, David Michael
    The reign of Mary Tudor.
    Bibliography: p. 528
    Includes index.
    1. Great Britain—Politics and government—1553–1558.
2. Mary I, Queen of England, 1516–1558.
3. England—Church—16th century. I. Title.
DA347.L58 1979   942.05'4'0924   79–16479
ISBN 0-312-67029-X

Contents

Preface

This book is in the nature of an interim report. Twenty years ago, when I began my researches into the reign of Mary Tudor, the whole period from the death of Henry VIII to the accession of Elizabeth had long been neglected except by ecclesiastical historians. The situation now is substantially different. The work of W. K. Jordan, W. R. D. Jones, D. E. Hoak, M. L. Bush, B. L. Beer, and a number of other scholars has brought the reign of Edward VI under careful and fruitful scrutiny. Mary has attracted less attention, except from romantically inclined biographers, but the recent appearance of work by P. S. Donaldson, R. H. Pogson, and Jennifer Loach indicates that the quantity of specific research being undertaken into different aspects of her reign has steadily increased, and that interest in the period is growing. It therefore seems to me appropriate that I should at this stage offer an interpretation of the government and politics of England from 1553 to 1558. In deciding to do this I was faced with many difficult choices, particularly of priority. Many books need to be written about the reign of Mary. Some I have already attempted myself; others I am simply not qualified to offer, while others again are already well advanced in the hands of younger scholars. As a result of these considerations, I have therefore chosen to say little about the detailed working of the institutions of government and administration, except for the privy council which is central to my main theme. This has meant that, for example, in the virtually unexplored field of Marian finance I have concentrated upon interpreting policy and assessing its consequences rather than investigating in detail the working of the receipt of the exchequer. For this purpose I have tended to rely upon the summary statements, memoranda, and accounts produced by the finance officers rather than upon the original departmental records. It is my belief that such accounts are accurate and appropriate for my purposes, while the original records are more relevant to the historian of the institution. Similarly, although I have discussed the attitude of Mary and her council towards the

Preface

discipline and control of the counties, I have said relatively little about the detailed working of the commissions of the peace, or about the attitudes of the provincial nobility. This is not because I do not believe such matters to be important, but because a proper assessment of them requires a number of specialized regional studies which it has been beyond my resources of time and energy to undertake. I have consequently chosen to write a certain kind of book, which has no pretensions to being a complete study of the reign, but which embodies what I want to say at this stage of my researches. I think that I have reached a point in my understanding of the period where my conclusions may be useful to students and to my fellow scholars, as well as possibly filling a gap in the historiography of Tudor England.

In preparing it I have incurred many debts of gratitude. For permission to read and cite their unpublished work, mainly in the form of doctoral theses, I am indebted to G. A. Lemasters, R. H. Pogson, R. C. Braddock, E. J. Baskerville, N. L. Jones, J. P. Marmion, Jane Dawson, and Jennifer Loach. The university of Durham gave me the financial support which enabled me to visit the archive at Simancas, and Dr C. J. Thewlis guided my footsteps there. I am grateful also to my colleague, Dr Peter Brightwell, and to the members of the Durham seminar for their helpful comments and suggestions. Several generations of undergraduates have contributed fruitfully to discussions of Mary's reign, and most particularly I am indebted to Mia Rodriguez Salgado, who has subsequently also helped me most generously from the results of her own research. Dr Ian Doyle and Beth Rainey of Durham university library have tracked down elusive books and given me most valuable bibliographical advice, while Dr Christopher Kitching has smoothed my path at the Public Record Office. To all of them I owe much; but my greatest debt, for years of encouragement, for giving most generously of his time to read this work in draft, for many helpful comments, and for agreeing to differ on some points, is due to Professor Geoffrey Elton. Like many other students of Tudor England, I have gained immensely from his knowledge and friendship.

Having made my acknowledgements, I accept full responsibility for the form and content of the work, and for such errors of fact or interpretation as further researches may reveal.

D. M. Loades

Durham
January 1979

Abbreviations

The following abbreviations have been used for works or locations frequently cited. For particulars of the works concerned the Bibliography should be consulted.

Aff. Etr.	Archives du ministère des affaires étrangères, Paris
AGS	Archivo General de Simancas
Bib. Pal. Real	Biblioteca del Palacio Real, Madrid
BL	British Library
CU	Cambridge University
GLRO	Greater London Record Office
LPL	Lambeth Palace Library
PRO	Public Record Office
APC	*Acts of the Privy Council*
ARG	*Archiv für Reformationsgeschichte*
BIHR	*Bulletin of the Institute of Historical Research*
Cal. For.	*Calendar of State Papers, Foreign*
Cal. Pat.	*Calendar of the Patent Rolls*
Cal. Scot.	*Calendar of State Papers relating to Scotland*
Cal. Span.	*Calendar of State Papers, Spanish*
Cal. Ven.	*Calendar of State Papers, Venetian*
CJ	*Journals of the House of Commons*
DNB	*Dictionary of National Biography*
DUJ	*Durham University Journal*
Ecc. Mem.	J. Strype, *Ecclesiastical Memorials*
EHR	*English Historical Review*
Foxe,	J. Foxe, *Acts and Monuments*
Harbison	E. H. Harbison, *Rival Ambassadors at the Court of Queen Mary*
HJ	*Historical Journal*
HMC	*Historical Manuscripts Commission*
Hughes and Larkin	P. L. Hughes and J. F. Larkin, *Tudor Royal Proclamations*
JEH	*Journal of Ecclesiastical History*
L&P	*Letters and Papers of the Reign of Henry VIII*

Abbreviations

LJ	*Journals of the House of Lords*
Machyn	*The Diary of Henry Machyn*
Mattingly	Garrett Mattingly, *Catherine of Aragon*
OL	*Original Letters Relating to the English Reformation*
OM	D. M. Loades, *The Oxford Martyrs*
P&P	*Past and Present*
PPE	*The Privy Purse Expenses of the Princess Mary*
Quirini	A. M. Quirini, *Epistolae Reginaldi Poli*
STC	*Short Title Catalogue*
TCBS	*Transactions of the Cambridge Bibliographical Society*
Tres Cartas	*Tres Cartas de lo sucedido en el viaje de Su Alteza a Inglaterra*
TRHS	*Transactions of the Royal Historical Society*
TTC	D. M. Loades, *Two Tudor Conspiracies*
Vertot	R. A. de Vertot, *Ambassades de Messieurs de Noailles*

Illustrations and maps

Acknowledgements

Plate 14, from the Royal Collection at Windsor, is reproduced by gracious permission of Her Majesty The Queen.
Plate 22, from the Public Record Office, is reproduced by permission of the Controller of Her Majesty's Stationery Office (PRO SP69/1/34 (i)).
Thanks are also due to the following:
The Society of Antiquaries of London: Plate 1
The Marquess of Anglesey: Plate 2
The Ashmolean Museum, Oxford: Plates 11, 12, 23
Musées de Besançon: Plate 3
The British Library: 18 (C.8 b.8), 19, 20, 21 (Cotton Augustus I.ii, f. 71)
The Trustees of the British Museum: Plates 24, 25
The Archbishop of Canterbury and the Church Commissioners for England (copyright reserved to the Church Commissioners and the Courtauld Institute of Art, London): Plate 6
The National Portrait Gallery: Plates 7, 10, 13
Lord Petre: Plate 8
The Earl of Scarbrough: Plate 10
Soprintendenza per i Beni Artistici e Storici della Campania, Naples: Plate 4
The Master and Fellows of Trinity Hall, Cambridge: Plate 5

1 The Background to the Reign: Mary's Personal History

The story of Mary's life properly begins many years before her birth, with the arrival in England of the young princess who was to be her mother. Catherine had been sixteen years old when she came to London in November 1501, the fifth and youngest child of Ferdinand of Aragon and Isabella of Castile. Her brother Juan had died in 1497, her sister Isabella, the wife of Emmanuel of Portugal, in 1498, and Isabella's son Miguel in 1500. An offspring of the ancient royal house of Trastámara, Catherine stood close to the Castilian succession when her mother died in 1504, and her marriage to the young prince Arthur was a diplomatic triumph which Henry VII of England had sought long and patiently.' However, Arthur died in April 1502, and it was not established beyond doubt until long afterwards whether or not the couple had consummated their brief matrimony. Ferdinand toyed with the idea of fetching Catherine home, but almost immediately rejected it in favour of a fresh negotiation for the hand of Arthur's brother, the eleven-year-old Prince Henry. This initiative was warmly welcomed by the king of England, who had no desire to lose the fruits of his earlier diplomacy, either the alliance or Catherine's substantial dowry. A papal dispensation would be required, but there was no reason to suppose that that would present any difficulty. Maria, Ferdinand's third daughter, had maintained the Portuguese alliance in a rather similar way by taking the place of her deceased sister as Emmanuel's queen. That marriage had been successfully negotiated in 1500. However, in this case the proceedings were to be protracted. Isabella was anxious for a swift conclusion, and made no difficulties about the dowry, but agreement was not reached until June 1503. On the 25th of that month Henry and Catherine were solemnly betrothed, and a formal request for dispensation was despatched to Rome. In order, as it was thought, to put the legitimacy of the forthcoming marriage beyond dispute, the parties to the marriage treaty had agreed to seek a full dispensation from consanguinity.

1

It is well known in England that the Princess is still a virgin [Ferdinand wrote to his ambassador in Rome on 23 August]. But as the English are much disposed to cavil, it has seemed to be more prudent to provide for the case as though the marriage had been consummated, and the dispensation of the Pope must be in perfect keeping with the said clause in the treaty . . .²

By the time this letter was written, Alexander VI had died, leaving the matter unconcluded, and his successor, Pius III, reigned for less than two months. Julius II, who was elected in October 1503, proved to be unwilling to make a hasty decision, and it was July of the following year before he eventually informed Henry VII that the dispensation would be granted.

Even then the matter hung fire, and it seems to have been an urgent request from Isabella, in the throes of her last illness in November 1504, which finally stirred Julius into action. On the 24th of that month, two days before she died, the queen received a brief of dispensation from the pope, misleadingly predated 26 December 1503.³ In spite of being *in extremis*, it seems that the queen was not satisfied with this document, which, in accordance with the terms of the treaty, assumed the consummation of Catherine's first marriage. When the bull was finally issued in its completed form in March 1505, the word *forsan* had been inserted, probably at Isabella's insistence.⁴ If this was the case, it is not surprising that Julius protested when he discovered that, contrary to his instructions, a copy of the brief in its original form had already reached England. When the bishop of Worcester, Silvester Gigli, eventually brought the bull to Henry it, too, was predated 26 December 1503, and in spite of the *forsan*, was a dispensation from full consanguinity. Perhaps for that reason, the alteration to the wording seems to have caused no comment. However, by this time three years had passed since Arthur's death. The king of England was having second thoughts, but Ferdinand, struggling to maintain his hold over Castile, had less desire than ever to see his widowed youngest daughter complicating the situation at home. Consequently, Catherine remained in England unwed, in a sort of unhappy limbo. Fortunately she was not aware of the full extent of her insecurity. When the dispensation reached England, in accordance with the terms of the original treaty she had been contracted to Prince Henry *per verba de praesenti*. If Henry had reached the age of majority, such a contract would have formed a canonically binding marriage, but since he was only thirteen, it had no more than the status of an espousal, in other words a mere repetition of the betrothal of two years previously. Shortly after this, on 27 June

1505, the day before his fourteenth birthday, and a year and a day before the marriage was due to be solemnized by the terms of the treaty, Henry made a formal protest that the contract had been entered into during his minority and without his consent, and that he had no intention of ratifying it.[5] This protest was almost certainly made on the king's insistence, perhaps with the advice of William Warham, the archbishop of Canterbury. It was kept secret, and never used, which was perhaps just as well since it had itself no canonical validity, having been made by a minor. Nevertheless, 28 June 1506, which should have been Catherine's second wedding day, came and went. The balance of her dowry had not been paid and the marriage did not take place.

The political reasons for these delays and uncertainties were numerous and weighty, and do not need to be explored here. At one stage early on, Henry VII, made a widower in 1503, considered marrying her himself. Later he planned alternative marriages for his son. His relations with Ferdinand fluctuated from month to month, and the latter, preoccupied with the problem of the Castilian succession and with wars in Italy, had neither time nor money to spare for his unfortunate daughter. After her brief excursion into the life of an English princess, Catherine had retired into the seclusion of her entirely Spanish household, ruled with a rod of iron by her *duenna*, Dona Elvira Manuel. Having renounced her dower rights by the terms of the second marriage treaty, she was in the invidious position of having to live on the bounty of Henry VII, and in such lodgings as he provided, whether at court or elsewhere. Her household, which initially numbered about fifty, grew restive and quarrelsome under the strain of continued poverty and the ill-concealed contempt of the English courtiers. Henry was not consistently forgetful, but his unpredictability only made the situation worse. From time to time he paid sums of money to her hard-pressed treasurer, Juan de Cuero, but never at regular intervals. Under this pressure several of her servants intrigued feverishly to get back to Spain. The men wanted proper rewards for their services and the women better prospects of acceptable marriages. To Catherine, however, her sufferings in England were all in the cause of duty, and she must remain at her post until her marriage to Prince Henry was an accomplished fact. It never seems to have occurred to her to blame either her father or the king of England for their neglect. In 1505 she quarrelled bitterly with Dona Elvira, and despatched her to her sister's service in Flanders.[6] By that time several other members of her threadbare retinue had made good their escape, and to those who remained Catherine became increasingly grateful and affectionate. In her unhappiness, and without a shred of justification, she blamed her predicament upon the unfortunate Spanish ambassador in England, Rodrigo González de Puebla. De Puebla was almost as poverty-stricken as Catherine herself, and had little influence either in England or in Spain, but because of his official position, and perhaps because of his humble origins, Catherine vented her wrath upon him, accusing him of misleading her father with lying despatches. Despite these unjust outbursts, isolation and poverty matured the young princess, and added political sense to her natural obstinacy. Also, in 1507 she found a welcome ally in the Spanish Franciscan Fray Diego Fernández, who became her confessor. Fray Diego encouraged her to stand firm, and countermined the efforts of others of her suite, such as Francesca de Carceres, who were determined to force her into retreat. In February 1508, in response to Catherine's repeated demands, De Puebla was recalled by Ferdinand, and replaced by Don Gutierre Gómez de Fuensalida. At first Fuensalida demanded the observance of the marriage treaty, but once again negotiations stuck over the payment of the dowry, and he moved swiftly through indignation at the princess's plight to intrigue with disaffected members of her household.[7]

When Catherine discovered the truth, she denounced her father's ambassador as a traitor in unmeasured terms, but Fuensalida had become genuinely convinced of the hopelessness of the situation, and was anxious for her personal safety. By the end of 1508 Henry VII was constantly ill, and his suspicion and dislike of Ferdinand increased week by week. Catherine put her trust in the young prince of Wales, not through any real knowledge of him, but simply because she must do so if she was to hope at all. As it became clear that the king was dying, Fuensalida assessed the situation gloomily. There was a pro-French party at court which wanted young Henry to marry Marguerite d'Alençon; there was also a pro-Habsburg party which favoured Catherine's child niece, Eleanor; but of Catherine herself there was no mention.[8] The best that could be hoped for was that the new king would allow his former betrothed, now a frustrated twenty-two-year-old, to make a dignified withdrawal. That the secluded prince would show any will of his own in the matter was not to be expected. In the event the stubborn princess was triumphantly vindicated. Henry VIII was determined to marry her, and the difficulties which had caused months of weary and inconclusive wrangling melted away overnight. Although he represented this decision as the result of his father's dying wish, the new king was probably indulging in a pious platitude, and Fuensalida, when he had recovered from his astonishment, was fully convinced that it was Henry's own. The old scruple of con-

4

sanguinity was not forgotten by the cautious councillors who continued to serve, but it was swept aside. On 11 June, six weeks after his accession, Henry and Catherine were married in the Franciscan church at Greenwich, and the new queen's faith in the goodness of God and the soundness of her own judgement were unshakeably confirmed.

The early days of their life together were calm and joyful, and it seems to have taken Henry some time to realize that he had married a resident ambassador. Catherine's loyalty to her father was unshaken by years of cynical indifference, and she never ceased to regard herself as a pledge of friendship and alliance between England and Spain. 'Among the many reasons which move me to love the king my Lord', she wrote to Ferdinand, 'the strongest is his filial love and obedience to Your Highness . . .'[9] Even allowing for the courtly exaggeration, this was hardly a sentiment which would have appealed to Henry. From the beginning Catherine was a queen to be reckoned with. Her small stature and demure good looks made her an excellent visual foil for her large and boisterous husband, but she was six years his senior, equally intelligent, equally well educated, and toughened by adversity and enforced self-reliance. She shared Henry's coronation on 23 June, and her influence over the court, although unobtrusive, was very strong. She was also suspected of exercising a powerful influence on England's foreign policy. This is impossible to prove, but Henry's determination to reopen the French war certainly made him amenable to Ferdinand's purposes. The king's bellicosity and search for glory distressed his older and more cautious councillors, but it provided a very necessary outlet for the frustrated energies of the English aristocracy, who had not yet ceased to regard themselves primarily as military leaders. Intentionally or unintentionally, Henry probably saved himself from a very difficult domestic situation by reviving his claim to the crown of France. Nevertheless, the war was vastly expensive and, for its declared purposes, an almost total failure. Moreover, it led to a total breakdown of relations with the king of Spain. Three times the unscrupulous Ferdinand betrayed his ally for his own advantage, and the third time, in 1514, Henry was so enraged that he contemplated allying himself with the French and putting forward Catherine's claim to the kingdom of Castile.[10] Such a proposal was quite unrealistic, but peace between England and France came quickly, and was followed by rumours that Henry would put away his Spanish wife and marry a French princess. There was no truth in these reports, but Catherine's hold over her husband was badly shaken. Ferdinand's duplicity was one reason for this; another was the rise of Thomas Wolsey. Wolsey had risen rapidly in the king's confidence after 1512, and he was probably the main architect of the peace of 1514 – a policy which at the same time strengthened his position at the *curia* by gratifying the pope. As a politician Catherine was no match for Wolsey, nor could her pious serenity disguise the fact that she had so far failed in her primary duty as queen.

Her first child, a daughter, was born dead early in 1510; a misfortune which soured her pleasure in the success of the Anglo-Spanish negotiations then being concluded. With exemplary promptness she conceived again, and on 1 January 1511 a prince was born, and christened Henry. This time the child lived for seven weeks: long enough for widespread rejoicings and the building of many hopes. Henry and Catherine shared their grief, and the queen multiplied her religious exercises. There was no hint of estrangement or recrimination. While the king was absent in France in 1513, fighting the futile campaign which culminated in the battle of the Spurs, Catherine governed England with calm efficiency, and supervised the defence of the realm against the Scots. Part, at least, of the credit for the crushing victory of Flodden should be given to her management of affairs. However, such successes, and even Henry's continued and ostentatious devotion, could not compensate for the failure of her annual pregnancies to produce a live and healthy heir. By the summer of 1514 Catherine had at last become thoroughly disillusioned with her father, and accepted commitment to her husband and her husband's kingdom. Fray Diego returned to Spain, and the last of her Spanish maids, the faithful María de Saliñas, left her service to become Lady Willoughby.[11] The queen put a brave face on her reactions to the French alliance, and refused to work against it, but indeed she had no option. With Elizabeth Blount and Thomas Wolsey eroding her influence on all sides, she could not afford to offend Henry, or cause him to remember her unwitting share in his diplomatic humiliation. In December 1514 she bore another son who lived only a few days.

When, therefore, on 18 February 1516, the queen was delivered of a daughter who lived and flourished, it was a matter for much more exuberant rejoicings than would normally have attended such an event. Henry treated the baby rather like a new toy, showing her off proudly to courtiers and diplomats; but he made it plain that her main significance to him was as a token of hope, '. . . by God's grace the sons will follow'.[12] However, Catherine was now thirty-one, and had endured five confinements. Her political influence had recovered somewhat since 1514, and the death of her father in Estremadura in January 1516 probably helped that process, but the cruel fact remained that she was rapidly becoming middle-aged. She looked much more than six years older than her still-youthful husband, and was becoming increasingly preoccupied with her devotions and works of piety. Although she had become progressively more English in speech and in allegiance, and had no Spaniards in her immediate entourage, in this respect her Trastá-mara blood was very evident. Her mother, Isabella, had been described as a 'crowned nun' in the later years of her life.[13] But Isabella had borne five healthy children, and did not have to please a husband even more her junior in spirit than in years. In some ways Catherine's dedication to good works bore abundant fruit. For many years her charity endeared her to the poor, and the story of her successful intercession for the perpetrators of the Evil May Day of 1517 was enshrined in popular ballads which remained current for half a century.[14] As Garrett Mattingly observed in his study of Catherine, prolonged belief in this story was more significant than its doubtful authenticity.[15] She was also a discreet but effective patron of learning, and this, like her piety, was to make a lasting impression upon her only child. Discretion was necessary because Henry was inordinately proud of his own scholarship, and Catherine knew better than to make it appear that she valued her judgement above his. Some contemporaries who were well placed to judge believed that the queen was the better scholar of the two, and she also seems to have been more consistently sympathetic to the humanists. The choice of Thomas Linacre as Mary's first tutor was hers; she was an early patron of Richard Pace and John Leland, and an enthusiastic admirer of Erasmus. She also identified the talents of her countryman Juan Luis Vives, and commissioned him to write *De institutione Christianae feminae* before he came to England in 1523 to take up a position at Wolsey's new foundation in Oxford. Vives's notions of upbringing were austere; a heavy programme of humanist Latin, Erasmus's *Paraphrases*, and the fathers of the church. '. . . Let not her example be wanton verses nor void nor trifling songs', he wrote, 'but some sad sentences, prudent and chaste, taken out of holy scripture or the sayings of philosophers'.[16] He admitted that the education of women was often held in suspicion, as providing 'a nourishment for the maliciousness of their nature', and was consequently insistent upon the strictest discipline. A 'daughter should be handled without any cherishing', he declared, 'for cherishing marreth sons, but it utterly destroyeth daughters'.

De institutione was written for Mary, but it was never rigorously applied to her. Except perhaps in music she was not a precocious child. By comparison with Henry's younger children she seems to have been placid and rather slow, never developing Elizabeth's

7

linguistic skills, or Edward's enthusiasm for theology. Indeed, her accomplishments never matched those of her parents; apart from Latin, the only language she mastered was French. Greek and Italian were attempted without much success, and surprisingly enough, she never learned to speak or write Spanish.[17] Catherine had not the slightest intention of bringing up her daughter to be anything other than an English princess, and Henry would certainly not have permitted it. It is possible that, in accordance with Vives's recommendation, Mary may have been educated in the company of other children of the court, but there were to be no younger brothers or sisters to share her classroom. Another child was still-born on 10 November 1518, and the queen did not conceive again in spite of years of prayer and pilgrimages. To make matters worse, in 1519 Elizabeth Blount bore Henry a healthy son, whom he promptly acknowledged by naming him Henry Fitzroy. Catherine does not seem to have become miserable or bitter in the face of these misfortunes, any more than she had done during her previous trials, but her mood of pious resignation deepened, and this had its effect upon her daughter. All the more so since the infant Mary spent far more time in her parents' company than was normal with royal children of that period. Unsatisfactory as it was in many ways, she was the heir of England, and likely to remain so. Her father continued to show her off on state occasions, and periodically shared in her musical instruction, but her mother set about the serious business of training her to be a ruling queen, such as her grandmother had been. We do not know how far Vives's suggestions were followed in the details of her reading, but Plutarch, Livy, Seneca, and Plato represented a typical programme for a renaissance prince, and Vives was at great pains to refute the common belief that women were by nature intellectually inferior to men, and unable to sustain the demands of a royal training.[18] For the first nine years of her life Mary lived under a strict but affectionate regime designed to make her worthy of her calling, but if she showed any notable aptitude for such exalted studies, there is no record of the fact. The main legacies of her early childhood in later years were a deep attachment to her mother, and a piety as conventional as it was profound.

During these years she also played her inevitable role in her father's diplomacy. In October 1518 Henry, still anxious for a *rapprochement* with France, swore to a treaty of marriage between Mary and the dauphin, a boy even younger than herself. Such solemn obligations were always at the mercy of circumstances, and Henry's pro-French policies did not survive the Field of Cloth of Gold. By 1522 the six-year-old princess was betrothed to her cousin

Charles, the Holy Roman Emperor, sixteen years her senior. This was more a pledge of alliance than a serious intention of matrimony, because although the age discrepancy was not a great obstacle in itself, it was unrealistic to expect the head of so important a dynasty to postpone the vital business of getting himself an heir for over eight years. In 1525 Charles determined upon a more mature bride, and married Isabella of Portugal. His relations with England had by this time noticeably cooled, and Henry was angered by the jilting of his daughter, so although Catherine continued to do her best for Anglo-Spanish amity, the king and Wolsey were swinging back towards France. The queen's political influence, still of some significance as late as 1522, had ebbed almost to nothing by this time. '. . . Her will is good', wrote Charles's ambassador, Mendoza, '[but] her means are small'.[19] Not only was she no longer an effective help to her nephew, she was now becoming an embarrassment to her husband's diplomacy. While there was still a prospect that she might bear a healthy son, her constant commitment to the Imperial alliance could be accommodated, but by 1525 she was forty, and would clearly have no more children. In 1526 fresh negotiations were opened with France, this time for a marriage between Mary and Francis I himself, a widower older than her own father. How serious these discussions were is debatable. In the summer of 1527 the eleven-year-old princess was discreetly paraded for inspection during a court masque, and the French envoys decided that so undersized a child would not be ready for the marriage bed in less than three years.[20] Moreover, it was being rumoured that there was some doubt of her legitimacy. Questions were again being asked about the ancient scruple of consanguinity in her parents' marriage eighteen years before.

Mary herself was scarcely conscious of these momentous-seeming deliberations about her future. She never saw the dauphin, or Francis, or James V of Scotland whose name was also linked with hers at one point. She did meet Charles, a grave and courteous young man who visited England in the summer of 1522, but was scarcely old enough to appreciate his qualities as a prospective bridegroom. The really important change which took place in her life came in 1525 when, with her own household and council, she took up residence at Ludlow as princess of Wales. Henry's motives in ordering this change were mixed. Increasing anxiety about the succession had caused him to bring his six-year-old son out of the relative obscurity of his early years. The boy was brought to court, knighted, and showered with titles and nominal offices. His major title, duke of Richmond, made it clear that the king was seriously considering the possibility of making him his heir.[21] Catherine, stung by the insult to herself and the threat to her daughter, had protested vigorously, and Henry decided to separate them. There was, as yet, no question of repudiating his queen or reducing Mary's status. An independent household and a separate residence at a relatively early age were normal provisions for the heir to a throne. The countess of Salisbury as lady governess presided over a worthy establishment, although it could be argued that the princess's schoolmaster, John Fetherstone, was hardly the equal of Linacre or Vives. Her council was headed by John Voysey, the bishop of Exeter, and there could be no complaint that either her dignity or her welfare was neglected. Nevertheless, as Catherine wrote assiduously and affectionately to her daughter, anxiety about the king's intentions was never far from her mind. If Henry had thought to reduce the intimacy of their relationship, he certainly failed. From time to time Mary naturally rejoined the court, particularly at major festivals. This could not be prevented without an open rupture, and her father was fond of her. In any case it was probably too late to cool her devotion to her mother by such means. Physical separation from her parents seems to have had little effect, either in making Mary a more independent person, or in redressing the balance of her loyalty. What it did give her was three more years to grow up in peace and relative contentment, away from the looming crisis which was about to break over the court. She did not spend all her time at Ludlow. Her household moved constantly, not only through the marches, but also to other royal residences nearer to London. In May 1528 she was at Greenwich, laid low with a mild attack of smallpox. How soon she learned of her mother's troubles is not known, but by the summer of that year not even the most sheltered seclusion could have protected her from the truth.

The king's 'Great Matter' has been the subject of so many special studies that there is no need to retell the story here.[22] However, it is important to emphasize that Henry's scruple of conscience was perfectly genuine, and that consequently none of the more or less sordid compromises suggested to him were satisfactory. At different times the pope professed himself willing to sanction bigamy, adultery, or even an incestuous marriage between Mary and the duke of Richmond as means of resolving the sexual and political problems of the king of England.[23] The one thing he could not grant was an annulment of his marriage to Catherine on the grounds which Henry wanted. Absolutely convinced that the premature deaths of so many of their children were the direct result of God's anger, the king would brook neither opposition nor half measures in what he considered to be his manifest duty of propitiation. His subjects never understood this fixation. They accused Wolsey of overweening ambition, and of leading the king astray. They accused Anne Boleyn of witchcraft, and called her a 'goggle-eyed whore'; but they never grasped that the crisis which they so much deplored was caused almost entirely by a clash of steel-tipped consciences. Catherine had endured her husband's infidelities for years with no more than the occasional touch of injured humanity. By 1527 she was accustomed to the more general estrangement which had fallen between them, in which Henry frequently avoided her company altogether for long periods, and no longer discussed his affairs either with her or in her presence. However, it was another matter altogether when he announced to her on 22 June 1527 that they were not, and never had been, man and wife. Catherine was both distressed and alarmed, but her main reaction was one of total and implacable denial. Her marriage to Arthur had existed in name only, and in any case the pope had granted a full dispensation. Never by any word or gesture or ambiguous silence would she admit that there could be any doubt about the validity of her wedding to Henry. Not only was the queen's worldly position at stake, and the fortunes of her dearly loved daughter, but far more important her honour and the honour of the Trastámara family were besmirched. Moreover, in challenging the validity of the dispensation, Henry was questioning the integrity of the papacy, 'to the high dishonour of Almighty God'.

There is no need to trace the painful course of the annulment proceedings here. Catherine repudiated them, and appealed to Rome, sustained through this ordeal by the same faith and courage which had upheld her during the long bleak months of waiting from which Henry had originally rescued her. Despite her widespread popularity, she had few open friends in England upon whom she could rely. Even Bishop John Fisher took some little time to pluck up the necessary courage to support her.[24] In this isolation the 'Englishness' which she had assumed during the previous fifteen years began to fall away from her. This was partly artifice; she could profess not to understand unwelcome news or advice.[25] But it was also partly genuine. When the crisis first broke, she sent one of her few remaining Spanish attendants, Francisco Felípez, post haste to Valladolid to solicit the aid of her nephew, Charles. The emperor responded almost immediately, despite his other preoccupations, and espoused her cause both directly with Henry and indirectly in Rome. The contrast between this warmth and the chill which the king's displeasure spread around her in England erased the memory of her father's duplicity, and revived her Spanish loyalties and affections. As her position deteriorated and her own servants were removed, she became increasingly dependent upon such contact as she could maintain with her nephew's envoys, first Iñigo de Mendoza, and later the energetic young Savoyard Eustace Chapuys. Charles, for his part, did not willingly court conflict with England, but so gross a challenge to the honour of his family could not be ignored, and fate had decreed that he was in an invincible position to frustrate Henry's every move in the *curia*.[26]

Curiously enough, Mary's position was not at first seriously affected by her father's conscience. Logically he should have regarded her as a bastard, and relegated her to obscurity. In fact she retained both her title and her household. The latter was reduced somewhat on grounds of economy, but the countess of Salisbury remained in charge, and it was not until 1533 that the princess's material circumstances were much altered. There seem to have been several reasons for this. One was that Henry was genuinely fond of his daughter, who had so far shown no sign of having a will of her own. Another was that even an illegitimate child could have her political uses. A third reason, and probably the most important of all, was that the king would not act without what he considered to be proper legal justification. Throughout the crisis Henry insisted that his conscientious scruples should be embodied in a formal and binding judicial decision. If it had not been for this insistence, the situation might have been resolved in a number of different ways. In the event, such a decision could only be provided by repudiating papal jurisdiction altogether, and within a few weeks of the decision of the archbishop's court, Mary was formally deprived of her title of princess of Wales. Little is known of her attitude towards the momentous events of the years 1527-33, the years during which she was growing from a child of eleven to a young woman of seventeen. She was seldom at court, and if she ever spoke frankly of her feelings, her servants were too wise or loyal to disclose the fact. Her attitude to her father may well have remained ambivalent, but it is clear that she hated Anne Boleyn and was fiercely loyal to her mother. Catherine's own position remained ambiguous for about four years. Convinced as he was of the unlawfulness of their marriage, Henry had not repudiated her. She continued to fulfil her normal duties at court, and the king occasionally passed the time in her company. However, between Anne Boleyn's impatience and Henry's periodic gusts of frustrated rage, her pertinacious attention to duty became increasingly difficult and painful. She was no more willing to make a voluntary withdrawal than she had been to quit England twenty-five years before, or to indicate by any gesture that she accepted the king's interpretation of their relationship. If he believed that he could insult her out of countenance, then he had misjudged her badly. Henry's own conscientiousness made matters worse for both of them. Their case was still *sub judice*, and consequently he would not take any definitive action against her, so he resorted to a long campaign of harassment and petty persecution. Meanwhile, her plight attracted the sympathy of his subjects at all social levels, the constant surreptitious intervention of intriguing diplomats such as Chapuys, and the heavy disapproval of the emperor.[27] It also progressively alienated Mary, who became not only totally committed to her mother's cause over the main issue of the annulment, but also heavily influenced by Catherine's reversion to her Spanish and Imperial loyalties.

These formative years of Mary's life are in many ways obscure. Until 1531 she lived under much the same regiment as before, working under her schoolmaster, riding, and learning the management of a great household. She moved from place to place as taste and circumstances dictated, seeing her mother from time to time, corresponding and sending messages frequently. Her marriage continued to be discussed, but there were no real negotiations because Henry did not know whether he wanted to continue using her in his diplomatic schemes or to neutralize her by disparagement. At the time in her life when a young princess should have begun to emerge as an important person at her father's court, Mary was kept in semi-retirement while Anne Boleyn emerged to play the leading female role, to the anger and embarrassment of everyone except her own family. Then in July 1531 the situation took a sudden turn for the worse. Henry finally abandoned Catherine and ordered her to retire to the More, Wolsey's old residence.[28] Mary, who was with her when the bolt fell, was ordered to withdraw at once and to see her mother no more. Thereafter pressure upon Catherine was steadily but unavailingly increased, and she became more and more dependent upon Chapuys for comfort, counsel, and support. Mary's reaction can only be deduced. Letters and messengers continued to pass between them, and the queen's distinctive blend of unshakeable obstinacy and pious resignation was firmly imprinted upon her daughter. It must have been a time of misery and uncertainty for the fifteen-year-old girl, and its main consequence seems to have been that she was steeled to defy her father long before any actual pressure was brought to bear upon her.

The long-maturing crisis finally came to a head in the early months of 1533. At the end of January, Anne Boleyn was discovered to be pregnant, and the king secretly married her.[29] By Easter the secret was out, and in May Archbishop Cranmer's court at Dunstable declared the validity of the marriage, and the nullity of that which Henry had contracted twenty-four years previously. The king then proceeded to take those formal steps for the degradation of his former wife and his daughter from which he had hitherto refrained. Catherine was restyled the 'Princess Dowager', a title which she furiously repudiated, and driven into remoter retirement with a decimated retinue.[30] Mary's humiliation did not come at once. Indeed, in May she wrote a correct and submissive letter to her father, but it contained no hint that she accepted the propriety of his actions. It was only after the birth of Elizabeth on 7 September that her title was transferred to the new arrival, her independent household discontinued, and the number of her servants substantially reduced. Her reaction was a carbon copy of her mother's. She would receive no message that did not come over her father's sign manual or with his duly sealed commission; and she would not accept designation as 'the Lady Mary, the king's daughter'. Henry's anger was fuelled by both apprehension and self-righteousness. He knew how widely and deeply unpopular his course of action had become, and Cromwell knew, even if the king did not, how assiduously Chapuys was encouraging the malcontents. The danger of rebellion in defence of the old legitimacies in church and state was real by the end of 1533, and Mary might have provided the pretext for such a movement. Also, to argue, as Mary did, that the king could not really believe in his own conscience that she was anything other than his lawful daughter, was to strike a particularly dangerous note. Henry had gone to immense pains to convince himself of the moral rectitude of his position, and this flat implication that he must be either a fool or a knave understandably exposed Mary to his full wrath. Richard Sampson, the dean of the chapel royal who was sent unavailingly to Newhall to reason with her, ended by telling her bluntly 'that she had worthily deserved the king's high displeasure and punishment by law . . .'[31]

The effects of that displeasure were not long in coming. During November her servants were gradually removed and replaced with others who were thought to be more amenable to the king's purposes. And then on 16 December she was peremptorily ordered to attend upon the Princess Elizabeth at Hatfield. The countess of Salisbury was finally relieved of her charge and Mary was deposited, without ceremony or status, in the hostile environment of a household dominated by the ladies of the Boleyn family and run by Anne, Lady Shelton. In this miserable situation of virtual imprisonment, Mary was soon enduring what she, her mother, and their sympathizers always regarded as a martyrdom. She would not acknowledge her rival's title, nor surrender her own, and until she did there was no prospect of relief. Marriage was now out of the question. Even a disparaging match, or one with some remote foreign prince, would have given too dangerous a lever to the king's enemies. Apart from the warmth of a good conscience, Mary's only comfort came from Chapuys, and in occasional smuggled messages from her mother – undergoing a martyrdom of her own in various draughty manor houses around the East Midlands. Although delighted by her daughter's constancy, Catherine was urgent with good advice: to depend wholly upon God, who was proving her in this time of trial; to obey the king in everything not repugnant to her conscience; and '. . . to keep your heart with a chaste mind, and your body from all ill and wanton company . . .'[32] She need not have worried. Adversity intensified Mary's piety, and since she never ceased to regard herself as a royal princess, she never wavered in the conviction that the consolations of common mortals were not for her. Nor was any attempt made to take advantage of her helplessness and isolation. Both Catherine and Mary feared assassination and conspiracies against their honour. Chapuys, who listened far too seriously to casual gossip, believed that such intentions existed.[33] However, they misjudged the king. Angry as he was, and precarious as his position might be, he was no less motivated by high principles than his victims. He might in time have sent his defiant daughter to the block, but he would not resort to sordid expedients.

Henry was caught in a dilemma of his own making. As 1534 advanced, and parliament legislated a new order of succession, Mary's defiance became technically criminal. She refused the oath required by 25 Henry VIII, c. 22, and continued to assert her own title, both actions constituting misprision of treason under the act. But although the king might make dark threats, which brought her to the brink of hysteria, and do his best to cut off her communication with her mother and Chapuys, he could not bring himself to more drastic action. When she fell ill in the late summer, he not only sent his own physician, William Buttes, to attend on her, but even allowed her to see Catherine's physician, under strict surveillance. Henry's affection for his elder daughter was by no means dead, and when, for a time in the autumn, his relations with Queen Anne seem to have cooled, pressure on Mary was significantly relaxed. Just after the new year she fell ill again, and Chapuys, in response to urgent pleas from Catherine, tried to persuade the king to send her to her mother. Henry refused, suspecting, rightly, that there were plans afoot to smuggle her out of the country. However, on this occasion Thomas Cromwell offered his services and managed to bring about a compromise whereby Mary was to be lodged close enough for Catherine's physician to attend her, without actually bringing them under the same roof. The secretary regarded

Mary with a cool political eye, bearing her no malice, and perhaps judging that her intransigence might have to be neutralized or accommodated if it could not be overcome. Henry may have bullied his daughter into a state of physical collapse, but the fact remained that he did not know what to do with her. Catherine's conscientious resistance was a nuisance because of her popularity and her relationship with the emperor. But Catherine was approaching fifty, and belonged to the past. Mary was eighteen and might constitute a serious threat, both to her father and to the secretary's reforming schemes, if some solution could not be found. 1535 was a dangerous year, which heard much talk of conspiracy and rebellion, as conservatives of all persuasions searched around for some means to check the king's inexorable progress into schism and 'innovation'.[34] Chapuys moved busily here and there among the disaffected, encouraging and inciting the bellicose, persuading the scrupulous, and comforting those whose resistance had already got them into trouble. The one thing he could not do, and which might have made all the difference, was to pledge his master's intervention in support of a rebellion. Charles had other things on his mind, and although he was quite prepared to allow his ambassador to act as an active conspirator, he could not afford to risk open war with the king of England. Chapuys, moving almost exclusively amongst the king's opponents, did not choose to recognize the fact that Henry also had much support in England. The emperor was not so easily deceived.

Inevitably Mary was a central factor in this ominous situation. Charles tried in vain to persuade first the French and then the Scots to bid for her hand in marriage. Neither would do so, although both professed to recognize her as the heir of England. English conservatives forlornly hoped to marry her to a scion of the White Rose, either Reginald Pole (who was an émigré in Italy) or his nephew Henry (who was a child).[35] The king even had some tentative plans himself for an alliance with the Lutheran Danes and Lubeckers, which would have involved a marriage with Duke John of Holstein. Meanwhile, Mary had returned to Elizabeth's household, where she continued to live in semi-confinement, sick, nervous, and occasionally hysterical. In April 1535 she begged Chapuys to aid her in an elaborate and rather wild plan of escape, and then fell ill at the critical moment, thus relieving him of the invidious responsibility. The possibility of spiriting Mary out of England had been talked about with too little discretion since 1533, and, like the constant rumours of incipient rebellion, it is very difficult to know how seriously to take such gossip. Perhaps like the emotional and not very intelligent adolescent that she was, Mary was taking refuge in fantasy. This certainly seems to have been the case when French envoys came in the autumn of 1535 to pay their respects to the infant Elizabeth. The king's elder daughter was firmly convinced that they had come to complete arrangements for her own marriage to the dauphin, and had to be forcibly restrained from demanding access to them.[36] Living in daily fear of poison, which no one had the slightest intention of giving her, by October 1535 Mary had followed her mother into explicit approval of rebellion and Imperial invasion. Such a course, she wrote to Chapuys, would be no less holy than a crusade against the infidel.[37] Neither rebellion nor invasion came, and Mary's lapse into treason presumably remained the ambassador's secret. Nor was any further attempt made to extort from her the oath to the new succession. By the end of the year there was no sign of a break in the deadlock, and even Cromwell appears to have been baffled as to what to do next.

However, 1536 was only a week old when the situation was changed by the death of Catherine in the gloomy isolation of Kimbolton. Henry, Charles V, and Anne Boleyn were equally pleased in different ways; Mary, who had been prevented from visiting her mother during her last illness, was deeply distressed. Increasingly she began to feed her imagination with fantasies of escape, which Chapuys encouraged only half-heartedly, fearing the emperor's disapproval. At one point he suggested to Mary that she should profess an intention to take the veil as soon as she reached full age, perhaps as a device to free her from immediate political pressure.[38] In the event, however, it was not Mary but Anne who first felt the full effects of Catherine's death. The circumstances of her fall are well known, and need not concern us here. As soon as the euphoria of being freed from the old queen's brooding presence had worn off, she had realized that a vital safeguard of her own position had disappeared. Henry need no longer fear that in casting her off he would be resurrecting his ties with Catherine. The king had long tired of her, and she had borne him no son. On 2 May she was arrested upon a specious charge of adultery, tried, and executed on the 19th. Her numerous enemies rejoiced, and sighs of relief could be heard all over the country. There now seemed to be no reason why relations with the papacy should not resume a normal course, and the strange policies of the last three years, generally blamed upon her influence, should not be consigned to the scrapheap. Mary anticipated a speedy end to her own troubles, and wrote cheerfully to Cromwell on 26 May:

Master Secretary, I would have been a suitor to you before this time to have been a mean for me to the King's Grace, to have obtained his Grace's blessing and favour; but I perceived that nobody durst speak for me as long as that woman lived which is now gone. . . .[39]

She then went on to ask for, and obtain, leave to write to the king. On 1 June she wrote a most humble and submissive letter to her father, begging for his forgiveness and blessing, rejoicing in his new marriage (to Jane Seymour), and praying that he may be blessed with a son. Such a confident change of tone can only be accounted for by the assumption that Mary blamed her father's previous harshness towards her entirely upon the personal malice of Anne Boleyn, and had no more understanding of his policy or state of mind than the man in the street. If this was the case, she was soon to be disabused. The king did not respond to her overtures, and she wrote again on the 10th and a third time on the 14th, with mounting anxiety.[40] Cromwell clearly monitored her letters, for on the 10th she wrote to him 'as one of my chief friends', claiming that she had followed his advice, and begging him 'to find means that I be not moved to any further entry in this matter than I have done; for I assure you I have done the utmost my conscience will suffer me. . . .'[41] Such a request reveals the depth of her misunderstanding. All that Henry wanted to hear from his daughter was that she was prepared to accept the royal supremacy and her own bastardization. Without that, humble submission and pleas for forgiveness meant nothing. The secretary tried again, this time sending a draft for her to copy, which did not specifically mention these obnoxious matters, but which professed submission to the king in everything, without qualification. Mary signed it gratefully. The rapid withering of her unfounded hopes had made her ill and depressed again; 'I have very small rest, day or night', she wrote. The king was not satisfied, and Cromwell could no longer evade the issue or soften the blow. At about this time he drafted an exasperated letter to Mary, calling her 'the most obstinate woman that ever was', and declaring that his own position was threatened by the friendship which he was known to bear her.[42] This draft was intended to be the covering letter for a set of specific articles of submission, but it was probably never sent because Henry decided to send the articles to Hunsdon by the hands of a powerful commission which would brook no refusal.

The urgency of the situation from his point of view can be gauged from the examinations of Sir Anthony Browne and Sir Francis Bryan conducted, probably, on 14 June.[43] Both were gentlemen of the privy chamber, and their testimonies reveal that Anne

Boleyn's execution had caused a flurry of gossip and speculation about the succession among the king's immediate entourage. Elizabeth would now be bastardized in her turn, and the general hope seems to have been that Mary would submit and be reinstated. The 'conventicles devised for the advancement of the Lady Mary' of which these gentlemen were accused do not seem to have amounted to much more than that. However, at a time when she could so easily have become the pretext for a conservative rebellion, the smallest suspicion of conspiracy close to the king's person demanded full investigation. Anne Boleyn's fall had led to the reappearance of the opinion that, although Mary was illegitimate, she had been born *in bona fide parentum* – that is when her parents were genuinely ignorant of their sin – and so could be regarded as legitimate for the purposes of the succession.[44] Browne and Bryan both professed ignorance of this doctrine, and denied that they had discussed the matter with Dr William Knight or any other learned man. Browne was examined again on 17 June, when he repeated with much emphasis that he and his fellows had only talked of what they hoped would be the king's pleasure, without any hidden or sinister intent.[45] Perhaps he was believed, because no further action resulted. In any case, within a few days the temperature of the whole issue had been cooled by Mary's submission.

The articles which the duke of Norfolk had presented to her were as explicit and complete as Mary's worst fears could have anticipated. She was required to acknowledge her father to be 'Supreme Head of the Church of England, under Christ'; to repudiate 'the pretended authority of the bishop of Rome'; and to acknowledge that the king's marriage to her mother 'the late Princess Dowager' had been 'by God's law and man's law incestuous and unlawful'. The exact sequence of events thereafter is not clear. In the course of a long despatch written on 1 July, Chapuys claimed that Mary had refused to submit, thereby provoking a crisis which lasted more than a week. During that time the council had been in almost continuous session, Henry had tried to bully the judges into condemning her for treason, and Cromwell had been on the brink of disgrace.[46] He, Chapuys, having been appealed to by the princess as her one true friend, had urged her to submit to save her life. However, the ambassador's account presents some problems of chronology, and Mary did not date either her letter of surrender or her next letter to Cromwell. As late as 14 June she had written anxiously about the reception of her general profession of penitence, so the commissioners cannot have reached Hunsdon earlier than the 15th. By 26 June, when she wrote a dated letter to her father, she had already received his first token of forgiveness and a letter from Jane Seymour.[47] Her actual submission is subscribed 'Thursday, 11 o'clock at night', so if any credence is to be given to Chapuys's dramatic account of crisis and strident bullying, this must have been 22 June.[48] In other words, the king's forgiveness was almost instantaneous. Mary's will had been broken by a mixture of nervous illness and intense pressure, but it was not her mother's death which had weakened her resolve so much as belated awareness that her father's insistence upon conformity was a genuine expression of his royal will and not a means of gratifying 'the Concubine'.

Having virtually destroyed her usefulness to his domestic enemies, Henry's natural affection for his daughter reasserted itself, actively encouraged by his new queen, who had begun her court career in the service of Catherine. Within a few days her household had been reconstituted to the number of 42, a process in which her own wishes were consulted, and such faithful familiars as Margery Baynton and Susan Clarencius reappeared.[49] In the first week of July her persistent requests for access to the king were answered during a short visit to nearby Hackney. She was graciously received, and came away the richer by 1000 ducats and a diamond ring. The news of her reconciliation quickly spread around Europe, and if anyone was inclined to blame her for the price which she had paid, they kept discreetly silent about the matter. On a Friday which must have been 30 June, Mary wrote to Cromwell thanking him for his good offices 'which hath not only travailed, when I was almost drowned in folly to recover me before I sunk and was utterly past recovery, and so to present me to the fire of grace and mercy, but also desisteth not sithence with your good and wholesome counsels, so to arm me from any relapse . . .'[50] She professed her heart to be entirely in the king's keeping; and disclaimed any views, even about the practice of her faith, which were not acceptable to him. Chapuys told a different story. The princess, he wrote, was conscience-stricken at her own weakness and betrayal, and in constant need of his own reassurances, with which he was generous, even on the pope's behalf.[51] Mary was now twenty, and fresh speculations about her marriage followed hard upon her reconciliation. The French were reported to be anxious to secure her for the duke of Angoulême; the emperor favoured Dom Luiz, the infante of Portugal; but Chapuys believed that Henry was still unwilling to allow her to marry outside the realm for fear that she would be used against him. The ambassador was almost certainly right. Pleased and relieved as he was by his daughter's dutiful submission, Henry's affection did not find much political expression. She was now honourably lodged and served, and a welcome visitor at court, but speculation that she would again be recognized as princess of Wales was quickly dashed. Even the lesser, but significant, title of duchess of York, which some expected, did not materialize.[52] As far as the succession was concerned, both Mary and Elizabeth were now in limbo while the country awaited the outcome of the king's new marriage.

The events of the autumn of 1536 showed that Mary was not yet out of danger. Early in October, simultaneously with the outbreak of rebellion in Lincolnshire, and perhaps as a result of it, the king insisted upon her writing to the pope, the queen of Hungary (Charles's regent in the Low Countries), and to Charles himself, reaffirming the terms of her submission, and insisting that they represented the genuine dictates of her conscience.[53] After another brief and painful struggle with herself, Mary complied. Chapuys realized perfectly well that these letters were propaganda exercises designed to inhibit any possible interference by the parties addressed in England's internal affairs. None of the recipients could afford to express doubts about the genuineness of the letters, or the sentiments expressed, because of the risk of harming Mary. Nor could they, in consequence, make representations in favour of a cause which she herself had ostensibly renounced. Chapuys wrote rather forlornly to Cifuentes, Charles's ambassador in Rome, suggesting that the pope would have to feign indignation with the princess, and requesting a secret absolution to salve her conscience.[54] Cifuentes was deeply troubled by this request. No such brief, he wrote to the emperor, could be issued in Rome without the French finding out about it, and if the French got wind of such a matter, they would immediately inform Henry. When Chapuys insisted, the best that Cifuentes could suggest was to ask the pope for a *vivae vocis oraculo in genere* empowering confessors to absolve all those who had fallen 'into these new English errors'.[55] Such verbal reassurances were all that could be obtained, and presumably Mary had to make the most of the consoling thought that the circumstances of her self-abasement were well known in both Brussels and Rome. The value of circumspection was soon demonstrated. Because of her new-found tractability the dangerous storm of the Pilgrimage of Grace passed her by virtually untouched. In spite of the rebels' demand that she should be reinstated in the order of succession, a demand which was probably central to the main thrust of the movement,[56] by Christmas 1536 she was able to play a leading role in the festivities of the court, and both Jane and Henry showed her great kindness and consideration. It was a quiet end to a stormy year; a year in which Mary had finally learned to cloak her thoughts in politic and submissive words, and

B

to hold herself in readiness for whatever future opportunities might arise. She had learned much from the diplomatic Chapuys, and although her conscience still troubled her, she had lived to fight another day.

Further relief of a kind came in October 1537 with the birth of Prince Edward. Although it cost the life of her friend Jane Seymour, even Mary's warmest supporters could no longer regard her as the heir to the throne. Nor was she in any further danger of disparagement at the hands of the duke of Richmond, who had died of consumption in July 1536. Henry had not persisted with the plan to make the boy his heir, but as a male and a titular duke he had taken precedence over Mary when they were both considered to be illegitimate. For the last decade of her father's life, Mary was withdrawn a little from the political firing-line. From her subsequent words and actions it is apparent that she viewed the reforming activities of her father's ministers with deep disapproval, loathed Thomas Cranmer, and maintained her secret allegiance to the papacy. However, she was wise enough not to allow any of this to appear. As long as Henry lived the conventional piety of the mass and the confessional would not be seriously challenged, and this had great importance for her in a life which otherwise remained without clear purpose or direction. Henry continued to talk of her marriage, and a number of negotiations succeeded one another, but for the most part they were unreal diplomatic exercises. The only suitor to visit her in person was the Lutheran Philip of the Palatinate, who came to England just before Christmas 1539.[57] His intentions were serious, and the Imperialists were temporarily alarmed, but his prospects (if they ever really existed) disappeared with the end of Henry's interest in a Lutheran alliance. Consequently the normal destiny of a royal princess was denied to Mary. Instead of a period of diplomatic usefulness, followed by marriage and subsequent dedication to the dynastic duty of producing children, it was as though her childhood had been indefinitely prolonged. Her illegitimacy in English law made little difference to her attractiveness to foreign suitors, but the years passed and nothing happened, until Mary herself complained '. . . . while my father lives I shall be only the Lady Mary, the most unhappy lady in Christendom'.[58]

The political events of these years affected her tangentially, rather than directly. In 1538 the so-called 'Exeter conspiracy' resulted in a selective purge of noble conservatives, notably Lord Montague and the marquis of Exeter.[59] They considered themselves to be her friends, and her name was often on their lips, but their indiscretions harmed only themselves. We do not know how severely Mary felt their deaths. Another, rather wild, intrigue in Yorkshire in 1541 cost the life of her old friend and governess the countess of Salisbury. Margaret, who had been in prison since her attainder in 1539 on a very dubious charge of treason, was executed and died vehemently protesting her innocence. Again Mary's true feelings can only be surmised, but the event seems to have forged a bond of sympathy and distress between herself and Margaret's exiled son Reginald Pole, himself by this time a cardinal and an attainted traitor. At long last, in 1544, the development took place which had been generally expected and desired by loyal subjects and malcontents alike since 1536. Mary was reinstated in the order of succession. Henry's third succession act (35 Henry VIII, c. 1) took advantage of his intended expedition to France to lay down

> that in case it shall happen the Kinges Majestie and . . . Prince Edwarde . . . to decease without heires of either of their bodies lafullye begotten . . . That then the . . . Imperiall Crowne and all other the premisses shalbe to the Ladie Marye the Kinges Highnes daughter and to the heirs of the bodye of the same Ladie Marye lawfullie begotten . . .[60]

The king was empowered to determine by letters patent or by his last will what conditions should be attached to this right, and if such conditions should be broken, then the crown was to pass to Elizabeth, standing next in line. Neither Mary nor Elizabeth was legitimated by this statute, which was a pure exercise in legislative sovereignty. At this stage no provision was made for the succession beyond Elizabeth and her heirs, but the king was granted

> . . . full power and auctoritie to give, dispose . . . and lymitt by his gracious letters patent under his Great Seale or els by his highnes laste will made in writinge and signed withe his most gracious hande . . . the Imperiall Crowne of this Realme . . . to suche person or personnes in remaynder or revercion as shall please his highnes . . .

Two years later, on his death-bed, Henry caused this final disposition to be made, and laid down the conditions under which both Mary and Elizabeth should inherit. In the event of a failure of heirs by any of his own three children the crown was to pass to the heirs of Frances Brandon, the elder daughter of his sister Mary by Charles Brandon, duke of Suffolk. Frances was already the mother of three daughters, but should her heirs also fail, then the heirs of her younger sister Eleanor were also named.[61] The descendants of Henry's other sister Margaret by her two marriages, to James IV of Scotland and Archibald earl of Angus, were passed over in silence.[62] The condition attached to Mary's right of inheritance was specific:

> . . . after our decease [she] shall not marry nor take any person to her husband without the assent and consent of the privy councillors and others appointed by us to our dearest son Prince Edward aforesaid to be of counsel, or of the most part of them, or of the most part of such as shall then be alive, thereunto before the said marriage, had in writing sealed with their seals.[63]

In the event of her marrying without his consent, so expressed, the succession was to revert to Elizabeth as though Mary were already dead without issue. Such a condition expressed no particular distrust of Mary. The same terms were applied to Elizabeth, and would have been applied to any unmarried inheritrix in a similar position. The real problem was the extraordinary dearth of males. Apart from Prince Edward, there was no man or boy in sight with a respectable hereditary claim. It was this fact rather than any sudden access of parental affection which caused Henry to provide for the inclusion of his two illegitimate daughters in the succession, with the consequent necessity to take whatever precautions he could to prevent this circumstance being turned to the advantage of his enemies, foreign or domestic.

During the last four or five years of her father's life, Mary was free from major storms, either personal or political. She did not get on with Henry's fifth wife, the flamboyant Catherine Howard, and during her brief ascendancy from 1540 to 1542 there was bickering and petty malice.[64] However, in July 1543 the king married for the last time, and the thirty-one-year-old Catherine Parr brought a measure of peace and happiness to his oddly assorted family. Mary liked her, and in spite of the differences in their opinions, probably respected her superior brain. Catherine coped admirably with a temperamental stepdaughter only five years younger than herself, and tried to find something constructive for her to do. For this the princess's sound early education provided an opening, in spite of her lack of intellectual tastes. The two women corresponded in Latin, as a useful form of mental exercise, and with Catherine's encouragement Mary undertook, but did not complete, an English translation of Erasmus's Latin paraphrase of the gospel of St John. The queen was a considerable patron of learning, and has been presented in at least one recent study as a key figure in the English renaissance.[65] Her influence on the upbringing of Prince Edward was important, and she was known to sympathize with 'the new sort' in religion. Mary did none of these things. Her privy purse expenses show her to have been generous with alms and with small gifts, especially to the country people who brought her fruit and other tokens of their affection.[66] But of patronage of learning or the arts there is no sign, except in her continuing fondness for music. She enjoyed dancing and hunting; played bowls and cards, and gambled modestly on both; and was diligent with her needle. Only on clothing and jewellery did she spend with anything like extravagance, and the inventory of her jewels with the marginal annotations in her own hand expresses the keenness of her interest. She loved interludes and entertainments of all kinds, keeping in her own household a female tumbler, and a jester, 'Jane the Fool', of whom she became extremely fond.[67] It was not only her adherence to the old faith that drew upon Mary the critical and somewhat contemptuous glances of the professors of the 'new learning'. Her tastes were those of an aristocrat of the old school, and in 1546 her eight-year-old brother expressed a solemn concern for the welfare of her soul, not on theological but upon puritanical grounds. Her life was comfortable and honourable, but unsatisfying. Not only did marriage elude her, but she had literally nothing to call her own beyond her personal accoutrements; no offices or official responsibilities, no estates, and no permanent residences. An unmarried royal princess approaching thirty and in full possession of her faculties was an unprecedented phenomenon, and her father could never bring himself to give her any measure of real independence. Consequently, although her wishes were normally respected, appointments to her household were made by the king, and her whole establishment was paid out of the royal household, to the tune of about £2000 a year.[68]

Henry died in January 1547, when Mary was nearly thirty-one, and her position underwent a radical change. Not only was she once again the heir to the throne, but for the first time she became a magnate in her own right. In his will the old king did what he had persistently failed to do in his lifetime, and instructed his executors to make proper provision for both his daughters. Each of them was to receive a marriage portion of £10,000, 'they being married to any outward potentate by th'Advise of the aforesaid Counsaillors ...' Moreover,

> ... from the first howre of our Death untyll such Tyme as the sayde Counsaillors canne provide either of them or bothe of sum honorable Mariages, they shall have eche of them thre thowsand pounds ultra reprisas to lyve on ...[69]

His wishes were not fulfilled literally, but at some time, probably before the end of 1547, Mary was put in possession of extensive estates in several counties to an annual value of £3819. These lands she held for life, or until a suitable marriage was provided for her, in return for fealty and a rent of £99 18s. 6d. in augmentations. They included the residences of Kenninghall, Hunsdon, and Newhall, from which it appears that Mary may well have been consulted before the grant was made. The patent was not enrolled until 18 May 1548, but issues were granted from Michaelmas 1547,[70] and for the first time the princess needed stewards, receivers, and all the extensive establishment of a great estate. According to her father's will his executors were supposed 'to limite and appoincte . . . sage Officers and Ministers for ordering thereof', but the protector seems to have allowed her to appoint her own officers for the most part. With the freedom of patronage and 'entertainment' which the assured income now gave her, Mary began to transform her modest household into a princely retinue, conspicuously devoted to traditional aristocratic virtues and the ancient faith.

Such a course was not pursued with any aggressive intentions, but in the circumstances of Edward's minority it soon became a political fact of considerable importance. Mary had stood in genuine awe of her father, and had sincerely mourned his death, but there is no reason to suppose that she had ever approved of his policies. Nevertheless, as soon as Protector Somerset began to show signs of introducing further religious change, in the autumn of 1547, she protested that the settlement which Henry had left must be upheld unchanged until Edward came of age.[71] This was also the opinion of Stephen Gardiner, the conservative bishop of Winchester, but whereas Gardiner's outspokenness landed him in prison, Mary received only a mild explanatory letter from Somerset, claiming that Henry himself had intended a further programme of reform.[72] There, temporarily, the matter was allowed to rest, and Mary's personal relations with the protector, the duchess of Somerset, and the increasingly protestant Edward continued to be good. However, by 1549 the princess's catholicism had become a symbol of her integrity, and a rallying-point for opposition to the regime. Under these circumstances it is not surprising that continuing negotiations for her marriage produced no result. Somerset was only interested in marrying her to a foreign protestant prince who might 'turn her opinions', while she herself had long since undertaken not to marry without the consent of her cousin the emperor.[73] As the English government got into increasing difficulties during the summer of 1549, Charles used his special relationship with Mary as a pretext for open interference in England's domestic affairs. A protestant England would be a natural ally for those German protestants whom he had defeated with such labour and to so little effect two years previously, a standing threat to the Low Countries and a probable ally for the French. If the princess could be encouraged to be intransigent, she might well provide a focus for opposition so powerful that the protector must either be overthrown or abandon his protestant policy.

Mary's old friend Chapuys had gone home in 1545, but his successor, Van der Delft, moved into action with suspicious promptness at the first sign of danger. On 25 January, within a few days of the passage of the first act of uniformity, and months before it was due to come into effect, he declared to Somerset that his master would not tolerate any pressure upon Mary to enforce conformity with this law.[74] Early in April the princess herself, who was clearly in regular consultation with Van der Delft, appealed to the emperor for protection, so that she might 'continue to live in the ancient faith, and in peace with my conscience'.[75] In May the ambassador responded to this by making representations to Somerset about the diplomatic difficulties which his religious policy was causing, and demanding a written guarantee of immunity for Mary. Such a demand was entirely improper, and suggests that the emperor, in collaboration with Mary, was determined to force an issue. Somerset was equally anxious to avoid one, and consistently returned soft answers, declaring his willingness not to pry into what went on in the princess's household. But he could not, and would not, make any guarantee of immunity.[76] The council, disillusioned with Somerset in many ways by this time, were not satisfied, and pressed for a tougher response. Mary's position was infinitely stronger than it had been thirteen years before when she had confronted her father. She could not now be summarily isolated and humiliated. Her servants might be bullied or bribed, but the princess herself could only be called to account by a full-scale judicial process. Quite apart from any possible action by the emperor, the government was simply not strong enough to risk that kind of showdown in the turbulent summer of 1549. Consequently Mary's defiance was almost entirely successful. The commission which visited her just before Whitsun to see the statute obeyed retired with its mission unaccomplished,[77] and on the critical day, 9 June, mass was celebrated at Kenninghall with unusual splendour. The council could not ignore such a challenge and on 16 June, Mary was commanded to discontinue her mass, and to send her chaplains and controller to receive the council's orders. Her reply was angry and haughty. She did not acknowledge the validity of this 'late law of your own making', notwithstanding the authority of parliament, and refused to send her officers.[78] This was dangerous indeed. The country was torn with rebellion, which Mary was strongly suspected of fostering and encouraging.[79] She denied the charges, which were not pressed, and ultimately, in spite of almost hysterical protests, sent her officers to the council. On the main issue, however, it was the government which gave way. A letter from the king, which must have been Somerset's way of circumventing the council, attributed her wilfulness (without a shade of justification) to 'want of good information and conference with some godly and well learned men', and under the colour of brotherly concern, allowed her 'weakness' to continue for the time being.[80] Van der Delft had not got his guarantee, but Mary still had her mass in defiance of the law.

If the emperor had intended by this means to get rid of Somerset, then he must have found the outcome satisfactory, for just over a month after Edward had written this letter, his uncle was arrested and sent to the Tower. For several weeks thereafter the political situation in England was confused. Many contemporaries thought that a religious reaction was inevitable, and Van der Delft flattered himself that he had played an important part in Somerset's overthrow. Conservatives such as the earls of Southampton and Arundel had helped to engineer the *coup*, and there were rumours that Mary would be made regent. On the other hand, the earl of Warwick had never disguised his sympathy with the reformers, and it seems that purely political and domestic discontents had played the dominant part in forming the alliance against the Protector.[81] A tense power-struggle between Southampton and Warwick followed, from which the latter emerged victorious some time before Christmas. Early in February the earl of Southampton was disgraced and dismissed from the council. Arundel was charged with abusing his office as lord chamberlain,[82] while the duke of Somerset was pardoned and released. If there had ever been a concerted plan between the Imperialists and the English conservatives to halt the advance of protestantism, then it had certainly failed by the end of 1549. A statement issued in the king's name on Christmas day gave the *coup de grâce* to any hopes of immediate reactions.

> . . . divers unquiet and evill disposed persons, since the apprehension of the Duke of Somerset, have noised and bruted abroad that they should have again their old laten services, their conjured bread and water, with such like vain and superstitious ceremonies. . . .[83]

Not only was the exclusive use of the prayer book reaffirmed, but the bishops and clergy were ordered in explicit terms to gather up and destroy all copies of former uses and services. Not only had the overthrow of Somerset failed to improve the situation in England, from Mary's point of view it had made it a great deal worse, since she now had to deal with the hostile and implacable Warwick instead of a man who, for all his mistaken policies, had still been an understanding friend.

The princess's mood at the beginning of 1550 was one of extreme despondency. She had kept her hands scrupulously clean during the crisis of the previous autumn, but she had certainly known what was afoot, and her closeness to Van der Delft makes it very probable that she had shared his hopes. By March, although no further steps had been taken against her, she was convinced that they were impending, and became increasingly apprehensive. As before the emperor responded by making powerful representations to the English council which, in effect, told him to mind his own business. All that seems to have been said to Mary at this time was an official warning to have mass celebrated in her closet and not in the chapel, which was virtually a public church. However, the princess, who had never shown very much grasp of political events and had become increasingly isolated since the protector's fall, was thoroughly unnerved. First she begged the emperor to bring pressure upon her brother's government to conclude the longstanding negotiations for her marriage with Dom Luiz, and then she returned to her adolescent fantasy of escape.[84] Charles was as unenthusiastic as ever about this latter course, which would have meant the end of her hopes for the succession, and the end of her usefulness as a diplomatic lever. Nevertheless, Van der Delft induced him to consent to such a plan by convincing him that Mary was desperate, and that her life was in real danger. The result was a fiasco which casts the gravest doubt upon the princess's stability of mind. The ambassador's secretary, Jehan Dubois, at considerable risk to himself, arrived at Maldon on 30 June with a small boat, and sent word to Mary of his arrival. At this point Robert Rochester, her controller, who seems to have had considerable influence over her, began to raise fears and objections.[85] Mary's hysterical determination dissolved into uncertainty, and Dubois was forced to leave without her. Rumours that she was already in Flanders alerted the council to what had happened, and a similar opportunity was never allowed to occur again. Van der Delft, who was a sick man, had already been recalled, and the matter was never mentioned to his successor, Jehan Scheyfve.

The main issue was never resolved as long as Edward lived. Mary's relations with the emperor continued to be close, and Charles exerted whatever diplomatic pressure he could upon the English council to extract a guarantee of immunity for her. In spite of their diplomatic weakness neither Warwick (duke of Northumberland from 1551) nor the young king himself would yield on this point, and there is some evidence to suggest that Edward's personal determination was responsible for this.[86] His relationship with his sister never broke down entirely, but he frequently reproached her, both in writing and to her face. The situation was, from the government's point of view, not merely intolerable in principle, but dangerous in practice. Mary was a great conservative noble, in close alliance with a foreign power. This point was emphasized, if it needed emphasis, by her arrival at court in March 1551 accompanied by a retinue of 130 knights, gentlemen, and ladies, all displaying rosaries as symbols of their allegiance.[87] So might their grandfathers have appeared, wearing the badges of Stafford or Percy. Protected both by the emperor and by her proximity to the throne, the princess was the acknowledged and powerful leader of all those who opposed religious innovation, and adhered either to her father's settlement, or secretly and discreetly to the papal authority and the ancient ways. In 1536 her defiance had been a symbol and an encouragement to others, now it was an intractable political fact in its own right. The government did the only thing it could, and resorted to pressure and harassment in the hope of breaking her will, since the straightforward remedy of judicial force could not be applied without running even graver risks. Fortunately for Northumberland, Mary was handicapped by her sex, and even more by political inexperience and lack of nerve. She was a leader more by virtue of what she was than what she did. She might lend herself, wittingly or unwittingly, to the schemes of others; but to conspire actively and purposefully for the overthrow of the existing government was not in her nature. Consequently she has always appeared as the victim of Northumberland's persecution; an innocent woman suffering for her conscience.[88] The truth was a great deal more complex, and Northumberland's failure to find any real solution to the threat which she presented was ultimately to prove fatal to him.

It appeared that the crisis was going to come to a head in March 1551, when, following her flamboyant entry into London, Mary was summoned before the council and informed by the king himself that her evil example could not be tolerated any longer. She refused to yield, and was immediately and collusively supported by Scheyfve, who threatened war if the matter was pressed. This was a risk which Northumberland could not afford, and he therefore temporized until the diplomatic situation seemed more propitious. In August he tried again. On the 14th the three principal officers of her household, Rochester, Francis Englefield, and Edward Waldegrave, were summoned to London and commanded to ensure that no illegal services were held in Mary's houses.[89] This attempt to circumvent the indignant princess failed. She appealed directly to the king, and as a result her officers were imprisoned in the Tower, and she herself was visited by a commission consisting of Lord Rich, Sir William Petre, and Sir Anthony Wingfield. The resulting confrontation was heated, and on Mary's part abusive. Her father, she declared, 'made the more part of you almost of noething'.[90] The interview reflected little credit on either her wit or her discretion. She was compelled at last to restrict the mass to her private rooms, and her officers remained in the Tower. That so much was accomplished can probably be attributed to the fact that much of the plausibility was taken out of the emperor's threats by the renewal of his war with France, and the fact that he was no longer prepared to risk a breakdown of relations with England. For the remainder of the reign an uneasy truce prevailed, with the honours about even. Mary still had her mass, and although it was no longer public, the fact that she had it was public knowledge. Her officers were released in the spring of 1552, and no further action was taken against her. Although he had accomplished as much as the circumstances permitted, in reality Northumberland had lost, because he had failed to discredit Mary sufficiently to break her hold on conservative opinion. Had Edward lived and fathered an heir this would not have mattered, but Edward did not live. It is not true to say that the council drove Mary into the arms of the Imperialists by wanton persecution.[91] She had looked primarily to the current Imperial ambassador for advice and support since her first great crisis in 1536. English conservatives may have looked to her for comfort and leadership under Edward, but she did not look to them for counsel. They had failed her in her previous need, and had only partially and belatedly redeemed themselves. Only Stephen Gardiner and Edmund Bonner might have got close to her in the latter part of Edward's reign, but, lacking her royal immunity, both were in prison.

By the summer of 1553 Mary was thirty-seven; tested and toughened, but not much instructed by adversity. She had just about given up hope of marriage, and the damage which that prolonged frustration may have done to her psychological make-up can only be guessed at. Together with her intense piety it must have given her something of the mentality of the nun. By long habit of thought she was detached, not from English politics but from English political and religious thinking; accustomed to making decisions on first principles, she had virtually no sensitivity to interests or loyalties which were alien to her own mind. She was also intensely conscious of her royal estate, to which she had clung through thick and thin, and which had been during the last six years bodied forth in great estates and extensive *manred*. Finally, and ultimately most significant of all, her health was poor. For years she had reacted to each succeeding crisis with bouts of neuralgia, toothache, fever, and other ailments; moving, whenever she was free to do so, restlessly from one residence to another to escape infection or enjoy purer air.[92] She was not exactly a hypochondriac because her illnesses were real enough, though probably no worse than those which many less demonstrative people suffered. She was, however, very conscious of her own physical well-being, or lack of it. When circumstances made her depressed or hysterical, or when pressures upon her became unendurable, she took refuge in sickness as another person might have taken refuge in drink. As a result, by the time that she came to the throne, her health was seriously undermined, a fact which not only reduced still further her chances of belated childbearing, but also made her prone to physical collapse in the face of critical decisions.

Notes

1 Henry had first moved for this marriage as early as 1488, when he had sent an embassy to Spain for that purpose, as a part of his campaign to win recognition for his dynasty from the established royal houses of Europe. Garrett Mattingly, *Catherine of Aragon* (1941), 21.
2 Ferdinand to de Rojas, 23 August 1503. *Cal. Span.*, I, 370.
3 *Cal. Span.*, I, 338. H. A. Kelly, *The Matrimonial Trials of Henry VIII* (1976), 104.
4 ibid., 97.
5 G. Burnet, *History of the Reformation in England*, I (1679), App., 10. *Cal. Span.*, I, 435.
6 For a full discussion of the circumstances of this quarrel, see Mattingly, 61-4.
7 ibid., 90-1, citing *Correspondencia de Gutierre Gómez de Fuensalida*, ed. El Duque de Alba (1907), 490-540.
8 Mattingly, 92-3; *Correspondencia de Gutierre Gómez*, 449, 484.
9 Cited Mattingly, 98.
10 ibid., 124-5.
11 Their friendship lasted as long as Catherine's life. Lady Willoughby was the only person, apart from her servants, who was with her when she died.
12 *Cal. Ven.*, II, 285.
13 Mattingly, 25.
14 The event was the subject of a pedestrian ballad by Thomas Churchyard published in *The Firste parte of Churchyardes chippes* (1575). A contemporary account confirming some of Churchyard's detail was given by the Venetian Chieragato. *Cal. Ven.*, II, 385.
15 Mattingly, 136.
16 Vives, *De institutione*, in Foster Watson, *Vives and the Renascence Education of Women* (1912), 55.
17 Mary's linguistic accomplishments have been the subject of some disagreement. Madden, quoting various sources, believed that she was

accomplished in French, Latin, Greek, Italian, and Spanish; F. Madden, *The Privy Purse Expenses of the Princess Mary* (1831), cxxxii-iii. However Michieli, one of Madden's sources, states clearly that she understood Italian but did not speak it, while an eyewitness account of her marriage to Philip in 1554 states with equal clarity 'the Queen does not speak Castilian, though she understands it'. *Cal. Span.*, XIII, 12. There is no evidence, outside panegyrics, that she had more than a smattering of Greek.

18 Mattingly, 141.

19 *Cal. Span.*, III, ii, 185.

20 *Letters and Papers*, IV, ii, 3105.

21 Mattingly, 173-4. He was created duke on 18 June 1525, and extensive estates were conferred upon him by act of parliament in 1531 (22 Henry VIII, c. 17). He was also made earl of Nottingham and lieutenant of the north.

22 Two of the best and most recent are: G. de C. Parmiter, *The King's Great Matter* (1967) and H. A. Kelly, *The Matrimonial Trials of Henry VIII* (1976). For a rather different interpretation of the canon law, see J. J. Scarisbrick, *Henry VIII* (1968), 163-98.

23 H. A. Kelly, 'Kinship, Incest and the Dictates of Law', *American Journal of Jurisprudence*, 14 (1969), 73.

24 For Fisher's role in the proceedings, see Kelly, *Matrimonial Trials*, 81-4; and Jean Rouchausse, *Saint John Fisher* (1972), 230-45.

25 Mattingly, 208.

26 In May 1527 a mutinous and unpaid Imperial army sacked Rome, and Clement VII was forced to take refuge in the Castle of Sant' Angelo. Although he had not planned this move, Charles was more than willing to take advantage of it. Bishop John Clerk to Wolsey, 28 May 1527, *L&P*, IV, 3136.

27 Mattingly, 218-19. For a full examination of popular reactions to Catherine's treatment see G. R. Elton, *Policy and Police* (1972), 278-9, etc.

28 Kelly, *Matrimonial Trials*, 192-3. Chapuys to Charles, 31 July 1531, *L&P*, V, 361.

29 The reasons which may have induced Anne to yield to her royal lover in December 1532 are discussed in Scarisbrick, op. cit., 309 and n.

30 First to Ampthill, then to Buckden, and finally Kimbolton. Mattingly, 258-73, 278-83. In March 1534 this designation was confirmed by statute, and a modest but adequate estate settled upon her for life. 25 Henry VIII, c. 28.

31 *Cal Span.*, IV, ii, 1186. H. F. M. Prescott, *Mary Tudor* (1952), 46.

32 *L&P*, VI, 1126.

33 e.g., Chapuys to the emperor, 27 December 1533. *L&P*, IV, ii, 1165. Prescott, op. cit., 44-50.

34 Elton, op. cit., 83-171.

35 The son of Lord Montague, who died without achieving his majority. Chapuys to Granvelle, 8 July 1536. *Cal. Span.*, V, ii, 72.

36 Prescott, op. cit., 66-7.

37 *Cal. Span.*, V, i, 218. Prescott, op. cit., 61.

38 Chapuys to the emperor, 21 January 1536. *L&P*, X, 141.

39 BL Cotton MS Otho C x, 283. *L&P*, X, 968. Thomas Hearne, *Sylloge Epistolarum* (1716), 140.

40 Otho C x, 268. *L&P*, X, 1109. Otho C x, 272. *L&P*, X, 1133.

41 Otho C x, 2696. *L&P*, X, 1108.
42 Otho C x, 280. *L&P*, X, 1110. Mary's subsequent correspondence with Cromwell gives no hint that she ever received this stinging rebuke. Hearne, op. cit., 137.
43 Otho C x, 172, 174. *L&P*, X, 1134.
44 Otho C x, 174. *L&P*, X, 1134.
45 PRO SP1/104/f.185-5. *L&P*, X, 1150.
46 Chapuys to the emperor, 1 July 1536. *Cal. Span.*, V, ii, 70. According to this account, Cromwell considered himself 'a dead man' for having acted as an intermediary with Mary. It seems certain that Cromwell deceived the ambassador on this point, however. He had used Mary's supporters to help destroy the Boleyns, and was fully secure in the king's confidence. G. R. Elton, *Reform and Reformation* (1977), 253-4.
47 Otho C x, 275. *L&P*, X, 1203. PRO SP1/104/f.223. *L&P*, X, 1204.
48 And not 15 June, the date tentatively assigned to it by *L&P*. Otho C x, 289. *L&P*, X, 1136. This would mean that her subsequent letter to Cromwell should be dated 30 June, not 23. *L&P*, X, 1186.
49 BL Cotton MS Vespasian C xiv, 245. *L&P*, X, 1187 (2). Susan Tonge, alias Clarencius, was a lifelong servant and familiar of Mary's. Her pseudonym, by which she was always known, derived from the fact that her husband was Clarence Herald.
50 *L&P*, X, 1186.
51 Chapuys to the emperor, 1 July 1536. *Cal. Span.*, V, ii, 70.
52 ibid.
53 Chapuys to the emperor, 7 October 1536. *Cal. Span.*, V, ii, 104.
54 Chapuys to Cifuentes, 8 October 1536. *Cal. Span.*, V, ii, 105.
55 Count Cifuentes to the emperor, 8 October 1536, referring to an earlier request by Chapuys, written in September. *Cal. Span.*, V, ii, 106.
56 The most recent interpretation of the Pilgrimage argues convincingly that it was engineered and led by political conservatives from the centre, to whom Mary was of crucial importance. G. R. Elton, *Reform and Reformation*, 262-4.
57 Prescott, op. cit., 93-4. He was the younger brother of Otto Henry, subsequently elector.
58 Marillac to Francis I of France, 3 June 1542. *L&P*, XVII, 371.
59 M. H. and R. Dodds, *The Pilgrimage of Grace and the Exeter conspiracy* (1915) remains the only full account of this episode. Montague and Courtenay were executed, along with Sir Edward Neville, on 9 December 1538.
60 35 Henry VIII, c. 1. A. Luders, *et al.*, *Statutes of the Realm* (1810-28), III, 955-8.
61 Thomas Rymer, *Foedera, etc.* (1726-35), XV, 112-14. Frances was the wife of Henry Grey, marquis of Dorset, and the mother of Jane, Catherine, and Mary. Eleanor was the wife of Henry Clifford, earl of Cumberland, and the mother of Margaret.
62 Margaret Tudor's son by her first marriage, James V of Scotland, was recently dead, and peace between the countries was new and precarious. He had been survived by his widow, Mary of Guise, and his infant daughter, Mary. Her daughter by her second marriage, Margaret, was the wife of Matthew Stewart, earl of Lennox, and the mother of Henry Lord Darnley.
63 Rymer, op. cit., XV, 114.
64 Prescott, op. cit., 92.

65 J. K. McConica, *English Humanists and Reformation Politics* (1965). Mary's works of translation, incomplete because of illness, was finished by her chaplain, Dr Mallet. John Strype, *Ecclesiastical Memorials* (1721), I, 45. *PPE*, cxxxiv-v.

66 Almost any page of the privy purse expenses will provide an example: e.g., 30-31 (June 1537). Mary's literary interests seem to have been confined almost entirely to works of piety. Three prayers by her, written during Edward's reign, are published in *Ecc. Mem.*, III, 2, 145, 550. Although Madden was at great pains to praise her accomplishments (*PPE*, cxxxiv-viii), books (title and subject unspecified) are mentioned only four times in the eight years covered by her accounts, during which time there are hundreds of references to items of clothing, food, and ornaments, as well as many references to cards, bowls, hunting dogs, and other items of use or relaxation. Nor was she ever (to my knowledge) praised by contemporaries as a patron.

67 There are a number of references to this Jane in *PPE*, including one payment made 'for the tyme of hir seeknes' (p. 123). See also Madden's explanatory note (p. 241). The new year gift list for 1557 records the gift of a silver salt to a woman living at Bury 'for healing of Jane the Fool her eye', and another gift to a Mrs Ayre 'for keeping of the saide Jane during the tyme of her helyng'. BL MS RP 294. The tumbler's name seems to have been Lucrece. *PPE*, 246.

68 Apart from the time of her greatest trouble in 1536, the allowance for Mary's household usually seems to have run at about £1100–£1400 a year. *L&P*, III, 3375 (1525-26); *L&P*, II, ii, App. 58 (3) (1517-18). Sir John Shelton, writing to Cromwell on 16 August 1536, declared that £4000 would be 'little enough' to cover the households of both Mary and Elizabeth. *L&P*, XI, 312.

69 Rymer, op. cit., XV, 116.

70 *Cal. Pat.*, Edward VI, II, 20.

71 *Ecc. Mem.*, II, i, 92-3.

72 BL Cotton MS Faustin C ii, 13; cited by W. K. Jordan, *Edward VI: the Young King* (1968), 207.

73 As early as 1536 she had assured Chapuys that she would never marry without Charles's consent, and 'except for some great advantage to the peace of Christendom, she would not care to be married at all'. Chapuys to Charles V, 3 August 1536. *L&P*, XI, 219.

74 *Cal. Span.*, IX, 330.

75 Mary to Charles V, 3 April 1549. *Cal. Span.*, IX, 361.

76 Van der Delft to Charles V, 28 May 1549. *Cal. Span.*, IX, 381-2.

77 Prescott, op. cit., 121-2. Van der Delft to Charles V, 13 June 1549. *Cal. Span.*, IX, 393-4.

78 Mary to the council, 22 June 1549. J. Foxe, *Acts and Monuments* (1877), VI, 7-8.

79 Council to Mary, 18 July 1549. PRO SP10/8/30.

80 Edward to Mary, August 1549. PRO SP10/8/51-3.

81 For a full discussion of this power struggle and its circumstances, see D. E. Hoak, *The King's Council in the Reign of Edward VI* (1976), esp. 246-51.

82 ibid., 59-60.

83 PRO SP10/9/57.

84 Van der Delft to Charles V, 2 May 1550. *Cal. Span.*, X, 80-6. As recorded by the ambassador, Mary's proposal was that of a very fright-

ened, or very foolish, woman. Neither Charles nor Van der Delft had much confidence in Mary's nerve, or competence, at this time.

85 For a full account of this episode, see Prescott, op. cit., 131-43.
86 For a discussion of this point, which is not entirely conclusive, see Jordan, op. cit., 256-64.
87 J. G. Nichols, *The Diary of Henry Machyn* (Camden Society, 1848), 4-5.
88 Most notably by Prescott, in what is still the fullest and best biography.
89 *APC*, III, 329-33.
90 PRO SP10/13/36. 'And I have (said shee) the Emperors hand testifying that this promise [concerning her mass] was made, which I beleeve better than you all of the Councell . . . yet should you show more favour to me for my fathers sake, which made the more part of you almost of noething . . .'
91 Jordan, op. cit., 262-3.
92 Not only are there innumerable references to her illnesses in the correspondence of Chapuys, Van der Delft, and Scheyfve, but her privy purse expenses bear plentiful testimony to the numerous occasions upon which she required the services of a physician. *PPE*, 90, 113, 123, etc.

2   The Background to the Reign: Political and Religious Developments after the Break with Rome

The years of the king's 'Great Matter', and indeed its aftermath down to 1540, had been years of crisis and upheaval. Changes and developments had taken place during those years which had aroused the fiercest passions at the time, and the significance of which was only to be gradually revealed during the succeeding decades. Mary had been close to the eye of the storm, but seems to have comprehended very little of what was passing. Even Sir Thomas More, who saw the full implications of the royal supremacy more clearly than any other person of the age, had been prepared to concede the right of parliament to alter the succession. Strongly as he had opposed Henry's plans to repudiate Catherine, the indications are that he would have accepted a pure legislative *fiat* to that effect.[1] Mary, untroubled by a legal education, had been no more prepared to admit the right of parliament to bastardize her or to deprive her of her royal title than she had been willing to accept the ecclesiastical supremacy. Her submission in 1536 had not altered this basic attitude. Her conscience had been just as troubled by the betrayal of her mother's integrity as by the betrayal of the universal church. She never accepted, or even understood, the expansion of statute law which had been brought about by the reformation parliament. Like Chapuys, and like other ill-informed English conservatives, she blamed the evil influence of specific people working upon the king – particularly Anne Boleyn and Thomas Cranmer. There is no evidence that she shared in the widespread execration of Thomas Cromwell, but the whole reform programme for which he worked seemed to her an integral part of the wickedness of the times: '. . . a happie florishing and most prosperous Common wealthe', disrupted by 'the malicious and perverse affections of somme a verye fewe persones . . . for their own singuler glorye and vayne Reputacion . . .', as one of her own early statutes later expressed it.[2] This 'conspiracy theory' of the

English reformation has always had its adherents, but, like most such explanations, it has served only to conceal the true course of events. A serious attempt had been made to implement a reform programme of sweeping extent and profound implications. Enmeshed in the problems of her own conscience, Mary had seen only the negative and destructive aspects of what was intended to be a positive and constructive policy. Some aspects of this policy had never got beyond the pamphlets and memoranda of idealistic writers; others were defeated or rendered nugatory in practice. But some were accepted and put into effect, not grudgingly but with energy and even enthusiasm.[3] These fragmentary successes had wrought considerable changes, not only in the fabric of the English church and state, but also in the attitudes and reactions of Englishmen. The situation which Mary inherited as queen had been profoundly affected by the crisis of the 1530s, but her own experience of that crisis had made her incapable of appreciating either the nature or the extent of what had happened.

Between 1533 and 1536 statutes had been made and successfully enforced which clearly transgressed the hitherto accepted limits of the positive law. The fourteenth-century acts of provisors and *praemunire* had created precedents for legislative meddling with the respective rights of the *regnum* and the *sacerdotium*, but such meddling had fallen a long way short of the total exclusion of papal jurisdiction. Similarly, although English kings had long since become accustomed to nominating bishops with a minimum of papal interference, it was a different matter to remove the ultimate safeguard of confirmation altogether. The bills embodying the submission of the clergy and the destruction of their jurisdictional autonomy had been fiercely contested, not merely by vested interests, but on the highest principles.

> This indictment [Sir Thomas More is alleged to have said at his trial] is grounded upon an act of Parliament directly repugnant to the laws of God and His Holy Church, the supreme government of which, or any part whereof, may no temporal prince presume by any law to take upon him, as rightfully belonging to the See of Rome. . . .[4]

Whether or not More actually used such words, they are an accurate expression of his opinion, and it was a view which was shared by others who lacked his courage. It was also an accurate view by previously accepted standards. Why then did parliament overturn it? The simplest explanation, believed by Chapuys at the time and by conservative chroniclers and biographers subsequently, was that

Henry packed the Commons and bribed or intimidated the Lords.

> In this Parlement the Common Howse was so parcially chosen, that the king had his will almost in all things that himself listed ...

wrote the Elizabethan catholic Richard Hall,[5] while Stephen Gardiner later claimed that the assembly had been 'constrained with great cruelty' to serve the king's purposes. Perhaps Henry would have been willing to employ such tactics if he had had the power. But he did not have the power, and in any case there was no need. Anti-clericalism had been strong among the Commons in earlier parliaments, and had reappeared again with the session of 1529. Nor did the lay peers have any great love for the clergy, and their resentment had been heightened by the career of Thomas Wolsey.[6]

The recent researches of Professor Stanford Lehmberg have shown that royal interference with elections to the Commons was confined to the normal operations of patronage, with the exception of a few by-elections between 1534 and 1536.[7] A considerable number of members were, as Edward Hall noted, 'the king's servants', placed by Cromwell or by peers operating in the king's interest, but the number was no higher than normal, and constituted only a small fraction of the 310 knights and burgesses. Nor did Henry make any attempt to swamp the Upper House with tame peers. Five new barons did indeed sit in this parliament, three of whom supported the king's policies and two opposed them.[8] The process whereby the lay peers had come to outnumber the spiritual was a long continuing one. In 1529 there had been 49 spiritual peers and 51 temporal. By 1534 the figures were 50 and 55 respectively, but there is no evidence to suggest that the king made any effort to reduce the attendance of mitred abbots, who were probably the least secure group in the House. All those who had traditionally received writs sat in this parliament and one or two additional ones as well. What Henry and Cromwell did do, indisputably, was to apply pressure to individual peers and commoners. Sometimes this was pressure to attend, or to stay away from, particular sessions; for example, Robert Acton, a burgess for Southwark who was presumably considered a reliable supporter, was called from his sick bed in 1533.[9] In the critical sessions of 1534 a number of knokn conservatives absented themselves: Fisher, Tunstall, and Edward Lee among the bishops, Lord Darcy among the lay peers, Sir George Throgmorton and Sir Marmaduke Constable among the Commons. In the cases of Tunstall, Throgmorton, and Constable government interference can be proved, in the other cases only suspected.[10] Nevertheless, of large-scale bribery or intimidation there is no evidence, and it must be presumed that the acquiescence of both Houses was secured by means which did not transgress the limits normally observed by a monarch whose interests were deeply engaged. Unfortunately there is little evidence of how the vital act in restraint of appeals fared, once it had gone through its prolonged and careful process of drafting.[11] It seems to have lingered in the Commons from 14 to 31 March, attracting prolonged debate, and probably the attentions of at least one committee. Such information as we have about these debates suggests that the burgesses were more concerned about the political and economic effects of such a measure than about the legal or moral principles involved. Fears were expressed that catholic princes might attack the realm, or impose crippling trade embargoes; fears which were countered by cheerful assurances that other princes would be only too willing to follow Henry's lead. The bill probably emerged from the Commons unscathed,[12] and passed the Lords within a week, also without amendment. It is arguable, at least, that the major acts establishing the supremacy passed because many of those in both Houses who disliked them did not believe that they represented a serious long-term policy. High-principled resistance, involving the risk of royal displeasure, must have seemed inappropriate to men who believed that they were dealing with a temporary royal whim arising out of a sordid matrimonial tangle. On the other hand, there is plentiful evidence that some members of each House supported the king with zeal, and even conviction. By 1533 Henry had become genuinely convinced that God had intended His church to be ruled by Christian princes. That view was shared by Cromwell, although not necessarily for the same reasons, and commanded a respectable body of aristocratic and popular support.[13]

Even the most clearsighted must have been uncertain at the time as to exactly what effects the body of legislation relating to the supremacy would have. Theoretically these acts enforced with penalties the recognition of a longstanding situation, '. . . that this realm of England is an Empire . . . institute and furnished by the goodness and sufferance of Almighty God with plenary, whole and entire power . . .'[14] In order to make this autonomy abundantly clear, judicial appeals to Rome were to cease, and no further taxes or revenues were to be sent thither. Instead the archbishops of the two provinces were to hold the final appellate jurisdiction, first fruits and tenths were to be paid to the king, and the king was to enjoy unrestricted control over episcopal appointments. It has been argued that these changes made little real difference to Henry's control over the church,[15] and had he made no further use of his supremacy than to administer ecclesiastical affairs in such terms, this argument would be justified. However, the king was not prepared to stop at this point. Further legislation gave the king's court of chancery the final right to hear ecclesiastical appeals, dissolved the religious houses, and laid down a standard of doctrinal orthodoxy. Direct use of the supremacy, through proclamations, injunctions, and the control of convocation, modified many of the traditional practices of the church, curtailed holy days, imposed ecclesiastical discipline, and authorized the English bible. The common lawyer Christopher St German, who approved of the supremacy in principle, regarded this direct application with grave suspicion, fearing that it might be used to circumvent the limitations traditionally imposed upon the king by the common law.[16] He strongly advocated the full participation of parliament in order to keep the supremacy within at least some traditional bounds, and saw more clearly than anyone, with the possible exception of Cromwell, the potential transformation which had taken place in the extent of the king's authority.

While Henry lived, much of this potential remained unfulfilled. Although he appointed bishops, he seems to have been unsure of his power to deprive them. The resignations of Latimer and Shaxton were forced in the aftermath of the act of six articles, but Edmund Bonner of London was the first bishop to be deprived by royal commission, on 1 October 1549.[17] Similarly, although Henry clearly believed, and stated, that it was his duty to defend orthodox catholic doctrine, it is not certain to what extent he believed that he had the responsibility to define it. His view may well have approximated to that of Stephen Gardiner, who believed that the supreme head had the right and duty to define orthodoxy in *adiaphora*, but not in fundamentals, which had been immutably decreed by the church.[18] Unfortunately there was considerable scope for disagreement over what constituted *adiaphora*, and Gardiner's own definition was to change dramatically after Henry's death. As a result of the king's conservatism, some of the most important issues concerning the supremacy were avoided, except as abstract points of principle, until 1547.

Since Edward succeeded at the age of nine, the nature of his supremacy was inevitably different from his father's. It could not be exercised in person, and this prompted the conservatives to claim that its full powers were in abeyance. Gardiner, who was the main protagonist of this view, realized that he was in a dilemma, since it could not be claimed that any other powers of the crown were in abeyance during a royal minority.

A king's authority to govern his realm never wanteth [he admitted in June 1547] though he were in his cradle. His place is replenished by his Council, as we have now my Lord Protector . . .[19]

On the other hand, alarmed by the threat of impending protestantism visible in the policies of Thomas Cranmer and Protector Somerset, he felt that he could not concede such plenary authority over the church. Until December 1547 he took refuge behind the act of six articles, and when that was repealed, argued with more commonsense than legal force that Edward's supremacy should be regarded as purely administrative and jurisdictional until he came of age. '. . . It is a difference in the judgement of the people', he observed, 'to direct and order things established, and to make in the highest innovations'. Mary's view was similar, but lacked Gardiner's professional caution. When her brother came of age, she declared, he would find her obedient in this as in all other matters. Until then she considered herself and the council to be bound to the settlement which Henry had left, to which 'all ye executors [were] sworn upon a book'.[20] As the reformation advanced, Gardiner's dilemma became more acute. His concept of *adiaphora* had been sufficiently flexible to embrace the dissolution of the monasteries and chantries, the use of the English bible, and the curtailment of ceremonies, but it could not embrace the abolition of the mass. Eventually he either had to accept the act of uniformity, or reject it as *ultra vires*. He did the latter, and was deprived of his see.[21] The necessity for this decision killed his belief in the royal supremacy altogether and he returned, albeit secretly, to the papal allegiance. For Mary there was no dilemma. The act of uniformity was '. . . no law, unless it be a late law of your own making . . . which in my conscience is not worthy to have the name of law . . .'[22] Whether she denied this act the status of law because of the king's minority or because of its content she did not make clear. Whether either Mary or Gardiner would have accepted a protestant settlement at the hands of a mature Edward must remain uncertain, but all the indications are that they would not and that their arguments about the minority were specious. Ultimately both denied, as Sir Thomas More had denied in 1535, that statute had any power to touch or alter what they considered to be the fundamentals of the catholic faith.

However, by 1549 it was too late to decide that parliament had no right to legislate on matters of religion. The conservative bishops in the Lords, who formed the only solid opposition to the passage of the act of uniformity, found themselves on slippery ground.

Having accepted the right of parliament to abolish the pope, and virtually to abolish purgatory, they had great difficulty in finding a principle upon which to deny its right to touch the mass. Ultimately they all fell back upon the distinction between fundamentals and 'things indifferent', and most of them were imprisoned or deprived for refusing obedience to the law.[23] Such a distinction was far too subjective to provide the basis for a theory of legislation, and Edward's parliaments went on, without any further opposition of principle, to carry out more drastic modifications in the doctrine and usages of the church. By the end of Edward's reign, inevitably, the supremacy was much less personal, and much more a normal function of the monarch's public authority than it had been at the time of Henry's death. In theory it was still possible to challenge a statute on the grounds that it transgressed some fundamental or divine law, but in practice such a possibility had become unreal.[24] By 1553 only someone as detached from English events as Reginald Pole could seriously maintain that it was the queen's duty to ignore as invalid all those acts of parliament which had affected the affairs of the church since 1532. Only those who believed that parliament had consistently followed the precepts of God's law in emancipating the realm from popery, on the other hand, could still believe that the traditional authority of such law had survived intact. In the 1530s Christopher St German had been able to juggle with his terminology in such a way as to support the royal supremacy while still claiming that if parliament erred in spiritual matters 'there was no man bounden to obey the parliament in that behalf'.[25] After 1553 some protestants took up this position, identifying the divine law with the scriptures, but by that time there was no substantial body of lay opinion, inside parliament or outside it, which denied the authority of statute law to regulate the affairs of the church. The reality of this situation was tacitly acknowledged by Mary herself in August 1553 when she was discussing religious affairs with Gian Francesco Commendone. It would be necessary, she admitted, 'to repeal and annul by Act of Parliament many perverse laws made by those who ruled before her'.[26]

As well as being a change of major importance in itself, the royal supremacy had brought in its wake a variety of other changes. Of these the most far-reaching affected the property of the church. The extensive secularization of ecclesiastical lands which occurred between 1536 and 1553 was probably the most revolutionary upheaval in the pattern of landholding to take place in England between the Norman conquest and the industrial revolution. Perhaps as much as a fifth of the usable acreage of the country changed hands at least once, and most of it more than once during these years. Thomas Cromwell's original intention seems to have been to carry out a drastic pruning of religious houses, probably by direct application of the supremacy rather than by statute.[27] After a brief period of uncertainty, however, two statutes, one in 1536 and the other in 1539, swept away the religious houses altogether, and transferred their landed estates, worth more than £150,000 a year, to the crown. Five new bishoprics, a number of secular cathedrals, and two lavishly endowed colleges, one in Oxford and the other in Cambridge, indicated that the reforming intention had not been lost sight of;[28] but to the audible disgust of the more determined reformers the demands of the royal treasury came first. Almost immediately these great new crown estates began to be sold. Perhaps this dispersion was the understood price for parliamentary co-operation; perhaps it was a deliberate attempt to create a vested interest in the royal supremacy; or perhaps it was undertaken reluctantly under the pressure of circumstances. The precise reasons for the policy remain uncertain, but its effects are clear and striking. Between 1539 and 1553 the bulk of this land passed by sale and grant into the hands of the existing nobility and gentry, and of that which remained in the hands of the crown the major part was leased to members of the same social groups.[29] The mechanics of distribution still require further investigation, because the common use of agents and middlemen in the negotiation of purchases has given rise to considerable misunderstanding. The great majority of the grantees or their agents paid the full market price of twenty years' purchase, and much land was alienated under licence, that is resold, soon after the initial grant.[30] Although small estates frequently ended up in the hands of yeomen or burgesses, the principal beneficiaries were the gentry and aristocracy. No social revolution resulted from the dissolution of the monasteries, but there was a marked increase in the number of armigerous families in most counties over the next twenty or thirty years, and a broadening and flattening of the pyramid of aristocratic wealth.[31] The financial gain to the crown was for the most part ephemeral, while that to the gentry and nobility was lasting, resulting well before the end of the century in a significant shift in the balance of political power.

A further consequence of this transfer of property was that large numbers of impropriated benefices also passed into the king's possession. Some of these 'spiritual revenues' were used by both Henry and Edward to extract valuable estates from the bishops by way of compulsory exchange, but most were sold along with the estates to which they naturally appertained. As a result there was a sharp increase in the proportion of livings under the patronage of laymen, including the king.[32] When we add to this the innumerable small properties acquired as a result of the dissolution of the chantries in 1547 and subsequently leased or sold, and the profits of first fruits and tenths accruing to the crown (about £25,000 a year), the extent of the vested interest becomes apparent. The whole of this enormous redistribution of wealth depended for its legal validity upon a small number of statutes which stood or fell with the royal supremacy. Whether by accident or design most of this property passed rapidly through the normal real-estate market, with the result that its possession passed under the jurisdiction of the common law and its possessors could legitimately argue that they had acquired a proper legal title. With these changes a whole facet of the religious life of the country disappeared.[33] There was no shortage of protest and complaint, but active resistance was scattered and isolated apart from its ambiguous role in the Pilgrimage of Grace. There were a number of reasons for this. Many of the gentry who might have led such resistance quickly became beneficiaries of the process. Monks who might have fought for their livelihood were decently, and sometimes generously, pensioned, a wise policy which initially cost the crown upwards of £30,000 a year.[34] Nor were the regular clergy uniformly popular, and in some places such as Tynemouth and Bury St Edmunds the local townsmen anticipated the king's commissioners with violent attacks upon their local priories. More typical was the cynical worldliness of the religious conservative who took his share, and justified himself with the remark 'I saw that all would away, and so did as other men did'. Significantly the dissolution of the chantries, which must have been far more hurtful to the traditional small pieties of ordinary people, passed almost without protest from the laity although there is every sign that such pieties were flourishing right down to the end.[35] By 1547 the economic and political power of the medieval church had been decimated. Twenty-nine mitred abbots had disappeared from the House of Lords, leaving their 26 episcopal brethren in a hopeless minority. Lands worth upwards of £800,000 had passed from the church to the laity, and more remained in the hands of the crown. For better or worse England was a very much more secular country than it had been twenty years before, and the meaning of law had changed. In November 1538 the abbot of St John's, Colchester, had declared: 'the king shall never have my house but against my will and against my heart, for I know by my learning that he cannot take it by right and law'.[36] Ten years previously he would have been right, but by the time he spoke his learning was obsolete.

Reform was not a conspicuous feature of these particular

changes, although it could be argued that the drastic reduction of mortmain was an essential step towards the creation of a prosperous land market. Certainly an immense amount of capital was invested, with incalculable economic consequences,[37] but there is no evidence that this was the result of a planned policy. At the same time the royal supremacy did result in reforms which were deliberately planned. Perhaps the most significant in the long run was the requirement in the royal injunctions of 1538 that every parish should possess an English bible, and should allow readers free access to it. Encouragement of preaching and catechizing, and the deliberate curtailment of pilgrimages and other traditional practices as 'superstition and hypocrisy', were moves in the same direction; towards an informed and self-conscious Christian community. Specific requirements were also laid upon the clergy for the support of the poor and of education; 'a fortieth part of the fruits and revenues of their said benefices' in the first case, and a 'competent exhibition to one scholar' for every £100 of income in the latter.[38] Traditional discipline in such matters as clerical dress and behaviour, the control of pluralities, and the payment of tithes was reinforced by the weight of the king's authority. The use of images and invocation to the saints were discouraged, and the keeping of parish registers initiated. Although it is not entirely clear what he believed, Thomas Cromwell was immensely serious about religious reform, and his programme shows many signs of protestant influence.[39] Without the foundations which he laid the legislated reformation of the following reign would have been impossible in every sense. Cromwell's fall was part and parcel of a reaction which halted the advance of the 'new learning' for about five years, but did little to recover the ground which the conservatives had already lost. Conservative ecclesiastics such as Gardiner and Stokesley had become thoroughly alarmed by the rapid spread of heterodox ideas under the patronage and protection of the reformers, and seem to have succeeded in persuading the king that if provocative innovations in religion were not checked, the security of the realm would be imperilled and the royal supremacy itself brought into disrepute.[40] Recent research on the city of London and on Essex has shown that such fears were not without foundation. Reforming preachers such as Latimer, Hilsey, and Barnes had stirred up furious controversy, particularly by attacking the doctrine of purgatory, and in response conservative clerics were denouncing the king and his ministers for permitting such 'knaves' to call the traditional verities in question.[41] Acting in alliance with Cromwell's secular enemies, such as the duke of Norfolk, Gardiner pressed home his advantage with the king by insinuating the idea that the lord privy seal was a 'sacramentary' – that is a Zwinglian. Henry had an irrational horror of this radical protestant doctrine, which was almost as objectionable to Luther as it was to the catholics, and although there is no evidence that Cromwell ever held it, the suspicion played an important part in his downfall.

Briefly the ecclesiastical pendulum swung back. The act of six articles and the *King's Book* were markedly more conservative than the earlier formularies. Several reformers resigned their offices; 'advanced' preachers lost their licences, and some were imprisoned; attempts were made to restrict access to the English bible. On the other hand, all attempts to dislodge or discredit Cranmer failed; the English bible was never actually withdrawn; and the revived persecution of heresy was shortlived and fitful. Although it did something to discourage the provocations of the 'new sort' and dampen the fires of controversy, the reaction was only partially successful even at its height, and with the advent of Catherine Parr and the rise to favour of Edward Seymour it fizzled out altogether. Just how 'protestant' most of the reformers were in the 1530s and 1540s will probably remain a matter of debate. Those who were radically and unequivocally so, such as Tyndale and Hooper, sought refuge abroad. Nevertheless, the reform movement which Cromwell protected and patronized, and which he associated so intimately with the royal supremacy, was all of a piece with the official protestantism of the following reign, showing extensive continuity both of ideas and personnel. It was a movement of genuine and constructive idealism, although its adherents were relatively few, but its tendency to proceed by methods of demolition and corrosive criticism caused this fact to be consistently ignored by the majority who opposed it. Observers such as Bucer noticed that protestant legislation had far outrun the government's capacity for effective enforcement, let alone the limits of willing acceptance.[42] By the reformers' own standards they failed. They failed to bring about a great spiritual regeneration, failed to impose protestant discipline, and failed to protect the revenues of the church from further drastic encroachments. For this last failure the more radical elements were partly at least to blame. Rejoicing to see the downfall of 'superstitious toys' such as chantries, and willing to see the bishops 'unlorded' in the interests of their pastoral zeal, they abetted a further round of secularization.

There was no really substantial transfer of assets from the purposes of the old church to those of the new. Very little was done to endow sermons or lectures, and virtually nothing to make the innumerable poverty-stricken benefices up and down the country more attractive to the learned ministry which the preaching of the word required. In spite of this, however, there was far more positive achievement during these years than the conservatives would ever admit. Although student numbers certainly declined, the universities were far from being the wastelands that hostile propaganda bewailed. Vigorous debate and discussion went on in both Oxford and Cambridge as the reformers dug themselves in to certain colleges, particularly Christ Church and St John's, and the influence of Peter Martyr and Martin Bucer long outlived their brief sojourn.[43] The printing presses disgorged, along with a lot of polemic, primers and manuals of reformed piety. Above all, particularly among the younger generation, a genuine and informed protestant spirituality began to spread, with its own vision of God and his purposes; a vision which transcended ecclesiastical politics and wranglings over church property. The acts of uniformity could be repealed, and the traditional canon law reimposed, but changes of this sort could not simply be unmade or ignored. Wherever the reformed ideas had spread, they had aroused fierce contention; passionate assertion and equally passionate denial. In the universities, in the Inns of Court, in markets and taverns the debates had raged, in spite of the efforts of the authorities, conservative and reformed alike, to quieten the dissensions. Whichever course it eventually settled to, the English church could never pretend that these boisterous, bitter, and invigorating quarrels had never taken place.

The vision of the king as the spiritual father and leader of his people – a 'Godly Prince' – which had inspired Cranmer and infused some genuine religious content into the stark politics of the royal supremacy, had also manifested itself in other ways. There was nothing new in the idea that the king was in a general way responsible for the common weal. The administration of justice and the enforcement of public order had always been among his principal concerns. However, the extensive and systematic programme of legislation which elaborated this responsibility in the reformation parliament was altogether unprecedented.[44] Enclosure, urban decay, the wool trade, encouragement of shipping, the repair of highways, and the relief of poverty were all made the subjects of carefully drafted official bills. Most, but by no means all, of these became acts, and were supported and extended by a considerable number of proclamations. Characteristic of the preambles of these enactments is the statement which introduced a proclamation of February 1539 on the rights of alien merchants: 'Forasmuch as it is the office and duty of chief rulers and governors of all civil commonalities to study, devise and practise by sundry ways and means to advance, set forth and increase their commonwealths committed to their cures and charges . . .'[45] It was a decade of earnest endeavour, and of serious and protracted debate on the subject of the common weal, when thinkers such as Starkey and Morison were urging upon the king and his servants a conception of his responsibilities at once more detailed and more extensive than that which had been familiar to previous generations. It has become customary to refer to these writers as 'the commonwealth men', and to imply that they constituted an organized lobby or pressure-group,[46] but the evidence suggests that they worked as individuals, and differed considerably in the details of the policies which they advocated. Some of them certainly began work under Cromwell's patronage, but they long outlasted him and should not be seen primarily as propagandists for his reforming legislation. After Cromwell's fall the thrust and energy went out of the practical programme of reform, but the extended view of the royal authority which it had embodied did not fade, nor did the king's awareness of the unique position of parliament. It was in 1542, according to Holinshed, that Henry declared '. . . we at no time stand so high in our estate royal as in the time of parliament, wherein we as head and you as members are conjoined and knit together in one body politic. . . .'[47]

The substance of this 'commonwealth' policy was not innovatory. In some respects it was, as A. B. Ferguson expressed it, 'a profoundly conservative ideal', aiming to preserve the existing social hierarchy, and that sense of paternal responsibility which was thought to have been one of the ancient virtues of aristocracy.[48] Its radicalism lay mainly in its conception of the action which could be taken to bring about such a desirable consummation. The same was true of other aspects of Cromwell's programme, 'In his hands', as G. R. Elton has recently observed, 'sumptuary legislation ceased to be the means for saving fools from extravagance and became an instrument of social control'.[49] The notorious statute of uses can also be seen in this light. Not only was this unpopular measure designed to prevent the aristocracy from cheating the king of his feudal perquisites, it was also intended to enforce strict entails, thereby hopefully reducing social mobility and stabilizing the existing gentry and peerage families. Such an intention could hardly be described as revolutionary, yet insofar as it involved an intrusion of statutory legislation into an area of customary and feudal law it was certainly radical.[50] As such it was resolutely resisted in application, and drastically modified by the subsequent statute of wills. This sequence of events is significant, because it was never claimed that parliament had no right to interfere with the laws of inheritance. The objectors were concerned about their own material interests, not about legal principles. The Pilgrims of 1536 also made this statute a regional grievance, albeit a minor one, claiming that the north was under-represented in the House of Commons (which was true) and that consequently local circumstances had not been taken into account.[51]

The Pilgrimage was a complex movement, interpretations of which have changed significantly in the light of recent scholarship, but there has never been any doubt that one of its features was the resentment of the northern aristocracy against government and infiltration from London.[52] Such centralizing tendencies were not an accidental consequence of Cromwell's other policies, but a deliberate and integral part of the reform programme. Wolsey had had similar ideas in the 1520s. The rise in the numbers and importance of the king's fee'd men in the northern marches; persistent attempts to diminish the authority and independence of the Percies; and the reconstitution of the councils in the north and in the marches of Wales bear witness to this.[53] In 1525, as we have already seen, the nine-year-old Princess Mary was sent with a council to rule the marches from Ludlow; and in the same year the six-year-old duke of Richmond was sent to York with a similar establishment. This latter attempt at extended conciliar rule did not prove particularly effective, but it contributed to the general irritation of the northern lords. Ironically it was the Pilgrimage itself, or rather its failure, which opened the way for real advances in royal control of the north. The power of the Percies was virtually destroyed, and new men such as Sir Thomas Wharton rose to prominence by the king's patronage. The council was reorganized and strengthened, and Henry was able to boast, with only a modicum of exaggeration, '. . . we will not be bound of a necessity to be served with lords. But we will be served with such men of what degree soever as we shall appoint to the same . . .'[54] That he continued, on the whole, to choose local men was common prudence, and corresponded with normal practice elsewhere in the country. Wales presented no such explosive problems, but rather a running sore of lawlessness which called for something more drastic than a reinforced council. This was provided in 1536 by two major statutes abolishing the marcher franchises, and reducing the whole of Wales to 'shire ground' – that is establishing government on the English pattern by sheriffs and justices of the peace.[55] The former act, which also abolished other surviving franchises such as the palatinate of Durham, was one of the major legislative achievements of the period. It was recognized that liberties and franchises had, in the first instance, been granted by the king; but the only acknowledged method of terminating them was by absorption through inheritance, as had happened with the earldom of Chester. There were admittedly minor precedents for the curtailment of liberties by statute, in the cases of Tynedale and Redesdale, dating from the reign of Henry VII. However, the act of 1536 must be counted as one of the boldest and most original measures to emerge from the reform programme. After it came into force, the king's writ ran uniformly throughout the realm as it had never done before. At the same time the counties and boroughs of Wales (but not County Durham) were granted parliamentary representation.[56]

In the Lordship of Ireland Cromwell's London-centred policies were less successful. Coming into a situation which had been largely created by the king's unwillingness to spend money, he endeavoured to create both a more effective means of enforcing royal authority in secular matters and a church amenable to the royal supremacy. To achieve these aims he established links with an energetic group of Anglo-Irish lawyers in the Pale, who had long been agitating for a reform of government.[57] However, success would depend upon his ability to reduce the autonomy of the great Anglo-Irish earldoms of Kildare, Ormond, and Desmond, and to achieve a *modus vivendi* with the native Irish. As soon as the drift of his intentions became clear, the FitzGeralds, the clan of the earl of Kildare, rose in rebellion led by the earl's son 'silken Thomas'. This rising took nearly a year to suppress, and the virtual destruction of the Fitz-Geralds which followed did little to strengthen the hold of the English government. It soon became apparent that the reformers of the Pale had different ideas of royal government from those of Cromwell's servants. They were quite willing to co-operate in the enforcement of the royal supremacy, but they had no intention of surrendering control of the 'obedient lands' to administrators or soldiers from England. Consequently although the Irish parliament of 1536 dutifully abolished papal authority and dissolved the religious houses, the Anglo-Irish remained determined to keep the benefits of these changes in their own hands. Lord Leonard Grey, appointed in 1535, proved to be an abrasive and inept lord deputy, while Cromwell refused to allow his agents to be drawn into the vastly expensive plans for the conquest of the 'wild Irish' which were being cherished by the gentry of the Pale.[58] These plans would have involved large-scale military effort from England for the benefit of the Anglo-Irish, and were firmly vetoed. Consequently, although much was accomplished to bring the 'Englishry' into line with England, the authority of the crown remained more apparent than real. Even the adoption by Henry of the title of 'King of Ireland' in 1541 did more for the independence of the Anglo-Irish establishment than it did for the power of the king. Only when

Cromwell's preference for direct rule was drastically modified by Sir Anthony St Leger as lord deputy after 1541 was significant progress made. St Leger's vision of a united Ireland was statesmanlike, and he enjoyed remarkable success in his relations with the gaelic chieftains. These had been so alienated by Lord Grey that they had launched the fierce attacks of the gaelic league in 1540; but by the following year some of them were sitting for the first time in the Irish parliament.[59] Eventually St Leger also failed, partly because his policies were too expensive for the taste of the English government, and partly because the protestantism which the council of Edward VI strove to impose upon the country was regarded as an alien intrusion. The Anglo-Irish had adopted the royal supremacy as their own, but the prayer book became another symbol of English pretensions and interference.

In Ireland, Cromwell's reforms failed to create, or to adapt sufficiently, instruments of government which were amenable to the royal will. This was partly because of the entrenched position of the aristocracy of the Pale, partly because of the inaccessibility of the country, and partly because he had too many more urgent tasks elsewhere. In England the executive and judicial machinery was swiftly and thoroughly overhauled. This aspect of Cromwell's work has become thoroughly familiar through the extensive researches of Professor Elton, and its details do not need to be reiterated.[60] At the highest level the composition and procedures of the king's council were clarified. The conciliar courts of star chamber and requests already enjoyed a distinct existence, but in its advisory and administrative capacities the council which Wolsey bequeathed in 1529 was amorphous. This was partly because of the highly personal nature of Wolsey's authority and his distaste for bureaucracy, and partly because of the vagaries of royal favour. What emerged before 1540, and probably by 1536, was a more limited and clearly defined group of about twenty to which was applied the title 'Privy Council' – a term hitherto used loosely to describe those councillors who happened to be highest in the king's confidence at any given moment.[61] This privy council met regularly and frequently all the year round, and after 1540 kept systematic records of its routine business. 'Councillors at large' did not disappear, but they became few and uncertain in their functions, dwindling to the status of assistant councillors who could be called upon for specific services, but who did not attend meetings. No fresh 'councillors at large' were sworn until Sir Thomas Pope in August 1553, but since the council oath was indelible, a dwindling number of earlier councillors must have existed outside the privy council. The privy council proper consisted, as the king's council had always done, of a mixture of magnates, courtiers, lawyers, and clerics. It acquired, however, a more 'professional' atmosphere in the sense that virtually every privy councillor was now an office-holder – that is a working politician or administrator in the royal service. One of the consequences of this reorganization was that the privy council held something much closer to a monopoly of the function of advising the monarch than had belonged to any similarly identifiable group in the past. Nevertheless, the significance of these changes should not be over-stressed. The privy council was not a cabinet. It had no constitutional or collective responsibility. Although it made, and enforced, routine decisions in its corporate capacity, its authority was the authority of the crown, and its members first and foremost individual councillors of the king. As long as Cromwell remained in office he managed the business of the privy council, using it primarily as an omnicompetent instrument of enforcement, transmitting orders from the king or the king-in-parliament to local justices and other officials. After his fall it retained this function, and the institutional features which he had developed, although its management passed into the hands of men who lacked his constructive talents. After Henry's death, and the end of his brief attempt to govern through a council of executors, Cromwell's work was progressively undone. Protector Somerset, while ostensibly preserving the integrity of a small, effective privy council, in reality paid progressively less attention to it, reserving important decisions to himself rather as Wolsey had done.[62] It was this emasculation of the privy council, rather than opposition to his social policies, which caused the majority of the councillors to support the earls of Warwick and Southampton in bringing about his overthrow in October 1549.

The much-maligned Warwick in fact returned to effective conciliar government early in 1550. However, as a result of this move he found it necessary to alter the composition of the council considerably, removing by one means or another conservative opponents such as Wriothesley, Tunstall, and Arundel, and replacing them with his own friends and supporters.[63] By 1553 there were over 30 privy councillors, several of whom held no significant offices, and the number of commissions and *ad hoc* committees being set up to handle different aspects of the council's work was multiplying. Although it had retained the formal definition and procedures of Cromwell's reforms, in substance the council had moved back towards the large, differentiated body of earlier years, with only a minority of councillors in frequent or regular attendance, and large variations in the status and effectiveness of members. Owing to the special circumstances of the minority, it is hard to compare the privy council of 1553 with that which Cromwell left in 1540, but at least some of the features introduced by his reforms had disappeared, leaving it less coherent and manageable than he had intended, in fact less of an institution.

Cromwell was a great believer in institutions, and nowhere was this more clear than in his management of the crown's resources which had, since the time of Edward IV, been mainly in the hands of household officials supervised (if at all) directly by the king. Not wishing to return to the moribund 'ancient course' of the exchequer, and faced with the diversity of new revenues acquired in the wake of the supremacy, he initiated the creation of a whole crop of new financial courts. General surveyors and wards and liveries were institutions which continued functions already existing, administering crown lands and the fiscal prerogative. Augmentations and first fruits and tenths were created to handle the new revenues. All were modelled on the duchy of Lancaster, with its defined jurisdiction, bureaucratic organization, and modern accounting methods.[64] Each of these courts functioned efficiently, but the need for so many was questioned almost from the first, and it may well be that the reason for such a proliferation was political rather than administrative. One new revenue court would have become immensely powerful, especially in view of the weakness of the exchequer, and Cromwell possibly felt that such a strong institution might have slipped from his control. As it was, he continued to manage the patronage of all the courts until his fall, and to use their officials as one means of keeping himself informed about the affairs of the country. After his death considerations of economy began to be more loudly urged, and in 1547 the court of general surveyors (which had in any case a diminishing responsibility) was absorbed by augmentations.[65] In addition to its fiscal functions each of these courts played its part in increasing the effectiveness of royal government. Most noticeably was this true of wards and liveries which gave the king an excellent machinery, strictly within the bounds of law and custom, to exert maximum control over the aristocracy by a judicious choice of guardians and marriage partners.[66]

The development of all these institutions, including the parliament itself, has to be seen in terms of improved methods of control. This was the unifying factor behind all Cromwell's administrative reforms, and the main reason why he has been represented as the servant, or architect, of 'Tudor despotism'. The debate over the exact nature of Cromwell's intentions, and the extent of his influence over the king, will probably never be concluded, but in the light of the evidence which has recently been presented for his religious and social idealism it is no longer possible to claim that he saw the increase of royal power simply as an end in itself. Some vision of an orderly and Godly society under a rule of law informed his actions, and it was a vision of the 'new learning', not the old. Some of his friends and correspondents were as critical of the traditional common law as they were of the church. Thomas Starkey and Richard Morison both urged drastic simplification, claiming that complexity and incomprehensibility were the parents of injustice.[67] Starkey, indeed, preferred the civil law, but some of Morison's ideas foreshadowed the Leveller pamphleteers of the following century. John Rastell, who had a common-law training, suggested a number of specific reforms to be the subjects of legislation: 'the reformation of pleading', the procedure of chancery, and the reduction of excessive fees.[68] Several utopian schemes of unknown provenance survive, one of the best known being that for a court of 'Conservators of the Common Weal', significantly also cast in the form of a draft bill. Cromwell's actual achievements as a law reformer were substantial. Apart from the immense implications of the royal supremacy for ecclesiastical jurisdiction in general, he dealt effectively with the ancient vexation of sanctuary. Probably the act of 32 Henry VIII, c. 12 was intended to abolish sanctuaries altogether; as it ultimately emerged, it abolished existing refuges and set up eight others in named towns, thus converting an ecclesiastical privilege into a secular and statutory provision.[69] The new financial courts, as we have seen, also had jurisdictional aspects, and were partly designed to speed up the administration of the law in fiscal cases. The statutes of uses and of wills, although in some respects contradictory, nevertheless between them revolutionized the law of real property. The statute of enrolments of 1536 improved the security of transactions by bargain and sale. A considerable number of reforming bills which were probably of official provenance failed in 1539 and 1540, but several important measures also relating to real property passed, as Sir Thomas Audley continued the initiative which Cromwell had begun.[70]

Ironically, Cromwell died, not by the common law, but by act of attainder. He had used the device himself, but not extensively,[71] and it could be argued that his greatest service to the common law was the extent to which he insisted upon its use. In this the king's conscience and the minister's principles seem to have coincided. During the tense and dangerous years between 1533 and 1540, when royal policy faced very widespread opposition of unknown political strength and determination, the law of treason had been expanded and elaborated several times. It became treason to (maliciously) deny the royal supremacy, to challenge the succession to the crown laid down by statute, to call the king 'in express writing or words . . . a heretic, schismatic, tyrant, infidel or usurper of the crown', or to forge his seals.[72] But these new laws were consistently enforced through the traditional procedures; presentment or indictment by the grand jury of the appropriate shire, trial by petty jury, also from the appropriate shire, and conviction or acquittal. The only significant modification was made by a statute of 1541 which permitted trial by commission of oyer and terminer outside the shire in which the offence had been committed.[73] By modern standards those subjected to this process were unjustly used, in that they were allowed no counsel and no opportunity to prepare a defence, but such deprivation was customary. Reliance upon one witness, made notorious by the case of More, was also the traditional practice, although it was very seldom that such exiguous evidence was used. In the case of Giles Heron in 1539 Cromwell preferred an act of attainder to the testimony of a single witness.[74] As in his dealings with parliament, so in his use of the law of treason, Cromwell resorted to pressure and manipulation, but never to gross abuse. Considering the danger in which the government believed itself to stand, this scrupulosity was remarkable. Out of about 500 people known to have been tried for treason during the eight years from 1532 to 1540, over 30 were acquitted and about a hundred subsequently pardoned.[75] All these trials were conducted either in the court of king's bench or through the well-tried device of a commission of oyer and terminer. Efforts were made to empanel compliant juries, but they did not always succeed, particularly against strong local influences, and juries do not seem to have suffered for returning unsatisfactory verdicts. No special courts were created, no new forms of action were invented, and no attempt was made to extend the jurisdiction of the conciliar court of star chamber.

Only a minority of those 'detected' for treasonable offences ever came to trial, and the care which was taken to investigate the truth of accusations is even more impressive than the legal correctness of the trials. There were genuine divisions of opinion about the king's proceedings at every social level, there was private malice and unscrupulous opportunism. As a result accusations, particularly of treasonable speaking, flew thick and fast.[76] Typically, denunciations came not from officials but from private citizens, motivated by everything from greed to a sense of duty. Once received, these would be investigated by the local magistrates, and if a *prima facie* case was established, the offender would probably be imprisoned and the privy council informed. A further examination was then ordered, either locally or, if the matter seemed serious, by bringing the accused person to London. Occasionally suspects might spend weeks or even months in prison without being formally charged, but in the great majority of cases which can be traced, trial or release followed swiftly. The meticulous attention to detail which characterized all these proceedings was the hallmark of Cromwell's administration. He was a man with an immense capacity for work, and a compulsive collector of information.[77] Knowledge was power, and Cromwell owed much of his unique influence to his capacity for keeping his hands on a wide variety of negotiations simultaneously. It was to facilitate this task that he developed the office of principal secretary, and turned it into a central clearing-house for business and information of all kinds. In this position he did not need a professional secret service. All those with favours to ask applied to him automatically as the controller of the king's patronage, as they had earlier applied to Wolsey. Bureaucratic as it was in some ways, Cromwell's system of government depended for its drive and effectiveness upon his own energy and talent. When he was gone, the privy council gradually lost its new-found coherence, although it remained in many respects different from the council which he had found. The office of principal secretary was divided and lost its powerful co-ordinating and controlling role, while remaining a developed office in a sense which it had not been before 1530.[78] Ironically, Cromwell's real legacy lay less in the institutions which he had created than in the attitudes of mind which he had fostered during his brief ascendancy. He knew, perhaps better than any other statesman of the century, how to create and mobilize the support which was needed to make royal government effective and political innovations acceptable.

He mounted a propaganda campaign of unprecedented intensity and skill, using both the traditional medium of the pulpit and the new power of the press.[79] He dramatically increased the work and responsibilities of the justices of the peace, building up the prestige of that office by multiplying its contacts with the central government and thus increasing access to the crown's patronage.[80] As a result, what was essentially an onerous and unpaid post became increasingly sought after, and by 1547 the council was expressing concern at the rapid expansion of the commissions of the peace. By that time the commission was already becoming the key institution in local politics, and the threat of removal or demotion a genuine sanction.[81] In seeking to make loyalty and service the keys to favour in place of existing status or blood relationships Cromwell was fighting an uphill battle against some of the strongest conventions of the age, and he was only partially successful. However, he did succeed in giving a pragmatic and constructive twist to royal patronage by building up wherever possible the strength of reforming interests both at court and in the localities. One of the results of this was that the reaction which swept him away was neither permanent nor complete. By the time of his fall, support for reforming policies and the royal supremacy was firmly entrenched among the noble and gentry families who ruled the English counties. Consequently such policies could no longer be regarded as a temporary aberration; they had become an established part of the political pattern.

In one important respect, however, Cromwell failed. He did not remedy the inadequacies of the king's revenues. As we have seen, the monastic wealth, which was very great, came and went for the most part as current income and expenditure. Whatever the original intention, there was no massive increase of capital wealth. Failing such an endowment, what the crown needed was a new or greatly enhanced source of ordinary revenue, and in 1534 a step was taken in that direction by requesting and obtaining a parliamentary subsidy without recourse to the normal pretexts of war or emergency. The preamble to the subsidy act of that year justified the grant by referring to the benefits conferred upon the realm by the king's excellent and pacific government.[82] This was a device of great potential significance, heralding the arrival of peacetime taxation. But the precedent was never fully exploited. Other peacetime grants were made subsequently, but the notion of parliamentary taxation as a regular and ordinary source of revenue was not to be accepted for a very long time. Whether Cromwell ever intended to negotiate such a far-reaching scheme with the parliament we do not know. If he did, it failed to get beyond the first stage.[83]

Henry's financial problems were never solved, and the ruinously expensive wars which were fought between 1540 and 1545 as the king strove to recover his energetic youth, left an indebtedness of £100,000 in Flanders alone. In 1544 the coinage was debased, a process which was repeated in each of the two succeeding years and at intervals down to 1551.[84] Henry took a profit of £363,000 from the mint in the last three years of his life, and Edward's minority governments a further £540,000 between 1547 and 1551.[85] As a result, the exchange value of the pound sterling collapsed from about 26s. Flemish in the early 1540s to 13s. Flemish in the spring of 1552. Prices and interest rates shot up, social and economic discontents were sharply exacerbated, and the crown sank further into debt. Somerset's stubborn pursuit of the French and Scottish wars was the main cause of this disastrous situation.[86] Attempts to finance his policy by introducing a new indirect tax on sheep, hopefully calculated to yield £156,000 a year, failed. The actual return proved less than the expectation and the relevant act (unpopular because of its association with Somerset's agrarian policy) was repealed after his fall. Normal parliamentary taxation, yielding about £180,000 in the first two years of the reign, was quite inadequate, and resort to the profits of the mint was the result. Northumberland faced up to the resultant problems only gradually. Henri II of France had taken advantage of the confused situation in England in the summer of 1549 to launch another attack upon Boulogne, and it was March 1550 before peace could be concluded on that front. Realistically, Boulogne was sold back to the French, who had failed to take it. Peace with Scotland came at the same time, although Mary Stuart did not ratify it until the following month, again at the cost of an almost total surrender of the English position. These important if unheroic retrenchments were accompanied, however, by a marked increase of domestic grants and annuities designed to strengthen Northumberland's own position. It was not until after a final round of debasement in 1551 that a serious attempt was made to get to grips with the crown's financial plight. By that time the accumulated debt was over £220,000.[87]

The decade which followed Cromwell's fall was characterized by war, chronic financial difficulties, and persistent political dissension. The wars were Henry's own doing, and did not in any sense spring from the adventurous policies of the preceding period. Charles V had been deeply offended by the king's behaviour, and had allowed his agents to intrigue persistently against him, but his intervention in English affairs never went beyond diplomatic bluster. Henry's foreign policy after 1540 was highly personal, and can be described as a mixture of nostalgia and paranoia.[88] Since the financial problems were directly caused by the war, they were only related to the earlier crisis in the indirect sense that Cromwell's reforms failed to provide against them in advance. On the other hand, the political dissensions resulted directly from the reforming initiatives of the 1530s and the reactions to them. In 1533 Cromwell had allied with the Boleyns and the Howards to overcome Catherine's friends. In 1536 he had allied with the Howards and the Seymours to destroy Anne Boleyn, while four years later the Howards had allied with Gardiner and other conservative churchmen to overthrow him in his turn. Cromwell's immense clientage scattered after his death. Several of his more substantial followers, such as Paget, Paulet, and Sadler, who were professional civil servants, remained in office.[89] Others allied themselves with the Seymours, who remained in favour thanks to the military talents of Edward Seymour, or later with the Parrs. In the early 1530s the basic division had been between those who actively supported the king's proceedings and those who accepted them reluctantly and hoped that he would change his mind. Those who actively opposed him – Catherine, Mary, More, Fisher – scarcely constituted a party in spite of the level of popular sympathy which they commanded. Later in the decade a more clear-cut antagonism developed between those who accepted the royal supremacy but would not willingly go further, such as Norfolk, Derby, Gardiner, and Tunstall, and those who supported the moves which Cromwell was continuing to initiate: Audley, Arundel, Hertford, Cranmer. To fall outside the limits of these categories was a perilous matter, as Exeter, Montague, Aske, Bigod, and Robert Barnes all discovered in different ways.[90] Between 1540 and 1547 the fortunes of the two main factions fluctuated. Until 1543 Gardiner and Norfolk dominated the council, but the indiscretions of the latter's niece, Henry's fifth queen, weakened his position, and by the autumn of that year the reformers were again gathering strength. From 1543 to 1546 the balance gradually tilted in their direction, thanks partly to Queen Catherine Parr and the sympathetic influence of Sir Anthony Denny at court, and partly to rising soldiers such as Sir John Dudley, Viscount Lisle. In the summer of 1546, with the king obviously ailing, the conservatives, who had never conceded defeat in the council although outweighted at court, seemed poised to recover the initiative. However, by August the reformers had overcome the challenge represented by the execution of Anne Askew, and were firmly in control of access to the king. Finally in the last weeks of the year the king turned fiercely on the Howards. Norfolk and his son, the earl of Surrey, were arrested on charges of treason for pretending a claim to the throne. In all probability they were the victims of a court conspiracy, as Cromwell had been, but the result was decisive. Surrey was executed, and Norfolk was in the Tower when the king died, an ineffectual onlooker at the dramatic events which were to ensue.

The executors nominated in Henry's will to act as his son's privy council were thus overwhelmingly of the reforming party.[91] With Gardiner excluded, the only conservative of real political weight to be named was Thomas Wriothesley, the lord chancellor. Wriothesley had earlier been a supporter of Cromwell, but had survived the latter's fall by adroitly changing sides. Others, such as Audley and Rich, had done the same, and then reverted to the reforming party, but Wriothesley stayed firm in his new allegiance. How genuinely the will published by Paget and Hertford represented the late king's wishes has always been a subject of controversy.[92] The reforming party made sure that they were close to Henry in the last hours of his life, and Cranmer was with him when he died. The ease with which Hertford was able to establish himself as protector, in violation of the will, certainly suggests careful planning and the reformers' control of the dry stamp in the last moments of the reign gave them the opportunity to make such last-minute alterations as suited their purposes. As soon as Henry was dead, there was a solemn distribution of new dignities, allegedly in accordance with Henry's wishes. Hertford became duke of Somerset, Wriothesley earl of Southampton, and Dudley earl of Warwick. Within a few weeks, however, Wriothesley had fallen. An intractable and opinionated man, his enthusiasm for the civil law caused him to commit a misdemeanour in delegating his authority in chancery to a commission of civil lawyers without the authority of a royal warrant.[93] For this he was deprived of his office and excluded from the council, having given his political opponents a weapon against him which they exploited with unscrupulous thoroughness. He was subsequently readmitted to the council, an act of generosity which the protector was to regret. For the next two years, as the reformers pressed cautiously ahead with their protestant programme and Somerset sought to realize his own concept of a Godly commonwealth, conservative opposition was fragmentary and unco-ordinated. Mary, Van der Delft, Gardiner, and some of the other bishops made their antagonism plain enough, but the royal supremacy had spreadeagled the conservative peerage and gentry. The failure of such powerful men as the earls of Derby and Shrewsbury to take any action against the spread of 'innovation' is a measure of the extent to which the Henrician reforms had been accepted by the aristocracy. The introduction of the prayer book caused widespread resentment, but the only movement of active resistance was a rebellion in Devon and Cornwall that was almost entirely confined to the lower orders.[94]

The duke of Somerset, however, had severe limitations as a statesman, and presumed upon his authority to an unwarrantable extent. His highhanded methods and obsessive pursuit of the war offended the aristocracy and had the effect of alienating most of his supporters on the council. As a result, the radical party split, the larger part, led by the earl of Warwick, making common cause with the conservatives, led by Southampton, to overthrow him. This took place in October 1549, and in the three-month power struggle which followed Warwick and his radical supporters emerged victorious. Although in the aftermath of this victory he managed to win back most of Somerset's erstwhile followers, Warwick's position was never really secure, hence his attempts to purchase allegiance which we have already noticed. Moreover, as he pressed on into a more radical and exposed religious position, his government became ever more obviously that of a faction. By the end of 1552, without any really striking successes to give his regime prestige, he was existing upon a precarious acquiescence which was maintained partly by fear of revolutionary disorders and partly by the known preferences of the young king.[95] Warwick had brought about his own elevation to the dukedom of Northumberland in October 1551 and had been generous with honours to his supporters. After a period of rehabilitation, Somerset had been destroyed in January 1552; Southampton had died in disgrace in 1550; and with Norfolk and Gardiner in the Tower, it is not, perhaps, surprising that no conservative challenger emerged from the ranks of the remaining peers. Northumberland had capitalized upon the successes of the reforming party going back to 1533, and neither his general unpopularity, nor the disgust of the conservatives for his religious policy, nor the thinly veiled hostility of the emperor seemed to offer any guarantee that his progress could be checked. His whole position, however, and that of his faction, depended upon the life of the king. Mary, the heir to the throne, had challenged her brother's governors only passively, but she had demonstrated clearly that her attitude had not changed since 1536. She remained a symbol and a cause of hope to all those who resented the persistent advance of radical policies, and by 1553 this category embraced a wide variety of different opinions from mildly conservative *politiques* like Paget and Arundel (both of whom had fallen foul of Northumberland) to strong reactionaries like Gardiner. When, in the early weeks of 1553, Edward fell seriously ill, Northumberland was consequently faced with a crisis. Fortunately for him the king, who was a staunch protestant, needed no urging to exclude his sister from the succession.[96] Probably in January 1553 he drew up an elaborate 'device' directing the succession, in the event of his own death without heirs, to the descendants of his aunt Mary by Charles Brandon, duke of Suffolk. Both his sisters he excluded on the grounds of their illegitimacy.[97]

This 'device' of course overturned his father's will; but the duke of Somerset had already set a precedent for doing that with impunity. More seriously it was by no means certain that Edward, who was still a minor, could himself make a valid will. Most seriously of all it ignored the succession act of 1544, which had empowered Henry to designate the crown by will, but not his son. Perhaps because of these weaknesses, and perhaps also because the king's health seemed to be recovering, the 'device' was not submitted to the parliament of March 1553, and its authority therefore remained untested. Soon after, but before the crisis had become imminent, Northumberland set out to strengthen his position by a series of carefully planned marriages: his son Guildford to Jane Grey, his daughter Catherine to Lord Hastings, and Jane's sister (another Catherine) to Lord Herbert, heir to the earl of Pembroke. Jane and Catherine Grey were the daughters of his ally the duke of Suffolk, and featured prominently in the succession laid down in the 'device'. However, if Northumberland was planning to 'capture' the crown for his own son, he moved both too blatantly and too late. There is no reason to suppose that at this stage he was planing any measures more desperate than he had already undertaken. Within a fortnight of these weddings being celebrated on 21 May he knew the king was dying and he had, at the most, three months to secure himself and the radical cause which he represented. The 'device' was hastily altered, perhaps by the duke, perhaps by the king himself, to exclude Frances Grey, the duchess of Suffolk, and cut out all reference to putative male heirs.[98] The effect of this tampering was to make Jane Grey herself the heir, and to convince everyone who knew what was afoot that Northumberland was setting himself up as a kingmaker. It was one thing to set up so eccentric a succession, however, and another to carry it out. As long as he lived, Edward did his best to commit his councillors, judges, and other leading subjects, such as the aldermen of London, to support the 'device'. Charged on their allegiance and bullied by the duke, almost all reluctantly complied, with the result that when Edward finally died on 6 July even such well-informed and unsympathetic observers as the Imperial ambassadors believed that Northumberland had won.[99] In reality he was skimming the surface of very thin ice. Without mercenary troops, he would stand or fall by the extent of the support or acquiescence he could command from the English aristocracy. Jane Grey represented, in a sense, the *reductio ad absurdum* of the radical cause; standing as she did for an unpopular protestantism and the pretensions of absolute power to overturn custom and law, her real support hardly extended beyond the families of Grey and Dudley. What might have happened had Northumberland succeeded in capturing Mary before the news of her brother's death was known, or had her nerve failed (as was not impossible), we cannot know. As it was, she retreated through friendly country to Kenninghall in Norfolk, and there, on 10 July, she proclaimed herself queen and wrote to the council in London demanding the allegiance of its members.[100] Over the next few days letters were sent out from Kenninghall commanding her loyal subjects to raise forces against John Dudley 'calling himself duke of Northumberland', and to join her in Norfolk.[101] The response to these summonses brought down the duke's house of cards without any further action on Mary's part. If Northumberland was the heir

63

of the tradition which Cromwell had initiated, as in a sense he was, then his overthrow might be thought to herald the overthrow of the whole reforming programme going back to 1533. To Mary, with her rigid and rather simple mind, this probably seemed to be the case. But the situation in fact lacked that kind of logic. The new queen had become the heir to all the hopes and aspirations that the rapidly narrowing radical party had shed under the pressures of Edward's minority, as well as to those of the conservatives and reactionaries whom she more truly represented. The rejoicings which accompanied her accession concealed a welter of incompatible expectations, and it remained to be seen how she would cope with the problems of disappointment.

Notes

1 W. Roper, 'The Life of Sir Thomas More', in *Two Early Tudor Lives*, ed. S. Sylvester and D. F. Harding (1962), 244-5.
2 1 Mary, st. 2 c. 1. 'An Acte declaring the Quenes Hyhnes to have bene borne in a most just and lawfull Matrimonie . . .'
3 For a full discussion of Cromwell's reform programme and its implementation see G. R. Elton, *Reform and Renewal* (1973). The same author explores Cromwell's religious motivation further in 'Thomas Cromwell Redivivus', *ARG*, 68 (1977), 192-208.
4 Roper, op. cit., 248. In 1506 a judicial decision had laid down explicitly that 'no temporal act can . . . make a temporal man have spiritual jurisdiction'; cited C. H. McIlwain, *The High Court of Parliament and its Supremacy* (1910), 277.
5 *The Life of Fisher* (1921), 68.
6 Wolsey's fall left his fellow bishops divided and in disarray, under the inadequate leadership of the aged Warham. Warham was a lifelong servant of the king, and his habits of obedience seem to have triumphed over his undoubted scruples in subscribing to the crucial 'Submission of the Clergy' in May 1532; A. G. Dickens, *The English Reformation* (1964), 155-6. A will to resist was not entirely lacking among the clergy themselves, see M. Kelly, 'The Submission of the Clergy', *TRHS*, 5th series, 15 (1965), 97-119.
7 S. E. Lehmberg, *The Reformation Parliament, 1529–1536* (1970), 13-30.
8 Andrew Windsor, Thomas Wentworth, Edmund Bray, John Hussey, and Henry Pole. Hussey and Pole subsequently opposed the king. ibid., 46-7.
9 ibid., 170.
10 ibid., 182-4.
11 ibid., 163-9. G. R. Elton, 'The Evolution of a Reformation Statute', *Studies in Tudor and Stuart Politics and Government*, II (1974), 82-105.
12 ibid., 105 n. 4.
13 For a discussion of Henry's personal convictions, see particularly J. J. Scarisbrick, *Henry VIII* (1968), 326-7. The extent of positive support for the king (outside the ranks of committed protestants) will probably remain controversial, but both Lehmberg (op. cit.) and Elton (*Policy and Police*) cite considerable evidence for it.

14 24 Henry VIII, c. 12. For brief discussions of the significance of this form of wording, see Elton, *The Tudor Constitution* (1960), 329-31, and D. M. Loades, *The Oxford Martyrs* (1970), 38-41.

15 G. L. Harris, 'A Revolution in Tudor History?', *Past and Present*, 25 (1963), 3-58, argues that Henry accomplished little more than had been achieved by the *praemunire* acts of the fourteenth century.

16 F. Le Van Baumer, *The Early Tudor Theory of Kingship* (1940), 120-91.

17 *The King's Book* asserted his right to remove unsatisfactory bishops, but Henry did not exercise such power. *OM*, 47-8.

18 J. A. Muller, *Stephen Gardiner and the Tudor Reaction* (1926), 101-10. Four statements of official orthodoxy were made between 1536 and 1543, which differed, but did not contradict each other.

19 Gardiner to Cranmer, 12 June 1547; J. A. Muller, *Letters of Stephen Gardiner* (1933), 299.

20 Mary to the council, 22 June 1549; Foxe, *Acts and Monuments*, VI, 7-8.

21 Gardiner's prolonged rearguard action, and subsequent trial and deprivation, are examined at length in Muller, *Stephen Gardiner*, 154-203.

22 Foxe, VI, 7-8.

23 Bonner (London), Gardiner (Winchester), Day (Chichester), Heath (Worcester), and Tunstall (Durham); the aged Voysey (Exeter) was induced to resign. W. H. Frere, *The Marian Reaction in its Relation to the English Clergy* (1896), Appendix I.

24 S. E. Thorne, 'Dr Bonham's Case (1609)', *Law Quarterly Review*, 54 (1938), 543 ff.

25 Christopher St German, *An Answer to a letter* (1535), sig. B vi; cited Elton, *Tudor Constitution*, 232 and n.

26 *Cal. Ven.*, V, 429.

27 'The History of the English Reformation' in D. M. Loades, *The Papers of George Wyatt*, Camden Society, 4th series, vol. 5 (1968), 159.

28 Trinity, Cambridge and Christchurch, Oxford; the bishoprics were Oxford, Bristol, Peterborough, Westminster, and Chester. Some savage denunciations of the shortcomings of the Henricians were later made by the reformers. Anthony Gilbey in his *Admonition to England and Scotland*, written in 1558, declared 'There was no reformation but a deformation in the time of that tyrant and lecherous monster. The boar, I grant, was busy rooting and digging in the earth and all his pigs that followed him. But they sought only for the pleasant fruits which they winded up with their long snouts . . .'

29 J. Youings, *The Dissolution of the Monasteries* (1971).

30 W. C. Richardson, *A History of the Court of Augmentations* (1961).

31 Alan Simpson, *The Wealth of the Gentry, 1540–1660* (1961). L. Stone, *The Crisis of the Aristocracy* (1965). The growth in the number of armigerous families is attested by the heraldic visitations of the late sixteenth century.

32 R. O'Day, 'Ecclesiastical Patronage: who controlled the church?', *Church and Society in England: Henry VIII to James I*, ed. R. O'Day and F. Heal (1977), 137-55.

33 M. C. Knowles, *The Religious Orders in England*, III (1959). G. W. O. Woodward, *The Dissolution of the Monasteries* (1966). Modern scholarship suggests that most of these institutions were decent, if easy-going, institutions, and that genuine vocations existed, but in small numbers.

34 The opinions of historians have varied over the adequacy, or otherwise,

of these monastic pensions; see Woodward, op. cit., 139-57; also G. Baskerville, *The English Monks and the Suppression of the Monasteries* (1937) and G. A. J. Hodgett, 'The Unpensioned Religious in Tudor England', *JEH*, 13, ii (1962). The pension list (including chantry priests) was still running at over £25,000 a year in 1555, see below, 345-6 and n.

35 S. E. Brigden, 'The Reformation in London, 1522-1547' (unpublished Cambridge PhD thesis, 1979).

36 Elton, *Policy and Police*, 156.

37 The means by which such large sums of money were made available for these purchases still remain something of a mystery. The most recent discussion of these land sales is in G. R. Elton, *Reform and Reformation* (1977), 246-9, etc.

38 The first royal injunctions of Henry VIII. W. H. Frere and W. M. Kennedy, *Visitation Articles and Injunctions* (1910), II, 1-11.

39 Elton, *Reform and Reformation*, 171-2.

40 Muller, *Stephen Gardiner*, 79-94; Gardiner's defence of orthodoxy in terms of the supremacy was a consistent theme with him before 1550. *OM*, 52-5.

41 Brigden, op. cit.

42 Bucer to Brentius, 15 May 1550. *Original Letters relative to the English Reformation*, Parker Society (1846), II, 542. The *Original Letters* contain large numbers of other complaints to the same effect; see particularly Peter Martyr to Bullinger, 1 June 1550, *OL*, II, 483. *OM*, 92-100; C. Cross, *Church and People: 1450-1660* (1976), 81-100.

43 H. Porter, *Reformation and Reaction in Tudor Cambridge* (1958). J. E. A. Dawson, 'The Early Career of Christopher Goodman' (unpublished Durham PhD thesis, 1978) is particularly interesting on Martyr's 'circle' in Oxford.

44 Elton, *Reform and Renewal*, 92-7. Lehmberg, op. cit. One of the highest expressions of the theory behind this policy appears in an anonymous 'discourse addressed to the king' of c. 1532. *L&P*, V, 635-6, cited W. R. D. Jones, *The Tudor Commonwealth* (1970), 18-19.

45 P. L. Hughes and J. F. Larkin, *Tudor Royal Proclamations*, I (1964), 281.

46 For an exposition of this view see Jones, op. cit., 24-42.

47 This statement was made in the context of the Ferrers case, the most recent examination of which is in S. E. Lehmberg, *The Later Parliaments of Henry VIII* (1977), 165-71.

48 A. B. Ferguson, *The Articulate Citizen and the English Renaissance* (1965).

49 Elton, *Reform and Renewal*, 121.

50 E. W. Ives, 'The Genesis of the Statute of Uses,' *EHR*, 82 (1967), 673-97.

51 'The Pontefract Articles' (*L&P*, XI, 1246), especially 12, 15, and 20. M. H. and R. Dodds, *The Pilgrimage of Grace* (1915). The whole north, from Lincolnshire and Cheshire to the borders, had only 48 members in the Commons.

52 A. G. Dickens, 'Secular and Religious Motivation in the Pilgrimage of Grace', *Studies in Church History*, IV (1967), 39-64; C. S. L. Davies, 'The Pilgrimage of Grace Reconsidered', *Past and Present*, 41 (1968), 54-76; M. E. James, 'Obedience and Dissent in Henrician England; the Lincolnshire Rebellion of 1536', *P&P*, 48 (1970), 3-78. Elton, *Reform and Reformation*, 270-1.

53 M. E. James, *Change and Continuity in the Tudor North* (1965); D. M. Loades, *Politics and the Nation, 1450–1660* (1974), 179-86.
54 ibid., 186.
55 27 Henry VIII, cs 24, 26. The process was completed in 1543 by 34 and 35 Henry VIII, c. 26.
56 Lehmberg, *Reformation Parliament*, 241-2.
57 B. Bradshaw, 'The Irish Constitutional Revolution, 1515–1557' (unpublished Cambridge PhD thesis, 1975).
58 ibid. Elton, *Reform and Reformation*, 208-10.
59 ibid., 302-3.
60 Elton, *The Tudor Revolution in Government* (1953); *The Tudor Constitution;* and numerous articles.
61 Elton, 'Why the History of the Early Tudor Council remains unwritten', *Studies in Tudor and Stuart Politics and Government*, I, 308-38.
62 For a full examination of Somerset's relations with the council, see D. E. Hoak, *The King's Council in the Reign of Edward VI* (1976).
63 ibid., 243-58. B. L. Beer, *Northumberland* (1973).
64 Strictly it was the court of duchy chamber, the council of the duchy sitting in its judicial capacity, which provided the model. Elton, *Tudor Constitution*, 156-7; R. Somerville, *History of the Duchy of Lancaster, 1265–1603* (1953).
65 The court of general surveyors was responsible for those lands (other than ancient demesne) which had come into the hands of the crown before the erection of augmentations. W. C. Richardson, *A History of the Court of Augmentations.*
66 H. E. Bell, *An Introduction to the History and Records of the Court of Wards and Liveries* (1953); J. Hurstfield, 'The Profits of Fiscal Feudalism, 1541–1602', *Economic History Review*, 2nd series, 8 (1955); Hurstfield, *The Queen's Wards* (1958).
67 *A Dialogue between Reginald Pole and Thomas Lupset*, ed. K. M. Burton (1948); Morison's scheme is in BM Royal MS 18 (*L&P*, XVII, App. A, 2). See Elton, 'Reform by Statute', *Studies*, II, 236-58.
68 Elton, *Reform and Renewal*, 138-40.
69 Sanctuary had already been whittled down by earlier statutes, 21 Henry VIII, c. 2; 22 Henry VIII, c. 14; and 26 Henry VIII, c. 13. I. D. Thornley, 'The Destruction of Sanctuary' in *Tudor Studies . . . presented to A. F. Pollard* (1924).
70 Elton, *Reform and Renewal*, 158-69; Lehmberg, *Later Parliaments*.
71 Elizabeth Barton and her associates died by attainder in 1534, and Giles Heron in 1539. Margaret countess of Salisbury was also attainted in 1539.
72 25 Henry VIII, c. 22; 26 Henry VIII, c. 13; 27 Henry VIII, c. 2.
73 33 Henry VIII, c. 23.
74 Elton, *Policy and Police*, 308, 390. Two witnesses were required by 1 Edward VI, c. 12 and by 5 and 6 Edward VI, c. 11, but the repeal of these acts by Mary returned procedure to its original form.
75 ibid., 387.
76 ibid., 48-82.
77 Elton, 'Thomas Cromwell Redivivus', *ARG*, 68 (1977).
78 F. M. G. Evans, *The Principal Secretary of State* (1923); Elton, *Tudor Revolution*, 124 ff, 299 ff.
79 Elton, *Policy and Police*, 171-216; W. G. Zeeveld, *Foundations of*

Tudor Policy (1948); E. Duff, *A Century of the English Book Trade* (1948).

80 There is no good study of the working of the commissions of the peace in this period, but Lambarde wrote in 1581 that 'the growing number of statute laws committed to the charge of the Justices of the Peace hath bene the cause that they are nowe againe increased to the overflowing of each shire' (*Eirenarcha*, 37-8). Many such statutes were passed during the reformation parliament, but Lambarde was clear that the process had begun 'long since'. The commission for the West Riding of Yorkshire, which had stood at 35 in 1513 and 38 in 1530, had gone up to 64 by 1538, R. B. Smith, *Land and Politics* (1970), 154.

81 ibid., 123-64. For a study of this process in operation at a later date, see A. H. Smith, *County and Court* (1974).

82 Elton, 'Taxation for War and Peace in Early Tudor England' in *War and Economic Development*, ed. J. M. Winter (1975), 33 ff.

83 Subsidies had, very occasionally, been granted in the past under similar circumstances, which might be termed apprehension rather than emergency. G. L. Harriss, 'Thomas Cromwell's "new principle" of Taxation', *EHR*, 83 (1978), 721-39.

84 C. E. Challis, 'The Debasement of the Coinage, 1542-1551', *Economic History Review*, 2nd series, 20 (1967).

85 F. C. Dietz, *English Government Finance, 1485-1558* (1921), 174-6.

86 M. Bush, *The Government Policy of Protector Somerset* (1975), makes clear the overriding importance of Scotland in Somerset's plans.

87 See below, .

88 L. B. Smith, *The Mask of Royalty* (1971).

89 These men remained broadly sympathetic to reforming policies, although not to protestantism. The same could be said of Sir Thomas Audley and Sir Richard Rich. Only the protestant preachers, Jerome, Barnes, and Garrett, shared Cromwell's fall, as the logic of the charges against him demanded.

90 Exeter and Montague executed for alleged catholic conspiracy in 1538, Aske for his share in the Pilgrimage in 1537, Sir Francis Bigod for an individual but essentially protestant revolt in Yorkshire in the same year, and Barnes as a 'sacramentarian' in the wake of Cromwell's fall.

91 Apart from Wriothesley, the only other 'strong catholics' were Tunstall and Sir Anthony Browne, neither of them strong personalities.

92 W. K. Jordan, *The Young King* (1968), 54-6, summarizes the evidence. For a more recent appraisal, see Elton, *Reform and Reformation*, 329-32.

93 Jordan, *The Young King*, 69-72.

94 The best and most recent account of the 'Prayer Book rebellion', which emphasizes the strength of the popular religious feeling and the strong element of provincialism, is in J. Cornwall, *Revolt of the Peasantry 1549* (1977).

95 B. L. Beer, *Northumberland* (1973), 124-46; Loades, *Politics and the Nation*, 213-15; Jordan, *The Threshold of Power*, 56-70.

96 ibid., 494-520. In his desire to exonerate Northumberland, Jordan almost certainly exaggerates the king's role in the alliance, but Edward's views were perfectly clear.

97 ibid. Mary had been bastardized by the first succession act of 1534, and Elizabeth by the second of 1536. In spite of being restored to the succession in 1544, neither had been technically legitimated.

98 For a full discussion of the text of the 'device' and its alterations, see J. G. Nichols, *Literary Remains of Edward VI* (1857), II, 571.
99 Ambassadors to the emperor, 10 July 1553. *Cal. Span.*, XI, 77-80.
100 *Chronicle of Queen Jane*, Camden Society, 48 (1850), 5.
101 e.g., Mary to the mayor of West Chester, 12 July 1553. *HMC Fifth Report*, App., 343 (Cholmondeley MSS).

3　The Structure of the Regime; Council, Court, and Administration

Superficially the circumstances of Mary's accession appeared to have placed her in a very strong position to shape her government freely in accordance with her own tastes and requirements. Virtually the whole of her brother's council, the officers of state, and the senior law officers had been implicated to some extent in Northumberland's conspiracy.[1] At the same time she had triumphed so rapidly that there had been no question of her becoming the candidate of a faction which would have attempted to monopolize the fruits of victory. She came to the throne remarkably free from obligations, either explicit or understood. Consequently the queen has been sharply blamed by some historians for failing to impose coherence upon her servants, and specifically for creating an over-large and factious council.[2] This latter charge is not without foundation, as we shall see, but the size and composition of Mary's council was not simply the product of her own foolishness or sentimentality. From the moment when she arrived at Framlingham and proclaimed herself queen, she needed the appurtenances of royalty, and had no option but to create a council from among the most substantial of those immediately to hand.[3] The murky nature of Mary's prospects during the preceding decade, and the strict religious tests which she had herself imposed, had meant that her household as heir-apparent had not attracted a very conspicuous array of talent. Her faithful servants Robert Rochester, Edward Waldegrave, and Francis Englefield did not make a very impressive royal council, but fortunately, as Mary's cause gathered momentum, they were swiftly reinforced. By 12 July they had been joined by the earl of Bath, Sir Thomas Wharton, and Sir John Mordaunt.[4] During the next week the tide turned decisively, and Mary's council recruited the earl of Sussex, Lord Wentworth, Sir Thomas Cornwallis, Sir Richard Southwell, Richard Morgan, and several other men of substance and experience. By the time that Lord Paget and the earl of Arundel arrived on the 19th to offer the submission of the lords in London, the queen already had a working council of nearly twenty members. She also had a *de facto* secretary in the person of John Bourne, who kept such notes of the business of the Framlingham council as have survived.[5] She did not, however, have the makings of a stable and successful government. Even if we include those who had clearly declared for Mary in other parts of the country, such as the earl of Oxford, Lord Rich, Lord Dacre, Sir Thomas Cheney, and Sir John Gage, she could still deploy only a fragmentary assortment of political talent. She could certainly have defeated the lords in London had it come to a military issue, and showed every sign of doing so, but whether she could have governed the country for any length of time without their loyalty and support is very much more doubtful.

For their part, the London council had never been solidly behind Northumberland. Indeed Lord Paget had been disgraced in 1551 and had been recalled only after the king's death.[6] He had been closely associated with Somerset, but was innocent of any involvement in the plot to crown Jane Grey. The earl of Arundel had also been excluded for opposing the duke, and recalled in an attempt to win his support earlier in the summer. He had signed the instrument recognizing Jane, but was not committed to her cause. The same was true of the earl of Pembroke, who had had his own quarrels with Northumberland,[7] and to a lesser extent of the earls of Bedford and Shrewsbury. There was also a conservative group among the less powerful members of Edward's council who had been profoundly unhappy about the duke's schemes and who had succeeded in avoiding more than a token involvement; Sir Thomas Cheney, Sir William Petre, Sir John Gage, Sir John Mason, Dr Nicholas Wotton, and one or two more. On the other side stood Northumberland himself; his faithful but rather ineffectual associate the duke of Suffolk; William Parr, marquis of Northampton; Sir John Gates; and Sir Philip Hoby. Rather more equivocal in their views, but still deeply entangled in the plot, were the earl of Huntingdon; Walter Devereux, Viscount Hereford; Thomas Lord Darcy; Sir William Cecil; and the two ecclesiastics Cranmer and Goodrich. When the crisis came, and it became clear that Mary could command, and was prepared to use, far more active support than her opponents had calculated upon, the council split. Arundel, Pembroke, and Paget naturally took the lead, since they had the most to hope for and the least to fear in declaring for Mary. After that it was a question of *sauve qui peut*, and the queen's main problem was to know how to react to the seasoned and powerful politicians who now hastened to Framlingham to offer their services. Paget and Arundel were promptly received into favour, and the latter was immediately given the responsible task of apprehending Northumberland.[8] They may well have been sworn of the council at the same time, since no council oaths are recorded for the Framlingham period, and neither appears on any subsequent list. The first record of a councillor's oath is that of Sir Edward Hastings on 28 July.[9] Sir Edmund Peckham, the treasurer of the mint, was sworn on the 29th, and thereafter the Edwardian councillors begin to appear; the earl of Bedford on the same day, and Sir William Petre, and Sir John Mason on the 30th.[10] By the time that Mary entered London on 3 August her council must have numbered about 25. They were already a somewhat ill-assorted team, because they had been recruited as opportunity and the needs of the moment dictated. However, the queen had had little alternative, not knowing at first from day to day who would offer their services, and latterly having to judge the truth of what had happened in London between 15 and 19 July.

In most cases she seems to have shown good sense and discrimination. Northumberland's belated and rather pathetic gesture of submission stood no chance of being accepted. The duke and all his five sons were rounded up and put on trial. Northampton, Gates, Sir Thomas Palmer, and subsequently Cranmer shared the same fate. Of those closest to Northumberland, only the duke of Suffolk escaped with a brief period of imprisonment.[11] Of the others who were deeply implicated, the earl of Huntingdon was committed to the Tower and the earl of Rutland to the Fleet. Viscount Hereford, Sir William Cecil, and Sir John Yorke were similarly imprisoned, while Lord Darcy was placed under house arrest.[12] Northumberland himself, Gates, and Palmer died immediately for their part in the conspiracy; Guildford Dudley and Jane Grey the following February. Suffolk was executed for a subsequent treason, and Cranmer for heresy.[13] All the rest made their peace with the queen in varying degrees, but none was received into high favour, or given a seat at the council board. Of the 33 members of Edward's last council, 22 were excluded by Mary, and of those only two, Lord Clinton and Dr Nicholas Wotton, subsequently regained their places.[14] Between 4 August and the end of October, when the construction of the privy council was completed, six Edwardian councillors took the oath: the marquis of Winchester, the earls of Shrewsbury and Pembroke, Sir John Gage, Sir Thomas Cheney, and Sir John Baker.[15] For all these appointments there was good political justification, both because of the administrative continuity which they provided, and because they represented Mary's willingness to come to terms with the existing establishment. The new queen could only afford to execute or disgrace a proportion of her most powerful subjects because she was willing to accept and employ the services of the rest. Similar reasoning would also justify the inclusion of the earl of Derby, a powerful conservative who had been kept at arm's length by Northumberland, and who had made only one brief and mysterious appearance on Edward's council.[16] He took the council oath on 17 August. However, it is very much harder to explain the appearance of the aged Thomas West, Lord La Warr, who was sworn on the same day. He was certainly a staunch catholic, but was more noted for being 'the best housekeeper in Sussex' than for any qualities of statesmanship. It seems that he was included more out of reward for his past constancy than in anticipation of good service, and indeed he died in the following year.[17] Similar sentiment probably accounts for the admission of Thomas Howard, 3rd duke of Norfolk on 10 August, and of Cuthbert Tunstall the octogenarian ex-bishop of Durham on the 14th. Norfolk had remained in the Tower throughout Edward's reign, until released by Mary on her arrival in London. Without waiting for the formality of reversing his attainder, the queen restored him to his former rank, and to the order of the Garter.[18] Tunstall was freed and rehabilitated at the same time, and with a similar lack of legal propriety.[19] Neither of these ancient servants of the crown represented a major political asset in 1553, although Tunstall was to outlive the queen, and do useful work in the northern marches. They owed their places on the council to the prestige of their former careers, and to Mary's keen sense of the injustice which they had suffered. Their principal significance was as symbols of that return to former ways and former values which was the queen's most deeply felt commitment.

By contrast, their fellow prisoner Stephen Gardiner was a politician and statesman of the first rank. Eclipsed by Thomas Cromwell in the 1530s, and by Seymour and Dudley in the 1540s, deprived of his bishopric of Winchester and imprisoned in 1551, he emerged in early August 1553 with his talents unimpaired, his thirst for power undiminished, and with his famous irascibility markedly increased. In the circumstances of Mary's accession Gardiner was a man whom it was impossible to ignore. On 22 July, during the uneasy calm which followed the submission of the lords in London, the Imperial ambassadors reported that he was refusing to leave the Tower without the queen's especial command, but that in the meantime '. . . the Council have conferred with him on affairs and are adopting his advice'.[20] Even before his release he showed every sign of bearing himself with a high hand, demanding from the earl of Pembroke the return of revenues previously confiscated from the see of Winchester, an act of presumption which several observers thought unwise.[21] Gardiner clearly anticipated favour and high office, although there is no evidence that he had received any prior assurances to that effect. When he had been excluded from the list of Henry VIII's executors in 1547, the dying king is alleged to have said '. . . if he were in my testament and one of you, he would cumber you all, and you should never rule him, he is of so troublesome a nature . . .'[22] However, troublesome or not, he was one of the few statesmen of outstanding ability available to serve Mary, and his self-assurance was swiftly justified. Released on the 3rd, he was sworn of the council on the 5th, and treated from the first as though his deprivation was null and void.[23]

In spite of her strong religious views, Mary cannot be accused of packing her council with clergy. Apart from Gardiner and Tunstall, only two prelates were appointed in this formative period, Nicholas Heath and Thomas Thirlby. Heath, bishop of Worcester from 1543, had suffered deprivation and imprisonment in 1551 for his opposition to the protestant ordinal. He took the oath on 4 September as bishop of Worcester, only a few days after John Hooper's arrest, and long before any legal steps could be taken for his reinstatement.[24] Thirlby, a professional survivor of considerable adroitness, had served on Henry's council as bishop of Westminster. Translated to Norwich when the see of Westminster was suppressed in 1550, he contrived to retain some favour with both Somerset and Northumberland. Although he was never a privy councillor during Edward's reign, he did serve as ambassador at the Imperial court, and was in Brussels at the time of the king's death. Mary at first retained him in that post, but he was recalled in October 1553, and admitted to the council on the 25th of that month.[25] By that time the privy council numbered 43, and at that level it was to remain with only minor fluctuations for the remainder of the reign.[26]

This was approximately twice the size of the tightly controlled privy council of 1540, or of Elizabeth's council at the same stage of her reign. It resembled more closely the council which Northumberland had assembled in 1552-53 when he was bidding for support,[27] and both its size and composition have been interpreted as evidence of Mary's weakness and political inexperience. The truth seems to be that at the beginning, when Mary made her first bid for the crown and before she had the benefit of any experienced advice, she raised to the status of privy councillors far more men than the situation required, several of whom could never have justified their inclusion by the standards applied after 1 August. Men such as Rochester, Waldegrave, and Englefield, who were personally close to the queen and clearly destined for high household office, would have been included by any monarch similarly placed. The earl of Bath, equally unimpressive as a public figure, was understandably chosen because he was the first peer to declare for Mary, and his example influenced others. On the other hand, such East Anglian gentry as Sir Henry Bedingfield, Sir William Drury, and John Huddlestone could have been more appropriately rewarded for their allegiance, and minor administrators such as Robert Peckham and Robert Strelly were quite out of place in a royal council.[28] Altogether about eight or nine of these early appointees can be classified as inadequate by previously accepted standards. Of the rest, several were to become important administrators, but only Rochester emerged as a significant political figure because of the trust which the queen reposed in him. Inevitably once Mary had entered London and begun to pick up the threads of government, most of these early councillors found themselves being elbowed aside by the more eminent and experienced recruits from Edward's administration. As we shall see, in the choice of her principal officers the queen's judgement was usually sound, but this did not prevent anger and frustration among some of those who felt that their loyalty was being disparaged. On 16 August the Imperial ambassadors reported

> Discontent is rife, especially among those who stood by the Queen in the days of her adversity and trouble, who feel that they have not been rewarded as they deserve, for the conspirators have been raised in authority . . .'[29]

This impression was confirmed by Scheyfve in conversation with the earl of Derby, but the implication that potentially dangerous disaffection would result seems to have been entirely without foundation. The ambassadors, and particularly Renard, were highly critical of Mary's council from the first; 'the said Council', they wrote on 27 August, 'does not seem to us, after mature consideration, to be composed of experienced men endowed with the necessary qualities to conduct the administration and government of the kingdom . . .'[30] Gardiner and Paget were jealous of each other, and the hostility between the Framlingham councillors and the rest was unappeased. In a private letter to the bishop of Arras on 9 September, Renard repeated these criticisms, along with a second-hand rumour to the effect that Pembroke, Paget, and Sir John Mason were about to retire from the court.[31]

Renard, as the successor of those Imperial ambassadors whom she had trusted in the past, was very close to the queen, and to the centre of affairs. He is not, however, necessarily a reliable witness. His consistent disparagement of the English council over the next two years was partly at least the result of his need to justify his own activities, and to magnify the success of his achievements.[32]

When Mary chose to confide in him, and to consult him secretly, as she did within a few days of her accession, he naturally claimed that this unusual course was made necessary by the unsatisfactory nature of the advice otherwise available to her. Renard needed a special relationship with the queen because it was his task to persuade her into a marriage acceptable to the emperor, and he found it highly convenient to be able to circumvent possible opposition in this way. In fact the ambassador's position was anomalous, and impeded the development of a proper working relationship between Mary and her council. Through him the emperor proffered his advice, not only about marriage, but about religious affairs, the late king's funeral, and the treatment of the imprisoned conspirators.[33] All these were matters which the queen should have decided with the advice of her council, but in each case she seems to have preferred to consult Renard, and there is no evidence that the council discussed them at all until after the queen's mind was made up. The most important of these issues, the marriage, must be treated separately, but it is worth noticing here that it was a major cause of the divisions and suspicions which Renard so much deplored.[34] At first Lord Paget was the only councillor to favour Philip's candidature; most, following the lead of Gardiner, would have preferred Edward Courtenay. Since the French ambassador for his own reasons also favoured Courtenay, it was easy for Renard to implant in the queen's mind the suspicion that several of her councillors were favourable to the interests of the French. Mary seems to have believed from the beginning that England's true interests could only be served by seeking the guidance and protection of the Habsburgs. This innocent trust was not shared by any of her councillors, not even the loyallest of her intimates, and consequently there always remained an element of tension and reserve in the queen's relationship with her council in one of its primary roles – as an advisory body for the formation of policy at the highest level.[35] Renard, whose whole task was to encourage Mary's trust and commitment, understandably regarded the council with suspicion, and was only too ready to disparage its members for incompetence or disloyalty. Neither the emperor nor Granvelle took the ambassador's complaints too seriously, and the latter warned him in April 1554 not to intervene openly in English affairs,[36] but by then the damage was done.

During and after the Wyatt rebellion, which admittedly concerned his mission very closely, Renard was a particularly intrusive presence. In a despatch of 31 January which contained several complaints about the council's dilatoriness in coping with the emergency, and insubstantial suspicions that some of them were implicated, he reported that the queen had sent for him in great perplexity and grief. She complained that she could not make her council provide her with a guard and 'begged your Majesty . . . to . . . remember her in her present need'.[37] A week later, when the rebels made their final bid to enter the city of London, Renard's reports reached a climax of self-congratulation. The council, he declared, were '. . . so . . . frightened . . . that they went to the Queen between two and three o'clock in the morning, to urge her to get up and fly by boat. She, without losing her presence of mind for a moment, sent for me . . .' According to his own account, the ambassador then persuaded Mary to ignore the craven advice of her councillors, and concluded by explaining how her consequent firmness had saved her crown.[38] Unfortunately, there is no means of checking the accuracy of many of these statements, with their colourful circumstantial detail. Mobilization does seem to have been slow, and for a few days the queen would have had no means of resisting a determined rebel attack – if it had come. However, this was not the fault of the council, which sent out its orders promptly enough once the real nature of the situation had become clear.[39] Mary's insistence that Renard should be consulted and informed at every stage was a hindrance and an embarrassment, and when she taxed Paget with negligence in this respect, he declined to explain, merely begging her to address her question to the whole council.[40] It is not surprising that the councillors were edgy and quarrelsome when the queen's words and actions constantly implied that she did not trust them either to defend her or to give her good advice, and that she preferred to look for both to the emperor and his servant. Gardiner was understandably chilly towards Renard's offer of Imperial troops, and the ambassador promptly decided that he lacked zeal in his mistress's cause, an opinion which was reflected in the eclipse of the chancellor's influence once the crisis was over.

Although he was unsuccessful in his campaign to bring Elizabeth and Courtenay to the block,[41] Renard's powerful influence continued to bedevil relations between the queen and her council during the spring and early summer of 1554. The ill-feeling between Paget and Gardiner, which was real enough, was exacerbated by the ambassador's tendency to take sides, and to represent the chancellor in a sinister light, not merely to the emperor and Granvelle, but also to Mary.[42] His concern over Philip's forthcoming visit was perfectly legitimate, but when it led him to lecture Gardiner over his dealings with the French ambassador, or to dictate the legislative programme of the parliament, it led him to transgress his proper limitations.[43] Unfortunately the queen listened to his constant complaints about the factiousness of her councillors, remonstrated with them collectively and individually, and eventually complained that she spent half her time shouting at them.⁴⁴ In early May, baffled by Paget's conduct during the parliament which had just ended, Renard changed sides, and almost immediately began to cast extravagant doubts upon his former ally's loyalty. By the middle of June he had come to the conclusion that Paget was conducting a sinister intrigue with the earl of Arundel and Sir John Mason, Mary's ambassador at the Imperial court. He thereupon persuaded Mary, who deferred to the emperor's judgement in all things, to allow Charles's agents in the Low Countries to intercept and open letters passing between Mason and Paget.⁴⁵ He himself also had access to Mason's despatches, and freely criticized their content as harmful to his master's interests. The queen's lack of confidence in her own councillors could hardly be better demonstrated than by this strange episode. Renard fostered that mistrust, sometimes deliberately, sometimes accidentally. That the English council might legitimately suggest policies which were not entirely subservient to Habsburg interests does not seem to have occurred to him, and in the face of his insistent representation of his master's wishes, it did not very often occur to Mary either.

Consequently in making any assessment of the working of Mary's council, particularly during the first year of her reign, we must treat Renard's statements with the greatest caution. Nevertheless, in some respects his criticisms were probably justified. The constantly reiterated statement that 'numbers cause great confusion' cannot be entirely discounted by pointing out, as one scholar has recently done, that the average attendance at council meetings between August 1553 and July 1554 was 13.6.⁴⁶ It is equally true that, with the single exception of Sir Anthony St Leger, who appeared only once before going to Ireland in October, every man who was eligible to sit at the council board appeared at at least two formal meetings between August and December 1553.⁴⁷ Attendance at individual meetings fluctuated widely, between 6 and 27, and since several of the less frequent attenders, such as Jerningham and Strelly, held offices in the court, it is reasonable to suppose that they were often present in the environs even when they were not actually attending meetings. Councillors were perfectly entitled to discuss the queen's business at other places than the council board, and with so many men participating more or less actively in the business of the council during these early months of the reign, Renard may have had some cause to feel that the situation was chaotic. Preoccupied with her secret marriage negotiations, Mary does not seem to have taken any effective steps to organize her council for the conduct of its normal business. Two memoranda 'of things to be done' survive from the earliest days of the reign, listing such matters as the better enforcement of the laws, the settlement of religion, the reduction of the crown's expenses, and the necessity to curb the growing number of JPs,[48] but unlike the comparable memoranda at the beginning of Elizabeth's reign they indicate no specific division of responsibility.[49] The more comprehensive of these is in the handwriting of Sir William Petre, and his biographer surmises that he was the main manager of business at this stage.[50] Someone certainly began a prompt examination of the crown's debts, but the view that this was the joint work of Petre and Gardiner seems to rest upon an unsupported statement by Froude.[51] Memoranda upon the state of the navy and upon the sale of crown land were also prepared in early August, but neither was followed by immediate action.[52] We do not even know which councillors were mainly responsible for the preparation of business to be discussed in the parliament which met in October. On 5 October, Renard reported that Paget had been specifically consulted by the queen about '. . . the articles of religion to be brought before parliament, which might cause trouble . . .', but who else had been involved in these discussions he either did not know or did not report.[53] We know that some councillors accompanied the queen to Richmond in mid-August, while others remained at Westminster, but this division was more determined by the nature of the offices they held than by any distinctions in importance. What seems to have happened during August and September was that the councillors were left 'to find their own level', as determined by their respective skills, ambitions, and experience. It is not surprising that there were complaints, both from Renard and from the less successful competitors. By the beginning of October a hierarchy of importance was clearly emerging. In his despatch of 5 October, quoted above, Renard listed six who had by then emerged as '. . . those who govern the Council of State and the Privy Council', Arundel, Gardiner, Rochester, Tunstall, Paget, and Petre.[54] A month later, on 6 November, he announced that the queen had 'reduced her council to six persons', and listed the same group save that Tunstall had by then been replaced by Thirlby.[55]

The formal records of the council bear no trace of this arrangement, and what it seems to mean is that Mary had returned to a situation common before 1536, by which an informal group of councillors enjoyed pre-eminence over their colleagues. As such it was a matter of confidence and convenience, not appointment, a working arrangement necessitated by the large numbers and unequal abilities of the remaining councillors. Consequently it had the disadvantages as well as the advantages of informality. The 'inner council' could not become an exclusive group, and when its members disagreed among themselves, they naturally looked for support to their less favoured colleagues. Unanimity in the council was always rare, and when sharp personal rivalry was superimposed upon genuine differences of opinion, protracted and bitter quarrels could result. This had happened when Norfolk and Gardiner had confronted Cromwell in the 1530s, and it was to happen again between Cecil and Leicester after the latter joined the council in 1562. In the early part of Mary's reign it happened between Gardiner and Paget, but unlike either Henry or Elizabeth, Mary seems to have been unable to remedy the situation by bestowing her confidence emphatically or consistently on either.[56] In ignorance of the queen's real intentions, Paget supported and Gardiner opposed the Spanish marriage, but Gardiner was always closer to the queen's mind on religious questions, and in his antipathy to Elizabeth. More fundamentally, Paget remained loyal to the secular priorities and administrative discipline of his Cromwellian training, while Gardiner, having repudiated the royal supremacy, seems to have hankered after the personal and unfettered authority of Wolsey. Paget had already shown a constructive interest in the organization of the council under Somerset,[57] and he soon made common cause with Renard in arguing for some division of function among the councillors which would effectively result in the emergence of a select 'council of state'. It is impossible to say how far the developments of October and November 1553 reflected his advice, or how long they lasted. Probably the upheavals of the Wyatt rebellion disrupted whatever working habits had become established, and certainly strengthened Paget's hand during the ensuing weeks.[58] It is not surprising, therefore, that under the date 23 February the council book records a scheme for the rationalization of its work. Eleven committees of the council were listed, to consider such matters as calling in crown debts, organizing supplies for Calais and Berwick, and examining the imprisoned rebels. Nine of the committees are listed in full, and include altogether the names of 24 privy councillors and two others.[59] Presumably all those who were considered to be active and competent, and were not absent on legitimate business, were allocated to one or more of these committees, so that at a time when the average recorded attendance at council meetings was no more than eleven, more than twice that number of councillors were thought to be available for official business. There is virtually no information about the working of this scheme, which bears all the marks of Paget's administrative brain, but it does not seem to have been intended as a permanent arrangement. Some of the committees, such as that to prepare for the parliament, were occasional in their nature. The scheme represents a method of tackling routine work rather than a structure, but is no less significant for that.

It also gives some hints of a policy in respect of the political functions of the council. The committee to consider the appointment of a council to remain in London included no councillor of major importance, an indication that the 'London council' was thought of as a purely routine and administrative body.[60] On the other hand, the committees which dealt with potentially sensitive subjects, such as the royal debts, parliament, and patents and annuities, were dominated by Gardiner, Paget, Rochester, Arundel, and Winchester. There was no question of creating a 'council of state', it was not that sort of scheme, but there are clear indications of the continued existence of an informal core substantially unchanged from that of the previous November, in spite of the conclusion of the marriage treaty and the upheaval of the rebellion which had intervened. By the end of March, when Renard's frustration over the punishment of the rebels produced a fresh crescendo of complaint,[61] it seems that another device for increasing the political effectiveness of the council was under consideration. Once again the core was to be a council of state consisting of Gardiner, Paget, Arundel, Rochester, Petre, and Thirlby who was to be recalled from Brussels for the purpose. This time the formality of the arrangement was to be increased by providing that 'the other councillors should have offices in the provinces given to them, and only the State Councillors should have chambers at Court'.[62] This, together with another attempt to negotiate a verbal *entente* between Gardiner and Paget, would, it was hoped, bring some much-needed coherence to the council as an advisory body. If such a plan was ever realized, it certainly did not work. There was no significant exodus of councillors from the court, and it was months before Thirlby was recalled.[63] Renard subsequently alleged that Gardiner had sabotaged the council of state because he found his views in a permanent minority,[64] but it was simply impracticable to separate the 'councillors of state' from the others in the way envisaged. If about three-fifths of the privy council were to be compulsorily exiled to the provinces, not only would the February committee scheme have collapsed, but the whole administrative work of the council would have ground to a halt. An informal 'inner ring' might be confused and complicated by the intervention of others, but a specialized council which '. . . only [took] cognisance of affairs of state . . .' would have been completely at variance with English custom. In any case the great majority of Mary's active councillors held offices either in the court or in the central administration, and would expect to serve on council committees and commissions as a matter of course.

The large number of councillors was, in fact, no handicap to the council as an executive or administrative body once an organizer had emerged who was capable of imposing some order and discipline. Both Paget and Petre were seasoned administrators, and between them they seem to have got the situation under control within the first six months, but neither enjoyed their sovereign's confidence to the same extent as Cromwell or Cecil, and the process was consequently both slower and more difficult to trace. Nevertheless, there is a variety of evidence to suggest that the administrative work of the council was proceeding with reasonable efficiency, whatever political storms may have been blowing. A major programme of financial reform was undertaken, which must be given separate consideration;[65] the tricky disciplinary problems created by the change in religious policy were handled with firmness and despatch;[66] and the privy councillors lent their weight and experience to a variety of commissions. Twenty-five councillors served on one or more commissions during the first year of the reign, their names corresponding closely with those of the active councillors appearing on the February committees. Winchester, Rochester, and Southwell emerge as the 'work horses' of these 21 commissions.[67] Neither Winchester nor Southwell were frequent attenders at formal council meetings, and it seems likely that many councillors tended to specialize in their forms of service, quite apart from those who might be candidates for the 'council of state'. Renard was interested in the disciplinary work of the council, and in its attempts to improve the financial situation, both subjects in which he was at pains to instruct the queen and her ministers in the performance of their duties. However, he never showed any real understanding of the way in which the council worked, persistently thinking of it in terms of the *conseil d'état* with which he was familiar.

He was also understandably reluctant to criticize the queen, and continually blamed the council for factiousness and disunity when the real problem was Mary's own failure to be frank with her advisers, or to make a decision when one was called for. Councillors were under no obligation to be unanimous in the advice which they proffered to their sovereign. Their oath bound them

> . . . in all matters to the uttermost of your witt and power [to] give such councill to hir Maty as maye best seme in your conscience to tend to the savety of hir Matys person and to the common weale of this realme . . .[68]

The responsibility was individual and not collective, and the influence of any minister of state depended upon his ability to win the confidence of his sovereign, not upon his capacity to muster majority support upon the privy council. Differences of opinion over policy and personal quarrels between ambitious rivals were commonplace in the history of the Tudor council, so there is no reason to doubt the substantial truth of Renard's running commentary, although the nature of his interest in the situation clearly led him into exaggeration. Gardiner was from the first a difficult colleague, tetchy and autocratic, who was determined to reverse the secular tendencies of the previous twenty years. His policy seems to have been one of restoring the wealth and jurisdiction of the church on a national basis before re-establishing the papal obedience. Such a priority was well calculated to increase his own power, a fact which was more apparent to his fellow councillors than it was to either the queen or Renard. Unlike Pole, the chancellor was quite willing to sacrifice the monastic lands, and to restore the catholic church by statute.[69] The restoration of episcopal revenues and authority, and the suppression of heresy, were much closer to his heart, both matters which directly affected his own position. While the Wyatt rebellion was in progress, it was his enemies who sought to blame the danger on his 'hastiness' in religion. As soon as it was over, Gardiner embraced this explanation himself, claiming that vigorous action against the heretics was essential for the security of the state.[70] So determined was he to make good the political losses which he had suffered over the marriage and the rebellion that he took the risk of double-crossing the other members of the council committee in preparing measures for the second parliament in April 1554. Having agreed that the marriage treaty was to be the main business, he then seems to have smuggled through the committee under a general and misleading description a series of highly controversial proposals for the abolition of the royal supremacy, the punishment of heretics, and the establishment of 'a sort of Inquisition'.[71] When these bills came before the parliament, they caused a furore and most of them were rejected or frustrated, angry councillors such as Paget, Arundel, and Rich leading the opposition.[72] Whether Gardiner had calculated upon such a reaction or not, we do not know, but in the event it played right into his hands. Insofar as we can reconstruct its contents, his bill on the royal supremacy seems to have been unrealistic, and bound to arouse the anger of established property interests,[73] but both it and a companion bill on ecclesiastical jurisdiction appealed greatly to the queen. When the latter was rejected, she was furious, and Gardiner's opponents speedily found themselves in disgrace. There were, as we shall see, other factors in this complicated situation,[74] but the outcome of the crisis was that by June 1554 Gardiner had emerged into a position of clear supremacy in the council, and it is hard to avoid the conclusion that he had sprung a crafty trap upon his enemies in the parliament. Renard's attitude to him changed completely, and he must have felt that he could now look forward to Philip's arrival with equanimity.

Much of the explanation for the 'factiousness' of Mary's council lies in this power-struggle between Gardiner and a formidable alliance of secular nobles.[75] This struggle was misinterpreted to her by Renard, and instead of controlling it by the imposition of her own will as her father or sister might have done, she allowed herself to be manipulated by the combatants. As a result, what was essentially a normal and manageable situation became a cause of major anxiety and political disruption. The queen did not normally invoke her father's memory, but she was right to point out to her councillors on one occasion that they would never have dared behave towards him as they did to her. And one of the first things that de Feria was to say about Elizabeth as queen was '. . . she seems to me incomparably more feared than her sister, and gives her orders and has her way as absolutely as her father did'.[76] Gardiner must have calculated on his ability to exploit a malleable and inexperienced ruler, but found the going unexpectedly hard. The confidential relationship which his sufferings for the faith might have entitled him to expect was immediately usurped by Renard, and the queen turned out to have an inconveniently long memory. On top of this he overreached himself in supporting the matrimonial pretensions of his suggestible young friend Courtenay, and found himself by November 1553 in considerable disfavour.[77] He was not alone in that position, several other important councillors having discovered the strength of the queen's Habsburg affiliations rather too late. While it would not be accurate to describe such men as Pembroke or Derby as Gardiner's supporters, they had reached a similar position independently, and the same may have been true of the household councillors, Rochester, Waldegrave, and Englefield. There was considerable discontent among these men by the end of the year, arising not so much out of frustrated ambition as from an awareness that they had unexpectedly misread the queen's mind. According to Renard, at the end of December, Rochester and Waldegrave were talking of leaving her service, as though her forthcoming marriage would leave them without a role.[78]

The ambassador's constant tendency to dramatic exaggeration makes it difficult to know how seriously to take his account of the 'split' in the council at the time of Wyatt's rebellion. According to him '. . . the Councillors reproached one another . . . quarrelling, taking sides and blaming one another . . .', some blaming Gardiner's religious zeal, others Arundel and Paget for arranging the marriage, and others 'those of the Council who stood for Courtenay and the Lady Elizabeth'.[79] However, as we have seen, there is good reason for saying that the council was not as inefficient as he represented it to be, so it was probably not as divided either. Gardiner lost ground because he misjudged the situation, recommending caution and conciliation when a show of strength was required. He was pilloried by Renard, and eclipsed in the queen's favour by Paget, Pembroke, and Clinton. Up to this point there seems to have been little substance in the complaint that the council was divided into two 'parties'. Gardiner was no doubt closer to staunch catholics such as Waldegrave, Englefield, and Bourne than he was to *politiques* such as Petre or Lord William Howard, but groupings changed according to the particular issue under discussion.[80] The only permanent hostility was between Gardiner and Paget. However, by the end of February the situation seems to have changed as Gardiner fought his way back out of the wilderness. The issues now were not the marriage, or even the punishment of the rebels, but the fate of Elizabeth and the menace of heresy. The nature of this controversy split the active councillors pretty evenly between those who accepted a religious priority and those who did not. The former group wished to take effective action against the princess, either by execution or exclusion from the succession, and supported Gardiner's plan to revive the jurisdiction of the church. The latter group regarded these plans as provocative and untimely, and wished to protect Elizabeth's interests as the rightful heir. Behind Gardiner in the 'ecclesiastical' camp stood Rochester, Waldegrave, Englefield, Southwell, Gage, Jerningham, and Bourne. Behind Paget on the 'secular' side were Arundel, Pembroke, Sussex, Hastings, Petre, Cornwallis, and Howard.[81] Thirlby was in Brussels, and Winchester seems to have remained aloof. Throughout March and April 1554 the struggle went on. Renard became increasingly despondent as he found his sympathies divided, so that on 22 March he wrote 'The confusion is such that no one knows who is good or who is bad, who constant or inconstant, loyal or treacherous'.[82] For weeks he strove officiously to heal the breach, and was eventually forced to accept the logic of Gardiner's victory. Mary characteristically failed to impose either peace or a decision upon the combatants until her anger was aroused by what appeared to be an open defiance of her wishes.

Gardiner scored an early success when he engineered Elizabeth's committal to the Tower,[83] but on that issue – the most important of all in the long run – he was ultimately defeated. In other respects,

D

events proved that he had chosen his ground with great skill, and by managing to keep the substance of his proposals secret until they were actually unveiled in parliament, he contrived to place his opponents in an impossible dilemma. As a result, by the summer of 1554 it appeared that the secular and 'Edwardian' bias noticeable among the most influential and powerful councillors since the previous September had been effectively neutralized. In reality this change was both temporary and superficial. Temporary because the coming of Philip brought about a new situation, and superficial because the 'Cromwellian' pattern of organizing the council's ordinary and routine business was not seriously disturbed. The 'division' in the council reflected to some extent a division in the queen's own mind, a fact which partly accounts for her failure to deal with it effectively. Equally committed to the restoration of the church and the Habsburg alliance, she found the demands of these policies, and of their particular supporters within her council, periodically in conflict. However, it is important to distinguish between differences of opinion which were legitimate within the normal practice of the privy council, and those which transgressed such limitations. The disputes over the queen's marriage which preceded her public decision were proper; so were the disagreements over the correct tactics to use against Wyatt. On the other hand, a public quarrel in parliament over several important pieces of legislation was another matter altogether. Gardiner deliberately abused the machinery which had been set up to initiate and manage an agreed legislative programme, and he succeeded because he read the queen's mind correctly. Instead of being enraged that measures had been introduced without the necessary conciliar backing and consent, her anger was aroused by the defeat of what appeared to be good and Godly proposals.

Mary's lack of judgement and confidence was a continual source of anxiety and distress to her servants, who rightly suspected her of being too easily influenced. Between a quarter and a third of her privy councillors were really superfluous, doing no noticeable good – or harm – to the government.[84] The remainder, all justifiable appointments as individuals, were deeply divided from each other and from the queen by their parts in the troubled events of the preceding decade, and Mary never succeeded in welding them into a team. Even her appointments to the highest offices of state show a divided mind, and a tendency to recognize past service or allegiance, without much thought for future coherence or co-operation. The element of continuity was strong. After a period of acute uncertainty, the marquis of Winchester was reappointed to the lord treasurership on or about 8 August,[85] although his favour remained precarious for some time, and he was compelled to surrender his lucrative mastership of the court of wards to Sir Francis Englefield. As late as 1 November there were rumours that his office would be conferred upon Sir Edward Waldegrave. 'The Treasurer is held to be the richest man in England', reported Renard, 'and he made his fortune by devouring church property and the substance of wards and minors . . .'[86] The earl of Bedford was similarly reappointed to the office of lord privy seal by 17 August, and the brief commission of Sir Nicholas Hare came to an end.[87] Sir William Petre, a principal secretary throughout Edward's reign, was occupying the same position in Mary's administration by the beginning of August.[88] Sir Anthony St Leger was returned to his post as lord deputy of Ireland, and the earl of Shrewsbury continued as president of the council in the North.[89] England's two most important resident embassies also remained in the same hands, Thirlby staying in Brussels until recalled to the council in October, and Wotton continuing in Paris until the outbreak of war nearly four years later. At a slightly lower level Mary also retained the services of her brother's attorney-general, Edward Griffen, his treasurer of the mint, Sir Edmund Peckham,[90] and his chancellor of the exchequer, Sir John Baker.

On the other hand, the number of displacements was significantly greater than was normal at the beginning of a new reign. Thomas Goodrich, Edward's chancellor, and two principal secretaries, Sir John Cheke and Sir William Cecil, were removed from office. The great seal was entrusted to Stephen Gardiner on 23 August, and John Bourne became principal secretary a few days earlier.[91] The duke of Northumberland's presidency of the council was bestowed upon the earl of Arundel, and the earl of Pembroke was replaced as president of the council in the marches of Wales by the bishop of Worcester.[92] Sir Edward Montague and Sir Roger Cholmley, chief justices of common pleas and king's bench, were replaced by Richard Morgan and Thomas Bromley.[93] John Gosnold lost his position as solicitor-general to William Cordell, and Sir Robert Bowes the mastership of the rolls to Sir Nicholas Hare.[94] In the north the disappearance of the warden-general necessitated a reorganization. For a few months Lord Wharton seems to have remained in command,[95] but his patent as deputy warden-general was not renewed and by the end of 1553 an earlier pattern of government had been restored. Lord Dacre of Gilsland became warden of the West and Middle marches and captain of Carlisle, while Lord Conyers was appointed to the East march and to the captaincy of Berwick.[96] Neither was a stranger to border government, but the issue of these two patents, almost simultaneously, marked a significant break with the immediate past. Military or semi-military posts like the wardenries naturally tended to be more sensitive than purely administrative offices. Sir Edward Warner was 'discharged of his office' as lieutenant of the Tower on 28 July in favour of Sir John Bridges,[97] Sir Philip Hoby lost the ordnance office to Sir Richard Southwell, and Lord Clinton was replaced as high admiral by Lord William Howard,[98] who had earned Mary's gratitude by holding Calais for her during the succession crisis. The new deputy of Calais was Lord Wentworth.

At the local level, in spite of the considerable number of individuals who fell under suspicion during July 1553, and were briefly imprisoned or confined to their houses, there seems to have been no significant upheaval in the administration. At first, while her position was still insecure, the queen showed a natural tendency to issue her instructions to catholics who were known to be her adherents, rather than to the local officials. In Essex, for example, various members of the Tirrell family were particularly active on her behalf.[99] Thereafter there seems to have been very little disturbance, except for the removal of those actually attainted of treason. In a county such as Kent this made a noticeable difference to the commission of the peace, but nationally the number of exclusions on political or religious grounds was small, the fluctuations in the membership and order of the commissions being mainly explicable in other ways.[100] The council certainly attempted to influence elections to important borough offices, and to parliament, but enjoyed only very partial success.[101] In the central administration the reform of the exchequer and the subsequent abolition of the court of first fruits and tenths caused significant displacement, but the holders of posts in the dissolved institutions were generously compensated, and these changes had in any case been planned well before Mary's accession. Except for a relatively small number of senior posts the entrenched interests of the 'civil service' were undisturbed. The queen did not dispense her favours indiscriminately, and her influence at that level was indirect and slow to act. As we shall see, there was a distinct pattern in her patronage, but she made no attempt to carry out an extensive purge of office-holders. A typical experience was that of Nicholas Bacon, the promising young attorney of the court of wards. A noted protestant under Edward and a close friend of Sir William Cecil, he made his peace with the queen, conformed to the religious changes, and kept his office.[102] On the other hand, he gained no favour and made no progress. His career stood still for five years and he consoled himself with scholarship and literature.

In her choice of councillors, and of officers at all levels, the queen's freedom of action was circumscribed by considerations of political wisdom and practicability. The more intimate environment of her court and household offered substantially more freedom, and it is here, as one would expect, that her personal predilections are most noticeable. With the exception of Sir Thomas Cheney, the treasurer, all the chief officers were replaced. The earl of Arundel became great master and lord steward, positions previously held by the duke of Northumberland. The earl of Oxford recovered his hereditary position of lord great chamberlain from the marquis of Northampton,[103] and Thomas Lord Darcy lost the functional chamberlainship to Sir John Gage. Robert Rochester continued to serve Mary as controller, replacing Sir Richard Cotton; Sir Henry Jerningham took over the sensitive position of vice-chamberlain and captain of the guard from the attainted Gates. Sir Edward Hastings became master of the horse, and Edward Waldegrave master of the great wardrobe. At a slightly lower level Sir Edmund Peckham, who, like Cheney, had swiftly declared for Mary and been received into her favour, was permitted to continue as cofferer.[104] The privy chamber was also completely purged, partly because Northumberland had exercised his political patronage on it to a very marked degree since Somerset's fall,[105] but also because a female ruler required female attendants. The gentlemen of the privy chamber, hitherto a numerous and influential group, were reduced to less than half a dozen, and in their place a team of seven ladies and thirteen gentlewomen appeared. Some of these, notably Susan Clarencius and Frideswide Strelly, had been with Mary for years, and were very close to her.[106] It was not long before their influence attracted the unfavourable notice of the emperor, who instructed his ambassadors on 23 August 1553 to mention discreetly to the queen '. . . that people are said to murmur because some of her ladies take advantage of their positions to obtain certain concessions for their own private interest and profit . . .'[107] His main anxiety seems to have been lest these women who 'did nothing but chatter of marriage' to Mary should be induced to use their influence in favour of Edward Courtenay, whose mother, the marchioness of Exeter, was a frequent and welcome visitor at court.[108] He need not have worried. Whether as a result of Renard's skill, or cash bribes, or out of a genuine understanding of their mistress's mood, the queen's gentlewomen came out strongly in favour of Philip.[109] Several of these ladies were widows, including Susan Clarencius, the mistress of the robes, who was probably the most influential of them all. Others were the wives of Mary's trusted servants – Petre, Jerningham, Cornwallis, Waldegrave. The privy chamber was swiftly and predictably transformed, to become an accurate reflection of the queen's personality. In her public service she felt constrained to employ many whom she did not fully trust, but in this intimate environment she was able to enjoy a measure of confidence and security.

The other departments of the court above stairs, the outer chamber and the great hall, were less affected. Here the interests of career courtiers predominated, and the main changes were brought about by the necessity to accommodate a small number of Mary's own servants. The same was true of the departments below stairs, with their much more numerous and humble staffs. Nevertheless, even there the impact of the new regime was noticeable. Whereas the accession of Edward had passed almost unnoticed, Mary added over thirty names to the 'check roll', and replaced no fewer than five of Edward's sergeants.[110] These were the long-serving and responsible heads of departments, and since there were only eleven such departments altogether, the disturbance at that level must have been considerable.[111] It was also temporary, since the queen was motivated mainly by the desire to reward those who had previously served her, rather than by any intention to punish delinquency, political or otherwise. Consequently after an interval of time the established interests reasserted themselves, as Mary's nominees allowed themselves to be bought out, or were given preferment elsewhere.[112] The household had a natural tendency to increase in size, and its expense featured regularly in the memoranda of financial reformers. Mary was not unaware of this problem, and began by abolishing or discontinuing several virtual sinecures which had been created by Northumberland for his own purposes – chief carver, chief cupbearer, and the four knights attendant.[113] However, the saving was not as great as it might have been, because such holders of these positions as escaped attainder or disgrace, like Sir Henry Sidney, continued to draw their fees as pensioners.[114] Mary also allowed the four masters of the household to disappear.[115] These were posts which had been created in the Cromwellian reforms of 1539, and had not been consistently filled since Henry VIII's death. In February 1554 a committee of the council was set up to investigate ways of reducing the charges, and at some point in the first year of the reign a new set of household ordinances were drawn up.[116] These did not show any very significant departures from the earlier ordinances, but in addition to the usual emphasis upon security and a tighter control over bouge of court, they declared:

It is the Queens pleasure that her Counsellors appointed to tend upon her grace from tyme to tyme as they shall think convenient send for the said Booke [of the Ordinances] and by their discretions note, hear and examine whether anie default be in due execution of the premises, which found shall pr[oc]eed to the reformation, correction or punnishment of such as shalbe found culpable or negligent . . . and if the default be in any of the said Councell, being head officers of the Queens Chamber or Household, the residue of them shall make relacion thereof unto ye Q[ueen's] Highnesse, for knowledge of her further pleasure in that behalfe . . .[117]

In spite of Mary's generosity to her old servants a measure of saving did result from these precautions. In the last full year of Edward's reign the household had cost nearly £66,000; in the first whole year of Mary it cost a little over £57,000.[118] However, as we shall see, the improvement was not to last.

After the privy chamber, it would be reasonable to expect that the 'military establishment' of the court, the gentlemen pensioners, yeomen of the guard, and gentlemen at arms, would have felt the impact of the queen's accession most strongly. However, this does not seem to have been the case. None of these 'bands' had been particularly subject to political appointments under the previous regime. The gentlemen pensioners, who would have been the most liable to such interference, had been protected by the creation of a group of reversionary pensioners at the end of Henry VIII's reign,[119] and by the stubborn independence of their former captain, Sir Ralph Fane, in whose gift the places in the company lay. Northumberland had succeeded in replacing Fane by the marquis of Northampton early in 1550, but the latter had been left very little room to manoeuvre, since he had to honour the reversions.[120] Nevertheless, the pensioners had been placed in a very exposed position during the crisis of July, and when put to the test, had split almost equally. A few dodged the issue by staying at home on one pretext or another, but twenty-one had remained loyal to Jane, while twenty-nine declared for Mary.[121] There is no comparable information for the yeomen, but some of them at least seem to have remained with Northumberland until the end.[122] In spite of this, with the exception of Northampton who was replaced by the earl of Sussex, there is no proof that any pensioner, gentleman at arms, or yeoman lost his place for his part in this campaign. Many were in prison or placed under restraint in late July and early August, and even those who had supported Mary had to petition for the right to attend Edward's funeral, but no action seems to have been taken against them. Only Clement and John Paston were summoned to give an account of themselves before the council, and they were discharged within a few days.[123] Mary's clemency in this respect was consistent with her general awareness of the danger of pursuing any kind of vendetta against the followers of her defeated enemies. As Renard wrote at the end of August, 'if she punished all those who are guilty of anything, she would have no subjects left'.[124] It may also have been partly due to the fact that she had not had a large staff of gentlemen in her earlier household, who would have been the natural claimants for this kind of promotion. Reward loomed larger than punishment in most of the changes which Mary made.

Most of those who were gentlemen pensioners or gentlemen at arms in July 1553 still occupied those positions at the end of the reign. 16 out of the 29 who had then espoused Mary's cause attended her funeral as pensioners, while 13 out of the 21 who had resisted her did the same.[125] Moreover, both the Marian lieutenants, Sir Humphrey Ratcliffe and Edward Fitzgarrett, had been on the losing side.[126] Sir Ralph Bagnall and Edward Underhill may have been deprived for displeasing the government subsequently. Bagnall was to have a turbulent career of opposition. He spoke out against the restoration of the papal jurisdiction in the parliament of November 1554, was in exile for a short time, and was actually attainted for his part in Thomas Stafford's ill-fated expedition in 1557.[127] The case of Underhill is much less straightforward. A convinced and distinctly puritanical protestant, he was interrogated and imprisoned by the council early in August 1553 for publishing an anti-catholic ballad.[128] Shortly after he was released at the beginning of October his place was given by letters patent to one Philip Brown, for the latter's loyal service at Framlingham.[129] However, according to his own account Underhill continued to receive his wages through the favour of Sir Humphrey Ratcliffe. In January 1554, at the time of the Wyatt rebellion, Underhill reported for duty at court, only to be challenged by John Norris, 'a rank papist and therefore Chief Usher to Queen Mary's Privy Chamber', who discharged him. The other pensioners may have resented Norris's interference, because Underhill, who had not hitherto been very popular with his colleagues, was able to reappear a week later and play his part with the others in the turmoil which prevailed during Wyatt's last advance, and which he graphically described.[130] The following July he duly turned up again at Winchester to take part in the wedding celebrations. This time he was challenged by the earl of Arundel, but Ratcliffe came to his defence, saying that he had served since the inception of the band in 1539 (which was not true), and had done good service.[131] This time he was allowed to continue, and although his career at court never prospered, he remained on the roll until he gave up of his own free will in Elizabeth's reign. It seems that Brown's patent never became effective. Underhill's experience not only demonstrates how chaotic even the more noticeable parts of the court could be, but how tenacious established interests were in the face of anything less drastic than conviction for felony or treason. Underhill was doubly *persona non grata*, and in an exposed position since he was well known by sight to many officers of the household, yet he clung on to his position even after it had been explicitly granted to someone else.

The clerical members of the household were less fortunately placed, because the protestant commitment which had been required of Edward's almoner, dean, and chaplains made them specifically unacceptable to Mary. Richard Coxe, the almoner, was indeed a conspicuous delinquent, having played a major part in organizing the prayer books and ordinal, and being generally suspected as a prime mover on Jane Grey's behalf. He was imprisoned in the Marshalsea on a charge of treason on 5 August 1553, but the charge was not proceeded with and he was released into house arrest on the 19th. In May 1554 he escaped into exile and remained abroad for the remainder of the reign.[132] His place in the household was taken, some time before September 1553, by George Day. Day had been deprived of his see of Chichester in 1551, but John Scory's incumbency was ignored, and Day is described as great almoner and bishop of Chichester from his first appearance in the records.[133] Henry Cole became dean of the chapel royal, and purged his domain of protestant sympathizers. The same was not, however, true of the court as a whole. Underhill, who was in a good position to know, later testified that there was 'no better place to shift the Easter time than Queen Mary's court'.[134] The majority of the queen's servants, like her subjects at large, conformed to her wishes in religious matters, but it is clear from the occasional cases in which offenders were later detected or denounced, that the household continued to contain a number of more or less convinced protestants throughout the reign.

Apart from Elizabeth, who spent most of the reign under suspicion and whose servants were under constant surveillance, the queen had no close blood relations, so there was no equivalent of the prince's household which Henry had set up for his son, and which had provided useful extra patronage.[135] Mary did, however, establish a full English household for Philip before his arrival on the lines of the consorts' provision made for Henry's queens, leaving him thereafter to modify it – and reward it – as he thought fit. Like her own, it provided both for chamber and household below stairs, the latter being relatively modest in size and ruled by the queen's lord steward, treasurer, and controller – which seems to suggest that it was never thought of as being completely separate from the main establishment of the court. The chamber, on the other hand, was lavishly staffed. Under Sir John Williams as chamberlain and Sir John Huddlestone as vice-chamberlain served the earl of Surrey and the eldest sons of the earls of Arundel, Derby, Shrewsbury, Pembroke, Sussex, and Huntingdon, as the principal gentlemen.[136] Twenty-three other gentlemen were designated as aids, cupbearers, carvers, servers, and ushers; while a hundred yeomen ushers, a guard of a hundred archers, and a dozen grooms and pages completed this honorific and largely superfluous ménage.[137] In April 1559 Philip's financial advisers calculated that he still owed 45,462 crowns to his English pensioners and servants, a sum amounting to over £11,000 sterling.[138] These accounts are certainly not complete, and since only a minority of those listed were owed for more than one year, this sum must represent a minimum estimate of the king's annual commitment in England for fees, wages, and annuities alone. A substantial inducement to the English aristocracy to be cooperative.[139]

As a monarch who had gained her throne by force, albeit swiftly and almost bloodlessly, Mary was always aware of the problem of security. Although the majority of those who had mobilized to defend her in July 1553 were swiftly disbanded and sent home with thanks, some at least seem to have been retained in response to the emperor's insistent warnings. On 16 August the ambassadors reported that the queen was 'arming 700 or 800 horse and 200 foot', and ten days later they explained that in addition to her 'normal bodyguard of mounted men', eight pieces of field artillery had been taken to Richmond '. . . for her greater safety and to make a show of her strength . . .'[140] These forces must have been additional to the gentlemen pensioners and yeomen of the guard, and were probably disbanded at the end of August, after the duke of Northumberland's execution.[141] The problem, however, did not disappear with the duke and his immediate adherents. Exaggerated fears of protestant and French intrigues were kept alive by the appearance of hostile pamphlets and the nervous promptings of Renard. Mary could not afford a standing army, even of modest size, and fell back instead on the ancient expedient of licensed retaining.[142] As early as August the ambassadors reported that Gardiner was keeping 200 men in his house because of 'tumults over the mass', and in November he was licensed to retain that number, over and above his household servants, with a retrospective pardon from 1 September.[143] At the same time the earl of Arundel received a similar licence, and Lord Paget one for a hundred men.[144] Apart from Nicholas Heath, who was licensed to retain ten men in his capacity of president of the council in the marches, no more were issued for over a year, but later in the reign it became a regular expedient, and was always a good indication of the confidence reposed in the recipient.[145] North-umberland had used the same device to arm his own adherents, and it was not a hopeful sign for the independence and stability of the crown. Nor were such small-scale precautions any use in the face of a real emergency. Confronted by the sudden crisis of the Wyatt rebellion the government was virtually without military resources. From 25 January onward warrants and orders were despatched to trusted nobles and gentlemen, ordering them to hasten to the queen's defence with whatever forces they could raise.[146] Meanwhile the councillors had to rely upon their own retainers, the royal house-hold, and the London trained bands which were on the spot. When the trained bands defected, the situation could have become disas-trous, because apart from Arundel, Gardiner, and Paget the coun-cillors do not seem to have had any useful men at their disposal. Renard's strictures upon their diligence and loyalty were unjustified, but they had been taken by surprise, and the ambassador's earlier criticisms concerning the lack of security were amply vindicated.

In the event, because of Wyatt's slowness an adequate military force of a sort was assembled before he made his final bid to enter London. It was made up of the hastily summoned contingents which we have already noticed, and its fighting qualities were highly suspect, but it was sufficient for the immediate task. Like the similar levies of the previous summer, most of these men were soon dis-missed, but the government was by now thoroughly alarmed, and could not ignore the possibility of further trouble. On 12 February the council drew up a scheme which combined some features of selective retaining with those of a small standing army. Ten of their own number and six other named noblemen and gentlemen were to maintain 2100 footmen and 680 horsemen at the queen's expense.[147] 300 of these horsemen were immediately deployed under the earl of Pembroke to round up suspects in Kent, and most of the infantry seems to have been used to garrison London. On 24 February Renard reported that the earls of Derby and Westmorland had been despatched to their 'countries' with commissions of lieutenancy and orders to raise troops, and that each of the queen's councillors '. . . is keeping up 100 foot and 50 horse, paid by her, for her ordinary guard . . .'[148] No more is heard of the provincial levies. If they were ever raised, they would have been impossible to maintain, except in the event of actual fighting. The 'ordinary guard', how-ever, seems to have been kept up for some time, although probably not at the strength which the council originally intended – let alone that suggested by Renard, which would have numbered over 6000. On 8 March the ambassador confirmed that the queen was keeping up her forces, and added that Lord Clinton had been appointed

'Lieutenant Governor' of the London region, with adequate troops.[149] On 13 March Mary demanded 6000 marks from the city towards the cost of its garrison,[150] and Clinton was still leading 'certain men of warre about London' on 10 May, when he was supplied with corselets, pikes, and guns by the master of the ordnance.[151] On 19 May, Sir Henry Bedingfield was paid £300 'in prest' towards the 'entertainment' of a hundred men, and supplied with weapons. On 24 May, the council recorded the payment of over £400 to the earl of Arundel for the service of his 'band' in terms which also implied that the service was expected to continue.[152] In the original plan he had been scheduled to provide a hundred footmen and 50 horse. The council authorized payment for 50 horsemen from 21 February to 8 May, and 200 marks 'in prest' for a hundred horsemen since 8 May.[153] From this it seems likely that a modified form of the original plan continued in operation well into the summer, probably until after Philip's arrival, when a marked lessening of tension followed the successful completion of the marriage. Despite the quarrels which afflicted the council in April and May, and the loss of favour which several councillors suffered as a result, not even the apprehensive Renard ever suggested that these 'bands' were more of a threat than a safeguard!

Despite the strong elements of continuity which are obvious between Mary's government and that of her predecessor, there was a very marked change in the distribution of power and favour. In the church, which must be subjected to separate examination, this was almost complete – continuity being provided only by the conformity of the humble and unprincipled. In the household it was substantial but patchy; among office-holders apparently significant only at the top, and there but partially. Among the political *élite* there were a remarkable number of survivors, and the observers might be excused for supposing that, with the exception of a few individuals, the pattern of favour and reward would continue very much as before. In fact this was very far from the case, and the queen's generosity showed some distinctly idiosyncratic features. She was generous with knighthoods. Fourteen Knights of the Bath were dubbed at her coronation, including Courtenay, Rochester, Jerningham, and the sons of several leading councillors.[154] The following day the earl of Arundel dubbed a further hundred knights, including Waldegrave, Bourne, Huddlestone, Robert Peckham, Freston, and Morgan, all councillors themselves.[155] With other titles of honour, on the other hand, Mary was distinctly sparing. William Howard became Lord Howard of Effingham on 11 March,[156] Sir John Bridges Lord Chandos, and Sir John Williams Lord Williams of Thame on 8 April, while Edward North was summoned to the second parliament of the reign as Lord North of Kyrteling.[157] On 6 September, also in 1554, Sir Anthony Browne was created Viscount Montague, and in January 1558 Sir Edward Hastings was raised to the peerage as Lord Hastings of Loughborough.[158] These were all the new peerage creations of the reign; the remainder were restorations of former titles lost by attainder or disfavour. Thomas Howard was restored to the dukedom of Norfolk and his attainder annulled in the first parliament of the reign, while his grandson and heir received the earldom of Surrey which his father had forfeited.[159] In September 1553 Edward Courtenay was created earl of Devon, a title which his father had lost by attainder in 1538,[160] while on 13 May 1554 Gerald FitzGerald received the earldom of Kildare, which his half-brother Thomas had forfeited in 1536.[161] Finally, on 1 May 1557 Sir Thomas Percy was raised to the earldom of Northumberland.[162] This title had died with Henry, the sixth earl, who, lacking issue, had made the king his heir in 1537; so the Marian creation was not a straightforward restoration. On the other hand, Sir Thomas was the nephew and heir general of the previous earl, and the queen's intention was clearly the same. Mary pursued a consistent policy in respect of her peerage. Wherever possible the old families, distrusted and broken by her father, reappeared: Howard, Courtenay, FitzGerall, Percy. Only Browne, Bridges, and Williams represent new peerage families, all loyal and diligent men, but distinguished mainly for their powerful religious conservatism. For some reason which is not readily apparent, none of her hardworking household officers and councillors were rewarded in this way – not even Sir Robert Rochester, although it is possible that his death in 1557 may have frustrated such an intention.

Mary herself broke three major families by attainder: Dudley, Parr, and Grey, and although she was not ungenerous in a small way, particularly to the widowed dowagers, none of them was restored in her lifetime.[163] Nor did she restore either of the Seymour titles lost by the attainder of the duke of Somerset in 1552, although her own relations with the duke had been reasonably amicable.[164] These attainders, together with the fall of lesser but still wealthy families such as Wyatt, Gates, and Carew, brought revenues to the crown well in excess of £20,000 a year. In addition to this the commissioners who received the movable goods of the offenders accounted for upwards of 12,000 ounces of plate and over £8000 in cash.[165] Compositions brought in at least another £20,000 in cash and obligations. So, although Renard was over-optimistic when he wrote in February 1554 'confiscations . . . will amount to over a million [crowns] in gold . . .',[166] these windfalls should have made a significant difference to her financial position during the first year.

97

On the other hand, her restorations were an expensive business. The Howards were re-endowed with lands to the value of nearly £2500, and the Courtenays to the value of almost £3000.[167] Other attempts to right what the queen clearly saw as her father's injustices were similarly costly. Henry Neville, earl of Westmorland, in addition to having a £10,000 recognizance annulled, received 27 manors which had once belonged to the duke of Buckingham, to an annual value of £1258 3s. 4d.[168] When the earldom of Northumberland was re-erected, the new earl received 82 manors which had belonged to his uncle – an endowment of over £3000.[169] Cardinal Pole also received a personal estate for his lifetime valued at £1252 *per annum* when his attainder was reversed in November 1554.[170] Sir John Lumley and Sir Walter Hungerford were each regranted substantial parts of their attainted fathers' estates, and Sir Edward Seymour, although not granted a title, did receive over £600-worth of land towards the end of the reign.[171] Henry Lord Stafford, Sir Matthew Arundel, Sir Thomas Stanley, and Thomas Heron were also among those who received grants of forfeited land – the last-named specifically 'for the discharge of the Queen's conscience'.[172] Altogether Mary's secular restorations, not counting the small grants made to those whom she had herself attainted, or their next of kin, committed lands to the value of more than £17,000 a year. If the restoration of religious houses, and the restitutions made to bishoprics, are included, then the crown must, on balance, have surrendered more than it gained.

Moreover, in none of these transactions was the reward of services to Mary herself a major consideration. The earls of Westmorland and Northumberland certainly performed such services, but neither was a councillor, or personally close to the queen. Those who were close to her and served her diligently seem to have been very variously rewarded, although the true profits of office are difficult to estimate, and need to be the subject of much further research.[173] On the whole Mary does not seem to have been generous with outright grants of land. The marquis of Winchester received over £400-worth; Sir Francis Englefield £330 per annum; and the earl of Rutland (not conspicuous for his service) upwards of £250 per annum.[174] Many others, including Lord Paget, the earl of Arundel, and Sir Henry Jerningham, gained estates to an annual value of between £50 and £150, but on their own these would have been meagre rewards, and compare unfavourably with many of the restorations. The real rewards of service came in the form of profitable supplementary offices, like Rochester's chancellorship of the duchy of Lancaster; small sinecures, preferential leases, annuities, wardships, remissions, and opportunities for purchase on preferential terms. In spite of her council's insistent advice to retrench in that direction, Mary seems to have been generous with annuities, particularly small ones, often given specifically for service against Northumberland or Wyatt.[175] The list of those who purchased the movable goods of Northumberland's family and friends – presumably at a discount – reads like a roll-call of the queen's established servants: Arundel, Rochester, Englefield, Hastings, Huddlestone, Mrs Clarencius, Petre . . .[176] Accurate calculations are impossible, but the impression is that Mary's loyal intimates did very well in this lottery. Rochester collected many subsidiary offices and sinecures, and was a rich man by the time he died. Waldegrave and Jerningham also did well in the same area, while Englefield with the court of wards and a substantial land grant probably did best of all. Outside the inner circle, Sir Edward Hastings and Sir Thomas Cornwallis were conspicuously enriched, while hardworking administrators like Southwell and Baker were given a good deal less. Of the peers who had first declared for Mary, the earl of Sussex was rewarded with the wardenry of royal forests south of the Trent, and with about £300 in annuities;[177] the earl of Bath got only 90 marks a year as captain of Beaumaris castle;[178] and Lord Rich nothing of note. Great offices of state, of course, gave many opportunities to their holders to enrich themselves without specific grant, but Mary was not notably generous to her most responsible servants. Winchester, admittedly, gained valuable land, but virtually nothing else; Gardiner gained nothing, neither a personal estate such as Pole was given, nor an archbishopric, nor the cardinal's hat which Noailles had heard in September 1553 was coming his way.[179] Perhaps his early death frustrated generous intentions. Bedford, Petre, Bourne, and Paget all made modest gains, but hardly commensurate with their services. Of the other magnates, Arundel received £1000 that was due to him in debts from the crown,[180] and a considerable selection of small benefits. Pembroke was paid over £400 in debts, and his family were granted the wardship of his heir when he went to fight in France, a potentially valuable benefit which was not in fact used.[181] Shrewsbury and Derby seem to have received very little, although the former's son George was appointed warden of the royal forests north of the Trent, and given a number of minor but potentially valuable offices in the north.[182]

It appears that in rewarding service, Mary was generous in breadth rather than depth, making many small grants and no really large ones. No fewer than 12 boroughs were incorporated in 1554, many of them ostensibly for loyal service in the crisis of 1553.[183] Innumerable annuities and grants of small parcels of land in possession or reversion specifically refer to service against either Northumberland or Wyatt – the beneficiaries varying from important councillors to minor gentry and yeomen. The queen cannot fairly be described as parsimonious. On the other hand, it is hard to avoid the conclusion that her largesse was more freely and lavishly bestowed upon those whom her father had disgraced, or their heirs, than it was upon the majority of her own servants and councillors. Complaints about Mary's 'unthankfulness', although not always justified in the mouths of those who uttered them, nevertheless had some foundation. We cannot know whether the queen's favour would have created great new dynasties if she had lived longer, but the indications are negative. The pattern of Mary's patronage did not very closely correspond to the structure of her regime. In choosing her councillors, her administrators, and to a lesser extent her household, the queen was circumscribed by established interests and unavoidable political realities. We can see to some extent through the working of her council in the first year of the reign, before Philip's arrival introduced a new element, the nature of her real ambitions and interests. But these are, I think, revealed more clearly when she felt free to pacify her troubled conscience by righting some of the innumerable wrongs of the world in which she found herself.

Notes

1 Jordan, *The Threshold of Power*, 517. See also above, 63.
2 Most notably by A. F. Pollard, *The Political History of England, 1547–1603* (1919), 94-5.
3 Mary's initial letter to the council was written from Kenninghall, and it must have been there, or during her flight, that the first meetings of her own embryonic council were held, although nothing was recorded until after her arrival at Framlingham.
4 *The Chronicle of Queen Jane*, Camden Society, 48 (1850), 5. C. Wriothesley, *A Chronicle of England*, Camden Society, n.s. 11 (1877), II, 87. Wharton and Mordaunt were the sons of the barons of those names.
5 Notes of the Framlingham meetings begin on 14 July. *APC*, IV, 415 *et seq*. The MS containing these notes is among the Cecil Papers at Hatfield House (245/1), and it has been convincingly attributed to Bourne by G. A. Lemasters. Lemasters, 'The Privy Council in the reign of Queen Mary I' (unpublished Cambridge PhD thesis, 1971), 255-6.
6 Paget actually joined the lords in London only a day or two before their decision to submit, and their invitation to him must be seen as a move in that direction. S. R. Gammon, *Statesman and Schemer* (1973), 186-7.
7 Scheyfve had reported friction between them in February. *Cal Span.*, XI, 13. The marriage of his son Lord Herbert to Lady Catherine Grey on 25 May was probably an attempt to secure his doubtful loyalty. See also Jordan, *The Threshold of Power*, 526.

8 *Chronicle of Queen Jane*, 10-11.
9 *APC*, IV, 418. By this time Mary was at Newhall.
10 ibid., 419.
11 Suffolk was committed to the Tower on 28 July and released on 31 July. *Diary of Henry Machyn*, 38. He was pardoned on 27 November for all offences committed before 1 October. *Cal. Pat.*, Philip and Mary, I, 194.
12 *APC*, IV, 306-8.
13 Cranmer was tried for high treason on 13 November, and convicted. PRO Baga de Secretis, KB8/23. His attainder was confirmed by parliament the following month and he was never pardoned, but the queen preferred to execute him on what was, to her, the major charge. *OM*, 120-1.
14 D. E. Hoak, *The King's Council in the Reign of Edward VI*, 79, lists 31 councillors in March 1552. To them must be added the earl of Arundel and Sir John Cheke. The survivors were Arundel, Baker, Bedford, Cheney, Gage, Mason, Pembroke, Petre, Rich, Shrewsbury, and Winchester. Clinton was readmitted in April 1557 and Wotton in August of the same year.
15 *APC*, IV, 311-60.
16 Hoak, op. cit., 66-70.
17 Thomas West had been born in about 1472, and was consequently over eighty by this time. He had been knighted during the French campaign of 1513, and inherited his peerage on the death of his father in 1525. Implicated in the western 'conspiracy' of 1538, he had been imprisoned and fined £3000. Thereafter he did not venture to oppose official religious policy openly, but remained a staunch conservative and was out of favour with Somerset. Curiously, Northumberland patronized him – perhaps because of a marriage connection between the two families – and he was made a Knight of the Garter in 1549. *DNB*.
18 *Chronicle of Queen Jane*, 14. *APC*, IV, 315. The attainder was declared void by Mary's first parliament.
19 Not only had Tunstall been deprived, but his see had been abolished by statute in 1552. For the circumstances of his restoration, see D. M. Loades, 'The Last Years of Cuthbert Tunstall, 1547–1559', *Durham University Journal*, 66, i, 10-22.
20 *Cal. Span.*, XI, 114.
21 Ambassadors to the emperor, 27 July 1553. ibid., 120.
22 J. Foxe, *Acts and Monuments*, V, 691.
23 *APC*, IV, 311.
24 *APC*, IV, 340. Hooper, described as 'Bishop of Gloucester', was committed to the Fleet on 1 September. ibid., 337. Hooper was not formally deprived until March 1554. See below, 158 and n. Both Heath and Thirlby had been reformers in the 1530s and seem to have become more conservative with age.
25 *APC*, IV, 358.
26 Altogether thirteen privy councillors died during this short reign, perhaps a reflection of the high average age of Mary's appointees. Eight new councillors were sworn between January 1554 and the end of the reign, although it is probable that Sir John Tregonwell, whose oath was recorded on 10 February 1555, was a councillor at large, since he does not seem to have attended any meetings as a privy councillor. *APC*, V, 96. Lemasters, op. cit.
27 Hoak, op. cit., 77-80. Northumberland had shown a tendency to recruit

councillors who were not office-holders, contrary to the Cromwellian practice. Eight of the 31 councillors in March 1552 held no significant office either in the court or the administration (ibid., 79). Mary carried this tendency further; seventeen of her initial 43 councillors held no significant office.

28 Peckham seems to have owed his place partly to the influence of his father, Sir Edmund, and partly to his strong catholicism. Strelly probably owed his to his wife.

29 Ambassadors to the emperor, *Cal. Span.*, XI, 172.

30 ibid., 189.

31 ibid., 228.

32 See particularly Charles's letters of 22 and 29 July, and 9 August. *Cal. Span.*, XI, 109-11; 123-5; and 159-60.

33 ibid.

34 See below, 115-16.

35 Mary's hostility to the French was repeatedly demonstrated, and was far more the result of Habsburg influence than of any rational appraisal of England's interests. For a full consideration of this aspect of her mentality, see E. H. Harbison, *Rival Ambassadors at the Court of Queen Mary* (1940).

36 Bishop of Arras to Simon Renard, 2 April 1554. *Cal. Span.*, XII, 193.

37 The situation was also complicated by the continued presence of the other ambassadors whom Charles had sent over to conclude the marriage treaty, and who were seeking assurances for their personal safety which the council was in no position to give. Ambassadors to the emperor, 31 January 1554. *Cal. Span.*, XII, 65.

38 Renard to the emperor, 8 February 1554. *Cal. Span.*, XII, 86.

39 There was at first some understandable doubt about Wyatt's intentions, and Sir Edward Hastings and Sir Thomas Cornwallis were deputed to communicate with him. This they probably did before 25 January, when Wyatt raised his standard at Maidstone. Loades, *Two Tudor Conspiracies* (1965), 54-7. The first warrants directed to particular individuals for mobilization against the rebels were issued on the same day. *HMC Seventh Report*, App., 610 (Molyneux (Loseley) MSS).

40 Ambassadors to the emperor, 29 January 1554. *Cal. Span.*, XII, 52.

41 See below, 128-9.

42 For example, during the rebellion Renard discovered that Gardiner had attempted to omit the name of Courtenay from the transcription of a captured French despatch, and used this fact in an attempt to persuade the queen that the chancellor 'approved of Wyatt's undertaking'. *Cal. Span.*, XII, 79.

43 Renard's own account of his attempts to bring pressure on the council are spread over a number of despatches, but particularly that of 3 April. *Cal. Span.*, XII, 197-206.

44 Renard to the emperor, 22 April 1554. *Cal. Span.*, XII, 222.

45 Renard to the emperor, 20 June 1554. *Cal. Span.*, XII, 280-3.

46 My own conflation of Lemasters's monthly averages, which varied from 22 for October 1553 to 8 for June 1554. Lemasters, op. cit., 303.

47 *APC*, IV, 318-81. The first attendance list recorded was for 13 August.

48 PRO SP11/1/4, 5.

49 PRO SP12/1/3. A memorandum in Cecil's hand.

50 F. G. Emmison, *Tudor Secretary* (1961), 160-3.

51 Emmison, ibid., 162, quotes Froude to this effect, but J. A. Froude

(*History of England from the Fall of Wolsey to the Death of Elizabeth* (1856–70), VI [*Mary Tudor*], 32-3 [1910 ed.]) quotes no source for his statement. The document he refers to for his figures contains no ascription.

52 PRO SP11/1/22, 23.
53 Renard to the emperor, 5 October 1553. *Cal. Span.*, XI, 265-72.
54 ibid.
55 Renard to the emperor, 6 November 1553. *Cal. Span.*, XI, 337-45.
56 The queen's lack of confidence in her own judgement is a constant theme below the surface of Renard's reports. On 15 March he wrote, '. . . she was greatly perplexed as to how she had better behave, and she wished his Highness [Philip] were already here to take matters in hand . . .' *Cal. Span.*, XII, 157.
57 BL Egerton MS 2603 ff. 33-4. 'The remembrance given to my Mr by my Lord Paget 23 iii 1549'. Hoak, op. cit., 163-4.
58 *TTC*, 89-127. Paget urged leniency in the punishment of the rebels, against both Gardiner and Renard.
59 *APC*, IV, 397-9. The two were Sir John Bridges, the lieutenant of the Tower, and Sir Thomas Pope. Pope was in the special position of having been sworn as a councillor at large (*APC*, IV, 419). Whether any similar oath had been administered to Bridges.
60 The members of the committee were Rich, Peckham, Hare, Pope, Mordaunt, and Bridges, *APC*, IV, 398.
61 He was particularly incensed that 'the heretic element' in the council had taken advantage of Gardiner's absence to persuade the queen to issue an 'Easter pardon' to six of the condemned rebels. *Cal. Span.*, XII, 167.
62 ibid.
63 Thirlby reappeared at the council board on 19 May. *APC*, V, 23.
64 The chancellor and his supporters also complained that the views of heretics were being preferred to those of good catholics. Renard to the emperor, 22 April 1554. *Cal. Span.*, XII, 220.
65 See below, .
66 The way in which the protestant leaders and preachers were rounded up, the expulsion of the foreign protestant congregations, and the effective enforcement of the ban on married clergy after December 1553 are all evidences of the council's efficiency. D. M. Loades, 'The Enforcement of Reaction, 1553–8', *JEH*, 16 (1965), 54-66. See also below, 154-5. Although we do not know who organized it, the repeal of Edward's religious legislation in the first parliament was also smoothly carried out. J. Loach, 'Parliamentary Opposition in the Reign of Mary Tudor' (unpublished Oxford DPhil thesis, 1973).
67 Lemasters, op. cit., 299-300. Southwell sat on 12 commissions during this time, Rochester 9, and Winchester 7.
68 PRO SP12/1/2. For a detailed consideration of the procedure by which the council arrived at decisions see Hoak, op. cit., 126-7. The presiding councillor might seek unanimity, but had no clear means of obtaining it.
69 J. A. Muller, *Stephen Gardiner and the Tudor Reaction* (1926), 217-35.
70 '. . . the rotten and hurtful members thereof [must be] cut off and consumed . . .', as he said in a court sermon on 11 February. *Chronicle of Queen Jane*, 54. *TTC*, 89-91.
71 *Cal. Span.*, XII, 216. When Paget was later justifying himself in an interview with the emperor, he declared that '. . . when the measures to

be laid before parliament were being discussed at the council board . . . the Chancellor had merely read over the headings of some articles on religion, disclosing a few points contained in them . . .' *Cal. Span.*, XIII, 88. Paget claimed that he had never made any secret of his opposition to any controversial religious proposals, and that the majority of the council had agreed that none should be introduced.

72 *Cal. Span.*, XII, 238-43. Lord Rich was the only peer to register his objection to the bill for the restoration of the see of Durham. *Lords Journals*, 10 April 1554, I, 451.

73 According to Renard the bill provided for the suppression of the title of supreme head, '. . . in exchange for which the possessors of the church property were to be confirmed therein by the consent of the Pope . . .' *Cal. Span.*, XII, 216. This was all very well, but Gardiner was in no position to pledge the pope's consent, as both he and his opponents must have known. The bill was probably that which appears in the Journals as providing 'that neither the bishop of Rome nor any other bishop shall convent any person for Abbey lands'. See below, 168-9.

74 Particularly the rejection of a proposal to extend the protection of the treason laws to Philip, which Paget '. . . had assured the Queen was reasonable and would pass'. See below, 136.

75 Arundel, Derby, Shrewsbury, and Pembroke tended to act as a group, except over the marriage, where Pembroke and possibly Derby initially supported Courtenay. In the spring of 1554 this group was supporting Paget, or perhaps pursuing its own quarrel against the chancellor, but only Arundel was a reasonably frequent attender at meetings. This struggle did not end with Paget's fall from grace, and should not be seen simply as an extension of the quarrel between Gardiner and Paget.

76 Feria to the king, 14 December 1559. *Cal. Span.*, Eliz., I, 7.

77 Harbison, 89-92. See below, 119-20.

78 Renard to the emperor, 29 December 1553. *Cal. Span.*, XI, 471. Rochester's relations with the queen seem to have been clouded at this point 'because of his pride', according to Renard.

79 *Cal. Span.*, XII, 77.

80 This was particularly true among the middle- and lower-ranking councillors such as Petre and Cornwallis. The former, normally associated with Paget, seems to have favoured Courtenay. The latter, normally a religious conservative, opposed the repeal of the Edwardine legislation. For a full discussion of this issue of 'parties', see Lemasters, op. cit., 103-230.

81 Renard to the emperor. *Cal. Span.*, XII, 220.

82 ibid., 164-70.

83 This course of action was strongly opposed, even by some councillors such as Rochester and Bourne, who supported Gardiner's religious policy, but the chancellor got his way because no member of the council was prepared to be responsible for the princess's safe-keeping. *Cal. Span.*, XII, 166-7.

84 In addition to the fact that 17 councillors held no significant offices, only 19 attended more than one-fifth of the formal meetings which took place during their membership. Lemasters, op. cit., 302. Several of the non-attendant councillors were useful local officials, but their nominal status was irrelevant.

85 A letter to 'the Lord Thresorer' is recorded under that date (*APC*, IV, 313), although Winchester did not attend a council meeting with that

title until 17 August (ibid., 323).

86 *Cal. Span.*, XI, 331.

87 Bedford's patent was dated 3 November, but he was attending council meetings as lord privy seal from 17 August. *Cal. Pat.*, Philip and Mary, I, 208; *APC*, IV, 323. Sir Nicholas Hare had been granted a warrant authorizing him 'to seale all kynde of processe . . .' on 30 July. *APC*, IV, 306.

88 Emmison, op. cit., 160.

89 St Leger had served as lord deputy from 1540 to 1548 and again from 1550 to 1551. His patent as lord deputy for Mary is dated 1 September 1553. *Cal. Pat.*, I, 165. The earl of Shrewsbury's patent bears the same date. ibid., 67.

90 *Cal. Pat.*, I, 240. Peckham had joined Mary as early as 13 July, and seems to have been continued in office at once. He was certainly acting as treasurer by 1 August, although his patent of appointment is dated 12 February 1554. *Cal. Pat.*, I, 87.

91 *APC*, IV, 329. Bourne first appears as secretary on 21 August (ibid., 323), but according to Edward Underhill he was already functioning as such by 4 August. 'The Narrative of Edward Underhill' (from E. Arber, *An English Garner* (1877–90)). *Tudor Tracts* (1903), 170, ed. A. F. Pollard.

92 Before 8 November 1553. *Cal. Pat.*, I, 321.

93 ibid., I, 65. ibid. Curiously, Bromley had been a member of Edward's privy council as a puisne judge, a dignity which was not conferred upon him by Mary.

94 *Cal. Pat.*, I, 71. Hare's patent is dated 18 September 1553. ibid., 209.

95 On 28 July a letter to him 'to contynewe in hys offyce untyll he shall knowe further of the Quenes pleasure'. *APC*, IV, 421.

96 *Cal. Pat.*, I, 177.

97 *APC*, IV, 422.

98 The date of this change is uncertain. According to Renard, Mary had already decided to deprive Clinton of the post by 23 September. *Cal. Span.*, XI, 255. On 14 November, Howard wrote to the council complaining that confusion had been created by his appointment, which had been made before Clinton's discharge. *Cal. For.*, Mary, 27. Howard's patent was dated 20 March 1554. *Cal. Pat.*, I, 148.

99 Sir Henry, George, and William. The last-named was appointed vice-admiral of the 'Narrow Seas' on 25 July. *APC*, IV, 417.

100 J. H. Gleason, 'The Personnel of the Commissions of the Peace, 1554–1564', *Huntington Library Quarterly*, 18 (1955), 169-77. Gleason's starting-point is the commissions of 1554, but his conclusions also apply to the earlier period.

101 For a full discussion of the various attempts made to influence the return of MPs, see Loach, op. cit.

102 R. Tittler, *Nicholas Bacon* (1976), 54-5.

103 Although supposedly hereditary in the De Vere family, this office had been held since 1547 by Somerset, Warwick, and Northampton in succession, and had become of considerable political significance. Hoak, op. cit., 82. After its recovery by Oxford, it relapsed into insignificance.

104 His tenure, however, was brief. By 18 October the office had passed to Sir Richard Freston. *APC*, IV, 357.

105 R. C. Braddock, 'The Royal Household, 1540–1560' (unpublished PhD thesis, Northwestern University, 1971), 80 *et seq.*

106 PRO SP11/1/15 'The order of the Queens Matys proceeding with her trayne through London' (to her coronation). H. F. M. Prescott, *Mary Tudor* (1952), 84, 271.
107 Emperor to the ambassadors, *Cal. Span.*, XI, 178-82.
108 Renard made a number of apprehensive references to her influence: e.g., Renard to the emperor, 27 August 1553. *Cal. Span.*, XI, 183-93.
109 ibid., 397.
110 Braddock, op. cit., 82-3 and Appendix.
111 Bakehouse, pantry, cellar, spicery, ewery (pitcher house), kitchen, achatry, larder, poultry, pastry, scullery, and woodyard. PRO LS13/279 f. 5. Household regulations, 1554.
112 Braddock, op. cit., 83-5.
113 ibid., 78-9.
114 ibid.
115 ibid., 85-6.
116 PRO LS13/279.
117 ibid.
118 BL Lansdowne MS 4 f. 19.
119 PRO LC2/2. There were twelve of these reversionaries at the time of Edward's coronation.
120 *APC*, III, 30. Northampton seems to have made about half a dozen appointments of his own. PRO E179/69/64.
121 R. C. Braddock, 'The Character and Composition of the Duke of Northumberland's Army', *Albion*, 8 (1976), 342-56.
122 ibid. Mary's decision to release the prisoners in early August makes positive information unobtainable, but their captain, Gates, had extracted a special oath of allegiance to Jane from them, and Northumberland still had a small force with him when he surrendered at Cambridge.
123 *APC*, IV, 306, 309, 330.
124 *Cal. Span.*, XI, 189.
125 Braddock, 'Northumberland's Army', 356; PRO LC2/4, ii.
126 'The Narrative of Edward Underhill', *Tudor Tracts*, 186, PRO LC2/4 ii.
127 *DNB*; PRO KB29/90 rex 26.
128 *Tudor Tracts*, 170-7.
129 *Cal. Pat.*, I, 198-9.
130 *Tudor Tracts*, 186-91.
131 ibid., 191-2. Underhill must have been appointed some time between 1540 (BL Add. MS 45716, in which he does not appear) and 1546 (PRO LC5/178, in which he does).
132 C. H. Garrett, *The Marian Exiles* (1938), 134-6.
133 i.e., 28 September 1553. *Cal. Pat.*, I, 199.
134 *Tudor Tracts*, 179.
135 Listed in PRO LC2/2 'The household of our Sovereign Lord the Kinge when he was Prince'.
136 *Cal. Span.*, XII, 397-9. See below, 137-8.
137 Philip brought a complete Spanish household with him, which caused considerable friction. See below, 211-12.
138 Archivo General de Simancas, E811 f. 124. These accounts are calculated at 4 crowns to the pound. In March 1554 'Themperor's Crowne' had been valued at 6s. 4d. *APC*, IV, 410; so these must be 'crowns English'.
139 Philip's pensioners included virtually all the politically significant

peerage and office-holders. The original list, drawn up in July 1554, envisaged pensions of £500 each for Arundel, Shrewsbury, Derby, and Pembroke; £250 each for Bedford, Sussex, Howard, Clinton, Gage, Rochester, Jerningham, Petre, Worcester, and Grey; and £150 each for Bourne, Englefield, Waldegrave, Hastings, Wentworth, Dacre, and Southwell. In addition Gardiner, Paget, Winchester, Tunstall, and many others were scheduled for unspecified rewards. *Cal. Span.*, XII, 315-16.

140 *Cal. Span.*, XI, 188.

141 On 4 September the ambassadors reported that the queen had 'disbanded the 2000 horse she had about her person for her guard, on the pretext that their cost was very high . . .' *Cal. Span.*, XI, 204.

142 For discussions of Tudor policy over retaining, see Elton, *Tudor Constitution*, and J. Hurstfield, 'The Revival of Feudalism in early Tudor England', *History*, 37 (1952), 131-45.

143 *Cal. Pat.*, I, 174.

144 ibid., 390, 409.

145 See below, 284-5.

146 e.g., *HMC Fourth Report*, App., 365 (Fitzhardinge MSS).

147 *APC*, IV, 392.

148 *Cal. Span.*, XII, 124.

149 ibid., 140.

150 Greater London Record Office, Guildhall Letter Book, 1549–54, 290.

151 *APC*, V, 20.

152 ibid., 24.

153 ibid., 26.

154 Machyn, 334.

155 ibid. Arundel would appear to have exceeded his commission, which set an upper limit of sixty upon his creations. *Cal. Pat.*, I, 72.

156 *Cal. Pat.*, I, 175. Howard had previously held the courtesy title of Lord William Howard as second son of the second duke of Norfolk.

157 Machyn, 59.

158 ibid., 67. *DNB*.

159 1 Mary, st. 2 cs 34, 22.

160 Henry Courtenay had held the titles of marquis of Exeter and earl of Devon. *Cal. Pat.*, I, 70. He was subsequently restored in blood by parliament; 1 Mary, st. 1 c. 3.

161 *Cal. Pat.*, I, 177. A portion of Fitzgerald's patrimony had already been returned to him by Edward in 1552. Jordan, *Chronicle and Political Papers of Edward VI*, 91 n. 187. He was related by marriage to Sir Anthony Browne.

162 *Cal. Pat.*, II, 495. He had been created Baron Percy the previous day. ibid.

163 Parr was restored in blood by 1 Mary st. 3 c. 47, but received little else until after Elizabeth's accession. Ambrose and Robert Dudley, Northumberland's surviving sons, were restored in blood by 4 and 5 Philip and Mary c. 12, and received small grants.

164 This was probably because the younger Edward Seymour was a minor for most of the reign. He was restored in blood by 1 Mary, st. 2 c. 23.

165 PRO E101/520/14.

166 *Cal. Span.*, XII, 107.

167 Thomas duke of Norfolk, £1626 10s.; Thomas earl of Surrey, £666 13s. 4d.; Edward Courtenay earl of Devon, £1242 6s. 8d.; Gertrude

marchioness of Exeter, £666 13s. 4d. PRO SP12/1/64. This document is probably the report of the council committee set up at the beginning of Elizabeth's reign 'to understand what lands etc. hath been granted by the late Queen during her reign'. PRO SP12/1/57.

168 *Cal. Pat.*, I, 72-3. PRO SP12/1/64.
169 ibid.
170 ibid.
171 ibid. Walter Lord Hungerford had been attainted in 1540 for unnatural vice and treasonously attempting to foretell the king's death by the use of magic.
172 *Cal. Pat.*, I, 472.
173 See, for example, R. C. Braddock, 'The Rewards of Office Holding in Tudor England', in *Journal of British Studies*, 14 (1975), 29-47. (On Sir Thomas Cornwallis.)
174 PRO SP12/1/64.
175 See the typical grants to Henry Lord Stafford, Sir Edward Hastings, and George Clarke of Wrotham. *Cal. Pat.*, I, 483, 85, 168.
176 PRO E101/520/14.
177 *Cal. Pat.*, I, 205-6.
178 ibid., 307.
179 M. de Noailles au Roi, 7 Septembre 1553; R. A. de Vertot, *Ambassades de Mss de Noailles* (1743), II, 143. Gardiner's 'normal' income as chancellor would have been in the region of £1300 a year. He also received a substantial income from the see of Winchester.
180 £743 of ordinary debt, and £300 for a legacy from Henry VIII which had never been paid. *Cal. Pat.*, I, 184.
181 Lemasters, op. cit.
182 *Cal. Pat.*, II, 49.
183 R. Tittler, 'The Incorporation of Boroughs, 1540–1558', *History*, 62 (1977), 24-42.

4 The Spanish Marriage

Following the victory of his army at Thérouanne, the unexpected ease and speed of his cousin's triumph in England restored the emperor's health and spirits to a remarkable degree. Not only did it seem obvious to a man of Charles's strong piety that the will of God had been directly manifest in the course of events, but the new opportunities open to Habsburg diplomacy were exciting and far-reaching. When he had drawn up the instructions for his extra-ordinary ambassadors on 23 June, the main drift of his intentions had been to prevent the French from using the impending succession crisis in England for their own purposes. The ambassadors were to assist Mary in securing her rightful inheritance, but should this prove impossible, they were to concentrate on gaining the confidence of the new government, emphasizing the emperor's affection for the late king, and the ancient enmity between England and France.[1] Whatever the outcome, the question of Mary's marriage could not be avoided. It was already being said in England that should she come to the throne, she would marry a foreigner and subject the country to alien rule. The ambassadors were to counteract such reports by declaring the emperor's preference for an English marriage, because

> . . . if they are reassured as to our intentions they may be less accessible to the schemes of the French, and cease to dread having a foreigner, loathed as all foreigners are by all Englishmen, for their king.[2]

Should Mary be successful, but her position appear to be weak or precarious, they were to continue in support of an English marriage. Only if her position seemed strong and the political situation stable, were they discreetly to suggest some delay in order to 'arrive at a better solution'.

By the end of July the emperor was sufficiently confident of his cousin's security to make the first move in the implementation of this latter plan. On the 30th he wrote to Philip in Spain, observing that now events had fallen out so favourably in England, it was possible that Mary might remember her erstwhile betrothal to himself.[3] He was quite sure, he wrote with more truth than modesty, that if the English could be brought to accept a foreign consort for their queen, they would prefer him to anyone else. However, he was now old and disinclined for further matrimony, so he hoped that it might be possible by a mixture of hints and delays to encourage the English to think of Philip, and even to introduce his name into the negotiations themselves. 'The advantages of this course are so obvious', he went on, 'that it is unnecessary to go into them'. His only fear was that Philip's negotiation for the hand of the Infanta Maria's uncle, the Infante Dom Luiz, had been frequently mentioned situation was indeed a delicate one in every sense. Not only was Philip's Portuguese negotiation a matter of common knowledge, but Maria's uncle, the Infant Dom Luiz, had been frequently mentioned in the past as a possible husband for Mary Tudor, and would inevitably expect to enter the lists in these new and favourable circumstances.[4] At the same time Charles was acutely conscious of the difficulties to be anticipated at the English end. The queen's enthusiasm for the old faith was a mixed blessing, and she had to be strongly dissuaded from ordering a requiem mass for her deceased brother, not before there were ominous rumblings of discontent.[5] Through his ambassadors he constantly urged her to proceed with caution, to keep a reliable guard about her, to treat her defeated enemies with firmness and moderation, and to show herself '. . . a good Englishwoman, wholly bent on the kingdom's welfare'.[6] The English were a violent and fickle people. Against all expectations they had swept Mary on to the throne on a wave of loyalty, and there seemed to be no guarantee that they would not remove her with equal ease if she displeased them sufficiently. In all probability Simon Renard, who was the working diplomat of the mission, had been secretly informed of the emperor's real intentions before he left Brussels, either by Charles himself or by Granvelle. On 29 July, in a private audience which was to set the pattern for subsequent discussions, Renard delicately opened his campaign. The queen, he later reported, disclaimed all personal desire for marriage, but recognized it to be her duty, and expressed her deep gratitude to the emperor for all his good offices in the past.[7] A few days later, after another private audience at Richmond, significant progress had been made. Mary distrusted her own subjects as 'variable, inconstant and treacherous' and was unlikely to marry within the realm. Meanwhile Lord Paget had taken the important step of mentioning Philip as a possible bridegroom in a secret conversation with the ambassador. Renard had responded with cautious interest, and energetically set about counteracting rumours that Philip was already married to the infanta. At this stage the French diplomatic presence was insignificant. Antoine de Noailles, who had sympathized strongly with Northumberland, kept discreetly out of the way until 6 August when he presented his new credentials.[8] Although resolute French opposition would be inevitable once Renard's real objectives became known, in mid-August the Imperialists were more worried by the powerful and popular rumours that Mary would marry Edward Courtenay.

Courtenay was the son of the marquis of Exeter, who had been attainted and executed in 1538, and was thus of the royal blood of the house of York. He was twenty-five and had spent most of his youth and early manhood in the Tower, where he was rumoured to have passed his time in worthy and pious studies.[9] In the event he turned out to be handsome, well educated, and courteous, but totally lacking in discretion and self-control. He rapidly became, and remained for several months, politically important as a patriotic symbol. He was the only remotely plausible candidate for the queen's hand among the English nobility,[10] and all those Englishmen from the lord chancellor downwards who strongly desired her to identify herself with the realm expressed this desire by urging his claims upon her. There is no evidence that Mary ever seriously contemplated following such a course, even before Courtenay's ill-concealed ambition and dissolute behaviour made him personally objectionable to her. Nevertheless, his popularity represented that strong xenophobic streak in the English character which the emperor had clearly identified, and which his envoys must either circumvent or subdue if his aims were to be fully achieved.

Fortunately for his own purposes, Charles had a decisive ascendancy over the queen's mind. She regarded him 'as a father', for reasons which we have already noticed, and soon resolved '. . . to follow his advice and choose whomsoever he might recommend'.[11] Mary was a woman of inflexible honesty and did not make such statements lightly, so there was no danger that she would voluntarily marry someone of whom he did not approve. At the same time, to disclose his hand too fully or too soon would have meant playing into the hands of those who, as Renard wrote on 15 August, were 'doing their utmost to discover means of robbing the Queen of her subjects' affections'.[12] These malign forces the ambassador identified as the French, the heretics, and 'the partisans', by whom he presumably meant Courtenay's supporters. Renard was almost certainly too apprehensive at that early date, and was working less from observation than from *a priori* assumptions, but his fears reinforced the emperor's reluctance to exploit his influence over Mary too obviously. In any case, he could do nothing until he knew the state of the Portuguese negotiation, and it was not until the beginning of September that Philip's letter, despatched on 22 August, reached Brussels. Far from being contracted to the infanta, his son wrote, he had already decided to break off the discussions because he deemed that the 400,000-ducat dowry which was being offered was insufficient.[13] Philip expressed due satisfaction at the news of his aunt's success in England, and a surprisingly complaisant willingness to contract the marriage which his father had in mind.

> I am so obedient a son [he wrote] that I have no will other than yours especially in a matter of such high import. Therefore I think it best to leave it all to your Majesty to dispose as shall seem most fitting . . .[14]

Since both the potential partners thus placed themselves in the emperor's hands, it is important at this stage to consider rather more fully what was in his mind. Mary was thirty-seven, politically and sexually inexperienced and keenly aware of her own shortcomings.[15] At such an age, and with a long record of poor health, she was an unpromising gamble from a dynastic point of view. Moreover, her kingdom was notoriously weak and impoverished; religiously divided and socially turbulent. Philip was his father's sole heir and the apple of his eye. Already a widower with one son, although eleven years younger than Mary, he had ruled Spain as regent since 1551 and was both loved and respected there. Had Charles merely been concerned to keep England out of the hands of the French, he had several relations and loyal adherents to whom he could have turned – his nephew Ferdinand, Emmanuel Philibert of Savoy,[16] or even Dom Luiz of Portugal. Instead he was determined to use Philip, although he knew perfectly well that Philip had made himself extremely unpopular during a two-year residence in the Low Countries between 1549 and 1551, and that the English shared many of the tastes and prejudices of the Netherlanders. Jehan Scheyfve, perhaps not unwilling to make his successor's task more difficult, told Renard at the beginning of September that '. . . the English did not at all want his Majesty or his Highness [Philip], but would prefer the King of the Romans or the Archduke [Ferdinand], partly because they dreaded the rule of Spaniards and partly for religious reasons . . .'[17] Not only did the emperor not respond to this hint, but he showed himself to be both worried and annoyed when Ferdinand's candidature was independently advanced soon afterwards.[18] Had he been primarily concerned to complete a ring of Habsburg alliances round France, as was claimed by the French themselves at the time, it is difficult to see why he should have taken unnecessary risks in affronting those English opinions of which he was so keenly aware. The explanation seems to lie in the tensions which existed within the Habsburg family itself. In 1551 after a long and difficult negotiation, a family compact had been arranged to determine the Imperial succession. For twenty years the emperor's designated successor – the king of the Romans – had been his younger brother, the elder Ferdinand. By 1550 Charles was regretting this arrangement and anxious to secure the future interests of Philip. Ferdinand on his side was equally anxious to advance his own son, Maximilian, the king of Bohemia. The settlement had not satisfied either side. The elder Ferdinand was indeed confirmed in his longstanding expectation, but thereafter the succession was to alternate between the two branches of the family, first Philip and then Maximilian. Moreover, Charles had made it clear that he was determined that Philip should succeed him in the Netherlands and in northern Italy. Both these areas were technically Imperial land, and their rule from Spain would require a legal fiction which Ferdinand was most reluctant to countenance,[19] since it was directly contrary to his interests. So far had relations between the two branches of the family deteriorated that neither Ferdinand nor Maximilian had moved to support Charles against the dangerous rebellion of Duke Maurice in 1552, and their complicity was even rumoured.

In later life Charles had become increasingly orientated towards Spain, and was willing to see his son grow up entirely Spanish in outlook and loyalties.[20] This, together with the behaviour of his Spanish troops, had alienated the German princes, so that in 1552 the rebels could speak of their desire to throw off 'this beastly, intolerable and continual servitude, like that of Spain'.[21] The electors refused to recognize the Habsburg family compact, and eventually refused to countenance Philip as his uncle's successor. In the summer of 1553, therefore, Charles not only saw the English marriage as an opportunity to advance Habsburg interests against the French, but equally and perhaps more urgently, to strengthen Philip's hand in his rivalry with Ferdinand and Maximilian. Both these issues centred on the Netherlands, and it was there that the key to the emperor's policy lay. When Renard wrote to Granvelle on 8 September

> . . . it has been represented to the Queen that his Highness will have great difficulty in keeping possession of the Low Countries after his Majesty's death, for the King of Bohemia is loved there, and his Highness and the Spaniards hated . . .[22]

he put his finger on the sensitive spot. Charles had already decided to abdicate, and Philip would stand a very much better chance of holding his own with the prestige of the English title, and with control over the fleet and havens of England, than he would as prince of Spain with no other resources north of the Pyrenees. In the latter case Ferdinand could have argued with justice that he and his sons were in a much better position to defend the Netherlands against the French, and had in every way a superior claim to the inheritance. The emperor's main object in initiating the marriage proposal was therefore to strengthen Philip's position by resurrecting the earlier Anglo-Burgundian-Spanish alliance, which had been represented by Catherine of Aragon. If there should be issue, such a union might produce a long-lasting Habsburg power bloc in northern Europe, independent of the Austrian branch. If it failed dynastically, and even if Mary were to die quite soon, there were crucial short-term gains to be made. As a ruling queen Mary was the most prestigious match in Europe. Such a match would enhance his son's honour[23] and hopefully give Philip the necessary strategic base to ensure his control of the Low Countries in the immediate aftermath of his own departure.

At the beginning of September Renard was marking time. He had succeeded in building up a remarkably confidential relationship with the queen; so much so that on one occasion she suggested that he should visit her in disguise in order to avoid arousing the suspicions and jealousy of her councillors.[24] The ambassador was gratified by such confidence, and by Mary's innocent avowals of dependence on her cousin, but her naivety also aroused serious misgivings. 'She is . . . inexpert in worldly matters, and a novice all round', he confided to Granvelle, 'I believe that if God does not preserve her, she will be deceived and lost, either by the machinations of the French or the conspiracies of the English . . .[which] will throw her off the throne one fine morning'.[25] Renard was also embarrassed by the continued presence of his diplomatic colleagues, with whom he was compelled to associate himself in formal reports to the emperor, but who did not share his *entrée* to the court. It was mid-September before Charles decided to recall them, and October before they eventually left.[26] More seriously, there was beginning to be talk about Philip as a possible bridegroom, particularly among those to whom the idea was obnoxious, and Paget, who had first mentioned the possibility, was now asking pointed questions about Luiz and Emmanuel Philibert. Then on the night of 6/7 September an English courtier, probably Sir John Leigh,[27] called on Antoine de Noailles and informed him that a firm proposal had actually been made. He supported his story with circumstantial details. If the marriage took place, Philip would live in England, renouncing all other titles, and would bring the Low Countries to the English crown as a dower. Presumably a mixture of apprehension and shrewd guesswork produced this story. Whether Leigh really believed it himself we do not know, but Noailles, who was desperately short of inside information, certainly did. His reaction was violent and immediate. The next day he wrote to Henri II

> . . . la chose me semble estre d'une extresme importance, estimant que ce seroit pour vous et les vostres une perpetuelle guerre estans tous vos anciens et presens ennemis joincts ensemble pour estre apres si fortz . . .[28]

The strongest representations must be made at once, he urged, even to an ultimatum declaring that Philip's landing in England would be an act of war. Fortunately for Renard, Henri was in no position to risk a war with England at this juncture, but the consequence of this alarm was that several weeks before the Imperialists were in a position to open formal negotiations, the French had committed themselves actively and fully to supporting the candidature of Edward Courtenay. They had no plausible candidate of their own to offer,[29] and rightly judged that there was no prospect of removing Mary in the interest of the young queen of Scots, but English sentiment was running so strongly in Courtenay's favour that it seemed possible to build up an irresistible pressure.

A more experienced politician than Mary, or a more intelligent one, might well have heeded the growing evidence of hostility to Philip during September, but the queen's mind was limited, conventional, and obstinate. She had no intention of marrying Courtenay, and the only real alternative to Philip was continued celibacy. Such a course was highly undesirable, partly because there was no obvious heir whose catholicism could be relied upon and partly because she fully shared the universal conviction that government was not woman's work. She needed the support of a husband, and accepted the emperor's guidance without question, so the real political issue which dominated the first six months of the reign was whether any combination of forces would prove strong enough to stop her, either by deposition or in any other way. This situation gradually became clear to those most directly concerned during September and October. Because Mary did not fully trust any of her own councillors, they all started by believing that the issue was open, and Stephen Gardiner, who disliked the French and the Spaniards impartially, emerged as the leader of Courtenay's supporters.[30] As the rumours of a Spanish marriage became stronger, Gardiner and his friends pressed for an early parliament, to precede the coronation which was fixed for early October. Just what such a parliament was intended to achieve is not clear. Presumably a show of strength in support of an English marriage was intended, but there were legal uncertainties in the position of a ruling queen which some may have wished to resolve before the crowning ceremony.[31] It was not difficult for Renard to represent such pressure in a sinister light, and Mary soon decided to adhere to the normal practice. The first English councillor to appreciate the true state of the queen's mind was Lord Paget. As we have seen, Paget inclined to a Habsburg alliance from the beginning, and when Renard at last received the emperor's letter of 20 September instructing him to propose Philip's name to the queen officially, he sensibly turned to Paget as a necessary ally. Renard knew well enough that Paget was ambitious to recover power and office, and was on bad terms with Gardiner.[32] He was also an experienced and skilful politician, and in a private interview at the end of September treated the ambassador to a shrewd analysis of the situation, pointing out the disadvantages to England of a king who spoke no English and who had other realms to care for. He warned Renard that the English had no desire to get involved in war with France, and would not allow Philip extensive powers within England.[33] In spite of a carefully expressed preference for Dom Luiz, it is clear from this exchange that Paget understood the direction in which events were moving, and his comments were intended to be constructive. He also suggested that the emperor should write direct to a selected group of Mary's councillors, commending the ambassador's negotiation to them, although he was too tactful to observe directly that the queen's tendency to confide in Renard behind their backs had already caused a good deal of ill-feeling.

Paget may have supported Renard out of personal ambition, but he might equally have done so out of a sense of duty as a councillor. An English marriage would have had many drawbacks, particularly with a king consort as weak and foolish as Courtenay was turning out to be. The disastrous marriages of Mary Stuart to Lords Darnley and Bothwell in the following decade were to provide striking illustrations of the kind of factional quarrels which some Englishmen foresaw in 1553 should the queen marry one of her own subjects. Not only was it desirable that the queen's consort should be independent of English family and sectional ties, but also that he should have prestige and resources of his own, and that he should be a man of political experience and judgement. In all these respects Philip was a suitable candidate, and he had the additional important advantage of providing strong ties with the Low Countries, which were essential for England's security and economic wellbeing. That Philip was also well known to be a zealous catholic was a more equivocal factor. To Mary it was a prime attraction, to Paget and his friends in the council it was a potential source of trouble. They were for the most part conformists, and could not openly display any lack of enthusiasm for the old faith, but they could and did argue strongly for caution. As early as the middle of October Renard had realized that the issue of secularized church property would be a stumbling block in any attempt to restore the papal jurisdiction, and Paget himself voiced the common opinion that a return to the Henrician situation would be the best solution.[34] The fear of French-backed protestant intrigues, which loomed large in the ambassadors' reports at this time, were exaggerated and unreal. The protestants certainly disliked the idea of Philip as king consort, but their political power was far less than either Renard or the emperor believed. The possibility of a reconciliation between England and the papacy was a subject studiously avoided in all the discussions we have been considering. As we shall see in another context, it was the constant theme of Cardinal Pole's correspondence from that moment in early August when a hopeful Julius had included England in his legatine commission,[35] but his enthusiasm was extremely distasteful to the emperor. Pole made no secret of his opinion that submission to the Holy See was Mary's first and unavoidable duty, and that neither marriage nor the political settlement of her kingdom should be allowed to take precedence over it.[36] Charles seems to have had his own ideas about the future of the English church, and was not prepared to tolerate the cardinal's high-principled interference.

An early memorandum prepared for Philip on the subject of the marriage described it as '. . . mui necesaria para la conservacion y augmento de los estados de su M. y la universal paz de la Xrianidad . . .',[37] and in the minds of both Philip and his father the peace of Christendom demanded the healing of the English schism. By the middle of November word of the emperor's intention had reached the *curia*, and Don Juan Manrique de Lara was able to report the pope's favourable reaction.[38] At the beginning of the following January, when the negotiations were approaching a successful conclusion and Charles applied for the necessary dispensation,[39] Julius was enthusiastic '. . . tiene por muy cierta la reduction de aquel Reyno'.[40] On 10 January the cardinal of Perugia wrote to Philip offering his warmest congratulations, and at about the same time Manrique de Lara reported with gratification '. . . la reputacion y grandeza que su M. haganado con este matrimonio de Inglaterra . . .',[41] and the improvement which had become noticeable in the state of Spanish and Imperial affairs in Italy. The reconciliation of England was a matter of the greatest interest to Charles, both as a thing desirable in itself, and as a means of strengthening his own and Philip's influence in the *curia*.[42] Since the peace of Passau in August 1552 it had become clear that a stable settlement in Germany would necessitate substantial concessions to the Lutherans. Charles was extremely reluctant to make such concessions, both because they offended his own conscience, and because he knew from his recent experiences over the interim that to offend the pope was to open the door to increased French influence and pressure in Rome, which would harm both his interests and his son's. Throughout 1553 the emperor was seeking ways to escape this dilemma, and the English marriage has to be seen in this context. It was essential for his purposes that the reconciliation of England to the church should be seen as a direct consequence of Mary's marriage to Philip, and preferably as a result of Philip's own initiative and management. By such a *coup* he would not only escape any unfortunate consequences of a settlement in Germany but would establish an unassailable reputation as a friend and defender of the church.[43] Eventually, in July 1554, Charles was able to shift on to his brother Ferdinand the invidious task of negotiating with the Lutherans, but that success did not in any way detract from the desirability of giving Philip a catholic triumph in England. No doubt when Renard, on the emperor's instructions, constantly urged Mary to caution in her religious policy, he was genuinely concerned lest she stir up tumults and disorders in her kingdom. Rebellion could have destroyed the marriage project, or even cost the queen her throne, as the ambassador gloomily predicted on several occasions. However, he also seems to have had another motive, which in the nature of things could hardly be acknowledged. Had Mary followed Pole's advice, or even the more cautious programme of Stephen Gardiner, and successfully restored England to the papal fold before the marriage had taken place, a valuable source of credit and prestige would have been lost. When Philip did at length arrive in England and the marriage was consummated, the emperor's caution disappeared not simply because English discontent was then less dangerous, but also because a speedy settlement was required by the new king's interests and honour.

It is not, therefore, surprising that the emperor stopped Pole's progress at Dillingen in Bavaria with specious arguments about the unripeness of the time,[44] or that he took pains to persuade the pope to postpone his legate's mission. In October 1553 Pole was a complication that Charles could well do without. Apart from Paget, whose aid and advice was becoming increasingly valuable to Renard, the Spanish marriage was not winning many friends. On 10 October the emperor wrote in personal but general terms to seven selected councillors, but with no noticeable results.[45] Part of the trouble was alleged to be resentment among the aristocracy at the heavy fines imposed upon some of their number for involvement with Northumberland,[46] but such an explanation is hardly necessary. Continued secrecy, the natural antipathy constantly referred to, and the propaganda efforts of the French gave Renard hardly any room for manoeuvre. The English had had little direct contact with Spain in the recent past. Less than twenty years previously Catherine of Aragon had been a popular queen, and it is not very easy to understand why Englishmen should have conceived a particular dislike for Spaniards by 1553, but such was the case.[47] Noailles and his allies were able to exploit a situation which already existed. Renard, who was a Franche-Comptois and had no great love of Spaniards himself, offered a number of explanations including merchants' quarrels at Antwerp and – more convincingly – '. . . the manner in which your Majesty's own subjects complained of their arrogance . . . and the unfortunate stories repeated by several exiled and refugee Spaniards who live over here'.[48] Probably it was the reaction of the Germans and Netherlanders, particularly the latter, which had communicated itself to England and initiated those extravagant fears of 'Spanish tyranny' which were to play such an important part throughout Mary's reign, and well beyond. Outside the court only the folly and boastfulness of the newly created earl of Devon[49] gave the Imperialists much cause for satisfaction. Inside the court the signs were more hopeful. Renard's personal relations with the queen continued to be excellent, and he was at length relieved of the embarrassing presence of his colleagues, the last of whom departed on 27 October. Mary's friendship with the marchioness of Exeter, Courtenay's mother, was a source of anxiety, but that lady's influence was more than counteracted by that of Susan Clarencius who supported the Imperial cause 'to the uttermost'.[50]

By the end of October the first decisive step had been taken. The queen had been showing an increasing, if somewhat coy, interest in Philip's personal characteristics, and Renard was able to say with some truth that he had 'almost caused her to fall in love with him'. On 29 October, in a scene of celebrated drama, she solemnly swore that she would marry Philip, repeated her expressions of daughterly trust in the emperor, and declared that 'she felt herself inspired by God'.[51] In this unstatesmanlike frame of mind the queen does not seem to have been much interested in the detailed negotiations which were now necessary. The council was formally notified of her decision on 8 November in a select session with the ambassador, and whatever misgivings individuals may have felt, no voice was raised to question the queen's will. There had been considerable opposition to the proposal, notably from Stephen Gardiner, whose distrust of the emperor's intentions was shrewd and cogent. Gardiner feared the inevitable reaction of France, for which there was already plentiful evidence; French intrigues with the protestants; French plots to supplant Mary by Elizabeth; open war.[52] Nevertheless, it was one thing to disagree with a suggested policy, and quite another to oppose the sovereign's decision. Had Mary openly asked the advice of her council, the majority voice would almost certainly have been negative, and both she and Renard probably realized this quite well. However, she had not done so, and whatever prudence might have suggested, no law or custom bound her to. The claim later made by rebels and conspirators that she had acted without the consent of her council was plausible but untrue. She had acted without advice, but not without consent. The chancellor's doubts were not allayed, but his loyalty to the queen was never in question, and Mary did him less than justice when she accused him of preferring the people's will to her own and stirring up opposition in the House of Commons.[53] This latter charge was brought about by the celebrated parliamentary petition of 16 November. This petition was the work of Courtenay's friends and besought the queen to marry within the realm. Quite possibly Gardiner had been involved, because it had been drawn up in late October, when only the most intimate of Mary's friends knew that her decision had been made. Other councillors, notably the earl of Pembroke, had also taken part in the discussions. However, the queen had put the petitioners off with talk of illness until the ground was cut from under their feet, and then publicly rebuffed them in an angry and intemperate speech.[54]

After this there could be no further secrecy. 'This news', the Tower chronicler wrote, 'although before they were not unknown to many, and very much myslyked, yet being now in this wise pronounced, was not only credited but also heveley taken of sundry men'.[55] There was a flurry of rumour and speculation. Courtenay seems to have toyed with the idea of rebellion, of marriage to Elizabeth, and of flight to France. In the event he did nothing. There were threats against Paget's life; Pembroke and Clinton were alleged to be plotting a rising; and Henri II was rudely awakened from the illusion that Mary would never dare to defy the powerful prejudices which he and his ambassador had been so assiduously fostering. By the end of November there was a conspiracy, but of all the powerful and important men who were reported to be disaffected over the marriage, only Courtenay eventually became involved. It is possible that Gardiner still hoped that argument would change the queen's mind, but the main preoccupation of the council by this time was the negotiations for the actual treaty. If the emperor was as enthusiastic as he appeared to be, it might be possible to secure very advantageous terms, and Mary's advisers were quite prepared to strike a hard bargain.

However large Philip may have loomed in the queen's mind, he had played no direct part in the discussions. The two envoys who came to England in September bearing formal greetings to his 'muy cara y muy amada tia' and congratulating her on her accession, were not permitted to raise the subject of the marriage.[56] From time to time both Renard and the emperor wrote briefly outlining the progress of events, and when he was informed of Mary's decision in early November, Philip replied to his father in terms of the warmest satisfaction,

> I implore you to order all necessary despatch to be used [he went on], if the Queen wishes me to go soon, I will start without loss of time . . .[57]

Charles, too, was anxious for haste, and at about the same time wrote urging Philip to prepare a fleet and set everything in readiness, so that he could set out as soon as he received word that the treaty had actually been signed. However, it was soon to transpire that this apparent unanimity of intention was deceptive. Philip might have been less enthusiastic had he known that it was being seriously suggested in London that he should be served entirely by Englishmen and Netherlanders while he was in England.[58] There was also misunderstanding about money. Philip, who was worried about his strained resources, was concerned to cut costs, but his father urged him to bring with him at least a million ducats in minted gold.[59] More important, the treaty itself was negotiated entirely between Brussels and London, and the four commissioners appointed in December to travel to England were all Netherlanders and servants of the emperor.[60] Charles had no hesitation in agreeing to the majority of the English conditions, and replied in careful and reassuring terms to a list of doubts and objections drawn up by Paget for the purpose of forestalling lengthy discussions in the council. He had, he claimed, fully provided against any possible claim on the Netherlands by the king of the Romans, and had no intention that his son should possess any claim to the English crown should Mary predecease him without heirs.[61] A draft treaty, based on these exchanges, was sent from Brussels at the end of November, and approved by the English council on 7 December. A general approval had already been given by the council of state in the Low Countries on 27 November.[62]

There is no doubt that the terms so swiftly agreed upon appear very favourable to English interests. The bulk of the documents[63] consists of a series of elaborate provisions for the succession. Should there be a son of the intended marriage, he is to inherit England and the Low Countries, but to advance no claim to Spain, Italy, or the Indies as long as Philip's existing son Don Carlos or his line survives. Should the only surviving child be a daughter, the same provisions are to apply, with the rider that she must seek and obtain her half-brother's consent before marrying. Should the senior Spanish line fail, the entire inheritance is to pass to the descendants of this marriage; on the other hand,

> . . . in cace that no Children being lefte, the sayd most noble Quene doo dye before him, the sayd Lorde Prynce shall not chalendge any Right at all in the sayd Kingdome, but without any impediment shall permytte the Succession therof to come unto them to whom yt shall belong and apperteine by the Right and Lawes of the sayd Realme.[64]

Under no circumstances can either Don Carlos or his descendants put forward any claim to the kingdom of England, unless the succession should fall to them by English law. Philip is to receive the title of king, and is to be joined with Mary in the exercise of sovereign power. At the same time he is bound to uphold the laws of England, to promote no aliens to English office, and to make no attempt to remove the queen or their children from the country without the consent of 'the Nobilytee of Englande'. Nor is he to possess any executive authority in his own right. England is bound to observe and uphold the existing treaties of friendship, which dated from 1543 and 1546,[65] but not in any other way to become involved in the war '. . . that is between the most Victorious Lorde Themperor . . . and Henrye the Frenche King'. On the contrary Philip is to labour to 'see the Peace between the sayd Realmes of Fraunce and Englande observed' and to give no occasion for any breach.

Charles had good reasons for being so accommodating. Fears that England would be subjected to rule by Spaniards, her laws subverted and her nobility slighted, had been among the main causes of opposition, and reassurance on those issues was absolutely essential. The same was true of the danger of immediate war with France, and the emperor also seems to have been rightly convinced that any loophole which might have enabled Philip to pretend a claim to the succession in his own right would have involved him in an English civil war, to the severe detriment of the Low Countries which it was his main objective to safeguard. He may also have considered that when Philip actually reached England, his political and emotional ascendancy over Mary would be so complete as to make many of these apparent concessions insubstantial. On at least one point Mary was prepared to give him a secret assurance, contrary to the wishes of her council,[66] and her whole attitude hitherto had suggested a willing compliance with any demands which her future husband might make. The same thought had, of course, occurred to the English opponents of the match. No matter how favourable the terms of the treaty might appear,

> In case . . . the bands should be broken between the husband and the wife, either of them being princes in their own country, who shall sue the bands . . .[67]

The arrival of the emperor's commissioners on 27 December provoked hostile demonstrations, and the proclamation of the full terms of the treaty on 14 January[68] seems to have done nothing to allay the widespread suspicion and discontent. Ironically, Philip's reaction was almost equally hostile. Although in correspondence with his father he continued to make smooth professions of satisfaction, the true state of his mind is revealed by an extraordinary document drawn up on 4 January, witnessed by the duke of Alva, Ruy Gómez de Silva, and Juan Vásquez de Molina, and inserted into every *legajo* of the Simancas archive that contains any reference to the negotiations.[69] It is in the form of a declaration, beginning with a recital of the terms of the treaty and of the fact that Philip is about to grant a power in due form to named commissioners to ratify and swear to these articles on his behalf. Until these articles had actually been drawn up, the declaration goes on, Philip had not known of them

> . . . and he intended to grant the said power and swear to observe the articles in order that his marriage with the said Queen of England might take place, but by no means in order to bind himself or his heirs to observe the articles, especially any that might burden his conscience.

So anxious was the prince 'to make valid this protest and revocation' that 'he protested once, twice, thrice, or as many times as was necessary to make the act legal' that 'the power and confirmation which was about to grant should be invalid and without force to bind him, as things done against his will and only in order to achieve the aforesaid object'.[70] The exact reasons for such a tortuous piece of perjury were never made clear. Philip later confessed that he regarded the clause excluding England from the war with France as very detrimental to Habsburg interests, but there was probably more to his indignation than that. The marriage was as unpopular in Spain as it was in England. The prince's courtiers and servants had no desire to follow him to a chilly land of barbarous heretics, and his other subjects had no desire to see him go. Those who knew the terms of the treaty felt that Philip's honour had been disparaged, and it is quite probable that he shared that view, although he never said so openly. Later, when they were actually in England, Ruy Gómez gave vent to his indignation, dividing the blame between Renard and Granvelle:

> The ambassador, far from succeeding in affairs here, gets everything into a muddle . . . However, I do not blame him, but rather the person who sent a man of his small attainments to conduct so capital an affair as this match, instead of entrusting it to a Spaniard . . .[71]

The emperor had been rather less than frank with his son about the negotiations, because he could hardly confess the anxiety which he undoubtedly felt about Philip's ability to maintain himself in the Low Countries. The prince's priorities were therefore different from his father's. He was more aggressive, more concerned to press home the advantage against France, and much more inclined to take his position in England for granted. He therefore found the emperor's willingness to defer to English demands incomprehensible, a reaction which at the same time makes it clear why Charles had felt it necessary to keep the negotiations entirely in his own hands. Philip never quite summoned up the courage to repudiate the treaty, partly because he still very much desired the English crown and partly because of his deep and continuing respect for his father's political judgement. Instead, his acute resentment expressed itself in the paralytic slowness with which he prepared to journey north, in long silences in his correspondence with Brussels, and in his total failure to communicate with his betrothed wife. He did indeed send the necessary authorization to enable the betrothal ceremony *per verba de praesenti* to be celebrated in London on 6 March,[72] but his proxy on that occasion was his father's councillor, the count of Egmont, and the magnificent ring which was presented to the queen came from the emperor and not his son. It was June before the marquis de las Navas at last arrived in England bearing the token which Mary had been expecting for about six months. At no time did Philip volunteer any explanation, either for his remissness in communicating or for his lack of energy in preparing his departure. In January and early February 1554, between Philip's anger and English disaffection, the whole fate of the project hung in the balance.

As we have already seen, a conspiracy among the opponents of the marriage had come into existence at the end of November.

Those whose complicity can be proved were mostly substantial gentry, some of them members of the House of Commons, some erstwhile followers of Northumberland, and some who had been among Mary's earliest supporters.[73] The original leader seems to have been William Thomas, at one time clerk to Edward's privy council, but he was quickly displaced and neither the leadership nor the objectives of the conspiracy thereafter is very clear.[74] The government subsequently accused them of being heretics who wished to restore the Edwardian church, and resurrect the claim to the throne of Jane Grey, who had been a prisoner in the Tower since the previous summer.[75] Detailed examination of the evidence has shown that the second charge was entirely false, and probably made for propaganda purposes, while the first had only a very slight justification. The main motivation of the conspirators was certainly dislike of the marriage, coupled with intense frustration at being unable to find any less drastic method of preventing it. During and after the consequent rebellion leaders such as Sir Thomas Wyatt claimed that their intention was a demonstration in strength, not a change of monarch.

> 'Sir', he was asked, 'is your quarrel only to defend us from over-running by Strangers, and not against the Queen?' 'We mind nothing less than anywise to touch her Grace', he replied.[76]

However, it seems likely that this was less than honest. Had the rebellion succeeded the beneficiary would have been Elizabeth. Elizabeth had been a thorn in the Imperialists' flesh from the beginning. As early as the end of August the ambassadors had coupled her name with those of Courtenay and the French ambassador in a warning to Mary against intriguers.[77] The queen disliked and distrusted her half-sister, believing, probably correctly, that her pose of religious conformity was a mere pretence. By 10 October the emperor was sufficiently alarmed to urge that a close watch be kept on her, so that '. . . such things might be discovered as would give just occasion to the Queen to . . . put her in the Tower'.[78] There were constant rumours that the princess's secret dealings with the French had come to light,[79] but not a scrap of evidence has survived, and probably none ever existed. The trouble was that, by the terms of their father's will, Elizabeth was Mary's heir until either the latter had children of her own, or the will, which rested upon a statute, was overturned by parliament. On 25 November the queen had summoned Renard and Paget to discuss the delicate issue of the succession, and Renard's subsequent report was frank and illuminating.[80] The best hereditary claim was recognized to be that of Mary Stuart, who was half French and betrothed to the dauphin.

There would be no difficulty about excluding her, because she was not mentioned in the will and had been born an alien. The Suffolk line could also be excluded, on the ground of illegitimacy.[81]

> As for the Lady Elizabeth, the Queen would scruple to allow her to succeed because of her heretical opinions, illegitimacy, and characteristics in which she resembled her mother.

Mary's choice had been the unpromising Margaret Douglas, countess of Lennox,[82] but Paget had pointed out the strength of Elizabeth's position, and expressed the frank opinion that parliament would refuse to bar her. His own solution had been to marry Elizabeth to Courtenay, and to recognize her as the heir for the time being, in order to conciliate English opinion and reconcile it to the queen's own marriage. Not surprisingly, this suggestion had aroused Renard's strongest suspicions, and the emperor had imposed an absolute veto as soon as he had heard of it.[83] Nothing had come of these discussions, and the princess's position was unchanged at the time of the revolt.

Had the conspirators been allowed time to mature their plans, it is probable that just before Easter there would have been four concerted risings; one in Devon, led either by Courtenay or Sir Peter Carew; one in Leicestershire led by the duke of Suffolk; one in the Welsh borders led by Sir James Croftes; and one in Kent led by Sir Thomas Wyatt. In the event, partly through the vigilance of Renard and Paget, partly through the weakness of Courtenay, and partly through sheer accident, enough of their scheme became known to force them into premature action,[84] and in the resulting confusion several things became apparent. In the first place, antipathy to the marriage, although widespread among all classes of society, was nothing like strong enough to provoke a general and spontaneous movement of the kind which had put Mary on the throne. Even the lurid reports put about in Devon that the Spaniards would land there and '. . . woold ravyshe ther wyves and daughters and robbe and spoile the commons' failed to produce the desired reaction.[85] Secondly, any association with the duke of Northumberland carried an uneradicable stigma; Suffolk, the only important nobleman to attempt an active part, could not raise more than a handful of his own tenants. Furthermore the orthodox protestant leadership resolutely refused to countenance involvement, some imprisoned ministers even refusing to accept release at the hands of the rebels.[86] On the other hand, the council was divided, and Gardiner's behaviour gave some grounds for suspicion that he still entertained hopes of using the situation to persuade the queen to change her mind. More seriously, the spontaneous loyalty of the previous summer had disappeared. When the Kentish gentry were summoned by the sheriff, Sir Robert Southwell, to meet the main thrust of the rebellion, some made excuses and others were mysteriously unavailable. The London trained bands deserted in the field, and the force which Lord Clinton and the earl of Pembroke eventually assembled was of uncertain temper and allegiance.[87]

Fortunately for the queen the French were not prepared to seize their opportunity. Noailles had been in touch with the conspirators almost from the beginning, and wished to give them full support, but they had no desire for open French intervention, and Henri II dithered. He was subjected to conflicting advice from the constable, Anne de Montmorency, and from the duke of Guise, anxious to take any chance to frustrate the marriage, but unwilling to commit precious resources to what might prove to be no more than another piece of English instability. On 22 January he decided to send ships and money, but by then it was too late.[88] Ironically, it was an unfounded rumour of French preparations on the Normandy coast which caused Renard to seek an urgent audience with the queen on 18 January and urge her to take immediate steps to protect herself. News of this audience, transmitted with suspicious rapidity, convinced the conspirators that they must act at once or not at all. The subsequent course of events is well known. Over-optimism and lack of preparation doomed the attempted risings in Devon and Leicestershire within a few days, but in Kent, thanks to their speed and resolution, Sir Thomas Wyatt and his friends at first held the initiative. The effort of one of them, William Isley, was typical. Riding into Igtham, near Maidstone, on 22 January he announced '. . . that the Spanyards was commynge into the realme wt harnes and handgonnes, and would make us Inglish men wondrous . . . vile . . .', and when the villagers protested that opposition was too dangerous, he urged them that the people were 'alredy upp in Devonshire'.[89] By such means, and by exploiting his well-established position in the county, Wyatt was able to raise a force of nearly 3000, while Renard, Paget, and Gardiner offered the queen conflicting advice and important noblemen such as the earls of Arundel and Shrewsbury withdrew from the court on the pretext of illness. The key to the situation, it was soon apparent, was London. January was an evil month for campaigning, and the rebels needed an early and striking success to give them the national status which they claimed. London was the political and financial heart of the kingdom, and Wyatt had many friends and sympathizers within the walls. By the end of January Renard was very gloomy. Mary had indeed reaffirmed her inflexible intention to marry Philip, and had extracted a special oath of allegiance to him from her household.[90]

On the other hand, the council had turned down his offer of military aid and were being very slow about raising their own forces.[91] There were constant reports of disaffection at the highest level, and the Venetian ambassador, Giacomo Soranzo, was hand in glove with the French.[92] In the event Wyatt failed to take the city, partly because of his own delays, partly because of the queen's resolute appearance at the guildhall on 1 February,[93] and partly because the Londoners feared an incursion of armed men. On 7 February, after a virtually bloodless confrontation at Temple Bar, the rebellion collapsed.

Philip, who had been belatedly and imperfectly informed about these dramatic events, displayed little reaction. When the emperor wrote to him on 16 February, he presented the official explanation in a dismissive tone.

> Certain discontented individuals have caused some unrest in England under the pretext of not desiring a foreign prince, but the real reason was religion . . .[94]

There is no reason to suppose that Philip's continued delays were the result of anxieties about his own safety. He was not a coward, and in any case neither Renard nor his father were frank with him about the continuing tension in England. Both had misgivings which they were careful not to communicate to Valladolid, and Renard certainly had no illusions about the real cause of the rebellion. From his point of view the main task was now to consolidate the advantage which the failure of the rising had given to the Imperial interest, and this consisted primarily in removing Elizabeth from the scene, either by execution or by an inconspicuous foreign marriage.[95] At first it seemed that he might succeed, in spite of the fact that he could expect no support from Paget on this issue, and Paget's prestige in the council had been greatly increased by the success of his tactics against Wyatt. The princess was arrested on 9 February, and for several weeks thereafter the imprisoned rebels and conspirators were rigorously interrogated in the hope of forcing them to incriminate her. Wyatt and several others confessed that they had communicated with her, but not that they had any intention of putting her on the throne, or that her replies had contained any expression of support.[96] Such evidence as could be collected against her was entirely circumstantial, and indeed it was never conclusively demonstrated what the exact objectives of the rebellion had been, beyond the frustration of the marriage. Nevertheless, and in spite of what Renard was told about English laws of evidence,[97] the reasons for Elizabeth's survival were political and not judicial. Gardiner, who would have welcomed her execution, found his hands tied by his determination to protect Courtenay, who was much more clearly implicated;[98] and Paget continued to believe that English opinion could be reconciled to the marriage by an explicit recognition of Elizabeth as heir in default of the queen's issue. By early April Renard had been forced to concede defeat. Neither Elizabeth nor Courtenay was ever brought to trial, and the progress of events in England during February and March had given the ambassador very little cause for satisfaction.

In spite of his clearly proved complicity, Noailles's recall was not demanded, and within a few weeks he had resumed his intrigues with discontented elements.[99] About ninety of the convicted rebels were executed, including nearly twenty of the gentry leaders. This was a high proportion of the 3000 or so involved, by comparison with the toll of other risings, such as the Pilgrimage of Grace, although both Renard and Noailles exaggerated its effect on account of their own preoccupations. The latter, who could now see little hope of using English resistance to frustrate the marriage, represented London as cowed by a deluge of blood, while the former claimed that 'A new revolt is feared because the people say that so much noble blood ought not to have been shed for the sake of foreigners . . .'[100] By the end of March Renard was expressing acute anxiety about the council's failure to complete the trials and executions of the rebels, a failure which he blamed with some justice upon the conflict between Paget and Gardiner. On the 27th he warned the queen that if she did not take steps to remedy the matter, he would have to advise the postponement of Philip's arrival, '. . . for his Highness could not bring forces to guard him, and must look to her for protection . . .' Having failed over both Elizabeth and Courtenay, he was particularly anxious to bring Wyatt to the block, and his persistence in this case was rewarded on 11 April, it being later reported that a special message had been received from Philip '. . . that he would not come in if the knight weare not first made awaie'.[101] Mary was acutely distressed by the ambassador's threats, partly because the majority of her own advisers were urging her strongly towards clemency, partly because of the popular temper which so enthusiastically welcomed the acquittal of Sir Nicholas Throgmorton on 17 April,[102] and partly because of understandable doubts about Philip's real intentions. On 3 April, Renard reported that '. . . the Queen assured me that anxiety for his Highness's safety prevented her from sleeping or taking any rest . . .', and that she had at last taken steps to reconcile the divisions in the council. Consequently he was proceeding with detailed negotiations about Philip's household, specific security arrangements, and the provision of fodder and accommodation.[103]

Henri seems to have been less surprised than Noailles by the failure of English opposition to the marriage to translate itself into effective action, nor did he have any illusions about his own popularity in England.[104] He may have regarded war as inevitable, and was certainly willing to offer all kinds of provocation, but would not entertain Noailles's suggestion for an invasion or seizure of Calais. He deliberately encouraged exaggerated reports of French naval preparations, and entertained English exiles such as Sir Peter Carew, turning a deaf ear to diplomatic remonstrations. Having earlier spread fanciful accounts of the rebellion, particularly for consumption in Italy, where they caused Peter Vannes, the English envoy in Venice, great embarrassment,[105] he later caused his agents to turn their attentions to Spain. Realizing that Mary and Charles were both trying to minimize the hostility of the English, the French naturally applied themselves to creating the opposite impression.

> It seems to me, Sire [wrote Noailles on 17 February], that it would be very necessary for the Prince of Spain and the nobles in his Council to be assured of the ill-treatment which has been accorded here to his father's ambassadors and which people are determined to accord to his own person if he comes here . . .[106]

Relations between England and France continued to be near breaking-point for over three months. Noailles provoked a stormy interview with the council on 15 March over the question of Carew's extradition, and Nicholas Wotton, the English ambassador in Paris, indulged in futile recriminations with Henri and Montmorency.[107] By the end of April Noailles was again expressing hopes that English opposition would revive with the imminence of Philip's coming, and that 'the road to their liberty' might tempt new Wyatts into the field.[108] However, by that time his master was no longer interested in such remote possibilities. The new campaigning season required all his energies and resources, and it would be foolish to risk a defeat at the hands of the emperor for the sake of a hypothetical advantage in England. Consequently, when Noailles again bandied words with the English council, on 10 May, this time over the belligerent status of Philip's escort to England, and declared that Henri did not consider himself bound by the previous treaties between the two countries '. . . otherwyse . . . then of his awne good will and enclinacion and as her Highness shall by her doynges and shewyng of friendship, gyve him cause to do . . .', he found his words repudiated and had to take refuge in explanations.[109] Nevertheless, his continued presence in London reflected, not only the weakness of the English government, but even more its extreme reluctance to admit that the efforts to dissociate England from the

Franco-Habsburg war which played such an important part in the marriage treaty might become dead letters before the marriage had even taken place.

Philip, his enthusiasm for the marriage somewhat cooled, as we have seen, also faced considerable difficulties. There was a sharp reaction in his own council to the prospect of alienating the Netherlands from Spain, since it was accepted as axiomatic that his patrimonial inheritance should be passed on intact to his heir – in this case Don Carlos.[110] It also appears that his Spanish advisers did not consider that the prestige of the English marriage outweighed the dishonourable limitations on the king's power. The treaty was certainly a great blow to the honour and power of France, but it was for the benefit of the emperor, and not his son. Moreover, having been compelled against their will to finance the emperor's policies in Germany for many years, the Spaniards now foresaw an extension of that liability to England. Mary's poverty continued to be a constant theme of Renard's correspondence, and by February she was urgently requesting a loan of 200,000 crowns.[111] Charles prevaricated, not being able to raise the money. Eventually Gresham managed to contract a normal commercial loan, but the money still had to come from Spain, and it was not until July that Philip was eventually prevailed upon to grant the *sacca*, or permission to export, 200,000 ducats.[112] Faced with considerable financial difficulties of their own, neither Philip nor his nobles relished an additional drain on their resources. The journey itself was an expensive project. As reports of French naval preparations became more alarming, the potential size of the escort fleet also had to be increased, and attempts to extract the ship service due from the ports of the north coast were slow and not always effective. Penalties for default at this time were still being discharged nearly a decade later.[113] Many Spanish courtiers had to raise money by mortgaging property or selling movable possessions, and in some cases the prince had to come to their aid.[114] All of this took time, as did the arrangements to hand over the government of Spain to his sister Juana, the princess of Portugal, who was to succeed him as regent. Philip, having originally contemplated coming quickly with a small escort, had changed his mind by January, although some of his servants still anticipated an early departure.[115] On 6 January he wrote that it would not be proper for him to set out until he had received confirmation that the marriage *per verba de praesenti* had taken place.[116] The queen had already decided that she would not marry during Lent, and since Ash Wednesday fell on 7 February, it is clear that by the time he wrote this letter the prince had already decided to delay his departure at least until April. By that time both

Renard and the emperor were impatient and apprehensive. The ambassador had to 'make what excuses [he] could' for Philip's failure to communicate with the queen, and Charles was justifiably afraid that his son was creating such a bad impression that his already difficult task of winning over the English would become impossible.

Unfortunately the situation was complicated still further by the affairs of the Netherlands, where military and financial assistance was urgently needed. On 4 February, Mary of Hungary, the regent, wrote to Philip,

> . . . this country cannot hold out longer unless it is supported . . . you will lose it, and if His Majesty stays here he would only expose himself to an insulting rebuff and you to great loss . . . Things have come to such a pass that the time for allowing yourself to be deceived has gone by . . .[117]

As we have already seen, Charles considered that at least a million ducats was needed for this purpose, in addition to reinforcements. Not only was the need to mobilize these resources a major delaying factor, but the urgency of the situation made Philip's own programme highly problematical. He had no desire to linger in England, and the emperor hesitated between the desperate need of the Netherlands and a clear awareness that both honour and practical politics demanded that time should be spent both on Mary and her kingdom. In January he wrote to his son suggesting a possible compromise:

> Y por esto me parece bien lo que apuntays que despues de vos llegado haviendo communicado y assentado las cosas de aca y la orden que alla se devia tener podria yrme y assy pienzo plaziendo a Nuestro Señor efforzarme quanto fuese possible y acerlo por Agosto o Septiembre.[118]

But such a timetable was soon made impossible by Philip's slowness, and Charles's anxiety about the English situation was compounded by worries about plots and rumours elsewhere

> . . . especialmente in Alemania donde los franceses entran y salen y caminan . . . mas seguramente que espanoles. Y en Saxonia se anda previniendo gente por todos, y el Rey de Francia tiene nombrados sys o siete coroneles.[119]

Eventually, at the end of June when Philip was already at Santiago, the emperor wrote that, in view of the emergency created by the capture of Marienbourg by the French, he was to stay only six or eight days in England,[120] trusting that the English could be made to understand that his honour required him to be at his father's side in such extreme danger. By that time it had already been determined that the troops who were to accompany Philip would not land in England but would proceed direct to Nieuport. The prince's journey began in early May, when the count of Egmont and the earl of Worcester arrived in Spain bearing formal confirmation of the betrothal ceremony two months previously, and he quitted Valladolid on a leisurely progress to the coast. A few days later an English embassy led by the earl of Bedford reached Coruña, where they awaited Philip's arrival. At length, having sworn another ratification of the marriage treaty in the presence of the ambassadors,[121] he sailed on 12 July, accompanied by upwards of a dozen grandees and a numerous retinue, the mood of the expedition being well captured in a contemporary Spanish verse.

> Que yo no quiero amores
> en Inglaterra,
> pues otros mejores
> tengo yo en mi tierra.
> ¡Ay Dios de mi tierra
> saquesisme de aquí!
> ¡Ay que Inglaterra
> ya no es para mí! [122]

While Philip thus gradually got himself to the point of embarkation through a welter of difficulties and uncertainties, the English remained in ignorance of the real state of his preparations. As early as the end of January it was being confidently reported in Antwerp that 140 sail had assembled for the journey.[123] On 8 February, after he had told his father that he would not come until the betrothal ceremony had been performed, he wrote to Simon Renard, claiming that he had despatched his majordomo, López de Padilla, to meet the expected English envoys, and announcing that he would be bringing 3000 men and 1500 horses to England in addition to the complement of the fleet.[124] A week later he wrote again, declaring his intention to make haste. He would come in advance of his suite, with only a few servants, because

> . . . when I arrive I shall have to accept the services of natives, in order to show them that I mean to trust myself to them as if I were an Englishman born . . . And . . . being few, my servants will the better be able to adapt themselves to English ways, which we must now consider our own . . .[125]

There then followed a long silence, and a still longer delay, which caused 'much astonishment'; and when he did come, he brought a full Spanish household, to the embarrassment and chagrin of all concerned. I can only conclude that Philip must have changed his mind not once but several times in response to conflicting advice and pressures from his father, from Renard and from his Spanish councillors. As a result, preparations were made in England, and then postponed or countermanded in a manner not calculated to increase enthusiasm.[126] Renard was so apprehensive in the midst of these discouragements that at one point he suggested that the English should be required to give hostages for Philip's safety,[127] and at another that the prince should bring with him soldiers disguised as servants, and seize some coastal fortress as a secure base. There was also friction between the English and the Imperialists over the provision of a naval escort. Both fleets were at sea from early April, anticipating the need to provide protection against a French threat which never materialized. By June the commanders were at loggerheads and the English crews mutinous. On the 29th of that month the sieur de la Capelle, the Imperial commander, reported that he was having trouble victualling his ships, and that Lord William Howard was incompetent, having no control over his men.[128] Repeated rumours of Philip's coming had turned out to be false. There was frustration in every line of La Capelle's letters, and Howard was reputedly blaming Renard for keeping the ships at sea unnecessarily, declaring that '. . . no ambassador was ever so deep in the counsels of Kings or Queens of England as this one . . .'[129] Equally serious was the fact that Philip's English household was kept for several weeks kicking its heels at Southampton. After yet another false alarm, on 9 July, Renard reported gloomily that the household officers '. . . are now beginning to leave that place, speaking strangely of his Highness . . .'[130]

The domestic political situation also continued to give grounds for concern. The Wyatt rebellion had been premature, and only briefly dangerous, but its collapse had resolved nothing. Neither popular dislike of Spaniards nor suspicions about the treaty were in any way diminished. On 7 January Renard reported that two unnamed English lawyers had expressed the view that '. . . by English law, if his Highness marries the Queen, she loses her title to the Crown and his Highness becomes King . . .'[131] This was presumably by analogy with the law of property since there was no specific law of the succession, but to anyone who remembered that the quarrel between York and Lancaster had arisen from a very similar application of the common law of inheritance to the crown, the argument was a disturbing one.[132] Renard was vehemently opposed to submitting the question to parliament, as some of the English council wished, and Mary concurred, declaring that '. . . even if the law

invested his Highness with such a right he would never use it otherwise than as the treaty provided, trusting entirely to the Emperor's
word'.[133] As we have already seen, the queen's confidence in Habsburg honour was misplaced. In the event, when the marriage treaty
itself came before parliament for ratification in April, it was accompanied by a brief act 'declaring that the Regall Power of this Realme
is in the Queenes Ma[tie] as fully and absolutely as ever it was in any
of her most noble progenitors Kinges of this Realme',[134] which must
have been partly intended to exorcise fears that Mary had only a
'woman's estate' in the crown. Parliament made no great difficulty
over the treaty, much to the ambassador's relief, but it was a source
of acute anxiety in other ways. At first Gardiner intended to summon it to Oxford, well away from the turbulent and heretical Londoners, but wiser counsels prevailed after it had been pointed out
that the city was already a hotbed of intrigue, and the additional
grievance of losing the profits of parliament would make the situation worse rather than better.[135] More seriously, the chancellor seems
to have resolved to press on with the policy of religious reaction, a
course which was bound to displease the emperor, for reasons which
we have already noticed. Gardiner was fighting hard to regain his
influence in the council after the setbacks of January and February,
and the religious interpretation of the rebellion, which he assiduously
promulgated, gave his policy plausibility.[136] Immediately after the
rebellion Pembroke, Paget, and Clinton were the idols of the court,
but divisions of opinion over the treatment of the prisoners, particularly Elizabeth, and the queen's growing desire to settle the religious
question played into Gardiner's hands. Renard grew increasingly
despondent about the effects of this quarrel, and until the end of
April Gardiner was his *bête noire*. Not only had Paget always been
his closest ally in the council, but those nobles who had, since
December, begun to show signs of supporting the marriage, such as
the earls of Arundel and Pembroke, were supporting Paget at this
juncture as well. On 22 April Paget even appealed to the ambassador to persuade Mary to dissolve parliament, because he had got
wind of a proposal to disinherit Elizabeth by statute.[137] Thereafter
the tone of Renard's letters began to change. By 1 May he was doing
his best 'to remain on good terms with both parties, and not be
caught up in their quarrels'; he noted that Paget was opposing the
chancellor's bill for the punishment of heretics, and, incomprehen-
sibly, a measure to extend the protection of the treason laws to
Philip.[138] By 13 May Paget had been disgraced by the queen for his
actions during parliament, and allowed to retire to his estates. The
chancellor, the marquis of Winchester, and Sir Robert Rochester
were now the queen's closest advisers, Renard reported, and there

were strong rumours that Paget, Arundel, and Pembroke would be placed under arrest.[139]

No such dramatic event occurred, and indeed soon after Paget was back at the council board, but a diplomatic revolution had taken place in Renard's relations with the council. He drew close to the chancellor, who was willing enough to efface all memories of his previous opposition to the marriage, and became almost pathologically suspicious of his former associate. It was reasonable enough for him to conclude that a man who had forfeited the queen's confidence as completely as Paget, would no longer be useful to him. However, to countenance reports that Paget was actively plotting rebellion with seditious heretics, reflects no great credit on his judgement. Indeed one of Paget's associates, Sir Philip Hoby, described by Renard as 'the craftiest heretic in England', was shortly after given by Mary a cordial letter of introduction to the Imperial court![140] There remains an element of mystery about Paget's conduct at this time, even allowing for the fact that he was a *politique* who feared the effects of Gardiner's religious zeal. So experienced a politician cannot really have opposed the extension of the treason laws to Philip out of 'ignorance and inadvertency', as he later claimed.[141] Perhaps he considered the proposed measures inadequate, or improper in the case of a prince who would not become king of England until he actually arrived.[142] Whatever his true motivation he was certainly outmanoeuvred by the wily chancellor, the veteran of many such conflicts. Paget never regained the queen's favour, but he continued to be highly regarded by Charles, and was soon to gain the confidence of his son.[143] Thus in the two months before Philip reached England the political pattern had significantly changed. The *politiques* who had worked with Renard during the previous six months or more, and who had been promised the emperor's rewards, were in the shadows. Apart from a generous distribution of gold chains and gifts to officials and minor dignitaries during March,[144] Charles had allowed only promises to be made, since he wished to leave as much scope as possible for Philip's generosity. Not only did Paget, Arundel, and Pembroke now doubt their rewards, but similar uncertainties must have afflicted other nobles who had been despatched to their 'countries' in early May, notably Sussex, Huntingdon, Shrewsbury, and Derby.[145] Noailles's correspondence makes it reasonably certain that neither Paget nor any other councillor was indulging in intrigue against the queen, or even against Gardiner at this time, but Renard was so much on edge that no rumour seemed too fantastic to be credited. The dowager queen of Scotland was reported to be advancing on the borders with a great army; French agents had suborned the Percies; Cardinal Pole was calling himself duke of York and advancing a claim to the throne.[146] In fact the ambassador had lost his sense of proportion, and committed himself much more fully than he need have done to the chancellor and his rather second-rate catholic allies. These mistakes were to be brought home to him after Philip's arrival. Indeed, he had enough real problems, without imagining others. He was short of money, as he had been for most of his stay in England. In March a former servant of Scheyfve's, Jehan Dubois, had accused him to Granvelle of accepting a bribe from the marquis of Northampton to obtain his pardon. He had defended himself vigorously, but the charge seems to have had some foundation,[147] and then in early May he had discovered that one of his secretaries was selling his secrets to the French.[148]

Antoine de Noailles also felt the strain of these weeks of uncertainty. He did not derive much comfort from the discredit of the *politiques*, knowing perfectly well that their loyalty to the queen was not in real doubt. But he did give credence to optimistic agents who still believed that the English would resist Philip's landing, and by the end of May he was firmly convinced that the English council would declare war as soon as the prince arrived. For these reasons he strongly urged Henri to contemplate no peace settlement with the emperor, and to stand prepared to give full assistance to the next English defence of their 'liberties'. He need not have worried on this score, since neither side really wanted peace at this juncture, and Cardinal Pole had made a complete mess of his delicate mission of reconciliation.[149] At what was to prove to be his last audience before the marriage, on 27 May, the ambassador again resorted to bluster and convinced the English that Henri meant to attack them, but was quite unable to persuade his government to do anything more positive than the encouragement of intrigue and propaganda which had been going on for nearly a year.

By the end of May the formal preparations for Philip's reception were almost complete. His English establishment amounted to some 350 individuals, under the overall control of the earl of Arundel, who was to be lord steward of both households.[150] The heirs of seven leading peers were appointed to serve as gentlemen of the chamber, supported by three 'aids', who were clearly interpreters.[151] The lord chamberlain and vice-chamberlain were those staunch and favoured catholics Sir John Williams and Sir John Huddlestone, while the latter was also to act as the captain of a hundred archers who were to serve as the prince's bodyguard. Every indoor duty was catered for, down to the scourers and turnspits, but there was no establishment for kennels, mews, or stables, beyond a note that the queen's master of the horse would 'work with his Highness master of the horse', and no provision for chapel or musicians. Presumably in these rather specialized areas it was realized that Philip would, at first at least, prefer to use his own servants.[152] Needless to say, he was expected to bear the full cost, in addition to the pensions which Renard had already promised in his name. Philip had been deluged with good advice from all sides about his conduct in England, but left no recorded reaction. Charles had earlier written to the duke of Alva, 'For the love of God . . . see to it that my son behaves in the right manner . . .'[153] and had urged that the Spanish courtiers should leave their wives at home 'as even soldiers would be more likely to get on with the English . . .' Friction between two proud and touchy peoples was inevitable, and the members of Philip's train had shown no sign of intending forbearance before they left Spain. It was therefore of the greatest importance that trouble, particularly violence, should be stamped out quickly by exemplary punishment. For this reason, at the beginning of April, Charles sent across to England Briviesca de Muñatones 'licencie es lois', who was to act as *alcalde* (or justiciar) of Philip's household, to work out an appropriate method of resolving disputes.[154] A set of articles for this purpose was drawn up early in May, providing

> First that ther be one commission made by the Lord Stewarde wherin thalcalde and one other lerned man of thenglishe nation be appoincted judges to enquire and determyn all criminall causes for all crimes and offenses to be committed by any of the trayne of the quene or prince that is to say either of any of the Spanisshe or other straunge nation amonge themselfes or against any naturall subject of the quene or of any suche naturall subject against any straunger being of the said trayn . . .[155]

Any capital offence coming under the jurisdiction of this commission was to be tried by English law, apparently by committal to the ordinary courts or to the court of the lord steward, as appropriate. Lesser offences were to be handled by the commissioners themselves, '. . . consideration [being] had to the nation of thoffender', and for the better enforcement of these summary penalties, '. . . two men of good reputation [shall be] appointed provost marshalls thone for the queen and thother for the prince to be aiding to the said commissioners . . .' If the offender was a nobleman, or other person of special consideration, then their cases were to be referred to the council at the lord steward's discretion.[156] Before the end of May Sir Thomas Holcrofte had been nominated as the English commissioner,[157] and sent down, with the *alcalde*, to Southampton to await Philip's arrival.

On 11 June Philip's harbinger, the marquis de las Navas, reached

Southampton, and on the 16th the queen left London and proceeded to Guildford, where she received him.[158] Then, by easy stages, she moved on to Farnham and Bishop's Waltham, where she remained awaiting her bridegroom's arrival and causing terrible problems to her commissariat, who found themselves having to cater for weeks instead of days. At length, on 20 July Philip and his seasick entourage dropped anchor in Southampton water. Leaving their ships at Portsmouth, they proceeded by barge to Southampton itself, where the prince was greeted by the assembled English nobility and received the insignia of the Garter.[159] Neither the French interception nor the threatened rebellion had taken place, and the time had now come when the value of the long and difficult negotiation which had thus been brought to a successful conclusion would be put to the test. The emperor had written to the duke of Alva three months before,

> So great were the difficulties . . . that God would seem to have guided it with his own hand, and I trust it will prove a factor of weight in our endeavours to serve Him and guard and increase our dominions . . .[160]

For Mary the moment was one of triumph, almost equalling that of twelve months previously, and, as for Charles, convincing evidence that her actions were acceptable in the sight of the Lord.

Notes

1 The emperor's instructions to MM. De Courrières, De Thoulouse, and Simon Renard, 23 June 1553. *Cal. Span.*, XI, 60-5.
2 ibid.
3 Emperor to Prince Philip, 30 July 1553. *Cal. Span.*, XI, 126-7.
4 See above, 20. Charles was later at great pains to explain, both through his ambassador in Portugal, Luis Sarmiento, and directly by letter to Dom Luiz himself, that Mary had insisted on choosing Philip. It is clear from the content of the latter document that Luiz had himself revived the project of his marriage to Mary, probably in a letter to the emperor of 31 August. *Cal. Span.*, XI, 374-5. The Portuguese royal family was considerably offended by this double rebuff.
5 Ambassadors in England to the emperor, 2 August 1553. *Cal. Span.*, XI, 129-34.
6 Emperor to his ambassadors in England, especially 23 August 1553. *Cal. Span.*, XI, 178-82.
7 Ambassadors to the emperor, 2 August 1553. *Cal. Span.*, XI, 129-34. After a public audience given to the four ambassadors in the presence of six of her council, Renard was deputed to speak to the queen alone, clearly in accordance with a prearranged plan.
8 Ambassadors to the emperor, 8 August 1553; *Cal. Span.*, XI, 155-8. A special French embassy, consisting of M. de Gyé and the bishop of

Orléans, arrived on 25 August to offer congratulations to Mary upon her accession and general assurances of friendship. Harbison, 71-2.

9 Ambassadors to the emperor, 22 July 1553. *Cal. Span.*, XI, 114.

10 Lord Maltravers, the son of the earl of Arundel, was mentioned in some quarters as a possibility, and so was Cardinal Pole (as yet only in deacon's orders), but the former was not acceptable to the queen, and the latter never contemplated such a course himself. Harbison, 57-8.

11 Ambassadors to the emperor, 2 August 1553. *Cal. Span.*, XI, 132.

12 Renard to the bishop of Arras (Granvelle), 15 August 1553. *Cal. Span.*, XI, 165-6.

13 *Cal. Span.*, XI, 177-8. Despite the explicit statements contained in this letter, Philip had already intimated to his ambassador in Portugal that he would accept the Portuguese terms, and only changed his mind after the receipt of his father's letters. AGS, E376 f. 43.

14 *Cal. Span.*, XI, 177-8. It is clear from later correspondence that Philip's compliance was due less to a sense of duty than to a desire for a crown. He was quite capable of defying his father on occasion, as over the appointment of Juana to succeed him. M. Fernández Alvarez, *Corpus Documental de Carlos V*, III (1977).

15 Ambassadors to the emperor, 2 August 1553. *Cal. Span.*, XI, 132.

16 Known as the prince of Piedmont, he succeeded his father Charles III as the titular duke of Savoy on 18 August. The French had overrun Savoy in 1537 and Emmanuel Philibert at this time commanded an Imperial army in the Netherlands. He regained his inheritance in 1559.

17 Renard to the bishop of Arras, 9 September 1553. *Cal. Span.*, XI, 227-8. According to Renard, Scheyfve had already shown 'some jealousy' over the special role which Renard had come to play in the embassy.

18 In the middle of August, Ferdinand sent his great chamberlain, Martin de Gúzman, to England, intending to raise the question of a marriage. However, Charles successfully vetoed the proposal, and Gúzman was only allowed to present formal congratulations to the queen. *Cal. Span.*, XI, 163-4. When Gúzman's secretary, Alonso de Games, returned at the end of October, he bore letters from the king to Mary specifically advancing his son's candidature. King of the Romans to Mary, 28 October 1553. *Cal. Span.*, XI, 318-19.

19 Philip eventually ruled in Milan as an Imperial vicar. The situation in the Netherlands was much more complex. In 1548 Charles had created the Burgundian circle, which left the provinces under the protection of the empire, and bound to contribute to Imperial subsidies, but not subject to Imperial law. The following year by a pragmatic sanction it was decreed that all the provinces should adhere to the same succession, which was then settled on Philip. In 1553 the issue was partly to maintain the pragmatic sanction, and partly to prevent any revival of Imperial authority over the Burgundian circle during Ferdinand's incumbency of the Imperial crown.

20 Philip was born and educated in Spain, and the Castilians particularly were fiercely loyal to him. Ironically, the Spaniards never reciprocated Charles's increasing regard for them, and the Castilian nobility studiously ignored him when he landed at Laredo in 1556, much to his chagrin. M. Fernández Alvarez, *La España del Emperador Carlos V* (1966), 813-14.

21 K. Brandi, *Charles V* (1939), 602-3.

22 *Cal. Span.*, XI, 212-14.

23 The struggle between Valois and Habsburg which dominated the first half of the sixteenth century was essentially one of emulation, in which honour and prestige played almost as great a part as territorial power, and indeed was very difficult to distinguish from it. See particularly articles by M. François, J. A. Maravall, and R. Menéndez Pidal in *Charles Quint et son temps* (1959). Also M. Fernández Alvarez, *Política Mundial de Carlos V y Felipe II* (1966).

24 Simon Renard to the bishop of Arras, 7 August 1553. *Cal. Span.*, XI, 153-4.

25 Same to same, 9 September 1553. *Cal. Span.*, XI, 227-9.

26 Mary prolonged Renard's agony by requesting them to stay for her coronation, as she explained to the emperor on 21 October. *Cal. Span.*, XI, 308.

27 Vertot, t. II, 142-3. Harbison, 76-7 and n.

28 M. de Noailles au Roi, 7 Septembre 1553. Vertot, II, 144-5.

29 There were no adult princes of the blood at this time, Henri's younger brother, the duke of Orléans, having died unmarried in 1545.

30 Gardiner and Courtenay had become close to each other during the period when they were both in the Tower, so that Courtenay spoke of him as his father. Vertot, II, 247. J. A. Muller, *Stephen Gardiner and the Tudor Reaction* (1926), 235.

31 It was felt necessary to pass a special act affirming the legality of Henry VIII's marriage to Catherine of Aragon, and repealing all statutes or parts of statutes which stated the contrary. 1 Mary, st. 2 c. 1. *Statutes of the Realm*, IV (i), 200-1.

32 Paget had begun his political career as Gardiner's protégé, but had then been an important prosecution witness when the latter was put on trial by Northumberland in 1550–51. Thereafter the two men were enemies. Muller, *Stephen Gardiner*, 198-200; S. R. Gammon, *Statesman and Schemer* (1973), 175.

33 Renard to the emperor, 5 October 1553. *Cal. Span.*, XI, 265-72.

34 Renard to the emperor, 19 October 1553. *Cal. Span.*, XI, 303-8.

35 Pole's original mission was to negotiate a peace between Charles and Henri, but the news of Mary's accession, which reached Rome in early August, caused Julius to give him a mission to England as well. From 13 August onward he bombarded Mary with letters of good advice. *Cal. Ven.*, V, 384 *et seq.* See also below, 171-3.

36 Pole to Mary, 27 August 1553. *Cal. Ven.*, V, 398.

37 AGS, Secretaría de Estado, E 807 f. 20.

38 AGS, E 879 f. 74. 18 November 1553.

39 The close blood relationship between the two had been one of the arguments used by opponents of the match. Philip referred to Mary as his 'aunt', but she was in fact his second cousin.

40 AGS, E 879 f. 95. 1 January 1554.

41 AGS, E 880 f. 34; E 881 f. 1.

42 For the complexity of Habsburg affairs in Italy, and the delicacy required in dealing with the pope, see especially Charles's letter to Don Juan Manrique de Lara of 7 April 1554. *Cal. Span.*, XII, 207-11. Among the archives at Simancas are several interesting memoranda of about this date, listing the cardinals by their French or Imperial allegiance; notably E 809 f. 1.

43 The French had long since attempted to gain Mary's sympathy by urging her to restore the old religion, promising from Henri 'all the

comfort and aid which she could expect and desire from a Christian Prince'. Vertot, II, 119-23; Harbison, 72 and n.

44 Pole to Mary, 2 October 1553. *Cal. Ven.*, V, 419.

45 Gardiner, Tunstall, Arundel, Shrewsbury, Rochester, Paget, and Petre. Half a dozen similar letters were sent with the names blank. *Cal. Span.*, XI, 284.

46 Ambassadors to the emperor, 14 September 1553. *Cal. Span.*, XI, 233-7.

47 '. . . the people and nobility will never put up with Spaniards in this country, for they call them proud and impertinent'. *Cal. Span.*, XI, 333.

48 Renard to the emperor, 11 December 1553. *Cal. Span.*, XI, 425.

49 Courtenay was created earl of Devon on 3 September 1553. There were rumours that he would be made marquis of Exeter and duke of York.

50 Simon Renard to the emperor, 6 November 1553. *Cal. Span.*, XI, 344.

51 Simon Renard to the emperor, 31 October 1553. *Cal. Span.*, XI, 328.

52 These doubts were expressed on a number of occasions, but see particularly Renard to the emperor, 4 November 1553. *Cal. Span.*, XI, 332-7.

53 Renard to the emperor, 6 and 20 November 1553. *Cal. Span.*, XI, 343, 372.

54 *Cal. Span.*, XI, 363-4; Vertot, II, 269-70; Harbison, 92-3.

55 *Chronicle of Queen Jane*, 35.

56 Diego de Acevedo (Philip's majordomo) and Diego de Mendoza arrived at the beginning of September, but Mary would only receive them in the presence of her council, in order to prevent them from pre-empting the negotiation. *Cal. Span.*, XI, 201.

57 *Cal. Span.*, XI, 389.

58 Renard to the emperor, 21 November 1553. *Cal. Span.*, XI, 381. Charles replied cautiously to this suggestion. He was prepared to offer the English '. . . every reasonable ground for satisfaction', but nothing more explicit. *Cal. Span.*, XI, 391.

59 Emperor to Prince Philip, 30 November 1553. *Cal. Span.*, XI, 404.

60 Lamoral count of Egmont; Charles count of Lalaing; Jehan de Montmorency, sieur de Courrières; Philip Nigri, chancellor of the Order of the Golden Fleece.

61 Emperor to Simon Renard, 28 November 1553. *Cal. Span.*, XI, 387-92.

62 A set of proposals, dated 25 November, were apparently submitted to the council for discussion on 27 November. Thereafter they are referred to as having been approved. Licentiate Games to the king of the Romans, 28 November 1553. *Cal. Span.*, XI, 397-8. The Netherlanders were as cool towards the proposals as the English. Harbison, 99-100.

63 Strictly there were two treaties. The first dealt with the dower and made provision for the succession; the second stipulated the various conditions and safeguards demanded by the English council. Rymer, *Foedera* (1726-35), XV, 377 *et seq.* PRO SP11/1/20.

64 PRO SP11/1/20.

65 ibid. By these treaties England was bound to come to the aid of the Netherlands with an army of 6000 men should those provinces be invaded by the French.

66 The English council insisted that the betrothal ceremony should be carried out *per verba de futuro*. Charles wished the present tense to be used, and Mary assured him secretly that this would be done. Emperor to Prince Philip, 21 January 1554. *Cal. Span.*, XII, 36.

67 J. Strype, *Ecclesiastical Memorials* (1721), III, 55.

68 Hughes and Larkin, *Tudor Royal Proclamations*, II (1969), 21-6.
69 e.g., E 807 f. 36 (i). *Cal. Span.*, XII, 4-6.
70 ibid. Philip's procuration is in AGS, Patronato Real, 7; *Cal. Span.*, XII, 6.
71 Ruy Gómez to Francisco de Eraso, 23 August 1554. *Cal. Span.*, XIII, 35. Eraso, who was the emperor's secretary, had already expressed resentment over this. Harbison, 100. Juan de Figueroa, in a letter to Granvelle on 26 July, naturally concentrated the blame on Renard. Biblioteca del Palacio Real, Madrid, MS II – 2285 ff. 70-1.
72 Count of Egmont and Simon Renard to the emperor, 8 March 1554. *Cal. Span.*, XII, 137-45.
73 *TTC*, 15-16. The names are listed in two indictments, PRO KB27/1174 Rex v, and KB8/29.
74 Probably Croftes succeeded Thomas as the main brain behind the operation, although there is no clear proof of this. The objectives have to be reconstructed from later testimony. It seems clear that the conspirators agreed among themselves that Mary would have to be deposed in favour of Elizabeth, but whether Courtenay was ever seriously intended for the crown matrimonial now seems to me rather uncertain. *TTC*, 19-20.
75 Hughes and Larkin, II, 27. John Proctor, *The Historie of Wyates rebellion* (London, 1554).
76 ibid., 48. The rebels' proclamation had invited the townsmen of Maidstone '. . . because you be Englishmen that you will join with us . . . in this behalf; protesting unto you before God . . . we seek no harm to the Queen but better counsel and councillors'. ibid., 50.
77 Ambassadors to Mary. *Cal. Span.*, XI, 194-6.
78 *Cal. Span.*, XI, 281.
79 e.g., Renard to Philip, 3 October 1553. *Cal. Span.*, XI, 261-4.
80 *Cal. Span.*, XI, 293-7.
81 Because the duke of Suffolk had allegedly been contracted *per verba de praesenti* to the sister of the earl of Arundel before he had married Frances Brandon. ibid.
82 Daughter of Margaret Tudor by her second marriage to Archibald earl of Angus. Married to Matthew earl of Lennox, she was the mother of Henry Lord Darnley.
83 *Cal. Span.*, XI, 454.
84 *TTC*, 23-4. On 21 January, Gardiner sent for Courtenay and extracted a confession of complicity, which he then suppressed.
85 PRO SP11/3/10 (ii). Sir Ralph Hopton was alleged to have declared that 'he wolde rather cutte off the kynge of Spaynes hed hym self' than allow such outrages, but in the event, like many others, he did nothing. SP11/2/33.
86 'The troubles of Thomas Mowntayne, rector of St. Michael TowerRyall, in the reign of Queen Mary, written by himself'; *Narratives of the days of the Reformation*, ed. J. G. Nichols (Camden Society, 1859), 218-33.
87 *TTC*, 59-62; 71-3.
88 Harbison, 124-5. La Marque, Noailles's agent and messenger, left Paris on 26 January bearing money and assurances of support. He did not reach London until after Wyatt had surrendered.
89 SP11/2/10. *TTC*, 52.
90 Renard to the emperor, 5 February 1554. *Cal. Span.*, XII, 77-82.

91 Ambassadors to the emperor, 31 January 1554. *Cal. Span.*, XII, 63-6. The council requested instead that the emperor should prepare a fleet to prevent arms or reinforcements reaching the rebels from France. ibid.

92 Soranzo had already been warned not to involve himself in affairs which did not affect the interests of the Seignory. *Cal. Ven.*, V, 448. He was shortly after recalled.

93 *TTC*, 66-7. In a speech to the assembled citizens she called for their loyalty, and declared that '. . . she never intended to marry out of the realm but by her council's consent and advice; and that she would never marry but that all her true subjects shall be content . . .' There are several versions of the speech, which agree in essentials. Proctor, op. cit., 77; Machyn, 53; Foxe, VI, 414-15.

94 *Cal. Span.*, XII, 100.

95 e.g., Renard to the emperor, 3 April 1554. *Cal. Span.*, XII, 197-206. It was important that any prospective husband should be catholic, an Imperialist, and not too strong in his own right. Emmanuel Philibert was suggested.

96 It was alleged that Wyatt had written out a full confession implicating her, but he denied it on the scaffold, and it was never produced. *TTC*, 91-3.

97 He was informed that she could not be convicted '. . . . because those with whom she plotted are fugitives'. *Cal. Span.*, XII, 201.

98 Gardiner had full charge of the investigations, and Renard was convinced that he suppressed a critical letter from the French ambassador, which had implicated both Courtenay and Elizabeth. *TTC*, 93-4.

99 Harbison, 153-66.

100 Renard to the emperor, 12 February 1554. *Cal. Span.*, XII, 96.

101 BL Wyatt MSS 10 f. 4. There is no other evidence that such a message was ever sent.

102 *TTC*, 97-8. W. Cobbett, *State Trials* (1816), I, 870 *et seq. Chronicle of Queen Jane*, 75. The verdict '. . . so much angered the Queen that she was ill for three days . . .' *Cal. Span.*, XII, 221. For a recent and very thorough examination of this case see the unpublished DPhil thesis by Jennifer Loach (Oxford, 1973).

103 *Cal. Span.*, XII, 206.

104 On 21 March he wrote to Noailles that the English had '. . . such an inveterate hatred for this crown of mine that the common people will find difficulty accepting any grace or favour from me'. Paris, Archives du ministère des affaires étrangères, IX f. 22. Harbison, 160.

105 *Cal. For.*, 24 February 1554. Peter Vannes to the bishop of Norwich. Thomas Gresham wrote at the same time in a similar vein, about the damage that the rumours were doing to English credit in Antwerp.

106 Noailles to Montmorency, 17 February 1554. Aff. Etr., IX ff. 137-8; Harbison, 159.

107 Wotton's despatches, over a number of weeks, are full of his accounts of Henri's double-dealing and evasiveness in respect of the exiles. *TTC*, 151-75.

108 Harbison, 167-8.

109 Council to Wotton, 10 May 1554. PRO SP69/4/185. Harbison, 178-9.

110 The Spanish council was very sensitive about the prospect of losing control over the Low Countries, because once Charles had guaranteed in 1548 that they were to pass to Philip, Spaniards seem to have regarded them as attached inalienably to the crowns of Spain. M.

Fernández Alvarez, *Política Mundial de Carlos V y Felipe II.*

111 *Cal. Span.*, XII, 115. The Imperial crown was worth 6s. 4d. sterling; Hughes and Larkin, II, 39.

112 *Cal. Span.*, XII, 304. Mary had asked for permission to export 500,000 ducats, but 'grave difficulties caused by the shortage of coin' made this impossible. See below, 198-200.

113 AGS, Diversos de Castilia, 6 ff. 65-8.

114 *Viaje de Felipe II a Inglaterra*, Andres Muñoz (Zaragoza, 1554).

115 One Ramón de Tassis wrote to Granvelle on 7 January: 'el principe neustro senor da toda la priesa posibile a su partida para ynglaterra y segun esto se trata de veras no se tiene duda sino que en fin de hebrero o a principio de Marco sera la salida de aqui . . . que ciento a dado gran contentamiento en general y particular el casamiento de su alteza . . .' This may indicate that Philip and his courtiers changed their minds very rapidly on learning the terms of the treaty, or that de Tassis wished to deceive Granvelle as to the true state of opinion. Biblioteca del Palacio Real, Madrid, II – 2251 f. 34. I am indebted to Miss M. Rodriguez Salgado for this reference.

116 *Cal. Span.*, XII, 6.

117 *Cal. Span.*, XII, 73-6.

118 Emperor to Philip, 19 January 1554. AGS, E 808 f. 122.

119 Emperor to Juan Vásquez de Molina, 30 April 1554. AGS, E 881 f. 124.

120 Emperor to Philip, 29 June 1554. *Cal. Span.*, XII, 291-3.

121 *Cal. Span.*, XII, 286-7. The conditions sworn to on these occasions were those of the second treaty.

122 Fernando Díaz-Plaja (ed.), *La Historia de España en sus Documentos* (Madrid, 1958), 149.

123 Francisco de Aresti to Juan Vásquez de Molina, 29 January 1554. *Cal. Span.*, XII, 57. There were a number of similar reports reaching England and the Netherlands at this time.

124 *Cal. Span.*, XII, 84.

125 Philip to Renard, 16 February 1554. *Cal. Span.*, XII, 103-5.

126 On 1 March a general proclamation was issued, ordering the courteous treatment of Philip's retinue in terms which suggested that its arrival was imminent. Hughes and Larkin, II, 33-4. Circular letters for the same purpose were prepared in February. BL Cotton MS Titus B 103. Renard reported that 'everything was ready' at Winchester by 13 May. *Cal. Span.*, XII, 153. The Spaniards were inclined to blame some of the delays on the slowness of the English ambassadors. Don Juan de Mendoza to Granvelle, 24 and 29 March 1554. Bib. Pal. Real, II – 2251, 225-6, 239-40.

127 *Cal. Span.*, XII, 197-206. Shortly after a rumour was current in France that Mary would marry in Bruges. Giovanni Capello to the doge and senate, 22 May 1554. *Cal. Ven.*, V, 486.

128 *Cal. Span.*, XII, 293-5.

129 ibid.

130 *Cal. Span.*, XII, 307-10. Several others, including Sir George Howard, had left earlier without licence, pleading poverty. ibid., 289.

131 Renard to the bishop of Arras, *Cal. Span.*, XII, 15.

132 Henry VI's title (apart from possession) depended upon the fact that he was the heir male of Edward III (via John of Gaunt); that of Richard of York upon the fact that he was the heir general (via Philippa, daughter of Lionel duke of Clarence). If the crown was con-

sidered to be a title, like that of a peerage, then Henry's claim was unchallengeable; if it was considered to be an estate, then Richard's claim was best. Legally, the position had not changed since that time. M. Levine, *Tudor Dynastic Problems* (1973).
133 *Cal. Span.*, XII, 16.
134 1 Mary, st. 3 c. 1. *Statutes of the Realm*, IV, 222. It would have been more logical to have passed this act in the first parliament, if it had not been a response to the doubt which Renard mentioned. According to the subsequent reminiscences of William Fleetwood this act caused some suspicion that there might be an intention to 'give unto Her Majestie the same power that her most noble progenitor William the Conqueror who had seized the lands of the English people and gave them unto straingers . . .' (doubt allegedly raised by Ralph Skinner). Fleetwood claimed that these doubts were inspired by an unnamed man who had been a servant of Cromwell's, had been imprisoned in 1539, and would have been charged with treason early in Mary's reign 'had he not been by great frendship holpen'. BL Harleian MS 6234 f. 20-21.
135 *Cal. Span.*, XII, 152.
136 See below, .
137 *Cal. Span.*, XII, 220.
138 ibid., 230-1. For a full examination of the affairs of this parliament see Loach, op. cit.
139 '. . . the Chancellor believes that the heretics mean to seize him, throw him into the Tower, and impose their will on the Queen . . .' Renard to the emperor, 13 May 1554. *Cal. Span.*, XII, 250-4. Whether it really was Gardiner who was so hysterically nervous, or Renard himself, is not quite clear.
140 Hoby had originally been nominated to accompany the earl of Bedford to Spain, but apparently fell under suspicion of involvement with Wyatt. At this time he was given leave to travel, and went first to Brussels and then to Italy. He was certainly out of favour, but there is no evidence that he was guilty of sedition, and in 1555 he returned to England with Philip's full approval. 'The Journal of Sir Thomas Hoby, Kt., of Bisham Abbey', ed. Edgar PPowel. *Camden Miscellany*, X (1902).
141 *Cal. Span.*, XII, 251.
142 When the marquis de las Navas arrived in England in June, he brought with him a number of letters addressed to members of the English council, and signed 'Philippus Rex'. Renard persuaded him not to deliver them, as 'unsuitable', but to convey their contents verbally. *Cal. Span.*, XII, 309.
143 See below, 217.
144 To the value of nearly 5000 crowns. *Cal. Span.*, XII, 158-9.
145 *Cal. Span.*, XII, 251. '. . . and all the others who may be of the plot shall be despatched hither and thither on the pretext of some mission or other . . .' Meanwhile, the queen would keep her own forces in readiness.
146 *Cal. Span.*, XII, 222.
147 ibid., 178-80. Dubois had been Scheyfve's secretary, and his charges related to the time when there was considerable ill feeling between Scheyfve and Renard, just before the former left England in October 1553. Renard had also severely reprimanded Dubois for altering one of his despatches without authority. Harbison, 152-3.

148 Wotton had picked up this information in France late in April. *Cal. For.* Renard wrote on 6 May that he suspected one Guillaume Mondrolois, whom he had already dismissed, but the true culprit seems to have been Etienne Quiclet, his *maître d'hôtel*. 'Vunière', *Etude historique sur Simon Renard* (Limoges, 1878), 103-5; Lucien Fèbvre, *Philippe II et la Franche-Comté* (1912), 156-8.

149 *Cal. Span.*, XII, xvii-xviii. Pole was particularly strongly denounced by the Imperialists, mainly because he had inadvertently made it clear that the emperor did not really wish to negotiate, and therefore revealed him to be less zealous for the welfare of Christendom than he wished to appear.

150 *Cal. Span.*, XII, 297-9.

151 ibid. 'Anthony Kempe, who has served the Queen of Hungary; Richard Shelley, recently at the court of the King of the Romans; Francis Basset, belonging to the Chancellor, a good man and a linguist'.

152 Charles warned his son not to bring aggressive or controversial theologians with him, and the supervision of his chapel seems to have been in the hands of Alonso á Castro, bishop of Cuenca, whom he subsequently referred to as 'my preacher'. *Cal. Span.*, XII, 317 and n.

153 *Cal. Span.*, XII, 185.

154 The emperor's instructions are dated 2 April. *Cal. Span.*, XII, 191-3.

155 PRO SP11/4/10.

156 ibid.

157 Ambassadors to the emperor, 22-25 May. *Cal. Span.*, XII, 258. Holcrofte, who was receiver of the duchy of Lancaster, had probably been one of those to receive a gift in March 1554. *Cal. Span.*, XII, 158.

158 *Cal. Span.*, XII, 283.

159 Don Juan de Figueroa to the emperor, 26 July 1554. *Cal. Span.*, XII, 316. Mary had had a special collar made for him, worth 7000 or 8000 crowns. ibid., 275.

160 *Cal. Span.*, XII, 185.

5 The Restoration of the Old Religion

Edward's death found the protestants in disarray. Instead of rallying to support the protestant claimant, in conformity with what had clearly been the king's wishes as well as Northumberland's design, they divided, and the great majority of those who took any action at all declared for Mary. Alone among the established leaders of the church, Nicholas Ridley preached publicly in support of Jane. Speaking at Paul's Cross on 9 July he declared that both Mary and Elizabeth were debarred by their illegitimacy, and that as the former was of 'the old religion', she would seek to overthrow all the Godly work of the last six years.[1] All the official pronouncements of Jane's council during her brief ascendancy emphasized the same points. Writing to the sheriff and JPs of Surrey as late as 16 July the council refuted Mary's claim on the grounds that Edward had foreseen her intention to subject the realm to Antichrist and to bring in the government of strangers.[2] Such arguments fell on deaf ears, and the few attempts which were made outside London to uphold the king's 'device' were the work of political supporters of Northumberland, not of zealous protestants.[3] The radical John Hooper, who minced no words in his condemnation of Mary's religious policy, nevertheless went to considerable trouble during his subsequent imprisonment to point out that he had actively furthered the queen's cause during this crisis.[4] There were two main reasons for this attitude, which seems to have taken Northumberland and his friends by surprise. One was the overwhelming conviction that Mary was the lawful heir, alike by birth, by her father's will, and by statutory confirmation. The English reformers had as yet developed no theory of resistance, let alone one of religious determinism, and were fully prepared to see the will of God in the vagaries of hereditary succession. The second reason was the strong feeling of failure and impending judgement which existed among many of the intellectual and spiritual leaders. This was no doubt partly the result of the extravagant expectations which some of them had enter-

148

tained, and of the slow and piecemeal progress which the gospel had made at the parochial level. However, it was also the result of a genuine disillusionment with their secular allies, and a growing frustration with the effects of a legislated reformation. Martin Bucer had been quick to see and comment upon this weakness in the English church, and in correspondence with Brentius and Calvin had felt free to express his doubts.

> Affairs in this country are in a very feeble state [he had written in May 1550], the people are in want of teachers. Things are for the most part carried on by means of ordinances, which the majority obey very grudgingly, and by the removal of the instruments of the ancient superstition . . .[5]

Most of the nobility were strongly anti-clerical, and had no appetite for reform, let alone for genuine ecclesiastical discipline.[6] Confusion and abuses of all kinds were rampant:

> The bishops have not yet been able to come to an agreement as to christian doctrine, much less as to discipline . . . and there are persons, even among the ecclesiastical order and those too who wish to be regarded as gospellers, who hold three or four parishes . . . You are well aware how little can be effected for the restoration of the Kingdom of Christ by mere ordinances . . .[7]

Bucer's vision had been one of apocalyptic foreboding. '. . . Unless the Lord look upon our most innocent and religious king and some other godly individuals . . . it is very greatly to be feared that the dreadful wrath of God will very shortly blaze forth against this kingdom . . .'[8] Other continental observers also found England a depressing spectacle, and were sharply critical of its lack of discipline. Influenced perhaps by the views of these respected theologians, their English friends concurred in such censures. 'I never saw so little discipline as is nowadays . . .', said Latimer in one of his outspoken sermons; '. . . the severe institutions of Christian discipline we most utterly abominate', agreed Richard Coxe. 'We would be sons and heirs also, but we tremble at the rod'.[9] With such views being commonly expressed, it is not surprising that the untimely death of the young king from whom so much had been expected was seen as a judgement upon the sins of the realm and the weakness of its ecclesiastical leadership. Antipathy to Northumberland was also strong, not only because of his political ambition and high-handedness, but also because of the frank secularism of his priorities. Having been hailed as 'an intrepid soldier of Christ' after his break with the conservative Wriothesley in 1550,[10] he had become by 1553

F

the outstanding example of a 'carnal gospeller' – one who paid lip-service to the faith but whose actions belied his words. Scarcely any of the 'superfluous' church wealth acquired by the crown had been channelled into education or charity, let alone the augmentation of poor livings. The reform of the canon law had been blocked in parliament, and the subjection of the church to secular jurisdiction and legislation constantly re-emphasized.[11] By the time that Edward died the duke's relations with Cranmer were cool and suspicious, and with Knox and Hooper frankly hostile. The established protestant leaders had also weakened their position in this crisis by the deeply rooted nature of their erastianism, going back to the earliest days of the royal supremacy. Consequently they had neither the will nor the conviction to make a political stand against Mary, although she made no secret of her religious conservatism and some at least suspected her of being a secret papist. Their position was aptly summed up by Hooper – a man of inflexible faith and courage – when he wrote from prison at the beginning of September,

> Our king has been removed from us by reason of our sins, to the very great peril of our church. His sister Mary has succeeded, whom I pray God always to aid by his Holy Spirit, that she may reign and govern in all respects to the glory of his name . . .[12]

God in His wisdom had seen fit to punish His elect, and to put them to the test. It was therefore their duty to accept this fate with gratitude, as an opportunity to testify to their faith.

This attitude of acquiescence was not born of feebleness or a desire to compromise, but it offered at first no clear ground upon which to stand. Humble protestants were discouraged and confused. Cranmer and John Scory of Chichester conducted Edward's funeral with reformed rites on 7 August, and rumours began to circulate that the archbishop would conform to the queen's wishes.[13] Richard Thornden, the suffragan bishop of Dover, was so anxious to prove amenable that he began to celebrate the mass almost at once, in spite of the fact that it was technically illegal and he had obtained no dispensation.[14] The defection of those who had adhered to the reformation out of ambition or greed was symbolized by the behaviour of Northumberland himself. After his conviction for treason on 18 August, together with Northampton, Gates, and others, he '. . . heard mass very devoutly in the Tower, and there received the sacrament, even as they were wont forty years ago . . .' The council laid on an audience of London merchants to witness this spectacle, and Northumberland improved upon the occasion with a very explicit speech of penitence and submission, declaring that he had been '. . . seduced these sixteen years past by the false and erroneous preaching of the new preachers, the which is the only cause of the plagues and vengeance which hath lit upon the whole realm of England . . .'[15] This phraseology, which closely resembles that of some official pronouncements, strongly suggests that the speech was put into his mouth. On the other hand, it is possible that he genuinely believed what he was saying, since the death of the king and the collapse of his ambitions could be regarded as a divine punishment in this sense as well as the sense in which it was accepted by Hooper or Coxe. Catholic polemicists such as John Christopherson made much use of the argument that God had testified against the whole 'innovation' of the reformers and had raised up Mary to be the instrument of His will.[16] Northumberland's apostasy was greeted with jubilation by the conservatives. His final speech on the scaffold 'edified the people more than if all the catholics in the land had preached for ten years . . .', as one observer reported.[17] The protestants were correspondingly cast down. '. . . Who would have thought he would have done so', lamented Jane Grey, 'woe worth him . . .'[18] In the long run they gained rather than lost by this apparent defeat, because it helped the 'true disciples' to dissociate themselves from the damaging embrace of such 'carnal gospellers', but this advantage could not be exploited until the former had devised some method of standing up to be counted.

Some protestants, indeed, were immediately impatient of the acquiescence of their bishops and leading preachers and refused to be silent in the face of what they took to be manifest ungodliness. There were angry murmurings among the yeomen of the guard when it was rumoured that a requiem mass would be celebrated for the late king, and one Richard Alleyn was committed to prison.[19] Before Mary even reached London some outspoken malcontents had been set on the pillory, and the reappearance of the mass in a number of city churches provoked disturbances during the first two weeks of August. 'This daye', wrote one commentator, 'an ould prest sayd masse in St. Bartholomewes, but after that masse was done the people would rave pulled him in peeces . . .'[20] Something like a campaign of agitation by pamphleteers and minor preachers culminated in a serious riot at St Paul's on 13 August, when an angry crowd attacked Dr Gilbert Bourne for denouncing the imprisonment of Edmund Bonner by Edward's council.[21] Significantly, Bourne was saved from possible injury by the intervention of the respected protestant John Rogers, who did his best to calm the mob and dissuade it from violence. The immediate consequences of this disturbance were a stinging rebuke to the city authorities, and a series of swift and effective moves by the council against leading protestants of all persuasions. On 20 August Renard reported,

> ... the popular commotions because of religion which were feared here are very much quieted since ten or twelve of the leaders have been taken prisoner, and all private assemblies forbidden under pain of death.[22]

Those arrested included several who were specifically accused of inciting the riot, but were not 'leaders' in any other sense, and others described as 'sedicious preachers', who included John Bradford, Thomas Becon, and, ironically enough, John Rogers.[23] At the same time steps were taken to expel the congregations of protestant refugees who had settled in London and elsewhere during the previous reign. Persuasion was sufficient for the most important of these groups, and by the middle of September both John á Lasco's church and the Walloon weavers from Glastonbury under Valerand Poullain had withdrawn.[24] Some smaller groups lingered on until they were ordered to depart in February 1554, but their influence on the situation was negligible. In late August and early September a number of other leading reformers, including John Hooper and Hugh Latimer, were imprisoned on grounds of sedition, and active protestant clergy from Buckinghamshire, Kent, and East Anglia were summoned or brought before the council.[25]

From the government point of view the situation at the end of August was reasonably satisfactory. Mary was much influenced by those who assured her that her triumph was a miracle, specifically brought about by God to enable her to restore the true church. She seems to have had no doubt that this was what the overwhelming majority of her subjects wanted, and expected her to bring about. She viewed protestantism with a mixture of anger and blank incomprehension. L. B. Smith wrote several years ago of Stephen Gardiner that he regarded the reformers

> ... in terms of cloaked conspirators and carefully planned tactics, controlled by clever and unscrupulous men whose avowed policy of social and religious reform was a veil behind which they concealed their ultimate aim of seizing control of the country for their own advantage.[26]

Mary shared this attitude, but she also believed passionately that heretics were the devil's agents, who ensnared the souls of the innocent and ignorant and confused the faithful with a babble of false and conflicting doctrines. The apparent tolerance of her earliest pronouncements upon religion, particularly the important proclamation of 18 August, did not rest upon any genuine willingness to permit the continuance of protestant worship or preaching, nor indeed upon any legal scrupulosity, but simply upon the assumption that coercion would be unnecessary. The total overthrow of their political mentors, by depriving the heretics of the temporal sword, had exposed them to swift and inevitable extinction by the liberated forces of truth. The queen's innocence in this respect suited her more pragmatic advisers well. Her council had been alarmed to discover that her intention was a full restoration of traditional catholicism '. . . as far as the Pope's authority'.[27] Like most other Englishmen, they had assumed during the crisis of July that she would restore the situation that her father had left in 1547. When they learned the truth, most of them were only too willing to encourage Mary's belief that positive steps to implement such a policy were unnecessary. Renard, too, was perturbed when he learned the queen's mind. Not only could he, like the councillors, foresee endless problems over property and jurisdiction which might have serious political repercussions; he could also anticipate dangerous complications for his master's policies, as we have already seen. As it transpired, the queen's early assumption that God would do her work for her contributed significantly to the disarray of her opponents. They had no suspicion of the true extent of her policy, most of them not believing, or not wanting to believe, extremist alarms about popery; and they were not subjected to the kind of sharp coercion which might have forced them to reconsider their acquiescent attitude. Even in London, where protestant influence was strong, there was some justification for Mary's optimism. Altars began to reappear in city churches 'not by commandment but by the devotion of the people'; mass was celebrated – not always with happy results – and the elaborate traditional rituals delighted the sight of Henry Machyn and the author of the Greyfriars Chronicle.[28] '[The v] of August a vii a cloke at nyght came home Edmond Boner byshoppe [from the Ma]rchelse lyke a byshoppe, that alle the pepulle by the way badde hym welcom home [both] man and woman, and as many of the women as myghte kyssyd him . . .'[29] Outside London, as many recent studies have shown, the pattern was much the same; frequent enthusiasm, occasional resistance, and a large amount of unchronicled indifference, the significance of which was not at first appreciated in high places.[30]

With this measure of encouragement and her own invincible convictions, the queen pressed steadily ahead, restoring deprived catholic bishops, removing and imprisoning their supplanters, and instructing the universities to return to their ancient statutes, abandoning all innovations which had been introduced since her father's death.[31] In Oxford the protestants were in confusion and despair, overwhelmed by the conservatives whom they had earlier barely managed to contain. Peter Martyr abandoned his chair in these hopeless circumstances, and after a brief period confined to his house moved to London, accompanied by several of his younger disciples to whom the university now offered neither refuge nor opportunity.[32] Meanwhile the council had begun to shape a legislative programme to 'take further order' for the church as the queen's proclamation had promised, and Thomas Cranmer had chosen the ground upon which to make his stand. At the beginning of September he wrote a forceful denunciation of the mass, and issued a challenge, in his own name and that of Peter Martyr, offering to defend in disputation the orthodoxy of Edwardian doctrine. This document, sealed with his archiepiscopal seal, was initially posted on the doors of London churches, and subsequently published.

> . . . by which means [Martyr wrote later] they were so confounded that they now declared in their discourses that it was not safe to dispute upon such matters; and that it was not to be allowed that any doubt should be entertained respecting those things which had been received by the universal consent of the church. They therefore cast the Archbishop of Canterbury into prison, but have dismissed me with licence to depart under the Queen's sign manual . . .[33]

Cranmer was committed to the Tower on 14 September, theoretically for his earlier treason, since his declaration transgressed neither the existing law nor the queen's proclamation. He was not allowed to dispute at this juncture, but his action had nevertheless served its purpose. Not only was he the acknowledged leader and patriarch of the English reformers, he was also the most committed erastian; and he had now declared unequivocally that the queen's authority did not extend to matters of conscience. The mass was not an indifferent ceremony, but the quintessential idolatry which no protestant could accept. The imprisonment of Cranmer, and the steady round-up of other noted protestant clergy which went on throughout September and October, caused Renard to suppose that there were '. . . many secret practices on foot for upholding the new religion', but he was mistaken.[34] What had happened was that Cranmer had given notice to the government that it could expect neither cooperation nor acquiescence from himself and his colleagues, even in the first stages of its religious policy.

The queen and her council may have been surprised by this display of conscience, but Peter Martyr deceived himself if he thought they were much impeded. Gardiner, who seems to have been mainly responsible for the direction of policy, cheerfully admitted to

Renard that he was deliberately frightening as many protestants as he could out of the country;[35] so that the ones he arrested were those who had refused to be intimidated. Robert Parkyn, the conservative Yorkshire cleric whose account is one of the best sources for the study of this period outside London, was disgusted by the way in which 'the new sort' took refuge behind statute law in their rearguard action against the mass.[36] Their leaders did not make that mistake, knowing that the Edwardian prayer book would not survive Mary's first parliament. Weeks before they were repealed, the Edwardian statutes were dead letters. Not only did the queen adhere to her expressed intention that none of her subjects should be hindered in the practice of their catholic faith; she also annulled, with only the most perfunctory of legal process, the deprivations of catholic bishops, and ignored the dissolution of the see of Durham.[37] Apart from James Hales, no one protested at this cavalier treatment of the law, because it was obvious that repeal was only a matter of time.[38] The real issue was not the fate of protestantism, but the extent of the reaction. Mary had already made it clear to her councillors that she intended to restore the papal jurisdiction. In this she was supported by Gardiner, and probably by Rochester, Waldegrave, and others of her household. Paget believed that a Henrician situation would be preferable, and hoped that the queen would not persist with her intention.[39] Thirlby agreed with him, and so too did Arundel and other secular peers. For the time being Renard sided with this latter group, and his arguments may well have been decisive. Before her coronation Mary had given secret audience to two papal envoys, Gian Francesco Commendone, who had come on behalf of Julius himself, and Henry Penning from Cardinal Pole. In conversation with the latter the queen made it clear that she had accepted the necessity to proceed through parliament, and indicated that a 'step by step' policy might be necessary.[40] Her councillors were not informed of these discussions, but it seems that Gardiner did not press his proposal to seek the repeal of the royal supremacy, probably because preliminary soundings convinced him that he would not succeed. His speech at the opening of parliament on 5 October 'touched on' the matter of reunion, but reactions were distinctly unfavourable, and the important bills subsequently introduced make no further mention of it.[41]

There is no reason to suppose that the House of Commons in this parliament was anything other than normally representative, and in most respects it did the government's business well enough.[42] However, if Mary expected loyal and enthusiastic endorsement for all her policies, she must have been disappointed. As we have already seen, the Commons presented a highly distasteful petition on the subject of her marriage, and the debate on the repeal of Edward's religious legislation got bogged down in early November 'on matters which would baffle a general council', as Renard commented.[43] If the discussion assumed a technical theological nature, as this remark suggests, there must have been a number of determined protestant laymen in the house; and the eventual voting figures – approximately 279 to 80 – also indicate a measure of determined resistance.[44] Mary informed Pole that the catholics had had to work hard for their victory, and on other measures they were not uniformly successful. An act providing imprisonment as a punishment for disrupting sermons and services passed without much difficulty, but a 'bill for such as come not to the church' was dropped after one reading.[45] As a result there was no statutory compulsion to attend any services after the Edwardian act of uniformity was repealed, and the matter being 'referred to the ecclesiastical power'. Finally, on 5 December the government's bill for the revival of Durham diocese was rejected, causing considerable embarrassment and annoyance both to the queen and to Cuthbert Tunstall.[46] The House of Commons was clearly much more worried about property and jurisdiction than it was about doctrine or the form of services, but it had effectively issued a warning to the government not to assume that the quietism of the protestant ecclesiastics represented the full extent of opposition. By comparison, convocation had lost the habit of making important decisions, and the stand of the protestant divines there was a good deal less effective than they later claimed. Having been accorded a disputation, Philpot, Haddon, Cheney, and Elmer laboured unavailingly to prevent a reaffirmation of transubstantiation.

> There came moche pepulle [declared the . . .] but they ware never the wyser and . . . the qwenes graces cowncell was fayen to send worde that there shulde be no more dy[spu]tacions but that it shulde be dyscussyd by the hole parlament.[47]

Renard was understandably worried by this noisy wrangle, disliking any course which drew attention to the existence of religious dissension. 'The French and the protestants are saying', he wrote on 4 November, 'that if the marriage takes place his Highness will try to reform religion by force . . .'[48] However, he misjudged the reformers, both in respect of their strength and their intentions. Crude demonstrations, like that of Robert Mendham the London tailor who tonsured his dog 'in despite of priesthood', or the 'lewd and seditious behaviour upon all hallows day', of which a group of Coventry craftsmen were accused, did not deserve to be taken so seriously.[49] When the act of repeal came into force on 20 December, to his considerable surprise there were no disturbances of any significance. Instead a conscientious and rather pathetic petition arrived from a group of protestants in Maidstone to be allowed to continue with the English services. Its bearer and prime mover, William Smith, spent a week in the Gatehouse for sedition.[50]

In spite of its quiet reception, the act of repeal marked a significant development in the government's religious policy. Up to this point the council had concentrated on silencing or removing outspoken protestants, and seeking by persuasion and example to encourage a return to traditional forms of worship. After 20 December a serious attempt began to restore some semblance of catholic discipline through the machinery of visitation, and some small but significant acts of restitution were made. At first the chief victims of orthodox zeal were those clergy who had availed themselves of the statute of 1549 abrogating the canon law against the marriage of priests.[51] It was very much simpler to ascertain who had married than to distinguish between shades of conformity and nonconformity. The statistics available from most dioceses are very incomplete, only London and Norwich having anything like full returns. In both these cases the number of deprivations was surprisingly high. In rather more than a year following the re-establishment of the canon law, 150 beneficed clergy in London lost their livings, and 243 in Norwich;[52] over a quarter of the total incumbents. In Norwich also a hundred unbeneficed clergy were disciplined for the same offence. The impression given is that the pursuit of such offenders was intense and prolonged; partly because of the queen's personal indignation, and partly because the sexual immorality of the reformers was a favourite theme with their conservative enemies.

> Hoo, it was ioye to here and see [gloated Robert Parkyn] how thes carnall preastes (whiche had ledde ther lyffes in fornication with ther whores & harlotts) dyd lowre and looke downe, when thay were commandyde to leave & forsayke the concubyns . . .[53]

The retrospective amnesty granted by the act of repeal to those who had celebrated heretical services did not extend to the married. Nor did it avail, as John Rogers was to discover, for one in that position to point out that his marriage had been lawful at the time when he contracted it. Ironically, deprivation, which was the automatic penalty in these cases, was a very much more severe punishment than that inflicted upon the orthodox for adultery. The removal of married clergy features in every set of visitation articles from March 1554 onward, and in certain cases special royal commissions were also issued for this purpose. When the Lower House of convocation petitioned for such action in March 1554, it asked merely that

'. . . such priests as were lately married and refuse to reconcile themselves to their order . . .' might be proceeded against,[54] and this seems to have been the queen's original intention, but the course eventually decided upon was more severe. However, with such large numbers involved there was a serious danger of parochial ministration breaking down altogether in the worst-affected dioceses, and the bishops had to be given discretion, in cases where the wives were dead, or where both parties were willing to accept complete abstinence '. . . after penance done . . . [to] . . . receive and admit them again to their former administration, so it be not in the same place . . .'[55] In the diocese of Norwich all but forty of those deprived were re-admitted in this way – and the backslidings of many of them continued to be a disciplinary problem for the remainder of the reign.

Restitutions and acts of pious generosity on the part of the queen began at about the same time. Among the first was the re-endowment of the collegiate church of Wolverhampton on 26 December. The lands of this foundation had come into the hands of the crown by the attainder of the duke of Northumberland, and Mary not only returned them intact to the new dean and prebendaries, but also granted issues from the date of dissolution, which had been Easter 1548.[56] Since the lands were worth over £113 a year, this benefaction cost the exchequer an initial outlay of about £600; and in addition all first fruits and tenths 'due or to be due to the Queen by virtue of the statute of 26 Henry VIII', were released to the incumbents. On the same day another grant was also sealed; a smaller but equally significant gesture. Ann More, the daughter-in-law of Sir Thomas, and her son, also Thomas, were given the reversion of lands in Hertfordshire worth just over £50 a year. These lands had been parcel of the estate of Sir Thomas, and were currently in the hands of Princess Elizabeth.[57] During March and April 1554 most of the queen's generosity was absorbed by her initial efforts to get some of her bishoprics off the financial rocks. Royal commissions on 13 and 15 March resulted in the deprivation of seven of the imprisoned protestant bishops, four of them – Holgate, Farrer, Bird, and Bush – on the pretext of marriage.[58] Since two bishoprics had been vacant since the previous reign, Mary now had the opportunity not only to appoint nine new bishops of her own choosing, but to relieve their poverty at the same time.[59] The effect of this action upon episcopal morale was noticeable and immediate. In January Sir John Mason was persuaded to surrender the deanery of Winchester. As an unqualified layman he could have been deprived, but since he was a privy councillor, this might have been embarrassing. His co-operation was rewarded with an annuity of £240, so although he must have lost on the transaction, once again the principal benefactor was the queen.[60] May saw a gleam of royal favour shine upon the universities. Both Oxford and Cambridge had been deeply disturbed by the recent ecclesiastical turmoil, and the royal grant declared Oxford to be '. . . so afflicted by the wrongs of the times that it lies almost uncultivated and in want of means to sustain its dignity'. The queen, went on this grandiloquent piece of propaganda, '. . . holds that it pertains to her royal office to raise up the academy, in which the orthodox faith overthrown by heretics cannot enter and be defended . . .' The grant itself, which consisted of a number of advowsons to the value of £131 a year, scarcely matched up to this preamble.[61] More substantial and less pretentious was the benefaction a few weeks later to Trinity College, Cambridge, of lands and advowsons worth £220 a year as a thank offering for her victories over Northumberland and Wyatt.[62] In the previous month the first English benefice was conferred on a Spanish priest, when the queen presented Alonso de Salinas to that canonry at Westminster from which the ex-Benedictine Humphrey Perkins had recently been ejected.[63]

Mary gave up using the offensive title of supreme head of the church at the end of 1553, and at about the same time, both in London and in Rome, the religious significance of her forthcoming marriage began to be earnestly discussed. As we have already seen, the impending reconciliation caused somewhat premature rejoicings in the *curia*. 'May your Highness enjoy the kingdom of England many years', Don Manrique de Lara wrote to Philip, 'and reduce it to the faith and obedience of the church, for this will be the greatest victory of all . . .'[64] Few reactions are recorded from leading English protestants, but they seem to have regarded the prospect with a certain grim satisfaction. A persecution much more severe than their present relatively lenient confinement was probable, but as Latimer had told Henry VIII as far back as 1530, '. . . where you see persecution, there is the gospel and there is the truth'.[65] To men of passionate conviction the opportunity to testify dramatically to their faith would not be unwelcome. Real alarm was more widespread among the Henrician conservatives, who foresaw the heavy political hand of the Habsburgs being used to re-endow the catholic church at their expense. The rebellion which broke out in January 1554, and conspiracy which preceded it, were the work of men who feared and hated the prospect of a Spanish king, for this and other equally secular reasons.[66] The protestant leaders gave them no scrap of encouragement, and Wyatt studiously avoided any public pronouncement on religion.[67] Inevitably some protestants were involved, because Kent was an area where they were relatively numerous. Walter Mantell, a friend of Sir James Hales,[68] was one such, and a handful of others can be identified, but the great majority of those whose religious allegiance can be determined were conservative or conformist. Among the leaders only Sir Peter Carew and the discredited duke of Suffolk could be described as openly hostile to the reaction. Nevertheless, official spokesmen and observers sympathetic to the government persistently claimed that one of the rebels' chief objectives was the re-erection of 'the new religion'. One of the reasons for this was the desire of Renard and Paget to demonstrate that dislike of the marriage was a mere pretext; another was the queen's natural inclination to think of treason and heresy as synonymous; a third was Gardiner's desire to use the rebellion as an excuse for harsher anti-protestant measures. After the collapse of the insurrection and Wyatt's arrest official propaganda predictably set out to exploit the situation. 'If she [the queen] had been an adversarye of his truth, and of his holy word', wrote John Christopherson, 'as some folkes report her, he would never have so ayded her . . .'[69] Protestantism must be false doctrine because it has failed,

> And thereby it well appeareth yt there cause is moste wycked and dampnable. For commonly whensoever men take any enterprise on hand, yf their cause be just, God will prosper them therein, but yf ther cause be naughte, then shal they spede accordinglye . . .[70]

For the time being protestant pamphleteers had little to say in reply. They also disapproved of rebellion, even against an 'ungodly' ruler; but they did not feel inclined to denounce such a demonstration against the marriage, or a leader who was by way of becoming a popular hero and martyr.[71] It was not until 1558 that Christopher Goodman drew the conclusion that Wyatt had failed precisely because he had not called upon the Lord more explicitly, and because the secular-minded nobility had thus been enabled more easily to shirk their responsibility to overthrow the idolaters.[72] Eventually the reformers were to gain far more than they lost from the misguided attempts of their enemies to tar them with the brush of treason. Not only was hostility to the marriage far more widespread than protestantism, but it continued to gain in strength, as we shall see. In the aftermath of the rebellion, with their foreign theologians and supporters banished, the protestants began to shed the disadvantages of their previous Swiss and German associations, and to be linked instead with the rejection of the unpopular Spaniards. Christopherson's argument that the failures of Northumberland and Wyatt proved that God had turned His face away from the protestants was blunted by the fact that neither had received much open or unequivocal protestant support – and by Northumberland's behaviour after his defeat. Indeed the future bishop of Chichester partly refuted his own case, and gave his opponents a useful lead, when he declared in another part of the same discourse: '. . . in Christes warre those wynne the fielde that beare awaye the strokes, he that suffreth most getteth ye moste noble victory . . .'[73] *The Historie of Wyates rebellion* by the Tonbridge schoolmaster John Proctor[74] succeeded in putting forward a plausible case for Wyatt's underhand religious purposes, but even he could not claim that the imprisoned bishops and preachers had given the rebels any countenance.

The protestant propaganda which appeared in print during these early months of the reign was almost entirely non-political, unless we include *The copie of a pistel or letter sent to Gilbard Potter*, which was an invective against Northumberland.[75] Typically these tracts and pamphlets called for steadfastness and repentance; even the fiery Knox confined himself to *An admonition that the faithfull Christians in London . . . may avoid God's vengeaunce.*[76] A new edition of *De Vera Obedientia Oratio* with a strongly protestant preface was produced just before Christmas 1553, probably in Rouen. This was a deliberate attempt to embarrass and annoy Gardiner, but could hardly be described as seditious while the queen still bore the title of supremacy.[77] The chorus was of considerable volume: *An humble supplication unto God, A letter sent from a banished minister,*[78] and many others, mostly published abroad by those who had already withdrawn into exile. Almost from the beginning of the reign there were some who chose this course in preference to compromising their consciences, and Cranmer and Ridley both urged it as an acceptable method of testifying to the faith. In February 1554 Peter Martyr wrote to John á Lasco from Strasbourg:

> English youths have come over to us in great numbers within these few days, partly from Oxford and partly from Cambridge, whom many godly merchants are bringing up to learning, that, should it please God to restore religion to its former state in that kingdom, they may be of some benefit to the church of England . . .[79]

Martyr probably gives an exaggerated impression, both of the scale and the purposefulness of this movement, but it was beginning to assume some importance as a source of encouragement and exhortation to those who had remained in England. Some of the handwritten broadsheets being passed around the streets of London, however, seem to have been a good deal more inflammatory than these pious exercises, and Renard periodically refers to documents urging open defiance, which must have been of this nature. Renard was also troubled, of course, by French-subsidized pamphleteering against the marriage, but there is no evidence to connect such works as *The discourse of an English Gentleman*[80] with the protestants, in spite of the official tendency to lump the two together. The government reacted conventionally to both these challenges. Three proclamations between July 1553 and April 1554 ordered that 'seditious bills and writings' should be destroyed, and that their authors and distributors should be imprisoned or set on the pillory.[81] These authors sometimes showed considerable ingenuity, and there was almost a diplomatic incident with Danzig when a certain William Hotson succeeded in persuading a printer in that city to produce copies of a 'libel' against Philip and Mary.[82] Official propaganda in support of the marriage was virtually non-existent, apart from the proclamation of the terms of the treaty and a printed genealogy demonstrating that Philip, far from being a stranger, was a lineal descendant of the English royal house.[83]

By contrast the catholics were active in their own interest, with only a modicum of government patronage and support. Apart from Proctor and Christopherson, the indefatigable Miles Huggarde produced two tracts, *The assault of the sacrament of the altar* and *A treatise declaring howe Christ by perverse preachyng was banished out of this realme.*[84] Huggarde, who had defended the faith in less auspicious days, had recently been given the position of queen's hosier, and the *Treatise* contains the rather touching dedication

> My dutie considered most noble quene
> Syth it has pleased your graciouse goodness
> Me a pore man to place as is sene
> In office to serve your noble highness . . .[85]

Not surprisingly, Mary came in for some lavish praise from this quarter, much of it in the dreadful doggerel of the popular ballad. Typical of this genre was *An Ave Maria in Commendation of oure moste vertuous Queene* by Leonard Stopes,[86] which contained the lines

> Marie the mirrour of mercifulnesse
> God of his Goodness hath lent to this land
> Our Iewell oure ioye, our Judith doutlesse
> The great Holofernes of hell to withstand . . .

Another popular writer greeted her accession as

> A wonderful miracle, ever to be remembered
> That God wrought for our Queene be He ever praysed . . .[87]

More substantial controversial works were less in evidence, but John Standish produced *A discourse wherein is debated whether it be expedient that the Scriptures should be in English.*[88] Sermons by Brooks and Weston were also published, and two polemics against heresy by John Gwynneth: one against Frith and the other *A declaration of the state wherein all heretickes dooe leade their lives,*[89] predictably accusing them of licence, debauchery, and every kind of uncharitableness. There was little in the way of positive catholic exhortation or instruction, and nothing to suggest spontaneous enthusiasm for a return to the papal jurisdiction. Indeed, the papacy is scarcely mentioned in these early tracts, being much more of a bogey to the protestants than a source of encouragement or hope to the faithful.

In terms of quantity there was little to choose between the catholic and protestant presses during this period, despite the fact that the catholics enjoyed the great advantage of being able to publish openly in England. In terms of quality, however, the protestants led from the start. In polemic against the mass, or against the 'Roman Anti-Christ', they displayed none of that reticence and uncertainty which kept them silent on political issues. In elaborating upon the theme of judgement they found hope, and a sense of purpose, in the very act of submitting to an ungodly oppression lawfully applied.

> . . . we shall finde mercie in time convenient [wrote the anonymous editor of *De Vera Obedientia*] and though he scourge us with these uncircumcised soldiers of Satan for a time yet (as David saithe) When he is angrie he will remember mercie . . . and in cace we will (like obedient children) take his chastisinge in good parte/ and paciently abide his leasure . . .[90]

William Turner's *The huntinge of the Romyshe wolfe* took up a familiar theme with zest, and John Bale displayed his remarkable talents for invective in *The vocacyon of Johan Bale to the Bishoprick of Ossorie.*[91] Such writers had no hesitation in lambasting catholic spokesmen such as Weston, or identifiable leaders like Bonner and Gardiner. Indeed the latter came in for specific attack in *The communication betwene my Lord Chauncelor and Judge Hales,* and even Cranmer did not scruple to denounce Richard Thornden as 'a false flattering and lying monk'.[92] Even in their perplexity, with so many of their leaders in confinement and apparently ineffective, the protestants had already begun to develop a flair for articulate self-justification which worried some of their more perceptive opponents:

> And yf they be troubled [wrote Christopherson], . . . and peradventure shutte up in prison, lette them not glorye in their fetters

as thoughe they were apostles, and write letters of comforte one
to another in an Apostles style . . . nor let them not exhorte one
another to sticke fast in theyre fonde opinion . . .[93]

By the early part of 1554 it was clear that those optimists who
had assumed that protestantism was no more than a cover for time-
serving and political ambition had misjudged at least a proportion
of their opponents. Since the queen had no intention of allowing
process for heresy to be initiated against the obstinate until proper
ecclesiastical jurisdiction had been restored, it thus became important to bring public discredit upon some leading prophets of the
'new religion'. Those protestants who had disputed unavailingly in
the convocation of 1553 had complained loudly at being deprived
of the services of their ablest champions, and even suggested that
the catholics had been afraid to face such champions. Such a jibe
demanded an answer, and the poor performance which Cranmer
had put up at his trial for treason in the Guildhall suggested an
effective one.[94] It was consequently decided at the beginning of
March to stage a new disputation in Oxford, in which Cranmer,
Latimer, and Nicholas Ridley would be confronted by the full theological talent of the two universities. Although an academic form
was used, this confrontation was in fact a trial, and as in trials for
treason every precaution was taken to make sure that the defendants were given no opportunity to prepare themselves. The catholic
disputants were nominated by convocation, and led by Weston as
prolocutor. Cranmer, Latimer, and Ridley were remitted to the
custody of the mayor and aldermen of Oxford, and lodged in the
town gaol, the Bocardo. On 11 April royal instructions to the city
authorities of Oxford made the real nature of the occasion abundantly clear. The prisoners

> . . . now remaining in your custody, by our appointment, have,
> besides other their great crimes, maintained and openly set forth
> divers heresies and erroneous and most pernicious opinions . . .
> to the great offence of Almighty God, and evil and dangerous
> example of all our faithful and loving subjects.[95]

They were therefore to be brought forth upon commandment '. . . so
as their erroneous opinions, being by the word of God justly and
truly convinced, the residue of our subjects may be thereby the
better established in the true catholic faith . . .'[96] Weston and his
colleagues were to act as both advocates and judges, with power to
condemn their opponents but not to impose any kind of sentence.[97]
The proceedings commenced in St Mary's church on 14 April, and
continued intermittently until the 22nd. Large crowds of students

and townsmen attended, and seem to have shown little sympathy with the victims of what was virtually a gladiatorial display.

Significantly, our knowledge of the disputation itself depends almost entirely upon protestant sources.[98] In spite of its concern to discredit the protestant leaders, the government made no attempt to publish a propaganda version of the debate. Weston formally pronounced his opponents defeated, and when they failed to make an orthodox submission, he excommunicated them and returned to London to make his report to convocation. In fact the two sides seem to have spent most of the time arguing at cross purposes upon different philosophical premises, and a futile deadlock would be the fairest description of the outcome.[99] Disadvantaged as he was in every way, Cranmer did not put up an impressive performance, apparently daunted and confused by Weston's blustering and aggressive tactics, but he made no concessions. Latimer refused to dispute at all, on the grounds that he was too old and unlearned, but he insisted upon making a declaration of his faith, and the prolocutor was reduced to making crude threats. 'Your stubbornness comes of a vainglory', he declared, 'which is to no purpose; for it will do you no good when a faggot is in your beard . . .'[100] Ridley, on the other hand, counterattacked his enemies with skill and some relish in an unavailing but impressive display of formal logic. The government had unintentionally complimented the reformers by ranging no fewer than thirty-three conservative theologians against them, and had ended by securing no more than a rather meaningless formal condemnation. Cranmer and his colleagues remained in prison in Oxford, where Ridley, in particular, began to build up an important network of communications with other protestant leaders both in prison and in exile.

During the long period of waiting which now ensued such communications sustained the morale of the prisoners – who included Bradford, Rogers, Hooper, and Rowland Taylor in London as well as the three in Oxford – and enabled many humble protestants to make a contribution to the cause. Some contributed money or acted as messengers, others, particularly such women as Ann Warcop, provided clean linen and other small necessities.[101] As a matter of general policy the council tried to keep the prisoners apart, and to prevent the exchange of letters. Latimer and Ridley were imprisoned in private houses in Oxford, while Cranmer remained in Bocardo; and periodically they were deprived of books and writing materials. However, such strictness was never sustained because very few of the gaolers and others who were immediately responsible for their safe-keeping bore them any ill-will. As a result letters, tracts of instruction, and pious exhortation flowed out from the prisons to encourage the steadfast and support the wavering, while the leaders corresponded amongst themselves, conducting theological discussions, and even controversies.[102] Latimer's Swiss servant and friend Augustine Behrner played a key role in the organization of this network, which by the summer of 1554 had already begun to play a vital part in keeping the scattered congregations of active protestants in touch with each other and with the preachers who could no longer address them directly or openly. The queen's decision to take no further judicial action using the royal supremacy meant that throughout 1554 the ecclesiastical and secular authorities were endeavouring to maintain discipline by the use of summary jurisdiction. Evidence of this activity is widely scattered. In January Sir John Arundel sent information to the council about 'disrespectful words' spoken by two Cornishmen 'against the Queen and the catholic religion'.[103] A month later Lord Rich and Sir John Wentworth were instructed to punish 'those who, at Colchester and thereabouts have tried to dissuade the Queen's people from frequenting Divine Service, as appointed'.[104] Frequent references to 'lewd books' and 'seditious bills' also provide evidence of protestant resistance. In July one Richard Smith, a yeoman of the guard, was dismissed and imprisoned for spreading such propaganda. There were also persistent rumours that Edward VI was not really dead, and the council twice examined men accused of spreading such reports, in November 1553 and January 1554.[105] Popular prophecies and other vague but pervasive gossip sometimes showed an alarming tendency to take specific religious or political shape. In May 1554 the earl of Sussex examined such a case, which provides a very good example, both of the content of such rumours and of the frustrating process of trying to trace and suppress them:

> Witness that one Lawrence Hunt of Diss came unto Robert Lowdall chief constable, and told him that he did here saye that the Queens Maiestie was with childe, and that his wife dyd tell hym so. And when his wyfe was examined before the said Robert Lowdall and others she tolde hym she harde it of one Sheldrakes wife. And when Sheldrakes wiffe was examined she sayde she heard yt of her husband. And when her husband was examined he saide he harde it of one John Wilby of Diss aforesayde. And when the said Wilby was examined he said he heard it of one Johan Smith thelder of Cockstreet. And when the said Johan Smith was examined he said he heard it of oon wydow Miles, wch cam to his howse and tolde yt two tymes. And when she was examined she saide she had heard it of ii menne, but what they were she could not telle, nor where they dwelt . . .[106]

At about the same time one of the canons of Peterborough was accused of '. . . giving abroad old prophecies',[107] but the content of his prognostications is not mentioned. The problem was an intractable one, and by no means confined to Mary's reign, but was aggravated by the existence of a determined religious minority which had every intention of harassing the authorities to the best of its ability.

Such harassment fell a long way short of open resistance, and was not touched by scruples of principle. It was one of the ways in which the rank-and-file protestants drew attention to their existence, although its impact as a form of religious dissent was lessened by the opportunities which it presented to troublemakers and hooligans of all kinds. In March or April 1554 'some wretched and develish disposed person . . .' hung up in Cheapside a dead cat dressed up as a priest. In June a rather simple-minded servant girl was induced to play the part of a 'hidden oracle', uttering cryptic phrases condemning the queen and the catholic church.[108] In July and August there were anti-catholic demonstrations in Ipswich, variously described as 'an intended commotion' and 'half a rising'. The ringleaders, John Ramsey and Peter Mone, were protestants, but after about three months in the Tower they were released on recognizance without, apparently, suffering any further punishment.[109] According to Renard they had 'tried to burn a church . . . with the entire congregation which was hearing mass . . .',[110] but the truth was probably rather less dramatic. Ribald remarks, small-scale iconoclasm, and foolish pranks were more typical of such dissidents than attendances at conventicles or other acts of identifiable protestantism. Nevertheless, some protestant clergy continued to minister to their flocks in secret, like Robert Samuels at Bergholt in Suffolk;[111] and in other places prayerbook congregations carried on as best they could without a regular ministry, as happened at Hadleigh. It is quite misleading to suggest, as some scholars have done, that opposition to Mary's religious policy was conducted almost entirely by vandals and anabaptists – antisocial forces which would have fallen foul of any sixteenth-century government.[112] In May 1554, while he was escorting Princess Elizabeth from the Tower to house arrest at Woodstock, Sir Henry Bedingfield wrote a series of perceptive letters in which he commented upon his charge's popularity, and upon the political and religious attitudes of those with whom he had to deal. One Christopher Cooke, 'a playne husbande man' who guided his party near Woburn, he described as 'a very p[ro]testante', and commented that most of the men of those parts '. . . be off the same opinion'.[113] Of the early part of his journey, between London and Windsor, he wrote:

. . . you shall right well perceyve . . . that men betwyxt London and theys partes be not goode and whole in matters of relygion. And surelie I did understand by conference with the noblemen whose assistance you did command in the same servyce that they be fully fixed to stand to the late abolyshynge of the Byshoppe of Romes authoritie as heretofore agaynst the order of all [that] hath been establyshed by statute lawes withyn this realme. Yet they and everye of them dothe to my judgement show themselves your heartie and servicable subjectes alle other wayes . . .[114]

Whether Bedingfield intended this letter as a warning to the queen we do not know, but coming less than a month after the unsatisfactory conclusion of her second parliament, it must have underlined the message of that session in striking fashion.

Stephen Gardiner had intended to use this parliament to carry his own religious policy a stage further. Just how far he intended to go is not certain, because so little of his programme was eventually translated into statutes, but it certainly included the revival of the heresy laws, and almost certainly some formula for the restoration of papal jurisdiction. These controversial proposals did not represent the agreed policy of the privy council, and indeed, as we have already seen, had to be smuggled through the committee which was preparing business for the parliament.[115] How much Mary herself knew of what was afoot is uncertain, but her desire to return to the papal fold was increasingly common knowledge, and Gardiner may well have counted upon her sympathetic support without consulting her over the details of his intended legislation. If she was in possession of such information, she succeeded in concealing the fact from Renard. In his opening address the chancellor declared that the parliament had been convened 'for the corroboration of the true religion and touching the Queen's Highness most noble marriage'.[116] The second of these objectives was attained with comparative ease, but the former made only fragmentary progress amidst a welter of abortive bills. Six or seven such measures were introduced into the Commons, beginning on 9 April with a bill to 'revive statutes repealed against Lollards and Heretics'.[117] This was followed on the 17th by a bill to revive the act of six articles, and another 'against Lollardy, Heresy and erroneous preaching'. On the 20th came two more, 'a bill that the Bishop of Rome, or any other bishop, shall not convent any person for any abbey lands', and 'a bill for Lollardy against eating of flesh on divers days forbidden'. Of these, the bill to revive the heresy acts passed all its stages in the Commons without recorded difficulty and was sent to the Lords on 26 April;[118] that concerning abbey lands passed its third reading on 27 April;

and that concerning fast days on 1 May. The others disappear from view and must have been either dropped or cut off by the early prorogation. A further measure, designed to deprive of their pensions ex-religious who had married since their foundations had been dissolved, was read for the first time on 28 April; but this was a rehash of a bill which had been sent down from the Lords on the 20th, and had received one hearing in its original form.[119] That also disappeared. Two relevant bills were introduced in the Upper House, and neither encountered serious difficulty there. One was that concerning clerical pensions, and the other for the re-erection of the bishopric of Durham.[120] This latter was essentially the same measure which had failed in the Commons in the previous parliament, and it again had a stormy passage in the Lower House, being strenuously resisted by the burgesses of Newcastle. After a tough contest extending over several days it eventually passed on a division by 201 votes to 120 on 19 April.[121] Of the measures sent up by the Commons to the Lords only that for the revival of the heresy acts came to a resolution. It was rejected by the Lords on 1 May, and it was this failure, which, as we have already seen, aroused the queen to fury and brought about both the prorogation of parliament and the fall of Lord Paget.

Unfortunately the evidence of the *Journals* and that of Renard's despatches does not fit together very well. It is not clear why the refusal of the House of Lords to revive three medieval statutes against heresy should have so angered the queen that she effectively abandoned the rest of Gardiner's programme. If the chancellor's intended bargain for the return of papal jurisdiction was included in any of the recorded bills, it must have been in that concerning abbey lands, and although that certainly disappeared in the Lords, it was not actually defeated. Mary must have been convinced that these two measures were so closely linked that the loss of the one gave the other no chance of success, although we have no means of knowing now why she should have believed this.[122] All that actually reached the statute book was the restoration of the see of Durham, and an act restoring the independence of the parish of Ongar in Essex, which had been united with Greenstead 'by the sinister labour and procurement of one William Morys Esq., . . . sometime patron of the parish church of Ongar . . . inordinately seeking his lucre and profit . . .'[123] This unsatisfactory outcome does not seem to have been due to any single factor. Although ultimately it was Paget and his allies in the Lords who frustrated Gardiner's intentions, allegedly out of fear for the security of their church property, only Lord Rich had voted against the Durham bill. The Commons, on the other hand, who reacted so strongly to the property implications of the latter, passed without demur the measures to which the peers were to object so effectively. Neither house seems to have objected to anti-protestant legislation *per se*, but where such laws would have either stated or implied a significant increase in the jurisdictional powers of the church, let alone the abrogation of the royal supremacy, resistance, unco-ordinated but extremely effective, was stirred up.[124]

Following this rebuff, in the summer of 1554, religious policy marked time, as the council and the bishops continued to apply such disciplinary pressure as they were able. The English aristocracy had made it clear that they were not prepared to carry the reaction beyond 'religion as king Henry left it' without specific guarantees for their material interests which could not, at that time, be given. The protestants, although still aggressively vocal, had been reduced to a pattern of scattered nonconformity at home and economically precarious survival abroad. Although they had shown a level of religious commitment which neither Mary nor Gardiner had expected, they had as yet formed no political alliance either with the opponents of the Spanish marriage or with the property-conscious Henricians. The flicker of such an alliance at the time of the Wyatt rebellion had not taken fire because of the determined opposition of the most respected protestant leaders to any form of overt resistance. Moreover, the tendency of observers such as Renard to lump the protestants and Henricians together as 'adherents of the new religion' – a tendency particularly noticeable during the second parliament – shows either semantic carelessness, or a serious misunderstanding of English ecclesiastical affairs. By June 1554 the future of the English church lay effectively in the hands of three men: Julius III, who had been seeking for almost twelve months for a formula of reconciliation; Philip of Spain, who had no intention of ruling over schismatics, let alone heretics; and Cardinal Reginald Pole, who had been bombarding Mary with good advice since the previous August.

Pole was a man whose birth, character, and previous history conspired to make him a major figure in the recatholicization of England. Born in 1500 of the Plantagenet royal blood;[125] carefully and thoroughly educated for the priesthood, he had seemed destined for a career of high office in the church and in the favour of Henry VIII. This prospect had been blighted by the king's 'great matter' to which Pole, strongly influenced by the London Carthusians, had reacted, at first hesitantly and then with mounting hostility.[126] Since 1532 he had lived in northern Italy, and his hostility to Henry VIII had become bitter and profound. His abortive mission in support of the Pilgrimage of Grace, and the appearance of *Pro ecclesiasticae unitatis defensione* in 1537, led to his attainder for high treason, and for years he went in dread of assassination by the king's agents.[127] He escaped, but his family in England had been less fortunate. Caught up in the so-called 'Exeter conspiracy', his brother, Lord Montague, had gone to the block in 1538 and his mother, the countess of Salisbury, in 1541. Pole's anguish over their deaths had been intense. His family were 'dearer to him than his own life', he later declared.[128] At the same time he was rising in favour at Rome, and an active member of that reforming group associated with the Oratory of Divine Love, being particularly close to the reforming leader Gasparo Contarini. In 1536, although only in deacon's orders, he had become a cardinal, and had collaborated in the preparation of the *Consilium delectorum Cardinalium . . . de emendenda ecclesia*. In 1545 he had been one of the three cardinals chosen by Paul III to preside at the council of Trent. It might be thought on this evidence that Pole was either a distinguished theologian or an ecclesiastical statesman of great skill. However, he does not seem to have been either, and the quality of his greatness is somewhat elusive. He was certainly no diplomat, as his subsequent well-intentioned blundering in Paris and Brussels makes plain. A recent, and sympathetic, scholar has described him as a 'reluctant theologian',[129] who got himself into acute difficulties over the doctrine of justification, and eventually took refuge in silence and in submission to authority. Nor was he an administrator of genius, although he had some experience of office as governor of the *Patrimonium Petri*, the largest of the papal states, a post which he had held from 1541 to 1547. The secret of his eminence seems to have lain partly in his royal blood, which automatically made him a person of consequence; partly in a mind which, without being distinguished, was nevertheless scholarly and acute; and partly in those pastoral gifts which he possessed to a remarkable degree. He was, *par excellence*, the guide, confessor, and friend of the great. Testimonies to the quality of his spiritual advice, the warmth of his friendship, and the saintliness of his character abound. Sir John Mason, not the most impressionable of men, was lavish in his praise of Pole shortly before the latter was eventually admitted to England. In him 'yt is to be thought Godd hath chosen a special place of habitacion', he wrote on one occasion; and on another '. . . it would be a right stony hart that in small tyme he could not soften'.[130]

Nevertheless, by the time that Mary's accession raised in Rome the first real hope of reconciling England since 1536, Pole was already in many respects a spent force. In particular his experiences at Trent had shaken him profoundly. Despite the failure of his friend Contarini at Regensburg in 1541, Pole had still approached the council with hopes of being able to heal the Lutheran schism by judicious reforms and conciliatory formulae. These hopes collapsed in the long debates which produced the draft decree on justification, a decree which made no concessions whatsoever to the *sola fide* position which was the doctrinal heart of Lutheranism. The outcome of these debates not only spelled defeat for Pole's policy at the council. they also placed him in an acute personal dilemma. During his time at Viterbo as governor of the *Patrimonium* he had been associated with a number of intellectual reformers whose zeal had subsequently carried them over into heresy: Peter Martyr Vermigli, Bernardino Ochino, and the authors of the intensely controversial *Beneficio di Christo.*[131] This latter work had been avidly read and commented upon in reforming circles even after it had been condemned by the inquisition. Pole avoided all pressure to be explicit about his views on justification, but he was certainly influenced by these scholars, and was strongly suspected of outright heresy by such conservative leaders as Gian Pietro Carafa. After what seems to have been an intense spiritual struggle which broke his health, Pole decided that the authority of the church must take precedence over the promptings of his private conscience, and he never openly questioned the correctness of received doctrine. Nevertheless, he had felt obliged to withdraw from Trent, his breakdown in health providing him with a genuine reason for doing so. Consequently, by the time he came to take up the English mission, Pole had become profoundly convinced that the authority of the church, and in particular of the papacy, was the keystone of the faith. Theological argument and discussion, as he knew to his personal cost, resulted only in doubt, strife, and confusion, even among the learned. The peace of the church and the salvation of souls depended, not upon the right convictions of the faithful, but upon their willingness to obey 'as little children'.[132] At the same time he believed himself to be in possession of a much deeper understanding of the English situation than he in fact had. Much had happened in the years of his exile. The anti-clericalism of the 1520s was still there, but it was no longer a dominant force. A new generation had grown up with the royal supremacy; a generation to whom it was no longer the whim of a single king, wicked or otherwise, but an established fact of political life. The depth of Pole's misunderstanding is clearly revealed in a letter which he wrote to the emperor's confessor in October 1553,[133] in which he pointed out that the English had always been most loyal to the holy see, and 'more disposed to that obedience than any other nation'. This situation had only been interrupted by the rebellious conduct of the late king, and since the people '. . . have not been benefited but injured by the change [they] cannot hold that obedience in abhorrence . . .' Being an Englishman, he claimed to 'know thoroughly the sentiments of the people with regard to obedience to the Holy See . . .' Moreover, there had developed in England over the previous decade a kind of popular heresy which Pole had never experienced. The cultured intellectual heretics whom he had encountered in Italy had been men whose convictions he could comprehend and respect, even if he did not share them. They had, moreover, been men whose convictions had led them swiftly into danger and exile, and who had seldom had cause to expect anything else. In England he was to be confronted with men whose professions of faith had brought them office and power in the recent past, and who had wrought great changes of which he bitterly disapproved. He could never bring himself to acknowledge any genuine faith or integrity in such men, believing implicitly that what he saw as evil consequences could only stem from wicked or perverted motives. He was also to be confronted with simple, unlearned men and women, who in his eyes were fit only to be humble and obedient sheep, not only professing convictions of their own, but offering to defend them in the most unseemly fashion. Such tragic and unnatural consequences could only stem from the deliberate wickedness of their erstwhile shepherds.

In spite of his high standing in the church, and his recent closeness to the formulation of what has since come to be known as the 'counter-reformation', by 1553 Pole was a man out of touch, and increasingly out of sympathy, with his own regiment. Just as he looked back to the England of the 1520s, so he looked back to the Rome of the 1530s; to the *Consilium . . . de emendenda ecclesia* and to Contarini at the height of his influence. When he solicited the English mission from Julius III in August 1553, it was with a confident expectation of success which nobody else at that time shared, and with very little understanding of the difficulties which would stand in his path.[134] Julius indeed, although believing him to be the obvious man to send to England, gave him the assignment only in conditional terms and as part of a more general mission to northern Europe, the main purpose of which was to make another attempt to mediate peace between the emperor and the king of France. Nevertheless, on 13 August, Pole wrote to Mary in terms of exaltation and thanksgiving, hailing her accession as the divinely wrought vindication of all that they had both stood, and suffered, for over the years.[135] This letter, which he sent by his privy chamberlain, Henry Penning, also informed the queen of his own mission, and urged her to show a proper gratitude to God by returning immediately to the obedience of the holy see, the repudiation of which had been the source of all England's miseries. A week later he wrote with almost equal enthusiasm to Charles V, congratulating him upon his cousin's triumph, and expressing his belief that '. . . il restituire quel regno all' obedientia della Sede Apostolica' was as close to the emperor's heart as it was to his own.[136] Even Pole, however, was not so naïve as to take Charles's co-operation entirely for granted. The bearer of his letter, his secretary Fiordibello, was given instructions which clearly reveal that he expected the emperor to urge caution and delay. Fiordibello was not only to argue the emperor's duty to God and the salvation of souls in England, but also the danger that if Mary was not given immediate recognition and support, the French might invade in the interest of the young queen of Scots.[137]

The cardinal's doubts were fully justified by the events of the next few weeks. Although he bombarded the queen with letters pointing out the dangers of delay, the expectations of christendom, and her manifest duty, the English mission made no progress at all. This was partly because, as we have already seen, Charles's ambassador in England, Simon Renard, had quickly acquired a great ascendancy over Mary, and the emperor's policy subordinated reconciliation to the marriage project. It was also partly on account of the report made by Gian Francesco Commendone who had been sent secretly into England by Geronimo Dandino, the legate in Germany, and who had obtained an audience with the queen by means of the Venetian ambassador.[138] Commendone seems to have been independently convinced of the need for caution, recommending that in the first instance the pope should merely ease Mary's task by the relaxation of ecclesiastical censures. When he learned the substance of Commendone's report, Pole was incensed, and expressed his disagreement forcibly to Dandino, declaring that compromise with worldly and unworthy considerations was not in his nature.[139] By this time Mary was distressed and alarmed by the legate's intransigence. She had already pointed out to Penning that she was a loyal daughter of the holy see, and would avow this publicly as soon as she deemed it to be practicable.[140] However, there could be no question of casting aside all considerations of worldly prudence, much as her private conscience might prompt her to do so. To regard her father's and brother's religious legislation as *ipso facto* invalid was in accordance with her own convictions, but to have acted upon such principles would have been politically impossible. Consequently on 11 September, Mary sent urgent representations to Dandino via the Venetian ambassador, that Pole should not as yet be sent to England in either a public or private capacity.[141] Her goodwill towards the holy see was unabated, but the time was unpropitious, and she did not wish to be placed in the embarrassing position of having to refuse him admission. On 23 September the

English ambassador in Venice, Peter Vannes, reported that Commendone's arrival in Rome the previous week had been followed by a meeting of the consistory at which the chamberlain had reported that 'the schismatics are greater in number than the heretics, and all enemies to the church of Rome' – a realistic assessment of the English situation.[142] The consistory had made no resolution on the matter, which meant that the pope had decided not to press the mission for the time being. Within a few days Pole had been given new instructions which clearly gave priority to his role as mediator in the Franco-Habsburg war, and despatched northwards.

The cardinal was obedient, but not really reconciled to this situation. He continued to write letters of earnest admonition to Mary, and entertained hopes of influencing the English situation from the Low Countries. In reply the queen was friendly, but firm. She sought absolution for the sin of continuing to bear a schismatic title, but the time to declare her mind openly had not yet come.[143] By this time Mary had eased her conscience in a number of small ways – obtaining a special dispensation for Gardiner, amending her coronation oath,[144] and importing special chrism for her anointing – but the main lines of her policy were laid down by the emperor and her lay councillors. Gardiner was in a dilemma. Zealous for 'the union of religion', he had no desire to see Pole in England, partly because he mistrusted his total commitment to the papacy, and partly because he feared his own eclipse. So in spite of the broad similarity of their aims, the chancellor at this time was no friend to the legate's mission, and did nothing to promote it. By the end of October, Pole was suffering further frustrations. With the marriage negotiations at a delicate stage, Charles had decided that Pole's presence in the north at all would be an embarrassment, and stopped his journey at Dillingen in Bavaria, thus effectively suspending both his missions.[145] The cardinal's protests and exhortations alike went unheeded:

> . . . for a woman to call herself head of that multitude which constitutes the church, is forbidden both by Divine as well as natural law [he wrote to Mary on 1 December] . . . [you] have received from God the spirit of council; let [your] Majesty now entreat the spirit of fortitude necessary for the completion of the undertaking . . .[146]

The queen did indeed cease to use the title of supremacy, thus casting doubts upon the legality of her official documents,[147] but more than fortitude was needed for the task Pole had in mind. He was kept at Dillingen until the end of December, when, with the marriage negotiations effectively completed, the emperor was prepared to allow him to proceed to Brussels. The emperor's suspicions of Pole's attitude to the marriage were not altogether unfounded, as the legate's letter to Cardinal di Monte on 10 February makes plain. Had he been asked for his opinion, he claimed, he would have advised against it on the grounds of the queen's age.[148] However, his opinion had not been sought, and he had not volunteered it. Faced with the fact of the treaty, he took the reasonable attitude that the marriage offered good prospects of advancing God's service, and should be used for that purpose.

Now that he was more readily accessible to messengers from England, Pole was able to make a small beginning with his task of reconciliation. On 23 January, Mary sought his advice and aid over the filling of innumerable benefices which were already or soon would be vacant, and a month later requested him to confirm twelve new episcopal appointments, which he did.[149] In acting so the queen was clearly contravening the existing law, but it had no doubt been for such a purpose that she had qualified her coronation oath. In March the legate opened his register, and began to record the resort to his jurisdiction of a steady trickle of private individuals, both laymen and clergy. Dispensations to say mass, to eat flesh in Lent, and to have altars in private houses form the bulk of these early entries.[150] By May there was anxiety among the queen's councillors about the possible consequences of condoning such breaches of the law, and Mary was urged to prohibit such resort until a general reconciliation had been negotiated.[151] Once again Pole fulminated against the dictates of 'worldly prudence', and no action was taken to prevent the practice. During these early months of 1554 most of the cardinal's energies were devoted to his diplomatic mission. The details of this do not concern us here, but it was not a success and Pole's incompetence was a contributory factor. Not the least inept of his suggestions was the involvement of Mary as mediatrix at a time when she was obviously committed to the Imperial interest, and according to Damula, the Venetian ambassador in Brussels, '. . . will not say a word . . . until receipt of the order hence . . .'[152] Charles was not at this moment anxious to pursue such a negotiation, and was quite prepared to blame either the French or the cardinal for the failure to make progress, and Pole was an easy scapegoat. However, better tidings were on the way. By the end of June Julius III had come to the conclusion that the repeated warnings which he had received about the intransigence of the English over secularized church property represented an unavoidable truth, and concessions would have to be made. He also anticipated, rightly, that Philip's impending arrival in England would open the way for direct negotiations. With the peace negotiations temporarily stalled, he instructed Pole to give priority to the English mission, and gave him increased discretionary powers to negotiate on the question of church lands and goods. By the time that Gardiner celebrated the royal wedding at Winchester, the prospects for a full reconciliation with Rome were brighter than at any moment since the beginning of the reign; and the protestants, although by no means either silenced or suppressed, showed no signs of being able to prevent that consummation.

Notes

1 Foxe, *Acts and Monuments*, VI, 389.
2 *HMC Seventh Report*, App., 609 (Molyneux, Loseley MSS).
3 For example, Robert Dudley's unsuccessful attempt at King's Lynn. *HMC Third Report*, App., 237 (Bedingfield MSS). In Northampton, where Mary was proclaimed by Sir Thomas Tresham, Sir Nicholas Throgmorton 'withstanding him to his power' was driven to fly for his life. *Chronicle of Queen Jane*.
4 *An apology made by . . . John Hooper*. Published in 1561 by Henry Bull (STC 13742). Part of Bull's preface runs 'Great was the care of this blessed man and other for the churche of god, and manye fruitfull workes did they write in prison . . . but fewe are come to light . . .' For the minority protestant view, see Richard Hilles to Henry Bullinger, 9 July 1553. *Original Letters relating to the English Reformation*, Parker Society (1846), I, 272.
5 Bucer to Brentius, 15 May 1550. *OL*, II, 542.
6 Among the nobility of the kingdom those are very powerful who would reduce the whole of the sacred ministry into a narrow compass . . .' ibid. For a fuller discussion of this point see *OM*, 87-100.
7 Bucer to Calvin, Whitsunday 1550. *OL*, II, 546.
8 ibid.
9 Cox to Bullinger, 5 October 1552. *OL*, I, 123.
10 See above, 53. For a discussion of this crisis, see Beer, *Northumberland*, 72-92.
11 *OM*, 67-9. This is also the main theme of Claire Cross's treatment of the period: *Church and People*, 81-101.
12 Hooper to Bullinger, 23 September 1553. *OL*, I, 100.
13 *Greyfriars Chronicle* (Camden Society, 1852), 82.
14 For which he was subsequently reprimanded by Pole. Foxe, VII, 297. *OM*, 139 and n.
15 *Chronicle of Queen Jane*, 18-19. *Cal. Span.*, XI, 184.
16 John Christopherson, *An exhortation to all menne to take hede and beware of rebellion* (STC 5207), 1554.
17 *Cal. Span.*, XI, 186.
18 *Chronicle of Queen Jane*, 19.
19 *APC*, IV, 306. Gardiner celebrated such a mass privately for the queen. *Ecc. Mem.*, III, i, 31.
20 From a newsletter in Starkey's collection. *Chronicle of Queen Jane*, 16.
21 There are descriptions of this well-known incident in Machyn, *Chronicle of Queen Jane*, and Foxe.

22 Renard to the queen-dowager, *Cal. Span.*, XI, 175.
23 Rogers had earlier preached openly against the revival of the mass. It was perhaps because of his intervention at Paul's Cross that he was at first confined to his house and not sent to the Tower. *APC*, IV, 321.
24 The council issued a collective passport to the Glastonbury congregation on 5 September, and on 16 September ordered the mayors of Dover and Rye to give passage to '. . . suche Frenchemen as have lately lived at London and hereaboutes under the name of Protestantes . . .' *APC*, IV, 341, 349.
25 *APC*, IV, 335, 336, 338, 340, 351, etc.
26 L. B. Smith, *Tudor Prelates and Politics* (1953), 99.
27 *Cal. Span.*, XI, 216.
28 e.g., 'Item, the next day [24 August] a goodly masse songe at sant Nicholas Wyllyams, in Laten, in Bredstrett . . .' Machyn, 42.
29 *Greyfriars Chronicle*, 82.
30 P. Hughes, *The Reformation in England*, II (1953), 200-2; A. G. Dickens, *The Marian Reaction in the Diocese of York* (1957); J. E. Oxley. *The Reformation in Essex to the Death of Mary* (1965), 179-90; C. Haigh, *Reformation and Resistance in Tudor Lancashire* (1975), 178-95.
31 *HMC Seventh Report*, App., 432 (Malet MSS); 20 August 1553 to the university of Oxford. *OM*, 113-15.
32 Foxe, VI, 393, 412. J. E. A. Dawson. 'The Early Career of Christopher Goodman' (unpublished Durham PhD thesis, 1978), 95-8. Julius Terentianus to John ab Ulmis, 20 November 1553, *OL*, I, 365-74.
33 Martyr to Bullinger, 3 November 1553. *OL*, II, 505.
34 *Cal. Span.*, XI, 233.
35 ibid., 217.
36 '. . . suche as was of hereticall opinions myghtt nott away therwithe butt spayke evill theroff, for as then ther was no actt, statutte, proclamation or commandmentt sett furthe for the sayme . . .' A. G. Dickens, 'Robert Parkyn's Narrative of the Reformation', *EHR*, 62 (1947), 79.
37 *OM*, 113-15. D. M. Loades, 'The Last Days of Cuthbert Tunstall, 1547–1559', *DUJ*, 66 (i) (1973), 10-21.
38 Hales, who had been the one judge to stand out against Edward's 'device' on the grounds of its illegality, insisted on respecting the law against the mass in defiance of the queen's wishes, and was imprisoned. W. Cobbett, *State Trials* (1816), I, 714.
39 Renard to the emperor, 4 November 1553. *Cal. Span.*, XI, 335.
40 Penning's report to the pope. *Cal. Ven.*, V, 429.
41 The chancellor's speech referred to 'reunion', but made no specific mention of the papacy. Mary subsequently informed Renard that the Lords had shown themselves willing to repeal Henry's religious legislation, but that the Commons had refused. How these soundings were taken is not known. *Cal. Span.*, XI, 297.
42 The queen had made the House of Lords more amenable by depriving or imprisoning nine protestant bishops before the session opened, and restoring five catholics – an instructive contrast with Elizabeth's proceedings in 1559. For a full discussion of the parliament, see Loach, op. cit.
43 *Cal. Span.*, XI, 322.
44 Renard was informed that those who voted against the measure were

'not of the most substantial sort'. No division figures are recorded. *Cal. Span.*, XI, 349.

45 *CJ*, 29 November 1553, I, 31.
46 ibid., 5 December. Loades, 'The Last Days of Cuthbert Tunstall'.
47 *Greyfriars Chronicle*, 85. 21 October 1553.
48 *Cal. Span.*, XI, 332.
49 *APC*, IV, 349, 368. Foxe, VI, 411.
50 *APC*, IV, 375, 377.
51 2 and 3 Edward VI, c. 21.
52 W. H. Frere, *The Marian Reaction in its Relation to the English Clergy* (1896), 46-71; G. Baskerville, 'Married Clergy and Pensioned Religious in Norwich Diocese, 1555', *EHR*, 68 (1933), 43-64, 199-228; in Essex 88 incumbents were deprived out of 319; in York diocese 53 out of about 1000 lost their livings, although evidence suggests that about 90 had married H. Grieve, 'The Deprived Married Clergy in Essex, 1553–61'. *TRHS*, 4th series 22 (1940), 141-69; Dickens, *The Marian Reaction in the Diocese of York*, I, 'The Clergy', 1-2, 14-15.
53 Dickens, 'Robert Parkyn's Narrative', 82.
54 D. Wilkins, *Concilia* (1737), IV, 95.
55 W. H. Frere and W. M. Kennedy, *Visitation Articles and Injunctions* (1910), II, 327. As a recent study has pointed out, the public penances and other humiliations inflicted upon the married clergy had the unintended effect of lowering the prestige of their order in spite of this precaution. Cross, *Church and People*, 104.
56 *Cal. Pat.*, I, 230-1.
57 ibid., 50.
58 ibid., 175-6. *OM*, 113-16.
59 The vacant sees were Rochester and Bangor. Gardiner, Bonner, Heath, Tunstall, and Voysey had already been restored. By the terms of an *inspeximus* granted to Bonner on 2 March 1554, he was deemed to have been restored to his see '. . . and to the estate in which he was' when called before Edward's commissioners. This had the effect of making all Ridley's grants and surrenders to the crown void, which meant that Bonner was entitled to repossess a number of estates which had passed into lay hands. *Cal. Pat.*, I, 121. Both Bonner and Gardiner succeeded in dispossessing a number of lay holders in this way, but, sensing the insecurity of their position, subsequently also obtained the cancellation of the offending grants in chancery. A protracted struggle in Elizabeth's first parliament reinstated the lay patentees. N. Jones, 'Faith by Statute' (unpublished Cambridge PhD thesis, 1977), 225-30.
60 *Cal. Pat.*, I, 243.
61 ibid., 165-6. The university of Oxford, as distinct from the colleges, appears to have had no endowment before this grant.
62 ibid., 203.
63 ibid., 384.
64 *Cal. Span.*, XII, 8.
65 *Sermons and Remains of Bishop Latimer*, Parker Society (1845), 303. Latimer's thinking on this point was not entirely consistent, as his comments upon the anabaptists make plain. *OM*, 88-91.
66 See above, 125. For a full discussion of the motivation of this rebellion, see *TTC*, 15-24.
67 According to Proctor, Wyatt declared that any mention of religion 'would withdraw from us the hearts of many', implying that he was

more protestant than he wished to appear. His indictment contained no hint of such a charge, but his widow, Jane, was one of those who later helped Ridley and Latimer in prison. *The Works of Bishop Ridley*, Parker Society (1841), 385. The question of the religious affiliation of Wyatt and his followers has recently been reopened by Malcom R. Thorp (*Church History*, 47, 4, 1978).

68 *HMC Ninth Report*, I, App., I, 155 (City of Canterbury MSS). Mantell's children were legatees under Hales's will.

69 *Exhortation*, sig. Qiiii.

70 ibid., sig. Fiv.

71 *TTC*, 116 and n.

72 *Howe Superior Powers oght to be obeyd* (1558). I am indebted to Dr Jane Dawson for drawing my attention to this point.

73 *Exhortation*, sig. Gii (v).

74 STC 20407. Reprinted by E. Arber in *An English Garner* (1903), vol. VIII.

75 STC 20188.

76 STC 15059. Knox also wrote *A faythfull admonition* (STC 15069) and *A Godly Letter* (STC 15073) at this time, in the same spirit of exhortation.

77 STC 11587.

78 STC 10384; STC 10016. For an informative discussion of the pamphlets of this period, with extensive bibliographical footnotes, see J. Loach, 'Pamphlets and Politics, 1553–8', *BIHR*, 48 (1975), 31-45.

79 *OL*, II, 513.

80 Harbison, 79-81.

81 28 July, 18 August, and 10 April 1554. Hughes and Larkin, II, 4, 5, 41.

82 *Cal. For.*, Mary, 105.

83 STC 17560.

84 STC 13556; Lambeth Palace Library, 1488.6.

85 LPL, 1488.6, 3.

86 STC 23292.

87 *A compendious treatise in metre . . . by G(eorge M(arshall)*, STC 17469.

88 STC 23207. Standish subtitled his work 'A question to be moved to the hyghe courte of Parliament', but there is no evidence that it ever was.

89 STC 12559; STC 12558.

90 LPL, 1553.07, sig. A iii.

91 STC 24356; STC 1307.

92 *OM*, 118; STC 11583; see also *An admonishion to the bishoppes of Winchester London and others* (STC 11593).

93 *Exhortation*, sig. K vi (v).

94 Cranmer had pleaded Not Guilty, and changed his plea during the trial; PRO KB8/23. For a discussion of this trial, see *OM*, 119-21.

95 Foxe, VI, 531-2.

96 ibid.

97 They had the power to excommunicate, but not to take any further action on account of the obscure jurisdictional position. *OM*, 129-36.

98 Primarily the account published by Foxe in 1563, suppiemented by letters and notes written by the participants themselves.

99 The arguments upon the nature of the presence in the eucharist were rendered futile by different assumptions about the nature of space. T. F. Torrance, *Space Time and Incarnation*, 25-6; J. McGee, 'The

Nominalism of Thomas Cranmer', *Harvard Theological Review*, 57 (1964), 189-206.
100 Foxe, VI, 510.
101 *OM*, 169. For a full discussion of the period of imprisonment in Oxford, see *OM*, 167-91.
102 The most active correspondents were Ridley in Oxford, and John Bradford in various prisons in London. Bradford also conducted a considerable controversy with Henry Hart and the 'freewillers'. *The Works of Bishop Ridley*; *The Writings of John Bradford*, Parker Society (1848), 53.
103 PRO SP11/2/2.
104 *APC*, IV, 395.
105 *APC*, IV, 363; 12 November 1553. ibid., 384; 13 January 1554.
106 BL Cotton MS Titus B II f. 174.
107 *APC*, V, 17; 3 May 1554.
108 *Greyfriars Chronicle*, 90; *APC*, V, 49; 30 June 1554.
109 Ramsey and Mone, or Moone, both wrote crude satires and plays against the catholic church, as well as some evangelical tracts (STC 18055-6; 20661-3). A. G. Dickens, *Notes and Queries* (1954), 513; also *The English Reformation*, 222-3. *APC*, V, 70, 88; 2 September and 26 December 1554.
110 Renard to the emperor, 3 September 1554. *Cal. Span.*, XIII, 46.
111 Foxe, VII, 371-4.
112 For this position see particularly P. Hughes, *The Reformation in England*, II (1953), 262.
113 BL Cotton MS Titus C VII ff. 6-65.
114 ibid.
115 See above, 83.
116 *CJ*, I, 33.
117 ibid.
118 ibid.
119 On 24 April. We do not know why it was redrafted.
120 *Lords Journals*, I, 450.
121 In fact two Edwardian statutes were involved, one of which annexed the borough of Gateshead to the city of Newcastle; it was this second measure which the citizens of Newcastle were anxious to retain. Various provisos were added to the act of repeal before it was passed. *CJ*, I, 31. Loades, 'The Last Days of Cuthbert Tunstall'.
122 One of the arguments which swayed the Lords against the revival of the statutes, which were presumably those of 5 Richard II, 2 Henry IV, and 2 Henry V, which were eventually resurrected in January 1555, was that they would have the effect of restoring autonomous ecclesiastical jurisdiction. In the absence of any specific recognition of papal authority this would have given the bishops a level of independence which the lay peers presumably considered intolerable.
123 1 Mary, st. 3 c. 10.
124 Loach, 'Parliamentary Opposition in the Reign of Mary Tudor'.
125 His mother was Margaret countess of Salisbury, daughter of George duke of Clarence and niece of Edward IV.
126 He had originally been used by Henry in canvassing the opinions of the universities, but by 1530 had demonstrated his hostility to the proceedings. W. Schenck, *Reginald Pole* (1950). For a full discussion of Pole's part in Henry's 'great matter', see W. G. Zeeveld, *Foundations of*

G   181

Tudor Policy (1948).
127 *DNB*; Schenck, op. cit.
128 R. H. Pogson, 'Reginald Pole, Papal Legate to England in Mary Tudor's reign' (unpublished Cambridge PhD thesis, 1972). At the same time he described himself as 'the son of a martyr'; D. B. Fenlon, *Heresy and Obedience in Tridentine Italy* (1972), 283.
129 ibid., 174.
130 Mason to Mary, 24 October 1554 and 5 October 1554; PRO SP69/5 ff. 77, 52.
131 Benedetto Fontanino and Marcantonio Flaminio. Fenlon, op. cit., 74-82.
132 For an extended consideration of Pole's attitude towards his mission, see Pogson, op. cit.
133 *Cal. For.*, Mary, 20.
134 See particularly his letter to Mary of 13 August, *Cal. Ven.*, V, 384-7.
135 *Cal. Ven.*, V, 384-7. '. . . those who, having been previously utterly given to the cause of human malice, now all devoted themselves to the honour and service of God and of her highness, and to the benefit of the whole kingdom'.
136 *Cal. Ven.*, V, 389. Pole to the emperor, 20 August 1553.
137 ibid., 391-3.
138 Commendone was sent on Dandino's authority, but his brief was to report directly to the pope, which he did. Dandino presumably instructed him to work through Soranzo. Giacomo Soranzo to the doge and senate, 11 September 1553. *Cal. Ven.*, V, 410-11.
139 Pole to the cardinal of Imola, 9 September 1553. *Cal. Ven.*, V, 409-10.
140 Penning's report. *Cal. Ven.*, V, 429-32.
141 ibid., 410-11.
142 *Cal. For.*, Mary, 14-15.
143 Pole to Mary, 2 October 1553; Mary to Pole, 8 October 1553. *Cal. Ven.*, V, 418-23; 425-6.
144 She had insisted upon inserting the words 'just and licit' into her undertaking to uphold the laws of the realm. Ambassadors to the emperor, 19 September 1553. *Cal. Span.*, XI, 239.
145 While he waited at Dillingen for safe conducts from the duke of Wurttemberg and the count palatine, he was met by Don Juan de Mendoza on 24 October. *Cal. Ven.*, V, 434.
146 *Cal. Ven.*, V, 447. Pole to Mary, 1 December 1553.
147 Jones, 'Faith by Statute', 133-4. It was argued by John Aylmer and others that the supremacy was inalienably vested in the crown, and that consequently all official documents lacking it were invalid.
148 *Cal. Ven.*, V, 463-6.
149 ibid., 453-4; 471-2. Pole had been given special powers of dispensation to enable him to cope with this 'mission at long range'. ibid., 464.
150 LPL; microfilm of Pole's legatine register, MS 292 in Douai Municipal Archive.
151 Pole to his agent in England, 25 May 1554. *Cal. Ven.*, V, 495-7.
152 Marc' Antonio Damula to the doge and senate, 7 June 1554. *Cal. Ven.*, V, 505. This suggestion had first been mooted some months before.

6   Financial Policy, 1553–1554

Mary's financial advisers were acutely aware of the predicament in which the new regime found itself, for the good reason that most of them had been struggling with it for the past two years. Stability and continuity in office were more marked in the financial departments than in any other aspect of the government,[1] and there was consequently no noticeable change of direction or emphasis in the opening months of the reign. The queen inherited a debt of rather more than £185,000, according to a calculation made early in August.[2] This was a marked improvement on the £220,000 which Edward had owed in October 1552,[3] but serious enough at a time when the ordinary revenue account could be expected to show a surplus of no more than £36,000 a year.[4] £61,000 of this debt was owed to foreign bankers, mostly in Antwerp, and with credit costing anything from 11 to 14 per cent per annum even the payment of the interest was a considerable burden. Nevertheless, Mary was not bankrupt, and the Imperial ambassadors' reports of her extreme poverty need to be treated with caution. Towards the end of August they reported that she had '. . . found the realm in debt for £500,000 sterling',[5] an estimate which by November had improved to £700,000.[6] Before she even reached London they had informed the emperor '. . . she has found no money for current expenses', which was not true since Thomas Mildmay, auditor of the court of augmentations, had joined her some days earlier, bringing with him the balance of the sum which he had drawn from the mint on 11 July to pay the duke of Northumberland's army. This amounted to over £2000.[7] At the same time about £550 remained in the hands of the tellers of the exchequer,[8] and an unspecified but probably small sum at the mint itself. Since it had not been unknown in the past for the coffers to run completely dry, this situation, if not exactly one of affluence, was far from desperate; especially in view of the quick and substantial returns which could now be expected from compositions and attainders.

Neither the queen nor her councillors were averse to exaggerating

183

the poverty of the realm, partly because the duke of Northumberland had become such a convenient scapegoat, and partly because the need for reform and retrenchment was real and urgent. A new reign always gave an opportunity for stocktaking, and it was possible that the energetic repudiation of Edwardian policies which was now fashionable could be exploited in the interests of improved solvency. A number of memoranda were drawn up in the first month of the reign, very much in the spirit of the royal commission of 1552, but covering rather different ground. The first of these, a series of hasty notes, is mainly concerned with 'the great debts which be owing many ways', and 'to seke all occasions to pay those debts and to take away all superfluous and new charges . . .'[9] Economies are suggested in the garrisons of Calais, Berwick, and Ireland, in bouge of court, in the numbers of gentlemen pensioners and men-at-arms, and in those pensions and annuities granted during royal pleasure. The second document, drawn up by Cecil just before his eclipse, urges Mary to take cognisance of Thomas Gresham's dealings in Flanders, and to accept responsibility for the outstanding obligations there.[10] The third is a careful list of transactions which are to be investigated with a view to detecting negligence or fraud: particulars of sales, gifts and exchanges of land; 'how the money is answered for the woods of the lands sold . . .'; all those who have received lead, bell metal, jewels, plate, or ornaments from abbeys or chantries are to be called to account; 'that the sums of money demanded for the fall of the money may be well and substantially examined . . .'; and that the goods which were foisted on English agents in the Low Countries as the price of renewing earlier loans should be properly accounted for.[11] All this adds up to a policy of careful and thorough supervision, the necessity for which had long been realized, and which Mary had inherited along with her lord treasurer and exchequer officers.

Several years ago, in a work which has since remained the only serious study of Mary's finances, F. C. Dietz argued that these memoranda were not only accepted by the queen and her council, but effectively implemented in most particulars. 'This was the constructive work of Mary's government', he decided, after a somewhat selective investigation of the evidence.[12] However, just as it now seems certain that the reforming proposals of the 1552 commission were never included in the final report,[13] it also appears likely that these admirable intentions remained very largely on paper. For example, the third memorandum pointed out that over £4500 was being paid out annually in pensions granted 'during pleasure' which could easily be stopped.[14] Mary certainly did stop many, perhaps cutting the bill by as much as a half, but she then proceeded to grant over £2800 a year in annuities to those who had joined her at Framlingham.[15] Apart from the major issue of exchequer reform, which seems to have occupied most of the energy of the financial reformers in Mary's first year, there is little evidence of any new or more effective attempts either to curb expenditure or to improve the exploitation of revenue. Once the succession crisis was over, frugal minds inevitably turned to military expenditure. The garrisons of the Calais Pale were reduced, in spite of the protests of Lord Grey, the captain of Guisnes;[16] the queen's additional guard was dismissed, and the lord treasurer headed an inquiry into the costs of the coastal forts and blockhouses.[17] The Edwardian practice of appointing special commissions to take the accounts of revenue officers was continued, and commissions were also used to compound with the followers of Northumberland and Wyatt, with denizens seeking naturalization, and with those who did not wish to take up the honour of knighthood.[18] In February 1554 when the council reorganized the conduct of its business, several *ad hoc* committees were set up to deal with different aspects of the financial situation. Four different committees supervised the victualling and establishments of the border garrisons, the fleet, and the Tower of London. Another set out to 'moderate the excessive charges' of the household and the chamber, while a particularly high-powered group headed by the lord treasurer undertook more generally 'to call in the debtes and provide for money'.[19] The most noticeable outcome of this conciliar activity was a resumption of the Henrician and Edwardian practice of selling crown lands. On 29 March Winchester and six others were commissioned to sell land to the annual value of £3000, paying the proceeds direct to Sir Edmund Peckham at the mint.[20] A month later a similar Edwardian commission of March 1553, authorizing sales to the annual value of £1000, was reactivated. Transactions entered into under the earlier commission were now to be completed, and the money again was to go to Peckham.[21]

One of the main problems was what a modern economist might call 'cash flow'. Many of the payments due from the crown had to be made promptly, particularly to foreign bankers, while revenue always came in more slowly than expected. Renard's guess in February 1554 that if the queen 'could get possession of the sums owing to her she would have 400,000 or 500,000 crowns in hand . . .' was an exaggeration, but it contained an element of truth.[22] A few months later Gardiner was to estimate the debts owed to the crown at over £200,000, irrespective of arrears on ordinary revenue.[23] The political troubles of January and February probably caused additional delays, so it is not surprising that the council was willing to forgive Sir Martin Bowes 3000 marks out of an 8000 debt in return for the immediate payment of the balance.[24] Nevertheless, the situation was never as bad as Renard represented it to be while he was trying to persuade the emperor to lend Mary 200,000 crowns, and his claim that '. . . she has no one in her Council who looks after her finances' was almost grotesquely inaccurate.[25] Not only was the queen well supplied with good advice, she was also well served by her officers and commissioners. There were no major financial scandals during her reign, of the kind that closed the Bristol mint under Edward, or afflicted the exchequer in the early part of Elizabeth's reign.[26] On the other hand, she was not an easy ruler to advise. Unlike Elizabeth, Mary was not much interested in finance, and never showed the kind of personal concern over her revenues that she showed over ecclesiastical affairs, or over the disputes within her council. She was always prone to put her conscience before her purse. It was sound economics as well as good sense to undertake the payment of her father's and brother's debts, but her decision to remit the subsidy granted by Edward's last parliament was little short of quixotic. As a public relations exercise this was a great success 'with marvellous giving of the Queen thanks', and the proclamation announcing it extracted the last ounce of propaganda advantage:

> Notwithstanding it is well known to the multitude of the said good subjects how by the evil government of the realm in these late years, specially since the said Duke [of Northumberland] hath borne rule, the treasure of the same is marvellously exhausted . . . yet having both a special mind to the weal of her said subjects, and accounting their living hearts and prosperity as her own weal . . . Her majesty . . . of her mere grace and great clemency . . . hath freely . . . pardoned and remitted . . . the said subsidy.[27]

In fact the gesture was not quite as generous as it was made to appear. Parliament had granted two fifteenths and two tenths in addition to the subsidy, and these were not remitted. Together they amounted to about £88,000. Moreover, although this is not clear from the proclamation, it was only the unpaid balance of the subsidy – about one-third according to a contemporary estimate – which was waived.[28] A full subsidy on this assessment (4s. in the £ on lands and 2s. 8d. in the £ on goods) should have produced about £153,000;[29] so about £50,000 was written off in this way. When we remember that Mary's councillors were carrying out laborious investigations for the purpose of saving a few hundred pounds a year in annuities or soldiers' wages, the significance of this gesture becomes fully apparent.

On a smaller scale the queen's generosity to the church also began to make itself apparent at an early date. At her accession the incumbent bishops owed nearly £10,000 in arrears of tenths and first fruits.[30] As these were replaced in the course of her first year, this collective liability should have increased. However, Mary was keenly aware of the extent to which financial pressure had been applied to the Edwardian bishops, and seems to have made a policy of remitting all such debts upon the appointment of a catholic incumbent. Henry Morgan, appointed to the poor see of St Davids, was forgiven almost £1000 in May 1554.[31] At the same time James Brooks, the new bishop of Gloucester, was granted an exoneration for over £500 owed by his predecessor John Hooper.[32] Edmund Bonner of London not only received remission of the £552 owed by Nicholas Ridley 'lately termed bishop of London', but a grant of lands valued at over £525 and exoneration for the future of all tenths in excess of £100 per annum.[33] Because of the diverse nature of such favours, and the fact that they varied greatly from one see to another, it is almost impossible to calculate how much this policy cost the crown in the first year of the reign, but it must have been several thousand pounds. The diminution of future income was less serious, but even that could be ill afforded. As we have already noticed, Mary also practised a similar generosity in her secular restorations. The Howards and the Courtenays, who were the earliest major beneficiaries, received lands to an annual value approaching £5500; which accounted for rather more than half of the massive gains accruing to the crown by the attainders of Northumberland, Warwick, Northampton, Gates, Palmer, Cranmer, and Andrew Dudley.[34] In the short term Mary's finances certainly gained more than they lost by this game of political 'Cox and Box'. When the substantial compositions are taken into account, followed by the attainders of Wyatt and the Greys, and the fines which followed that rebellion, despite a number of other small restorations the crown must have benefited to the extent of over £10,000 *per annum* in lands, and at least £10,000 in ready money and plate. However, the policy of restoration went on, and there were no more major attainders.

By comparison with the great efforts which had been made in the last year of King Edward, both to reduce the debt and to clear up the long backlog of peculation and inefficiency, the activity of Mary's council in the first year of her reign was not particularly impressive. Occasional notes in the records about suspected minor frauds; summonses to treasurers and receivers to 'make their indelayed appearance'; and orders to local officials to investigate complaints, indicate a reasonable level of vigilance.[35] But the only

187

major defaulters to be dealt with in the first year had been detected before Edward's death. Richard Bunny, the treasurer of Berwick, was committed to the Fleet in November 1553 for malpractices in office, and was later judged to owe the crown £2800. He forfeited his position, and early in 1554 underwent another period of imprisonment, being finally released upon bond to pay £2000 and surrender his lands, worth £53 *per annum*.[36] Sir John Williams, the treasurer of augmentations, who had already had to make up an £826 deficit in the jewel house, was discovered in 1552 to have presented no accounts for his major office in almost a decade. Eventually, in March 1554, seven weeks after the court of augmentations had ceased to exist, a commission was appointed for this purpose.[37] The commissioners discovered that Williams had failed to disclose receipts of over £30,000, extending over a number of years, until, presumably realizing that detection was imminent, he had entered the whole lot as a lump sum at some time between September 1552 and September 1553. By so doing he seems to have escaped any formal charges, and was called upon to pay no more that £2100 when the council finally 'took order' for his debt in June 1556.[38] Not only did he suffer no punishment, his career prospered and flourished, as we have already seen. Presumably he had also made good use of the unauthorized loan of the crown's money which he had enjoyed for so long. The other commissions to take accounts which were issued during this year were mostly in response to requests from the prospective accountants themselves,[39] and revealed no irregularities of any significance. The numerous commissions for the collection and delivery of church goods which had been set up in the last few months of Edward's life were stalled in mid course by the king's death; but instead of immediately calling them to account, the council sent out piecemeal instructions for restitution.[40] In the resulting confusion a considerable quantity of what had been collected seems to have vanished into the personal possession of the commissioners and their friends, so that neither the exchequer nor the parish churches received their due. It was not until November 1555 that William Berners, Thomas Mildmay, and John Wiseman were commissioned to '. . . call before them all persons who have meddled by commission or otherwise with the receipt, charge, sale or order of any lead, bell metal, plate, jewels, etc. to which the Crown has been entitled since 4 February 27 Henry VIII, and to compel them to give full accounts of the same . . .'[41] Much was recovered, but a great deal less than might have been realized by prompter action.

The financial situation in this early part of the reign is complicated and obscured by the major organizational changes which took place in the exchequer, but there is no reason to suppose that any marked improvement took place as a result of the change of regime. In spite of all efforts the charges of the household showed no signs of diminishing: £65,923 in the last full year of Edward's life, they came down to £57,358 in the first year of Mary, only to rise to an enormous £75,043 in the second year.⁴² The wardrobe, upon which Sir Ralph Sadler had 'ordinarily spent' £5373 3s. 10d. in 1552–53, cost £12,307 12s. 6d. in the following year, and £7681 15s. in 1554–55.⁴³ Ireland, which had absorbed £42,609 (including a special payment of £5700 for fortifications) in the last year of Edward, cost Mary £37,916 in her first year and £38,524 in the second – regular payments remaining almost unchanged.⁴⁴ At the same time clear revenues remained static, or even dropped. The English customs, which had yielded £23,386 in the fifth year of King Edward, produced £22,407 in the first year of Mary.⁴⁵ Ordinary exchequer revenues, which had cleared a meagre £5477 in 1551, were actually overspent in 1553–54, and the modest sum in the hands of the tellers went down by £2679. This setback may, however, have been due to the political disturbances, since the exchequer cleared £22,222 in the second year of the reign, and £8672 in the fourth.⁴⁶ In the case of augmentations the method of calculating 'clear' income seems to have changed with the reorganization.⁴⁷ In 1550–51 the 'clear' yield of the court was recorded as £29,337, and in 1552–53, the last year of its existence, as £26,883. In 1556–57, the fourth year of the reign, the 'clear' income of the augmentations office was, according to one computation, £47,723, and according to another £80,000.⁴⁸ In the latter case it is quite clear that expenses normally charged on the old augmentations account have not been included, and had the calculations been carried out in the traditional manner, it seems that the true equivalent of the earlier figures would be in the region of £32,000.⁴⁹ The court of wards and liveries, which was not affected by the reorganizations, had produced £6045 'clear' in the fourth year of Edward VI, and £2665 in the sixth; but in the second year of Mary it produced only £189 7s. 5d., and in the fifth year £65 9s. 1d.⁵⁰ Here again it was the level of payments and allowances which changed, rather than the level of revenue, which stood at £16,526 in the sixth year of Edward, and £15,147 in the second year of Mary, so the explanation may lie in the fact that the real surpluses accruing to the court had been transferred elsewhere before these 'clear' returns were made.

In April 1554, after about nine months of the reign, Stephen Gardiner drew up another summary of the crown's debts, similarly itemized to that of August 1553 but estimated in round figures.⁵¹ According to his calculation the enormous Irish debt had been almost halved – from £36,095 to £20,000 – while the Calais debt had improved even more satisfactorily – from £21,187 to £10,000. Arrears in the admiralty and at Berwick had been marginally reduced – from £16,639 to £15,000 in the latter case; but closer to home the situation had deteriorated very markedly. The household debt had gone up from £21,025 to £32,000; that in the chamber from £17,968 to £40,000; and the ordnance from £3134 to £10,000. Equally seriously the debt to foreign bankers, which had fallen steeply in the last year of Edward's reign, had begun to creep up again: from £61,064 to £69,000.[52] Altogether the chancellor calculated that the crown owed £239,000. From the way in which the summary is drawn up it seems likely that Gardiner included in this estimate about £40,000 in current expenditure which was covered by the ordinary revenue. Given the benefit of this doubt, and a real indebtedness of about £200,000, it is still clear that the position had deteriorated rather than improved since Mary came to the throne. In the same memorandum Gardiner went on to claim that this debt could be covered by realizing existing assets: £60,000 by the sale of crown land already undertaken, £82,000 for the sale of lead and bell-metal, and £60,000 in good debts. However, of these only the first sum could be collected with anything like ease. Prolonged and intensive administrative pressure would be necessary to produce even a proportion of the other two, and time could only be bought in Antwerp at a high rate of interest. The deterioration revealed by these estimates does not mean that the council and the revenue officers were relaxing their efforts, or even that the queen was indulging in irresponsible generosity, but simply that the government could not be carried on without either the discovery of a major source of new 'ordinary' revenue, or periodic resort to parliamentary taxation. The only really serious mistake which Mary made early in her reign was to remit the balance of Edward's last subsidy, because this meant that the slow process of collecting arrears of direct taxation virtually stopped. It also meant that the queen could hardly ask her first parliament for a new vote.[53]

During the first year of the reign the realm was at peace, and the cost of putting down the Wyatt rebellion cannot have been of major significance.[54] No major economies were effected, and revenue declined because there was no way of compensating adequately for the temporary renunciation of direct taxation. On the other hand, the council commenced a new round of investigations, into the Irish situation, the customs, the household, and the mint, which were to bear fruit in due course. None of these seem to have owed anything to the personal interest of the queen. For the most part they represent the continued efforts of those who had been struggling with the situation since about 1550, particularly Winchester, Baker, Peckham, Mildmay, and Gresham. The same was true of the reorganization of the exchequer, the one event which made the year 1554 significant in the history of government finance. As we have already seen, the multiplicity of revenue courts which had been created in the 1530s had reduced both the exchequer and the treasury of the chamber to relative unimportance. Not only was this situation much resented by the entrenched vested interest of the exchequer officials, who were losing large sums in fees on the diverted business, it was also unsatisfactory on more objective grounds. By 1540 there were five departments – exchequer, augmentations, general surveyors, first fruits and tenths, and wards and liveries – doing similar work with different aspects of the royal revenues. Each had its own jurisdiction, and a full staff of fee'd officials with the usual tendency of such staffs both to increase and to compete for business. In 1547 the court of general surveyors had been absorbed by augmentations, at a cost of over £2000 a year in compensation for the profits of the abolished offices,[55] and by 1552 augmentations itself was clearly under threat. In spite of the fact that the commission report of that year showed that it was handling well over half the gross revenues of the crown,[56] conservative arguments for the 'certainty' of the exchequer procedure, linked to the real need to rationalize and simplify financial administration, had prompted a plan to reabsorb the whole of this great volume of business into the 'ancient course'. It is not known exactly when this plan was accepted, but it was almost certainly before March 1553, when Edward's last parliament passed an enabling act, empowering the king to reorganize the revenue courts by letters patent – and containing a guarantee that any officials losing their positions in such a process would be compensated.[57] The king's death might have brought a reprieve, but Mary's decision to continue Winchester in office sealed the fate of augmentations. On 17 October a commission headed by the lord treasurer took over the seals of the court, and thus the management of its affairs during the period of transition.[58] In order to facilitate this the chancellor, Sir Richard Sackville, resigned his office at about the same time. He was reinstated on 20 January 1554, three days before the court was dissolved, presumably to enable him to qualify for his pension as an officer.[59] Edward's enabling act was repeated by Mary's first parliament in almost identical terms, and the consequent letters patent became effective on 23 and 24 January.

During the final period of its existence the business of augmentations was kept to an absolute minimum, and on 5 December, Sir Edmund Peckham was commissioned to receive and disburse all the crown's revenues for a limited but unspecified period – not only those of exchequer and augmentations, but also of departments not affected by the reorganization.[60] Peckham's special role seems to have continued until the autumn of 1555. In the period from Easter to Michaelmas 1554 the block warrant to Peckham accounted for £32,848 out of £33,926 spent by warrant; and in the corresponding period of 1555 £45,582 out of £48,105.[61] The abstract of payments by privy seal shows that payments by direct warrant were resumed on 23 October 1555.[62] The appointment of Edmund Cockerell as clerk of the pells, and the consequent commencement of the *Brevia Recepta* on 21 January 1556 were probably results of this return to normal procedure.[63] The court of augmentations ceased its legal existence on 23 January 1554, and along with it was dissolved the court of first fruits and tenths. Since this court had not been included in Winchester's supervisory commission, the decision to do away with it may have been a late one, taken perhaps in light of the queen's developing religious policy which must have already foreshadowed a decline in its work. The assets, records, and business of both these courts were then transferred to the exchequer the following day. At the same time complex schedules were drawn up and annexed to the letters patent, setting out the manner in which the revenues were to be administered under the new system.[64] It had already been provided in the enabling act that if any court should be amalgamated with the exchequer under its provisions '. . . that then all things within the survey of the said Court so conveyed shall be ordered in like manner to all intents as the said Court of Exchequer is or ought to be by the common laws and statutes of the realm . . .'[65] In theory this meant a complete return to the 'ancient course', with all crown properties in England accounting through the sheriffs, and those in Wales through the chamberlain there. The sheriffs were to account from Michaelmas to Michaelmas, and to be granted allowances in proportion to the sums for which they were responsible. Sums due to be paid at Michaelmas had to be delivered, in person or by authorized deputy, by Christmas; those due at Martinmas similarly by 20 February. All audits were to be held during the Hilary term, and completed by 24 February, being sworn to by the accountant or his agent 'according to thauncient usage'. The completed accounts were then to be delivered to the pipe office.[66] This should have meant the disappearance, not only of the twelve districts through which augmentations revenue had been collected, but of the whole system of accounting 'augmentations wise', with its modern double-entry methods. All that should have been left of augmentations was an 'augmentations office' – a record repository to enable the exchequer officials to keep track of the obligations which they had undertaken. A similar but smaller 'office of first fruits and tenths' was designed to perform the same service in respect of that department.[67]

In the event, however, the triumph of exchequer conservatism was much less complete than these schedules promised. Article 32 of the schedule had given the lord treasurer and barons 'full power and auctoritie from tyme to tyme to amende refourme and correcte any clause or article aforesaid . . .' in the light of their experience. Winchester seems to have exercised this discretion from the beginning, perhaps with the assistance of less conservative officials such as Mildmay. The 'office of first fruits and tenths', in addition to being a record repository, was actually a small department of the exchequer managing the business for which the court of that name had been responsible and controlled by its own remembrancer. This, contrary to the original intention, became the model for the very much larger augmentations office, except that the latter was not accorded the official recognition of having its own remembrancer. Augmentations revenues never passed through the hands of the sheriffs, and the receivers and 'country officials' continued to function as before.[68] Nor were the accounts submitted to the 'ancient course'; the simpler and more efficient augmentations methods continued in use. On the other hand, the auditorships of the prests and of the foreign accounts were abolished. In fact the practice of presting, or advancing lump sums to royal agents, continued, and both these auditorships were restored early in the reign of Elizabeth.[69] How the foreign accounts were audited in the meantime is not quite clear, however. These were accounts such as the hanaper of chancery, the butlerage, the staple of Calais, the great wardrobe, and the mint which had become attached to augmentations in the course of its development. They were not absorbed by the 'ancient course' and continued to account 'augmentationswise'; but seem to have done so, like the treasury of the chamber, independently and not as part of the augmentations office.[70] Probably the greatest benefit of the reorganization was unity of control. Apart from the duchy of Lancaster and the court of wards and liveries, all the revenue departments were now under the jurisdiction of the lord treasurer and barons of the exchequer. Another advantage, not envisaged by those who had proposed the reform, was the increased influence of augmentations methods, even within the traditional exchequer departments themselves. However, one of the main benefits sought in the original proposals, economy in administration and the reduction of 'superfluous charges', was not achieved to any great extent. This was partly on account of the failure to dismantle the augmentations structure of receivership and subordinate offices, and partly because of the necessity to provide pensions for those made redundant by the changes. In the case of first fruits and tenths pensions and new offices came to £733 13s. 4d. a year, as against an earlier bill for salaries and allowances of £956 15s. 1d.[71] In the case of augmentations discontinued offices saved a wages bill of £3769 6s., while pensions alone amounted to £3302 13s. 4d.[72] Taking into account the two new auditorships in the exchequer which had to be created to take on the new work, and which were salaried at £20 a year each, the annual saving on the reorganization was in the region of £650; well short of the £3775 which the optimistic commissioners of 1552 had envisaged from such a reform.[73] Of course the pensions were a diminishing liability, and sooner or later an additional £4000 a year would accrue to the crown, but this would not happen quickly and it was only too likely that increasing costs would absorb these savings even before they were realized. The commissioners had originally projected a reversionary saving of £6466, making a total economy of £10,242 a year.[74] The actual saving, even on the most optimistic computation, was well under half that sum, and in the short term can hardly have been noticeable.

Considering the amount of planning and effort involved, the reorganization of the exchequer cannot be regarded as a success from an economic standpoint, and administratively it would have been more efficient to have absorbed the exchequer into augmentations. Nor were the conservatives happy. In the fourth year of the reign an anonymous memorandum on the management of the crown estates again urged that the sheriffs rather than the receivers should account for the crown lands. The author's reasons included ancient usage, and the fact that sheriffs 'are of the best rank', as well as the more substantial argument that the sheriff '. . . whose office is annual cannot conceal the king's money as officers for life who pay the debt of the first year with the revenue of the second . . .'[75] The same memorandum also went on to urge that the duchy of Lancaster should be absorbed by the exchequer, pointing out that since the duchy was permanently vested in the crown, there was no reason for the separation. However, such arguments fell on deaf ears and the exchequer, although remaining an extremely conservative institution, was never again the homogeneous medieval department which it had been before 1554.

Any scrutiny of the ordinary revenues of the crown was bound to include the customs, and this was always a sensitive area. Customs rates were fixed and archaic. Theoretically the rates on most commodities except cloth were *ad valorem*, but in practice a system of official valuations had long since put all duties on to a specific basis.[76] A book of rates had been produced for London in 1507. The use of this was extended to the whole country after 1536, but

194

the rates had not been changed. Consequently the merchants, and particularly the merchant adventurers who handled the great bulk of the Low Countries trade, were paying far less in real terms than their predecessors had done. On the other hand, it was essential for the crown to maintain good relations with the adventurers. Northumberland had squeezed a loan of £40,000 out of them shortly before his fall, for repayment in October, and Mary was constrained to ask them to accept over £15,000 of this debt in Antwerp rather than London.[77] They agreed, but not without a great deal of virtuous protestation over the losses they were suffering. The adventurers were a regular source of medium-sized short-term loans, but were not to be taken for granted in that capacity, as they demonstrated in September 1554 when, according to Renard, they met such a request with 'a flat refusal'.[78] The adventurers may well have been in an unco-operative mood by that time, having had nearly a year to experience the restored privileges of the Hanse. These privileges went back to the fourteenth century, and basically allowed the Germans to export unfinished cloth, wool, tin, and other commodities at preferential customs rates.[79] They also enjoyed monopolistic control over the import of such Baltic produce as flax, iron, and copper. The merchant adventurers had long resented the position of the Steelyard, as the London Hanseatic headquarters was called, and the sharp decline in the cloth trade in 1551 brought about a crisis. It was argued, correctly, that the Hanse merchants were using their privileged position to gain an ever increasing share of the diminished trade,[80] and were able to undercut both English and Dutch merchants in general trade because they paid less custom. Edward had confirmed the Hanse privileges at the beginning of his reign, but a series of controversial incidents had already created a tense situation before the crisis of 1551, and on 9 February 1552 the dispute had been brought to a special session of the privy council.[81] The English merchants had then complained of losses amounting to over £20,000 a year, of the fraudulent use of privileges by Germans who were not of the Hanse, and of the complete failure of the Hanse towns to grant that reciprocity to English merchants which had been stipulated in Edward's grant of confirmation. The council had upheld these complaints, and on 24 February 1552 had declared the privileges abrogated. The Hanseatic community had fought a rearguard action lasting into the summer, but had succeeded only in gaining clearance for cargoes already loaded.[82]

For the remainder of Edward's reign the Steelyard merchants had been permitted to trade on equal terms with their competitors, but the confederation did not give up hope of regaining their earlier position, and its envoys soon gained a more sympathetic hearing from Mary's council. The matter was discussed at the end of August, and then or soon after the decision of Edward's council was reversed. On 24 October a new agreement was drawn up with the Hanse commissioners restoring the traditional privileges, and repeating the provision for reciprocity which had earlier proved ineffective.[83] On 15 and 16 January following, the queen issued instructions to her customs officers not to levy tonnage and poundage from the Hanse merchants, and to permit them to export unfinished woollen cloth of the value of £6 per cloth at their privileged rate of 12d. per cloth.[84] What prompted this volte-face is not clear. Perhaps it is significant that of the five English commissioners who signed the new agreement only Petre had been a member of Edward's council early in 1552, and only he had any particular expertise in finance, or connection with the city of London.[85] The terms of the agreement itself suggested that the Edwardian decision had been of doubtful legality, and that the Hanseatic appeal had not received proper consideration 'because of the troubles and difficulties which then prevailed'.[86] It is possible that the skilled diplomats of the Hanse had succeeded in appealing to the virtues of ancient custom – an appeal to which Mary and Gardiner were both susceptible – or in impugning the motives of Edward's council, which was a favourite activity in official pronouncements of this period. Neither the merchant adventurers nor the city authorities were pleased, and at a time when rumours of the queen's marriage plans were first becoming current, it was being said in London that the council '. . . intended to enrich foreigners by opening the gates of the country to them and impoverish its unfortunate inhabitants . . .'[87]

The Hanseatic merchants did not, in fact, enjoy a very significant advantage over the adventurers in the export of cloth; they paid 12d. per cloth while the adventurers paid 14d. They did, however, enjoy a major advantage over other aliens, who paid 5s. 9d., and over both aliens and English for the goods which they imported. Where aliens paid 15d. in the pound on the latter, and the English 12d., the Hanse paid only 3d. In an anonymous memorandum drawn up towards the end of December 1554 it was argued that in the eleven months from 20 January to 24 December these privileges had cost the exchequer £9360 in lost customs revenue, and business worth over £150,000 had been taken out of the hands of Dutch and English merchants.[88] The Dutch, indeed, 'since the enlargement of the Easterlings have shipped never a cloth . . .' The memorandum was a piece of special pleading, which also accused the Hanse merchants of causing a decay in cloth-making standards by forestalling the clothmarket in Blackwell Hall; a decay in English shipping by using their own vessels; and a 10 per cent fall in the value of the pound. Not all these arguments need be taken very seriously, but they are evidence of the continued animosity of the English merchants – an animosity which was to boil up again into a privy council case at the beginning of 1556.[89] It is also clear that, irrespective of the accuracy of the author's figures, all the business which the Hanse recovered after the restoration of its privileges represented money lost to the exchequer, at least until such time as there was a major improvement in the volume of trade.

Other aspects of customs administration also gave cause for dissatisfaction. Smuggling was a perpetual problem. Early in 1554 a servant of the Venetian ambassador told Mary that she was losing 10,000 crowns (£2500) a year through peculation,[90] and the activities of Henry Dudley's friends in 1556 were to demonstrate once again how easy it was to bribe the 'searchers'.[91] Traditional privileges and perquisites were inimical to efficiency in this as in so many other respects. In July 1555 Simon Low, Sir Francis Englefield's deputy in the management of the London wool customs, reported that almost 30 per cent of the revenue from that source was being lost '. . . by giving to the merchants in every pocket an overdraught called a laste, which they saye hath of long tyme bene used to be given . . .' Low calculated that the crown had lost, and the merchants gained, £4135 by this means during 1553, and £3538 in 1554.[92] Eventually the customs were to be subjected to almost revolutionary change by Mary's council in one of its few really successful attempts at reform, but little was achieved through piecemeal retrenchment or closer administrative control. After reaching a peak of £29,315 in the fourth year of the reign, the 'old customs' sank again to £25,797, in the first year of Elizabeth.[93] Customs revenues were always to some extent at the mercy of trade fluctuations over which the government had no control, but it appears that Mary's willingness to respect and restore traditional privileges just about neutralized the efforts of her servants to improve the methods of collection. And both activities strained relations with the merchant adventurers.

The adventurers were the most important element in the economic structure of the city of London, and as such played a vital part in the maintenance of the government's credit, quite apart from the direct loans which they could occasionally be induced to grant. It was the resources of London which guaranteed to the bankers of Antwerp that the sums of ready money which they advanced to the English crown would eventually be repaid. Usually such loans were assured by bonds issued by the city under its own seal, covering those issued under the great seal of England, although sometimes 'assurance' of a less formal kind was made.[94] London could not supply the government's need for specie itself, as its banking facilities were relatively small-scale and rudimentary, but even after the crisis of 1551 English cloth continued to be a major element in the prosperity of Antwerp. In January 1554 Thomas Gresham estimated that the adventurers' fleet which was then expected would bear a cargo 'richly worth £300,000',[95] and that its arrival would improve the exchange value of the £ sterling from 22*s*. 4*d*. Flemish to 23*s*. It was upon this basis that Mary's credit rested, and since the Antwerp bankers would not accept repayment in London, it sometimes also fell to the adventurers or to the city to supply the necessary cash in the Low Countries against actual or promised repayments at home. Occasionally loans were requested from the adventurers, or on a smaller scale from the staplers, to repay debts which had fallen due, and to be reimbursed in Antwerp from other loans as they were taken up.[96] For such business services the crown paid normal brokerage dues as appropriate, but the real bill was settled in terms of privileges and protection. In the last analysis the indispensability of the London companies to the shaky finances of the crown spelled the doom of the Steelyard, the decline of the outports, and the rise of the regulated and joint-stock companies.[97]

Because of this sound foundation, English credit upon the Bourse was in a surprisingly healthy condition in the autumn of 1553 when Mary's council recommenced operations there. The queen's undertaking to honour her brother's bonds, and the promptness with which this pledge was redeemed, inspired confidence, as did her decision in early November to renew the service of Edward's conspicuously successful agent, Thomas Gresham. Between April 1551 and the summer of 1553, Gresham had first reorganized and then reduced the crown's massive indebtedness, spreading out the repayment dates upon obligations, and making practical arrangements to fund such obligations in advance. He had also, between July 1551 and May 1553, raised the exchange rate of sterling from 13*s*. Flemish to 20*s*. 4*d*., mainly by the skilful use of cloth credits.[98] Gresham returned to Antwerp in mid-November with instructions to take up a loan of £50,000 for one year at 11 or 12 per cent,[99] and was active there until March 1554 when he returned to England for the audit of his last Edwardian account. Gresham was much annoyed on reaching Antwerp to discover that the council had already authorized one Christopher Dawntesey to 'take up' 200,000 florins – that is 100,000 ducats or about £33,000 – from Lazarus Tucher at 13 per cent.[100] Dawntesey was a laughing-stock, he claimed, as there was plenty of money to be had at 11 per cent, or even 10 per cent. However, the damage was done. No one would now lend to the English at less than 13 per cent, and to make matters worse, Dawntesey had agreed for a repayment date only 11 months away, thus making the effective interest-rate 14 per cent.[101] On the other hand, to dishonour an agreement made in the queen's name would be even more damaging, and Tucher was an ill man to cross. Eventually on 30 November the council instructed Gresham to go ahead with the first 100,000, and out of that sum to repay £15,427 to the merchant adventurers who had agreed to receive it in that manner.[102] Subsequently the second 100,000 was also taken up, and Tucher received the queen's bonds for 226,000 florins – £37,666 13s. 4d. – due on 1 November 1554.[103] In all probability most of this sum was absorbed in Antwerp itself, and later in December the council wrote again to Gresham to raise £100,000 over and above the sums already borrowed from Tucher, and not to pay more than 12 per cent.[104] Such a task was impossible. Money was not to be had at less than 13 per cent, and was getting scarce at that. On 24 December, Gresham reported that he had raised 60,000 florins from Gaspar Schetz and a similar sum from Andrew Lixalls, both at 13 per cent, and asked hopefully if that was not enough.[105] The council replied on the 28th, sending bonds from the queen and the city for 120,000 florins, and asking urgently for 60,000 more.[106] By 8 January Gresham had managed to find another 50,000 from Michael Deodati of Lucca,[107] but it is clear that the supply was temporarily drying up and the council's reiterated demand for the full £100,000 was unrealistic. Not only was money getting short, by the end of January news of Wyatt's rebellion – exaggerated by French-inspired rumours – had paralysed English credit entirely. On 6 February Gresham reported that Deodati would not honour his agreement until the political news improved, and everything else was at a standstill.[108]

By the time that the crisis was over, Gresham had found a means of circumventing the difficulties of the Antwerp market. A group of Genoese bankers led by Antonio Spinola and Federigo Imperallo had offered a loan of 300,000 ducats to be taken up at the fair of Villálon in Spain and repaid in Antwerp.[109] Since a fair proportion of the specie available in Antwerp came from Spain in any case, and the rate offered was favourable, the bargain seemed a good one.[110] Gresham returned to England early in March to render his account, and the agreement must have been concluded with the Genoese either just before or just after that date.[111] Payments commenced at Villálon at the end of March, and the repayment date agreed upon was 20 April 1555. However, at this point the plan began to go astray. The export of bullion or minted coin always required a licence from the ruler of the exporting territory, and Gresham had never experienced much difficulty in getting Imperial licences from Antwerp, partly because it was his policy to make frequent but small shipments. To bring a large sum of money out of Spain was a different matter. On 4 May, while Gresham was still in England, the emperor wrote to Renard explaining that news of the English agent's activities had reached him, which suggested that Gresham was taking the *sacca* – that is, Philip's export licence – for granted. There might well be difficulties about this, he went on, as it would have to be handled by the Spanish officials, and money was short in that kingdom. So in spite of his anxiety to oblige Mary, he wished to communicate with Gresham as soon as the latter returned to Antwerp.[112] On 26 May, Gresham reported that difficulties had arisen over the 'passport', and, perhaps as a result, on 7 June, Mary wrote directly to Charles explaining that she was about to send her agent into Spain to collect the money, and requesting him to grant permission '. . . to take the sum of 500,000 ducats out of Spain'.[113] This was the sum which Gresham had originally suggested in January, and was well in excess of the real need – perhaps to allow room for compromise. On the same day Renard also wrote urging compliance on the grounds that delay could have unfortunate political repercussions.[114] In view of the dissatisfaction then being expressed over Philip's own dilatory and uncommunicative attitude, this was a point of some substance. These importunities were partly successful. By the time that Gresham received instructions for his voyage to Spain on 12 June, and Mary wrote a letter of credence for him to the princess of Portugal, he had received an Imperial 'passport' for 200,000 ducats.[115] On 3 July Philip, already at Coruña on his way to England, issued his own licence for the same amount, apparently without knowing of his father's action.[116] For the time being all efforts to improve upon this situation failed, and the money, upon which the English government was contracted to pay interest, remained uselessly in Spain.

On 3 August Princess Joana wrote to Queen Mary, acknowledging her letters of 12 June, and Gresham's request for a licence of 500,000 ducats, and regretting that it was impossible to comply. Philip had granted 200,000 and 'the representatives of the Kingdom' had begged him not to permit any further exports.[117] The Spaniards were indeed in great difficulties. They had been partly financing the emperor's international policies for many years, and the latest example, Philip's voyage to England, was itself a costly venture, as we have already seen. A memorandum drawn up by Francisco Eraso at the end of August and relating to the English request, made the point forcibly.

. . . there is great shortage of coin in Spain, caused by the large sums exported in recent years by his Majesty and by private persons, as well as what recently came over in the fleet. The country is in such straits now that his Majesty had decided to buy out various persons who have had permission to export money granted to them; for he has decided to suffer serious loss rather than allow any further exportation of coin.[118]

Nevertheless, the English council persisted. On 15 August they wrote to Gresham that he was to continue pressing the regent for an additional licence, now modified to 120,000.[119] Early in September this pressure was rewarded, not in Spain but in Brussels. The emperor decided to gratify his son's new subjects at the expense of his own, and gave orders that Gresham was to be allowed another (and final) 100,000 ducats.[120] Philip's opposition was thus overruled, and on 12 September he wrote to his half-sister endorsing his father's decision, merely stipulating that the operation must be conducted quietly to avoid inflaming Spanish opinion.[121] Nevertheless, it was still some time before Gresham got most of the money out. His instructions had authorized him to take up some of the money from merchants trading into Spain, and it is possible that as much as 90,000 ducats may have been obtained in this manner.[122] At the end of November he wrote from Seville that 100,000 ducats had been packed and were ready for despatch, while the remainder, amounting to 110,000, had still to be delivered.[123] He eventually accounted for 300,750,[124] so the balance may well have been obtained before November. The atmosphere in Seville was distinctly hostile. The expected Indies fleet had not arrived, and at least one major bank had failed. Gresham was being blamed for this bankruptcy, and feared that other failures would also be laid to his account because of his strict instructions to accept only specie. With the exception of one bond for 65,000 ducats taken up at the October fair, all Gresham's obligations had run for a matter of eight months before the money to which they related reached England.[125] It is not surprising, therefore, that in February 1555 Mary wrote to John Gresham and Nicholas Holborne, who were still acting for her in Antwerp at this time, to seek a prolongation of the loan for twelve months.[126]

In September or October 1554 a 'note of the Queen's Highness debts in Flanders' showed a total indebtedness of rather more than £150,000.[127] This dramatic increase was partly caused by the Spanish loan itself, and partly by the fact that the English government could not fund its other loans while so much money was tied up in Spain. For example, the loan which Dawntesey had negotiated with Lazarus Tucher fell due on 31 October, amounting to £37,666 13s. 4d. Earlier in the month the queen, dealing directly with Tucher in Gresham's absence, had requested a prolongation, with the result that repayment of half was deferred for one month, and the other half for three.[128] At the same time the council had pressed Gresham hard to raise money between November 1553 and March 1554, and had not encouraged him to take up loans for less than twelve months, with the result that repayments became 'bunched' in a manner similar to that which had prevailed before Gresham's advent. It was to take him over a year to rectify this situation, and in spite of his constant, and on the whole successful, efforts to meet repayment dates, the crown's indebtedness in Flanders had risen steadily. Both Philip and Charles considered that they had made great sacrifices to help the English, and one of Philip's courtiers, presumably misunderstanding the nature of Gresham's transactions in Spain, reported in October 1554 that his master had paid the queen's debts to the tune of 250,000 ducats, in addition to the 30,000 which he had distributed among her lords.[129] In fact neither Philip nor his father gave any direct financial assistance to England during this period, for the simple reason that their own resources were stretched to the limit. The English council dropped sufficiently broad hints, which were dutifully transmitted by Renard. On 3 February 1554, in the midst of the Wyatt rebellion, he reported that the council had told him '. . . that the time when Her Majesty ought to receive her revenues was now up, and that she had as yet received none of it, so that if your Majesty was willing to lend her 200,000 crowns, she would be exceedingly grateful . . .'[130] Charles had been listening to lamentations about English poverty for over six months, and this first specific request for aid crossed in the post with some cool and shrewd comment.

> Your letters also say that the Queen has no money, and no means of raising any in England. It seems to me that she must have credit at Antwerp on the strength of having paid the debts of her late brother, King Edward, and that if she sent someone thither to borrow a goodly sum, she would find the bankers willing to listen.[131]

Gresham had certainly been working quietly, and shipping money over secretly, but he was not smuggling and it is hard to believe that Renard knew nothing of his activities. Presumably he realized that his master's commonsense was not an adequate response, for on 17 February he resumed the same theme unabashed, claiming that 100,000 crowns in aid were absolutely necessary if the security of the regime was to be preserved.[132]

How far Renard was acting as an accomplice of the council in this matter is uncertain, but his importunity certainly embarrassed the emperor. The latter's instructions to Egmont, who was to visit

England as Philip's proxy for the betrothal ceremony, included a directive to evade any renewal of the request for a loan, and to insist that the queen must concentrate on collecting her own revenue.[133] On 5 March, Granvelle wrote confidentially to Renard '. . . to tell you the truth an attempt was being made at Antwerp to raise a loan of 100,000 crowns for the Queen of England . . .', but the bankers were not satisfied with the emperor's terms, and the money had not been obtained.[134] Charles was probably right in thinking that Mary's credit on the Bourse was at least as good as his own. On 15 March the queen sent for Renard and begged him to convey a personal plea to the emperor; she really was doing her best to raise money, but she desperately needed the 100,000 crowns. 'In short', the ambassador concluded, 'she was greatly perplexed . . . and wished his Highness [Philip] were already here to take matters in hand . . .'[135] Even this well-flighted arrow missed its mark, however, and the emperor replied on 2 April that attempts were being made, but without any guarantee of success. Granvelle was slightly franker. The following day he wrote to inform Renard that there was no real likelihood of the sum being raised.[136] After that the attempt seems to have been abandoned and English hopes switched, as we have already seen, to the Genoese bankers. Even allowing for the fact that the emperor's finances were in their usual parlous state, it is hard to believe that he could not have responded to this plea had he really wished to do so. On the other hand, in the light of Gresham's success it is difficult to see why Mary should have striven so hard to extract an additional loan from Antwerp via her cousin, unless it were to reassure herself of his fatherly concern.

As we have already seen, one of the main purposes of such extensive borrowing was to obtain a supply of specie. England had virtually no natural source of precious metals, and much of the cash which Gresham obtained went to supply the mint. For this reason the passports which were periodically requested for the export of coin sometimes specified the bullion weight rather than the value.[137] On occasion Gresham actually had coin melted down into bullion before shipping it,[138] but for the most part it was sent in the form of whatever coin could be most readily obtained. On 31 December 1553 he wrote that he was sending over a consignment of 8211 'philippines' which had been amongst the money received from Lazarus Tucher 'which are as good to be melted as the French or Imperial crowns . . .'[139] The money shipped from Spain late in 1554 was sent in the form of silver rials. Since there were 11 rials to the ducat, the sheer bulk of this consignment was great – the first instalment consisted of 50 chests with 22,000 rials in each – and this added considerably both to the risk and cost of transportation.[140]

The problem of bullion supply was aggravated by the bad state of the English currency. As we have already seen, large quantities of base silver coin had been minted between 1546 and 1551, which had then been arbitrarily 'cried down'. The efforts to reform the coinage which had begun in October 1551 resulted in good-quality coin being minted, and promptly exported as every foreign creditor sought payment in the improved currency. This situation continued when Mary decided in August 1553 to go on minting silver at 11 oz. fine,[141] so that as the good coin was minted from imported bullion, it was very largely re-exported in settlement of foreign debts, while the base coin continued to circulate within England. Renard was correct when he observed in November 1553 that 'quantities of gold and silver are being fetched out of Flanders by ships arriving from your Majesty's ports', but his belief that this was due to the profitability of the exchange was almost certainly mistaken.[142] Towards the end of 1553 the rumour got about in Antwerp that the English government was about to 'cry down' the debased currency yet further, in the hope of making it more attractive to foreign creditors. On 1 January, Gresham wrote in considerable anxiety, saying that such reports were unsettling the exchange, which had already dropped from 22*s*. 4*d*. to 21*s*. 8*d*. as a direct result. If the proposal were really implemented, he predicted that the £ would drop to 20*s*. Flemish, '. . . in which case it were better for the Queen and realm to have given £100,000 besides the great loss she shall thereby receive' and all his plans would be 'clean frustrated'.[143] In the event the debased coin continued to circulate at the former rates, and forgery continued to be a major problem, both at home and abroad. Confidence was as important to the exchanges as to a modern stock market, and by the end of 1554 Mary's government had taken all the steps which it could, short of a full recoinage, to ensure that confidence. Edward's debts had been paid, sound money had been minted, and the exchange values of the main French and Imperial coins fixed by proclamation.[144] Domestic prices also seem to have been stabilized to some extent by the council's decision to continue minting fine coin – although it is hard to believe Renard's assertion that some prices dropped by as much as a third when the decision was announced.[145]

On the whole Mary's advisers showed good sense both in policy and administration during the first year of the reign, but reform and retrenchment existed more in intention than in execution. A major reform of the exchequer was indeed carried through, but to no very great financial advantage. Economies were made in annuities and in military expenditure, and large sums gained by forfeiture, but these advantages were largely offset by new rewards, restorations, and the forgiveness of debts. At the same time there was no adequate compensation for the remission of the subsidy, and no direct financial advantage could be extracted from the Imperial alliance. Moreover, the council's instructions to Gresham to 'take up' almost £150,000 in the space of about three months, resulted in his unsatisfactory Spanish venture, which further strained relations between the two peoples, and left the crown's foreign debt in as bad a condition as it had ever been at the worst period of her brother's reign.

Notes

1 See above, 86-7.
2 PRO SP11/1/14.
3 Estimates of the crown's indebtedness at that date vary from £219,686 to over £241,000. The former figure comes from a contemporary calculation made by Cecil, the latter was taken by Strype from an unknown source. W. C. Richardson, *The Report of the Royal Commission of 1552* (1974), xxv, n. 52.
4 This was the figure calculated by the 1552 commissioners as the surplus 'in possession'. It was probably very optimistic. ibid., 157.
5 *Cal. Span.*, XI, 193.
6 *Cal. Span.*, XI, 373.
7 *Cal. Span.*, XI, 124; 29 July 1553. Thomas Mildmay's account, rendered 16 March 1555. PRO E351/21.
8 PRO E405/499. Rough book of receipt, 1 Mary.
9 PRO SP11/1/3.
10 '. . . that her highness letters may be written to the merchauntes to observe the promises made with the kings highness that ded is, and to promise repayment of the same within iii months . . .' PRO SP11/1/4.
11 PRO SP11/1/5. In some cases, particularly in the earlier loans, items of merchandise had been included in the loans themselves.
12 F. C. Dietz, *English Government Finance, 1485–1558* (1921), 202. Dietz dealt with Mary's finances in one short chapter, and his work has long been recognized as incomplete.
13 G. R. Elton, 'Mid-Tudor Finance' (a review of Richardson), *HJ*, 20 (1977), 737-40.
14 PRO SP11/1/5.
15 BL Cotton MS Titus B IV f. 133. The sum quoted is £2821 19s. 8d.
16 *APC*, IV, 319, 335.
17 ibid., 369.
18 *Cal. Pat.*, I, 75, 78.
19 *APC*, IV, 397.
20 *Cal. Pat.*, I, 265.
21 ibid., 301. This had been the last of a number of such Edwardian commissions. When, on 28 June 1554, Peckham presented his accounts for the period 1 April 1552 to 13 May 1554, he accounted for £337,952 of which £144,878 had been received in 6 and 7 Edward VI for the sale of lands. PRO E351/2080.
22 *Cal. Span.*, XII, 89.

The Reign of Mary Tudor

23 PRO SP11/4/6. 'An estimate made for the payment of debts, by My Lord Chancellor'. n.d., but probably April 1554.
24 *Cal. Pat.*, I, 265.
25 Renard to the emperor, 14 February 1554. *Cal. Span.*, XII, 99.
26 Sir William Sharrington, the vice-treasurer of the Bristol mint, was deeply involved with Sir Thomas Seymour, and his extensive speculation was uncovered by Seymour's fall. Jordan, *Edward VI: The Young King*, 382-5.
27 Hughes and Larkin, *Tudor Royal Proclamations*, II, 10. 1 September 1553.
28 *Cal. Span.*, XI, 214.
29 BL Lansdowne MS 4 f. 9. 'A brief note of all and singular subsidies as well of the clergy as of the laity . . . granted to the late Queen Mary'.
30 PRO SP11/1/2. 'Arrears . . . due at or before Christmas last', 20 July 1553.
31 *Cal. Pat.*, I, 112, 8 May 1554.
32 ibid.
33 ibid., 119. 3 March 1554.
34 Northumberland's lands were valued at £4300 *p.a.*, those of Northampton at £2800, Andrew Dudley at £555, Gates at £796, and Palmer at £309. Beer, *Northumberland*, 191.
35 The council also showed a marked interest in improving the administration of the crown lands. A memorandum on this subject was drawn up at the beginning of the reign (PRO SP11/1/22). On 18 January 1554 the council also drew up an eight-point plan, which included a prohibition of grants and exchanges and a ban on all leases over 20 years. *APC*, IV, 387.
36 Richardson, *History of the Court of Augmentations*, 262.
37 *Cal. Pat.*, I, 265. Richardson, *Augmentations*, 266-8.
38 *APC*, V, 279.
39 See below, 199, relating to Sir Thomas Gresham. The delinquency of Thomas Egerton at the mint concerned the minting of the Spanish silver, and was not uncovered until 1555.
40 *APC*, IV, 360, 362, etc.
41 *Cal. Pat.*, III, 116.
42 BL Lansdowne MS 4 f. 19.
43 PRO E351/3027, 3028, 3029.
44 BL Add. MS 4767 f. 125.
45 BL Add. MS 30198; PRO E405/499.
46 BL Add. MS 30198; PRO E405/499, 510; BL Cotton MS Titus B IV f. 133. A different set of figures was quoted by Joseph Stevenson in Appendix I to the *Calendar of State Papers, Foreign*, Elizabeth, vol. II. Stevenson shows a deficit of £2330 2s. 8d. on 1 Mary, a surplus of £1701 4s. 9d. on 2 Mary, and a deficit of £2701 9s. 4d. on 4 Mary. No source is given for these figures. I am indebted to Mr Christopher Coleman for this reference.
47 The augmentations office accounts, as these were rendered after 1554, do not appear to have included the 'foreign accounts' which had been rendered through the court. See also below, 303 and n.
48 BL Add. MS 30198; Dietz, op. cit., 206 and n.; BL Cotton MS Titus B IV f. 133.
49 In addition to the foreign accounts, the 'clear' figures for the court of augmentations had also included money spent by warrant (dormant and

otherwise) on the household, the garrisons of the borders, the admiralty, and other causes. This makes an exact equivalent hard to calculate.

50 PRO SP11/14/16.
51 PRO SP11/4/6.
52 At about the time this summary was drawn up, the foreign debt was more than doubled by Gresham's Spanish negotiation. See below, 199-201.
53 In fact no subsidy was demanded until the third parliament in November 1555.
54 A payment of £2000 is recorded 'To Matthew Colthurst, treasurer of the wars against the rebels in the county of Kent'. PRO E405/484. Peckham's account also records £2245 2s. 0d. as a payment 'parcel of the charges against the rebels of Kent', but whether these sums overlap, or should be added together, is not clear. PRO E351/2080.
55 Richardson, *Augmentations*, 258.
56 £160,671 out of £271,912. BL Add. MS 30198.
57 7 Edward VI, c. 2.
58 *Cal. Pat.*, I, 300.
59 *Cal. Pat.*, I, 73; Richardson, *Augmentations*, 250. Richardson considers that Sackville's last-minute reinstatement was to enable him to make a formal hand-over.
60 *Cal. Pat.*, I, 72; Richardson, *Augmentations*, 249. The mint had functioned as a treasury before, but not to this exclusive extent.
61 PRO E405/484.
62 PRO E405/511.
63 PRO E405/241.
64 PRO C54/500; Richardson, *Augmentations*, 251-2. BL Cotton MS Titus B IV f. 62.
65 1 Mary, st. 2 c. 10; *Statutes of the Realm*, IV, 208-9.
66 PRO C54/500 ms. 3-6.
67 Richardson, *Augmentations*, 444-5.
68 Of the field officers, only the ten district auditors were discontinued and pensioned. Richardson, *Augmentations*, 256-7; BL Cotton MS Titus B IV f. 140.
69 Richardson, *Augmentations*, 466 and n.
70 The hanaper of chancery, great wardrobe, Calais staple, chamber, and duchy of Cornwall are listed separately, along with the exchequer (ancient revenues), augmentations, wards and liveries, and duchy of Lancaster in a statement of the crown revenues for 1556-57. BL Cotton MS Titus B IV f. 133.
71 Richardson, *Augmentations*, 252, 255.
72 ibid., 256-7.
73 Richardson, *Royal Commission*, 216; BL Add. MS 30198.
74 ibid.
75 BL Cotton MS Titus B IV f. 135.
76 N. S. B. Gras, 'Tudor Books of Rates', *Quarterly Journal of Economics*, xxvi (1912), 766-75.
77 Scheyfve to the emperor, 24 June 1553, *Cal. Span.*, XI, 66; *Cal. For.*, Mary, 30.
78 Renard to the emperor, 18 September 1554; *Cal. Span.*, XII, 49.
79 See below, 196-7. For a brief survey of the background to this situation, see W. K. Jordan, *The Threshold of Power* (1970), 482-8.
80 ibid., 485 and n. 2.

The Reign of Mary Tudor

81 *APC*, III, 475-6.
82 ibid., 487-9; PRO SP10/14/47.
83 *Cal. Span.*, XI, 315.
84 ibid., note; PRO SP11/4/36.
85 Petre was a member of the merchant adventurers. *Cal. Pat.*, II, 55-9.
86 *Cal. Span.*, XI, 315.
87 Renard to the emperor, 8 November 1553; *Cal. Span.*, XI, 347.
88 PRO SP11/4/36. 'A brief declaration of the discomoditie and hynd-rance [to] this realme [and] the subvertion of the laudable trade and traphique of English Merchauntes . . . by the usurped trade and trafick which the Easterlinges manye yeres have used . . .' 'Dutch' in this context was used to mean Netherlanders in general.
89 *APC*, V, 252-7. BL Lansdowne MS 170. See below, 238-9.
90 Renard to the emperor, 8 March 1554; *Cal. Span.*, XII, 138.
91 *TTC*, 191.
92 PRO SP11/13/49; 'A declaration shewing what losse the Q. Marie hathe susteyned by lack of diligent circumspection of the weight of wolles transported oute of this realme'.
93 BL Cotton MS Titus B IV f. 133; BL Lansdowne MS IV f. 182.
94 The loan from Lazarus Tucher, for example, was guaranteed in this way. PRO SP69/2/85, 89. The normal practice also required the issuing of 'counter bonds' by the crown to the city. GLRO, Repertories of the court of aldermen.
95 PRO SP69/3/130.
96 PRO SP69/2/81. The more normal method was to repay such loans in London. Gresham accounted for over £50,000-worth of these in 1557. PRO E351/18.
97 The best general survey of these developments is G. D. Ramsay, *English Overseas Trade in the Centuries of Emergence* (1957). A useful brief summary is R. Davis, *English Overseas Trade 1500–1700* (1973). For a more specific study of the situation of London, see Ramsay, *The City of London in International Politics at the Accession of Elizabeth Tudor* (1975).
98 H. Buckley, 'Sir Thomas Gresham and the Foreign Exchanges', *Economic Journal* 34 (1924), 595-6. Jordan, *Threshold of Power*, 465. J. D. Gould, *The Great Debasement: currency and the economy in mid-Tudor England* (1970), 89.
99 PRO SP69/2/73.
100 ibid., 69, 77, 83. At this point the florin stood officially at 3s. 4d. sterling, and the ducat at 6s. 8d.
101 PRO SP69/2/83, 88, 89, 104.
102 ibid., 90, 98.
103 PRO SP69/6/320.
104 PRO SP69/2/103.
105 ibid., 111.
106 ibid., 112.
107 PRO SP69/3/130.
108 ibid., 146.
109 ibid., 135.
110 The exact rate of interest is not mentioned. A contemporary observer in Antwerp reported that 10 *gros* a ducat was being mentioned, which would have been about 16 per cent, at a time when 20 per cent was not uncommon in Spain. Gresham hopefully calculated that by converting

the debt into cloth credits, the queen would be able to make a profit at about the same rate. PRO SP69/3/135; Francisco de Aresti to Juan Vásquez de Molina, 29 January 1554. *Cal. Span.*, XII, 57.

111 Aresti wrote of the bargain as already concluded at the end of January, while Paget was still speaking as though the outcome was uncertain at the beginning of April. This may reflect no more than the time taken to translate an undertaking into a binding obligation. *Cal. Span.*, XII, 57, 205.

112 ibid., 232.

113 ibid., 269.

114 ibid.

115 Mary to the princess of Portugal, 12 June 1554. *Cal. Span.*, XII, 274. Gresham's instructions are printed in R. H. Tawney and E. Power, *Tudor Economic Documents* (1924), II, 144-6.

116 Philip's letter speaks of 'an agreement arrived at by her Majesty with certain merchants . . .', but makes no mention of the emperor's decision. *Cal. Span.*, XII, 304.

117 *Cal. Span.*, XIII, 15. Royall Tyler glossed this to mean the *cortes*; but the *cortes* were not in session at the time.

118 ibid., 38.

119 PRO SP69/5/254.

120 *Cal. Span.*, XIII, 42.

121 ibid., 47.

122 PRO SP69/4/220. Some of the details of this transaction remain obscure, particularly the calculation of interest. As we have seen, about 16 per cent was mentioned by one observer. On the other hand, Gresham contracted to repay in Antwerp at 6s. 5d. Flemish the ducat at a time when the official exchange rate was about 6s. 11d. Flemish the ducat. Subsequently Gresham rendered a sterling account for the disbursement of the whole sum of £89,598 8s. 9d. sterling, or £97,878 10s. Flemish; both sums calculated at 6s. 5d. Flemish and 5s. 11½d. sterling to the ducat. It may therefore have been that the difference between these valuations and the official ones (6s. 11d. and 6s. 8d.) represented the interest, which would have been low at 10½ per cent. On the other hand, it may have been that Gresham, having borrowed silver, had secretly undertaken to repay in gold.

123 PRO SP69/5/297.

124 PRO E351/18. Gresham's account rendered before the queen's commissioners, August 1557.

125 *Tudor Economic Documents*, II, 144-6. There were two bonds to Gaspar Schetz, one for 35,000 at Villálon, and one for 65,000 in October.

126 PRO SP69/6/332.

127 PRO SP59/6/219. The first bond to Schetz is omitted from this account.

128 PRO SP69/5/282.

129 *Cal. Span.*, XIII, 61.

130 ibid., XIII, 70.

131 ibid., 77.

132 ibid., 106.

133 ibid., 114.

134 ibid., 134.

135 ibid., 155.

136 ibid., 193-5.

137 PRO SP69/3/132.
138 ibid.
139 PRO SP69/2/116.
140 PRO SP69/5/297. The carriage and porterage costs came to more than £3000. PRO E351/18.
141 *APC*, IV, 340.
142 *Cal. Span.*, XI, 366. C. E. Challis, *The Tudor Coinage* (1978).
143 PRO SP69/2/123.
144 *APC*, IV, 410; Hughes and Larkin, II, 39. Gresham later claimed that these valuations had been forced through by the bishop of Winchester against his advice, but that was in a letter of self-justification to Elizabeth. *Tudor Economic Documents*, II, 146-9.
145 *Cal. Span.*, XI, 214.

7 Philip as King of England, 1554–1557

Philip's safe arrival in England was in itself a source of great satisfaction to the Imperialists. French intrigues and English hostility alike had failed to thwart this great project for the revival of Habsburg fortunes and morale. However, the fruits of victory were still to be gathered, and to judge from the number of reports which were made, many anxious eyes were on Philip in the last days of July. One of the main causes of his failure in the Low Countries six years earlier had been his unwillingness to appear in public;

> Rarissime volte va fuora in Campagna, ha piacere di starsi in Camera, co suoi favoriti a ragionare di cose private; et se tall'hora l'Imperatore lo manda in visita, si scusa per godere la solità quiete

as the Venetian Marino Cavallo had reported.[1] It was not a genial image. In England he did very much better, and his affability was favourably commented upon by all. His friends and servants such as Ruy Gómez were particularly lavish in their praise; which was partly courtly tact, and partly a measure of their relief. The English nobility were pleased, and gratified by the emperor's tactful gesture in conferring the titular sovereignty of Naples upon his son before the marriage was celebrated. Most important, his dealings with Mary herself were exemplary:

> Entretiene muy bien a la Reina y save muy bien pasar lo que no es bueno en ella para la sensualidad de la carne, y tiénela tan contenta que cierto estando el otro día ellos dos a solas, casi le decia ella amores, y él respondía por los consonantes. . . .[2]

This was an art in which the king had some experience, and his bride was not disposed to be critical. A woman starved of affection and personal attentions since her early childhood, she responded to Philip's skilful and discreet advances with a wholeheartedness which must have been both gratifying and embarrassing. 'I daily discover

211

in the king my husband and your son', she wrote to Charles a few days later, 'so many virtues and perfections that I constantly pray God to grant me grace to please him and behave in all things as befits one who is so deeply embounden to him. . . .'³ Mary had been 'half in love' with Philip before she ever saw him, but it was nevertheless of great importance that he was able to secure this kind of personal ascendancy over her from the beginning of their marriage. She may not have been very pleasing 'para la sensualidad de la carne', but there were other kinds of gratification to be obtained from a wife who was a ruling queen, if she could be made sufficiently suggestible.

During his first few weeks in England Philip did what he had conspicuously failed to do in the Netherlands, and was never seriously to attempt again. He set out to win friends and to make a good impression. He chatted (as best he could) with the English lords and with the ladies of the privy chamber; he drank beer, and even learned a few words of English. Above all, he distributed pensions and gifts with a generous hand; more than 15,000 ducats to the privy councillors who had attended the marriage, and as much again to other courtiers and gentlemen.⁴ Apart from his total conquest of the queen, the benefits which he reaped from these efforts were modest. The foolish misunderstanding over his two households, which took a long time to resolve, undid much of the goodwill which Philip was striving so hard to create. Quite apart from the expense which, as Ruy Gómez complained, fell entirely upon the king, the amalgamation which was at first decided upon caused bitter complaints on both sides. Renard, whose optimism about the marriage had evaporated in a few days, commented at the beginning of September that '. . . very few Englishmen are to be seen in his Highness's apartments'.⁵ Eraso, who no doubt drew his information from Ruy Gómez, informed the emperor that this was because the Englishmen who were appointed to serve had absented themselves, but Lord Fitzwalter, who spoke Spanish, complained that he had so little access to the king and his entourage that he was getting out of practice with the language.⁶ On the other hand, the Spaniards, many of whom had gone to great personal expense and inconvenience to follow their prince to England, felt slighted and superfluous.

> Doña María de Mendoza tuvo razón [one of them grumbled] de decir que no habiamos de servir ya más; todos andaramos bien vagamundos y sun hacer falta; podriamos ir á servir á S.M. en esta guerra.⁷

The war provided an excellent excuse to escape from what was rapidly becoming an unpleasant and frustrating situation. Quite apart from the misunderstandings at court, the English people were perfectly explicit in their hostility to Philip's Spanish servants whenever they got the chance. When the king and queen moved to Richmond early in August, some of them ventured into London, where they were jeered and insulted. By 17 August, according to one anonymous account, over eighty Spanish noblemen and gentlemen had sought and obtained leave to withdraw; the marquis of Pescara and his Italian followers had also gone, and so had the Flemings.[8] Only the duke of Alva, the counts of Feria and Olivares, and a handful of household servants remained. 'We are all desiring to be off', the correspondent concluded, 'with such longing that we think of Flanders as a paradise'. Even allowing for the jaundiced exaggerations of this letter, it is clear that mutual hostility appeared almost at once, and that the size of Philip's retinue was a major contributory factor.

In fact the military situation in the Netherlands had improved, and Charles had recovered from the momentary panic which had seized him after the fall of Marienbourg. By 2 August, Henri was retreating towards St Quentin, and the emperor decided that it would not do his son's reputation any good to arrive at the tail end of a campaign which was just about to fizzle out. 'You had better stay where you are', he wrote to Philip, 'and be with the Queen my daughter, busying yourself with the affairs of England, settling the government there, and making yourself familiar with the people. . . .'[9] This respite was timely, because the treasury was exhausted, and Charles can hardly have regarded an influx of Spanish and Italian noblemen with much enthusiasm, but it was preferable to leaving them kicking their heels and stirring up trouble in England. By the middle of October, Renard was able to report that the king had resolved the problems of his household, sharing the offices between English and Spaniards equally.[10] There were still rumours of discontent after this, but no major quarrels. Outside the court, however, hostility between the two nations raged unabated. The English were churlish and provocative, overcharging their unwanted visitors for every service they required, and robbing or beating up individuals who were rash enough to venture out alone or unprotected. 'At this time', wrote one observer shortly after the wedding, 'there were so many Spaniards in London that a man should have met in the street for one Englishman above four Spaniards, to the great discomfort of the English nation. . . .'[11] At one moment Philip was accused of bringing in an army to seize the crown, at another of planning to take all he could get and leave the realm to its own devices. In their own way the

H   213

English were as sensitive of their honour and reputation as were the Spaniards.

> Se dice publicamente [commented one of the latter] que no dexar salir á S.A. deste Reino sy ellos no son contentos, porque este reino dicen ser grande para un Rey, que le basta éste sin tener otro.[12]

The campaign of vilification which had been going on since the autumn of 1553 had created an atmosphere of suspicion in which even the most exemplary behaviour would have been misrepresented. And the behaviour of the Spaniards was not exemplary, in spite of Philip's efforts and the emperor's copious advice. Part of the trouble was caused by the fact that the Spanish courtiers had not only brought their own servants, but an indeterminate number of hangers-on, 'artisans and vagabonds', who were presumably on the look-out for what they could pick up.[13] There was also a rooted conviction in Spain that the English were all heretics and savages, a preconception which seems to have informed many of the earliest comments made by Philip's followers.

> Creo y tengo para mí [wrote one nobleman to a solicitous friend at home] que si no fuese por las muchas processiones é contínuas oraciones que (según de allá nos escriben) se hacen in España, ¡ Nuestro Señor nos guarde! creo que seriamos ya todos muertos, porque estos ingleses, como gente bárbara é muy herética, no tienen cuenta en sus ánimas é consciencias, ni temen á dios y á sus sanctos.[14]

So alarming was the news from England that on 13 September Juan Vásquez de Molina wrote anxiously to Philip from Valladolid, suggesting that a fleet might be despatched to rescue him on the pretext of reinforcing the army in the Netherlands.

No less responsible an official than Don Fernando Enríquez, the admiral of Castile, had caused this panic; describing to the regent the indignities suffered by his countrymen, representing the confusion over the households as a refusal on the part of the English to allow the Spaniards to serve their king, and broadly hinting that Philip would grasp at any pretext to withdraw.[15] Enríquez, like other Spaniards, seems to have been horrified by the lack of deference shown to the king. They commented sourly that even at the wedding the queen's throne had been higher and more ornate. 'Neither the king nor the queen have any authority over these lawless barbarians', wrote one; and de Molina suggested that Philip should at least withdraw until he could persuade the English to allow him to live in the country '. . . as befits their King and sovereign Lord'.[16] Some of these grievances stemmed directly from the nature of the marriage treaty, and had been brought from Spain ready-made; others sprang from the open hostility of the English, which both alarmed the Spaniards and offended their *amour propre*. Philip's attempts to calm the situation were themselves misrepresented; '. . . his Majesty has commanded', wrote one courtier resentfully, 'that while we are here no one shall say a word, but put up in silence with all the provocations of the English; so they ill treat us without fear'. The joint commission which had been set up before Philip's arrival to deal with the anticipated disputes between the nationalities, seems to have worked well enough as a purely judicial machinery, but it entirely failed to defuse the mutual hostility. As early as 15 August the privy council was calling upon the lord steward to investigate a disturbance, and at the same time the Spaniards were complaining bitterly to the *alcalde*,[17] with what result is not recorded. This situation did not change during the remainder of Philip's sojourn in England. In September 1554 there was a fracas near the court, in which several lives were lost; in October rumours of rebellion in London caused alarm at Richmond, and rumours of the king's intention to seize the Tower caused panic in the city.[18] Both these latter reports were thought to have been spread by deliberate malice. According to Michieli, who had no particular reason to distort his picture, there were at least two serious incidents in the summer of 1555. One, towards the end of May, involved 'upwards of 500' men, and resulted in five or six deaths. The other occurred on Corpus Christi day, 13 June, when a mob attacked the church in which a number of Spaniards were worshipping.[19] The number of casualties on that occasion is not mentioned. These were certainly not the only acts of violence, although they may have been the most dramatic. According to Michieli '. . . the English almost always give the provocation' and Philip used exemplary severity on any Spaniard who got involved in an affray, whether it was his fault or not. However, it seems clear that the foreigners were not always innocent victims. On 14 September 1554 one Griffin Middleton was set upon near St Clement Danes by Alonso Martine and Luis Medina, and subsequently died of the injury received. Martine and Medina were convicted of murder, and the former was probably hanged.[20] Henry Machyn recorded three such executions between September 1554 and January 1555, as well as the punishments of various Englishmen for robbing Spaniards.[21] At least one Spaniard died at the hands of his own countrymen, and on 10 August 1554 Peter López

Sapato and his wife were assaulted and robbed by a gang led by one Gonsales Salvedra. This latter offence was committed on the highway near Moorfields, Salvedra presumably hoping that the incident would be taken for yet another example of the lawless violence of the English.[22] As Ruy Gómez commented sardonically soon after his arrival,

> There are some great thieves among them [the English], and they rob in broad daylight, having the advantage over us Spaniards, in that we steal by stealth, and they by force. . . .

Gómez was a good deal more realistic in his assessment of the situation than many of his countrymen, perhaps because of the nature of his position, and never gave way to the bitter tirades which characterized the letters of some of the Spanish courtiers. His qualified optimism was also shared by Giovanni di Stroppiana, a special envoy from the duke of Savoy who wrote a number of chatty letters from England in the autumn of 1554. As he admitted, being an Italian he did not have to bear the brunt of English dislike, but the stories of hatred and violence being circulated by those Spaniards who had withdrawn to the Low Countries were grossly exaggerated.[23] The English were certainly bold robbers and had no great love for Spaniards, but they were very favourably impressed by Philip, particularly by his tender regard for the queen. The king's English and Spanish servants were making friends, he reported in October, and relations were gradually improving, greatly helped by well-authenticated reports that Mary was pregnant. At the opening of parliament in November there were many demonstrations of loyal affection.[24] The opposite point of view was represented, as might be expected, by Antoine de Noailles, who gleefully relayed every report of animosity to the French court. At the beginning of September 1554 he picked up a plot to slaughter all the Spaniards in London and at Hampton Court in a concerted nocturnal massacre. If such a desperate venture had actually been discussed by English malcontents, it never went beyond words, and since it was a part of Noailles's task to sow suspicion and mutual fear in this fertile soil, he may well have been responsible for the alarming rumours which, as we have already seen, were circulating soon after.[25] There was a half-hearted conspiracy in November 1554, when Philip and his nobles gave a demonstration of 'the play . . . called the cane' in Whitehall. Eighteen months later, when they were being interrogated about another plot, a group of minor courtiers confessed that they had plotted to shoot the participants, but had lost their nerve at the last moment. Since they were indulging in an orgy of confession and mutual recrimination when these statements were made, it is difficult to know how seriously to take them. Nobody, not even Noailles, got wind of their intention at the time.[26]

Renard was an early victim of the situation which he had done so much to create. His confidential relationship with Mary had come to an end with Philip's arrival, and he rapidly became a convenient scapegoat for everything that went wrong. Already vilified by the Spaniards for landing them in such a difficult and dishonourable situation, he was immediately blamed for the confusion over the households,[27] and for the fact that the English gentlemen appointed did not measure up to Philip's exacting religious standards. Sir Anthony Browne, who was a good catholic if little else, was dismissed as the king's master of the horse in early September, and once again Renard was blamed for his shortcomings.[28] Lord Paget made haste to ingratiate himself with Philip, and it was soon believed in Brussels that the ambassador had been guilty of the grossest ingratitude, and even that he had engineered Paget's temporary fall from favour.[29] Some of these charges may have had substance, but basically Renard was the victim of the resentment felt by Philip and his servants over the terms of the treaty. Since the emperor was above criticism in that respect, their indignation was vented on Granvelle, and on Renard as his agent. Philip almost literally froze his father's servant out of public affairs, conducting his business with Brussels through Ruy Gómez and Eraso. Charles, however, refused to take these broad hints, and did not respond to Renard's pleas for recall. He was ordered to remain at his post, ostensibly to give Philip the benefit of his unrivalled knowledge of English affairs, but perhaps more realistically to give the emperor a perspective upon his son's progress which the king's own servants could not have been expected to provide. Mary at least was not unmindful of the services which Renard had rendered her. On 23 September she presented him with over 1200 oz. of plate as a token of her gratitude.[30]

On one matter, however, Ruy Gómez, Renard, and Stroppiana were in complete agreement: the calming and beneficial effects of the reports of Mary's pregnancy which were circulating by the end of September. Even the most disgruntled Spaniard was prepared to admit that, if the queen had a child, their own and their prince's sacrifice might have been worthwhile. English attitudes are harder to understand. If the Spaniards were so much detested, why should the advent of an heir who would be three-quarters Spanish be a matter for rejoicing? Part of the answer can be found in simple affection for the queen:

> Wee all (as one) do love her Grace
> That is our Queene, this Marigolde

as one popular ballad expressed it.[31] Her marriage, so bitterly denounced in some quarters, had also found a welcome in the doggerel verses of such writers as John Heywood:

> This meete met matche, at first meeting
> In theyr aproche togither neere
> Lowlie, lovelie, lyveli greetinge
> In eche to other dyd appeare. . . .[32]

The news of her supposed pregnancy was similarly greeted:

> Nowe singe, nowe springe, oure care is exil'd
> Oure vertuous Quene is quickened with child.

Another reason for satisfaction in England was that the birth of an undoubted heir would remove the threat of civil strife in the event of Mary's own death, and place another life in the way of any attempt by Philip to obtain the succession for himself. If the terms of the marriage treaty were adhered to, the child would be brought up and educated in England, and would thus not appear to be a foreigner, whatever its blood. The small amount of popular affection which Philip ever won in England was entirely in the queen's account: 'Oh, what a good husband he is. How honourably and lovingly he treats the Queen!' were typical of the remarks which the optimistic Stroppiana claimed to have overheard when the king appeared at the opening of parliament.[33] Whether the birth of such a child would ever have reconciled the nationalities must remain open to doubt. After a lull during the winter (which usually had the effect of cooling hot blood), incidents began again, as we have seen, long before the reality of Mary's condition was seriously called in question. There had been some on both sides who had been sceptical of the queen's ability to conceive, but the visible evidence of her distended body appeared to be conclusive. In January 1555 the doge and senate offered their official congratulations, and it was not until May that the physicians began to take refuge in explanations. As early as March some protestants in London were spreading rumours of a substitution plot; '. . . The Queen's Grace is not with child, and another lady shall be with child, and that lady's child, when she is brought in bed shall be named the Queen's child . . .'[34] Such views were probably not widespread, but by no means all Englishmen rejoiced at the prospect of a royal birth, even a genuine one. When the people of Hereford were dutifully and mistakenly celebrating the arrival of a prince on

3 May, a certain John Gillam was alleged to have declared

> Now that there is a prince born, his father will bring into this realm his own nation, and put out the English nation . . .[35]

Although Gillam and his kind cannot have known it, his words were being given substance in Brussels at the same time by those members of the emperor's council who were urging their master to prepare an army in case the queen's miscarriage should place Philip and his interests in jeopardy.[36] Charles had no desire to heed such advice even if he could have spared the resources, but the apprehensions on both sides emphasize the extreme importance of what was at stake.

In January 1555 parliament had extended the protection of the treason laws to Philip, and had conferred upon him the guardianship of the realm during the minority of his expected child should the queen die.[37] The debates on this issue had not gone altogether smoothly, if Renard is to be believed, because the persistent suspicion that any increase in Philip's power would lead directly to war with France could not be silenced. Nor, in the midst of all this concern over Mary's child, did Elizabeth's friends forget that she remained the heir until such a child was actually born. Gardiner was once again forced to abandon a scheme to get her excluded. Since the provision for regency powers was accompanied by a reaffirmation of the marriage treaty, the king gained little in power and rather lost in prestige from this demonstration of continuing mistrust. As May passed into June, and the physicians continued to argue lamely that they had mistaken their calculations, rumours of every kind were circulating. The queen was bewitched, sick, or already dead. According to Foxe a certain Isabel Malt, who was safely delivered of a son on 11 June, was approached by Lord North to part with him in secret.[38] Although many of them had begun by regarding the prospect of issue as a remote contingency, by the early summer of 1555 the Imperialists were relying upon the birth of an heir to give Philip's title of king some reality. Michieli was echoing their thoughts when he wrote that after the birth 'King Philip will not live in this realm so much like an alien as he does . . .', but would be able to rule and command in a manner befitting a sovereign.[39] That opportunity was never to come. For months Mary had been the victim of sickness and her own desires, and by July this fact was being tacitly acknowledged. Without any official statement the trappings of confinement were gradually removed, and the queen began to transact business again. As soon as it became clear that his hope had been illusory, Philip began to prepare quietly to join his father in the Netherlands. He left at the end of August, with every outward sign of affection and solicitude for his queen. Many of his household remained behind, and the English did not know quite what to think or hope for. An alarmed note by one Spaniard who remained declared that it was common talk in England that the king would never return, although whether this was said in joy or in anger is not clear. The reporter was more interested in the accompanying threats of 'to kill all Spaniards', and his animadversions on the national characteristics of the English indicate that a year of close association had brought neither tolerance nor understanding.[40] The robberies, incidents, and recriminations continued. Apart from the king himself no Spaniard had found a bride in England during that year, perhaps the most eloquent testimony of all to the estrangement between the peoples.[41]

Nevertheless, Philip's first year as king of England had not been without its achievements. As soon as the marriage was concluded, reconciliation with Rome became the top priority, and his role in that negotiation was positive and crucial. Discussions held during August and September convinced Philip that it would be a mistake to allow Pole to enter England with the brief which he then possessed. Although Julius had become convinced that the English aristocracy would have to be satisfied over the matter of church lands, the instructions which he had issued to his legate gave the latter far too much discretion to enable the king to make the firm undertakings which would be required. He therefore turned a deaf ear to Pole's renewed pleas for admission, and launched instead a fresh diplomatic campaign in Rome to obtain a more satisfactory brief. On 12 October he wrote to Eraso, announcing his decision to make direct representations to the pope, and at the same time sent Renard to the Low Countries to reason with the legate.[42] The latter was a shrewd move, since the task was well suited to the ambassador's diplomatic talents, and did not require an emissary who was high in the king's confidence. By the end of October, Renard had succeeded in convincing Pole that the restoration of England to the church, and even Mary's survival as queen, depended upon the willingness of the legate to surrender his discretion entirely to the king. Haste was now imperative, since Philip had decided early in October to meet the parliament on 12 November, and that assembly could not be put off without great inconvenience.[43] Early in November word was received from Rome that the necessary powers would be granted, but there was no prospect of their arriving before parliament met. Philip consulted with his theologians and other advisers, both English and Spanish, and decided to go ahead on his own responsibility, '. . . feeling sure that the Holy Father would ratify and approve my course, and indeed be very glad that I had adopted it'.[44] Pole was consequently invited to return to England, and the negotiation proceeded to a successful conclusion. Although he did not depart substantially from the policy which his father advised, it was Philip and not Charles who was in command. The emperor was so sick by early October that he abandoned his plans to leave for Spain in January, a decision which relieved Philip of a difficult dilemma. His presence in Flanders at the time of his father's departure would have been imperative, and the effect of his leaving England in the middle of the reconciliation negotiations could only have been detrimental to their success. Mary's wishes were well known, and she seems to have played no direct part in the diplomatic proceedings, happily leaving the initiative in her husband's hands. When she wrote to the emperor on 7 December to inform him 'of the frank consent given by our subjects of every estate to return to the obedience of Holy Church and the catholic faith', she attributed this success 'largely . . . to the wise guidance of my said Lord . . .', which was no more than the truth.[45]

Whatever doubts might have been entertained by those who knew the English situation intimately, in the eyes of catholic Europe Philip had made a triumphant beginning as king of England. In December 1554 and January 1555 a spate of propaganda pamphlets celebrated his achievement. Many of these were published in Italy, and included *I successi d'Inghilterra dopo la morte di Eduardo Sesto* by Giulio Rosso, printed in Ferrara, and a set of five tracts beginning with *La partita del serenissimo Principe* which appeared at Rome.[46] Apart from the account of the voyage, this included a most interesting eyewitness description of the king and queen's entry into London on 18 August, complete with congratulatory verses by Nicholas Harpesfield, and a full account of the ceremony of reconciliation entitled *Il Felicissimo ritorno del regno d'Inghilterra alla cattolica unione*. Similar, but much briefer, tracts appeared in German and in Dutch, and *The Copie of a letter sent into Scotlande*, ostensibly by John Elder to the bishop of Caithness, dated 1 January 1555 and printed in London, belongs to the same genre.[47] All these works took great care to link the reconciliation with Philip's arrival, representing these events as two stages in the same process. The Spaniards also rejoiced, accepting the news as further proof of the Divine favour enjoyed by the prince they loved so well:

> Ya se recoge el ganado
> Inglés, que andaba perdido
> Por el pastor que allá es ído.

Recójase ya Albión
Y conozca el bien que tiene
Pues es tal, que le conviene
Para la fé y salvación.
Penitencia y communión
De nuevo ha constituido
Por el pastor que allá es ído.[48]

Congratulations and solemn thanksgivings were the order of the day. *Te Deum* was sung in Rome, and in Lisbon all the religious of the city went in procession to celebrate '. . . la bien aventurada nueva de la reduction del Regno de Ynglaterra al obediencia de la sancta madre yglesia . . .', as Luis Sarmiento reported in February, 'que ciertamente ha ayda una bien afortunada Jornada lo que han hecho sus magd. en servicio de nuestro señor . . .'[49] Philip's first venture as an independent sovereign had brought him honour and prestige, and one of the immediate objectives of the marriage had been achieved.

Within England, however, the king's cautious campaign for greater political freedom and authority made little progress. Having taken the initial precaution of assuring the English council that he did not intend to make any 'innovations' in the government, he set out to establish a working relationship with as many of the members as possible. In London it was being rumoured in August that Paget, Arundel, and other 'politique' lords were intriguing with the French, but in Brussels, Paget was regarded as a misused man to whom the king owed a considerable obligation. Perhaps in order to avoid renewed strife with Gardiner, Philip seems to have consulted him mainly about foreign affairs, and appointed him to lead the English delegation which was sent to escort Pole to England in November.[50] In the course of that trip he took the opportunity to re-establish his good standing at the Imperial court, and to present his own version of his relations with the chancellor. Nothing could overcome Mary's distrust, but the marked favour shown by Philip to Paget, Pembroke, and Arundel particularly was clearly intended to conciliate them, and was successful. During the autumn of 1554 Philip had both a Spanish and an English council, and consulted both over important matters such as the nature of Pole's instructions. The duke of Alva and the counts of Feria and Olivares were the principal Spanish noblemen to remain in England, along with Ruy Gómez and Don Pedro de Córdova, although they probably did not meet together with the English council because of the difficulties of communication.[51] The king's name was carefully included in all official documents, and some important commissions – notably those for the sale of church lands – were reissued in August, presumably for that reason.[52] Some Englishmen even presented petitions to the king alone, notably one John Fox 'late of Loughborough', on behalf of a group of copyholders who had forfeited their holdings for supporting the duke of Suffolk, and now sought relief.[53] Instructions sent out to the justices of the peace in March 1555 bore the signatures of both monarchs, and the indications are that Philip involved himself actively, but discreetly, in English internal affairs, working mainly through those councillors in whom he had confidence. However, the parliament which he had insisted upon calling so promptly was in some ways a disappointment. Responsive to his shrewd handling of the issue of church lands, it did nothing to improve the strength of his position. A surprising suggestion to accord him the succession in full sovereignty, possibly designed to test the wind, disappeared rapidly and without trace, and the matter of his coronation, greatly desired by the Spaniards, was never formally raised at all. The full protection of the treason laws, and the guardianship of his heir in the event of the queen's decease, were, as Renard pointed out, more in the nature of rights than concessions.[54] Moreover, on the day before parliament rose, 15 January, an address was presented to the king and queen, requesting confirmation that Philip would employ no foreigners in the government of the realm during the period of his protectorate.[55]

The matter of Philip's coronation was a continuous grievance. At first the fact that he had not been crowned was regarded as a slight, a reflection upon his honour akin to the fact that he was served off silver while the queen was served off gold – or so the jealous Spaniards reported. Renard pointed out to Mary that her own mother had been crowned as consort, and argued that it was incumbent upon her to crown her husband. However, the issue did not at once assume major political importance, being regarded as 'more a matter of satisfaction than of necessity'. The exact significance of such a step was, in any case, uncertain because of the lack of precedent. In November 1554 Renard declared that 'in England the coronation stands for a true and lawful confirmation of title, and means much more than in other realms',[56] but the marriage treaty made no mention of such a confirmation, and legally it would have made no difference to his position. As long as it appeared that Mary might bear a healthy child, the coronation was a secondary matter, although occasional murmurings about the Spaniards 'fetching away the crown' indicate that its symbolic significance was equally great for both sides. As early as January 1555 opponents of the coronation had succeeded in linking it with fears of involvement in the Franco-Habsburg war, and it seems to have been for that reason that Renard's attempts to get the matter discussed by parliament came to nothing.

The king was a shrewd politician, and dissembled his feelings of frustration and disappointment. He spoke flatteringly to the parliament of his confidence in its loyalty and prudence, and did his best to reconcile quarrels among the councillors. A further shadowy attempt to reduce the size of the council in the autumn of 1554 seems to have come to nothing because of the long-standing jealousies, but in the early part of 1555, while the chancellor's party was exploiting the reconciliation to launch a vigorous persecution, the king was making studied gestures of confidence in the *politiques*, particularly Paget and Pembroke. It was during these months that Gardiner, perhaps realizing that his victory of the previous summer had been largely undone, and that he was not high in favour with Philip, made a studied attempt to ingratiate himself by writing *A discourse on the coming of the English and Normans to Britain*. This work, which has been fairly described by its modern editor as a 'Machiavellian treatise',[57] survives only in an Italian translation by George Rainsford which was presented to Philip after Gardiner's death.[58] Explicitly it is an historical study, implicitly it is a piece of political advice to the king on the best methods of retaining control over England. While the author emphasizes the importance of discreet and conciliatory policies to prevent rebellion, the work is full of flattering allusions to Habsburg power and virtue, making only passing references to the queen.

> . . . nothing remains for me to say [he writes in the penultimate paragraph] . . . having shown how William subjugated the realm of England and left it in trust to his successors until the coming of the powerful and most merciful Philip, son of the Emperor Charles V. This I do not call change or alteration in the kingdom, but legitimate succession, confirmed by all orders for the restoration of religion, the honour of the kingdom and the benefit of the people.[59]

This treatise casts a good deal of light on the chancellor's attitude during the year which followed the marriage, and makes it probable that he was responsible for the otherwise mysterious suggestion to recognize Philip's title made in the House of Commons. His implacable hostility to Elizabeth, and broad hints that the king should circumvent an unco-operative aristocracy by appealing to the clergy and common people, were aspects of the same policy. What Gardiner really believed about the wellbeing of England is obscure, and perhaps irrelevant. Having once accepted the marriage, he set out to exploit the situation with all the political cunning at his command, quoting Machiavelli at considerable length as to the ways in which a 'stranger prince' can make his rule effective.[60] Once before the chancellor had salvaged his career by writing a tract designed to please his sovereign. *De Vera Obedientia* had succeeded brilliantly, but the 'Machiavellian treatise' was completed too late to serve its purpose. What Philip thought of it we do not know. He may not even have read it, since Rainsford was compelled by his own limitations to offer it in Italian and not Spanish. In one important respect it might even have displeased him. Generously as he flattered the king in misrepresenting the acceptability of his rule in England, Gardiner did not pretend to believe that it would be possible to employ other Spaniards for that purpose. Referring ostensibly to the massacre of the intruding Danes by the Saxons, he wrote:

> I do not marvel at all at the cruelty of the English when the causes which moved them to it are considered, for it is an extreme grief to men of any nation or province to see other men, foreigners, possess those honours, offices and dignities which in past time their fathers or predecessors enjoyed . . .[61]

In urging Philip to take warning by the example of Canute, the chancellor revealed that his political judgement had not entirely deserted him, and he endorsed Machiavelli's opinion that it was prudent for a king to respect the laws of his realm, but his priority was the preservation of Philip's power for which, if necessary, the king might act 'contrary to mercy, religion and faith'.

There is no reason to suppose that the contents of this tract ever became known in England, but it gives some substance to the stories later popularized by Foxe, relating how Gardiner organized two attempts upon the life of Elizabeth, one during her imprisonment in the Tower and the other after her withdrawal to Woodstock.[62] He is certainly on record as saying on several occasions that Philip's position in England would never be secure while she was in the country; an opinion which was shared by Renard and Charles but not, apparently, by Philip himself. The princess petitioned for release from her confinement shortly after the marriage, and the king seems to have been favourably inclined, but Mary was not disposed to be merciful, at least until she was convinced of the sincerity of her sister's catholicism. While he was on mission to the emperor in November 1554 Paget suggested that she should be married to some minor German prince who could be relied upon to neutralize her both religiously and politically.[63] Another similar proposal, naming the duke of Savoy as the prospective bridegroom,

225

was made in March 1555, but nothing was done, perhaps because the princess herself refused to entertain any thought of marriage. Early in April she and the earl of Devon were both released, and Courtenay immediately departed for Brussels *en route* to Italy.[64] Elizabeth came to court, where she remained for some time in semi-seclusion, having rejected all suggestions of a continental tour. It was reported that she was being kept as a hostage for the king's safety in the event of Mary's death, and at the end of April, Michieli had heard that 'the nobles who are thought to be faithful have brought up their retainers'.[65] However, at the same time both Noailles and Michieli picked up rumours that Philip was much attracted by the princess, and would marry her himself should his wife miscarry, a plan which she was thought to favour. The eventuality did not arise, and she was still at court in August when it was being predicted that the king would take her with him to Brussels, perhaps as a preliminary to sending her on to Spain.[66] She may have refused to go – or possibly Mary vetoed that particular plan! The subject of Elizabeth's marriage continued to be a favourite topic of gossip and speculation in the courts of Europe. In September 1555 Ferdinand's agent in Brussels decided that no English lord would dare to take the risk, and that the duke of Savoy would be rejected by the English council for fear of the French. His candidate was, naturally, the younger Ferdinand, but his master did not respond to the suggestion.[67]

Without relaxing his efforts, either to please the queen or to conciliate the English lords, by July 1555 Philip had long been anxious to proceed to the Low Countries. Partly because of his own ill-health, and partly because of the complexities of the situation in the Netherlands, Charles had decided in September 1554 to put off his departure until January. By that time, it was hoped, the English parliament would be over, the reconciliation concluded, and Philip free to spend some time in consultation with his father before the actual hand-over of authority took place. However, by October the emperor's health had deteriorated further and the prospect seemed less clear. Philip was apprehensive of his reception in the Low Countries, and complained that the governors of Naples and Milan were still applying to the emperor for instructions, rather than to himself. Moreover, he believed that he had 'made a good start' with affairs in England.[68] When January came, Charles showed no sign of going. Pole was trying to initiate peace negotiations between the Imperialists and the French, and perhaps more important, Mary was pressing Philip very hard to stay in England until after her lying-in. Quite apart from humane considerations, there were sound political reasons for yielding to this pressure, and the king stayed. The end of the queen's 'pregnancy', tacitly acknowledged by late July, galvanized Philip into action and opened the way for his departure. He spent long hours in consultation with the English council, consultations in which Gardiner significantly played a prominent part. Three main issues were discussed: the enforcement of religious orthodoxy; means of ensuring a tractable parliament to meet in the autumn; and the establishment of a council of state.[69] Philip's views on the religious situation are not clear from the surviving evidence. He was certainly in favour of the strictest enforcement of the law, but seems to have placed more faith in inducing the aristocracy to set a good example than in severe punishment. In a letter of 2 August, probably to Ruy Gómez, he outlined a plan whereby election to the forthcoming parliament should be made conditional, not merely upon the orthodoxy of the individual, but upon his willingness to co-operate in the policy of enforcement.[70] Since Gardiner is known to have been favouring the use of civil disabilities against heretics, this idea may have originated with him. The council of state was to consist of Gardiner, Thirlby, Paget, Arundel, Pembroke, Winchester, Rochester, and Petre, with Pole in the ill-defined status of attending if he wished.[71] This late burst of activity on Philip's part seems to have pleased and impressed the English, and was probably in marked contrast to his former attitude. On 11 June, Michieli reported that he took no part in the government, whereas on 27 August the same writer predicted that 'with the king's departure, all business will cease'.[72] When Philip bestirred himself, he could exercise a powerful and constructive influence on the government of England, and his tact and judgement in handling the council were warmly praised after his departure. However, it appears that these moods were neither frequent nor prolonged, and once he had reached the Netherlands his main recollection of England was as a place where he had been disparaged, insulted, and denied powers proper to his office.

He left on 29 August, leaving Mary deeply distressed, and completely uncertain about the length of his intended absence. 'The rumours', Michieli reported, 'are very contrary'. Some believed that the king would be away only a few weeks, and would return for the parliament, which was already summoned for 21 October. Others, on the other hand, were saying that he would go on from the Netherlands to Spain, and that the Spanish courtiers and servants left behind in England were only a blind to deceive the queen into false expectations.[73] It is possible that Philip had not as yet decided upon his course, and was keeping his options open, but his subsequent attitude suggests that he had no intention of returning except upon his own terms. Nevertheless, he maintained a gracious demeanour, taking an affectionate farewell of Mary, and distributing £40 among the poor people of Canterbury on his way to the coast.[74] The summer of 1555 had seen a general withering of Habsburg hopes. Although Philip had achieved something in gaining the co-operation of the English aristocracy, and had managed to recruit an uncertain number of English captains and soldiers for his father's army, popular hostility to Spanish rule in general had been constant and unremitting. One of the main reasons for this seems to have been the religious persecution, which, as we shall see, began in earnest as soon as the papal jurisdiction was restored. Within a few weeks both Renard and Michieli were commenting upon the unfavourable public reactions to the burnings, and the former was making urgent pleas both to the emperor and to Philip himself to curb the enthusiasm of 'the bishops'. Philip must have realized that he, Bishop á Castro, and the friars who had accompanied them were being generally blamed for this severity, but he did nothing to check it, either directly or by exercising his influence over the queen. Since hardly any Englishmen, even amongst his own servants, measured up to the king's exacting standards of orthodoxy, and he profoundly distrusted Renard's judgement, this is perhaps not surprising. Tellechea Idigoras has argued that, on balance, Carranza and the other Spanish divines exercised a moderating influence upon 'los inquisidores ingléses',[75] but he admits that the same cannot be said of the king. Protestant and anti-Spanish grievances and demonstrations were frequently associated together, as in the obscure 'conspiracy' at Cambridge that Renard and Michieli both reported in March. This seems to have been mainly the result of religious discontent, probably triggered off by the burning of the popular Rowland Taylor at Hadleigh on 5 February, but it swept up fears of Spanish rule and rumours of a substitution plot into a messy protest, which was probably not nearly as serious as was at first believed.[76] Renard believed that the matter had been hushed up because great men were involved, but there is no evidence to support him. Later in the summer there were further alarms. In the middle of July, when Philip's departure was common gossip, the council acted to disperse a suspicious gathering of gentlemen in London. They were reported to be friends of Elizabeth, and one of their number contacted Noailles with vague talk of 'recovering their liberties' by the end of August.[77] If this was a conspiracy designed to take advantage of the king's journey, then it came to nothing, possibly because the French were not interested. However, it was symptomatic of a hostile political climate, and Renard was not alone in believing that 'there cannot be so much smoke without fire'. Two of the most violent and outspoken pieces of anti-Spanish propaganda to appear in print also belong to these months: *A supplicacyon to the Quenes Majestie* and *A warnyng for Englande*.[78] Both these pamphlets were probably printed abroad, although the former contained a bogus colophon 'Imprynted at London by Iohn Cawoode Prynter to the Queenes Majestie, with her most gracious Lycence', a piece of impertinence which stung the council to particular fury. The *supplicacyon* was clearly a protestant work, which lamented, among other things, the evil consequences for 'religion' of the queen's marriage. *A warnyng*, on the other hand, scarcely mentioned religion, being an account of

> The horrible practices of the king of Spayne in the Kingdom of Naples, and the miseries whereunto that noble realme is brought. Whereby all Englishmen may understande the plage that shall light upo[n] them yf the Kyng of Spayn obtaine the dominion of Englande.

Full of invective against Philip, it was typical of an attitude which caused Mary acute distress, and tested the king's self-control to its limits. In July 1555 Michieli reported that he was still struggling to contain the fury of his followers, 'Not choosing that . . . they should come to blows at the risk of . . . insurrection . . . but rather to put up . . . with any affront or persecution'.[79] If anything, the fiasco of the queen's phantom pregnancy had left relations between the peoples even worse than they had been in the previous August.

Philip's honour and interests had also suffered setbacks on the wider European stage. Immediately after the marriage the French had been convinced that it was only a matter of time before Philip brought England into the war against them, and destroyed the advantages which Henri had secured in July 1554. Noailles wished as he had wished in the previous year, to frustrate this possibility by stirring up trouble in England. However, Montmorency believed that his contacts with the English malcontents, particularly Edward Randall, lacked 'substance' – and he was probably right.[80] The alternative was to negotiate peace, or at least a truce, while the going was good, and Noailles was instructed to sound out the possibilities of Pole renewing the mediatory offer which he had made unsuccessfully the previous year. Mary was anxious for peace partly on principle and partly because a settlement might persuade Philip to remain longer in England. Gardiner and Paget were both of the same mind, because both feared involvement if the war should continue. The English malcontents, of course, felt differently. Not only would a continued war give them fresh opportunities of undermining Mary's government with French help, but would also keep the emperor's hands occupied and prevent him from attempting to consolidate Philip's position in England by force. Intermittent and exploratory contacts were maintained throughout the autumn, Noailles being considerably assisted by his tactful young brother, François, but it was not until the beginning of 1555 that any real progress was made. On 19 January Vincenzo Parpaglia, abbot of San Saluto, was sent by Pole to Brussels to propose a conference to the emperor. Military successes in Italy and Piedmont, coupled with acute financial difficulties and persistent rumours of incipient English intervention, had made the French more anxious than ever to capitalize on their gains. Philip, besieged in London by exiled Italian nobles petitioning for aid, by February had come to add his voice to those of Mary and Pole in requesting Charles to negotiate. The emperor was reluctant to negotiate from a position of weakness, and it was early March before he verbally agreed to a conference. It was probably shortage of money rather than any desire to gratify his daughter-in-law which induced this change of mind, but by the middle of April it appeared that Philip and Mary were on the point of securing an important and prestigious diplomatic breakthrough.

When the conference actually assembled at La Marque, a small village in the Calais Pale, on 23 May, these hopes were quickly dashed. Each side seems to have come to La Marque convinced that the other was exhausted to the point of collapse, and neither was prepared to make any significant concession.[81] To make matters worse the English mediators, determined to occupy a dominant position, proposed to act as the sole channel of communication between the two sides, and had produced no agenda or other plan for the conduct of business. The French also knew that, greatly as Mary and her councillors desired peace, there were many in England who hoped that the conference would fail. Of the three principal English negotiators, only Pole was genuinely impartial. Both Paget and Gardiner conferred privately with Granvelle, and professed to be the emperor's 'good servants', each presumably hoping to induce the French to make some concession which would gratify the emperor in the process of agreeing to a peace which would gratify Philip and Mary. After two weeks the conference broke up in acrimony, partly because Pole's tactlessness gave the French an opportunity to blame the failure of the negotiations upon Granvelle,[82] and partly because of the news that the papal conclave had elected Philip's arch-enemy Gian Pietro Carafa. The political situation had moved markedly in favour of the French while the discussions went on. Mary still failed to produce the hoped-for heir which would have been the Habsburgs' trump card; the Lutheran princes in the German diet were refusing to budge; and the conclave was a disaster for Imperial hopes. Both sides denounced the English mediators for incompetence and partiality, and the diplomatic venture which had been intended to restore English prestige to the high days of 1518 resulted only in ignominy and helplessness. Some shrewd observers had forecast this outcome before the meetings began, but Mary was bitterly disappointed and Philip felt chagrined because he had lent himself to an enterprise which had turned out so badly. In fact semi-official contacts between the two sides went on, and Pole continued to be involved, but there was little likelihood that English mediation would be called on again in the near future.

The English could not, however, be blamed for the failure in Rome. At some time, probably just after the death of Julius III on 23 March, the Abbot Brizeno in Rome drew up a memorandum for Philip's benefit, listing the existing cardinals as 'Franceses' or 'Imperiales'.[83] This revealed a disturbing state of affairs, for whereas 25 appear under the former heading as 'cierto' and a further 3 as 'dudoso', there are only 19 and 5 respectively under the latter, with 3 'neutrales'. Even allowing for the fact that 6 assured French supporters and 3 Imperialists were away from Rome, victory for the French interest still seemed likely. In an attempt to redress this situation, on 8 April, Philip wrote a strongly worded letter to his father's ambassador in Rome, Manrique de Lara.[84] Credit for 20,000 crowns was being supplied immediately to assist in securing a suitable verdict, and Manrique was commended to the good offices of Cardinal Santa Fiora for the management of the Imperial campaign within the conclave. Cardinals Pole, Carpi, Santiago, and Morone would all be acceptable as pope. Santa Croce, who was rumoured to be ambitious and a favoured candidate, could be tolerated if necessary, but 'You are particularly to consider that the Theatine Cardinal [Carafa] would be entirely unsuitable . . .' Such blatant and unsubtle interference reflects the extent to which Philip was already in command of Habsburg policy. When a copy of his son's letter reached him in Brussels, Charles contemplated forbidding its despatch, but then recollected how angry Philip had been over the slow transfer of Italian jurisdiction, and decided not to upset him further. By the time these explicit instructions reached Manrique the conclave was over and Santa Croce had been duly elected as Marcellus II. Unfortunately the new pope quickly became seriously ill, and in the early hours of 1 May he died. The new conclave assembled on 15 May and Manrique strove to put Philip's instructions into effect. Writing on that day to the emperor, he declared that the Imperialists ought to be able to muster at least 22 votes, but that would not be enough for a clear-cut victory.[85] The best solution would be for Philip to make up his mind to put his weight behind Pole, instead of wavering between four candidates; as king of England he was still at peace with France, and could suggest Pole to the French with some hope of reaching an agreement; 'It would be better than to wait until the Cardinals, out of pure exhaustion, agree on some devil who will be no good to anyone . . .', he concluded gloomily. However, Pole had already decided not to attend, declaring in his unworldly way that if God wished him to be elected, then his presence or absence was irrelevant.[86] Moreover, neither Philip nor Charles was wholeheartedly in favour of the Englishman, distrusting both his sympathies and his judgement. In the event, Manrique's worst forebodings were realized. Pole failed by two votes, and so did Morone; at that point the Imperial party broke ranks and some, including the cardinal of Santiago, voted for Carafa, perhaps because he was a very old man and they had hopes of another early conclave. On 25 May, Manrique reported the outcome sadly, blaming Santiago with bitterness, and commending to the emperor's generosity the 14 cardinals who had remained loyal to the Imperial interest throughout.[87] The defeat itself was serious enough, but someone in the Imperial camp also betrayed the very forceful terms of Philip's instructions, and the fury of the new pope knew no bounds.

By the beginning of September 1555 the emperor was deeply immersed in his plans for the hand-over of power. When Philip reached Brussels on 8 September, they spent several days closeted together 'quite alone', as Eraso later reported, doing 'nothing but talk and look at papers which his Majesty had prepared'. Charles was again in poor health, and increasingly disposed to leave all policy decisions to his son.[88] It was confidently predicted that he would leave for Spain in October, and certainly by the end of the year. For his part, the king of England began to make his presence felt at once. Before the end of September he had taken the important decision not to press his candidature for the Imperial succession after Ferdinand's death. In view of the forcibly expressed opinions of some members of the German diet this was a sensible gesture which improved relations within the Habsburg family at no real cost to himself. On the other hand, his relations with the political establishment in the Netherlands showed immediate signs of strain. Eraso got on well with Philip, probably because of his nationality, but both Granvelle and Francisco de Vargas were discontented at being excluded from negotiations, and the Flemings proved to be almost as intractable about their internal affairs as were the English, insisting that no Spaniard was to have any share in the government of the provinces.[89] On 25 September the effective end of Charles's thirty-six years of Imperial rule was signalled by the signing of the religious peace of Augsburg, and exactly a month later in a moving ceremony at Brussels he handed over the lordship of the Netherlands to his son. In spite of all efforts, Philip did not make a good impression. He managed a short speech of acceptance in French, but was unable to address the estates general in that language, and Granvelle spoke on his behalf. The English seem to have expected Charles to hand over Spain at the same time, and to leave very soon after. In fact he did neither of these things, and the English fleet which had been prepared to escort him down the channel with suitable pomp stood by in expensive idleness for about two months.[90] By the beginning of January there was speculation in Brussels about the reasons for the delay. Charles was rumoured to be disappointed in his son, either for political reasons or because he was 'altogether too fond of masking and revels'. They had not lived in close proximity for several years, and this may have been an aspect of Philip's character of which his father was not aware; but in all probability the only reason for the delay was the old man's methodical caution. He did not hand over Franche Comté until April 1556. The crowns of Castile and Aragon and the grandmasterships of the Castilian military orders were transferred on 16 January, without fuss but in the presence of Spanish and Italian jurists. Philip had become the master of a great empire, and whatever his English subjects might think, England was no longer his principal dominion.[91]

Meanwhile affairs in England were going their own way, and Mary waited in almost daily expectation of her husband's return. The select council sent regular memoranda of its business (in Latin), and Sir John Mason discussed with the king such business as appeared to require his personal intervention. By the middle of October, Philip's household servants were drifting quietly away, and it was the common opinion in London that the king would not come back for a long time, if ever. Pole wrote movingly of the queen's grief, and declared that she was endangering her health by over-work, but it was being reported in Brussels 'on good authority' that Philip had written to his wife explaining that he could not possibly return to England on the former terms, and demanding an increased share in the government.[92] The real nature of Philip's attitude is hard to judge from the surviving evidence. He sought relief from the puritanical constraints of the English court. In early December, Federico Badoer, the chatty Venetian ambassador at the Imperial court, reported that he had been to several masked

233

balls, despite the wretched weather, and 'seemed much enamoured' of a certain Madame d'Aler.[93] He added that news of these escapades was being kept from Mary 'because she is easily agitated'. English couriers were constantly coming and going as Mary referred decisions and appointments to his judgement, consulted him about the affairs of parliament, or enquired solicitously about his health. Philip seems to have attended to English business in due proportion to the other business which pressed upon him, but he had no desire to return to England. He wanted the English parliament to agree to his coronation, but when Mary wrote at the end of October to explain how strongly such suggestions were being resisted, he apparently advised her to drop the matter rather than risk defeat.[94] By mid-November Charles had added his voice to Mary's, urging him to return by pointing out that there might still be a chance of his getting an heir. More realistically the emperor argued that his son would be more likely to obtain the things that he wanted in England – coronation, a greater share in the government, money, and possibly a declaration of war against France – if he went and demanded them in person.[95] However, Philip may well have felt that the year which he had already spent in England gave no grounds for such a hope, and that he would do better to hold out on Mary and persuade her to use her own authority on his behalf. At any rate, he continued to withdraw his servants from England, and the soothing half-promises which he continued to make to the queen carried less and less conviction. The parliament was dissolved with anger and recriminations on 11 December, and it was believed in Brussels that Mary was the helpless prisoner of the English factions, not daring to move in any direction. There were rumours as far away as Zürich that the emperor would assemble a fleet upon the pretext of his journey to Spain, and would use it to obtain Philip's coronation by force.[96] Neither Charles nor Philip ever had any such intention, but there was a further upsurge of anti-Spanish propaganda in England, much of it specifically directed against the king's crowning, the symbolic significance of which seems to have been increasing month by month.

By Christmas an extensive plot was being woven, involving a group of English exiles in France, led by Henry Dudley, and an uncertain number of discontented gentlemen and others in England.[97] Some members of the House of Commons, such as Sir Anthony Kingston, were certainly involved, and it was later to be rumoured that 'great men', including some members of the council, were implicated. The details of this plot need not concern us, but its ostensible aim was to make an armed demonstration with French support against the coronation. The real purpose of most of the conspirators seems to have been to depose Mary in favour of Elizabeth. During November and December, Henri and Montmorency were prepared to listen to such plans because they still believed that an open rupture with England was likely in spite of the peace feelers which had gone on throughout the autumn. French policy may well have been confused by the fact that there were considerable differences of opinion within the Imperial camp. Philip wished England to declare war on France because it was derogatory to his honour that she should hold back. He had no interest in English mediation after the failure at La Marque, and did not wish to use either Pole or his indefatigable agent, Parpaglia. On the other hand, he was willing, and even anxious, to reach a settlement by direct negotiation. In this he was supported by his Spanish advisers and by Renard, who after leaving England on 20 September had been appointed to the council of Flanders and was very active in negotiating an exchange of prisoners with the French. After his conspicuous failure to win Philip's confidence in England, he was clearly trying to salvage his career. Charles and Granvelle, on the other hand, were suspicious of direct negotiations, prepared to hold out for better terms, and anxious not to offend Mary and Pole. On 27 December, when Charles and Philip issued a joint statement on their desire for peace, it appeared that the former had prevailed.[98] They 'called upon the Queen and the Legate to take the matter in hand and call another conference', suggesting Vaucelles as a suitable venue. However, the French flatly rejected English involvement, and Philip consequently had his way since the emperor, notwithstanding his misgivings, was no longer in a position to insist upon his own terms. Consequently the five-year truce of Vaucelles, concluded upon 6 February, was negotiated without even a token English participation, since the English were neither belligerents nor mediators.

Reactions at the English court were bitter. Although it seems clear that the eventual mode of negotiation was determined by the French, Philip was generally blamed in England for the heavy blow to national prestige and self-esteem which the truce represented. Even Mary was hurt and resentful. The English council were also disposed to blame Pole for his clumsiness, a feeling shared by Parpaglia, whose intensive efforts had received neither recognition nor reward. However, there were tangible advantages in the new situation. As long as the truce endured, fear of English involvement in continental war receded, and an important source of irritation against the Habsburgs was removed. Also Henri's enthusiasm for adventures in England was sharply reduced. Before Christmas, Dudley and Ashton had received warm encouragement both from

Noailles and the king,[99] but when Dudley presented himself at the French court in the second week of February, he was dismissed with empty words.[100] The conspirators did not give up. There were upwards of 200 English exiles in France, most of them bored and anxious for action. If enough money could be obtained to equip them, the leaders believed that their extensive contacts in England would give them a good chance of success. It had been money that they had expected Henri to provide, and after his defection they turned to a wild-seeming plot to rob the exchequer. After coming within an ace of success, this end of the conspiracy was detected in early March, and the subsequent investigations occupied, and alarmed, the council for several weeks.[101] In May, Antoine de Noailles, discredited both in London and in Paris as conclusive proof of his involvement in the conspiracy emerged, was allowed to withdraw, and was replaced by his more subtle brother, François.[102] A complete breakdown of diplomatic relations was rumoured, but did not take place. England could not fight France alone, and Philip at this point had no intention of breaking the truce. The break-up of the conspiracy gave Charles and Granvelle renewed hope of Philip's coronation, but the king himself was losing interest in the possibility as he became increasingly immersed in the business of his other dominions. The French remained convinced that Philip intended to return to England with an army, and that Mary's repeated and well-known entreaties for his presence were an appeal to him to put down the English malcontents by force. In April the French ambassador in Brussels, Bassefontaine, accused Paget, then on mission to Philip in the Low Countries, of such an intention, warning him that

> . . . should they purpose doing this without the consent of the people of England, His most Christian Majesty . . . would be compelled to favour it [England] in order that it should not be forced to do anything against its will . . . [103]

In other words, Henri was threatening to treat Philip's coronation in England as a breach of the truce, and might even treat his return thither as a pretext, if it suited him. In view of the calculated provocations which Henri was offering to the English by continuing to harbour such men as Dudley and the piratical Killigrew brothers, the effrontery of this remark speaks volumes for his contempt of the English government.

For his part, Philip responded to his wife's pleas and his father's suggestions as before, with vague promises. At the end of January the arrival of some of his Spanish servants in London provoked rumours that he would be back 'at the latter end of next month'.

In March, while he was giving further assurances to Sir John Mason, the Spaniards in Brussels were openly saying that he had no cause to gratify a wife who had done nothing to gratify him, and that England was nothing but a nuisance and an expense.[104] In April there were rumours that Mary was becoming exasperated, and Henri was speculating pleasurably upon the possibility of Philip repudiating his queen.[105] However, the beseeching letters continued to arrive, full of personal unhappiness and political apprehension. It seems that Mary had given up thinking of the coronation as a real possibility, and was concerned with the fundamental problem of preserving her authority. 'Consider the miserable plight into which this country has now fallen', she wrote to the emperor on 10 September, 'Unless he [Philip] comes to remedy matters . . . great danger will ensue from lack of a firm hand'.[106] Hostile propaganda continued to belabour both Philip and his countrymen.

> Will ye crowne the king to make him live chast with his wife [asked John Bradford rhetorically] contrary to his nature; peradventure his majestie after he were crowned would be content with one woman, but in the mean time his Grace will have every night v or vi . . .[107]

Bradford, who professed to write out of pure love to the queen and the catholic faith, claimed to have learned the 'vile nature' of the Spaniards when '. . . for the space of ii or iii yeres my frendes put me to learne their language'. He denied all sympathy with heretics, but his attitude to the coronation and succession was identical with that of the authors of the *Warnyng* and the *Supplicacyon*; 'there is no law confirmed and past by which the Queene may lawfully disinherit the realme of the crowne. . . .'[108] The duke of Northumberland had tried to alter the succession by prerogative power, he pointed out, and had received his just deserts. Elizabeth was the rightful heir, and

> . . . if ever the king should have a iust title to the crown, and obteine it, he would knoke that most vertuous Ladi Elizabeth's Grace sure . . . either banished the land or els put to deth miserably . . . and when she is ded, do not you look to live long after . . .

There were also, he hinted, dark conspiracies to remove those English nobles who had no love for Spaniards, notably the lord treasurer. If Bradford was sincere in his professions of catholicism, then his work is all the more significant.[109] Philip's absence from

England may have been regretted by some of his rasher opponents who believed that '. . . if the Spaniard be absent, the common people will not so readily adhere unto [us] . . .', but there is no evidence to suggest that absence had made the hearts of Englishmen grow any fonder.

An early sixteenth-century Italian observer had written that the English considered themselves to be the most important people in Europe, and even those councillors and others most committed to the alliance found it hard to take an absentee king seriously. Not that communication was in any way inadequate. The select council continued to send memoranda of business, at least until the summer of 1556, and Philip periodically sent trusted servants across to consult with them. Feria was employed in this way at least twice. Similarly English councillors made frequent trips to the Low Countries, and certainly discussed other business apart from the perpetual topic of his return. Much of the limited evidence which survives relates to friction or disagreements, but that is commonly the nature of historical evidence. In February 1556, following Philip's acquisition of the crowns of Spain, he was in dispute with the English council over his new regnal style. The matter was not resolved until April, and the new style does not seem to have been proclaimed.[110] More significantly, the king intervened twice during this period against English commercial interests. Before leaving England, in July 1555, he had accepted Portuguese protests against English attempts to infiltrate the Guinea trade, and in October, Michieli reported that he was seconding John III's demands that the English merchants be checked.[111] The quarrel rumbled on for months, and it was not until the following summer that the English council made any determined effort to carry out his wishes.[112] At about the same time, on 28 June 1556, the council, in response to a petition from the merchant adventurers, decreed a suspension of all cloth exports to the Low Countries, whether by English or alien merchants, until 1 November.[113] The petition seems to have been a manoeuvre on the part of the adventurers to improve their competitive position, and there was an immediate outcry, particularly from the Flemings and the Venetians. The former appealed to Philip, and he supported them wholeheartedly. On 17 October, Charles Quarrentyne, 'councellor of the council of Brabant', presented a set of articles to the English council 'by commandment of the Kings Majestie', complaining not only about the embargo but also in general about the activities of the merchant adventurers in Antwerp, which Philip claimed to have investigated and found to be true, and contrary to the ancient treaties between the countries. The ninth article ran

His Majesty findeth this to be the trewe way wholy to deverte the saide traphique from his said low countries and to transport it into some other place and to seperate the subjectes of both partes from all mutual traphique communication and affection. A thing contrived by certyn privat persons of the said nacion for ther singular proffyt and conveynience. And may be by some evel disposed persons myndyng some other evel purpose, chiefly by those that be fledd into the said Hambourg, Empden and other places, the which go about for to bring the said realme of England into disorder to marre and destroy it . . .[114]

The English council was understandably put out by the suggestion that the adventurers, upon whom the government continued to depend for sizeable loans, were lending themselves to a protestant conspiracy. The charges, both of substance and intention, were rebutted not only by the adventurers, but also by the council, in a letter signed by Heath, Winchester, Arundel, Paget, Pembroke, Thirlby, Rochester, and Petre.[115] By the time this letter was sent the suspension had in any case expired, but the reverberations of the quarrel went on. On 14 February 1557 in a letter to Mary, Philip conceded that there was some justice in the English position, but he should have thought of that earlier. It was much too late by then to undo the harm which had been caused in England by his partisan approach. The king was also blamed, probably correctly, for the kidnapping of Sir John Cheke and Sir Peter Carew in May 1556. Cheke was a wanted man, but Carew had ostensibly been pardoned, and Badoer reported that his arrest was regarded by the English as a typical piece of Spanish duplicity and bad faith.[116] The summer of 1556 also saw a fresh outbreak of rumours concerning the future of Elizabeth, the most persistent being that she would be carried off in the emperor's entourage to Spain – when he eventually went – and perhaps married to Don Carlos. '. . . The affections and wishes of the majority [are] already inclining towards her', wrote Michieli in April.[117] Ferdinand still hankered after her for his son, but neither Philip nor Henri would tolerate such a suggestion, the latter even threatening to marry Mary of Scotland to Edward Courtenay if such a plan was to be put into effect.[118]

At long last, in September 1556, Charles embarked for Spain, and the last influence of his enormous, if somewhat stultifying, experience disappeared. For several weeks it was rumoured in England that he would visit the queen on his way, but such reports were rightly discounted by the council, and Mary seems to have entertained no false hopes. She did, however, believe that Charles's withdrawal would be the signal for Philip's return, and after a summer of wretchedness and frustration during which she had more than once given vent to her feelings, in September her spirits began to revive. Towards the end of October the arrival of some of his household appeared to confirm these hopes; 'Nothing is thought of, nothing expected, save this blessed return of the king . . .', wrote Michieli on 2 November.[119] Throughout that month the couriers passed to and fro, but Philip did not come. Observers on both sides of the channel were surprised by this continued dilatoriness, because quite apart from the need to attend to English affairs and gratify the queen, Philip was again in urgent need of all the assistance he could get on the continent. A final bid by Charles to secure the Imperial succession for his son had failed in July, and Philip's bad relations with the pope had resulted in the outbreak of open war on 1 September. The history of this breach went back almost a year to the secret Franco-papal treaty of December 1555. This had been negotiated by the militant Guises, and the cardinal of Lorraine had spent much of 1556 endeavouring to foment trouble between the pope and the Imperialists in Italy.[120] Ironically, Charles had risen to this bait more readily than his son, who was acutely aware of the exhausted state of his treasury. Nevertheless, it was Philip who had to sustain the resulting war, and it remained to be seen how long the fragile truce in northern Europe could withstand the pressure of this fresh development. Mary and Pole were both acutely distressed by this rupture, which boded no good for the restored catholic church, and the English waited apprehensively for fresh pressure from Brussels for financial and military aid. When Philip prolonged a loan from the English merchants in September, and as the privy council began to apply pressure to secure payment of the forced loan demanded in July, there were mounting complaints that the money would be used to 'favour the foreigner'. Naturally the French took what steps they could to exacerbate this feeling, and genuinely believed, as they had done since 1553, that Habsburg policy was directed to a full mobilization of England against them.

> I assure you [wrote Bassefontaine in August 1556] that their whole aim, counsel and plan has no other end but to occupy this kingdom and so install themselves there that they may use it against us . . .[121]

Whether any money actually reached Philip out of England seems uncertain, but rumours to that effect were widely believed, and were reflected in lampoons such as *Maria Ruyna Angliae*, which Gilles de Noailles reported having seen in London.[122]

The English government had its own reasons to quarrel with the French, and these increased the rumours of impending war during the autumn. The French had never entirely disbanded their forces in the north, and by October, Wotton was reporting from Paris that Henry Dudley was intriguing with traitors in Calais, Guisnes, and Hammes:

> Orator utrasque maiestii in Gallia significat quomodo profligatus illorum proditor Dudlarus et alli perditi fugitivi iam ante duos menses clam solicit' certis militis in Guisnes et Hammes . . .

as the select council reported to Philip on 22 November.[123] Wotton was also convinced that the French were deliberately prolonging a boundary dispute over the Pale in order to have a pretext for military action. At the beginning of December the earl of Pembroke was sent across with some troops to strengthen the garrison, and since Pembroke was high in favour with Philip, the French in turn read this as a sign of an impending breach. On 11 January 1557 Michieli reported that the French had finally broken the truce in Flanders, and although this was not directly aimed against England, it would force the queen to declare herself.[124] It may have been this development which prompted Mary to lay the whole dilemma before her council, and produced the memorandum, a draft of which now survives among the Cotton MSS.[125] In response to the question whether England was bound to furnish aid to the king under the treaties of 1542 and 1546, the authors replied in the negative, because the war 'which is now going on' is the same war from which England was excluded by the marriage treaty, having been broken only by a truce. Even if the treaties had been in full force, the queen would only have been bound to render aid if an invasion of the Low Countries had been 'certified', and if the king had requested it, '. . . and considering that the Queens Majesty is not hable to do that the treaty requireth it is to be hoped that his majestie will not require that which cannot be done'. Should Mary, then, offer to mediate a continuation of the truce? Certainly not, replied the authors, unless Philip should request such mediation; otherwise it would 'touch his majesties honour', causing him to lose service. It would also, they added, touch the queen's own honour, since she had made such an offer before, unsuccessfully. Even a proposal to threaten intervention as a deterrent to French aggressiveness was firmly rejected;

> The warres the Queenes Majestie is utterly unable to mayntayn and therefore to saie to the Frenche king that her Majestie will give aide and further doe for the kings Majestie according to the

treatie not being able to performe it in deed is both dishonorable and may be many waies daungerous to this realme.

If England should become involved in the war, the blame will fall upon the king, who will be held to have broken the marriage treaty,

> . . . It is considered also that the Common people of this realme being partly many wayes greived some pinched with famine and want of payment of money due to them, some miscontented for matters of Religion, and generally all yet talking of the smarte of the last warres, it might be very daungerous to entangle them now with new warres, especially where necessitie of defence shall not require the same . . .

Philip certainly desired the English to declare war on France, but he was not entirely unaware of this sort of danger, and refrained from invoking the treaties openly. At the beginning of February he sent Ruy Gómez across to inform Mary of his impending return, and to negotiate secretly with Paget about the prospects of engineering a break with France.[126] The French anticipated such a move, and Wotton warned the council that more plots were brewing to send an expedition, or at least a raiding party of English exiles to seize some coastal fortress.[127] The council ordered an inspection of coastal fortifications, sent reinforcements to the Scottish borders, and ordered musters. But these were purely defensive precautions, and otherwise it remained firmly opposed to war. By March, Henri believed that, as usual, the English council was divided, and would eventually compromise with Philip, supplying him with money but not declaring war. He was right insofar as Paget had now come out openly for war and one or two of the other Imperial pensioners were looking to their own interests, but they remained a small minority. In spite of Mary's obvious desire to gratify her husband, in the middle of March there did not seem to be much prospect of her being able to do so. However, the king himself landed in England on the 18th, and reached London on the 24th. A few days later the new Venetian ambassador in England, Michel Surian, reported that '. . . the king has all the grandees of this realm in his pocket. They are so venal they will do anything for money . . .', and continued that he believed that Philip would content himself with money and a fleet.[128] Surian was wrong on both counts. The 'war party' in the council still numbered no more than three or four, and Philip was determined upon an open declaration. It was uphill work. On 1 April, Mary summoned the select council, and in Philip's presence set out the arguments for war. Two days later the council returned a written answer, similar to its previous one, only at greater length, stating that England 'ought not and could not declare war'.[129] On 14 April in a letter to Granvelle the king expressed himself hopeful, but admitted that he found 'a little more hardening' than he had expected. By that time he had obtained an undertaking to supply 7000 troops and a possibility of war in the autumn. This was not good enough, and he kept up his pressure. At the end of April, Henri apparently came to his rescue by offering a piece of blatant provocation in supporting and financing Thomas Stafford's raid on Scarborough,[130] thus undermining one of the council's arguments. Although as late as 4 May, Philip was still writing cautiously that more time would be needed to bring about an open declaration, he had won.[131]

Desperate necessity, as well as the need to satisfy his own honour, had brought Philip back to England in 1557. He was bankrupt; with his revenues committed three years ahead and loans costing as much as 54 per cent. In these circumstances no pleas of poverty or hardship, however justified, were likely to impress him. The emperor's worst fears had not been realized. Philip's position in the Netherlands themselves had not been seriously challenged, but otherwise his situation was so bad that England's resources, no matter how small, were indispensable. The declaration of war, therefore, which came eventually upon 7 June, had for the Habsburgs a significance out of all proportion to England's fighting capacity. One of the major drawbacks of the marriage treaty had been overcome, and reluctantly the English had accepted their obligations as Philip's subjects. Nevertheless, the price was likely to be high. In two and a half years as king, Philip had gained neither power nor respect in England. In all probability Gardiner's death in November 1555 had deprived him of the services of the one English politician of the first rank who was prepared to promote his interests without reservation. It was commonly believed both in Brussels and in England that there was a party among the conservative English lords who were prepared to work for Philip's coronation, and by implication for the augmentation of his authority, but they made no effective move and their very identity is uncertain. Paget, Arundel, and Pembroke were probably his most consistent supporters, and the former certainly took the opportunity to ingratiate himself further with the king during his visit to Brussels in April 1556. He seems to have undertaken to arrange for Philip to enjoy a larger share in the government, and no doubt to enjoy a larger share himself, but he could do nothing while the king remained in the Low Countries.[132] Mary always preferred to rely upon Pole or Rochester, and neither man was sympathetic to Habsburg pretensions. Consequently, although Philip

243

retained a potentially strong foothold in English politics, he did virtually nothing to exploit it, and his prolonged absence almost certainly destroyed whatever chance there was of establishing himself in control of English affairs. This failure was epitomized by his inability to do anything decisive about Elizabeth. In the summer of 1556, following the Dudley conspiracy, the princess's household was reorganized under the catholic control of Sir Thomas Pope, and a number of her former attendants were arrested or otherwise removed, including Mrs Katherine Ashley.[133] However, in spite of repeated pressure, she refused all suggestions of marriage. At the end of 1556, it was confidently believed in Brussels that she would be married to the duke of Savoy, and that parliament would declare her incapable of succeeding. The French had heard the same rumours, and Renard reported that they would 'move the Pope to proclaim [her] a bastard'.[134] As late as April 1557, when Philip was already in England, Soranzo believed that the king would bring her back with him to the Netherlands. Yet nothing was done. It may be that Elizabeth's popularity deterred any move against her for fear of rebellion, but such an explanation is hardly necessary. Unless or until Mary produced a child, she was the heir, and if Philip was ever to challenge his own exclusion by the terms of the marriage treaty, then he would need to devote himself to the affairs of England much more wholeheartedly than he had shown any sign of doing since August 1555. A cautious politician such as Paget could not be expected to further any designs against the lawful heir unless the alternative was a convincing one. Consequently Paget and his friends, willing as they were to work in Philip's interest, were equally concerned to protect Elizabeth, at least until they were firmly convinced that the king was willing to make the kind of effort which would bring him success. That time never came.

Notes

1 Cited by W. H. Prescott, *A History of the Reign of Philip II* (1859), I, 50.
2 *Documentos inéditos para la Historia de España* (1842–95), ed. M. Fernández de Navarete, III, 531. Ruy Gómez to Eraso, 12 August 1554.
3 *Cal. Span.*, XIII, 28.
4 Renard to the emperor, 3 September 1554. *Cal. Span.*, XIII, 45.
5 ibid.
6 *Cal. Span.*, XIII, 50. Fitzwalter, whose remarks were taken in bad part, was also complaining of the general unwillingness of the Spaniards to attempt any communication with the English.
7 *Tres Cartas de lo sucedido en el viaje de Su Alteza a Inglaterra* (La

Queen Mary I; a woman uneasily poised between an intense awareness
of her royal destiny and a strong sense of unworthiness.
Portrait by Hans Eworth

King Philip; to whom England was first an attractive opportunity, second a political convenience, and thirdly an expensive nuisance.
Portrait by Titian

William, Lord Paget of Beaudesert, Lord Privy Seal. A skilled and tenacious administrator, his vision of Philip as King of England failed to materialize.
Artist unknown

Simon Renard, Charles V's ambassador in England from 1553 to 1555. As the chief negotiator of the marriage, he was made the scapegoat for Spanish disappointment, and his confidential relationship with the Queen hampered the Privy Council.
Portrait by Antonio Moro(?)

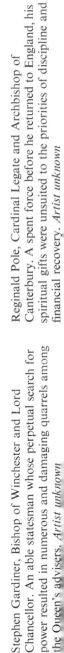

Stephen Gardiner, Bishop of Winchester and Lord Chancellor. An able statesman whose perpetual search for power resulted in numerous and damaging quarrels among the Queen's advisers. *Artist unknown*

Reginald Pole, Cardinal Legate and Archbishop of Canterbury. A spent force before he returned to England, his spiritual gifts were unsuited to the priorities of discipline and financial recovery. *Artist unknown*

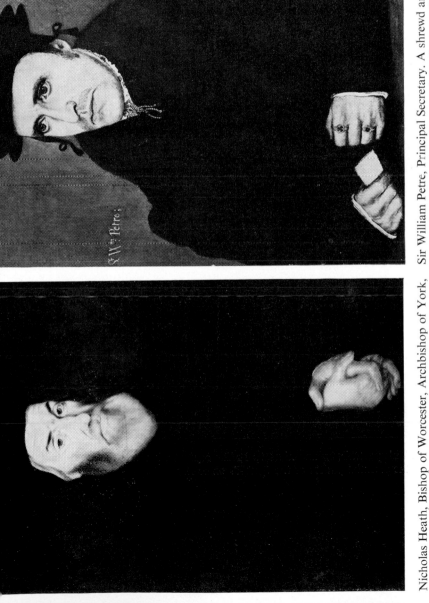

Nicholas Heath, Bishop of Worcester, Archbishop of York, and Lord Chancellor. A competent and peaceable man who made little impact upon political events.
Portrait by Hans Eworth

Sir William Petre, Principal Secretary. A shrewd and pragmatic conservative who served the Queen well, and left office under circumstances of some mystery.
Artist unknown

Mary (bust). This portrait, by an unknown Italian sculptor, is unique
in capturing the essential pathos of the Queen's character

Mary. An unflattering but beautifully executed portrait by the leading medallist Jacopo da Trezzo

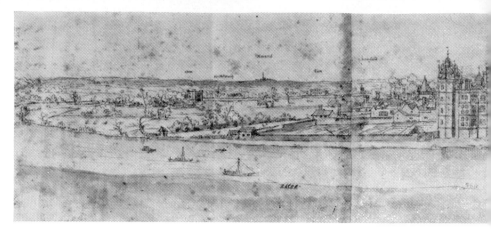

The Palace of Richmond. *Drawing by Antonius van den Wyngaerde*
The Palace of Hampton Court. *Drawing by Wyngaerde*

Sir Thomas Gresham, a financial adviser to three Tudor monarchs,
whose exceptional abilities almost justified his own opinion of them.
Artist unknown

I Russell L. Privy Seale.

with one Eye

John Russell, Earl of Bedford, Lord Privy Seal. A tough political survivor who managed to serve Henry VIII, Edward VI, and Mary in high office.
Portrait by Holbein

Bonner's *Homilies.* A serious attempt to grapple with the problems of re-education in the catholic faith, which found a ready market but few imitators

Huggarde's *Displaying.* The only extended work of catholic prose polemic to match the protestant tracts in liveliness and wit

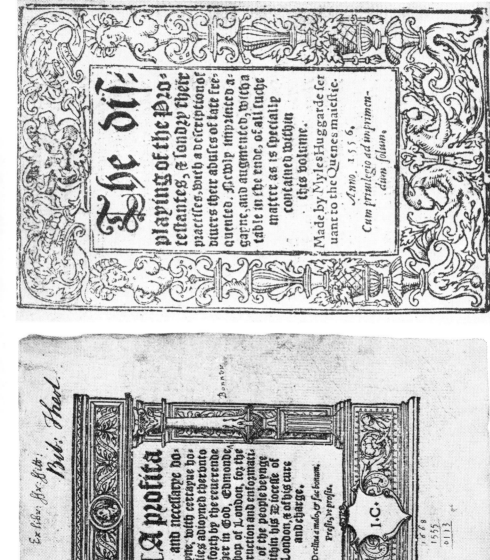

The Copye

of a letter, sent by Iohn Bradforth to
the right honorable lordes the Erles
of Arundel, Darbie, Shrewſburye,
and Penbroke, declaring the nature
of Spaniardes; and diſcouering the
moſte deteſtable treaſons, which thei
haue pretended moſte falſelye as
gaynſte our moſte noble kingdome of Englande.

Uſe beleue the trueth, ye
ſaue your liues. &c.

HOW
SVPERIOR

POWERS OGHT TO
BE OBEYD OF THEIR

ſubiects: and wherin they may lawfully by Gods Worde be diſobeyed
and reſiſted.

Wherin alſo is declared the cauſe of all this pre-
ſent miſerie in England, and the onely way
to remedy the ſame.

BY CHRISTOPHER GOODMAN.

The Lord hath brought vpon them a nation from a
farre countrey, an impudent nation and of a ſtrange
langage. Baruch 4. Deut.28.

Printed at Geneua by John Criſpin.

M. D. LVIII.

Goodman's *How superior powers*. A tract of great importance, breaking away from the non-resistance theories in which English protestantism had been reared

Bradford's *Copye of a letter*. A work of popular anti-Spanish abuse, ostensibly from the pen of a loyal English catholic

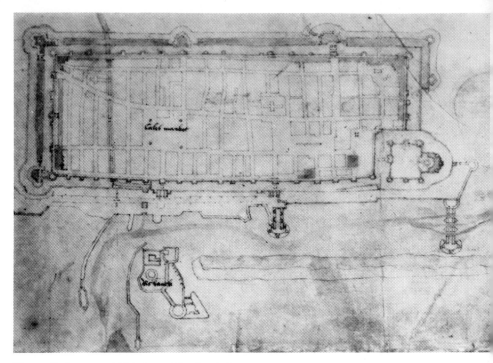

The walled town of Calais and Rysbank fort

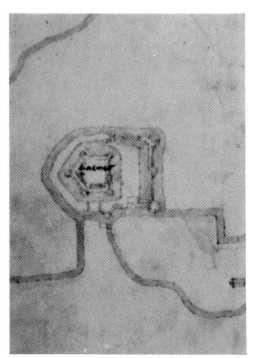

Hammes. An important fort which was not defended because of a mutiny in the garrison

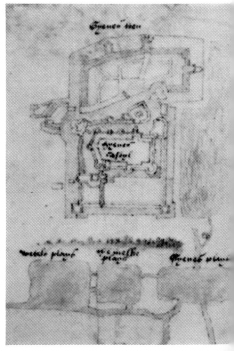

Guisnes. The only point in the Pale to offer significant resistance, it fell to a brief siege, being inadequately supplied and garrisoned

Master Wotton, for so muche as myn embassador
wch I came laste out of ffrance, hathe tolde me that the
ffrenche kyng did talke wt theym a farre of, as it
shulde seme, to prove if I wolde be a meane to procure
any peace betwen thempeoure and him. for the good
will that I beare to the comune welthe and univer-
sall peace of all crystendom, to escheu also the effusion
of blood and the evills and inconveniences wch alwaies
do procede of warre desiryng to do as muche as shall lye
in my power that thyng wch shalbe agreeable to bothe
the prynces and also to gratifie the ffrenche kyng
I have dispached theyse letters unto you to cause
you to demande audience assone as you maye, of
the ffrenche quene, or suche as have auchorite in the
sayde kyngs absence and the constable of ffrance and
to geve theym understandyng on my behalfe, that if
the ffrenche kyng be still in that mynde, that I shulde
be any meane to procure the sayde peace, I wolde
gladly knowe by what means I myghte do it and
uppon what foundacion and condicions I myghte
entre into that matter, wherin I wolde do my best
and asmuche as may be requyred at my hande
to persuade the sayde peace

Mary writes to Nicholas Wotton, her ambassador in France, about a
suggestion that she should mediate peace with the Emperor
(autograph letter)

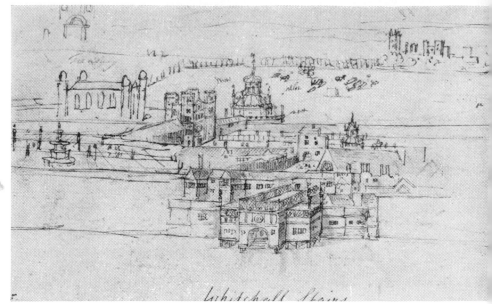

Westminster. Henry VIII's great palace by the Thames, which was a constant wonder to visitors for its size and complexity.
Drawing by Wyngaerde

Gold ryal. A fine coin, minted in 1553–54 as a part of the Queen's campaign to restore confidence in the currency

Philip and Mary shilling. Minted in 1557–58. 'The effigies of Ahab and Jezebel', as Bishop Hooper's widow commented acidly. This was the coin to which Samuel Butler referred more gently in *Hudibras*:

> Still amorous and fond and billing
> Like Philip and Mary on a shilling

Sociedad de Bibliófilos Españoles, 1877), Primera Carta, 91.

8 *Cal. Span.*, XIII, 30. According to *La partita del Serenissimo Principe* four Italian noblemen accompanied Philip to England, the marchese di Pescara, the marchese di Berges, the conte di Agamonte Fiamengo, and Cesare Gonzaga.

9 *Cal. Span.*, XIII, 13.

10 Renard to the emperor, 13 October 1554. *Cal. Span.*, XIII, 67.

11 *Chronicle of Queen Jane.* According to one contemporary estimate there were as many as 2000 Spaniards in England in August 1554, which is roughly consistent with Philip's expressed intention.

12 *Tres Cartas*, Primera Carta, 111.

13 Emperor's instructions to Eraso, 1 October 1554. *Cal. Span.*, XIII, 56. Several Spaniards set up unauthorized shops or booths in the vicinity of the court. On 12 October, Francis Yaxley wrote to Sir William Cecil : 'The artizans Spaniards were commanded yesterdaye to shutte up theyr shoppes, I think because by the order and lawes of the citie they maye not open the same being not free denyzens'. BL Lansdowne MS 3 f. 92.

14 *Tres Cartas*, Tercera Carta, 102.

15 Juan Vásquez de Molina to Philip, 13 September 1554. *Cal. Span.*, XIII, 47. Ruy Gómez seems to have been responsible for misleading Enríquez, since the admiral admitted that he did not have Philip's authority to speak as he did.

16 ibid. One Hernando de Rojas was sent to ascertain the king's wishes.

17 *APC*, V, 61-2. *Cal. Span.*, XIII, 32.

18 Count Giovanni di Stroppiana to the bishop of Arras, 6 October; Renard to the same, 13 October. *Cal. Span.*, XIII, 62, 64.

19 Michieli to the doge and senate, 27 May and 1 July 1555. *Cal. Ven.*, VI, 85, 126. Mary was as distressed by these affrays as Philip was angered. 'It is a cause of great sorrow to the Queen if they maltreat a Spaniard, greater than if she herself had to suffer . . .', wrote Juan de Barraona. *Four Manuscripts of the Escorial* (1956), ed. C. V. Malfatti, 92-3.

20 Medina was subsequently pardoned. *Cal. Pat.*, II, 243.

21 Machyn, 69, 72, 79, etc.

22 Salvedra was pardoned in July 1555. *Cal. Pat.*, II, 97.

23 *Cal. Span.*, XIII, 51-2.

24 Stroppiana to the bishop of Arras, 13 November. *Cal. Span.*, XIII, 81.

25 Noailles, Advis au Roi, 5 September 1554. Aff. Etr., IX ff. 261-2. Harbison, 197.

26 PRO SP11/7/47, etc. Confession of Thomas White 'concerning Hinnes', 30 March 1556. These were the confessions following the detection of the Dudley conspiracy.

27 Ruy Gómez was not alone in this opinion. Juan de Figueroa wrote to Granvelle on 26 July '. . . para hablar a V.S. verdad aunque no queria culpar a nadie los enbaxadores con los demas que aca estavan ninguna cosa tenien proveida de la necessaria para la disenbarcacion y asi anda una gran confusion . . .' Bib. Pal. Real, II – 2285 ff. 70-1. This reference was kindly supplied by Miss M. Rodríguez Salgado.

28 *Cal. Span.*, XIII, 49, 58, etc. Browne's dismissal became 'une affaire' because the English tried to use it as proof of the fact that Philip was

I   245 trying to avoid his obligation to employ Englishmen, under the marriage treaty.

29 Queen-dowager to the bishop of Arras, 14 August 1554. *Cal. Span.*, XIII, 26. Gammon, op. cit., 211-13.

30 BL Cotton MS Titus B II f. 162.

31 *A newe ballade of the Marigolde by William Forrest Preest* (STC 11186). Broadsheet 36 in the Library of the British Academy.

32 *A Balade specifienge partly the maner, partly the matter, in the most excellent meetyng and lyke marriage betwene our Sovereigne Lord and our Sovereigne Lady, the Kynges and Queenes highnes.* Broadsheet 37.

33 *Cal. Span.*, XIII, 81. Stroppiana also claimed to have been told by 'a great personage' that plans for his coronation were well in hand.

34 *Cal. Pat.*, III, 184. Pardon of Alice Perwicke of London. Mrs Perwicke had also added darkly 'that there be some about the Queen's Grace that will soon make her away, and that shortly . . .'

35 Deposition of Ralf Coles before the mayor and justices of Hereford, 13 May 1555. *HMC Thirteenth Report*, App., IV, 321 (City of Hereford MSS).

36 Federico Badoer to the doge and senate, 15 May 1555. *Cal. Ven.*, VI, 71. Some troops were redeployed by the emperor's orders, but Badoer was probably wrong in thinking that this had anything to do with the situation in England.

37 Statute 1 and 2 Philip and Mary, c. 10. Philip was also to enjoy the protection of such laws during his regency. For a full discussion of these debates and their significance, see Loach, 'Parliamentary Opposition in the Reign of Mary Tudor'.

38 Foxe, VII, 126. Foxe added 'This much, I say, I heard of the woman herself'.

39 Michieli to the doge and senate, 11 June 1555. *Cal. Ven.*, VI, 107. 'He has hitherto not only abstained from interfering and commanding as master, but would scarcely hear about anything at all, leaving this care to Queen Mary and her Council . . .'

40 *Cal. Span.*, XIII, 247.

41 The marriage between Count Feria and Jane Dormer, one of the queen's maids and the daughter of Sir William Dormer, did not take place until after Mary's death, although the couple had been betrothed for some time. Henry Clifford, *Life of Jane Dormer, Duchess of Feria*, ed. J. Stevenson (1887), 69-80. Spanish comments upon the attractiveness of English ladies were consistently unflattering.

42 *Cal. Span.*, XIII, 63-4. Charles seems to have been willing to leave the initiatives entirely to Philip, perhaps out of policy, or perhaps because of his poor health.

43 Philip seems to have interested himself considerably in the calling of this parliament, and later wrote as though the decision to call it had been his alone. See his instructions to Eraso. *Cal. Span.*, XIII, 92-5.

44 ibid.

45 *Cal. Span.*, XIII, 117.

46 Rosso had been a servant to the late duke of Ferrara, and had travelled to England in his service. His account, which he claimed had been read and approved by Michieli and Badoer, was dedicated to Lucretia and Leonora D'Este. It includes an oration on the reunion with Rome by Albertus Lollius. The five Roman tracts, bound in a single volume in the BL copy (G.6124), are: (i) La partita del serenissimo Principe con

l'armata di Spagna, & l'arrivata sua in Inghilterra, & l'ordine tenuto dalla Regina in ricevere Sua Altezza. (ii) La Vera capitulatione e Articoli passati e conclusi infra il Serenissimo Philippo d'Ispagnia, e la serenissima Regina Maria d'Inghilterra con il consenso de Principi Baroni e Popoli del detto Regno. (iii) La Solenne et felice intrata delli serenissimi Re Philippo et Regina Maria d'Inghilterra, nella Regal citta di Londra alli xviii d'Agosto. (iv) Copia delle lettere del Serenissimo Re d'Inghilterra e del Reverendissimo Card. Polo del la S. Sede Apostolica alla Santita di N.S. Iulio Papa III sopra la reduttione di quel Regno alla unione della Santa Madre Chiesa. (v) Il Felicissimo ritorno del regno d'Inghilterra alla cattolica unione. The authors or editors of these tracts are not known.

47 STC 7552.
48 *Viaje de Felipe II a Inglaterra* by Andres Muñoz (1554), ed. Sociedad de Bibliófilos Españoles, 15 (1877), 83-4.
49 AGS, E 377 f. 126; Luis Sarmiento to Francisco de Eraso, 25 February 1555. The cardinal of Siguenza was even more fulsome in his praise of the achievement, comparing Charles and Philip to Constantine in their service to the church. 'Yo no se por donde me comencasse encarecer esta Reducion de Inglaterra a la obediencia de la iglesía y creo que su magd. y la magd. del Rey se pueden tener por los mas bien aventurados hombres que ha havido grandes tiempos . . .' Siguenza to Granvelle, 22 December 1554. Bib. Pal. Real, II – 2286 ff. 326-9.
50 Paget's employment in this connection seems to have been a studied gesture of confidence. *Cal. Span.*, XIII, 87-92.
51 There is one mention only of them conferring directly with the English council, over the problems of finding lodgings for Spaniards in London. *Cal. Span.*, XIII, 60-2.
52 *Cal. Pat.*, II, .
53 PRO SP46/8/24.
54 Renard to Philip, undated but probably early January 1555. *Cal. Span.*, XIII, 128-31.
55 PRO SP11/5/2. Draft in the handwriting of Sir William Petre.
56 Renard to the emperor, 23 November 1554. *Cal. Span.*, XIII, 101.
57 *A Machiavellian Treatise by Stephen Gardiner*, edited and translated by P. S. Donaldson (1975). The ascription of the authorship of this work to Gardiner has been challenged by D. Fenlon in *Historical Journal*, 19, 4 (1976); and convincingly defended by Donaldson in a paper as yet unpublished.
58 There are two surviving MSS, the presentation copy itself (Escorial MS I. III. 17) and a less formal version at Besançon (MS 1169). For a discussion of the way in which Rainsford may have obtained and transmitted the work, see Donaldson, op. cit., Introduction, 4-15.
59 f. 135r-v; Donaldson, op. cit., 149-50.
60 ibid., Introduction, 16-21. Approximately 3000 words of Gardiner's text was taken verbatim from *The Prince* and *The Discourses*.
61 f. 86r – 87r. Donaldson, op. cit., 133.
62 Foxe, VII, 592; VII, 618. Gardiner seems to have been torn between his desire to see Elizabeth dead and his unwillingness to tamper with the judicial processes. Donaldson, op. cit., 33.
63 *Cal. Span.*, XIII, 90. The Margrave Charles of Baden was mentioned as a possibility. Charles expressed agreement with this idea, but warned

that the prince selected ought not to have territories on the coast.

64 After leaving England, Courtenay became convinced that he was being pursued by Habsburg assassins, and some of the attacks upon Spaniards in England may have been instigated by his friends out of revenge. He seems to have had some grounds for his fears, because according to the testimony of Marco da Risano the latter was hired by Ruy Gómez in August 1555 to kill him. *Cal. Ven.*, VI, 294. Whether Courtenay's death in Venice in September 1556 was natural or not remains a matter of dispute. M. Firpo, *Pietro Bizzari esuli italiano del cinquecento* (1971), 35n. Granvelle suggested sending Elizabeth to the queen-dowager's court, but his advice was not acted upon. Granvelle to Renard, 1 March 1555. *Cal. Span.*, XIII, 143.

65 Michieli to the doge and senate, 29 April 1555. *Cal. Ven.*, VI, 57.

66 Badoer to the doge and senate, 8 August 1555. *Cal. Ven.*, VI, 152.

67 Licentiate Games to the king of the Romans, 29 September 1555. *Cal. Span.*, XIII, 251.

68 Philip to the princess-regent of Spain, 18 September 1554. *Cal. Span.*, XIII, 48.

69 Draft letter in Philip's hand, 2 August 1555. *Cal. Span.*, XIII, 239. Michieli to the doge and senate, 9 September 1555. *Cal. Ven.*, VI, 182.

70 'First . . . that only catholics and persons not subject to suspicion should be elected; the second that they should take great care in their districts to punish offences against religion from now on; and the third that they should hear mass every day . . .' *Cal. Span.*, XIII, 239.

71 According to Michieli, the select council was to consist of Pole, Gardiner, Arundel, Pembroke, Winchester, Thirlby, Paget, and Petre. Harbison (259) follows this. However, according to a Latin memorandum preserved in the BL, Pole was only to be present for important matters, when he was able and willing, and Rochester is also named. Apart from Pole, this memorandum declares that all the named councillors were to be present for all business of state, finance, and debts. BL Cotton MS Titus B II f. 160, dated 29 August 1555.

72 *Cal. Ven.*, VI, 106, 173.

73 *Cal. Ven.*, VI, 167, 173, 199.

74 Anne Lady Capel to the earl of Rutland, 11 September 1555. *HMC Twelfth Report*, App., IV, 66 (Rutland MSS). The people again showed loyal enthusiasm at the sight of the queen, who had been in seclusion for some weeks.

75 J. I. Tellechea Idigoras, 'Bartolomé Carranza y la restauración católica inglesa (1553–1558)', *Anthologia Annua*, 12 (1964), 159-282.

76 *TTC*, 144-7.

77 This was Edward Randall, a very 'busy head' in conspiracy, and possibly a double agent. Noailles to Montmorency, 15 July 1555. Aff. Etr. IX, 489. Harbison, 271-2 and n.

78 STC 17562; STC 10024.

79 Michieli to the doge and senate, 1 July 1555. *Cal. Ven.*, VI, 126.

80 Montmorency to Noailles, 27 July 1555. Aff. Etr., IX, 498-9. Harbison, 271-2.

81 'Neither side had reached the point of preferring a compromise peace to continuation of the war; but each was persuaded – thanks to the pressure of exhausted resources, of public opinion and of Anglo-Papal mediation – that peace was worth discussing in the hope that the other side would yield'. Harbison, 245. This is the fullest and best discussion

of the negotiations.
82 Pole made the naïve suggestion that both sides should submit the dispute to an independent judge. The French agreed, hoping that a lengthy adjudication would give them the benefit of the *status quo*; Granvelle was forced to take refuge in equivocations, and the French took this opportunity to blame him for the breakdown. Early in August the English government protested that broadsheets, printed in France, were circulating in England, declaring that the emperor was responsible for the failure of the talks. Peace commissioners to the emperor, 30 May and 2 June; *Cal. Span.*, XIII, 198-206, 207-12. *Cal. Ven.*, VI, 149.
83 AGS, E 809 f. 1.
84 *Cal. Span.*, XIII, 154-6.
85 *Cal. Span.*, XIII, 171. Thirty votes were needed for victory.
86 Michieli to the doge and senate, 8 April 1555. *Cal. Ven.*, VI, 43.
87 *Cal. Span.*, XIII, 183-7.
88 Eraso to Juan Vásquez de Molina, 15 September 1555. *Cal. Span.*, XIII, 244.
89 Same to same, 23 September. ibid., 245.
90 Michieli reported on 1 October that such a fleet was being raised. It was in readiness by 14 October, and by 18 November the 15 ships and 2800 men had already cost £9631. Victuals were still being taken up by requisition in London at the beginning of December. *Cal. Ven.*, VI, 199. PRO SP11/6/61, 82, 83.
91 Philip clearly considered that his Spanish titles should have priority, but technically there was no crown of Spain – only the crown of Castile and the crowns of Aragon. The English council refused to yield precedence and the king eventually gave way.
92 PRO SP11/16-21, 82, 83. Some of Philip's replies are preserved in BL Cotton MS Titus B II ff. 114, 115, 116. Badoer to the doge and senate, 13 October 1555. *Cal. Ven.*, VI, 212.
93 *Cal. Ven.*, VI, 277-8.
94 Badoer to the doge and senate, 27 October 1555. *Cal. Ven.*, VI, 227.
95 Same to same, 19 November. *Cal. Ven.*, VI, 253.
96 Bullinger to Calvin. *OL*, II, 751.
97 For a full discussion of this plot and its outcome, see *TTC*, 151-217.
98 *Cal. Span.*, XIII, 255.
99 *TTC*, 186.
100 Wotton to Mary, 12 April 1556. *Cal. For.*, 222. *TTC*, 192 and n.
101 ibid., 218-37.
102 Harbison, 292-4. François was not immediately available and a third brother, Gilles, was sent over 'to keep the seat warm'.
103 Badoer to the doge and senate, 26 April 1556. *Cal. Ven.*, VI, 419. What this vague threat might have meant in the aftermath of Henri's failure to support the Dudley conspiracy is not clear.
104 Badoer to the doge and senate, 15 March 1556. *Cal. Ven.*, VI, 376.
105 Same to same, 8 April 1556. ibid., 401. '. . . la Regina desidera il marito, et lei se ne cura poco'. Giacomo Soranzo, ambassador in France, to the doge and senate. *Cal. Ven.*, VI, 410.
106 *Cal. Span.*, XIII, 276. This was Mary's final plea to Charles, who had probably embarked before it arrived.
107 *The Copye of a letter sent by John Bradforthe to the right honorable lordes the Erles of Arundel, Derbie, Shrewsburye and Penbroke, declaring the nature of Spaniards, and discovering the most detestable treasons*

which thei have pretended moste falselye agaynste our most noble Kingdome of England (1556) (STC 3480).

108 ibid. At the same time John Ponet was writing in Strasbourg: 'But thou wilt saie; it is the Queenes owne, and she maie lawfully do with her owne what she lusteth . . . But I answer that albeit she have it be enheritaunce yet she hath it with an othe, lawe and condicion to kepe and mayntene it, not to departe with it nor diminishe it . . .' *Shorte Treatise of Politike Power*, sig. E iiv.

109 There are two versions of this pamphlet. The BL and CU Library copies contain the anti-protestant disclaimers referred to. The version reproduced by Strype (*Ecc. Mem.*, III, 2, xiv) is much more protestant in tone. For a discussion of the relationship between these versions, see my note in *TCBS*, III, 2, 1960.

110 PRO SP11/8/43.

111 *Cal. Ven.*, VI, 218.

112 *APC*, V, 305, 315, etc.

113 ibid., 295-6.

114 BL Lansdowne MS 170 f. 129.

115 ibid., f. 141. The position of the adventurers was particularly strong at this time in view of the assistance which they were providing for the discharge of the foreign debt.

116 Badoer to the doge and senate, 17 May 1556. *Cal. Ven.*, VI, 452. See also *TTC*, 122-4.

117 Michieli to the doge and senate, 21 April 1556. *Cal. Ven.*, VI, 417.

118 Badoer to the doge and senate, 19 July 1556. *Cal. Ven.*, VI, 530.

119 *Cal. Ven.*, VI, 768.

120 Paul was persuaded to declare Philip deprived of the kingdom of Naples on the pretext of non-payment of feudal dues. For a good brief account of these events, see Ramón Menéndez Pidal, *España en el tiempo de Felipe II* (Historia de España, t. XIX, 1958), 387-404.

121 Bassefontaine to Gilles de Noailles, 2 August 1556. Aff. Etr., XIII f. 35; Harbison, 299.

122 Gilles de Noailles to Montmorency, 30 August 1556, Aff. Etr., XIII f. 46. Harbison, 304.

123 PRO SP11/9/50.

124 *Cal. Ven.*, VI, 907. The incident concerned had occurred on the night of 5/6 Jan.

125 BL Cotton MS Titus C VII ff. 198 *et seq.* This draft is without date or ascription, but the reference to 'the present situation' as one of war probably places it after 11 January 1557. Whether it is a sort of 'consulta' from either the select council or the privy council as a whole, or merely the opinion of two or more individuals, is not clear, but the advice which it gives corresponds very closely with the line taken by the council over the following three months. Although not specifically so directed, it was clearly intended for Mary alone.

126 Philip's instructions to Ruy Gómez, 2 February 1557. *Cal. Span.*, XIII, 285. Paget had not taken a markedly pro-Habsburg line during the discussions before Christmas, and only moved cautiously in favour of war after Ruy Gómez's visit.

127 See particularly Wotton's letters to Petre and the queen of 21 January 1557. *Cal. For.*, Mary, 284-5. The ambassador himself half suspected that these plots were more designed to spread confusion in England than produce real action.

128 Surian to the doge and senate, 3 April 1557. *Cal. Ven.*, VI, 1004. Feria had told Surian that '. . . it is in his Majesty's power to make the country wage war against France when and in what manner he chooses . . .'

129 François de Noailles to Montmorency, 5 April 1557. Aff. Etr., XIII ff. 182-3. Harbison, 324. This reply was also translated into Latin for Philip's benefit. Froude, [*Mary Tudor*], 286, quotes from a different version in BL Sloane MS 1786.

130 One of the arguments which the council had used consistently against war was that Henri had offered no challenge or provocation. For a consideration of the circumstances of this incident, and its interpretation, see below, 363-7.

131 Philip to the bishop of Arras. *Cal. Span.*, XIII, 291.

132 Paget apparently argued, during a week of audiences with Philip, that it would be possible for him to create a 'magnate' party which would support him fully, but only if he was prepared to return. Paget was not only fighting an uphill battle against the king's reluctance, but also against the full influence of his Spanish servants and courtiers. According to Badoer, Philip again attempted to make his coronation a condition of his return. *Cal. Ven.*, VI, 415. BL Sloane MS 147 f. 178. Gammon, op. cit., 228-9.

133 Michieli to the doge and senate, 16 June 1556. *Cal. Ven.*, VI, 484.

134 Simon Renard to Philip, 12 January 1557. *Cal. Span.*, XIII, 285.

8 The Government at Work 1554–1557

When the ceremonies attendant upon the marriage, the progress to London, and the solemn entry there upon 18 August had been completed, and the participants suitably rewarded by the king, the majority of the English nobility withdrew temporarily to their estates. 'At present', wrote Soranzo on the day of the entry, 'the bishop of Winchester has the management of everything . . .',[1] and his judgement is confirmed by the fact that Paget was one of those to withdraw. However, the latter had not been idle, or unsuccessful in his bid for rehabilitation. Renard's attempts to brand his erstwhile ally as a heretic and intriguer were already redounding painfully upon the ambassador's head. Ruy Gómez, who had such a low opinion of Renard's abilities, was inclined to give Paget whatever credit there was for bringing the marriage to a successful consummation, and his voice carried weight both with Philip and in Brussels.[2] Paget had also made it his business to gain the sympathetic ear of the king himself. However, Philip had no intention of rekindling the quarrel between Paget and the chancellor, so the latter's ascendancy in the council was only gradually eroded over the following twelve months.

In his recent study of the working of Mary's council, Dr Lemsaters has argued that Philip supplied what had hitherto been lacking, a strong and coherent royal will;[3] and consequently the council worked very much more efficiently as an advisory body after his arrival. There is, however, very little direct evidence of how the king dealt with his English advisers. On 27 July it was recorded in the council minutes '. . . that a note of all such matters of Estate as shuld pass from hence should be made in Laten or Spanyshe from hensefourth and the same to be delivered to suche as it shuld please the Kinges Heighnes tappointe to receyve it'. Whether such notes were ever made is uncertain, because none survive,[4] and it seems likely that Philip soon developed a different method of communication. He never attended formal sessions of the council, any more than Mary had done, but from his own letters and from the comments of observers, it is clear that he conferred frequently, and perhaps regularly, with certain chosen members. The membership of this 'inner group' was probably not fixed or formalized in any way at this stage. According to Soranzo the most influential councillors after Gardiner were Arundel, Paget, and Petre.[5] The names of Thirlby, Pembroke, Bedford, and Rochester are also mentioned as being in high confidence and regard; in other words, almost exactly the same men who had formed the political core of the council since the beginning of the reign. On 23 November 1554 Renard, not by this time a very well-informed source, reported that Paget's attempts to persuade Philip to formalize this 'select council' had provoked violent dissension '. . . especially as the new list did not include the High Treasurer, the Controller, Walgrave, the Lord Warden, Inglefield, Southwell, Baker, Peckham and Secretary Bourne, who consider themselves to be as deserving as those who, as they say, rebelled against and resisted the Queen . . .'[6] Perhaps this year-old grievance was still smouldering, or perhaps Renard was extrapolating from his previous experience to disguise his increasing ignorance of the real situation. If the latter, it was a foolish and dangerous course because Charles had many other sources of information, including the king himself. For this reason it does not do to discount entirely the ambassador's continued talk of divisions and jealousies, although it is very likely that he exaggerated. The French certainly continued to feed their hopes with talk of feuds and factions. After the failure of the negotiations at La Marque, in August 1555, Henri delivered himself of the judgement that it was impossible to negotiate with the English '. . . because what one does the other undoes by reason of their partialities and disunion, most especially between the right reverend Chancellor and Lord Paget'.[7] At the end of the following year, when reporting advices out of England from the French court, Soranzo ended by saying casually that the English council was divided 'as usual', the latest quarrel being between Paget and Pole.[8]

Philip very seldom consulted his English and Spanish advisers together, and was usually careful to talk to the former as a group only in the presence of the queen. Theoretically '. . . all matters of Estate passing in the King and Queenes name shuld be signed with both their handes', but in practice Mary seems to have asserted herself very little in the conduct of business during her husband's residence in England. On the other hand, as we have seen, Philip's Spanish servants continued to speak of his humiliating position, his exclusion from the government, and lack of real power – a picture which is supported to some extent by the testimony of the Venetian ambassador. What seems to have happened is that the king concerned himself intensively with certain kinds of business, notably negotiations over the reconciliation with Rome, but for the most part was content to ensure that the council functioned as efficiently as its composition and the cross-grained nature of some of its members would permit. The hostility with which he was generally regarded in England quickly persuaded him that in all domestic matters it must at least appear that decisions came from the queen and council, and that his own role was merely supporting. Two developments might have changed that situation: the birth of an heir or his own coronation, and from September 1554 to May 1555 the queen was believed to be carrying a child. Paget and his noble associates, particularly Arundel and Pembroke, seem to have been convinced that only Philip's active and increased involvement in English affairs could guarantee stable and efficient government,[9] but without an heir the king's authority was uncertain and possibly of short duration. They envisaged an active partnership between Philip and themselves, in which he would provide the controlling will, and they would give it an acceptable English face. They were not, however, prepared to risk abrogating the marriage treaty by allowing the king to exercise the full rights of sovereignty which belonged by inheritance and English law to Mary. How far they were prepared to abet his schemes for a coronation is uncertain. Rumour credited Arundel, Derby, Shrewsbury, and Pembroke, particularly Shrewsbury, with such designs, but if they ever existed, they must have been pursued with great discretion and not too much determination. To judge from the report of his interview with the emperor in November 1554, Paget planned to keep his political options open, ostensibly committing himself to Philip's cause, but carefully refraining from suggesting any course of action which would have specifically altered his position, such as excluding Elizabeth from the succession or declaring war on France.[10]

Gardiner, who felt his control of affairs to be slipping away in the face of Paget's continued hostility and the queen's obvious regard for Pole, seems to have decided by the summer of 1555 to work unreservedly for Philip's sovereignty, but he had accomplished nothing of significance before sickness and death supervened. During his first year in England the king was very much divided between his desire to exploit every opportunity of increasing his authority and his instinct to let events take their course, in the hope that the birth of an heir and the self-interest of the English politicians would give him the position which he desired, without running the obvious risks attendant upon a more overt search for

power. In the event he was disappointed, not only by Mary's failure
to bear a child, but also by the fact that the parliament did virtually
nothing to emancipate him from the restrictions of the marriage
treaty. Consequently the effect of Philip's presence upon the
government of England can only be inferred. He almost certainly
increased the *de facto* distinction between the inner council and
the privy council as a whole, dealing with the latter only through
the former, mainly by means of the principal secretary, Sir William
Petre.[11] The decision in May 1555 to create a council seal was a
reflection of this development. Council letters were normally
authenticated by the signatures of the councillors present, and this
practice continued, the use of the new seal being confined to the
more important and confidential documents emanating from the
'council of state'.[12] At the same time the king intervened effectively
to subdue the personal quarrels and rivalries which Mary had
found so intractable. These were not removed, but the protagonists
knew better than to allow their feelings to hold up business in
which the king was taking an interest. To outside observers it was
clear that Philip had a following of a sort among the English lords,
many of whom were his pensioners,[13] and that the queen, although
diligent in her application to affairs, was content to play a secondary role. On the other hand, it was by no means clear what benefits he had derived from this situation. He had no patronage of his
own in England, and there is no evidence to suggest that he made
any serious attempt to influence that of the queen or of the major
English office-holders. No Englishman was promoted to any title
of honour, either in England, or Spain, or the empire by his means,
and his only assiduous clients seem to have been unemployed
soldiers and sea captains, many of whom had been in trouble for
sedition and who, like Cuthbert Vaughn and Edward Randall,
sought pardon and service at his hands.[14] Even allowing for the fact
that much of his time and attention was taken up with affairs outside England, contemporaries can be forgiven for feeling that his
position was not that of a king as they understood it. Imperialists,
French, and Venetians alike blamed this upon the intractability of
the English, and their hatred and suspicion of foreigners. But it
may well have been that Philip, inhibited by problems of communication and regarding his island subjects with the liveliest distate,
simply did not apply himself with sufficient consistency or diligence
to make the most of his ill-defined authority.

The fact that he could act decisively and effectively when he
chose was demonstrated, as we have seen, by the provision which
he made for the operation of the government during his absence.
This consisted in the formal establishment of a council of state

255

quibus specialem Curam omnium causarum Status, Finantiarum aliarum Causarum Graviorum Regni, committendam duximus committimus . . .

which was almost certainly the existing inner council which had been functioning since the previous autumn. 'Decisions', Michieli noted on 9 September 1555, 'are made as hitherto'.[15] The privy council proper was now specifically relegated to formal and routine business, and the queen, significantly enough, was nowhere mentioned. The council of state was to report direct to the king, and to meet together with the remainder of the council on Sundays, when it might communicate to the larger body such of its special business as it thought fit. This select council seems to have worked very much as Philip intended, and fragments of its correspondence with the king survive, indicating not only that it kept him informed about English domestic affairs, but that it periodically felt it necessary to defend the country's interests against the demands of Philip's *Weltpolitik*.[16] The membership also remained substantially unchanged. Gardiner was a very sick man by the time the king left, and although he was consulted about business during his last illness, he can have played little part in the work of the council before his death on 12 November. His place was eventually taken by his successor as chancellor, Nicholas Heath, and there seems to have been no other change of membership until Sir William Petre's retirement in March 1557.[17] Presumably it was this council of state rather than the privy council as a whole, which so strongly resisted the united pressure of the king and queen for war in the early months of 1557. Pole is mentioned frequently as an active opponent of war, but his participation in the work of the council 'in Causis magnis, ubi voluerit, & commode poterit' had been provided for in its formal establishment. It may be that, under the pressure of this crisis, the distinction between the two councils again became blurred, but more likely the debate proper was confined to the select council, and the 'divisions' referred to by commentators signified mainly a difference of opinion between Pole and Paget. Paget, with the possible support of Arundel and Pembroke, seems to have maintained a minority position in favour of war until circumstances came to the king's aid at the end of April, as we have seen.[18]

In one respect, however, Philip's plan was clearly not carried out. Contact between the council of state and the privy council remained a great deal closer than he had intended. The provision for Sunday meetings suggests that the king did not envisage his councillors of state maintaining a regular presence at routine administrative meetings, but they certainly did so. Petre, Rochester, Heath, and Thirlby continued to be the most assiduous attenders, and on several occasions when the only recorded business was of a purely routine nature members of the select council formed either a large majority or the whole of 'Thapparaunce'. There were also 'grey areas' where the jurisdiction of the two councils overlapped. For example, when the merchants of the Steelyard, pursuing their intermittent feud with the city of London, brought a complaint against the mayor and aldermen for breach of their privileges and unjust detention of goods, it was heard and adjudicated by the privy council on 23 March 1556, and duly recorded in the council register.[19] However, when the merchants of Brabant complained against the council's order suspending cloth exports, their complaint was heard by the select council on 17 October, a day on which no routine council meeting is recorded.[20] Both complaints were heard by the same group of men – except that Rochester was present at the latter meeting, but not at the former. The senior council clerk probably attended upon the select council, and wrote whatever letters or other documents resulted from its deliberations, while the junior clerk kept the minutes of the privy council.[21] This must have been slightly tidier than the old practice of excluding the clerks whenever important or controversial political matters were under discussion – but the effect was exactly the same. Since the average attendance at recorded privy council meetings between June 1554 and June 1557 was no more than ten, in practice the two councils must have consisted substantially of the same body of men, conducting rather imperfectly differentiated business, but distinguished clearly by the presence or absence of official records.

The administrative functions of the privy councillors become slightly clearer when we look away from council meetings proper to the *ad hoc* committees and commissions which continued to occupy a considerable proportion of their working time. Seventeen privy seal commissions including one or more councillors were issued between July 1554 and June 1557, and a total of twenty-five councillors served on one or more of them. The hardest workers were Englefield, who belonged to twelve of them, Waldegrave with eleven, and Baker and Thirlby with ten each. Every member of the select council served on at least one, and Thirlby, Winchester (8), and Rochester (8) were among the most assiduous. During this period nine councillors died, and only three were appointed, so the total number dropped from 43 to 37. Of the latter number, 16 did not serve on any commission, 22 attended less than one-fifth of the possible privy council meetings, and 13 did not function in either capacity. Several of these inoperative councillors, such as Shrewsbury, Cheney, and Wentworth, were absent because of official duties or active in the service of the crown in other ways. Others, such as Strelly and Robert Peckham, were not active in any way which can be readily traced. In fact Philip's preference for working with a small 'inner council' for all important business, and the consequent establishment of the select council upon a formal basis, seem to have made virtually no difference to the working of the council in its administrative capacity, and less than might be expected to its advisory functions. The 'reduction in the numbers of the council', so warmly advocated by Renard and others from the early days of the reign, was accomplished by continuing the gradual process of establishing distinctions of function. The select councillors handled all kinds of business in the manner of the Cromwellian or Elizabethan privy council; and they were joined by others, mostly professional administrators or men experienced in financial affairs, for the more routine work of administration. In March or April of 1555 Renard, who was still trying to maintain a toehold near the centre of affairs, sent the king an unsolicited memorandum upon the government of England, in which he advised that

> . . . the choice [for a reduced Council] should fall upon the Chancellor, the Treasurer, Arundel, Paget, Petre, the Bishop of Ely, the Controller and Inglefield for routine matters and questions of state. It should also be declared that when the great lords of the country, like the Earls of Shrewsbury and Pembroke, are at court, they should be admitted to the Council, and that when they are absent they will be consulted.[22]

This is close enough to what actually happened to make it seem likely that the ambassador was trying to claim a share of the credit for reforms which he knew were already in hand. However, the suggestion of Englefield rather than Pembroke for the 'inner ring' indicates that Renard was still very alive to the rivalry between Paget and Gardiner, and was supporting the latter. There is no evidence to suggest that the 'great lords of the country' were consulted in any systematic fashion, but some of them did attend routine council meetings when they were in London for other reasons, such as attendance at parliament.

Philip's residence in England was important for the functioning of the council in two ways. Firstly, as we have seen, his presence subdued the personal feuds which had previously disrupted business, and secondly the confidence which he reposed in Paget enabled the latter to resume the function of management which he had exercised in the first year of the reign, but had temporarily lost during his disgrace in the summer of 1554. At the beginning of August 1555 Federico Badoer reported from Brussels that Paget had lost all favour with the emperor because of his alleged secret dealings with the French at La Marque, but even if Badoer was right, Philip does not seem to have been influenced by his father's change of attitude.[23] When Gardiner died, the king did his best to persuade Mary to appoint Paget to the chancellorship, but after a long hesitation, she refused, perhaps because she still distrusted him, but more likely because she believed that the office should go to an ecclesiastic.[24] Paget did, however, receive the lesser but still prestigious office of lord privy seal, which had been vacant since the death of the earl of Bedford on 14 March 1555. As a contemporary somewhat caustically observed, it was from Philip that 'all favours shown to him proceed, nor does he fail to seek them by all means and with all his might'.[25] Paget's right-hand man on the council was Sir William Petre, with whom he had collaborated closely since the beginning of the reign. When there was talk of Petre's resignation in November 1554, Paget had said that '. . . he ought not to be allowed to do so, but kept in office, for he had been there so long that he was as good as a Council register . . .' Petre had probably played an important part in bringing Paget, Pembroke, and Arundel back in September 1554 to their seats at a board which was still dominated by Gardiner and his friends.[26] He had never been caught up in the rumours of conspiracy, or diminished in the queen's confidence, and one or two otherwise unexplained journeys at that time may indicate that he was acting as a peacemaker or go-between. His assiduity as a councillor was unsurpassed by any save Gardiner, and he handled all the diplomatic correspondence, first of the 'inner ring' and then of the council of state. Wotton particularly addressed many letters and reports to Petre alone rather than to the council as a whole, especially if he was uncertain as to the validity or use of the information he was sending, referring its presentation to Petre's experience and discretion. Like Paget, Petre was unenthusiastic about the policy of religious persecution, although he made pious benefactions and was never referred to as a heretic even by the most zealous romanist. Unlike Paget, however, the secretary tended to be personally hostile to the Spaniards, and finally parted company with his friend over the issue of war in the early part of 1557. The circumstances surrounding his resignation of the secretaryship in late March are obscure. Ill-health may have been the pretext, but is not substantiated by other evidence. To have resigned as a protest against the pressure towards war, as his biographer suggests, would have been a most dangerous move, bordering on sedition.[27] Perhaps the most likely explanation is that the indignant Mary, angered by Petre's opposition to her wishes, allowed him to resign as an alternative to dismissal. However, he retained his seat on the council, continued to be a frequent attender, and continued to draft a considerable proportion of the council's correspondence. Whether he retained his place on the select council is not clear, but since his drafts of diplomatic letters continue without a break, it is possible that he did.

The nature of Petre's position in the spring of 1557 is only one of a number of unresolved problems. For example, Cardinal Pole, who was the closest person in England to Mary after Philip's departure, and exercised great influence over her, never seems to have taken a councillor's oath, despite his active intervention in the deliberations of the select council over the war issue. Nor is it clear in what sense Henry Lord Abergavenny and George Lord Cobham were 'the King's and Queen's councillors', as they were described in a commission of 25 April 1556.[28] Cobham had taken a council oath in 1550, but Abergavenny is not on record as having done so, and neither served Philip and Mary in that capacity. Were there then three categories of councillor after August 1555: select (who could attend all meetings, and were required to be present 'in Aula' to deliberate matters of high policy); privy (who could attend formal meetings but who were not necessarily expected to do so unless they were at court for other reasons); and 'miscellaneous' (who did not attend meetings, but who were expected to be available for specific services when called upon)?[29] If so, then the concept of 'the council' as a single governing body is hardly applicable. The distinctions of status, very noticeable in the first year of the reign, have become increasingly formalized, to the point at which the omnicompetent Cromwellian council has really disappeared. Paget was a Cromwellian in the sense that he accepted his mentor's priorities, and believed in 'government under the crown', but the initiative for this hierarchical structure came from him, and seems to have produced a system of government significantly different, both from that of the 1530s and from that which Elizabeth and Cecil were subsequently to create.

In terms of personnel, this middle period of the reign was one of stability. By far the most significant change in high office was wrought by the death of Stephen Gardiner. On 14 November 1555 the great seal was put into commission to Sir Nicholas Hare and others, and after a lengthy debate, which provoked some critical comment abroad, he was succeeded on 1 January 1556 by Nicholas Heath, the archbishop of York. Heath was a very different kind of man from his predecessor; a competent and irenic administrator, without any of Gardiner's capacity for intrigue, or his forceful political intelligence. He had no ambition to exercise a dominant voice in decisions of policy, and was scarcely referred to by observers of the English scene, either foreign or domestic. The second important change in high office, however, was a different matter. On 14 March 1555 John Russell, earl of Bedford, died at the age of seventy; and for the next nine months the office of keeper of the privy seal was discharged by Sir Robert Rochester.[30] Rochester received no patent of appointment, and the position remained vacant throughout that period. The reasons for this long delay are obscure, but there may well have been a disagreement between Philip and Mary, and the former for diplomatic reasons did not wish to be too insistent. Eventually, on 31 December, as we have seen, Lord Paget was appointed with Philip's support, having failed to secure the chancellorship. Whether the possession of this office really made much difference to his power may be doubted. No doubt the additional income of £365 a year was welcome, but the real gain was in honour and prestige, and in the formal reconciliation with the queen which his appointment signified. Petre was replaced as principal secretary on 30 March 1557 by the insignificant John Boxall,[31] but the formal loss to the government which this change represented seems to have been mitigated by the fact that Petre continued to discharge many of the functions of the office. Other changes were of a minor nature, and seem to have had no political significance. Sir John Bridges, Lord Chandos, resigned as lieutenant of the Tower, perhaps because of ill-health, and was replaced on 28 October 1555 by Sir Henry Bedingfield.[32] On 8 October 1554 Sir Richard Morgan was replaced as chief justice of common pleas on the grounds of his infirmity; his successor was Sir Robert Broke.[33] Sir Thomas Bromley, the chief justice of queen's bench, died in 1555 and was replaced by Sir William Portman, who in turn was replaced by Sir Edward Saunders in May 1557.[34] Only in the northern marches did changes take place which seem to be traceable to shifts in royal policy. As we have seen, after serving in the early months of the reign in an undefined capacity, Thomas Lord Wharton had been displaced from office at the end of 1553. On 30 July 1555 he was reappointed to the wardenry of the Middle March, the keepership of Tynedale and Redesdale, and the stewardship of Hexhamshire. At the same time he became constable of Alnwick castle, still at that time in the hands of the crown.[35] On 16 December 1555 he became again warden of the East March and steward of Rothbury, posts to which he added the captaincy of Berwick on 16 August 1556,[36] thus completing his establishment as a dominant figure in the English Marches. However, by May 1557 his position had been heavily undermined through the re-erection of the earldom of Northumberland, and on the 5th of that month he wrote to the king and queen complaining that he was being defamed by private enemies.[37] His request for a clarification of his position was not answered until 2 August, when the earl of Northumberland was joined with him in commission in all his major offices – the wardenries of the two Marches, the keeperships of the Dales, and the captaincy of Berwick. A week later all these offices were granted to Northumberland alone, Sir James Croftes being given by the council the thankless task of breaking the news to Wharton and '. . . to persuade him to be satisfied therewith'.[38] The reason for this revival and rapid extinction of Wharton's authority is not clear, unless it can be explained by fluctuating influences at court, which may be deduced from his own letter. The queen's decision to restore the Percies to their former glory was fatal to him, but why she waited until 1557 in order to do so is not apparent, unless it was a response to the prospect of open war with Scotland.

Rather surprisingly, the marriage at first made no difference to England's diplomatic representation. It was not until December 1555 that Michieli reported the queen's decision to recall all her ambassadors, except from France, and to rely henceforth upon her husband's agents.[39] If the Venetian was right, the decision took a long time to implement. Sir John Mason was not recalled from Brussels until Charles departed for Spain in September 1556, and Peter Vannes returned from Venice at about the same time, neither being replaced.[40] On the other hand, Sir Edward Carne remained at his difficult and invidious post in Rome, technically as an ambassador from both Philip and Mary, throughout the period of war between Philip and the papacy. After Wotton's recall from France on the outbreak of hostilities in June 1557, Carne was the only English diplomat resident abroad for the remainder of the reign. Conversely, when Michel Surian replaced Michieli in March 1557, he was accredited to the person of King Philip, and remained in England only as long as the king remained.[41] Renard having withdrawn in September 1555, and François de Noailles on the declaration of war, there was thus no diplomatic representation of a permanent nature in England during the last eighteen months of the reign, a situation not calculated to flatter English pride or self-esteem.

Philip's arrival, as we have seen, caused great and unexpected complications in the court because of his double household. The mere problems of feeding and accommodating such a multitude overtaxed the available resources, in addition to the quarrels and misunderstandings. Although the English palaces are enormous, wrote one disgruntled Spaniard, no rooms had been provided for the duchess of Alva, and in spite of the great profusion of food available, the earl of Arundel as lord steward had ordered economies in the number of dishes served.[42] The king's whole retinue, disregarding the soldiers who were not allowed to land, numbered between two and three thousand, although this multitude must have been rapidly reduced as some lords were allowed to withdraw, and others were sent on missions. As we have seen, Philip gradually sorted out the problem of his household, although not to everyone's satisfaction. Sir Anthony Browne, whose removal provoked particular discontent, was dismissed without, apparently, being replaced. On the other hand, Sir John Williams, Lord Williams of Thame, 'camerera mayor', continued to serve throughout the reign; and Sir John Huddlestone, the vice-chamberlain, until his death in 1557. At the end of the reign the former was owed £673 in arrears of wages, and the heirs of the latter £136 5s.[43] Of the hundred archers of Philip's English guard, 96 were still on the payroll in 1558, and sums were noted as being due to the heirs of the remaining 4 who had died.[44] Similarly, of the 7 young lords who had been appointed to serve as 'chamberlones', Fitzwalter, Strange, Hastings, and Talbot were still in office when Mary died, in spite of the fact that the first named had succeeded to the earldom of Sussex in the meantime.[45] Maltravers had died, while Herbert and Surrey had ceased to serve, the latter possibly because of his succession to the dukedom of Norfolk within days of the king's arrival. Below this level, the discrepancies between the list of June 1554 and that of late 1558 become considerable. Of the 8 'gentiles hombres de la boca' who appear on the latter, 5 can be readily identified upon the former; but of the 4 'gentiles hombres de la cassa' and 5 'castilleros', only one in each category. Altogether 49 persons were originally named to serve 'above stairs', and 57 are recorded as being owed money for similar services in 1558, but only 15 can be identified with certainty on both lists.[46] This may be partly because the Spanish forms of English names are frequently so eccentric as to be unrecognizable, and partly because the king's needs were not correctly assessed. For example, a veritable team of six interpreters made their appearance in addition to the three 'aids to the chamber' originally provided. Of the latter, one had died, and the other two were still in receipt of wages.[47] What happened to the considerable household 'below stairs' which had been named in 1554 is not clear, but it was probably never required and never functioned. How many of those who remained on the payroll actually attended upon the king regularly, or for any length of

263

time, is another matter. The early disputes were resolved by compromise, and it is very unlikely that Philip ever had as many as 50 English noblemen and gentlemen attending upon him at one time, since he never dispensed entirely with the Spanish advisers and servants. When he left England in August 1555, as we have seen, he left a number of these servants behind,[48] but there is no reason to suppose that he took any substantial part of his English household with him. He was accompanied by an unspecified number of 'English lords', who were soon grumbling and wanting to come home, but only Maltravers and Hastings are named as 'his Majesty's chamber attendants'. An honorific escort consisting of Pembroke, Huntingdon, Paget, Wentworth, and Howard accompanied the king as far as Brussels, but did not remain long. Maltravers and Hastings may have stayed for several weeks, along with 'some others of inferior grade', but essentially the household was 'stood down' until Philip returned to England in March 1557.[49]

The queen's household had been carefully constructed in the first year of the reign, and thereafter showed few changes other than those brought about by the deaths of office-holders. Thus the chamberlain, Sir John Gage, died in the summer of 1556 and was replaced by Sir Edward Hastings, Jerningham becoming master of the horse, and Bedingfield vice-chamberlain. Sir Robert Rochester, the controller, and Mary's long-serving confidant, died in the autumn of 1557 and was replaced by Sir Thomas Cornwallis; and Sir Richard Freston, the cofferer, also died in 1557, his place being given to Richard Ward. Below stairs there was some rationalization as long-serving yeomen who had been displaced in the early reorganization regained their places, either by purchase or by waiting until their supplanters had been promoted elsewhere.[50] In spite of constant urging from the council, no significant economies were achieved until the fourth year of the reign. Indeed the year of Philip's residence saw many expensive entertainments in addition to the marriage itself,[51] and expenses rose by almost 30 per cent. In the following year, which was much quieter and during which the queen's health was frequently poor, there was a slight improvement, but not enough to be satisfactory.[52] As a result, economies were planned in the autumn of 1556. On 22 September, Michieli reported

> They have commenced regulating the expenses of the court . . .
> having already broken the 50 gentlemen pensioners of the axe
> . . . and with them also the other 50 yeomen of the guard. . . .[53]

What the ambassador meant by 'broken' is not clear. The implication of his letter is that the pensioners and yeomen had been dismissed, but this was certainly not the case. Since he had also been informed that the pensioners were paid £50 a year each and the yeomen £25, the whole report seems to be mistaken. However, there was a very marked reduction in the cost of the household during the year 1556-57, which at £47,552 was the lowest since the third year of King Edward VI.[54] The germ of Michieli's story was probably a considerable reduction in the number of days attendance required of each individual. The pensioners and gentlemen at arms attended on average only 20 days during the fourth year of the reign, and the whole bill for the bouge of court of these two groups was no more than £208 12s. 6d.[55] There are no visible signs of factions or parties in the court during this short period, although the French ambassador continued to have sources of inside information, and Edward Lewkenor, a groom porter who was responsible for the supply of playing-cards, died in prison as a result of his involvement in the Dudley conspiracy of 1556.[56] After Philip's departure Pole was given regular accommodation at court, and became an increasingly important influence upon the queen, but there is no sign that he attempted to exercise any control over the personnel of the household. The discipline of the court had always been a problem, and Mary had been compelled to issue a proclamation in December 1553 expelling vagabonds and masterless men from the environs.[57] After Philip's arrival this problem had been compounded, as we have seen, by the number of hangers-on with no official standing who had followed the Habsburg train. On 15 September 1554 a further proclamation was directed against

> . . . such vagabonds and idle persons, as well Englishmen as strangers, as under the name of servingmen (being nevertheless masterless) do lurk about the court and the cities of London and Westminster . . .[58]

ordering them to depart within five days. Not only were such men a nuisance and possibly an expense, they also constituted a threat to law and order, and even possibly to the security of the monarch's person. In the public atmosphere of a sixteenth-century court such risks could never be eliminated, and theoretically the sovereign's personal servants continued to have the quasi-military responsibility of defending him against brawl, insurrection, or assassination. On 6 August 1556 '. . . my Lordes of the Counsaill, upon consideration of the state of thinges at this tyme . . . for the preventing of all inconveniences that might happen, and saveguard of the King and Queenes Majesties persones' decided to overhaul this antique security system. The controller, the treasurer, and the vice-chamberlain were ordered to muster the household '. . . and to enquire what armour and weapon eache of them hathe, giving them streight charge and commandment . . . that every of them do prepare suche armour and weapon . . . as shalbe prescribed unto them . . .' not later than Michaelmas next.[59] This may have been no more than a sensible routine precaution, but the widespread ramifications of the Dudley conspiracy which had recently been unravelled point to a more specific source of apprehension.

With the probable exception of the promotion of Lord Paget to the office of lord privy seal, Philip had no demonstrable influence upon the personnel of either the government or the court. In this respect the marriage treaty was very strictly observed. Not only were Spaniards and other Habsburg subjects carefully excluded from office in England, no grants of land were made to such aliens,[60] and the small number of pensions and trading concessions which can be traced were no greater than in other periods of comparable length. As we shall see, a small number of academic and ecclesiastical posts were given to Spanish theologians, but this was in accordance with precedent and caused no political comment. The extent to which the king attracted the loyalty and support of Englishmen who were already in office is hard to assess because except for pensions the rewards which he had to offer were uncertain. Englishmen who were out of favour with the queen, on the other hand, frequently sought out Philip as a means of repairing their fortunes, and in spite of the exacting religious standards which he imposed upon his household servants, they often received a favourable hearing. For example, on 24 November 1555 Federico Badoer reported that Sir Philip Hoby had been graciously received in Brussels, and that Sir Peter Carew had been pardoned by Mary on the king's intercession, 'who confers any favour he can on any Englishman, however ill-disposed he may be, with a view to obtaining their services in the affairs of that kingdom'.[61] It would be interesting to know how much of the queen's supposed clemency was due to this kind of interested pressure. Ambrose, Henry, and Robert Dudley, all pardoned in January 1555, fought at St Quentin in 1557, where Henry was killed. Sir James Croftes and Cuthbert Vaughn, both of whom had been convicted for their part in the Wyatt conspiracy, were not only pardoned and rehabilitated, both were on Philip's pension list at the end of the reign.[62] Francis Lord Russell, the earl of Bedford's heir, and perhaps the most committed protestant of all the peers, received his pardon and discharge on 12 September 1554.[63] Lord Bray, Sir William Courtenay, and Sir John Pollard, all of whom received pardons after indictment for their alleged parts in the Dudley conspiracy, subsequently served in the Low Countries, as did Sir Nicholas Throgmorton, who had needed a pardon for leaving the realm without licence after his controversial acquittal in 1554.[64] Other examples could be quoted which tend to support Badoer's judgement, although Philip's intervention can very seldom be proved conclusively. It was at best a hit and miss policy. Some of the king's clients served him well, particularly those who fought in the campaign of 1557, others, like Thomas Woodman, betrayed his trust completely.[65] Within England, perhaps because of his increasingly straitened circumstances, his pension list never extended beyond the most obvious figures in the council and the court: Paget, Derby, Arundel, Pembroke, Shrewsbury; Howard, Clinton, Rochester, Petre, Waldegrave, Englefield, and others to the number of about two dozen. His own household extended this list, but the rewards there were modest, and both pensions and household salaries were seriously in arrears by the end of the reign.[66] The majority of the English peerage, to say nothing of the major knightly and gentry families who dominated the counties, got, and could expect to get, nothing directly from the king. Mary continued to be generous with annuities and small grants, so that a favoured servant like Sir Thomas Cornwallis could advance from about £300 a year to about £2300 in the course of the reign without ever receiving any conspicuous grants or gifts.[67] But there is very little evidence to suggest that Philip influenced, or tried to influence, the workings of normal royal patronage.

It is hard to avoid the conclusion that Philip's familiarity with English affairs stopped short at the council and the parliament. Apart from his journeys from Southampton to London and London to Dover, his movements within England were restricted to the royal residences in the home counties: Windsor, Hampton Court, Richmond, Oatlands. He seems to have made little attempt to understand the workings of English local government, and had no contact with the provincial nobility and gentry who did not come to court. Debarred from employing his other subjects in England, he made no attempt to employ Englishmen in his other dominions, except in a humble military capacity. The composition and preparedness of the fleet was a matter of constant interest to him, and he was aware of some, at least, of the problems of defending the borders;[68] in such matters he was prepared to intervene. On the other hand, over questions of domestic order or the enforcement of religious orthodoxy, both close to his heart, he seems to have felt unable to take any direct action beyond restraining his Spanish followers. This was not simply the result of the shortness of his reign. Having expressed an intention not to be bound by the limitations of the marriage treaty, he actually adhered closely to its terms until the crisis of April–May 1557 over the declaration of war. He may have despaired of deriving any lasting benefit from the marriage after the failure of Mary's pregnancy, or he may have feared to provoke a major insurrection in England which would have invited French intervention, and which would have damaged both his resources and prestige, even if unsuccessful. Nevertheless, there were political opportunities in England which the king did not exploit, and his impact upon the government of the country was patchy and superficial.

Nowhere is this better illustrated than in his failure to overcome the persistent suspicion and hostility of parliament, particularly the House of Commons. Philip was fully aware of the importance of these assemblies. He played an active part in the preparations for that which met in November 1554, and attended in the House of Lords, with the queen, on 12, 15, and 22 November.[69] However, because of his inability to speak (or understand) the language, he was unable to address the members either collectively in the House or in delegations summoned to wait upon him. Mary herself spoke to parliament only rarely, and then not always to good effect, so that neither was able to resort to the kind of direct personal appeal or pressure which both Henry VIII and Elizabeth used successfully on occasions. Also, although he showed a lively concern over the need to secure a tractable assembly in 1555, and was kept well informed of the subsequent progress of business, Philip was not in the country for either that or the last parliament of the reign. This fact, coupled with his very imperfect understanding of procedure, meant that the king was unable to exercise any significant influence over the fourth and fifth parliaments, and since his interests did not correspond exactly with those of any group of English politicians, he obtained little satisfaction from either of them. The records of the parliaments themselves show very little trace of efforts being made on his behalf, but diplomatic observers saw, or thought they saw, such efforts. Noailles reported that Gardiner's opening oration to the third parliament contained a broad hint that the king's coronation was intended, and his letters later during the session reflected persistent anxiety that members were being prompted to demand a declaration against France.[70] More tangibly, there were strong disagreements and debates over the bill 'for the government of the king and queen's issue', which resulted, as we have seen, in a rather grudging concession of regency powers to the king. Renard believed that several important peers had absented themselves from the final debate in order to avoid giving their consent to a measure which would diminish the traditional authority of the Lords 'to appoint a protector'.[71] Since, however, statute was also a traditional way of making such provision, and Renard's list included Arundel and Pembroke, two of the peers highest in favour with Philip, his interpretation probably had little basis. The real anxiety seems to have been that the king would take advantage of his regency powers to employ 'strangers' in England, perhaps on the pretext that such a contingency was not covered by the marriage treaty. Notwithstanding '. . . the manifold vertues of his Majestie, his godly disposition and great favours to us all . . .' such a course of action would have been unacceptable to both the council and parliament.[72]

The fourth parliament was accompanied by even more conjecture and speculation. Before it met, Noailles, who was in close touch with malcontents of various kinds, reported

> . . . l'on dict que l'occasion pour laquelle ledict parlement a este assemblé ne tend a l'aultre fin que pour faire, s'il est possible, tumber le gouvernement absolu de ce royaulme entre les mains de ce roy, et pourvoir par ce moyen disposer des forces et estates d'icelluy a sa volunté.[73]

Michieli, on the other hand, had heard that one of the main purposes of the session would be to determine the succession in the event of the queen's death without heirs, some believing that Elizabeth would be 'utterly excluded', others that her right might be confirmed upon conditions. Many years after, it was related how a bill had been debated in this parliament entailing the crown to Philip and Mary, and the heirs of Mary's body, in such a way that Philip would have retained a life interest in the event of Mary's death without issue, and that the bill was 'dashed' in the Commons;[74] but the records contain no entry which could be construed in such a way. After the session was over, Noailles wrote with satisfaction that the queen had intended

> . . . de couronner le roy son mary d'avoir puissance et autorité de l'instituer son heretier encores que elle n'eust enfans de luy . . . Neantmoings elle n'eu a pu estre satisfaicte en un seul poinct . . .[75]

Badoer, in Brussels, believed that Mary had toyed with the idea of effecting the coronation 'with a number of peers' after parliament was over, but that Philip had dissuaded her, being more interested in gaining English support against France.[76] He also believed that the queen's failure to make any progress on Philip's behalf was a direct consequence of the king's failure to return to England for any part of the parliament. The final parliament of the reign, held in wartime and under the shadow of the fall of Calais, seems to have attracted less speculation of this kind, perhaps for the simple reason that there was no Venetian or French ambassador to report it. The celebrated outburst of the otherwise obscure Mr Copley, however, demonstrates that anxiety still lurked beneath the surface. This young member, it was recorded,

> . . . hath spoken unreverent words of the Queens Majestie concerning the bill for the confirmation of Patents, saying that he feared the Queen might give away the Crown from the right inheritors . . .[77]

He was imprisoned by order of the House, and there is no means of knowing how many shared his fears. In neither of its sessions was this parliament called upon to consider either the succession or the king's position, which may have been one of the reasons why the queen found it so satisfactory an assembly.

As a recent scholarly study has pointed out, it is difficult to assess Mary's relations with her parliaments precisely because some of the most important issues of the reign, of which everyone was aware, were never openly debated.[78] When matters of first-class importance were brought to parliament – the repeal of the Edwardian religious settlement, the marriage treaty, and the reconciliation with Rome – they were approved without serious difficulty. It is also a mistake to place too much emphasis upon the turbulence of the Commons in the fourth parliament, or upon the rejection of the 'exiles' bill'. Nevertheless, government-sponsored measures of some importance ran into serious difficulties in every parliament. In the first the Durham bill was lost in the Commons, in the second Gardiner's religious proposals were defeated in the Lords. The generally co-operative third parliament saw long wrangles over the inclusion of the pope's dispensation in the act of repeal, and over the 'government of the royal issue'. Two bills against married clergy, which were probably officially sponsored, also disappeared after numerous redraftings.[79] In the fourth parliament the defeat of the exiles' bill was only the tip of the iceberg. The subsidy bill, and the bill to return first fruits and tenths to the church, were almost as fiercely contested, and the normally co-operative Lords rejected by a majority a government bill to forbid (again) the wearing of private liveries by justices of the peace.[80] Even the fifth parliament refused to cancel the denization of duly authorized French residents. That there was opposition to government policies, and that it sometimes succeeded, is therefore undeniable; but whether there was 'an opposition' is a different matter. The substantial minority in the Commons who had voted against the first act of repeal in 1553 did not reappear a year later to vote against the second act. Nor did the Lords who had resisted Gardiner under Paget's leadership in April 1554 show any sign of repeating the performance in the autumn. In the autumn of 1555 there is evidence that 'opposition' members were in regular consultation outside the chamber, both with each other and with outsiders like the French ambassador.[81] There is also a list of unknown purpose which contains 106 names of MPs who resisted the crown in some unspecified way in this parliament.[82] However, if there was an embryonic 'party' in 1555, it had vanished by 1558 in spite of what seems to have been a normal level of continuity. To deduce the existence of a crypto-protestant group in the Commons from the behaviour of individuals during the reign of Edward VI or Elizabeth is also a hazardous hypothesis, bearing in mind the pressures of opportunism and conformity. There is, in fact, no evidence to support the notion of a continuous and organized opposition in the Marian parliaments, either of a political or religious nature. On the other hand, there was widespread suspicion of Mary's intentions, not only in respect of Philip's position and the succession, but also in respect of ecclesiastical property, and the restored endowments and jurisdiction of the church. Virtually every issue that came to a contest or a vote was a matter of property rights or financial provision. It was no coincidence that the troublesome fourth parliament had been opened with the reading of Paul IV's bull exempting England from the provisions of *Rescissio Alienationum*.[83] The reassurance was explicit, but that it should have been needed at all was deeply disturbing. Neither the queen's marriage nor her religious policy was much resisted in parliament *per se*, but each had implications for the vital interests of the Lords and Commons, and for those whom the latter represented, which were reflected in these expressions of discontent. Whereas Edward had met only two parliaments in six years, and had prorogued one of them three times; and Elizabeth was to meet two parliaments in seven years, proroguing one of them once; Mary met five different parliaments in five years. Since it was the normal Tudor practice to prorogue parliaments which were reckoned to be satisfactory, and to dissolve those which were not, the fact that Mary prorogued only her last parliament in March 1558 tells its own story.

Given a situation in which most members of the House of Commons came to Westminster to represent the interests of their localities, it was not necessarily easy to excite them about national issues. Many members owed their places to noble or municipal patronage, but were not by that fact committed to any kind of 'party line' on political or religious issues. As in the earlier parliaments, so in the third and fourth, circular letters were sent out to sheriffs and others urging the return of men of the 'wise, grave and catholic sort', and privy councillors exercised their patronage to secure amenable members, sometimes requiring the election of specific individuals. Nevertheless, the unsatisfactory Sir John Perrot sat for the Cinque Ports in 1555, under the patronage of Sir Thomas Cheney, the lord warden, and the earl of Cumberland put in John Holmes, the erstwhile secretary to the duke of Northumberland, at Ripon in October 1554.[84] As we have seen, Philip took great pains before he left England to insist that the council of state ensured the return of loyal catholics for what turned out to be the most turbulent parliament of the reign. Duchy of Lancaster patronage, under the control of the reliable Rochester, seems to have returned consistently sound men, and was probably extended for that reason.[85] Occasionally, as in the case of Alexander Nowell, the prebendary of Westminster in 1553, an unsatisfactory member could be legitimately removed, but on the whole, control of returns was very much less significant than the management of the House in being.

In 1553 prolonged uncertainty about the marriage, unease about the future of ecclesiastical property, and the queen's inept personal intervention had created an element of disaffection in what was otherwise a reasonably well-managed session. By April 1554 ecclesiastical property had become a dominant issue, and government management collapsed when Paget led the opposition in the Lords. In November 1554, on the other hand, with the king taking a strong interest and control firmly in Gardiner's hands, the same issue was handled effectively and without significant dissent. Perhaps the best proof that the initiative remained firmly in the hands of the council during that session is the fact that the strong feelings which were aroused over both the act of repeal and the regency bill were contained in committee and in debate; so that at the cost of several redraftings and some concessions, both measures were passed without a division in either House.[86] There certainly was discontent in the Commons in January 1555. When the House was called on 14 January, only 193 members were present, and, shortly after, writs of *venire facias* were taken out against 106 named individuals for absenting themselves without licence. Further legal proceedings were subsequently taken against 62 of them, and 25 were eventually fined.[87] It cannot be proved, however, that these had any political motive for their action, since many of those whose antecedents can be traced were loyal catholics. Dr Loach has concluded that indignation at being kept in London over Christmas and anxiety to return home were probably the true causes of their behaviour.[88] In 1555 the select council had a specific brief

... deliberabunt de Parliamento, quo tempore habendum sit, & quae in eodum agi & proponi debeant; Et quae agenda & proponenda videbuntur in Parliamento, in Scriptis redegi volumus ante Parliamenti initium

and in accordance with this, proposals were sent to Philip, who dutifully but not very helpfully commented upon them.[89] Gardiner's death early in the session was believed by observers to have weakened the government's control considerably. The chancellor was subsequently accused of having bribed and bullied members in earlier parliaments to secure compliance with his wishes, an ironic echo of his own complaints about the reformation parliament, but there is no clear evidence to support such charges.[90] For whatever reason, council leadership in the Commons was weak during this session, and the initiative was temporarily lost. This was partly a matter of numbers. Whereas the average council presence in the Commons for the first three parliaments had been 16.3, for the fourth it was only 10. There was also a group of disaffected west-country gentry, Sir Anthony Kingston, Sir William Courtenay, Sir John Pollard, and others, who were prepared to take the risk of openly defying the queen's wishes. It later transpired that several of these members were involved in actual conspiracy, and were thus opponents of the government in the full sense, if only for a short time. After seeking unsuccessfully to block the subsidy bill, and forcing a division over the bill to restore first fruits and tenths to the church, they eventually rallied enough support to defeat on its third reading a measure to confiscate the real property of those who had left the realm without licence, and refused to return.

A number of circumstances had combined to produce this rather-too-famous victory. A great atmosphere of resentment against Mary's attempts to re-endow the church seems to have been aggravated by the queen's address to a summoned delegation of the House on 19 November, in which she expressed her intention '... for to depart with first fruits and tenths; and my Lord Cardinal spake for the Tythes and Impropriations of Benefices to be spiritual . . .'[91] The tactics used to pass the relevant bill through the House also caused anger.[92] The council leadership was less than adroit, Sir Edward Hastings virtually coming to blows with Sir George Howard.[93] The confiscation of real property for absence, without a due process of indictment and conviction by the common law, raised an important issue of legal principle which affected many interests. And there was a quality and determination about the leadership of opposition in this session which was quite exceptional. Even the discreet Sir William Cecil, who occasionally assisted the councillors in the House, 'told a good tale', for the opposition in this debate.[94] Consequently, although it would be an exaggeration to claim that the events of this session marked a significant advance in the development of organized opposition, they did constitute a sharp reminder that the combination of an unpopular policy and ineffectual management could turn the Commons into a very obstructive body. Michieli's well-known description of this House as being '. . . quite full of gentry and nobility (for the most part suspected in matters of religion) and therefore more daring and licentious . . .' was a distortion of the truth, but a shrewd comment nevertheless. It did not need a very large number of 'licentious' gentry to cause serious trouble for a government whose policies commanded less than overwhelming support.

Mary's parliaments were not particularly productive in legislative terms. Whereas the five sessions of Edward's two parliaments had resulted in 164 statutes, and the four sessions of Elizabeth's first three parliaments were to add 122, Mary's passed only 104 in six sessions. Of these 15 were repeals of attainder or restitutions in blood, and a further 9 repeals of other statutes of an administrative, political, or religious nature. Although these latter figures were not large in absolute terms (Edward's parliaments had carried out 14 restitutions, for example), they did represent an unusually high proportion of the acts passed – 23 per cent. Treason legislation, domestic security, particularly in the form of comprehensive provision 'against unlawful and rebellious assemblies',[95] and the confirmation of attainders accounted for another 9 acts. Three more resolved specific problems arising from the circumstances of Mary's accession.[96] Routine continuations and financial provisions of a standard kind, such as tonnage and poundage and subsidies, formed the subject-matter of a further 10 statutes. Of the remaining 58 acts passed during the reign, the form and subject-matter of 30 point to origins in private interests; for example, 'An Act for the inhabitants of Halifax concerning the buying of wools' (2 and 3 Philip and Mary, c. 13), or 'An Act touching the Sea Sands in Glamorganshire' (1 Mary, c. 11). Among those acts of a public nature which were not directly concerned with restoration or the security of the regime, the largest group provided reforms in the content or administration of the law. Several of these were of a technical nature, such as that 'for the limitation of prescription' (1 Mary, st. 2 c. 5) or 'touching proclamations upon fines' (1 Mary, st. 2 c. 7), and reflect a proper care on the part of the council for the administration of justice. Others reaffirmed existing legislation, particularly relating to the workings of the commission of the peace. For example, 1 Mary, st. 2 c. 8, 'That Sheriffs shall not be Justices of the Peace during office', confirmed a part of 1 Edward VI, c. 7, and 2 and 3 Philip and Mary, c. 18 'for Commissions of the Peace in corporate towns not counties' protected the existing interests of mayors and burgesses.[97] Two acts were to have particular significance for the future working of the commission of the peace, 1 and 2 Philip and Mary, c. 13, controlling the bailment of felons by justices, and 2 and 3 Philip and Mary, c. 10, instructing justices to examine persons accused of felony and to certify the examinations in writing within two days. Although it is doubtful whether these acts were intended to be as far reaching as is sometimes claimed, they did express a determination to discipline procedures which were much open to abuse, and in the long run had a noticeable effect, particularly upon the working of juries of presentment.[98]

The rather smaller group of statutes which dealt with matters of social discipline and control show a similar pattern: 'reformation of Excess in apparel' (2 and 3 Philip and Mary, c. 2), 're-edifying decayed houses of husbandry' (2 and 3 Philip and Mary, c. 2), and 'punishing abduction of heiresses' (4 and 5 Philip and Mary, c. 8), were all matters of traditional concern in which the acts reaffirmed existing policies. Two statutes restricted the taking of purveyance, an ancient and recurring grievance; one enforced parochial responsibility for the maintenance of highways; and one provided 'for the relief of the poor' by reiterating the provisions of 22 Henry VIII, c. 12 and 3/4 Edward VI, c. 16.[99] Insofar as these acts expressed deliberate policies formulated by the council, as distinct from acceptable private initiatives, they show a conscientious preoccupation with the pursuit of existing means towards traditional ends.

However, it is not sufficient to label the legislation of these parliaments as conservative and unimaginative. In addition to the bailment and committal acts a number of individual measures were also passed which embodied significant reforms. The enabling act of 1 Mary, st. 2 c. 10 continued an initiative begun under Edward and resulted in the reconstruction of the exchequer. 2 and 3 Philip and Mary, c. 20, 'An Act enlarging the Duchy of Lancaster', also pointed towards a potential change of some importance. All duchy lands which had been alienated since the beginning of Edward VI's reign and which had returned to the crown were reunited to the duchy, but, more important, the crown was authorized to annex other lands to the duchy in the same way as they came into possession. The effect of this could have been to turn duchy chamber into a new court of augmentations, and greatly to increase its patronage. In fact the duchy does not seem to have been greatly enriched in the remaining three years of the reign,[100] but the time was too short to allow any real conclusions to be drawn and Elizabeth did not take advantage of the act. The subsidy act of 1555 ordered a complete reassessment, and set out a new schedule of graded payments on both goods and lands. Enthusiasm for reform (if such it was) was short-lived in this case, for the 1558 act reverted to the traditional pattern; nevertheless, the 1555 subsidy was significant in another way, for it renewed the practice of peacetime taxation, and was neither questioned nor challenged upon that ground. Rather belatedly under the pressure of war the last parliament also saw the passage of two important acts intended to reorganize the mobilization and equipment of the militia: 'An Act for the having of horse armour and weapons' and 'An Act for the taking of musters'. It was upon the basis of these two statutes that the Elizabethan militia ordinances were laid, and they remained significant until the following century.[101]

Looking at the whole corpus of Marian legislation, the overwhelming impression is one of thorough and systematic restoration; not only of the traditional church, but of families broken by attainder, and of privileges threatened by earlier reforms. The second impression is of real concern to improve the workings of the law by removing abuses in practice and ambiguities in existing legislation. The third impression is of a consistent willingness to support established economic interests, and an unwillingness to give any fresh thought to social problems. The fourth impression is of a constant anxiety about sedition and public order. The relatively small number of acts passed was not the result of unprecedented mortality among bills. The Commons rejected 17 and Lords (probably) 6.[102] A further 134 disappeared in one House or the other, so that an average of just over 31 bills died in each parliament, which compares very favourably with the 48 which were lost in the first session of Edward's first parliament, let alone the 75 which vanished in the second session, or the 52 in the third.[103] In fact the ratio of acts passed to bills lost was slightly more favourable than in the previous reign, but the government was clearly less willing to resort, or to allow others to resort, to legislation. There were no significant advances in parliamentary privilege, and no change in the position of the speaker as a trusted servant of the crown. The major advance which did occur was in the authority of statute, and was quite unintentional. Each stage of religious reform from 1533 to 1553 had been defended by its protagonists on the ground that it conformed to the will of God, and it could therefore be argued that parliament had never emancipated itself from the necessity to obey divine law, however that was defined. But, by accepting parliamentary repeal in 1553 and 1554 Mary had accepted the validity of the earlier statutes in law, irrespective of their standing in the sight of God. This decision was politically unavoidable, as we have seen, but it placed the religious settlement upon a strictly statutory basis, and thus made it vulnerable to further change. In certain respects, particularly over the administration of the law, Mary's advisers can fairly be described as continuing, and in some cases completing, initiatives which had begun in the 1530s. Paget and his friends also continued to retain, to a remarkable degree, the secularizing achievements of that decade. However, they clearly did not follow Cromwell in his enthusiasm for statute as a medium, and insofar as they had a coherent vision of policy as a whole, it was one of stability and discipline rather than reform.

When we look away from parliament to other evidence for the shape and direction of government policy during these years, the picture is naturally somewhat different. Proclamations, for instance, could not be used to bring about reforms in the law, or rehabilitate the attainted, and the queen was also reluctant to use them in straightforward ecclesiastical matters which belonged to a different jurisdiction. On the other hand, disciplinary matters of all kinds, social and economic regulation, and declarations of a political nature were normally handled through that medium. Mary issued 64 proclamations during her reign, markedly fewer per year than Edward, who had issued 114 in six and a half years.[104] Of these only three dealt directly with religion, in marked contrast to the 16 which Edward had issued in enforcing his progressive reforms. Political and administrative declarations, such as announcing the coronation pardon, the marriage settlement, or the outbreak of war with France, accounted for a further 16, a rather higher proportion than in the previous reign. Social and economic control, apart from the coinage, prompted 13 proclamations, a very much smaller proportion of the total than Edward's 35; while the vexed problems created by inflation and debasement were the subject of 8 edicts from Mary and 14 from Edward, a very similar level of activity. The largest single group of Mary's proclamations, however, 20 in all, was concerned with rebellion and sedition; at over 30 per cent this figure represents more than double the 14 per cent which were devoted to similar matters during the notoriously troubled years of the previous reign. During the first five years of Elizabeth 71 proclamations were issued, of which 11 concerned religion, 11 the coinage, 25 social and economic control, and a mere five sedition and domestic security.[105] Counting and classifying proclamations in this fashion does not, of course, prove anything in itself, because government strategy and the nature and intensity of the problems dealt with were all variables. Mary's concern with religion was no less than that of Edward or Elizabeth, but she was much more reluctant to appeal openly to

K

her own jurisdiction. On the other hand, in an area where the problem remained much the same, and the government's perception of its duty did not appreciably change, as in dealing with the coinage, the level of activity remained remarkably consistent. Bearing this in mind, the most significant pattern to emerge from Mary's use of proclamations is the relatively low level of concern with straightforward economic and social regulation, such as the control of trade or the punishment of vagabonds, and the very high level of concern with sedition. It could be objected in general that Mary treated as sedition what Edward or Elizabeth would have regarded as a religious or social issue, but in making this classification I have been careful to apply the same criteria to all three reigns, treating 'seditious preaching', for example, as sedition throughout.

A similar preoccupation emerges very strongly from the administrative records of the privy council. Orders to arrest suspects, the committal and interrogation of prisoners, the taking of recognizances, and letters of thanks and instruction to local justices, are of daily occurrence, forming much the largest single category of business. Only military and naval affairs, such as provisions for the garrisons of Calais or Berwick, victualling the fleet, or authorizing payments for these purposes show anything like a comparable level of activity. In her examination of the standing of members of parliament, Dr Loach has come to the conclusion that the exaction or pardoning of debts due to the crown was a standard method of penalizing offenders or rewarding faithful service.[106] For example, Sir Thomas Cawarden, Lord Grey of Wilton, and Lord Cobham were severely mulcted, while the earl of Pembroke, Sir Maurice Dennis, and several others were forgiven equally considerable sums.[107] Substantial recognizances were also used to ensure good behaviour, or the performance of specific duties. For example, Sir Thomas Golding was bound in £100 on 16 February 1556 to '. . . doo what lyeth in him for the recoverie of one Rooke of Braynetree, lately escaped . . .'[108] At the time of the Dudley conspiracy, in May 1556, Sir John St Low and Sir Arthur Champernowne were bound in their own recognizances of £1000 each to attend upon the council during pleasure, while Sir John Chichester had to find four sureties to put up £2000 for the same purpose.[109] Scores of such recognizances were recorded in the council register, and many were subsequently cancelled 'per mandatum consilii', 'ex mandato commissionariorum', or 'ex mandato Domini Cancellarii', but what proportion was actually forfeited will not be clear until further studies have been made. Letters of thanks seem usually to have been sent by the council itself to commissioners or individual officials who had displayed commendable zeal, whereas exhortations and reprimands, particularly the latter, bore the royal signature.[110] In April 1557, while Philip was in England, he signed with Mary a sharp letter to the justices of the peace for Yorkshire, castigating them for neglect of their duties, and sending them a list of fifteen articles devised by the council of the North to be implemented by them. These articles included provisions for overseeing the poor, keeping men in work, punishing slanderous rumours, and notifying heretics.[111] Two years earlier, in March 1555, the king and queen had signed a rather similar but less censorious letter to the justices for Norfolk, instructing them to set a good example in religious matters, to set careful watches upon all suspects, to aid good preachers, and to set a spy in every parish.[112] Such letters may well have followed a standard pattern, and although they covered a number of duties, the usual concern with sedition and religious dissent was very much to the fore. A similar letter, also of March 1555 but addressed to an unnamed commission of oyer and terminer, may stand as typical of the official attitude towards civil order and discipline.

. . . where of late tyme partly for want of the feare of god in mens hartes and partly also for lack of good order and due execution of the lawes the common sort of people within this our realme have growne to suche liberte insolency, as they have not let at sundry tymes to attempt divers stirres and rebellions contrary to their duetyes of allegyeance to the great trouble and disgust of us and oure whole realme . . .[113]

This may have been no more than the standard rhetoric of authority, but loyal writers such as Christopherson and Huggarde were at great pains to point out the peculiar iniquity of disturbing the peace of so Godly a queen.[114] Not only did the catholics blame the disturbed state of the country on those who had ruled before them, they clearly expected their own triumph to exorcise the evil spirits of dissension, since the wrath of God would no longer be turned upon a land where He was truly honoured. Consequently it is possible that the concern which Mary's government showed over questions of order and sedition was the result of higher expectations rather than of any increase in the incidence of the problems themselves. Indeed there is no reason to suppose that casual disorders such as enclosure riots, protests against the price of grain, or private brawls, were more common during these years than in the rest of the mid-century period. Nor was there any repetition of the upsurge of large-scale social violence which had occurred during the years 1548 and 1549. There were, however, one major rebellion, one minor invasion, and four or five conspiracies of varying seriousness, all of which were thought to have political aims. The Wyatt rebellion, as we have seen, was primarily a 'gentleman's matter', arising out of opposition to the Spanish marriage and fears of its consequences.[115] Ostensibly intended to persuade the queen to change her mind, its real objective had probably been to depose her in favour of Elizabeth. By contrast the 'insurrection' at Ipswich in July 1554, reported by the Tower chronicler, seems to have been the work of a small group of townsmen, and its purpose is unclear. The justices for Suffolk and the bailiff of Ipswich were thanked by the council for their pains in detecting and suppressing it. However, in March 1555 there was again trouble in East Anglia. On the 18th Henry Machyn reported: 'this day was browth to the Towre out of Cambryge shyre master Bowes master Cutt and master Hynd, and dyvers odur, for a nuw conspyrase the wyche shuld have byne done in Suffolke and odur plases'. Michieli, in commenting upon these arrests, expressed the opinion that the culprits would be dealt with severely, 'for not only was there a similar plot in Ipswich last year, but only last month the execution of Dr. Rowland Taylor was made the excuse for tumults in Norfolk . . .' By the end of the month Renard was in possession of many circumstantial details, which seem to indicate another attempt to promote the interests of Elizabeth and Courtenay, although Michieli was convinced that it was directed against 'the faithful and catholics, termed by them Papists',[116] and included plans for a march on London and an attack upon the court. On 1 April the Venetian complained that he was unable to obtain any more reliable information because of the secrecy with which the whole matter was being handled, and that nobody seemed to know whether it was serious or '. . . mere suspicion, which, if of usual occurrence elsewhere, may here be said to have dominion'.[117] Perhaps it was a similar suspicion, relating to another part of the country, which caused the king and queen, on 8 March 1555, to send orders to the earl of Cumberland to muster his servants and tenants 'to repress any sudden tumult, stir or rebellion'.[118]

The summer of 1555 saw a sequence of 'lewd' tumults. In May a young man named Edward Feltonstone appeared in Essex, claiming to be King Edward VI. In June the lord warden of the Cinque Ports was instructed to investigate a 'commotion practiced in Kent', to set strict watches, and to allow no May games. Early in July 'a new tumult in Sussex' called for an inquiry by the lord chancellor, and on the 12th Raynold Robson, 'oone of the chief conspiritors of the intended rebellion in Sussex', was delivered to the Tower.[119] Later in the same month William and Francis Clopton were sent up to the Fleet 'to be examined touching the conspiracy intended in Essex and Norfolk by Cornewall and others . . .' At the same time there were rumours of disturbances in Warwickshire, Devon, and Corn-wall, which turned out to be no more than minor agrarian riots.[120] It is not very easy to know how seriously to take the constant use of the alarming terms 'conspiracy' and 'rebellion', with their implication of deliberate sedition, but since there were plenty of other disorders which were not so described, it seems that the words were used advisedly, if not always very precisely.

There can be no doubt, however, about the nature of the intrigues which began with clandestine meetings of disaffected gentry in London in July 1555 and which were eventually betrayed to the government in March 1556. I have discussed the so-called 'Dudley conspiracy' in detail elsewhere, and there is no need to tell the story again, but its objective was certainly the overthrow of the queen's government by foreign invasion and domestic insurrection.[121] How serious a danger it actually represented is a matter of debate, but there is no doubt that the council, and the queen herself, were desperately worried in the spring of 1556. As the councillors and commissioners laboured day after day through March, April, and May, piecing together the story, the ramifications seemed to spread further and further. Some of those most deeply involved, such as Henry Peckham, had impeccable antecedents of loyalty,[122] others like Sir Ralph Bagnall and Sir Thomas Cawarden had been under suspicion before. A number of influential west-country gentry were involved, although how deeply was never established, and Elizabeth's household again came under suspicion.[123] As in the case of the Wyatt conspiracy, there was a clear and well-established link with France, on this occasion both through Noailles in London and directly through the numerous English exiles in France. The central theme of the conspiracy was opposition to Philip's coronation:

> yf ther were . . . that woold make a flagg ther woold be V^c, ye & V^c more that woold dye in this quarrell that no stranger shuld have the Crown . . .

as one of the humbler supporters declared.[124] This was a theme which commanded such widespread sympathy, as we have seen, that only the queen's oldest and most trusted servants were given the task of interrogating the prisoners.

Hardly had this alarm died down when there was another, although much less serious, scare. A certain Cleobury 'wch sometyme kept a scoole at Dis in Norfolk' went to Yaxley church in Suffolk one Sunday in July and read a bogus proclamation, declaring that Mary was dead, '. . . and did proclaim ye Ladye Elizabeth Queene, and her beloved bedfelloe Lord Edward Courtenay king . . .' According to the account in Sir Symonds D'Ewes's papers, Cleobury had arranged with three brothers named Lincoln to support his bid with a hundred horsemen, but they did not turn up, and Cleobury 'seeing his partye was so weake . . . beganne to flee . . .'[125] He was captured at Eye, and Thomas and Nicholas Lincoln were also subsequently imprisoned.[126] When the privy council wrote to inform the earl of Bath of the episode, they linked Cleobury with the Dudley conspirators, on what evidence is not clear, and claimed that he had actually represented himself to be the earl of Devon, then in Venice. They also, understandably, stressed the spontaneous loyalty of the local people who 'wt out any commandment dyd of themselves apprehende as manye of the attempters of thys develyshe practice as they could come by . . .', and instructed the earl '. . . to cause the willingness of the people shewed in those parts . . . to be bruited abroad . . . for the better encouragement of the Kinges and Queenes Majesties good subjects in those partes'.[127] The council also wrote carefully to Sir Thomas Pope to acquaint the Lady Elizabeth of the way in which her name had been taken in vain.[128]

When we add to these incidents the innumerable cases of verbal sedition which can be traced through the council records, through pardons, and occasionally through trials in king's bench; the pursuit of the authors of 'heretical and seditious' books such as *The Copye of a letter*; the performers of 'lewd interludes' and plays; and the activities of such men as Trudgeover, who in spite of his protestantism was eventually charged with treason, we are faced with impressive evidence of disaffection.[129] The great majority of Englishmen could be relied upon to behave loyally when it was fairly clear that the traitors were weak, as in the case of Cleobury and his friends or the foolhardy group who accompanied Thomas Stafford to Scarborough. But when they appeared to be numerous or well connected, as with Wyatt and Dudley, the crown was not conspicuously well served either with arms or information. Consequently, although the council seems to have acted with consistent diligence and efficiency against the malcontents, it never came near eradicating them, or frightening them into silence. In spite of her reputation for clemency in secular matters, Mary was not noticeably reluctant to execute traitors. About 90 died for their part in the Wyatt rebellion,[130] 10 for involvement with Dudley, 27 for Stafford's raid,[131] and five or six for the other conspiracies which I have mentioned. There were certainly others, sent to the local assizes to be 'ordered according to law', and further investigation is needed to produce more accurate figures. However, the minimum number of executions for treason in the three and a half years from January 1554 to the summer of 1557 (exclusive of such remainders of Northumberland's plot as Guildford Dudley and Jane Grey) is 132, which should be thoughtfully compared with the much more definitive figure of 308 calculated by Professor Elton for the nine years from 1532 to 1540.[132] Rumour naturally inflated the number of victims. Noailles wrote feelingly of the 'bloodbath' in London in February 1554, when about 50 men were hanged,[133] and in September 1556 Bullinger was informed that Cleobury's adventure had 'occasioned the execution of at least sixty or eighty people by an ignominious death on the charge of treason'.[134] The true figure in this latter case was between two and six. About a dozen of the ringleaders in the Dudley conspiracy were indicted and saved themselves by flight to France, where they remained, unpardoned and unreconciled, until the end of the reign.[135] Whereas the four men arrested for the conspiracy at Ipswich in July 1554 all seem to have been released, the misguided Feltonstone, who pretended to be Edward VI, was hung, drawn, and quartered, although he was probably simple-minded. Michieli was probably right when he wrote in the spring of 1556 that the queen was disillusioned with the results of clemency, and determined to make examples of future offenders.[136]

Because we do not possess the kind of detailed information for this period which is provided by Cromwell's correspondence for the 1530s, we cannot tell what proportion of the cases of disaffection and sedition investigated by the council was brought to light by the zeal of private citizens. Justices and other officials were thanked for their efforts, required to make regular reports of 'the state of their countries', and sometimes, as in July 1555, generally admonished for not doing so,[137] but we know little of how offences were brought to the attention of the justices. In theory, as we have seen, the commissioners were not only required to keep good watch for the disaffected themselves, and to investigate religious backslidings as well as other 'infractions of true obedience', they were required to place a spy in every parish. This was, apparently, done, at least in some places. As Edward Underhill reported,

> This Banberry . . . was the spy for Stepney parish; as John Avales, Beard and such others were for London, who caused my friend and neighbour Master Ive to be sent unto the Marshalsea . . . Wherefore I thought it best to avoid because my not coming to the church there, should by him be marked and presented . . .[138]

Although it is intrinsically unlikely that such 'parish spies' functioned generally, or for any length of time, they may have accounted for a number of denunciations from areas such as Suffolk and Essex, where there were both zealous justices like Lord Rich and Henry Tirrell, and a considerable number of malcontents. Underhill's experience also emphasizes the close connection between religious dissent and general disaffection, a connection automatically assumed by the government, and one which caused the more conscientious protestants acute discomfort, as we have seen. Although there is nothing to suggest that most of the ringleaders of the important conspiracies of 1554 and 1556 were zealous protestants, the undercurrent of discontent which manifested itself in so many minor incidents was strongly reinforced by 'mislike of religion'. Propagandists like Huggarde could write that all traitors were heretics since the days of Thomas Cromwell: 'What was the cause of the deaths of oure late traytors', he asked rhetorically in 1556, 'but heresie the foundresse of their conspiracie . . .'[139] This belief being widespread, it follows that zealous catholics, whether or not they had any official position, would form the eyes and ears of the council in dealing with sedition. According to Foxe this was the case, and the conservative clergy, as might be expected, played the leading role. Not only were they often motivated, like Robert Parkyn, the Yorkshire chronicler, by a certain spirit of revenge, they also had the most to lose should Mary's government fail. Consequently, in looking at the extensive evidence of disaffection, we must remember that, as in the 1530s, both the energy of the government and the willingness of citizens to act as informers contributed substantially to the shape of the picture.

By 1555 the council was under no illusions about the difficulty of combating disaffection, and in addition to maintaining a close watch on the justices, carried out a considerable extension of the practice of retaining. Loyal peers, such as the earls of Shrewsbury and Pembroke, arrived in London for the parliament of November 1554 with retinues of 120 and 200 horsemen in splendid liveries, the latter company wearing the badge of the green dragon.[140] A small number of licences to retain had been issued earlier in the reign, as we have seen, but between the summer of 1555 and the summer of 1557 this policy was much extended. 23 such licences were issued during those two years, varying from middle-ranking courtiers like Roger Ligons, a gentleman of the privy chamber, with 16 men,[141] to magnates such as Pembroke and Westmorland with a hundred each.[142] 18 of the 23 men licensed were privy councillors, and among the others were such prominent loyalists as Sir William Dormer. Although there is no obvious reason why Westmorland should have received a licence, while Shrewsbury or Derby did not, or why Englefield should have been licensed for one hundred and Rochester only for 60, the general pattern is perfectly clear. When we also take into account the evidence of selective mustering, such as the instructions to the earl of Cumberland in March 1555, it is apparent that the government was deliberately building up the strength of those nobles and gentlemen who were considered to be the most reliable in their 'countries'. These retainers were intended, not only to serve as nuclei for the armed forces which might be necessary to put down rebellion or disorders, but also to form a reliable element in their localities, who would be active in supporting official policies. As such they would supplement the work of the local justices, particularly where the latter were not of notable zeal, and back up the efforts of the catholic clergy. There was, of course, nothing new in using such methods; they were time-honoured, and probably effective. On the other hand, they perpetuated and formalized the association of the government with a party or interest. That association had clearly existed under the partisan regime of Edward VI, but Mary had started by trying as far as possible to avoid it, and the great increase in licences of retainer which began in 1555 probably represented a retreat, or at least an acknowledgement that such specific and organized support was necessary.

Notes

1 Soranzo's report, *Cal. Ven.*, V, 532-63.
2 Ruy Gómez to Eraso, 23 August 1554; *Cal. Span.*, XIII, 35.
3 Lemasters, op. cit.
4 *APC*, V, 53. The surviving communications of this kind all date from after Philip's departure.
5 *Cal. Ven.*, V, 532-63.
6 *Cal. Span.*, XIII, 101. Other evidence suggests that both Winchester and Rochester were of the 'inner ring'.
7 Soranzo to the doge and senate, 14 August 1555. *Cal. Ven.*, VI, 161.
8 Same to same, 27 December 1556. *Cal. Ven.*, VI, 881. This disagreement was almost certainly over the war issue.
9 Gammon, *Statesman and Schemer*, 228-30. *Cal. Span.*, XIII, 88-9.
10 *Cal. Span.*, XIII, 88-9. Paget seems only to have begun advocating war when he was already sure that Philip was determined on it.
11 F. G. Emmison, *Tudor Secretary* (1961), 182-5.
12 *APC*, V, 130. The decision that '. . . all lettres passing this Boorde' should be so sealed was never implemented.
13 See, for example, Federico Badoer to the doge and senate, 15 December 1555, *Cal. Ven.*, VI, 283-4. The Calendar translation of this letter (the relevant part was originally in cypher) is not very clear, but Badoer believed that there was a group within the council '. . . who now advise her Majesty to demand this [Philip's] coronation . . .' Both he and Soranzo also made references to 'the lords' who supported the coronation. There are several lists of Philip's pensioners: AGS, E 811 f. 121, f. 124; *Cal. Span.*, XIII, 373, 454-6.
14 On Randall, who was involved both with Wyatt and Dudley before entering the king's service, see *TTC*, 207-8. Vaughn's service under Philip is recorded in AGS, E 811 f. 14.

15 G. Burnet, *History of the Reformation in England*, III (1714), ii, 256. *Cal. Ven.*, VI, 182-4. The role of Arundel as titular president of the council does not seem to have been particularly significant. Although he is always mentioned as an influential councillor, this was not on account of his office. In the attendance records of formal meetings he appears simply as 'the Lord Steward'.

16 e.g., in the matters of the trade dispute with Brabant, and the royal title. See above, 238-9.

17 See below, 259-60. It is not certain that Petre ceased to be a member of the select council when he resigned the secretaryship.

18 Cardinal Pole's position in relation to the council was highly individual. On at least one occasion early in 1556 Mary seems to have solicited his advice, and he drew up for her guidance a memorandum of items to be discussed with the council, so presumably he was not, at that time, in the habit of attending meetings. Burnet, op. cit., II, ii, 255-6.

19 *APC*, V, 252-7.

20 BL Lansdowne MS 170 f. 129.

21 There were by this time three clerks of the council. The third, Bernard Hampton, was employed as Spanish secretary. *Cal. Pat.*, II, 72.

22 *Cal. Span.*, XIII, 150-3. The figures here are based on *APC* and *Cal. Pat.* The councillors who died were Bedford, Freston, Gage, Gardiner, Hare, Norfolk, Sussex, Morgan, and Huddlestone; the new appointments Boxall, Clinton, and Tregonwell.

23 *Cal. Ven.*, VI, 146. A man described as a servant of Paget's had been arrested in the Low Countries as a spy. Paget disclaimed all knowledge of him, but the emperor was not convinced.

24 According to Badoer, Mary wished to appoint Thirlby, so it may have been that the rather colourless Heath emerged as the 'compromise candidate'. *Cal. Ven.*, VI, 257-8. There were also rumours that Pole would be appointed.

25 *Cal. Ven.*, VI, 415-16.

26 Emmison, op. cit., 178-9.

27 ibid., 200-2.

28 *Cal. Pat.*, III, 24. The style is repeated in a further commission of 31 October 1556. ibid., 368.

29 This category would have included those, like Sir Thomas Pope, who had taken the oath as 'councillor at large'; those like Cobham who had taken an oath before 1553; and possibly others who had never been sworn, but who had particular skills or experience to offer.

30 F. M. Powicke, *Handbook of British Chronology* (1939), 76.

31 John Boxall, STP, was a clerical pluralist of the second rank, but on a large scale. He was warden of New College, Winchester, and a canon there; archdeacon of Ely and dean of Peterborough.

32 *HMC Third Report*, App., 238 (Bedingfield MSS).

33 *Cal. Pat.*, II, 221.

34 *Cal. Pat.*, II, 301; III, 363.

35 *Cal. Pat.*, III, 27. This appointment may have been connected with the unsatisfactory conduct of Lord Dacre, who had held the Middle March along with the West, and who was to receive a stinging rebuke for his negligence the following year. *APC*, V, 326.

36 *Cal. Pat.*, III, 182, 547.

37 PRO SP15/8/5. Some, at least, of the northern gentry did not wish to serve under him when a Percy was available.

38 *Cal. Pat.*, IV, 194. *APC*, V, 138. Relations between Northumberland and Wharton were understandably strained, and Shrewsbury had to try and mediate. The exact sequence of events is not clear because on 20 August the council wrote again to Wharton, refusing his request to be relieved of responsibility at Berwick. *APC*, V, 155.

39 Michieli to the doge and senate, 3 December 1555. *Cal. Ven.*, VI, 270.

40 The last letter from Vannes, while he was waiting to start his return journey, was dated 24 October 1556. *Cal. For.*, Mary, 267.

41 *Cal. Ven.*, VI, 991, 1195.

42 *Cal. Span.*, XIII, 30-4. The Venetian reported at about the same time that 22 'upper' tables were kept at court, and that the cost of feeding the household was 180,000 ducats a year – a considerable exaggeration. *Cal. Ven.*, V, 553.

43 AGS, E 811 f. 119.

44 ibid., f. 124.

45 ibid., f. 122. Henry Radcliffe, earl of Sussex, died on 17 February 1557.

46 ibid., and *Cal. Span.*, XII, 297.

47 Thomas Dennis, Robert Moffet, Thomas 'Vol', Peter Gage, John Brett, and John 'Panon'. AGS, E 811 f. 122. Anthony Kempe and Francis Basset were each owed for two years. *Cal. Span.*, XIII, 373.

48 See above, 227. Diplomatic observers recorded the gradual departure of the king's household between September and December, but according to Jean de Vandernesse 'the greater part of the household' under Don Diego de Acevedo left London together on 20 December, and sailed from Dover on Christmas day. *Journal of the Travels of Philip II, Cal. Span.*, XIII, 444-5.

49 False alarms about Philip's movements caused considerable effort and expense. For example, in August 1556 the council wrote to Sir John Huddlestone: '. . . the Queenes Majestie is advertised that the Kinges Majestie shortly returneth hither, and that he with His Majesties Garde shall meate with him at Calys, he is willed to repair thither and also to see the Garde put in a rediness . . .'. At the same time letters were sent out summoning Lords Talbot, Strange, and Hastings to the court 'to thende that they may put themselfs in a rediness to attende upon the Kinge at his return . . .' *APC*, V, 380-1.

50 Braddock, 'The royal household, 1540–1560',

51 Interesting particulars of masques, etc., between 17 October 1554 and 26 March 1555 are presented in the More–Molyneux MSS at Loseley. *HMC Seventh Report*, App., 606.

52 Household expenses for the third year of Mary's reign were £69,524. BL Lansdowne MS 4 f. 19.

53 *Cal. Ven.*, VI, 638-40.

54 Edward Underhill as a gentleman at arms was paid 40 marks *p.a.* (*Cal. Pat.*, I, 199), but a pensioner proper seems to have received 70 marks ('Underhill's Narrative', 186). The yeomen were paid £9 2*s*. 6*d*. a year (SP12/7/55). Neither band numbered a neat 50. BL Lansdowne MS 4 f. 19. The apparent economies of this year may have been partly the result of allowing wages to run into arrears.

55 PRO E407/1/1.

56 *TTC*, 266.

57 Hughes and Larkin, II, 18.

58 ibid., 46-8.

59 *APC*, V, 320. A large quantity of armour had been issued to the court

and household at the time of the Wyatt rebellion, and was not accounted for until after Elizabeth's accession. PRO SP12/1/53.
60 Even leases were extremely rare. The only one which I have come across was of a messuage at Brundish, Suffolk, for 21 years to Christopher Gamboa, one of Philip's couriers. *Cal. Pat.*, III, 469.
61 *Cal. Ven.*, VI, 258. On Carew see above, 126 and *TTC*, 122-5.
62 AGS, E 811 f. 121. They served mainly on the Scottish borders.
63 *Cal. Pat.*, I, 204.
64 BL Stowe MS 571 ff. 85-94. *Cal. Pat.*, III, 476.
65 On 27 August 1554 Philip wrote to his father commending Woodman, who, he claimed, 'is now going at the head of 300 men to offer his services to your Majesty'. *Cal Span.*, XIII, 36-7. It was later alleged that Woodman, a servant of the earl of Pembroke, obtained this commendation by false pretences, and after a series of misdeeds, by July 1555 was in prison in the Low Countries on charges of piracy. ibid., 230-1.
66 AGS, E 811 ff. 119-24. *Cal. Span.*, XIII, 373.
67 R. C. Braddock, 'The Rewards of Office Holding in Tudor England', *Journal of British Studies*, 14 (1975), 29-47.
68 Vaughn, Edward Randall, and other English captains in Philip's service were employed by him at Berwick. AGS, E 811 f. 14. The king's interest in the English fleet is reflected in the very full list of ships, with their tonnage and manning, preserved at Simancas. E 811 ff. 21 *et seq.*
69 *Lords Journals*, I, 465-9.
70 Vertot, IV, 26-8, 76, 113. Harbison, 220-1.
71 Renard to the emperor, 17 January 1555. *Cal. Span.*, XIII, 134.
72 PRO SP11/5/2.
73 Vertot, V, 171.
74 Michieli to the doge and senate, 1 October 1555. *Cal. Ven.*, VI, 199. Bodley MS Tanner 391.
75 Vertot, V, 880.
76 Badoer to the doge and senate, 27 October 1555. *Cal. Ven.*, VI, 227.
77 *CJ*, Saturday, 5 March 1558, I, 50.
78 Loach, 'Parliamentary Opposition in the Reign of Mary Tudor'.
79 *CJ*, 4, 5, 6, 8, 10, 13, 19 December 1554, I, 38-40.
80 *LJ*, 18 November 1555, I, 502.
81 Harbison, 273-79. *TCC*, 180-6.
82 Guildford Museum, Loseley MS 1331/1. This list is transcribed, and commented upon in detail, by Loach, op. cit., 175-84.
83 The original bull, annulling without exception all alienations of the old ecclesiastical possessions, had been one of Paul IV's first acts. Pole had written to Morone in August to say that '. . . some members of the Council had already commenced murmuring greatly about the revocatory Bull . . .', and asking Morone to obtain a confirmation of the original dispensation of Julius III. *Cal. Ven.*, VI, 154.
84 *HMC Third Report*, App., 37 (Devonshire MSS). Earl of Cumberland to Holmes, 17 October 1554. Francis Yaxley reported to Cecil on 12 October that a letter had been sent out to sheriffs 'for the better electing of knights and burgesses' – and sent him a copy. BL Lansdowne MS 3 f. 92.
85 Loach, op. cit., 37.
86 *LJ*, I, 464-90; *CJ*, I, 37-41. *CJ* records 'arguments touching the supremacy' on 30 December, and the whole day on 2 January was given over to further arguments. 7 and 8 January were similarly given over to

'arguments touching the government of the issue etc.'

87 PRO KB27/1177 Rex 25; KB27/1179, etc.
88 Loach, op. cit., 141.
89 Burnet, op. cit., III, ii, 256-7. PRO SP11/6/16, 19, 22.
90 Foxe, VI, 604. The charge was made by Rogers.
91 *CJ*, I, 40-1.
92 *TTC*, 182-3.
93 Michieli to the doge and senate, 16 December 1555. *Cal. Ven.*, VI, 283. There was also a good deal of hostile propaganda in circulation among the members. Badoer reported from Brussels that 'Both the Lords and Commons have displayed the worst possible will in printed books . . .' *Cal. Ven.*, VI, 272.
94 Francis Peck, *Desiderata Curiosa* (1732), I, 9.
95 1 Mary, c. 12, continued by 1 Mary, st. 3 c. 12.
96 1 Mary, st. 2 c. 1 (the queen born in lawful matrimony); 1 Mary, st. 2 c. 4 (legalizing documents written during the usurpation); 1 Mary, st. 3 c. 2 (regal power vested in the queen).
97 Separate commissions of the peace were by custom issued to many corporate towns which were not counties, and this custom had presumably been challenged. In the 'Liber Pacis' of 1555 the two types of town are distinguished by 'Mayor and Bailiff' commissions, as opposed to 'Mayor and Sheriff' commissions. PRO SP11/5/6.
98 J. H. Langbein, *Prosecuting Crime in the Renaissance* (1974) claims that they were intended 'to facilitate organisation of the prosecutional function' (34), although in the course of a long study he admits that they did not have that effect, both because of obscure drafting and the strength of traditional practices.
99 2 and 3 Philip and Mary, c. 5.
100 Duchy of Lancaster receipts for 1 Mary were £12,669 and for 5 and 6 Philip and Mary £14,429. PRO DL28/9, 14.
101 4 and 5 Philip and Mary, c. 2, 3. L. Boynton, *The Elizabethan Militia* (1967), C. G. Cruickshank, *Elizabeth's Army* (1966).
102 The Lords Journals are missing for the first parliament.
103 W. K. Jordan, *Edward VI: the Young King*, 179-81, 307-8.
104 Hughes and Larkin, II; F. A. Youngs, *The Proclamations of the Tudor Queens* (1976), 253-5.
105 ibid., 255-7.
106 Loach, op. cit., 39.
107 *APC*, V, 343, 372, 345. *Cal. Pat.*, III, 520; II, 118.
108 *APC*, V, 370.
109 ibid., 373.
110 e.g., BL Cotton MS Titus B II f. 99, f. 100. There were exceptions, however. On 16 July 1555 the council wrote to all justices '. . . marveyling that they have not certified monethly hither thestate of the shires according to the former lettres and instruccions sent unto them, whiche they are required fromhensforth to do, as they tendre the King and Queenes Majesties pleasures'. *APC*, V, 161.
111 *HMC Reports*, 55, ii, 89 (Wombwell MSS).
112 BL Cotton Titus MS B II f. 100.
113 ibid., 99.
114 J. Christopherson, *An exhortation to all menne to take hede . . . of rebellion* (1554), STC 5207, sig. P vi, 'If we dyd wundre what grevause oures, what broken slepes, what fearfull dreames, what doubtfull coun-

seylles, what stormes and troubles she hathe for oure sakes . . .'

115 See above, 124-7 and *TTC*.

116 Machyn, 83. *Cal. Ven.*, VI, 31-2. *Cal. Span.*, XIII, 147.

117 *Cal. Ven.*, VI, 35.

118 *HMC Third Report*, App., 37 (Devonshire MSS).

119 *APC*, V, 122, 151, 155, 157, 158.

120 *APC*, V, 165; *Cal. Ven.*, VI, 144, 147-8. For an examination of the troubles of the summer of 1555, see D. Loades, 'Subversion and Security, 1553–58' (Cambridge PhD, 1962), 158-210.

121 *TTC*, 176-218.

122 As well as being the son of a privy councillor, Sir Edward Peckham, he had 'manned a gate' against Wyatt. Attempts by his brother, Sir Robert, to argue that he had entered the plot as a spy were unsuccessful. PRO SP11/8/52, 53.

123 Michieli to the doge and senate, 9 and 16 June 1556. *Cal. Ven.*, VI, 479, 484.

124 Examination of William Crowe, 11 May 1556. PRO SP11/8/70.

125 BL Harleian MS 537.

126 ibid. *APC*, VI, 6. They were caught in Calais.

127 John Gage, *Antiquities of Hengrave* (1822), 158.

128 BL Cotton MS Titus B II f. 139.

129 Loades, 'Subversion and Security'. For Trudgeover, alias George Eagles, see Foxe, VIII, 393-7.

130 *TTC*, 116-17.

131 Four ringleaders were executed in London, and 27 others (of whom four were Scots, whom I have not counted) in various parts of Yorkshire. *Ecc. Mem.*, III, ii, 67-9.

132 Elton, *Policy and Police*, 387. 132 were executed for their part in the Pilgrimage of Grace, which probably involved almost 30,000 men at its peak.

133 Noailles to Montmorency, 17 February 1554. Aff. Etr., IX ff. 137-8.

134 Horne and Chambers to Bullinger, 19 September 1556. *OL*, I, 132.

135 *TTC*, 265-7.

136 Michieli to the doge and senate, 12 May 1556. *Cal. Ven.*, VI, 446-8. The Ipswich quartet of Goodwin, West, Ramsey, and Moone, were released on recognizance on 26 December 1554. *APC*, V, 88.

137 *APC*, V, 161.

138 'Narrative of Edward Underhill', in *Tudor Tracts*, ed. A. F. Pollard (1903), 186.

139 *Displaying of the Protestantes*, 102.

140 Machyn, 74.

141 *Cal. Pat.*, III, 228.

142 *Cal. Pat.*, II, 79; III, 294. In both these cases, and probably in several others, these licences regularized (to some extent) an existing situation.

9 Financial Affairs, 1554–1557

When Thomas Gresham returned from Spain early in 1555, he picked up the reins again almost at once. His main account commences on 20 March 1555, the date upon which he resumed responsibility for dealings in Antwerp.[1] Since 6 September 1554 John Gresham and Nicholas Holborne, who had been acting in his absence, had 'taken up' over £71,000 Flemish, of which £20,000 had come from the English merchants. They had also received from Sir Edward Peckham nearly £35,000 sterling, and had dispensed virtually the whole sum, almost £100,000 sterling, in discharging obligations upon the Bourse.[2] Their brief had presumably been to reduce the level of debt, and in that they had succeeded. Apart from their own diets and expenses they discharged only one warrant of £13 6s. 8d., so that during these six months the crown obtained no usable funds as a result of its agents' activities. As we have already seen, in February 1555 the council had instructed Gresham and Holborne to negotiate for a prolongation of the Spanish loan for one year.[3] They may have failed, or Thomas Gresham on his return may have persuaded the council to change its mind, because on 16 June 1555 he personally delivered to the privy council all the ten obligations in which the debt had been acknowledged for cancellation.[4] He also accounted for the whole sum himself, no part of it appearing on the account of John Gresham and Holborne. If there had been any prolongation, it was not explicitly mentioned, and can have been for no more than a few weeks, since most of the bonds had fallen due on 20 April. Thereafter he made a regular practice of sending discharged obligations to the foreign bankers for cancellation by the council and delivery to the lord treasurer or the city of London. The massive increase in foreign indebtedness which had resulted from the council's own instructions was now causing serious alarm, and the delivery of these discharged bonds seems to have been part of a strenuous effort to improve the situation. In November 1555 three bonds amounting to over £15,000 were surrendered.[5] These seem to have been taken up in April, and had

291

probably formed part of the means whereby the Spanish debt had been discharged. On 7 December six further bonds which had fallen due in October were delivered, a total of nearly £55,000 sterling.[6] Similar cancellations were also recorded upon 2 March 1556 (one obligation, £10,500);[7] 8 May 1556 (two obligations, £15,600);[8] 19 June 1556 (12 obligations, £97,000);[9] 24 November 1556 (three obligations, £10,600);[10] 24 December 1556 (7 obligations, £78,000);[11] and 30 May 1557 (6 obligations, £69,000).[12] In the two years from June 1555 to May 1557 the council therefore recorded payments of nearly £470,000 to the foreign bankers. Gresham's main account, running from March 1555 to August 1557, shows repayments upon bonds to the sum of £312,094 Flemish, that is, about £290,000 sterling. John Gresham and Nicholas Holborne had also discharged over £100,000 sterling, and the foreign debt before their account began in September 1554 had stood at about £70,000 without the Spanish money.[13]

When Gresham closed his main account in August 1557, the Antwerp debt, as such, no longer existed. John Gresham and Nicholas Holborne had received £34,495 from the mint and the exchequer and, as we have seen, had provided the government with virtually no usable income. Making due allowance for expenses, brokerage, and interest they had probably reduced the overall burden by about £25,000. Thomas Gresham himself received £174,448 Flemish from the mint and the exchequer, that is about £160,000 sterling, and raised in Antwerp £234,733 Flemish, of which £97,878 was the Spanish loan already considered. Out of these sums he spent £22,800 Flemish on provisions and commodities, mostly gunpowder and weapons, in the Low Countries, and paid £80,454 (£73,626 sterling) to Thomas Egerton, the under-treasurer of the mint.[14] Of the £312,094 which he paid out on bonds £34,333 was for 'old debts' which were not covered by new obligations, and he also managed to convince his auditors that he had 'by his wisdom and diligent travail' made a profit of £6421 on his exchange dealings. Nevertheless, with interest and brokerage charges amounting to over £35,000 he cannot have reduced the overall debt very greatly by his own efforts. In January 1556 he calculated that the queen's debts in Flanders amounted to £109,013,[15] and although this showed a marked improvement from the end of 1554, it was still almost twice what she had inherited. At about that point there seems to have been a change of policy. Hitherto the staplers and merchant adventurers had been used mainly to supply short-term or 'bridging' loans to cover payments to the Antwerp bankers when the latter were unable or unwilling to extend. In later years Gresham was to develop a technique for minimizing the effects of a capricious exchange by using the adventurers and staplers to deliver money in Antwerp at artificially fixed rates. The crown then repaid them in London.[16] As we have already seen, a transaction of a similar kind had taken place in the first year of the reign, and it is likely that Gresham had, in fact, developed his 'device' several years before 1558, when it was first specifically mentioned. On 4 May 1555 he reported to the council that the adventurers had advanced £18,000 for one month, which must have been a contribution towards his efforts in paying off the Spanish loan.[17] In October 1555 he reported receiving another £12,000 from the same source; by the following month this had been augmented to £25,085, while the staplers had also agreed to provide £12,000.[18] Altogether Gresham received £51,433 from these sources, and repaid to them £55,727 – an interest of about 8½ per cent. John Gresham and Holborne had similarly received £20,000. However, at the beginning of 1556 Mary seems to have compelled the two companies to take over the liability for the great bulk of the foreign debt. On 6 February, Michieli reported that the queen had demanded £100,000 from the two companies, to be paid in Flanders, 'Her Majesty being debtor there for that amount, which she received in Spain on account of the loan contracted there two years ago . . .' No excuse had served, the ambassador continued, and the adventurers had been compelled to pledge themselves for £60,000, while the staplers provided the balance.[19]

The Spanish debt itself had long since been paid off, but its legacy in the form of consequent bonds to Schetz, Lixhalles, and others must have been a burden of approximately that size. Just how the transaction worked is not clear, because it did not pass through Gresham's account, but it seems likely that a considerable proportion of the £290,000-worth of bonds delivered to the council between March 1556 and May 1557 were discharged by this means. Probably the companies were forced to use their own credit in Antwerp to discharge the queen's obligations to her creditors, accepting repayment by instalments from the receipt of exchequer. Gresham continued to work alongside this system in a relationship which is not entirely clear. He received from the exchequer for transmission to the merchants sums well in excess of the £55,727 which appears under that heading in his account.[20] He was also still transacting business as the queen's agent. In November 1555 he had taken the unusual step of bringing £45,000-worth of new obligations to the council for endorsement, presumably in an attempt on the government's part to increase control.[21] However, the expedient was not repeated, and in the following year he was conducting his business with the bankers much as before. His position was clearly not an easy one. In August 1555 he had written cheerfully that the queen's credit in Antwerp was good, and must be kept so, but within a month he was negotiating the prolongation of the bulk of the debt for six months, usually a sign of pressure.[22] In November he managed to discharge a series of obligations totalling £38,085 with the aid of the staplers and adventurers, who supplied sums which were duly recorded in his accounts, as we have seen. Only £1000 had been taken up at interest to meet these bonds, a situation which he described to the queen as 'much to her honour',[23] but it had cost him considerable effort, and perhaps helped to persuade the council that other methods must be tried. At the end of February 1556 he was instructed to prolong the whole of the outstanding loan for six months. On 24 February he reported that he had prolonged £40,000, but could get only half of the balance at 7 per cent.[24] By the middle of March he had succeeded, and on the 15th reported that the whole £70,000 was now prolonged, and no more obligations were to fall due until October.[25] Presumably this represented the debt for which he was at that date still responsible, the £97,000-worth of obligations presented to the council in June being cancelled through the agency of the two companies. When the £40,000 which Gresham had prolonged in February fell due, it seems that the council again succeeded in transferring liability to the companies, although perhaps not without a struggle. In October, Michieli reported that the adventurers had paid off another £40,000 debt for the queen in Antwerp,[26] and these obligations must have been included among those delivered for cancellation in November and December 1556, all of which had fallen due between 30 September and 31 October.

The remaining £30,000 had probably been discharged by Gresham with the aid of fresh obligations, according to his usual custom. Meanwhile he had incurred another obligation, probably solicited, through the helpful intervention of the king. On 25 April 1556 Ortel, the Fuggers' agent in the Low Countries, had agreed to provide 541,000 ducats for the king for one year at 14 per cent. Of this sum 105,800 ducats, about £35,000, had been paid to Gresham at the same rate.[27] At the end of 1556, therefore, in spite of two substantial interventions by the London merchants, the foreign debt still amounted to between £65,000 and £70,000. However, on 21 December, Michieli again reported that the queen had called upon the aid of the merchant adventurers, contracting with them to meet another debt for £40,000 which was due in April, and agreeing to repay the money to them in three months by means of assignments.[28] As we have already seen, obligations to a total of £69,000 which had fallen due in April were surrendered to the council in May 1557. All these sums were paid in the Low Countries, so presumably Ortel had accepted discharge through intermediaries there, rather than at the Spanish fairs as originally specified. No fresh bonds were sealed at this point, so the debts which remained were domestic ones, owed by the crown to the staplers and adventurers, particularly the latter. The discharge of so formidable a foreign debt was a considerable achievement, and one which seems to have been the culmination of a policy shaped between the summer of 1555 (when the council first started receiving cancelled obligations) and the spring of 1556 when a high-powered commission headed by Winchester and Paget was set up 'to take order for the better and speedier payments of the Crown's debts to merchants and other strangers dwelling beyond the seas, and to the merchant staplers and adventurers . . .'[29] Borrowing abroad had proved an extremely expensive expedient. Thomas Gresham, John Gresham, and Nicholas Holborne had received about £195,000 from the mint and the exchequer between September 1554 and August 1557. Against that they can only be shown to have paid in, or otherwise profitably employed about the queen's business, about £100,000 sterling. Of course they were repaying a proportion of the capital borrowed as well as interest and brokerage charges. Thomas Gresham's account, which is the more explicit on this point, claimed £41,900 for interest, brokerage, and his own expenses; between 17 and 18 per cent on the money which he borrowed. The interest rates charged by the bankers varied from 11 or 12 per cent up to 15 per cent, with occasional concealed rates as high as 18 per cent, so an average of 17 per cent including all expenses was not excessive.[30] However, it did mean that over a period of slightly less than three years the mint and the exchequer had to cover an expenditure of about £95,000, or nearly £32,000 a year, on these accounts alone, in addition to the sums which had to be reimbursed direct to the staplers and adventurers. These are hard to calculate because of the danger of double jeopardy involved in the complex relationship between the companies and Gresham, but cannot have amounted to less than £80,000 sterling if the whole debt was cleared, as it almost certainly was. This sum may well not have been completely discharged by August 1557, and a proportion of it at least was paid in assignments, so the direct impact upon the exchequer during the period under consideration may not have been as great as the total might suggest – which was no doubt why this course of action was chosen.

There was, however, a debt of a different kind to be paid to the merchants. It is not surprising that Gresham constantly urged the council to 'be good' to them, and backed them strongly in their perpetual struggle with the Hanse. Nor is it surprising that the council felt under an obligation to respond. In the summer of 1556 they placed a general embargo on the Low Countries trade for about three months in response to the wishes of the adventurers, stirring up in the process a series of quarrels with the Venetians and with Philip's subjects in Brabant, as we have seen.[31] A few months later, when he was reporting the bargain of December 1556, Michieli added

> . . . on account of these and other conveniences received by the Court, the Royal Council has conceded to them that henceforth woollens exported by aliens to Flanders shall not be landed elsewhere than at Bruges, under heavy penalties . . . This is extremely inconvenient and detrimental to the merchants of all nations, many of whom, although they have already been to complain of it, were answered that the order cannot be repealed . . .[32]

In May 1558, after the loss of the Calais staple, the staplers wanted permission to sell their wool anywhere in the Low Countries 'without a particular place assigned', and again the council backed them, to the king's great annoyance.[33] The strong backing which the English council gave to its merchants was the direct cause of a sharp deterioration in relations with the Hanseatic League at the end of 1557 and beginning of 1558. So bad had the situation become by February 1558 that the English were convinced that the league, in alliance with Denmark, was fitting out a fleet against them. The league in fact had no such intention, but it again appealed to the king, who urged the justice of its cause upon the English council. Neither the council nor the queen, however, were in any position to listen to such arguments, and the continuing quarrel played an important part in chilling relations between Philip and his wife's advisers during the last six months of the reign. On the other hand, the crown's financial difficulties considerably assisted the merchant adventurers in their struggle to recover from the serious trade slump of the early 1550s.

The original decision to increase the foreign debt in the first year of the reign had probably been inspired by a belief that the crown's financial difficulties could be overcome by a policy of retrenchment and reorganization at home and by the conviction that it was preferable to meet the immediate problem by short-term borrowing abroad rather than by seeking new grants of direct or indirect taxation. If this was the calculation, it turned out to be unsound for two reasons. In the first place the reforms which were carried out benefited the exchequer both less and more slowly than had been anticipated, so that without the benefit of the last instalment of the Edwardian subsidy there was no surplus to discharge the 'Spanish loan' when it fell due. Secondly, the necessity to continue the debt in Antwerp, at a high level, cost the mint and the exchequer at least

£32,000 a year in the second, third, and fourth years of the reign, a burden which the ordinary revenue was quite unable to sustain. Between Easter 1554 and Easter 1555 the summary of expenditure from the receipt of exchequer, which was by this time recording all payments except those of the mint, shows a total of £138,326.[34] There is, unfortunately, no comparable summary of income during this period, but a memorandum drawn up at some time during 1555 calculated the landed revenues of the crown in England and Wales at £82,741 'ultra reprisas'.[35] A very rough computation of the year's income can thus be made by adding an estimated £25,000 for customs revenues (£22,407 in the previous year) and £25,000 for the revenues of the Duchy of Lancaster and wards and liveries (£14,000 and £10,000 in 1557) to produce a total of around £132,000. Although it is impossible to trust such an approximation very far, it is thus probable that, even during a year without exceptional commitments, the government was slightly in deficit. Of course the receipt of the Spanish silver by the mint transformed the immediate 'balance of payments' situation, particularly in view of the fact that none of the consequent bonds were discharged until the next accounting year. On the other hand, it would be entirely misleading to include the whole of that loan in the income for a single year; also Egerton paid an equivalent amount into the hands of Peckham, who was acting, as we have seen, the part of a national treasurer at this time. Commentators, both foreign and domestic, certainly believed that England was still in deep financial difficulties. In November 1554, during his visit to Brussels, Paget admitted the seriousness of the situation,

> . . . whereas the country was formerly so well off as to be able to supply its friends and neighbours, it was now sorely embarrassed itself, and the Queen unable to find money for her household expenses or her officers' pay.[36]

Paget professed to believe that the situation could be righted in eighteen months, but he did not explain how. In March 1555 Sir John Mason complained bitterly from Brussels that he was always in arrears with his pay and allowances. There was continual talk of retrenchment and improvement, he went on, confiding in Petre, but never any real improvement, in spite of the opportunity created by peace. The situation was a disgrace, to the 'dishonour, shame and displeasure of Almighty God'![37] At about the same time a certain John Potter in London wrote gloomily to his correspondent in the north that money was acutely scarce in the capital, and that there were 'many merchants bankerowts'.[38]

The summer weather of 1555 was bad, and there was general

scarcity and hardship, so that the council's preparations for the parliament were made against a background of conflicting political and financial pressures. On 15 August the earl of Cumberland wrote to his agent John Holmes to say that he had received a privy seal demand for a loan, and would have to try and borrow the money to meet it, a difficult operation in view of the general scarcity. How many such demands were sent out at this stage is not clear, or what sort of sum was raised. It may have been a pilot scheme for the much bigger operation of the following year, or a forlorn attempt to escape the necessity to ask parliament for a subsidy.[39] However, by September it was as obvious to the Venetian ambassador as it must have been to the council that only direct taxation could provide any remedy for the queen's debts, and when parliament opened on 21 October, the ailing Gardiner performed his last public service to the crown in a major speech describing the urgency of the situation. If Michieli is to be believed, the chancellor wasted no opportunity of embroidering his story. Not only had Mary on her accession 'found the revenues of the Crown so exhausted and consumed' that she was unable to avail herself of them for her necessary and heavy expenses, but she had required further loans for their discharge. King Philip, he went on with careful vagueness, 'whilst in England had spent much more than her Majesty', and the queen had also been graciously pleased, not only to pardon many rebels of whose estates she could have availed herself, but also to forgive and remit 'upwards of 1,200,000 ducats' of Edwardian taxation.[40] If this was actually the figure named by Gardiner – £400,000 – he exaggerated wildly, and this may have been one of the reasons why many of the Commons were openly unimpressed by his oration. This was an occasion upon which Philip's presence in England was needed, and the courteous letter of apology which was read on his behalf was no substitute. A few days later, on 27 October, Michieli reported again at length, describing the setting-up of a joint committee of both Houses to consider the subsidy, and also the care which was being taken at the same time to reassure the holders of church property. 'Meanwhile', he went on, 'the English of inferior grade, even the members of the Lower House . . . give it freely to be understood with regard to this pecuniary supply, that there will be much ado before obtaining it . . .'[41] At such a time of poverty and scarcity, it was being argued, the country could not stand further taxation.

> Her Majesty should rather compel all the debtors of the Crown to pay up their arrears, there being [many] great personages here who owe, some five, some six, some eight thousand pounds sterling and upwards . . .

Also, since she was so heavily in debt, the queen ought to abandon all plans for returning spiritual revenues to the church.[42] The hardships were real enough, violent storms at the end of September having ruined what was left of an already poor harvest, but the debts owed by 'great personages' are less easy to verify. As we have seen, there were many recognizances, but these were not debts in the ordinary sense, and when debts to the crown were formally forgiven, they were nearly always for much smaller sums than those mentioned.[43] Wishful thinking, it seems, lay behind this suggestion for a way to remedy the crown's financial problems.

Sensing a political opportunity, Antoine de Noailles assiduously encouraged opposition to the subsidy bill, '. . . if my intrigues and spies prove of service', he wrote, 'she will get nothing'.[44] Such optimism, however, soon proved to be misplaced. The original proposal, which was probably contained in one of the draft bills which the select council agreed to have ready by 11 October, seems to have been for a subsidy and three fifteenths.[45] By the time this emerged from the committee of both Houses, it included only two fifteenths, and in that form it was debated by the Commons on 28 and 29 October.[46] According to Michieli the fifteenths caused particular discontent because they were thought to press most heavily upon the poor, and on 31 October Sir William Petre delivered a message from the queen agreeing to forgo these taxes, '. . . whereupon the motion passed without the slightest opposition'.[47] Noailles allowed himself the indulgence of some sarcasm at the expense of his English friends who had not proved either numerous or determined enough to force a division, and was soon to find them in a tougher frame of mind over the spiritual revenues.[48] The subsidy act, 2 and 3 Philip and Mary, c. 25, ordered a new assessment by commissioners with an extremely detailed brief, and provided a sliding scale for payments on moveable property: 8*d.* in the £ from £5 to £10, 12*d.* up to £20, and 16*d.* over £20. Goods worth less than £5 were exempt. Lands from 20*s.* per annum upwards were rated at 2*s.* in the £, and, as usual, a higher scale was imposed upon aliens. The subsidy was to be paid in two instalments, one by 1 March 1556 and the other by 20 May 1557.[49] Since the assessment was to apply to each instalment, it should be doubled to get a true picture of the level of taxation. At the same time a second statute, 2 and 3 Philip and Mary, c. 22, confirmed the grant of a clerical subsidy by the two convocations. This was to be levied according to the valuation 'now in the Exchequer', presumably the *Valor Ecclesiasticus,* and was to be 'taken and levied of all and singular . . . spiritual promotions', or rather on nine-tenths of their value. Stipends below £5 per annum were exempt, up to 20 marks paid a flat rate of 6*s.* 8*d.,* and over that level 2s. in the £. Monastic pensions of over 40s. were taxed at the same rate, and the subsidy was to be paid in three instalments over three years, making a total burden of 6s. in the £. The clergy were thus slightly more generous in their grant than the laity, but not as much so as might at first appear.[50]

This taxation was to be the sheet anchor of the crown's revenues over the next two years. Out of approximately £430,000 received by the exchequer between Michaelmas 1555 and Michaelmas 1557, over £181,000, or 41 per cent, came from the subsidies.[51] Unfortunately even this was not enough to keep the government out of difficulties. During the same period (which included the first six months of the war) the expenditure recorded in the receipt of exchequer was £537,432;[52] so that, allowing £25,000 a year for income from non-exchequer sources, there was still a deficit of about £57,000 over the two years.

This account also included the collection and part at least of the repayment of £42,000 in privy seal loans, which had been demanded during the autumn of 1556. These letters seem to have requested a uniform £100 from each recipient, so presumably about 420 of the queen's richest subjects were solicited in this manner.[53] There was considerable resentment, and several of those approached endeavoured to evade or refuse payment. On 18 August, John White, the sheriff of Hampshire, wrote to the council to acknowledge receipt of 13 privy seal letters, all but one of which he had succeeded in delivering. On the whole, he reported, those who had received the letters were willing to pay, but some had been misdirected to men who were too poor, and in general the gentlemen were short of cash, so that it would have been better policy to send the letters to 'rich farmers' – presumably yeomen.[54] White's experience was less trying than that of many who were given the task of handing out the demands. As early as 24 August, Thomas Chafyn of Salisbury had provoked a sharp rebuke from the council, and in early October, Thomas Mildmay was sent letters of admonition to pass on to the recalcitrant.[55] By the middle of October 'refusers' were being called before the council itself, and in November the governor of the merchant adventurers was instructed to punish (in some undefined way) those who had not subscribed.[56] The sanctions which the council were willing to impose were limited. In January 1557 six Gloucestershire men were ordered either to pay or to remain in attendance upon the council, and since they make no further appearance in the records, presumably they paid. In spite of the complaints and obstructiveness, the manoeuvre appears to have been a success, and although it is unlikely that the whole sum was repaid when it became due on 1 November 1557, it was discharged during the accounting period of the following loan, as we shall see in due course. If the ordinary income for 1 and 2 Philip and Mary can be accepted as approximately £132,000, then the income for 2 and 3 Philip and Mary – £184,279 – confirms that the subsidies increased revenue by about 40 per cent. The following year the comparable figure was £211,515, the accounting period terminating conveniently at Easter, just before the outbreak of war.[57] At the same time, expenditure for the year 2 and 3 rose sharply to £213,702 as the loan repayments began to bite, and that for the year 3 and 4 to £216,273, so that even with the benefit of parliamentary taxation and without the excessive demands of war, there was an inexorable tendency for the annual balance to be in deficit.[58] There was little or no resistance to the payment of the 1555 subsidies, an early Elizabethan account of 1559 noting that they had been paid in full before the 1558 subsidy began to be due.[59]

This endemic problem was not the result of negligence in administration. In two areas in particular the lord treasurer and the council were noticeably diligent, in the taking of accounts and the management of the crown lands. We have already seen that defaulters like Bunny were being pursued from the previous reign, and some of those who were proceeded against had undischarged debts going back forty years. Lord Grey of Wilton, Lord Cobham, the earl of Pembroke, and the earl of Worcester were among those proceeded against in exchequer chamber, along with a great many lesser men, mostly for debts between £200 and about £2000.[60] Two special commissions, one in the autumn of 1554 and the other in the summer of 1556, found Sir Thomas Egerton, the under-treasurer of the mint, indebted to the crown for £7497.[61] Another revealed that Sir Maurice Dennis, 'late Treasurer of Calais', owed £7486.[62] Andrew Wise, the under-treasurer and receiver-general in Ireland, was found guilty of malpractices in star chamber in September 1555, and bound in sureties for no less than £10,000, although the extent of his default was probably far less.[63] In November 1555, as we have already seen, a rather belated commission was set up to call in the accounts for chantry property and other church goods; while in 1556 another team, led by Paget and Thirlby, was given the task of investigating 'all embezzlements and concealments' of rents chattels etc., late of Edward, late Duke of Somerset . . .'[64] Collectively negligence and malfeasance, both by officials and by private individuals, presented a gloomy picture, although it seems likely that deliberate fraud on a large scale was comparatively rare. Whether the government's conscientious efforts during this period were well rewarded is not very clear. On 10 May 1555 it was recorded that Dennis had paid £4906 of his debt.[65] Egerton, after a period in the Tower, probably paid in full, while in September 1556 lands which had belonged to Thomas Wriothesley, earl of Southampton, who had died in 1550, were seized from his heirs in satisfaction for a £1000 debt to the crown which his executors had failed to discharge.[66] On the other hand, as we have seen, substantial debts were forgiven to those in political favour, such as Pembroke or Lord Williams. Some debtors, moreover, were simply unable to pay, and did not have adequate assets. Edward Pease of London, for example, could pay only £500 out of a debt of £2310, and the period which he spent in the Fleet by way of punishment did nothing to replenish the royal coffers.[67] Income from 'debts upon obligations', which presumably included the fruits of this administrative and judicial pressure, ran at a substantial £31,105 in the third year of the reign, and £36,498 in the fourth, although it is impossible to discover what proportion of this income accrued in such a fashion.

Tighter control of the crown lands is similarly easier to illustrate from orders and commissions than it is to assess in terms of financial advantage. At some stage Winchester, who seems to have been apprehensive of the effects of Mary's generosity, extracted from her a promise 'not to determine the gift of any land' without his consent. The queen took this in good part, and in an undated letter which survives among the Cotton MSS she sent a 'bill' for his approval, endorsing it 'mylorde I moste hartely thancke you for your dayly paynfulnes in my service . . .'[68] In 1555 a council committee recommended that surveys be made of the crown lands, with a view to increasing their value, and this was done. As we have seen, the revenues of these lands were carefully listed, county by county, no distinction being made between those which had accounted to augmentations and the 'ancient demesne'. At the same time a list of all forests, parks, and chases in the queen's hands, together with their officers, was also drawn up.[69] In the following year a memorandum of fifteen articles recommended that all manors and casualties be 'placed to farm', that urban properties be fee farmed, that no lease should be made for more than 21 years, and that every lease of more than 10 marks should pass the great seal.[70] Whether this memorandum was the work of a council committee or of some self-appointed adviser is not clear. It was summarized and annotated in Latin, possibly for the king's benefit, and also contained some administrative proposals which expressed the views of conservative exchequer officials: all crown lands should account through the sheriffs, and the duchy of Lancaster should be 'reduced to the exchequer' to save the unnecessary expenses of a separate establishment. Similar, but not identical, proposals were also contained in a treatise on the organization of the exchequer drawn up at about the same time, and it seems likely that both documents originated among the officers of that institution. Not many of the proposals were implemented. There was no universal policy of leasing or 'farming'; stewards and other officials continued to account 'augmentationwise'; the duchy of Lancaster was not absorbed. Nevertheless, the administration was overhauled. In January 1557 a special commission was set up, not only to survey afresh all the possessions and revenues of the crown, including the duchies of Lancaster and Cornwall and the earldom of Chester, but also to investigate concealments, under-leasing, and the maintenance of husbandry.[71] This was a major stock-taking operation, necessitating the appointment of many deputies to assist with the work county by county. Shortly after, on 4 May, a further commission, including many of the same councillors, was instructed to take surrender of indentures, patents, grants, and leases of crown property, and to grant renewal for adequate fines. This appears to have been a comprehensive operation, since the commissioners' brief instructed them

> To take surrender of any manor, lande, tenement (etc.) of any person having estate for term of lyfe, lives, yeres or otherwyse, and therupon to make newe leases of the same for fynes or other considerations . . .[72]

However, this was not to be a full implementation of the 1556 proposals. 21 years was to be the minimum rather than the maximum term for such leases, and the commissioners were also given discretion to 'devise', other than by lease, 'any manor or land being within the survey of thexchequer' for 21 years or more 'or for life or lives, in possession or reversion'.

The effect of these efforts upon the financial return from the crown lands does not appear to have been as great as was once believed. In the fifth year of King Edward VI (a year of heavy sales) the overall income from the crown lands, in exchequer, duchy, and augmentations, was just over £192,000 before deductions.[73] A comparable calculation for the fourth year of Mary shows about £123,000, and for the third year of Elizabeth £106,000.[74] Net figures or 'clear revenue', appear to present a totally different picture: £42,000 in 5 Edward VI; about £60,000 in 4 Mary; and £85,000 in 3 Elizabeth.[75] It is difficult to say which picture is the more meaningful in terms of estate management, because, as we have already seen, the methods of calculating 'clear revenue' changed, and fluctuating sales distorted the figures still further. However, at this point we are really concerned with income, not with expenditure policy, which shifted liabilities from one account to another, so it seems reasonable to conclude that, with sales continuing throughout

Mary's reign, the efforts of the reformers did not make a significant difference to the crown's income. Fresh sales, as we have already seen, had been authorized in the spring of 1554. On 8 October in the same year Sir Anthony St Leger was commissioned to sell crown lands in Ireland to the modest total of £1000 per annum.[76] and thereafter there was a pause. The next sales were undertaken in March 1557, as part of the 'tidying-up' operation also expressed in the general survey. Winchester, Thirlby, Rochester, and three others were commissioned to undertake a survey of castles and houses belonging to the crown, and to discharge by composition all officers where the premises were ruined or out of use, at the same time leasing off the sites for whatever could be obtained. The same commission was also to survey the royal parks, to dispark 'such as they shall think needful', and

> . . . to bargain and sell for ready money any messuages or houses not having above 12 acres of land and being no part of the demesnes of any of the Crown manors.[77]

We do not, unfortunately, know how successful this operation was. Fragmentary lands of this kind were not very marketable, which had been one of the reasons why much chantry property had been leased rather than sold by augmentations in the first place. Also stewardships of royal manors, constableships of castles, and keeperships of parks were much sought-after local preferments, not so much for their income but for the honour which they conferred upon their holders. Indeed local gentlemen, and even courtiers, were sometimes willing to undertake them at a loss for that reason. The crown always needed this kind of patronage to bind men to its service, and there was never enough of it, so it is quite likely that the good intentions of this policy of retrenchment were not realized to any great extent. A further commission on 20 April 1557 carried the sales policy further, empowering Rochester, Petre, Englefield, Baker, and Waldegrave to 'sell and conclude for ready money . . . any honours lands advowsons liberties etc. of which the Crown is seised of any estate of inheritance . . .' without limit until the commission should be cancelled under the great seal.[78] Since the lands so sold were to be held of the crown in chief by knight service, there was clearly no unexpressed assumption that these, too, would be fragments, and the openendedness of the terms suggests a pressing anxiety to make sales.

The evidence as to the intentions of the council is quite clear: retrenchment and reorganization to maximize profits and cut waste, plus a flexible sales policy designed particularly to dispose of properties which might be difficult to administer. The evidence of implementation is confusing and contradictory, and some of the commissions seem to have accomplished little or nothing. On the other hand, there is tangible evidence that the commissions issued to Sir Edmund Peckham as high treasurer of the mint were implemented. Peckham had, as we have already seen, acted as general treasurer of the kingdom during and immediately after the reorganization of the exchequer. Under the terms of this commission £73,626 of the 'Spanish loan' came into the mint between 13 February and 26 March 1555, and £17,735 in Spanish reals was recoined into current English money at a standard of 11 oz. fine.[79] The mint was active throughout 1554 and 1555, producing altogether £59,000 in fine gold coin, and about £155,000 in silver to the standard 11/1.[80] Thereafter there was a lull, but two commissions, of June and August 1557, resulted in the minting of a further quantity of fine angels, half-angels, sixpences, groats, and pennies by the end of the reign.[81] Following the example set by Northumberland in the last years of his authority, Mary minted only good-quality coin for use within England and in international commerce. She did not, however, resist altogether the temptations of debasement. In March of 1555, £6674 in base English money was recoined into £13,382 of 'rose pence' at 3/12 fine – a profit of about £6500.[82] This exceedingly base coin was then sent over for use in Ireland. Four further commissions for similar debasement were issued on 28 February and 24 March 1556, 4 September 1556, and 19 May 1557.[83] Altogether about £32,000 of base English money was treated in this way, realizing a profit to the crown of approximately £39,000; not a great deal spread over four years, but enough to be some help to the exchequer and a considerable nuisance to the Irish.

Mary's failure to tackle the question of a general re-coinage may not, as Feaveryear believed, have caused all the good coin to escape abroad,[84] but it did leave a great deal of base-metal circulating in England. This continued to cause problems by encouraging inflation, creating uncertainties in the exchange rates, and providing golden opportunities for forgery. The council had announced its intention to mint good coin in a proclamation of August 1553 which had fixed the values of the coins to be issued, and confirmed the devalued rates declared for the base money in the last relevant proclamation of Edward VI.[85] In March and May of 1554 three further proclamations had laid down official exchange rates for French, Spanish, Imperial, and Portuguese coin, although these seem to have borne only an approximate resemblance to the rates which prevailed in Antwerp.[86] In December 1554 another new coinage was announced, presumably that which was to bear the king's image as well as the queen's. This was to be of the same high standard of fineness as the first, in a hopeful attempt to counteract

> . . . the great and intolerable charges grown and chanced to her highness specially and also to all her loving subjects, as well by reason of the base moneys made within her realms and dominions as also by the great quantities of the like base moneys made and counterfeit both in this her Highness realm and in other foreign realms conveyed hither and issued out . . .[87]

The economic misfortunes of 1555 and 1556 aggravated all these problems, and an indignant proclamation of December 1556 denounced those who were spreading rumours that the teston was to be devalued.

> . . . their Majesties be heartily sorry that any man . . . should in this unmerciful sort (in this time of dearth wherewith it has pleased Almighty God presently to plague the world for the sins and wickedness thereof) seek upon this pretence their own gains with so great an injury and oppression of their poor needy neighbours . . .[88]

However, to judge from the level of official reaction, by far the greatest plague was forgery. The reasons for this are not far to seek. With the mint producing coin of good quality, the temptation to melt such coin down and issue a counterfeit of the base Henrician and Edwardian issues which were still current was irresistible. Coining became a widespread industry, not only in England but also abroad, particularly in France. Counterfeiting the coin of the realm was ancient treason, but until the statute of 1 Mary, c. 6 there was no adequate penalty for forging the coin of other realms which was allowed to pass for current. This offence also became treason by the terms of the act, a law which was confirmed in almost identical terms in the following year by 1 and 2 Philip and Mary, c. 11.[89] Armed with these laws, the government made strenuous efforts to hunt down and punish the coiners. In December 1554 a committee of the council was set up headed by Sir Edward Hastings 'to have the examination of all such as counterfeit coin',[90] and thereafter the council records are liberally sprinkled with orders to investigate, letters of thanks for information and arrests, and records of offenders imprisoned or sent for trial. Such trials were sometimes conducted in king's bench, sometimes at the assizes, and sometimes by commission of oyer and terminer. In April 1556, for example, the commissioners in Buckinghamshire were sharply ordered to proceed against offenders in accordance with their powers, and not to bother the council.[91] In January 1557 it was suspected that coining was actually going on within Newgate,[92] and there was no diminution of activity on the part of the authorities during the latter part of the reign.

It is against this background that we must see the plan of the Dudley conspirators to abstract bullion from the exchequer and to mint it in France. At least one and probably two mints were set up by the conspirators or their agents with the tacit permission of the French authorities. Patriotic motives were claimed; '. . . for the ayde of his countrymen against the spanyardes . . .', as one of the agents explained.[93] Engravers and other workmen were recruited, not a difficult task since the vigilance of the council had caused several known forgers to take refuge across the channel. When the conspiracy collapsed, the mints remained, discharging considerable quantities of false coin into England. On 3 April 1556 a proclamation warned all loyal subjects to be on their guard against the '. . . great quantity of forged and counterfeit coins of gold as well of this realm as of other realms being current within the same [which] hath of late and daily is counterfeit, forged, and brought in . . . by divers naughty and ill-disposed persons . . .'[94] On the 27th of the same month a further edict offered 'the whole penalty and forfeiture of every such offence' by way of reward to those laying information which should lead to the apprehension of the smugglers – an indication of the council's anxiety.[95] In August 1556, as a result of persistent diplomatic pressure, the French agreed to suppress a mint operating near Dieppe,[96] but there seems to have been another at Rouen, which continued working at least down to the outbreak of war. Criminals working for their own profit conveniently served the purposes of English political conspirators and French foreign policy alike. The French tried throughout the reign to 'de-stabilize' the English domestic situation, and aggravating the country's economic problems in this way had the double advantage of being easy to operate and apparently too trivial to cause major diplomatic incidents.

The actual scale of the problem is very hard to judge. We have no means of knowing how much counterfeit coin was put into circulation, or how many offenders were tried or executed. In the Hilary Term 1558 a certain John Chapman and his wife Jane, of Babraham in Cambridgeshire, were sentenced to death in king's bench, and subsequently pardoned.[97] A thorough examination on the plea rolls, however, reveals only a handful of other cases, so it seems likely that the majority of offenders, if they were brought to trial at all, appeared before commissioners of oyer and terminer. No statistical conclusions can be drawn from the surviving evidence, but we can obtain a few instructive glimpses of the process of smuggling in operation. The confession of one Bawcriffe, taken in March 1556, and that of William Hinnes from the same month, explain in some detail how the Dudley conspirators went about recruiting workers for the Dieppe mint.[98] Also, on 6 September 1558 a pardon was issued for one Henry Savell 'late of Halifax . . . merchant' who had, on 11 November 1556, attempted to pass in Norwich 66 false coins produced in Rouen and Dieppe.[99] The government had also created problems for itself by the policy of minting base coin for Ireland, and on 16 September 1556 issued a proclamation forbidding the circulation of 'rose pence' in England and declaring that they were '. . . no more to be taken for lawful or current money within this . . . realm of England'.[100] The accounts of the eventual recoinage of 1561 do not suggest that the absolute quantity of base English coin counterfeited during this period was very great, although the evil effects of counterfeiting upon the balance of payments were one of the main reasons adduced for the decision to call in the base coin.[101] This may well have reflected the consequences of counterfeiting for confidence in the money rather than any major quantitative effect. Most of the forgers operating within England seem to have been small-scale practitioners operating for their own profit; while the mints in France, which seem to have had a much larger output, concentrated upon counterfeiting French and Imperial coins. The bullion content of these was, of course, well below that of the genuine article, and they could be detected by their light weight. When they were so detected, English magistrates were under orders to 'break and deface' them. The traditional crime of 'clipping' coin also continued, although it aroused much less anxiety than counterfeiting, and the fact that the base coin was found to be only $3\frac{1}{2}$ per cent light on average when it was called in, suggests a manageable level of activity.[102]

Although statistical conclusions are impossible, the state of the coinage created nagging and consistent problems throughout the reign. The reasons why Mary's council failed to grasp the nettle which was to be seized so swiftly by her successor can only be guessed at. Perhaps Winchester, who was the obvious element of continuity in financial policy, moved only slowly towards the view that a recoinage was both necessary and feasible. The technical expertise was certainly present, as many of the officials were the same, and at some date which was probably in the autumn of 1556 a detailed memorandum was submitted to the council containing an analysis of the fineness of the existing money and proposals for a recoinage very similar to that which eventually took place.[103] It may well have been awareness of the scheme contained in this document which provoked the rumours of devaluation which the council denounced in a sharp proclam ition of 22 December. The most likely explanation for the decision not to proceed with the recoinage at that stage is that it was judged to be politically impossible in the context of dearth, hardship, and discontent then prevailing to 'cry down' the debased coinage to the extent which would be necessary if the operation was to be financially practicable.[104] At the same time the mint itself was scrutinized with a view to economy. Four years earlier the delinquencies of Sir William Sharrington had helped to bring about the demise of the Bristol mint, and now Thomas Egerton's indebtedness seems to have contributed to a plan for the drastic reduction of the establishment of the Tower mint itself. In close proximity to the memorandum mentioned above there exists among the state papers a draconian scheme to reduce the number of officials 'on the establishment' from 25 to 5.[105] The author commenced by outlining 'the old order' which had prevailed before 1545, in which every 'bringer in of silver' had paid 12*d*. in the pound troy. Of this 12*d*. the king had taken 2*d*. to pay the wages of the warden and five other officials, a total outlay of £145 a year; the mint master had taken 5*d*., to bear the charges of waste and to pay the wages of the inferior officials; and the moneyers themselves had taken 5*d*. 'for their workmanship', finding their own victuals and implements. By the 'new order' the charge was 17½*d*. in the pound, and the king took the whole sum, bearing in return a wage bill of £857, plus £304 for diets, coals, and instruments, a total outlay of £1161 per annum. The proposed reform amounted to nothing more than a careful resurrection of the 'old order'. The charge was to be 18*d*. in the pound, of which the queen was to take 6*d*., providing in return five officials at a total cost of £141; the mint master was to have 6*d*., and the moneyers 6*d*., on the same terms as before 1545. The rate for gold was to be 4*s*. in the pound, of which the queen was to take 12*d*., the mint master 2*s*., and the moneyers 12*d*. The scheme was never implemented, although it bears a strong resemblance to that which was to be adopted after Sir Thomas Stanley's death in 1572.[106] Its main significance lies in the evidence which it offers of conservative thinking on retrenchment. Whereas the changes of 1545 were designed to bring the whole operation of the mint under royal patronage and control, those proposed in 1556 would have returned the bulk of it to the private enterprise of contractors. This would not have been any less costly to the customer, and its effect upon the royal balance of payments would have been small as long as the mint was busy. But it would have meant a significant fall in the number of offices in the gift of the crown, and a considerable economy when the mint was standing idle. By September 1556 the mint was idle '. . . as there have not byn of long

L

tyme any coynage', and as a partial substitute for the economies proposed, the council discontinued the diets of all the mint officials, at a saving of £104 *per annum* and an unknown cost in annoyance.[107]

Retrenchment was more successful in other areas of royal finance which had long caused anxiety, such as Ireland and the household. In the latter case there are, as we have already seen, two sets of figures, differently computed but not incompatible. According to the first set, household expenditure, having risen to £75,043 in the second year of the reign, fell only slightly to £69,524 in the third, and then sharply to £47,552 in the fourth. There are no figures in this account for the fifth year of the reign, or the first year of Elizabeth, but they resume in 2 Elizabeth with a total of £46,800.[108] The other set is calculated by financial years, not regnal years – Michaelmas to Michaelmas, and shows for the year 1554–55 an expenditure of £59,453 and a deficit of £10,251. For the year 1555–56 the equivalent figures are £52,766 and £7717; for 1556–57, £54,411 and £4858; and for 1557–58, £36,208, with a surplus of £1744.[109] Clearly the discrepancies between these two sets of figures are rather greater than can be explained by the different methods of computation, but they tell the same story of increasingly effective economies over the second half of the reign. In the case of Ireland important reforms seem to have originated with the decision in August 1554 to set up a special committee of the council headed by Winchester and Thirlby to take order '. . . as well for the disburdeyning superfluous charges and discharging of the debtes there as allso for the staie and good ordre of the said realm'.[110] This committee sent articles of inquiry to the deputy and council in Ireland, and probably sent its own agents over to view the situation at first hand. As a result, military expenditure was slashed – from £35,251 in the first year of the reign and £36,046 in the second to £16,062 in the third, and probably about £15,000 in the fourth, for which the equivalent figures are missing.[111] This dramatic improvement was not merely the result of improved surveillance. The return of St Leger to Ireland, and more particularly the return of England to the catholic fold, reduced the need for an expensive military establishment. Down to the fourth year of King Edward VI expenditure under that head had never exceeded £18,500 a year, but with the advent of Sir James Croftes and a 'forward' protestant policy, the cost had gone up to £40,150.[112] Greater administrative care played a part, however. In March 1554 a commission had been set up to take the account of the Irish officials, and Andrew Wise, the former treasurer, was discovered to be heavily in default. So bad was the general situation in the summer of 1554 that the privy council was at one point forced to admit that it had no money to spare for Ireland, and instructed the deputy and council there to borrow £6000 from the executors of the late Justice Lutterell.[113] Thereafter the situation steadily improved, and the cost of Ireland to the exchequer in the fourth year of the reign was only £12,000 – not much more than a third of what it had been in the first year.

In a sense, however, this was a fragile achievement because there was no marked improvement in the ordinary revenues of the kingdom, and by the second year of Elizabeth, when war and the revival of protestantism in England had again created a need for a considerable military presence there, the exchequer was faced with a bill for £25,251.[114] This is not the place to discuss the Irish policy of Mary's council in general, but on balance it seems to have reflected the interests of the Anglo-Irish of the Pale rather than of the expatriate English or of those (like St Leger) who were anxious to accommodate the 'wild Irish' within the commonwealth.[115] Paul IV's bull elevating Ireland to the status of a kingdom was promulgated in England on 16 September 1555. However, as in the case of Henry VIII's assumption of the title (which it tacitly confirmed), the main benefits of this accrued to the Anglo-Irish lawyers and administrators rather than to the crown. The final withdrawal of St Leger and his replacement by the earl of Sussex in 1557, marked the end of the 'greater Ireland' policy for which he had worked, and paved the way for the later Elizabethan policies of conquest and colonization which were to follow. A memorandum of about 1560, while acknowledging the economies achieved by Mary's commissioners, was sharply critical of many features of the existing situation.[116] The constant absences of the lords deputy and their failure to supervise the other officers with sufficient strictness were singled out as two of the main causes of '. . . the great charges and also of the disorder of the said realm . . .' The treasurer, instead of riding round and collecting the revenues, stayed in Dublin '. . . not calling for any more than hath been brought to him. Whereby much arrearages hath growen and become desperate'. The tribute due from the wild Irish had been neither paid nor called for, and the queen's lands and manors 'have upon private suit by the said Lords Deputy been let under the old and just value thereof . . .' The 'great garrisons' which had cost so much had been, it was alleged, largely unused, and the 'good laws' against vagabonds, rumour-mongers, and those who used Irish dress and language were negligently enforced. There was great lack of 'some learned man of English birth' to have 'the chief ordering touching the same laws', and it was a serious disadvantage to Ireland that its money was not current in England. The author judged that now Elizabeth had recovered control of the ecclesiastical property which Mary had alienated, she could by proper administrative reforms make Ireland pay for itself.[117] Clearly such expressions of opinion must be treated with caution, but the author seems to make a good case for saying that the Marian commissions had achieved very little towards improving the returns from the Irish revenues, and that the policy of providing Ireland with a special base currency was deleterious. The Edwardian administration, which had been responsible for many of the problems of Ireland as they appeared in 1560, had at least maintained the coinage on the same basis as England and had avoided compounding the problems of the Irish merchants.

Attempts to augment the royal revenues by improved efficiency of administration and the elimination of waste and corruption enjoyed only marginal success. Neither land revenues nor customs showed improvements commensurate with the amount of work and thought which were put into the various schemes of reform. In addition to the schemes which we have already noticed, a set of articles was drawn up by the council of state at the end of September 1555, proposing not only the familiar survey of the crown lands but also reforms in the collection of customs dues, and other measures of retrenchment.[118] These articles, which were drafted in Latin for the king's benefit, may have been intended to lead to legislation in the forthcoming parliament, but if so, the intention was never carried out. In April 1557 another set of articles concentrated on preventing fraudulent evasion of the customs on cloth, proposing that no cloth should be removed from Blackwell Hall until the duty had been paid.[119] This was presumably aimed at the merchant adventurers rather than the foreigners who had been the target of earlier reforming schemes, but if it was implemented, it made little difference to the 'old' customs. As we have already seen, a lengthy memorandum had been presented in December 1554, blaming the decay of shipping, the scarcity of money, and many other evils upon the Hanse. One of the suggestions then made had been that all clothiers should be compelled to resort to 'their accustomed market' in Blackwell Hall, the argument being that the merchant adventurers were being cut out by the clothiers taking their wares direct to the Steelyard. The government responded to pressure from the adventurers because of their strong financial and political position, not only granting them a new charter in February 1555, but also licensing them to export considerable quantities of 'white' cloth, and periodically placing selective embargoes upon the trade of their rivals. In March of 1556, for example, bonds were taken from a number of foreign merchants not to unload more than a third of the kerseys which they were shipping at Antwerp,[120] and this was followed in July, as we have seen, by a total prohibition of exports to the Low Countries which lasted until November. The initiative which had resulted in the Muscovy voyage of 1553–54 had originally been backed by the Edwardian council, but Mary's government was equally co-operative, and one of the main purposes of the new charter of 1555 was to grant to the adventurers monopolistic rights in the trade which was then in prospect.[121] Shortly after the company received that extensive grant of privileges from Ivan IV which was to be the mainstay of the Elizabethan Muscovy company.[122] The time taken by extended overseas voyages meant that there was little chance for Mary's council to develop a distinctive policy in respect of long-distance trade, even if it had been disposed to do so. However, the failure of various reform projects to make any significant difference to the customs revenues must have contributed to the decision of 1556 or 1557 to venture upon radical change. The new book of rates which resulted in the last year of the reign was to be the outstanding positive achievement of Marian fiscal policy.

Attempts to curtail expenditure by tighter control were appreciably more successful, as we have seen in the cases of the household and Ireland. Similar success seems to have attended efforts to keep down the bills for wages, pensions, and annuities, which had exercised the council in the first year of the reign. The patent rolls give the impression that Mary continued to be generous with new pensions, but the figures for expenditure from the receipt of exchequer tell a rather different story. For the first half-year for which the exchequer controlled the whole account (Easter to Michaelmas 1554) disbursements under this heading totalled £22,119.[123] The following half-year saw a huge increase, to £34,079, but thereafter the improvement was marked: £21,205 from Easter to Michaelmas 1555, £21,778 from Michaelmas 1555 to Easter 1556, £17,271 from Easter to Michaelmas 1556, and £19,440 from Michaelmas 1556 to Easter 1557. Throughout the period wages were running fairly steadily at £14–15,000 per half-year, so we must either assume that some annuity payments were being disguised under other headings, or that they were falling into arrears, or that some genuine and effective economies were being made. The latter seems to be the most rational explanation.[124] At the same time Mary was rewarding some of her servants with grants of land, and although these grants were not necessarily alternatives to annuities, she may to some extent have been saving cash expenditure at the cost of landed income. Not only did the queen restore landed estates to the annual value of nearly £10,000, she also made new grants from former ecclesiastical property, and from lands which had come to the crown by attainder, which totalled £10,250 *per annum*.[125] Over and above

The Reign of Mary Tudor

this, lands to the value of £3982 were conferred upon the restored religious houses, making a total surrender of income amounting to over £24,000 a year. In the light of this it is not, perhaps, surprising that strenuous efforts to improve the returns from the crown lands, although aided by substantial forfeitures early in the reign, failed to halt the decline in gross income.

Mary also insisted upon returning spiritual revenues to the church, and was willing to fight a sharp political battle in her fourth parliament to accomplish it. The details of this transaction need not concern us here, but it was vehemently objected to on the rather curious grounds that the queen could not lawfully diminish the revenues of the crown.[126] The issue was politically sensitive because the laity were always suspicious of any attempt to restore property to the church, and because it coincided, as we have seen, with a demand for a subsidy. The income of first fruits and tenths had been in the region of £25,000 a year, so the concern is understandable, but since the relevant statute also transferred to Cardinal Pole the responsibility for paying monastic and other ecclesiastical pensions, the short-term loss to the crown was hardly discernible.[127] The queen continued her policy of forgiving outstanding debts to newly appointed incumbents, and of making piecemeal restorations of lands and revenue to her bishops, but the results of this after the first year are impossible to quantify, and probably had little effect upon the overall financial situation.

By late 1556 the coming war was casting its shadow before it. In January 1557 a new programme of works was undertaken at Berwick, for which masons were pressed from as far away as Kent,[128] and at the same time the finances of the navy were put on a more regular footing. On the 8th of that month Winchester himself took over responsibility for signing naval warrants. In doing so he undertook to see that the ships were repaired, refurnished, fitted, and victualled, and that the wages of the mariners and workmen were paid. In return he required that Gonson, the treasurer, and Bushe, the surveyor, should account to him at least once a year, that he should have as much timber as might be required from the crown lands, and that £14,000 a year should be placed at his disposal in half-yearly instalments.[129] Within two days a standing warrant had been issued to the exchequer to pay £7000 every six months direct to Gonson.[130] This probably did not represent any significant increase in the naval budget,[131] but it guaranteed Gonson a regular income, and provided against the situation which had arisen in November 1555, when he had found himself nearly £5000 short when confronted with the bills for keeping 15 ships uselessly at sea in anticipation of the emperor's passage. Contrary to what is sometimes supposed, Mary looked after the navy carefully, and it was Elizabeth who reduced the budget to £12,000 a year in 1559.[132] 1556 was in many ways a hard year; by October farmers in Leicestershire were dismissing their servants on the grounds that they could no longer afford to pay their wages, and the council wrote in alarm to the earl of Huntingdon, ordering him to forbid such social irresponsibility and to allow no man to be dismissed without sufficient cause.[133] There were complaints against the oppressive subsidy, and allegations of negligence and corruption in its collection.[134] There were also, as we have seen, complaints against the first privy seal loan, and these were aggravated by rumours (apparently unfounded) that the money was being raised for Philip's benefit. In September, Michieli reported that the fact that the money was to be delivered to Rochester rather than to the lord treasurer had added to the discontent and suspicion.[135] Alarms of this sort were persistent. The Dudley conspirators had been convinced that one of the reasons for Philip's non-return to England was that he was blackmailing the queen for £200,000, and they had formed contingency plans to intercept any such sum, should it be sent out of the country.[136] In fact those who claimed that Philip never drew a penny from England were almost certainly right. On the other hand, the claims of the same writers that he subsidized the queen's government had very little substance. He gave presents and pensions, paid for his own English household, and on two occasions facilitated Gresham's attempts to raise money, once in Spain and once in Antwerp, but no money from his own treasury ever found its way into the English exchequer. Indeed the king's own financial problems were desperate, culminating in the bankruptcy of 1557. No doubt he would have liked money out of England, but Mary was straining every nerve to keep her own head above water, and quite apart from the political unpopularity of such a move, no sum which England could conceivably have sent would have been more than a drop in the ocean of Philip's debts. In May 1557 Surian wrote that the queen was 'diligently intent' on raising money, having decided to sell crown lands to the value of £10,000 a year.[137] The whole of the 800,000 crowns thus realized 'will all pass to the king, as the Queen thinks solely of giving his majesty every possible assistance . . .' It seems that the Venetian was reflecting the fears of his English informants rather than the facts. His predecessor Michieli had been more accurate when he had written only a few days earlier that Mary was

. . . harassed by the poverty in which she sees the Crown, owing not only to the past debts and disorders but to the many expenses

315

and to the wants incurred in her own time, which prevent her from showing courtesy and liberality such as become a sovereign, either to her own subjects or to others. She is compelled . . . daily to repeat her demands for loans and subsidies, which have now become such a grievance . . . as notwithstanding all the subsidies the creditors remain unpaid . . .[138]

Although the gloom of this report was exaggerated, Mary was undoubtedly in debt in early 1557, and had never been free from it. The protestations of the council in April that England could not afford foreign war were entirely justified, but war was a political decision, and a financial system which could barely cope with the demands of peacetime administration found itself faced with further heavy and unpredictable burdens.

Notes

1 PRO E351/18.
2 Account of John Gresham and Nicholas Holborne. PRO E351/19.
3 PRO SP69/6/332.
4 *APC*, V, 149. These obligations correspond to the ones listed in Gresham's own account.
5 ibid., 190, 193.
6 ibid., 199-200.
7 ibid., 244.
8 ibid., 269.
9 ibid., 286-7.
10 *APC*, VI, 23.
11 ibid., 35-6.
12 ibid., 94. On 6 June, when the discharge of these bonds was reported to the court of aldermen of London, they were described as 'the laste undyscharged bondes to the merchaunte strangers'. GLRO. Repertories of the Court of Aldermen, 13, ii, 515.
13 PRO SP11/4/6.
14 This money was paid in instalments between 1 February and 26 March 1555. Egerton's account; PRO A01/1670/497.
15 PRO SP69/8/461.
16 R. B. Outhwaite, 'The Trials of Foreign Borrowing', *Economic History Review* (1966), 289-305. In 1560 Gresham was urging Elizabeth to borrow from her own subjects rather than on the foreign exchange, presumably, although he did not say so, convinced by the success of Mary's example. *Cal. For.*, Elizabeth, III, 384.
17 PRO SP69/6/354.
18 Gresham to the queen, 27 October 1555. SP69/7/429. Gresham to the council, 11 November 1555. ibid., 438.
19 *Cal. Ven.*, VI, 338. Unlike the obligations to foreign bankers, the queen's debts to her own merchants were not recorded in the London repertories.

20 PRO E405/484. Various warrants paid to Gresham to the use of the merchant adventurers.
21 *APC*, V, 195-6.
22 SP69/7/403; ibid., 406, 420, 5 October 1555.
23 SP69/7/429.
24 Gresham to the queen, 24 February 1556. SP69/8/474.
25 ibid., 483.
26 *Cal. Ven.*, VI, 718.
27 AGS, Contadurías Generales, L84.
28 *Cal. Ven.*, VI, 878-80.
29 *Cal. Pat.*, III, 81.
30 Outhwaite, op. cit.
31 e.g., Gresham to the queen, 24 February 1556. SP69/8/474. See also above, 238-9.
32 *Cal. Ven.*, VI, 879.
33 Feria to Philip, 1 May 1558. *Cal. Span.*, XIII, 379.
34 PRO E405/484 ff. 1-3.
35 PRO SP11/6/86. This is broken down by counties.
36 *Cal. Span.*, XIII, 90.
37 PRO SP69/6/333.
38 *HMC Third Report*, App., 37 (Devonshire MSS).
39 ibid. As far as I know there is no other reference to a privy seal loan being raised at this time. The letter may simply be misdated, and belong to August 1556; on the other hand, peers do not seem to have been included in the 1556 operation, and may therefore have paid their contribution quietly in the previous year.
40 Michieli to the doge and senate, 21 October 1555. *Cal. Ven.*, VI, 216-18.
41 ibid., 228-31.
42 ibid. For a discussion of this point, see also Harbison, 275-8.
43 W. C. Richardson, *History of the Court of Augmentations*, 262-5. Those who did owe large sums were normally financial officials, such as Dennis or Egerton, but they do not seem to be meant in this context.
44 Vertot, V, 171. Harbison, 276.
45 PRO SP11/6/22; ibid., 6/18.
46 *CJ*, I, 42-3.
47 Michieli to the doge and senate, 4 November 1555. *Cal. Ven.*, VI, 239. *CJ*, I, 43.
48 Advis au roi, 26 November 1555. Aff. Etr., IX f. 565. Harbison, 277.
49 *Statutes of the Realm*, IV, i, 301-12.
50 ibid., 297-300. The rate on each instalment is slightly less rigorous than for the laity, but there are 3 instalments, not 2.
51 PRO E405/241. Brevia Recepta. According to a calculation made at the beginning of Elizabeth's reign, the sum paid during this period was £172,031; £144,279 from the laity and £27,742 from the clergy (2 instalments). BL Lansdowne MS 4 f. 9.
52 PRO E405/484.
53 BL Cotton MS Cleopatra F IV f. 327 (draft letter, dated Eltham, 30 July).
54 PRO SP11/9/23.
55 *APC*, V, 335; ibid., VI, 5.
56 *APC*, VI, 20.
57 PRO E405/241 ff. 23-108.
58 PRO E405/484.

59 BL Lansdowne MS 4 f. 9.
60 Richardson, *Augmentations*, 264.
61 ibid., 263. *Cal. Pat.*, III, 23. PRO A01/1670/497; Egerton's account from Christmas 1 Mary to Christmas 2 and 3 Philip and Mary.
62 *Cal. Pat.*, II, 118.
63 Richardson, *Augmentations*, 265.
64 *Cal. Pat.*, III, 25. ibid., 83. This latter was the third inquiry of its kind. The duke's creditors had complained, and a previous commission with very similar terms of reference had been set up on 21 May 1555. *Cal. Pat.*, II, 342.
65 *Cal. Pat.*, II, 118. Richardson, *Augmentations*, 263-4.
66 The capital value of the land seized must have been well in excess of £1000 since it was leased to his widow for £400 *p.a. Cal. Pat.*, III, 107.
67 *APC*, VI, 281, 297-9. Richardson, *Augmentations*, 264-5.
68 BL Cotton MS Titus B 11 f. 136. Mary to Winchester, 4 July (no year), 'For so muche as at your departure frome me I made you a promyse not to determyne the gyfte of anye lande withowte your consent, wherefore I doe sende you here enclosyd . . .', etc.
69 PRO SP11/6/85.
70 BL Cotton MS Titus B IV f. 135.
71 PRO 30/53/9/16. *Cal. Pat.*, III, 313.
72 PRO SP11/10/58, 59. 4 May 1557.
73 BL Add. MS 30198.
74 BL Cotton MS Titus B IV f. 133. Lansdowne MS 4 f. 182.
75 These figures are calculated from the same sources, taking the phrase 'remaineth clear' at its face value. As we have already seen, there was a change in the accounting system between 5 Edward VI and 4 Mary, and the use of 'clear revenue' figures to estimate the crown's solvency is fraught with difficulties. See above, 193.
76 *Cal. Pat.*, II, 103.
77 *Cal. Pat.*, III, 315.
78 *Cal. Pat.*, III, 314.
79 Egerton's account; PRO A01/1670/497 (which shows that the actual coining was carried out in April and May 1555). Peckham's account; E351/2080.
80 PRO A01/1670/497. C. E. Challis, *The Tudor Coinage* (1978), 114, 306-7.
81 *Cal. Pat.*, III, 369; IV, 194. The mint accounts for this period are missing so the total sum coined is not known, but according to Stanley's estimate of 1559, approximately £156,000 in fine coin were produced in the two periods of the reign for which no accounts survive, July – December 1553 and December 1555 – November 1558. BL Add. MS 40061 ff. 11-12.
82 PRO A01/1670/497. Egerton was not allowed any wastage on this transaction.
83 *Cal. Pat.*, III, 82-3, 532, 369. On 7 November 1556 Sir William Fitzwilliam accounted to the council for £35,000 of base money for Ireland. *APC*, VI, 15.
84 A. Feaveryear, *The Pound Sterling* (rev. ed., 1963), 73-4.
85 Hughes and Larkin, II, 8. A token start was made immediately by coining £5050 of plate. *APC*, IV, 340.
86 Hughes and Larkin, II, 34, 39, 44. For the vagaries of the exchange at this time, see above, 197-8.

87 ibid., 51. 26 December 1554.
88 ibid., 72. 22 December 1556. On 14 December, Michieli had reported the confusions caused by these rumours, which he attributed to the queen's use of the money obtained by the privy seal loan to pay off some of her debts. *Cal. Ven.*, VI, 868.
89 *Statutes of the Realm*, IV, i, 258.
90 *APC*, V, 85. 3 December 1554. The committee consisted of Hastings, Bourne, Wharton, Southwell, and Peckham.
91 *APC*, V, 258. 1 April 1556.
92 *APC*, VI, 39. 8 January 1557.
93 Examination of William Hinnes, 28 March 1556. PRO SP11/7/39. For a discussion of this operation, see *TTC*, 191-2.
94 Hughes and Larkin, II, 67.
95 ibid., 68.
96 Wotton to the queen, 4 August 1556. SP69/8/523.
97 *Cal. Pat.*, IV, 379. 9 July 1558.
98 Confessions of Bawcriffe, SP11/7/58; of Hinnes, SP11/7/39.
99 *Cal. Pat.*, IV, 451.
100 Hughes and Larkin, II, 70.
101 For an analysis of the significance of Fletewood's and Stanley's accounts (PRO E351/2185; E101/303/20; SP65/6) see J. D. Gould, *The Great Debasement: currency and the economy in mid-Tudor England* (1970), 57-70, and Challis, op. cit., 112-28. The reasons for recoining are quoted from R. Ruding, *Annals of the Coinage of Great Britain* (ed. 1840), 334.
102 Gould, loc. cit.
103 PRO SP11/14/19. Undated.
104 On 27 September 1560 an arbitrary devaluation of all base coin by about 25 per cent was decreed. Hughes and Larkin, II, 150-4. This covered coins of various levels of debasement, and enabled the crown to make a small profit on the transaction. W. H. Cunningham, *The Growth of English Industry and Commerce* (new imp. 1968), 2, 127 *et seq.* Conyers Read, 'Profits on the Recoinage, 1560–61', *Economic History Review*, 6 (1936), 186-92. Challis, op. cit., 112-28.
105 PRO SP11/14/18. Undated.
106 Challis, op. cit., 134-40. The post-1572 scheme proved to be inefficient, and resulted in no notable economy.
107 *APC*, V, 348. 2 September 1556.
108 BL Lansdowne MS 4 f. 19.
109 PRO E351/1795, which gives both expenditure and receipt figures, but without specifying the sources of income.
110 *APC*, V, 59. 10 August 1554.
111 BL Add. MS 4767 f. 125. 'A brief memorial of the yearly charge of the said realm (of Ireland) from anno 33 Henry VIII to Michaelmas 6 Mary'.
112 ibid. For a full discussion of the development of English policy in Ireland during these years, see B. Bradshaw, 'The Irish Constitutional Revolution, 1515–1557'.
113 Richardson, *Augmentations*, 265. *APC*, V, 36; 10 June 1554.
114 BL Add. MS 4767 f. 73. 'A survey of the Queen's revenues and charges in Ireland'. 1559 or 1560.
115 Bradshaw, op. cit.,
116 BL Add. MS 4767 f. 125. On the effects of the replacement of St Leger by Fitzwalter (Sussex) see also SP62/1/10 and BL Add. MS 4763 f. 109.

319

Treatises on the state of Ireland in 1558.

117 ibid. In fact the Irish restorations had probably cost the crown well under £1000 a year. See below, 413.

118 PRO SP11/6/22. 30 September 1555.

119 PRO SP11/10/55.

120 PRO SP11/4/36. *Cal. Pat.*, II, 55-8. PRO SP11/10/9-54.

121 *Cal. Pat.*, II, 55-8. T. S. Willan, *The Early History of the Russia Company 1553–1603* (1956), Sir William Foster, *England's Quest of Eastern Trade* (1966), 11-12.

122 Printed in Tawney and Power, *Tudor Economic Documents*, II, 37-42.

123 PRO E405/484.

124 It also has to be remembered that the queen was granting some annuities which were paid directly by assignment, e.g., £200 to the earl of Sussex in 1556, from the petty customs of London. *Cal. Pat.*, III, 520. Such grants do not seem to have been numerous.

125 PRO SP12/1/64.

126 Michieli to the doge and senate, 11 November 1555. *Cal. Ven.*, VI, 243. J. Bradford, *The Copye of a letter . . .* (1556).

127 2 and 3 Philip and Mary, c. 4. PRO SP12/1/64. According to Pole's pension book, dated 24 February 1556, which is a complete survey of pensions, annuities, and corrodies, the total due under all heads was £36,808, PRO E164/31. The actual sums paid out seem to have totalled rather less, and according to Priuli, Pole found the difference himself. See below, 439.

128 Accounts of William Ridgeway, surveyor of the works. PRO E191/483/16.

129 PRO SP11/10/1.

130 PRO SP11/10/2. The annual £14,000 was to be allocated as follows: provisions, £2000; rigging £1000; wages and victuals, £600; building and repairs, £5000.

131 Gonson had received £13,204 between Easter 1555 and Easter 1556. PRO E405/484.

132 BL Lansdowne MS 4 f. 182.

133 *APC*, VI, 9. 12 October 1556.

134 Council to the earl of Rutland and Sir John Chatsworth, 31 January 1557. *HMC Twelfth Report*, App., IV, 67 (Rutland MSS).

135 *Cal. Ven.*, VI, 588-9. Michieli had been informed that all substantial subjects, lay and clerical, had been compelled to contribute to the loan which was expected to raise £400,000. Certain clergy did contribute, but the source of these inflated figures is unknown. According to the original letter, Thomas Mildmay was to be the recipient. BL Cotton MS Cleo. F VI f. 372.

136 Statement by Roger Carter, 13 May 1556. PRO SP11/8/73. Examination of John Dethicke, 18 April 1556. PRO SP11/8/13.

137 *Cal. Ven.*, VI, 1096-7. This presumably referred to the commission issued in April, but no total was mentioned in the commission, and the source of this figure is unknown.

138 *Cal. Ven.*, VI, 1057. Michieli's relation, 13 May 1557.

10   The Religious Reaction—
Pole as Legate

In August 1554 the future of Pole's mission to England still appeared uncertain. Julius III had done everything in his power to make his legate acceptable, and in writing to congratulate the emperor upon his son's English marriage had taken the opportunity to suggest that the time was now ripe to bring the English schism to an end.[1] Pole's commission was now addressed to the king as well as to the queen of England, and the cardinal sent one of his own household, probably Ormanetto, to Granvelle as early as 1 August to plead the cause of his mission. Ormanetto had just returned from Rome, and the sense of urgency which he sought to convey came as much from the pope as the legate;[2] not only was it conducive to Philip's honour to restore the church immediately after his arrival, but the souls of Englishmen were going unnecessarily to perdition by every day's delay. Granvelle, acting upon Charles's instructions, was cool. The emperor had as yet received no reliable information about the new situation in England, nor had he had a chance to examine the cardinal's fresh brief or to ascertain how he intended to implement his instructions.[3] In seeking to overcome this familiar reluctance, Ormanetto was indiscreet:

> The Cardinal well understood how to use moderation where church property was concerned [he declared], but care must be taken not to set a bad example to the rest of Christendom, or certain catholics who had laid hands on ecclesiastical belongings might invoke this precedent to keep them; and as for leaving all church property in the hands of the actual holders, that would make it look as if the apostolic see were buying back its authority in England with money . . .[4]

This was an accurate reflection of Pole's own mind, and did nothing to reassure the emperor. In communicating news of this interview to his ambassadors in England the following day, Charles expressed his continuing doubts about the cardinal's friends and associates, and declared that he would do nothing until he knew the wishes of the king and queen.[5] This placed Philip in a very difficult position. Every consideration of policy and personal piety urged him to end the schism as soon as possible, and Mary passionately desired it, but the cardinal's intractability made immediate progress impossible. Rather surprisingly in view of the self-righteous admonitions which he had received from Pole during the previous twelve months and of his former attitude, Gardiner was in favour of inviting the legate to England almost at once. 'Neither the Council nor Parliament, he thinks, ought to be allowed to dictate in this matter, for they would never consent to his coming at all . . .', reported the Imperial ambassadors.[6] However, the king rejected his advice, and decided that no invitation should be sent until a settlement had been negotiated which could realistically be brought before parliament for ratification. Illogical as it might appear in a spiritual context, the policy of re-catholicization must continue to have a sound constitutional basis.

In the middle of August the Imperial ambassadors drew up a *consulta* for Mary's benefit, apparently in response to a request from her, in which Renard's pessimistic mind can be clearly discerned. They advised her to obtain a secret unconditional absolution for the realm from the pope, and not to invite Pole, or make any other public reference to papal authority until she had been able to ascertain how much parliament would be prepared to concede. Not only was the papal authority odious and the question of church property explosive, but the queen was also bound, they urged, by her proclamation of the previous year not to introduce coercion in religious matters.[7] The ambassadors seem to have been more impressed by evidence of English anti-clericalism and the strength of the 'new religion' than either Philip or the council, so it is not surprising that, at about the same time, Damula in Brussels should have concluded that Pole's mission was irretrievably stalemated.[8] The legate himself hovered between despair and passionate entreaty. In three separate letters written during the last week of September he begged Charles and Philip for permission to proceed to England, urging the sacred nature of the task and the gratitude which they both owed to God for the successful consummation of the marriage.[9] To Philip he compared himself to St Peter knocking on the door of Mary the mother of John, and reproached the king with giving entry to all envoys 'while the Legate of St Peter's successor . . . is alone denied admission' – neither arguments likely to promote his cause. Writing to Julius on 13 October, Pole allowed his frustration and sense of political helplessness to show through his careful phrases about the emperor's conscientious concern for the welfare of the church.

. . . to wait until all became spontaneously well disposed [in England], and until every impediment was removed, would be to protract the conclusion for ever, as the parties concerned most especially desire nothing more than to continue in the present state having and holding what they possess.[10]

However, by the time this letter was written, Philip had moved decisively to break the deadlock, as we have already seen. Realizing that only the pope could force Pole to give the specific undertakings which were required, he opened direct negotiations in Rome through Don Manrique de Lara. At the same time, presuming upon the success of this initiative, Renard was sent across to exercise his persuasive gifts upon the legate, bearing with him a friendly and hopeful letter from the queen to her 'good cousin'. Thereafter events moved quickly. Renard met Pole on 22 October, and again on the 25th.[11] At the first meeting he learned that the legate would be quite content to come to England in the first instance as papal ambassador, should there be any difficulty in recognizing his legatine status, and that he would not take any action without consulting the king and queen. At the second meeting Renard explained the fears of the English property-holders: firstly that the wording of his existing brief implied an intention to summon each of them individually before a legatine court to defend their actions; and secondly that 'in gravioribus causis' he would refuse to exercise his own judgement and would refer such cases to Rome. Pole, according to his own subsequent report, was reassuring on the latter point, showing Renard the bull in which Julius had given him full discretion and had promised to ratify his decisions;[12] but on the former he was silent. The ambassador professed himself fully satisfied, and declared that he could see no remaining obstacle to the successful prosecution of the mission.

Nevertheless, problems did remain. Renard had not pressed the matter of possible legal process against the 'possessioners' because he saw that this could be covered by the legate's promise not to exercise any jurisdiction without the king and queen's consent, in other words to be bound by the statutes of *praemunire*.[13] Pole soon realized this, too, and was deeply unhappy about the possible consequences of his undertaking, as he confided to Morone on 28 October:

Facendo io da poi come è debito mio intendere alle Maestà loro et agli altri ancora, il debito loro in questa parte de' beni. Da un canto si può sperar nella pietà delle loro Mtà. che habbino a risolversi di fare, massime di quel che è in man loro, cosa che

323

convenghi con la pietà et obligo che hanno con Dio, ma quando per altri humani rispetti non si venisse a questo fine, io per me dubitarei forte della disgratia di Dio, sopra esse et quel regno, ancora che sì fusse tornato alla obedientia, non temendo tanto per rispetto di quello che non si potesse condure gli altri privati a fare.[14]

The only remedy, he concluded, would be to persuade the king and queen to do their Christian duty, although he clearly did not hold much hope that this would extend beyond restoring what was still in the hands of the crown. Presumably Renard's astute analysis was sufficient to persuade Philip, eager as he was for progress, that he could now give on his own responsibility the assurances which would be necessary to persuade the now-imminent parliament to repeal the schismatic statutes of Henry VIII. Perhaps Renard was also right in saying that if Pole's attitude and the legal situation had been better understood, there would have been no need to send to Rome for a new brief.[15] On 5 November, Mary announced to Sir John Mason, her ambassador in Brussels, that it had been decided to admit Pole, and that Lord Paget and Sir Edward Hastings were being sent to the Low Countries to escort him to England.[16] At the same time Philip informed his father of the same news, specifying only that the cardinal should not at first bear the insignia of his legateship, and that he should not immediately enter into detailed negotiations over church property.[17] To both these conditions Pole agreed without difficulty, and on 13 November began a stately and triumphant progress back to the homeland that he had not seen for twenty years. From Calais across the Channel, and by easy stages through Kent to Gravesend he was accompanied by an increasing train of English noblemen and councillors: Paget and Hastings, Montague and Thirlby, Tunstall and Shrewsbury.[18] At Gravesend he took to the river, and at noon on 24 November arrived at Westminster where he was received with great joy by the king and queen, and with seemly attention and respect by the remainder of the court.[19] The same night he was lodged across the river at Lambeth, confirmation, for those who wanted it, of the long-standing reports that he was destined for the metropolitan see. Stroppiana, who announced his arrival laconically to the bishop of Arras the next day, believed that he had been well received by 'the country people' of Kent. Owing to his mode of arrival the Londoners had been given no chance to make any demonstration of their feelings.

In the short time which had elapsed since their decision to summon him, Philip and Mary had taken two important steps to smooth the cardinal's path. On 10 November a proclamation had been issued commanding all their subjects to recognize and submit to his legatine authority

> . . . in such cases of spiritual jurisdiction for the reformation of their souls as in the time of the said 20th year of the reign of our said father King Henry VIII was, or with his consent might have been, used and expressed in this realm.[20]

Perhaps Mary was less cautious in this matter than her husband, or perhaps Philip had decided not to insist upon his conditions, but this proclamation certainly anticipated the decision of parliament by several weeks, and provoked no recorded protest. The second step was to rush through, between 17 and 22 November, all the stages of a bill to repeal Pole's attainder. On the latter day, at 3 o'clock in the afternoon, the king and queen took the unusual step of going to the parliament chamber in the middle of a session to give their assent and thus make the bill a complete act, about 48 hours before the cardinal arrived in London.[21] Meanwhile the pope had also been fully co-operative. On 7 November he declared to Charles that in the light of Don Juan Manrique's representations, and after due consultations in the *curia*, he had decided '. . . that it would be far better for all reasons human and divine to abandon all the church property [in England] rather than risk the shipwreck of this undertaking . . .' He had therefore directed fresh instructions to Pole in that sense; that is to say, not merely authorizing him but directing him to give a collective dispensation to the 'possessioners'.[22] These instructions reached the legate during the brief interval between his arrival in London and his first appearance before parliament on 28 November. Philip was greatly pleased when he learned their contents, because he was now absolved from the invidious task of having to interpose his own and Mary's authority between the cardinal and the English aristocracy.

Pole's address to the two Houses, in the presence of the king and queen, was a manifesto. Although losing no opportunity to castigate those whose avarice and sensuality had brought the schism into being, he nevertheless went on,

> My commission is not to pull down but to build; to reconcile, not to censure; to invite but without compulsion. My business is not to proceed by way of retrospection, or to question things already settled . . .[23]

Peace was his theme. Peace and the restoration of 'normality', which seems to have meant for him a somewhat idealized recollection of the 1520s, when, he told his hearers (many of whose memories must have been somewhat different), England had dwelt in 'glorious peace' under her Godly and as yet uncorrupted king. He could not, however, commence his ministry until parliament had removed the 'obstructions' which it had itself imposed between England and the apostolic see. After that, what was past 'shall be all overlooked and forgotten'. With this reassurance in their ears, on the following day the Lords and Commons conferred together, drawing up a petition to the king and queen, beseeching their Majesties, as persons unspotted by heresy or schism, to intercede with the legate for the absolution of the realm. This petition had presumably been prepared in advance by the council, and was carefully worded to avoid any suggestion of conditions. Church property was not mentioned, merely an expression of confidence in the judgement of the king and queen.[24] On 30 November the members of both Houses repaired to the palace and there, in the presence of the legate, Gardiner presented their petition with a suitably penitential speech, and after a show of conference with Philip and Mary, Pole pronounced a solemn absolution. The scene was an emotional one on both sides. As a member of the cardinal's household reported the following day:

> S. S. R. ma, parlando in inglese, diede l'assolutione, nel modo che vedrete dalla copia d'essa tradotta in latino, benedicendoli nel fine in nomine Patris et Filii et Spiritus sancti, et all'hora tutti con segni di grande allegrezza ad alta voce gridarno: Amen. Amen.[25]

Both for Mary and for Pole the joy of this moment was supreme. Apart from the scruples of Sir Ralph Bagnall, who claimed that he could not dishonour his oath to Henry VIII, no dissident voice had been raised in public debate.[26] Suddenly it seemed that there were more, and more enthusiastic, catholics in England than had ever been suspected. On 2 December the king and the cardinal attended a high mass sung by the bishop of London in St Paul's cathedral. 'The crowd', wrote Stroppiana, 'both in the church and in the streets was enormous, and displayed great joy and piety, begging the Cardinal for his blessing'.[27] After mass Gardiner preached at Paul's Cross to a packed throng, choosing as his text *iam nos de somno surgere*, and concluding with lavish expressions of gratitude to God, to the pope, to Pole, and to the king and queen. Detailed accounts of these stirring events were penned by zealous eyewitnesses and soon after published in many languages to the glory of God and the Habsburg dynasty.

In such a euphoric atmosphere, when English heresy appeared to be a feeble spectre, which could soon be exorcized, political realities tended to be forgotten, but the property issue never entirely disappeared from view. Pole had spent many hours closeted with the king since his arrival, and despite the public displays of harmony and affection they had not reached full agreement.[28] On the day after the cardinal's arrival Dr John Feckenham, the dean of St Paul's, had preached a controversial sermon arguing that no matter what dispensation they might receive, the 'possessioners' would be in conscience bound to give up their plunder. The council, annoyed and embarrassed, had sent for Feckenham on 29 November and reprimanded him, realizing perfectly well that he had articulated Pole's own views.[29] Collusion between Feckenham and Pole is most unlikely, but convocation was certainly prompted to present a petition to Philip and Mary on 7 December asking for the restitution of its traditional jurisdiction, and acknowledging

> . . . nos optime cognoscere, quam haec bonorum ecclesiasticorum difficilis et quasi impossibilis esset recuperatio, propter multiplices ac pene inextricabiles super hiis contractos et dispositiones; et quod si ea tentaretur, quies et tranquillitas regni facile perturbaretur.[30]

In spite of the cardinal's reluctant agreement to grant a general dispensation, there was still uncertainty as to the exact form which it would take, and recognition in some quarters that there could still be a last-moment breakdown in the negotiations. Pole's position was clear. He was obliged by his instructions to grant a general dispensation which would free the holders of church property from any threat of ecclesiastical censures. On the other hand, he

> . . . condescended in such a way to the retention of this property that everyone might very easily perceive that his dispensation was a mere permission ob duritiam cordis illorum, as in this dispensation he would never consent to add the clause 'quod absque aliquo conscientiae scrupulo possent huiusmodi bona retinere' although he was several times urged strongly to insert it.[31]

On its own this scrupulosity need not have mattered, although the threat of spiritual blackmail was a serious one. More worrying to the common lawyers was the cardinal's absolute refusal to concede the validity of the property-holders' title. This emerged at a council meeting on 21 December, the day after the bill for repeal of the Henrician acts had been read for the first time in the House of Lords.[32] The dispensation, Pole argued, was a permission only, granted by the charity and mercy of the pope, and in no way acknowledged the right of parliament to transfer ecclesiastical property to the crown. The queen concurred in this opinion, and declared that she would sooner abdicate than concede such a right. The common lawyers, on the other hand, argued that land was, and always had been, under the jurisdiction of the temporal authority. Whether they cited the statute of mortmain we do not know, because Priuli, who reported the discussion, had no interest in legal technicalities.[33]

The property-holders wanted the text of Pole's dispensation to be included in the act of repeal, presumably as a means of reinforcing its authority. The lawyers seem to have opposed this on the grounds that the powers of the crown under the statutes of *praemunire* might be called in question by such deference to an outside authority.[34] Pole also opposed such a move because he did not want it to appear that Julius's dispensation depended for its validity upon the endorsement of parliament. As far as we know, nobody mentioned the fact, of which many must have been aware, that if the pope's concession was a 'mere permission' granted by his own grace, there could be no guarantee that it would be recognized by his successor. The meeting broke up without resolving the problem, and Philip, who was very anxious to see the property-holders appeased, must have been somewhat embarrassed by the queen's forceful interjections. Agreement was finally reached on 24 December. Pole signed and promulgated the dispensation, making no specific recognition of title or absolution of conscience; and the text was inserted into the draft bill, read for the second time in the Lords that day.[35] Thereafter its passage was straightforward. Passed by the Lords on 26 December, it was sent to the Commons on the same day. On the 27th it was read for the first time and committed. The whole of 2 January was devoted to discussion, and it was read for the third time, and passed, on the 3rd.[36] The wording of the act in its final form was very careful, reciting the text of parliament's petition to the king and queen, as well as that of the dispensation. Thus it was recorded that the two Houses had asked that

> . . . all persons having sufficient conveiance of the said Landes and Hereditaments Goodes and Cattelles as is aforesaid by the Common lawes Actes or Statutes of this realm, may without scruple of conscience enjoy them . . . ,

a request which had not been granted. On the other hand, it was firmly declared that

> . . . the title of all Landes Possessions and Hereditaments in this your Maiesties Realme and Dominions, ys grownded in the Lawes Statutes and Customes of the same, and by your highe Jurisdiction Aucthoritie Royall and Crowne Imperiall and in your Courtes onley to be empleaded ordered tryed and judged and none otherwise.[37]

328

So although no statute could be made binding upon the pope, or convert his dispensation into law, the English legislature had firmly given notice that in acknowledging the authority of the apostolic see it had no intention of surrendering control over any aspect of property jurisdiction. In giving her assent to such a bill Mary was in fact surrendering the position which she had taken up on 21 December. Presumably, like Pole, she was prepared to make concessions in order to see the Great Reconciliation finally and incontrovertibly completed.

One further step remained to restore the jurisdictional position of 1529: the resurrection of the statutes against Lollardy originally passed between 1381 and 1415. These acts had not created the death penalty for heresy, but they had provided 'a definite legal procedure linking the sentence given in the bishop's court with an execution by the king's officers'.[38] They had also provided for the arrest of suspects by the lay magistrates, and for the forfeiture (to the crown) of the goods of those convicted. A bill for this purpose went rapidly through both Houses between 10 and 18 December, arousing only a faint echo of the storm which a similar proposal had aroused nine months earlier. Parliament's contribution to the catholic restoration was completed on 4 January, when the Commons accepted a bill to repeal the attainders of Richard Pate, William Peto, and a few others who had been exiled for their loyalty to the papacy.[39] When the session ended on 16 January, and the royal assent had been given to all these acts, Pole was in a position to assume full responsibility, as *legatus a latere*, for the conduct of ecclesiastical affairs in England, with the assurance of royal support. The alliance between protestants and property-holders, so much feared by the pragmatic Imperialists, had proved to be a mere association of convenience. The contemptuous assessment of protestant strength made by Mary and Gardiner at the beginning of the reign appeared to have been amply justified. Convinced that she was pregnant, with the church restored and her husband at her side, in January 1555 Mary stood at the apex of success.

At some uncertain date, but probably in early December, she had formulated her own views about the reconstruction of the church in a memorandum drawn up for the benefit of her council. As long as the parliament was in session those who had originally been commissioned to discuss the question of church property with Pole were to continue to meet with him at least once a week in order to pilot through the necessary legislation. Thereafter the consultations were to continue '. . . to understand of him which way might be best to bring to good effect those matters that have been begun concerning religion'.

. . . touching good preaching [the queen continued], I wish that may supply and overcome the evil preaching in time past. And also to make a sure provision that none evil books shall either be printed bought or sold without just punishment therefore. I think it should be well done that the universities and churches of this realm should be visited by such persons as my Lord Cardinal with the rest of you may be well assured to be worthy and sufficient persons . . . Touching punishment of heretics me thinketh it ought to be done without rashness, not leaving in the meanwhile to do Justice to such as by learning would seem to deceive the simple, and the rest so to be used that the people might well perceive them not to be condemned without just occasion, whereby they shall both understand the truth and beware to do the like. And especially within London I would wish none to be burnt without some of the Council's presence and both there and everywhere good sermons at the same. I verily believe that many benefices should not be in one man's hands but after such sort as every priest might look to his own charge and remain resident there, whereby they should have but one bond to discharge towards God whereas now they have many, which I take to be the cause that in most parts of the realm there is overmuch want of good preachers and such as should with their doctrine overcome the evil diligence of the abused preachers in the time of the schism; not only by their preaching but also by their good example without which in mine opinion their sermons shall not so much profit as I wish. And like as their good example on their behalf shall undoubtedly do much good, I account myself bound on my behalf also to show some example in encouraging and maintaining those persons well doing their duty (not forgetting in the meanwhile to correct and punish them which do contrary) that it may be evident to all this Realm how I discharge my conscience therein and minister true justice in so doing.[40]

If this document is genuine (and there must be some doubt since it survives only in copies), it suggests that the queen's priorities were rather different from Pole's, and from the policy which was subsequently followed. Although both were equally concerned about pluralism and the need to improve the quality of the clergy, Pole did not share Mary's insistent concern about preaching. For him order, discipline, and the administration of the sacraments were more important. Above all, the reconciliation must restore peace and harmony to the church. Sermons, however wholesome, were liable to be controversial, and the true role of Christian subjects was to obey, not to argue about theology, which was the function of the clergy.[41]

Consequently his first preoccupation was with how people behaved rather than with what they believed. Regular attendance at mass, participation in the numerous processions and other traditional rituals which had been revived since the beginning of the reign, and a seemly reverence towards the church and its ministers, would restore the faith more effectually than many expositions of the necessity of good works for salvation. However, such a policy required enforcement. A year and a half of catholicism under the royal supremacy had demonstrated convincingly that many Englishmen would not return to the old ways willingly. Considerable pressure had already been applied, as we have seen, but with only partial success, and Gardiner had been advocating sterner measures for several months. Particularly he wanted to put the imprisoned bishops and preachers on trial for heresy, confronting them with the alternative of surrender or execution. The Lollards had not had an heroic record under that sort of persecution, and Henry VIII's campaign against the sacramentaries had been too sporadic and political to provide much guidance as to what was likely to happen in this new situation.[42] The completion of the reconciliation enabled Pole to issue legatine commissions for the trial of heresy, and the first batch of prisoners was arraigned within days of the dissolution of parliament. On 22 January, between the dissolution and the first trial, Gardiner made a revealing move. He had all the imprisoned preachers in London (about eighty in number according to Thomas Sampson) brought to his house at St Mary Overy's. There he threatened and cajoled them to sign recantations, but only two yielded to his persuasions.[43] The bishop of Winchester saw the persecution in terms of policy – a policy aimed at enforcing submission to the authority of the church on the part of all those who had made protestantism their excuse for defiance and disorder. Such burnings as might take place would be intended mainly to prove that the government was in earnest – a proof which was clearly needed in the light of what had happened since August 1553. The queen's view was less detached, as might be expected. Burning was the punishment of a wicked individual, and the elimination of the threat which he represented to the simple, as well as a warning to possible imitators. Pole was probably less concerned with the purely punitive aspect, but even more anxious to protect the flock entrusted to his charge from such 'wolves'. The elimination of heresy was therefore uppermost in the minds of all those most directly concerned with the management of ecclesiastical affairs at the beginning of 1555.

The subsequent persecution has been the subject of many scholarly studies, and there is neither space nor necessity here for a lengthy investigation.[44] Between February 1555 and November 1558 almost 300 individuals were executed, and many others died in prison. An uncountable number were threatened or imprisoned and submitted. Over the longer period from the beginning of 1554 about 800 took refuge on the continent, mainly in Switzerland or Germany, while others left their homes in hard-pressed Essex or Suffolk and made temporary homes in counties where the authorities were less anxious and vigilant.[45] The great majority of those who died were laymen (and women) of the artisan class, although there was a significant minority of clergy. Most of those who fled were gentry or merchants, although again there were many clergy, and more theological students. Those who moved within the realm (a much more elusive and indeterminate group) seem to have been mainly humble folk, but including a few yeomen and others of substance.[46] Geographically the persecution was extremely uneven, 85 per cent of the burnings taking place in the four south-eastern dioceses of London, Canterbury, Chichester, and Norwich.[47] In the whole of the northern province there was only one execution, with three in Wales and five in the south-west. Whether all these victims were 'orthodox' protestants or not is still a subject of some controversy. Fr Philip Hughes, in his massive and learned *Reformation in England*, argued that most of the humble people who died were radicals whose confused and extreme beliefs would have been similarly punished by any contemporary government, catholic or protestant.[48] In support of this thesis it can be demonstrated that Foxe did not always tell the whole truth about his martyrs, and that in what he did reveal there was a good deal which would not have pleased Cranmer or Ridley.[49] On the other hand, the evidence of radical dissent in England before 1553 (which caused the protestant authorities much anxiety) suggests that it was on far too small a scale to support such a major role.[50] Also, where there is actual testimony of the practices of secret protestant congregations 'under the cross', it refers to '. . . all the English service without any diminishing, wholly as it was in the reign of King Edward VI' or '. . . the English communion in all points as it was used in the latter days of King Edward VI'.[51] With the exception of the celebrated controversy between John Bradford and the 'freewillers' the evidence rather suggests that the erstwhile radicals took part in Edwardian services during the period of persecution than that they assumed a dominant role. The persecution involved a massive administrative and judicial effort by both the ecclesiastical and secular authorities in East Anglia and the home counties, with thousands of detections, investigations, and interrogations behind the hundreds of trials.[52] This pressure had its effect. 'Many men', as Latimer had forecast, 'went with the world', and the protestant leaders were deeply distressed by the number of defections. On the other hand, their opponents were equally afflicted by a sense of failure, of fighting with a hydra which constantly sprouted fresh heads.

> Would to God the honorable couwnsell sawe the face of Essex as we do see [it] [wrote Chedsey to Bonner in April 1558], We have such obstinat heretikes anabaptists and other unruly persons here as was never harde of . . .[53]

As a policy designed to bring peace and stability to the church by the elimination of disruptive elements, the persecution failed, and could be seen by contemporaries to be failing well before 1558. However, after Gardiner's disillusioned withdrawal in the summer of 1555,[54] it was not primarily a policy but rather the discharge by the queen and the cardinal of a clearly conceived pastoral duty. As such, it cannot really be discussed politically in terms of success or failure, but must be seen simply as an aspect of the restored catholic church, inseparable from the whole process of restoration. One of its main effects was to define the protestants as a minority and dissident group; another was to reinforce their sense of eschatological purpose – of being tried and tested by the Lord. Neither they nor their persecutors knew what was going to happen when the first trials began on 28 January 1555. Ridley and other leaders still in prison watched with acute anxiety, and hailed the execution of John Rogers as a glorious victory. 'And yette againe I blisse god in our deare brother and of this time protomartyr Rogers . . .', wrote Ridley to an anonymous correspondent a few days after the event.[55] Within a few days Rogers had been followed to the stake by Laurence Saunders in Coventry, John Hooper in Gloucester, and Rowland Taylor in Hadleigh. Each met his end with great fortitude, and in Saunders's case with almost theatrical bravado.[56] Quite suddenly, what had appeared to be a discredited and ineffectual movement had become a cause that brave men would die for, and testify to in the face of death. Once this pattern had become established there were very few recantations among the established leaders, and morale among the committed rank and file rose appreciably. It was particularly important in this connection that the protracted saga of the proceedings against Cranmer, Ridley, and Latimer should have ended in all three going to the stake. Not only had these men been in the forefront of the Edwardian church, they had been singled out from the beginning for special pressure. Cranmer might perhaps have yielded, had it not become apparent that Mary intended to burn him whether he recanted or not, and the confused story of his eventual death was embellished by protestant propagandists in a spirit of triumphant relief.

England had no Inquisition to put down determined and organized heresy, and public opinion was ambivalent and unpredictable. We know that some of the apparently spontaneous demonstrations of sympathy made by the large crowds who habitually watched public executions were 'primed' by fellow protestants.[57] Also several of the most circumstantial accounts of crowd reactions come from the pen of Simon Renard, who was still pessimistically convinced of protestant strength.[58] On the other hand, Michieli, who had no axe to grind, was also convinced that the burnings were unpopular, at least in London, which saw the greatest number. On 1 June 1555 he reported

> . . . two days ago, to the displeasure as usual of the population here, two Londoners were burned alive, one of them having been public lecturer in Scripture, a person sixty years of age, who was held in great esteem. In a few days the like will be done to four or five more; and thus from time to time to many others who are in prison for this cause and will not recant, although such sudden severity is odious to many people.[59]

Unlike contemporary Spaniards, Englishmen in general did not regard heresy as a terrible crime, and there was nothing of the spirit of *auto dá fe* about these executions. They demonstrated to anyone who was willing to see that English protestantism had a genuine religious integrity, which its enemies had long denied. They also presented an excellent opportunity for skilful propagandists to cast the blame for such unprecedented severity upon the unpopular Spaniards, and thus by implication to represent the protestants as martyrs to the cause of English liberty, as well as to their faith. When Cranmer signed an abject recantation not long before his death, the first published version had to be suppressed because it was thought to have been witnessed by two Spanish friars.[60] Those who died gained so much credit from their steadfastness that catholic propagandists such as Miles Huggarde were driven to bitter mockery of the 'false stinkinge martyrs', whom they represented as madmen desperately casting themselves into the flames.[61] Even Latimer, shortly before his own execution, warned his co-religionists of the temptation of seeking a martyr's crown, and several of Foxe's stories reveal a pathological streak to the modern reader.[62]

Had the persecution continued longer, it seems unlikely on the evidence available that English protestantism could have been stamped out. It had taken root too firmly at a popular level, mainly, but not exclusively, in the south-east of the country.[63] On the other hand, it would certainly have been radically changed. Martyrs are no substitute for leaders, and leaders in exile could be a very mixed blessing, as the catholic recusants were later to discover. The majority of the clerical leaders of the Edwardian church had been driven into exile or had perished in the flames by 1556; a few had conformed, and a few had gone into hiding. The lay leadership, on the other hand, produced no martyrs, with the dubious exception of the duke of Suffolk, who made no secret of his protestantism but who had died for treason. Some whose convictions were particularly strong, such as Sir Francis Knollys or the dowager duchess of Suffolk, had joined the exodus of clergy and lesser gentry, but most conformed with more or less dissimulation. These men, who were variously denounced as 'heretics', 'neuters', and 'favourers of the new religion', were strongly represented in parliament and on the commissions of the peace.[64] Some of them were involved in the Dudley conspiracy, but most kept assiduously out of trouble, merely doing as little as they possibly could to further the cause of religious reaction. The acknowledged leader of this powerful but unheroic element was Princess Elizabeth. In the event these men were to revert happily to established protestantism in 1559, but how long their concealed and ambiguous allegiance to that faith might have survived in other circumstances, we cannot know. The persecution was effective enough to prevent any open religious dissidence by the nobility or upper gentry, and thus differed markedly from the contemporary efforts of Henri II of France.[65] Among the exiles the sufferings of their brethren in England produced guilty consciences, a spate of propaganda to which we must return in due course, and the progressive crystallization of some new and altogether more radical ideas.[66] The unprecedented freedom which they now enjoyed to experiment with forms of worship and church government caused endless particular disagreements, and a broad division of opinion over the future of the English church. One group, led by Coxe, Aylmer, and Grindal, looked for a return to the Edwardian situation, strove to maintain the traditions of the prayer book, and inevitably pinned their hopes on Elizabeth. Among the members of this group should be counted John Bale and John Foxe who had already, before 1558, begun to formulate an historical explanation for the English persecution, and to look beyond it to the glorious triumph of a new Constantine.[67] The other groups, centred on Geneva and led by Knox, Whittingham, and Goodman, gradually abandoned the non-resistance theories to which the earlier generation of protestant leaders in England had been committed. After those leaders were dead, they produced their manifesto – Goodman's *How superior powers oght to be obeyd*, published in 1558. In this remarkable work Goodman advanced his vision of the English as the covenanted People of God, bound by solemn religious duty to overthrow their idolatrous rulers. Should the nobility fail in this sacred task, as they had conspicuously done so far, it devolved upon the people as a whole, and whatever action contributed to so Godly an end became Godly in itself.[68] In the event it was the vision of Aylmer and Foxe, rather than that of Goodman, which was realized, but had Mary lived and the persecution continued, the more radical thinking would certainly have prevailed.

Speculation is an unhistorical indulgence, but any assessment of the Marian persecution must contain some comment on the likely consequences of its continuance. To me two points seem particularly significant, the elimination of the bulk of the Edwardian leadership, and the increasing association of protestantism with resistance to Spanish domination. That missionaries from Geneva would have endeavoured to create an insurrectionary alliance between the rank-and-file protestants and the anti-Spanish gentry seems highly probable. The outcome of that situation would have depended upon how hard Philip was prepared to fight for his wife's inheritance, and the indications are that he would not have given it a very high priority.

Although the general aim of the persecution was the elimination of heresy, it sought to achieve that end in numerous ways. The execution of the obstinate was only one part of the process, although by far the most conspicuous. Another part was the day-by-day battle against petty iconoclasm and the small demonstrations of the vulgar and irreverent which detracted from the dignity and authority of the church.[69] This proved to be an endless and massive task which could only have been crowned with success in the wake of a massive resurgence of catholic piety. A third part was the suppression of heretical writings and books, and it was probably in this respect that the persecution was least successful, despite the well-established tradition of censorship and licensing upon which the legate and the queen's council could call. During the first year and a half of the reign three proclamations had contained denunciations of those who spread heresy or sedition by words or writing, and ordered them to be committed to gaol or the pillory.[70] The same session of parliament which revived the heresy laws also passed a draconian act against the publishing of libels against the king and queen, which for the first time made the full machinery of the law available for the punishment of pamphleteers.[71] All such libels, if not within the categories of treason laid down in 1352, became felony both to write and distribute – punishable by the loss of the right hand. In June 1555 an index of prohibited authors was proclaimed, containing the names of 24 prominent reformers, and finally, on 6 June 1558, the council proclaimed the penalty of death by martial law for the possession of any heretical or treasonable book, imported or printed in England.[72] There seems, however, to have been a considerable gap between these fearsome penalties and the actual treatment of offenders. At least three commissions were set up between February 1556 and February 1557 'To enquire concerning all heresies, heretical and seditious books and all conspiracies against the King and Queen . . . with power to seize all such books and writings . . .'[73] These acted on the royal authority, and were additional to the normal ecclesiastical machinery of each diocese, and to such visitations as the legate might himself make or order. Nevertheless, the number of offenders known to have been proceeded against in any way is remarkably small. Eighteen individuals were examined and imprisoned by the council itself, and the correspondence of the council with local authorities adds a further five or six names to the list.[74] None of these seem to have suffered the ultimate penalty for treason, heresy, or felony, although the absence of assize records makes it impossible to be certain about the last category. Heretical and seditious writing was of course included among the charges made against such prominent leaders as Cranmer and Ridley, but George Eagles, the notorious Trudgeover, was probably the only man to be executed primarily for the distribution of literature.[75] As we have already seen, the council spent a great deal of time and effort upon the police work of which this was a part, but once the offenders had been caught, they were often treated with surprising leniency. For instance, Paul Bacton was committed to the Fleet in December 1555, having confessed himself to be the author of an 'heretical and seditious writing'. On 2 March following, 'being penitent' he was released without further process.[76] Sometimes the unco-operative attitude of local authorities may have been responsible. In March 1557 six men were examined for being concerned in the production of a number of seditious books, including *The Copye of a letter sent by John Bradforthe*. They were handed over to the city of London for trial, but five months later the trials had still not taken place. Three of the six were subsequently released upon recognizances of £40 each; one, John Capstocke, was indicted and almost immediately pardoned, and the other two seem simply to have been released.[77]

The printing trade itself does seem to have been effectively overseen. Known protestants such as John Day and Hugh Singleton were imprisoned, and subsequently escaped into exile.[78] William Rydall, William Copland, Richard Lant, Owen ap Rogers, John

Kingston, Thomas Marsh, and even the queen's own printer John Cawood were all under suspicion at one time or another and had their work suppressed or their premises searched.[79] Moreover, in March 1557 the stationers' company was granted a charter of incorporation. By the terms of this charter the 97 named freemen were given a monopoly of printing and bookselling within the realm (excepting only a small number of royal patentees), and the master and wardens received powers similar to those exercised by the officers of other companies to

> . . . make search in any place, shop, or building of any printer, binder or seller of books for any books printed contrary to statute or proclamation, and . . . seize or burn the same.[80]

The company did not become simply an agency of government control, but the wardens could not afford to tolerate any large-scale evasion of the censorship regulations. Whether the members of the company made any contribution to the detection or suppression of illicit presses in England during the short part of the reign remaining is not clear. There is no mention of such a press being located or broken up, and surreptitious printing probably continued.

On their own these domestic productions would have been little more than irritating. However, taken in conjunction with the considerable quantity of protestant and protestant-inspired writings produced abroad, they constituted a serious and disturbing challenge, as Miles Huggarde acknowledged when he wrote denouncing the growing martyrology of the heretics, and declaring

> . . . the deaths of our cranke hereticks lye dead and are buried in the grave of cankered oblivion, covered with perpetual infamy, except they be enrolled in a few three-halfpenny bookes which steal oute of Germany, replete with treasons against the King and Queenes Majesties, as with other abominable lies.[81]

Between January 1554 and November 1558 almost a hundred works of protestant propaganda and polemic were published, mostly in Germany or Switzerland, in addition to the unknown number of manuscript letters and treatises which circulated among the faithful, several of which were subsequently to be printed or incorporated in the works of John Foxe.[82] The peak years were 1554 (27 titles), 1555 (23), and 1556 (27). After that there was a marked falling-off, with 10 titles in 1557 and 11 in 1558. The significance of the decline is not clear, but since there was a similar, and even more marked, decline in catholic polemic, it cannot be attributed to more effective methods of prevention. At first, as we have already seen, these works tended to take the form of pious exhortation or reportage, such as *A Brief and Faythfull declaration of the true fayth of Christ*, *A Dialogue . . . concernyng the chyfest ceremonies . . .* , and *A communicacion between Fecknam and the Lady Jane Dudley.*[83] However, by 1555 a more overtly political note was being sounded, and along with such purely pastoral works as *An epistle wrytten by John Scory . . . unto alle the faythfull that be in pryson in Englande*, we find the fiercely polemical *A supplicacyon to the Quenes Majestie*, John Olde's *Acquital or purgation of the moost catholyke Christen Prince Edward VI*, and *A warnyng for Englande Conteynyng the horrible practises of the Kyng of Spayne*,[84] the last of which scarcely handles religious questions at all. Denunciations of catholic idolatry and cruelty, and expositions of protestant doctrine, continued to form a substantial proportion of the output, but criticism of the queen herself became increasingly uninhibited, and the appearance of John Ponet's *Shorte Treatise of politike power* in 1556 heralded a new and radical departure in protestant thinking.[85] By the beginning of 1558 Goodman and Knox were openly advocating religious revolution, and in his *Warning to England . . . by the terrible example of Calece* Bartholomew Traheron indulged in a violence of language against Mary which would have horrified Hooper or Cranmer.[86] It is difficult to be certain how much influence these books and pamphlets had in England, but they were imported and circulated in considerable numbers. Foxe later related a number of stories illustrating the workings of this illicit trade, and it is probable that financial backing for the enterprise came from wealthy sympathizers both in England and Germany, as well as from some of the exiles themselves. The thesis of Miss C. H. Garrett, that there was a single campaign, orchestrated in Germany by Sir John Cheke and financed by a committee in England led by Sir William Cecil, will not stand close examination;[87] moreover, the pamphleteers on the continent were slower to take advantage of events in England than might have been expected and did not always agree among themselves. Nevertheless, there was planning and organization of a sort, and the frequent messengers who passed to and fro between England and the exiles no doubt concerted the arrangements for the distribution of each work as it became available.

Both the government and the protestants themselves took this propaganda very seriously, believing that it both sustained the convinced and persuaded the unconvinced. The author of *A trew report of the dysputacyon in the convocacyon hows at London* explained this thinking clearly in his address 'to the Chrysten Reader'.

And as by readyng and weyng the reasons and answers of thys dysputation I dowt not but that thow shalt be sufficyently confirmed in the truth of the artycles therein reasoned and debated/ evyn so in a little treatise of the trew sacrifyce of a christen man which by gods grace shall shortly also be set furthe/ thow shalt be instructed what to judge of other artycles as of the masse/ or altaurs/ and ... such like.[88]

Similar thinking prompted the ephemera which soon began to celebrate and record every burning, from the moving and detailed journals of Hooper or Saunders to homely ballads, like that 'concernyng the death of Mr. Robert Glover' which was addressed 'to maystrys marye glover his wyf by a frende of heres'.[89] Moreover, every word and gesture of the victims themselves was observed and commented upon. As Miles Huggarde related sarcastically,

> ... when Rogers their pseudomartyr (protomartyr I would say) was burnt in Smith field, were there not divers merchant men and others, which seeing certain pigeons flying over the fire that haunted to a house adjoining ... were not ashamed boldly to affirm that the same was the Holy Ghost in the likeness of a dove ...[90]

Not only did the protestants have an extensive and edifying martyrology long before it was put into its final and compelling form by John Foxe, they were also well provided with devotional literature specifically designed to meet their current needs, and with batteries of theological arguments with which to refute their persecutors should the need arise. Unlike the Lollards of an earlier generation, the Marian protestants at first had no concept of a clandestine church, operating in defiance of the law. The interval between Mary's accession and the commencement of full persecution, however, had given them a chance to learn from the survivors of the earlier dissident tradition, and their leaders had set them an excellent example in resisting the blandishments of conformity. During the brief penal period they consequently survived in numerous underground groups and congregations wherever they had previously been strong: London, Essex, Kent, Sussex, Hertfordshire, Suffolk, and many other places.[91] Sometimes, as in London, they were regularly served by ordained ministers, sometimes they read the bible, the prayer book, and the literature of the persecution among themselves.[92] Stripped of the trappings of establishment, and most of the aristocratic patronage which went with it, they did not represent the political force which Renard and some other observers believed. But instead they discovered a genuine spiritual identity, and a sense of divine purpose in their sufferings which could probably have survived a very much longer martyrdom than they were actually called upon to endure.

Mary and Pole have been accused of excessive legalism in their fight against heresy; of relying too exclusively upon judicial weapons of suppression and punishment, and too little upon persuasion and argument. Pole's experiences in Italy, where he had dealt mainly with educated and cultivated heretics, had given him no great hope of the success of persuasion,[93] and observing the first few cases to be tried under his legatine authority in England must have confirmed him in that opinion. The lengthy and detailed exchanges recorded by Foxe indicate that many ecclesiastical officials, including Bonner, did seek to redeem those arraigned before them by argument, but that the results were often undignified and almost always unavailing.[94] As Latimer acknowledged, the fear of punishment was very much more effective:

> Will you give me leave to tell what hath caused Mr. Doctor [Cartwright] to recant here? It is poena legis, the pain of the law which hath brought you back, and converted you and many more; the which letteth many to confess God. And this is a great argument, there are few here can dissolve it.[95]

Pole's view was substantially the same. Having restored ecclesiastical jurisdiction, his main task was to restore discipline, and this was not to be accomplished by allowing the heretics to choose their ground, intoxicated as they always were by 'the singularity of their own wits'. It was partly for this reason that catholic propaganda and polemic were less, both in quality and quantity, than that of the protestants. There is little sign of the kind of intensive and purposeful official campaign which Cromwell had mounted against the papacy in the 1530s, or Cecil was later to conduct against the recusants. Nevertheless, a considerable amount of catholic literature of various kinds was produced, as the researches of Jennifer Loach and Edward Baskerville have recently demonstrated[96] – 64 titles between January 1554 and November 1558, as against 98 by the protestants. Again the peak years were 1554 (22 titles), 1555 (20), and 1556 (13). 1557 with five titles and 1558 with four were quiet years, perhaps because of the hardships caused by war, dearth, and sickness. Many of these works were devotional or homiletic, such as Thomas Watson's *Twoo notable sermons . . . concerninge the reall presence of Christes body and bloode in the blessed sacrament*, or Miles Huggarde's *Mirrour of love*.[97] In the early part of the reign a considerable number of sermons and ballads celebrated the catholic victory, with titles like *An oration gratulatory . . .* , or *The pathe of obedience*.[98] Specific controversial points were taken up and argued

M

The Reign of Mary Tudor

by Thomas Martin in *A Traictise declaryng and plainly provyng, that the pretensed marriage of Priestes . . . is no marriage* and by John Standish in *A discourse wherein is debated whether it be expedient that the scriptures should be in English.*[99] Also, as might be expected, the ascription of treasonable purposes to the heretics was freely made and exploited, particularly by John Proctor, John Christopherson, and the author of *The saying of John late Duke of Northumberland uppon the scaffolde.*[100] Sir John Gates, executed with Dudley, is quoted as saying

> I was the greatest reader of scrypture that mighte be of a man of my degree and a worse follower therof there was not livyng. For I did not rede to the yntent to be edifyed therebye, nor to seke the glorye of God, but contraiwise to be sedytious, and to dispute therof and privately to interpret it after my own witte and affection . . .[101]

Straightforward polemical works denounced heretical errors in general, often at tedious length and with a noticeable lack of the cutting wit and humour which their opponents sometimes displayed. Only the prolific Miles Huggarde in his main prose work, *The displaying of the protestantes,* showed any real gift for mockery or satire.[102] The catholics also showed a marked tendency to resurrect old controversial works, some of them of very dubious relevance, perhaps to demonstrate that there was nothing new in contemporary heresy. In October 1554 John Cawood reprinted an English translation of a sermon originally preached before the university of Paris in 1537 by John Venaeus. The following month Robert Caly similarly reprinted John Fisher's 1521 sermon against Luther, and during the same year John Gwynneth produced two lengthy and exceedingly tedious dialogues devoted to the refutation of John Frith.[103] The first of these dialogues had originally appeared in 1536. Of that systematic and elementary instruction in the catholic faith which was so much needed after twenty years of schism and heresy, there was remarkably little. The outstanding exception was Bonner's *Profitable and necessarye doctryne, with certayne homilies* by Bonner himself, John Harpesfield, Henry Pendleton, and others. There were two editions of this work, and two more of the homilies alone, so there was clearly a considerable demand,[104] but Bonner found few imitators. Richard Smith published *A Bucklar of the Catholyke fayth* in 1555, and in the same year also appeared *A plaine and godlye treatise concernynge the Masse . . . for the instrucion of the simple and unlerned people.*[105] Although the overwhelming majority of the catholic tracts appearing during these years (44 out of 64) were printed by Caly and Cawood, only a few of them seem to have been officially inspired. Bonner's *Homilies*, some of the sermons, a few of the political tracts, such as John Elder's *Letter sent into Scotlande*, and the recantations of Northumberland and Cranmer probably come into this category. However, the resources of the press were not exploited either as extensively or as intensively as they might have been by the party in power. Bearing in mind the enormous advantages which were conferred by patronage and judicial control, the superiority of the protestant polemic was a remarkable achievement, and one which worried Gardiner acutely in the last months of his life.[106] Characteristically, the only account which was published of the important debate in convocation of November 1553 was that of Archdeacon Philipot; virtually all that we know about the Oxford disputations with Cranmer, Latimer, and Ridley in March 1554 comes from protestant accounts;[107] and the same is true of all the more important trials, although hardly any of these were actually published during Mary's reign. Conversely, important government successes like the recantation of Sir John Cheke in 1556 passed unexploited for propaganda purposes.[108] It must be presumed that the priorities of official policy lay in a different direction. Perhaps it is also significant that one of the major publishing ventures of the reign was the first complete edition of the English works of Sir Thomas More, edited by his nephew William Rastell and printed by Cawood, Whaley, and Tottel in 1557.[109] The rehabilitation of More was a natural consequence of the return to catholic policies, and Huggarde explicitly pointed to him, and to Fisher, as examples of true christian martyrs, to set against the 'false martyrs' of the protestants. However, the initiative seems to have come mainly from the More family, pressing for the recognition of their kinsman's sacrifice, rather than from Pole, the queen, or the council. This pressure was reflected in the appearance of Roper's *Life*, as well as Rastell's work, but the English government seems to have made no particular attempt to exploit More in its general campaign of denigration against the policies of Henry VIII and his advisers. Pole in particular was more inclined to use his fate as an example of the king's wickedness than as an inspiration to catholic loyalty and devotion.

Both Mary and Pole saw the future in terms of the past, and this meant not only restoring the church to health by eliminating the recent disease of heresy, but reviving the traditional pieties, and as far as possible rehabilitating its material resources. The restoration of ceremonies, church furnishings, and images consequently played an important part in all the visitations ordered or conducted by the legate. The painstaking and beautifully recorded visitation of the diocese of Canterbury by Archdeacon Harpesfield in 1557 makes scarcely a mention of heresy, but picks up every missing chalice and altar cloth, every leaking roof and missing patronal saint.[110] In material terms alone the task which is revealed by surviving returns such as that of Harpesfield was immense. Not only did the results of deliberate iconoclasm and the Edwardian confiscations have to be overcome; there was an extensive backlog of sheer neglect in many places; innumerable cures were vacant (partly as a result of Mary's own policies); tithes and other dues were unpaid, charities in debt, and other obligations undischarged. To Pole these matters were not secondary or peripheral, but essential to the proper conduct of the Christian life. He set about his task in January 1555 without any illusions about its magnitude or difficulty; 'res non est parvi consilii et magni laboris', as he wrote to Morone.[111] One of the main problems was the poor state of the clergy themselves, and the contempt in which they were held:

> You have [he was later to tell an audience in London] above all other nations that I know, dishonoured the ministers of the church and priesthood itself; so you should now honour both the order instituted of God, and the persons for the order's sake, and him that they do represent, remembering ever what Christ sayeth, Qui vos spernit, me spernit. Above all obey their word speaking in God's name, whatsover their lives be . . .[112]

This was quite consistent with his general emphasis upon obedience, which we have already noticed, but it was also a counsel of perfection. As a recent study of Pole's legatine mission has pointed out, the cardinal was looking not merely for a return to the situation before the schism, but for 'an exemplary restitution of the law'.[113] It was for this reason that he had fought so hard against a general concession on church property, and for this reason also that he never gave up his attempts to attract voluntary restorations. His vision of the restored English church was inseparable from its material wellbeing. Not only did seemliness and order depend to a great extent upon whole buildings and proper equipment, but, more important, a respectable and authoritative priesthood depended upon suitable remuneration, and an effective episcopate upon wealth and patronage of the traditional kind.

Not even his worst enemies accused Pole of excessive worldliness, yet from the beginning of his mission he spent an immense amount of time upon financial investigations and administration, and received a personal estate of £1250 a year from the crown, as well as grants from the exchequer towards the cost of his household.[114] Slowly and painfully the royal commissioners, William Berners, Thomas Mildmay, and John Wiseman, pieced together what they could of the story of the Edwardian confiscations, a task in which they faced every kind of evasion and self-interested obstructiveness. In some places, such as the archdeaconries of Taunton and Wells, progress was quite promising, and about 25 per cent of the missing silver had been located and restored by April 1555.[115] The situation in Norwich diocese also showed some hopeful signs, but elsewhere even major churches were still without their silver pyxes and cruets, their candlesticks and censers, as late as 1558, unless they had gone to the great expense of providing them afresh.[116] In 1557 Harpesfield found that in many parishes of Kent local gentry and others were still retaining goods and money taken from their local churches, and refusing to make restitution. Pole knew from the outset that the task of restitution and reconstruction would be enormously complicated. In the opening weeks of 1555 he conferred regularly with the council upon the queen's instructions in order to get the measure of the situation. A more politically minded man might at that stage have taken account of the uncertain future, with the queen apparently carrying a child at a dangerously advanced age, the king about to take up a major continental inheritance, and no certain prospect of a catholic heir, and realized that time was not necessarily upon his side. However, Pole was a man of faith and he made no attempt to alter his planned priorities, or hasten the inevitably slow processes which he had initiated. Nothing positive could be done about the condition of the clergy until proper information had been obtained about, for instance, the state of impropriations, and until additional funds could be made available to provide supplementation for the poorer livings. In spite of continued urgings and promptings, the lay aristocracy showed few signs of being willing to supply the church's need, and even the crown was neither quite as generous nor quite as prompt as Pole had hoped. Mary spoke as though she intended to give back all the former ecclesiastical property which remained in her hands, but even if she had seriously intended this, her own financial problems would have precluded such generosity.[117] It was only after a sharp political battle in her fourth parliament that her councillors managed to put through an act to restore the spiritual revenues, tenths, tithe, glebe, and advowsons; and the queen continued to sell former monastic property for her own profit. It was not until the beginning of 1556, therefore, that Pole could even begin to plan a programme to reduce pluralism and non-residence by making it possible for a competent priest to live off a single cure. Even then the first stage had to be an assessment of liability, because along with the spiritual revenues, the cardinal had taken over the task of paying pensions to the surviving ex-religious. A survey of these obligations, completed in February 1556, shows a total of

£36,372 per annum, but as a recent examination of the listed pensioners by Dr R. H. Pogson has shown, there are some curious anomalies and it is unlikely that the actual sums paid out came to so large a total.[118]

Detailed knowledge of the assets acquired under the statute 2 and 3 Philip and Mary, c. 4 was equally necessary, and very much harder to come by. At the beginning of 1556 Pole granted to each diocesan bishop the power to collect first fruits and tenths, and to pay the pensions falling due within his jurisdiction. The accounts for these two processes were to be presented by Michaelmas 1556, and it was clearly intended that these accounts should provide the basis for a planned assault upon clerical poverty. At the same time visitations were ordered to discover the exact nature and extent of the problem, with prescribed and detailed questions about the value of livings, the state of buildings, and the numbers and wealth of the parishioners.[119] Although in an efficient diocese like London response to the cardinal's orders was almost immediate, the task was far too great to be completed within the time originally intended. When Pole had originally convened his legatine synod on 4 November 1555, he had hoped to present it with a full programme of reform, but in the event little could be done beyond expressions of intention.[120] On 10 February 1556 the synod was adjourned, ostensibly for Lent but in fact to await the financial details without which it could not proceed. By the end of October, in spite of everything that Pole could do to hasten matters, it was apparent that information could not be available by 10 November, the intended date for reconvening the synod, and so it was adjourned until 10 May 1557. By February 1557 enough progress had been made to enable a central committee of audit to be appointed for the episcopal accounts. Bonner, Thirlby, Griffith of Rochester, Henry Cole, and William Pye were named and began work,[121] but it was the autumn before Pole really had very much to go on, by which time he was no longer legate, and the synod was dead. One of the main difficulties was the paralysing slowness with which the spiritual revenues were paid. Even in dioceses where there should have been a surplus, there was deficit because of the impossibility of extracting the sums due. Nevertheless, some success was achieved. Norwich was discovered to have an actual surplus which could be diverted to relieve overburdened London, and a start could be made on the problem of poverty by releasing all benefices worth less than 20 marks from the payment of tenths.[122] Given the complexities and resentments with which they were faced, Pole and his bishops could not be expected to have moved faster or more effectively. They were not slack or inept, but they were committed to a long-term policy which

346

ignored certain important features of the immediate situation.

One of these features was the desperate need for spiritual leadership of a high calibre. The English bishops whom Pole found in office were of the most part able men, whose loyalty to the church could satisfy so demanding a critic as the queen, but they had all been to some extent involved in the schism, and had to seek personal absolution from the legate.[123] The men appointed under his auspices, such as White, Christopherson, and Oglethorpe, were competent theologians and administrators, and devoted pastors, but none of them was an outstanding personality. As Fr Hughes observed, what England needed, but failed to find, was another Canisius.[124] As we have seen, the cardinal was unenthusiastic about preaching. It was duly included among the pastoral responsibilities of the bishops enjoined by the legatine synod, but given no special emphasis. He seldom preached himself, and when he did, his main theme was exhortation to gratitude and obedience. There was also a marked tendency for official sermons to revert to the ornate, scholarly style which had been fashionable in the 1520s.[125] Not only did the restored catholic church not have a Canisius, it did not have a Latimer either. This failure was not accidental, nor simply the result of being cut off in the bud in 1559. Pole was keenly aware of the importance of education. He patronized scholars, encouraged the foundation of schools and colleges, and visited both universities with great care and thoroughness.[126] Moreover, his legatine synod took the pioneering step of ordering the establishment of diocesan seminaries for the training of clergy, an example which was to be followed with important consequences by the council of Trent.[127] Nevertheless, offers of help from Loyola and Ribadeneyra, and suggestions that young Englishmen should be sent to the highly successful Jesuit colleges on the continent, were studiously ignored.[128] Pole simply did not want men with the fire of the counter-reformation in their bellies trying to implant in his flock a vision of the church and its doctrines which he did not share. He belonged to an older generation. His spirituality had been formed by the London Carthusians, with whom he had lodged on several occasions in his youth, and his models for reform were Giberti's injunctions for the diocese of Verona and the *De Ecclesia Emendenda*, of which he had been a part-author in 1537. He had virtually no pastoral experience, or connection with the problems of ordinary men, and his instinct was for contemplation and withdrawal, to such an extent that he had been accused in the past of avoiding practical duties and responsibilities.[129] He certainly did not shirk his responsibilities in England, but his gifts were not those of an inspiring leader. His relationship with Mary had been likened to that which he had earlier enjoyed with Vittoria Colonna, the relationship of a private and intimate counsellor. The queen depended upon him heavily, and trusted him entirely. He also enjoyed a good personal relationship with Philip, in spite of the latter's dissatisfaction with his efforts as a peacemaker. Neither Mary nor Philip ever showed impatience or resentment over his handling of the English mission. They gave him the full support of their own authority, and subsequently protected him from the wrath of Paul IV. In spite of the evidence provided by obstinate and argumentative heretics, and by irrepressible pamphleteers and polemical writers, Pole never seems to have accepted that he was fighting a battle of convictions. Significantly, the doctrinal work of his legatine synod, which was not in any case very extensive, was modelled upon the council of Florence rather than the council of Trent.[130] Admittedly Trent had so far produced only draft decrees which were not binding, but the reason for Pole's preference lay in the bitterness of his own experiences in 1545 and 1546, experiences which were also reflected in his preoccupation with obedience, and in the suspicion with which he was still regarded in some quarters at Rome. So there was no emergency training for catholic preachers – no crash courses in Tridentine theology – and no attempt to flood the market with up-to-date devotional literature, manuals, or primers. As a recent scholar has written, after a careful study of the 1555–56 synod and its context, 'There is no reason to suppose that the London Synod could have done more than create a certain order and discipline. Spiritual vision and a high clerical esprit de corps is somewhat beyond the aims and objects of canon law'. The spirit which was to inform the foundation of Douai a decade later was not awakened by a conscientious programme of reconstruction.

Not only did the cardinal suffer from certain temperamental defects in approaching his task, he was also constantly distracted. His mission had always included a responsibility to seek peace between the Habsburgs and the French, and the first half of 1555, just when he was getting to grips with his ecclesiastical task, was full of busy and eventually fruitless negotiations which not only occupied his own time and energies but also those of trusted members of his household such as Pate and Ormanetto.[131] Equally disturbing in a different way was the death of Pope Julius III in March 1555. Not only had Julius created the English mission, he had also been a staunch personal friend of Pole's, who had done everything in his power to support him and facilitate his work. In the ensuing conclave it was widely expected that Pole would be elected, but, as we have seen, the emperor was not prepared to support him, and the cardinal was unwilling to promote his own cause. In a letter to the marquis de las Navas on 8 April he declared that he would not go to Rome, since both the state of affairs in England and the peace negotiations demanded his continued presence in the north.[132] He was in a quandary, as this letter makes clear, because although he had no desire to be elected pope, it was also of the utmost importance to him that whoever was elected should continue to promote and support the English mission. The outcome appeared to be satisfactory to all. Marcello Cervini was also a good friend to Pole, and on 1 May the latter wrote with joy and enthusiasm to acknowledge the renewal of both his commissions by the new pope.[133] However, by the time this letter was written Marcellus II was already dead, and although Pole's name was again freely mentioned, it seems that he had little chance of election. This time Mary decided to back him herself, since neither Charles nor Philip seemed anxious to move. On 30 May she wrote to her commissioners for the peace negotiations, Gardiner, Arundel, and Paget, commanding them

> . . . in our name to speake with the Cardinal of Lorraine and the Constable and the rest of the Commission of our good brother the French King, praying them to recommend unto oure sayde good brother in oure name oure sayde dearest cousin to be named by him to suche Cardinals as bee at his devocyon . . .[134]

She went on to commend Pole's 'syncerite of lyfe' and his lack of worldly preoccupations. What Henri (or Philip) thought of this innocent intervention we do not know; by the time it was written the conclave had been over for a week, and the new pope was Gian Pietro Carafa. Carafa had been for years deeply suspicious of the orthodoxy of the cardinal of England, and although he did not hesitate to confirm the mission, Pole could not hope to enjoy with him the kind of friendly *rapport* which he had enjoyed with Julius. As political relations between Philip and the papacy deteriorated through 1555, the restored English church found itself facing further difficulties.

By August, Paul IV had expressed a strong desire to have Pole back in Rome 'for the need of the reform',[135] and the cardinal had replied (as his principles dictated) placing himself entirely at the pope's disposal. For the time being this threat did not materialize, and Pole was also able to obtain a bull exempting England from the terms of *Rescissio Alienationum*, the news of which had caused serious alarm there. Paul confirmed his legate's decrees, erected Ireland into a kingdom, and waived the customary annates for the confirmation of episcopal appointments. Indeed he made no direct move against Pole, but on 16 December 1555 he concluded a secret treaty of alliance with the king of France, and a few days later

Pedro Pacheco, the Imperialist cardinal of Siguenza, reported pessimistically upon the repeated evidence of the pope's ill-will towards Charles and Philip.[136] Rumours of this ill-will had fluctuated through the autumn, causing both Pole and the queen grave anxiety and 'encouraging the malignants', as the former wrote to Philip. The spectre of Pole's recall also lurked ominously in the background, reappearing in November when the pope warned his legate against becoming too deeply involved in the affairs of the realm.[137] However, on 11 December, Morone was able to write cheerfully from Rome to say that the eventual condemnation of Cranmer had been followed by the nomination of Pole to the vacant archbishopric of Canterbury, a nomination made by the pope himself 'with many kind words'.[138] Such an appointment had been long expected, but Paul had earlier withheld his approval on the grounds that he might wish to employ the cardinal's services in other ways. Consequently, in spite of the darkening political horizon, it looked at the end of 1555 as though the earlier fears for the future of the mission had been much exaggerated. After Cranmer's execution on 21 March, Pole was duly installed in the archbishopric, but his position became increasingly difficult as Paul's hostility to the Habsburgs grew more overt. On 10 April the pope appointed two fresh legates, one to Paris and the other to Brussels, ostensibly to promote peace; but since both were known to be Francophile, this was interpreted as a hostile move by the Imperialists, and by implication superseded Pole in one of his functions.[139] On 24 June he wrote to Philip in great distress, begging him not to make war on the vicar of Christ, but the king was being provoked beyond endurance, and early on the morning of 6 September 1556 troops under the command of the duke of Alva marched into the papal states.

On 14 September, Pole wrote anxiously to Rome for instructions as to how to conduct himself in these difficult circumstances. He seems to have received no reply, and from then on communications with the *curia* became fitful and uncertain. At the beginning of December Pole confided to Michieli that he had

> . . . been many months without ever receiving any reply of any sort from the Pope or his ministers to any letters and offices performed by him; . . . thinking this strange, and being of the opinion that such constant and prolonged taciturnity is derogatory to the post of Apostolic Delegate.[140]

Having found correspondence useless, on 7 December he despatched his chamberlain, Henry Penning, in an attempt to reopen communications. Before Penning could reach his destination, a letter had arrived from Morone, explaining that the pope would not despatch English business, since he blamed Mary for siding with her husband, and regarded them both as 'monarchs who had incurred censures'.[141] The new year saw no improvement in the situation. On 12 February the pope set up a special commission to try Philip and his father as rebels against the holy see, presumably emboldened to this move by the open involvement of the French on his behalf. Philip had already set up machinery to run the Spanish church without reference to Rome, but neither Mary nor Pole could have endured such an echo of the royal supremacy in England. Consequently when, on 9 April 1557, Pole's legatine commission was revoked, along with the powers of all other papal representatives in Philip's dominions, the English church was left in a difficult and anomalous position. Ironically, it had been Pole's reluctance to associate the restored church with Spanish power which had done most to increase the force of this blow. As we have seen, the cardinal had always had his doubts about Mary's marriage and was under no illusions about the unpopularity of the Spaniards. With the exception of Juan de Villagarcía and Pedro de Soto, who were appointed to the chairs of Divinity and Hebrew at Oxford, no Spanish clerics were promoted in the English church, or appeared in any official capacity outside the court.[142] Not only did Pole always insist upon the strictest priority in acknowledging papal authority, he had been in the habit of constantly referring back for support and instruction, and emphasizing the direct dependence of the English church upon Rome. In the atmosphere of hostility which prevailed after September 1556, the restored church consequently suffered more damage to its efficiency and morale than would have been the case in a more Gallican establishment. However, given the issue which had been made over the reconciliation, and the need to depart as far as possible from the appearance of the royal supremacy, it is difficult to see what else he could have done.

Beset with administrative and political difficulties, Pole nevertheless stuck doggedly to his task and achieved a good deal more than he has sometimes been credited with. Diocesan administration was improved, with many good and worthy appointments being made at the level of dean and archdeacon, as a deliberate effort was made to strengthen the cathedrals as centres of catholic piety. The numbers of young men offering themselves for ordination also seem to have improved generally,[143] perhaps as a result of the cardinal's deliberate attempt to rebuild clerical prestige. The legatine register is also a revealing document.[144] On the one hand, it shows Pole scrupulously examining and absolving individual clerics before allowing them to say mass (a task later delegated to the bishops), which must have held up the process of restoration. On the other hand, it reveals the substantial number of influential laymen who sought dispensations, permission to have private altars consecrated, or personal absolution. On this evidence it seems that traditional piety was still very much alive, not only among the humble people who welcomed the return of the mass and the colourful ceremonies of the old order, but also among their social betters, and that consequently a policy of reviving neglected habits might have enjoyed considerable success in due course. At the same time the evidence of private benefactions – surely the acid test for the property-owning classes – is extremely thin. Seven or eight licences to found and endow schools survive on the patent rolls; two new colleges were established in Oxford, Trinity and St John's, and Gonville Hall in Cambridge was refounded as Gonville and Caius College.[145] However, there was nothing distinctively catholic about this sort of provision, and in that respect nothing to distinguish Mary's reign from the years immediately before and after.[146] There were some specifically religious foundations for the relief of the poor. Lord Rich set up one in the parish church at Felsted, Sir William Petre another at Ingatestone, while at Kirby Ravensworth in Yorkshire the rector, Dr John Dakyn, endowed an almshouse in honour of St John Baptist.[147] Some chantries were also founded, or money bequeathed for that purpose. William Bendelowes founded one at Great Bardfield; Viscount Montague two, at Battle and Midhurst in Sussex; while Sir Robert Rochester established one at Terling specifically to offer prayers for the king and queen. Recent researches have revealed others in several parts of the country, but not in significant numbers.[148] Viscount Montague, a man of conspicuous piety, also set an excellent example by releasing no fewer than twelve impropriations, in which he was followed on a more modest scale by William Bendelowes, and possibly one or two others.[149] There may even have been one privately restored religious house. In January 1557 it was recorded that Thomas Bowes, citizen and merchant of London, had made over the site of the former Observant Friars house in Southampton to William earl of Pembroke, who intended to restore it to its former estate; but there is no clear evidence that he ever did so.[150] As a response to the cardinal's constant hints and exhortations, this level of reaction must have been extremely disappointing, and although it would no doubt have improved in time, it does not suggest a high level of commitment, especially in view of the fact that the majority of those who did respond were councillors or others closely associated with the government.

Overwhelmingly the material rehabilitation of the church depended upon the crown, not only through the restoration of spiritual revenues and the forgiveness of debts, but also through specific benefactions. Piecemeal remission of first fruits seems to have continued down to the passage of the general act. In May 1555, £315 owed by the royal foundation of St Katherine was remitted 'because of the charges and difficulties of the House', and in March of the same year Richard Pate, newly appointed to the see of Worcester, was granted all the first fruits and tenths of his diocese, with release of all claim by the crown, an arrangement which presumably came to an end when all such revenues passed into the hands of the legate.[151] The cause which was closest to Mary's heart, however, was the restoration of the religious life. This presented all manner of difficulties. When the final renunciation by the church of its claims to the secularized monastic lands was technically completed by the bull *Praeclara* of 20 June 1555, all the English religious houses became canonically defunct.[152] Moreover, all those ex-religious in receipt of royal pensions were apostates, and most of them were long since settled into a different way of life. The embers, however, were not cold, and in March 1555, greatly to the queen's joy, sixteen ex-Benedictine monks, clad in the habit of the order and led by John Feckenham, the dean of St Paul's, appeared at court and announced their desire to return to the religious life.[153] It took some time to gratify this ambition, not only because of the need to disentangle the canonical status of the men themselves, but also because the queen wished to make the foundation which was now in prospect part of a wider policy of restoration. A commission consisting of Gardiner, Winchester, Rochester, and Petre was set up to confer with Pole for this purpose, and it was not until early 1556 that it was finally decided to settle the community in the available premises at Westminster. Two instruments of 7 September and 10 November 1556 gave the new monastery legal existence and an endowment of £1460 *per annum*.[154] On 20 November the monks solemnly took possession of their house and were almost immediately joined by ten or a dozen more.[155] Westminster was, and remained, by far the largest of the revived houses, but there were a number of others. The first to be refounded was that of the Franciscan Observants at Greenwich, to which came the survivors of those English friars who had fled to the continent twenty years before, and the handful of those who had joined them as recruits in exile. They returned on 7 April 1555, with a modest provision of £133 6s. 8d.[156] In June a small group of Carthusians also reappeared out of exile, and, warmly backed by Rochester, secured possession of the house at Sheen, which they occupied on 25 November.[157] On 26 January 1556 the twelve named members of the community were granted legal status and a landed endowment. At some time during the summer of 1555 a group of Dominicans had also been established at St Bartholomew's, Smithfield, but it is not clear whether they received any endowment other than the premises they occupied. There were also two houses of religious women; a community of 19 Bridgettines, most of whom had returned out of exile, were granted their old premises at Syon on 18 April 1557, and a small group of Dominicanesses, formerly at Dartford, were housed at King's Langley in Hertfordshire. The latter received legal recognition and an endowment of £216 a year on 25 June 1557, while the community at Syon, which had received the more modest grant of £180, was solemnly enclosed by Bonner and Feckenham on 1 August.[158]

There were thus six religious houses in existence by the summer of 1557, housing rather more than one hundred religious, at a cost to the crown of rather more than £2000 a year. Apart from Westminster we know very little of their brief period of existence. They attracted a few recruits, and a handful of young novices, but there is no evidence to suggest that a backlog of unsatisfied religious vocations existed in England, and the impact of these houses on the spiritual life of the church, even in their immediate neighbourhood, seems to have been small. Both the Franciscans at Greenwich and the Dominicans at Smithfield were subjected to hostile demonstrations which required the intervention of the council.[159] All the founding members of the Westminster community were upwards of forty years of age, and most of those who subsequently joined them were equally mature.[160] Apart from a small number of novices, all had worn the Benedictine habit before the dissolution. Eventually there were nearly fifty of them, and many years later Fr Augustine Baker, who had known some of the survivors as old men, recorded that

> Dr. Fecknam had not insisted much upon monastick regularities, at what time he was restored to the Abby of Westminster, but had contented himself to have sett up there a disciplin much like to that he saw observed in cathedral churches, as for the Divine Office; and as for other things he brought them to the laws and customs of colledges and inns of court.[161]

The regiment, as Professor Knowles noted, was sober and dignified rather than austere, and backward-looking, as one might expect from an ageing community. Pole tried to bring two Cassinese reformers from Italy to stiffen the discipline, but for some reason they did not come, and the only outstanding personality was Feckenham himself, whose revived vocation was no doubt genuine but hardly rigorous. In fact the restored religious houses were little more than a gesture, and an indication of how much things had changed in

England since the 1500 or so surviving religious had left their cloisters.

Although these re-endowments were the crown's most expensive benefactions (except for the restoration of the order of St John of Jerusalem, which did not come until 1558), they were by no means the only ones. Almost every kind of pious gift can be found among the royal grants. In May 1556 the archdeaconry of Wells, extinguished by statute in 1 Edward VI, was re-erected by letters patent.[162] In July Manchester college was re-established, for a warden, 8 fellows, 4 clerks, and 4 choristers, and became an important centre of religious life in Lancashire.[163] In the same month the guild and chapel of St Faith's, London was granted the status of a body corporate and £100 a year in lands. In November 1556 the hospital of the Savoy was restored and re-endowed at the same level.[164] Later, in 1558, we find the queen restoring two messuages to the rector and churchwardens of St Mary le Bow to maintain a light before the altar, and refounding the hospital of St Leonard's at Stoke by Newark in Nottinghamshire. Mary set an indefatigable example, but her subjects, particularly the wealthier ones, were slow to respond. Although it could be argued that the only way to re-create traditional religion was to restore the traditional setting, such constant preoccupation with material wealth played into the hands of protestant and anticlerical critics. This was equally the case with Pole's constant and protracted financial inquiries, although their objective was the improvement of pastoral care. Unfortunately Paul IV added to this bureaucratic tangle by demanding to know the 'true value' of all the English dioceses for the purposes of papal taxation. This necessitated another round of detailed surveys and assessments, and a thorough inquiry into the diocese of Winchester alone occupied several experienced officials throughout the summer of 1556.[165] Witnesses disagreed, accounts were missing, and yet the resulting survey is a monument to meticulous and efficient administration.[166] Ironically in the light of this additional burden which he had placed on the struggling English church, it was Paul IV's withdrawal of the legatine commission which made Pole's policy of 'total restoration' temporarily impossible. To him the papal authority, the jurisdiction and the material endowments of the church were all part of the seamless fabric without the protection of which the doctrine and ceremonies of the church could not survive or have meaning. His work was not ruined by the quarrel between Philip and the pope, but it was severely damaged because he had made so much contingent upon correct legal and administrative procedures.

Notes

1 Charles to his ambassadors in England, 4 August 1554. *Cal. Span.*, XIII, 14.
2 Marc' Antonio Damula to the doge and senate, 4 August 1554. *Cal. Ven.*, V, 526.
3 *Cal. Span.*, XIII, 14.
4 ibid.
5 Julius's anxiety not to arouse the emperor's hostility seems to have led him into a certain deviousness. Pole was obviously convinced that the pope urgently wished him to proceed, while Charles could write, on the basis of his own correspondence with Julius, 'We know the Cardinal has no commission to press onward so hotly . . .' *Cal. Span.*, XIII, 15.
6 Ambassadors to the emperor, *Cal. Span.*, XIII, 22. Gardiner had received at least two lengthy and patronizing admonitions from Pole during the previous year, and it was not only Renard who believed that there was personal animosity between the two men. Pole to Gardiner, 28 August 1553; *Cal. Ven.*, V, 399-402; 22 March 1554; BL Add. MS 25425 ff. 204-6. Pogson, op. cit., 33.
7 *Cal. Span.*, XIII, 28-30. This document is described by the editor as being addressed to Philip, but it seems clear from the contents that Mary was the recipient.
8 *Cal. Ven.*, V, 529, 12 August 1554.
9 21 September, to Philip, *Cal. Ven.*, V, 573-5. 24 September, to Philip, *Cal. Span.*, XIII, 53-5. 28 September, to the emperor, *Cal. Ven.*, V, 575-6.
10 *Cal. Ven.*, V, 578-81.
11 Reports by Pole to Julius III, 23 and 26 October 1554. *Cal. Ven.*, V, 582-3; 584-6.
12 ibid., 585.
13 These statutes had never been repealed, and it remained an offence in English law to exercise any ecclesiastical jurisdiction without the king's consent, a situation which Pole could not have accepted in principle. ibid., 585-6 and Renard to the emperor, 6 November 1554. *Cal. Span.*, XIII, 78.
14 Pole to Morone, 28 October 1554. *Cal. Ven.*, V, 588-90.
15 *Cal. Ven.*, V, 585.
16 PRO SP69/5/286.
17 This letter, which does not seem to have survived, is referred to in Philip's instructions for Francisco de Eraso, drawn up about 14 or 15 November. *Cal. Span.*, XIII, 92-5.
18 There are several accounts of this journey, but the fullest and most informative is that contained in a letter written by Donato Rullo, a member of Pole's household, to Cardinal Seripando, and printed by Carlo de Frede in *La Restaurazione Cattolica in Inghilterra sotto Maria Tudor* (1971), 49-54.
19 Both Rullo and Renard emphasized the attentions paid to Pole by the Spanish courtiers and members of Philip's household. Renard to the emperor, 30 November, *Cal. Span.*, XIII, 107-9. Rullo to Seripando, 30 November, de Frede, op. cit., 53.

20 Hughes and Larkin, II, 48-9. On the same day a licence was issued under the great seal to Pole to enter the realm and exercise his jurisdiction. *Cal. Pat.*, II, 311.

21 *CJ*, I, 38.

22 *Cal. Span.*, XIII, 79-80.

23 Biblioteca Vaticana, Rome (MSS on microfilm at the Bodleian Library, Oxford), Vat. Lat. 5968 f. 348. J. Collier, *An Ecclesiastical History of Great Britain*, II (1714), 372-3.

24 ibid. Quirini, *Epistolae Reginaldi Poli*, V, 1-4. *CJ*, I, 38. For a penetrating analysis of Pole's conception of his mission see R. H. Pogson, 'Reginald Pole and the Priorities of Government in Mary Tudor's Church', *HJ*, XVIII (1975), 3-21.

25 Rullo to Seripando, 1 December 1554; de Frede, op. cit., 57.

26 Foxe, VI, 776. *Cal. Span.*, XIII, 108.

27 Da Stroppiana to the bishop of Arras, 3 December 1554. *Cal. Span.*, XIII, 112. De Frede, op. cit., 58.

28 *Cal. Span.*, XIII, 112.

29 *APC*, V, 85. *Cal. Span.*, XIII, 108.

30 E. Cardwell, *Synadolia* (1842), II, 440-1.

31 Memorandum on developments concerning church property. *Cal. Ven.*, VI, 10.

32 Letter and postscript by Alvise Priuli, 22 and 24 December 1554. BL Add. MS 41557. J. H. Crehan, 'The Return to Obedience', *The Month*, n.s. XIV (1955), 221-9. *LJ*, I, 479.

33 The relevance of the Statute of Mortmain was fully appreciated, as is shown by the dispensation from its terms granted to William Roper when he was licensed to found a chantry in Canterbury, *Cal. Pat.*, II, 225.

34 BL Add. MS 41577. Loach, op. cit.

35 *LJ*, I, 480.

36 *CJ*, I, 40. According to Renard a group of members 'who possess no church property' had earlier tried to sabotage the bill by moving that no dispensation should be granted, but they had not prevailed 'because of the promise the King and Queen have given . . .' *Cal. Span.*, XIII, 125.

37 Statute 2 and 3 Philip and Mary, c. 8, section xiii.

38 P. Hughes, *The Reformation in England*, II (1953), 226 and n.

39 Statute 2 and 3 Philip and Mary, c. 19.

40 BL Harleian MS 444 f. 27; Cotton MS Titus C VII f. 120. These versions differ slightly, and both are contemporary, or near contemporary, copies. *Ecc. Mem.*, III.

41 Pogson, op. cit., 3-21. Pole was nothing if not patronizing to those of inferior social status. Several years after his death a member of his household (possibly Ormanetto) wrote that he '. . . used often to say that the schism of King Henry could not have come about had the bishops been of the nobility, or related to the barons of that kingdom and the parliament. But the bishops, finding themselves despised by the nobility all . . . supported the lusts of the king . . .' Vatican Library Misc. Arm. II ff. 34-5. Quoted by J. P. Marmion, 'The London Synod of Cardinal Pole 1555-6' (unpublished Keele University MA thesis, 1974), 104.

42 J. A. F. Thomson, *The Later Lollards: 1414–1520* (1965). *OM*. On Gardiner's attitude, see *OM*, 124-5.

The Reign of Mary Tudor

43 Thomas Sampson to John Calvin, 23 February 1555. *OL*, I, 170. The two who were 'thought to have yielded', Barlow and Cardmaker, had both recanted. Barlow subsequently escaped into exile, while Cardmaker withdrew his recantation and was burned. Foxe, VII, 77-9.
44 P. Hughes, op. cit., II; A. G. Dickens, *The English Reformation*; *OM*.
45 C. H. Garrett, *The Marian Exiles* (1938); D. M. Loades, 'The Essex Inquisitions of 1556', *BIHR*, XXXV (1962), 87-97.
46 ibid. J. E. Oxley, *The Reformation in Essex* (1965), 199-200, etc.
47 London, 112; Canterbury, 49; Chichester, 41; Norwich, 31. *Ecc. Mem.*, III, ii, 554-6.
48 P. Hughes, op. cit., II, 262. Hughes quotes the similar opinion of C. H. Smyth, but both were making the double assumption (a) that many of the victims were radicals (which cannot be proved) and (b) that Edward's government would have changed its policy had the king lived. In fact Edward's government had burned only two radicals in six years, and Cranmer's fierce canon law had failed to gain parliamentary endorsement.
49 For example, the case of William Branch, alias Flower, who attacked the celebrant in St Margaret's, Westminster, with an axe in March 1555. Foxe, VII, 74-6.
50 For a discussion of this question, see C. Burrage. *The Early English Dissenters* (1912), II; I. B. Horst, *The Radical Brethren* (1972); B. R. White, *The English Separatist Tradition* (1971); also J. W. Martin, 'English Protestant separatism: Henry Hart and the Freewillers', *Sixteenth Century Journal*, VII, ii (1976), 55-75.
51 Foxe, VII, 324.
52 The scale of the operation is made clear by both Foxe and the *Acts of the Privy Council*. No statistical analysis of the investigations and interrogations has ever been made to discover the number of man-hours absorbed, and it is very doubtful whether such an exercise is feasible. The most thorough modern study is by P. Hughes.
53 BL Harleian MS 416 f. 77.
54 Foxe, VI, 704, says he 'gave over the matter as utterly discouraged'. Thereafter he tried unsuccessfully to persuade Mary to introduce a policy of fines and civil disabilities.
55 BL Harleian MS 416 f. 16.
56 Foxe, VI, 628. The biggest impression was probably made by the death of Rowland Taylor. ibid., 697. At this stage the government was following an 'exemplary' policy of burning men in the places where they had ministered. In Taylor's case this misfired badly.
57 For example, Thomas Bentham. *Ecc. Mem.*, III, i, 133-5.
58 Renard to Philip, 5 February 1555. *Cal. Span.*, XIII, 138-9. Renard to the emperor, 27 March 1555. *Cal. Span.*, XIII, 147.
59 *Cal. Ven.*, VI, 93-4.
60 *APC*, V, 247-9. Michieli to the doge and senate, 24 March 1556, gives this reason for the suppression, although probably only one of the witnesses was Spanish. It was believed in London that Villagarcía and de Soto had forged the recantation. *Cal. Ven.*, VI, 386. *OM*, 230-2.
61 M. Huggarde, *The Displaying of the Protestantes* (1556), ff. 62, 127, etc. J. Christopherson, *An Exhortation* (1554), sig. I iii. A similar line was taken by Rowland Taylor's catholic successor at Hadleigh (one Newall) in a sermon on the day after Taylor's execution. BL Harleian MS 425 f. 119.

62 For example, the cases of John Bland (VII, 287) and Lawrence Saunders (VI, 628).
63 Dickens, *English Reformation.* For protestant influence outside this area see C. Haigh, *Reformation and Resistance in Tudor Lancashire* (1975); Dickens, *Marian Reaction in the Diocese of York*; K. G. Powell, 'Marian Martyrs and the Reformation in Bristol' (Historical Association, Bristol Branch, pamphlet no. 31 (1975)).
64 One of the consequences of the disappearance of the old leadership was an increasing tendency among the protestants to regard their persecution as being in itself evidence of election. Latimer had firmly rejected that interpretation (*The Sermons of Bishop Latimer*, ed. G. E. Gorrie (Parker Society, 1844, 160), but Ponet in 1556 took a different view. In *A shorte treatise of politike power* (sig. E v) he wrote '. . . to be slaughtered, spoken evil of, Whipped, scourged, spoiled of their goods, killed of the worldly princes and tyrants, rather than they would disobey God and forsake Christ; this can neither papists nor Turks, Jews nor gentiles, nor none other do, but only the Elect of God'.
65 R. M. Kingdon, *Geneva and the Coming of the Wars of Religion in France* (1956); R. J. Knecht, *Francis I and Absolute Monarchy*, Hist. Assoc. pamphlet (1969); N. M. Sutherland, *The Massacre of St. Bartholomew and the European Conflict* (1973).
66 J. W. Allen, *A History of Political Thought in the Sixteenth Century* (1928); W. Haller, *Foxe's Book of Martyrs and the Elect Nation* (1963); V. N. Olsen, *John Foxe and the Elizabethan Church* (1973); for a sensitive analysis of the exact relationship between the pressures of exile and the theology of these ideas, see J. E. A. Dawson, 'The Early Career of Christopher Goodman' (unpublished Durham University PhD thesis, 1978).
67 Haller, op. cit.; L. P. Fairfield, *John Bale* (1976).
68 Dawson, op. cit.
69 To be an effective instrument for the rebuilding of the faith, the obedience of the people had, in Pole's eyes, to be total and unquestioning. Pogson, 'Reginald Pole and the Priorities of Government'. See also, Loades, 'The Enforcement of Reaction, 1553-8', *JEH*, XVI, i (1965), 54-66.
70 28 July and 18 August 1553; 10 April 1554. Hughes and Larkin, II, 4, 5, 41.
71 2 and 3 Philip and Mary, c. 9.
72 Hughes and Larkin, II, 57-60, 90.
73 *Cal. Pat.*, III, 24.
74 Loades, 'The Press under the Early Tudors', *TCBS*, IV, i (1964), 29-50.
75 On Eagles, see Foxe, VIII, 393-7. Oxley, op. cit., 206-8.
76 *APC*, V, 244.
77 Loades, 'The Authorship and Publication of . . . (STC 3480)', *TCBS*, III, ii (1960), 155-60.
78 Machyn, 72. Garrett, *Marian Exiles*, 142-3, 288-9.
79 Loades, 'The Press under the Early Tudors'.
80 *Cal. Pat.*, III, 480.
81 *The Displaying of the Protestantes*, 70. Huggarde returned repeatedly to this theme, writing in another place 'Perceive advisedly with yourselves what cause the protestants have to shorten their lives by fire, and what cause they have to call their just punishments persecution . . .' ibid., 127.
82 Ridley specifically requested that his own writings should not appear in

print until after his death, and this wish was observed. Only *Certain godly learned and comfortable conferences* (STC 21048) appeared before Mary's death, and several of his letters, and those of the other martyrs, appeared for the first time in Foxe. Others were not published until the Parker Society volumes appeared in the nineteenth century.

83 Joseph Ames, *Typographical Antiquities* (1790), III, 1574; STC 10383; STC 7279.5. The fullest catalogue of the polemical literature of this period is E. J. Baskerville, 'A Chronological Bibliography of Propaganda and Polemic published in English between 1553 and 1558'. This bibliography has not yet been published, and I am grateful to Mr Baskerville for the opportunity to see it in typescript.

84 STC 21854; STC 17562; STC 18797; STC 10024.

85 STC 20178. W. S. Hudson, *John Ponet, Advocate of Limited Monarchy* (1942). Dawson, op. cit.

86 STC 24174. Robert Pownall's *Admonition to the towne of Callays* of April 1557 had been almost as savage. See below, 440-41.

87 Foxe, VIII, 576. Garrett, *Marian Exiles*, Introduction. Loades, 'The Press under the Early Tudors'. On the question of marketing and distribution, see also J. Loach, 'Pamphlets and Politics, 1553-8', *BIHR*, XLVIII (1975), 31-45.

88 STC 19890.

89 BL Stowe MS 958 ff. 8-17. The clearest exposition of the part which these ephemera and popular works played in the thinking of the protestant leaders is contained in a letter by John Ponet, written to an anonymous correspondent late in 1555: '. . . ballets Rymes and shorte toyes that be not deare and will easily be borne away doe much good at home amongst the rude people. To the whiche studies I mynd not to pluck yow from your other more weighty purposes, but wishe that you would pryck other men to suche easy exercises, who either cannot or will not travell in larger purposes. The papistes show ther faces so shamelessly, and being destitute of all godly weapons presse so sore upon us that it is an easy matter for any yt hath ben a scholar in Gods servyce to wounde them where he lyste. Blynd fury that hath made them witles . . .' BL Add. MS 29546 f. 25.

90 *Displaying of the Protestantes*, 64.

91 One of the most difficult problems which the earlier leaders had faced after losing power was that of justifying their defiance of the royal supremacy. As Dr John Story put it to Cranmer: '. . . the same laws, being put away by a parliament, are now received again by a parliament, and have as full authority now as they had then; and they will now that ye answer to the Pope's holiness; therefore by the laws of the realm ye are bound to answer him'. (Foxe, VIII, 54). Latimer had attempted, not very successfully, to find a reply: 'In the King's days that dead is, who was the church in England? The King and his fautors, or massmongers in corners? If the King and the fautors of his proceedings, why not we now the church, abiding in the same proceedings? If clandestine massmongers might be of the church and yet contrary to the King's proceedings, why may not we as well as they be of the church contrary to the Queen's proceedings?' (Ridley, *Works*, 124). It was left to Knox and Goodman to argue unequivocally that the truth of a church depended upon its covenant with God and not upon its recognition by any earthly society or authority.

92 Foxe, VII, 324; 371-4; *APC*, V, 150; BL Harleian MS 419 f. 131:

'This yere [1555] the xxiiii daie of June a priest was put into Newgate for sayng the litany in Englysh in hys parish church at Charyng Cross . . .'

93 For a discussion of Pole's experiences in Italy, see D. B. Fenlon, *Heresy and Obedience in Tridentine Italy* (1972).

94 G. Alexander, 'Bonner and the Marian Persecutions', *History*, 60 (1975), 374-92.

95 Latimer, *Works* (Parker Society, 1844-45), II, 272.

96 Baskerville, op. cit.; Loach, 'Pamphlets and Politics'.

97 STC 25115; STC 13559.

98 Reported by C. L. Oastler, 'John Day, the Elizabethan Printer' (unpublished Oxford B.Litt thesis, 1965); STC 4564.

99 STC 17517; STC 23207, 23208.

100 *The Historie of Wyates rebellion*, STC 20407; *An exhortation to alle menne to take hede and beware of rebellion*, STC 5207; STC 7283.

101 BL Harleian MS 284 f. 127.

102 Particularly in his description of the antics of 'Father Browne, the broker of Bedlam'. *Displaying*, 122-30.

103 *A notable oration . . .*, translated by John Billingham; *A sermon very notable Fruicteful and Godlie*, STC 10896; *A Declaration of the state wherein all heretickes dooe leade their lives*, STC 12558; *A manifeste detection of the notable falshed of that part of John Frithes boke . . .*, STC 12559.

104 STC 3282-5. Bonner's *Injunctions* of 1555 were also printed, STC 10249.

105 STC 22817; STC 17629. The same year also saw *An honest godlye instruction . . . for the . . . bringinge up of children*, published under Bonner's auspices, STC 3281.

106 J. A. Muller, *Stephen Gardiner and the Tudor Reaction*, 278-85.

107 STC 19890; Foxe, VII and VIII, accounts written by the defendants themselves.

108 Cheke's recantation, which Michieli ascribed to Pole's personal intervention, was carried out at court with maximum publicity. Great care was taken over the exact form of words used, and according to one account 30 heretics who were in danger of burning were persuaded by this example to recant also. *Cal. Ven.*, VI, 536. In spite of this, no account of the recantation was published. Feckenham's 'Oration in favour of Sir John Cheek' made before the queen at the time (4 October 1556) survives in BL Harleian MS 353 ff. 48-9.

109 STC 18076.

110 Edited for the Catholic Record Society by L. E. Whatmore and W. Sharp; XLV and XLVI (1950-51). This visitation was almost certainly one of those ordered by Pole as part of his general survey of the state of the church (see below); there are numerous cases recorded of individuals failing to attend church, but in only a few cases is suspected heresy given as the cause.

111 *Cal. Ven.*, VI, 5.

112 *Ecc. Mem.*, III, ii, 484-5. Christopherson, *Exhortation*, sig. Tv, made the same point forcefully. Denouncing the contempt with which the clergy had been treated in the past, he went on 'Yea as yet thys maliciouse mockers cease not in manye places when they can spie a prieste, to playe the like part . . .' and quoted Chrysostom on the reverence due to those who have the power to bind and loose. Every surviving visitation shows numerous cures vacant, and in Suffolk it was noted 'This

yeare [1554] the xi or xii daie of September in Ypswich, being xi
parishe churches, there was but ii priests to serve them, and in all
Suffolk very few in comparison to the townes . . .' BL Harleian MS 419
f. 131.

113 Marmion, op. cit., I, 48.
114 In addition to the main landed estate, Pole received annuities to the
value of £290 18s. 4d., and a pension from the king. *Cal. Pat.*, III, 69;
See below, 439 and n.
115 R. H. Pogson, 'Revival and Reform in Mary Tudor's Church: a question of money', *JEH*, XXV, 3 (1974), 249-65.
116 ibid. See also the evidence of Pole's visitation of Lincoln diocese in
1556, printed in *Ecc. Mem.*, III, ii, 389-413. There are numerous examples of churches refitting at considerable expense; e.g., Bridport,
Dorset. *HMC Sixth Report*, App., 497 (Town of Bridport MSS).
117 Foxe, VII, 34. According to Foxe, Mary unburdened her conscience to
her council on 28 March 1555, announcing her intention to return all
property.
118 PRO E164/31; Pogson, 'Revival and Reform in Mary Tudor's Church'.
119 Bonner's Register, Guildhall Library, London, MS 9531/12 f. 399.
Pogson, 'Revival and Reform', 259.
120 *Reformatio Angliae ex decretis Reginaldi Poli* (1565). Bodleian MS film
33 (Vat. Lat. 5968); R. Ancel, 'La réconciliation d'Angleterre . . .',
Revue d'Histoire Ecclésiastique, X (1909); J. I. Tellechea Idigoras,
'Bartolomé Carranza y la restauración católica inglesa', *Anthologia
Annua*, XII (1964), 159-282 (which presents the case for Carranza's
influence on the work of the synod); Marmion, op. cit.
121 Legatine Register (LPL microfilm of Douai MS 922), VI, ff. 7-8.
122 In April 1558 this was carried a stage further, when all taxation of a
tenth of the clergy was halved. Pogson, 'Revival and Reform', 261.
123 W. H. Frere, *The Marian Reaction in its Relation to the English Clergy*,
Appendix I. Apart from Cranmer, who was in possession only technically, eleven of these bishops were Henrician or Edwardian appointments
(several of them restored), eleven were Marian appointments, and three
sees were vacant. The absolutions are recorded in the legatine register.
124 *The Reformation in England*, II, 243.
125 J. W. Blench, *Preaching in England in the late XVth and XVIth Centuries* (1964).
126 W. Schenk, *Reginald Pole, Cardinal of England* (1950). Fenlon, op. cit.
Pole became chancellor of both universities, and his injunctions for
Cambridge are printed in Frere and Kennedy, *Visitation Articles and
Injunctions*, II, 415-21. Pole's interest in the running of Cambridge can
be seen from a number of letters relating to the university affairs preserved in BL Harleian MS 7037 ff. 247-59.
127 *Reformatio Angliae*; G. Alberigo, *Conciliorum Oecumencicorum decreta*
(Rome, 1962); Hughes, op. cit., II, 235.
128 Feria to Ribadeneyra, 22 March 1558. *Cal Span.*, XIII, 370. J. H.
Crehan, 'St. Ignatius and Cardinal Pole', *Archivum Historicum Societatis
Iesu*, XXV (1956), 72-98.
129 Marmion, op. cit., I, 3, 22-3; Pole had defended himself against charges
of evading responsibilities in a letter to Morone of 28 May 1554, but in
terms which acknowledged that there was some truth in the accusation.
Quirini, IV, 135-8; *Cal. Ven.*, V, 497-501.
130 Marmion, op. cit., I, 240-2.

131 See above, 229-31.
132 *Cal. Ven.*, VI, 46.
133 *Cal. Ven.*, VI, 59.
134 BL Cotton MS Titus B II f. 97.
135 Michieli to the doge and senate, 12 August 1555. *Cal. Ven.*, VI, 160.
136 Renard to Philip, 7 December 1555 (reporting the arrival of the cardinals of Lorraine and Tournon in Rome); and Siguenza to the emperor, 23 December 1555. *Cal. Span.*, XIII, 252-3.
137 Michieli to the doge and senate, 25 November 1555. *Cal. Ven.*, VI, 259-62.
138 *Cal. Ven.*, VI, 278-9. For the lengthy proceedings leading up to Cranmer's condemnation (and Pole's part therein) see *OM*, 192-233.
139 Cardinal Carafa and the cardinal of Motula. Don Diego Laso to the king of Bohemia, 11 April 1556. *Cal. Span.*, XIII, 266.
140 Pole to Morone, 14 September 1556. *Cal. Ven.*, VI, 618. Michieli to the doge and senate, 7 December 1556. ibid., 847.
141 *Cal. Ven.*, VI, 880.
142 The influence of such important clerics as á Castro and Carranza was exercised almost entirely behind the scenes, and is difficult to assess. Tellechea Idigoras, art. cit.
143 C. Haigh, *Reformation and Resistance in Tudor Lancashire* (1975), 200, makes the point specifically for the conservative diocese of Chester, but the tendency was similar in other dioceses where the records have survived.
144 The original of this document is in the municipal archive at Douai (MS 922) but there is a microfilm in LPL. It was first noticed and commented upon by C. H. Garrett in the *Journal of Modern History* (1941), 189-94.
145 *Cal. Pat.*, I, 204; II, 192; III, 51, 460; IV, 166, 225, 323 (confirmation). Sir Thomas Pope was licensed to found Trinity College, Oxford, and a school at Hokenorton, on 8 March 1555. *Cal. Pat.*, II, 90. Sir Thomas White was licensed to found St John's on 1 May 1555. *Cal. Pat.*, II, 322. And Dr John Caius to refound Gonville Hall on 4 September 1557; *Cal. Pat.*, IV, 160.
146 J. Simon, *Education and Society in Tudor England* (1966); W. K. Jordan, *Philanthropy in England, 1480–1660* (1959).
147 *Cal. Pat.*, II, 42; III, 542; III, 118. Oxley, *The Reformation in Essex* (1965), 184.
148 *Cal. Pat.*, IV, 91; III, 440; III, 363-4. Haigh, op. cit., 200-3.
149 *Cal. Pat.*, III, 290; IV, 91.
150 *Cal. Pat.*, III, 360. In her will, Mary was to leave £200 to the Friars Observant at Southampton, but I have found no reference to the community in existence. BL Harleian MS 6949.
151 *Cal. Pat.*, II, 117; II, 168.
152 M. C. Knowles, *The Religious Orders in England*, III (1959), 423. The Marian houses were consequently not restorations but new foundations. They had no entitlement to their former sites, let alone their former endowments.
153 *Cal. Ven.*, VI, 24-8.
154 *Cal. Pat.*, III, 546; III, 354. PRO SP12/1/64.
155 Knowles, op. cit., 424-5.
156 ibid., 439; *Cal. Pat.*, III, 354; SP12/1/64.
157 Knowles, op. cit.; John Rochester, Sir Robert's brother, had been one

of the Carthusian martyrs. E. M. Thompson, *The Carthusian Order in England* (1930), 500-9.

158 Knowles, op. cit., 440; *Cal. Pat.*, III, 403; SP12/1/64.

159 *APC*, V, 169.

160 Knowles, op. cit., 431-3.

161 'Life of Father Baker', in *Memorials of Father Augustine Baker*, ed. J. McCann, and R. H. Connolly. Catholic Record Society, XXXIII, (1933) 95-6.

162 *Cal. Pat.*, III, 15.

163 *Cal. Pat.*, III, 413; Haigh, op. cit., 203-4.

164 *Cal. Pat.*, III, 274; *Cal. Pat.*, III, 543; PRO SP11/9/8 (warrant for grant, 15 June 1556).

165 Pogson, 'Revival and Reform', 262-3. Heath and Thirlby were delegated to carry out this work.

166 Arch. Vat. Instr. Misc. 4008. Pogson, 'Revival and Reform', 263.

11 War and Government, 1557–1558

The episode which eventually enabled Philip and Mary to push the English council into war with France has never been satisfactorily explained. There were many English exiles in France at the time, and over the previous three years Henri had periodically encouraged these men with small subsidies and with facilities for carrying out their piratical activities in the channel.[1] At the beginning of 1557 the exile community was seething with rumours of conspiracy and impending war, but the only tangible information which Wotton was able to pick up related to a plot to fire the Calais magazine, and that had collapsed by the end of January. Henri was seriously alarmed, the ambassador wrote, by the prospect of Mary declaring war against him, and was unlikely to support any further exile adventure unless war became absolutely certain.[2] In early January Thomas Stafford had been received at court, and his inflated claims to English royal blood apparently recognized.[3] On 13 January Wotton had speculated that the king might have it in mind to use him for some 'great enterprise', but Henri drew back, as he had done so often before, and there was no further alarm in that direction for three months. In early April the rumours began again. The talk of war continued, and there was a new plot against Guisnes; also a servant of Thomas Stafford had disclosed that his master was planning to seize a castle on the English coast. An agent of Wotton's, designated as 'P', had managed to obtain a map of the place, which appeared to be Scarborough, although either Hull or Plymouth was also possible. 'It is thought', Wotton continued, 'the French King will not interfere . . .'[4] On 14 April the ambassador reported that Stafford had left the court, where he was rumoured to have received money, and was gathering arms and men at Rouen. Nine days later he appeared off Scarborough with two French ships, and landed a small force variously estimated between 30 and a hundred men, 'some French, some English rebels'.[5] The castle was partly ruinous, and the nominal garrison of about a dozen men surprised and quickly overpowered. Immediately thereafter Stafford issued a lengthy and carefully worded proclamation, declaring that he had

> . . . perfect knowledge by certaine letters taken with Spanyards at Depe that this same castle of Scarborow with xii other of the most chiefest and principal Howldes in the realme shall be delivered to xii thousand Spanyards before the kings coronation . . .

Because she was handing the country over to foreigners, Mary was no true queen. The crown must be kept in English blood, and the 'lawes lybertes and customes' established by Henry VIII restored. He proclaimed himself rightful duke of Buckingham and protector of the realm.[6]

News of this incursion travelled with incredible speed. By 10 o'clock the following morning the earl of Westmorland had been alerted, and decided to 'go upon' the rebels at Scarborough with the militia force which he had been about to lead to Newcastle, apparently on his way to the border.[7] By 27 April, two days later, the council had been informed, both of the invasion and of Westmorland's response, and issued an order to the mayor of Newcastle to fit out four or five ships to intercept Stafford's two before they could either escape or do any more damage.[8] On Wednesday, 28 April, Westmorland retook the castle without any serious fighting, and by the following day Surian could report from London that the crisis was over.[9] The contrast between the speed and decisiveness with which this incident was handled, and the manner in which the council had reacted to the news of Wyatt's rising and other lesser disturbances, is extreme. Part of the explanation lies in the fact that musters had been in hand for some weeks in anticipation of renewed hostilities from Scotland, and consequently there was a force in being only three days march away. Also Wotton's warnings, although they had not resulted in any alert being sent out, as far as we can tell, had presumably informed the council of the nature of the enterprise to be expected. Nevertheless, the episode shows some puzzling and suspicious features. It is almost 200 miles from Scarborough to London, and even if Surian misdated his letter by a day, it is still remarkable that he should have heard on the morning of the 30th of a success in Scarborough less than 48 hours previously. Also, he commented that, despite the brevity of the insurrection,

> . . . it has nevertheless revealed the disposition of many persons who could not refrain from showing themselves desirous of a change in the present state of affairs . . . but as this opportunity has placed within the power of the law, not only this ringleader but others likewise who were with him . . . it has freed the Queen from suspicion of them.[10]

In fact, Stafford had attracted virtually no support, and those captured with him were no more than the handful of adventurers who had accompanied him from France. It looks very much as though Surian was 'fed' a prepared story, which was communicated to him the moment the messenger arrived from the north. A proclamation was also issued in London on 30 April announcing Stafford's capture and denouncing his intentions in terms which make it clear that a copy of his proclamation was in the hands of the council. In the light of these circumstances, and of the results which followed, it is natural to wonder whether Stafford's apparently harebrained and provocative venture was not connived at, or even prompted, by Paget and his agents.

Henri naturally denied that he had been any party to it. His virtuous disclaimers have never carried much conviction, but in this case he may well have been right.[11] Noailles had no knowledge of any such involvement, and Henri knew enough of what was going on in the English council to have realized the likely consequences of such a move at that moment. Shortly after Stafford had left France, Wotton had written that he had a force of four or five hundred men with him 'and as many more promised'. Had the French king seriously intended to make a diversion in the north of England, that was about the scale of enterprise to be expected. When they heard what had happened, Dudley and the other English exiles in France laughed over Stafford, 'calling him King of Scarborough'; meanwhile Ashton was busy with a design of his own against Portland castle.[12] The evidence from the French end seems to suggest that Stafford acted entirely on his own initiative, and for his own purposes; and this is supported by the fact that he put himself forward as protector instead of invoking the popular name of Elizabeth. On the other hand, his own resources would hardly have sufficed to hire two ocean-going ships and their crews, let alone to arm them and his men. Perhaps he and his small band 'hitched' a lift on two French vessels that were going to Scotland about their own business.[13] On the other hand, the fact that the larger vessel was commanded by John Rybawde, alias Jean Ribault, makes such a relatively innocent explanation unlikely. Ribault was a known adventurer who had earlier served the duke of Northumberland, and was later to be involved with the notorious Thomas Stucley.[14] Only a short time after Stafford's raid Noailles reported that Paget was planning a similar attack on Normandy with the aid of the Spaniards, and of maps supplied by Jean Ribault.[15] Noailles seems to have been unaware of Ribault's part in the Scarborough episode, but knew that his connection with Paget went back to the time of his service in England. If Ribault was in fact in Paget's service at this time, and had lured the foolish Stafford to his doom, it would not only explain how the young man managed to find suitable shipping so quickly without the king's aid (and how he managed to afford it), but also how the English council came to be so accurately informed about the scale of the operation by 27 April, when alarms and conflicting first reports might have been expected. Wotton's earlier letter had warned them roughly what was afoot, but the confidence and *panache* with which the whole affair was handled strongly suggests that someone on the council had inside information about the true extent of the danger. That this was never mentioned nor admitted would be entirely consistent with the secrecy which would be necessary if the action was to be successfully represented to other councillors as a piece of wanton provocation on the part of the French. The evidence is not conclusive, but Paget, Philip, and Mary were playing hard for a big stake in April 1557, and if Thomas Stafford's intervention was entirely unsolicited, then it was an extraordinary coincidence.

War was not declared at once, but the decision to do so was taken within a week of Stafford's capture, while he and his accomplices were still awaiting trial.[16] Writing to the duke of Savoy from London on 28 April, before the defeat of the raid was known, Don Bernardino de Mendoza was already certain that the incident would mean war. 'As for the breach of the truce', he commented, 'the French have spared us the trouble . . .'[17] During May, Wotton continued to report from Paris on the activities of the other exiles, and to send such news as he could of French intrigues in Scotland. The type of letter which he had previously directed to Petre he was now sending to Bourne and Boxall, and the council responded to his warnings by issuing special instructions for the defence of the Solent and the Dorset coast to Lord Howard on 22 May.[18] At the same time Lord St John and Sir Hugh Paulet were ordered to strengthen the garrisons of Poole, Weymouth, and Portland. Musters and other military preparations were pressed ahead energetically under Philip's supervision, for the time being on the pretext of honouring existing treaty obligations for the defence of the Low Countries. On 13 May, Surian reported

> . . . a great part of the nobility of the kingdom are preparing, some from a longing for novelty . . . some from rivalry and desire of glory, some to obtain grace and favour with his Majesty and the Queen . . .[19]

The whole operation was being conducted with such promptness and energy that it was very much to the king's honour, as well as boding well for the fortune of the war. The council's opposition to the war was clearly not shared by those nobles and gentlemen who hoped to use it for their own purposes, and there was also, as Surian pointed out, the additional benefit of diverting the energies of so many potential troublemakers into a useful channel, leaving a much more governable realm behind them. By the end of May reinforcements had been despatched to the Calais Pale, although on an inadequate scale, as events were to show, Wotton had been recalled, and Norroy King of Arms issued with a special commission to bear the defiance of the queen of England to the court of France.[20] When he received the herald on 7 June, Henri laughed and declared that Mary would go to any lengths to gratify her husband, while Norroy insisted, in accordance with his instructions, that it was the queen's own grievances which had led her to such a course. He named Stafford, and the harbourage given to other English exiles and rebels over the years.

In England most people seem to have agreed with Henri. Apart from the fighting men themselves, reaction to the news was generally hostile. In two despatches, on 7 and 8 June, Surian reported their displeasure:

> . . . as besides the suppression of their trade, on which the kingdom may be said to subsist, they will have to pay constant subsidies for the maintenance of the war – and what weighs more with them than anything else, is to see that all this is being done for the benefit of aliens whom they detest, and most especially Spaniards . . .'[21]

The official pretexts given for the breach were regarded as either thin or stale: '. . . it is not for the interest of the Kingdom, but for the particular benefit of the King'. The Scots were even more disconcerted by the news, in spite of the fact that the earl of Shrewsbury was instructed to maintain the peace with his northern neighbours.[22] Mary of Guise, regent since April 1554, was firmly committed to a French policy in Scotland, but such a policy needed the pressure of English hostility to make it acceptable to most of the Scottish nobility, and that pressure had been absent since 1551. By the summer of 1557 hostility to the regent and her French advisers was growing rapidly, and the Scots no more relished making war on England for Henri's benefit than the English relished making war on France for Philip's. On 11 June, Thomas Martyn, one of Mary's commissioners for the settlement of routine border disputes, reported on their latest conference with their opposite numbers:

> . . . my Lord of Westmorland said to the Earl of Cassillis 'My Lord I think it but folly for us to treat now together, we having broken with France and ye being French for your lives'. 'By the mass', quoth the Earl of Cassillis, 'I am no more French than ye are a Spaniard' . . .[23]

Martyn's report naturally placed a suitably dutiful reply in the mouth of the earl of Westmorland, but he went on to make it perfectly clear that the border Scots had no desire to break the peace. They were quite prepared to pass on news about French troop landings, and to obstruct the operations of such troops to the best of their ability. Occasions for quarrels could always be found in that sensitive region, and there were still recriminations over a destructive raid which had taken place on the Scottish West March in July 1556,[24] but at this juncture Mary's instructions corresponded with the wishes of the borderers on both sides, and the continuation of peace between the realms was solemnly proclaimed at Carlisle and Dumfries on 18 July.[25] As soon as news of this reached the queen-regent, she recalled her commissioners, and entered into consultations with D'Oysel, the French ambassador. Before the end of July several bands of Scots and French had raided into the English East March, and on 1 August the English council informed all its officers in the north that the Scots had 'alredie entered into the warres with us'.[26] Whether any formal declaration was made is not clear, but the English and Scottish governments regarded themselves as belligerents. The regent ordered a general mobilization, and the English council diverted part of its fleet from the channel to the North Sea in order to prevent the movement of heavy guns from Leith to the anticipated siege of Berwick. A letter was also sent to Philip informing him of this new development, and requesting the assistance of his own fleet. The king was not pleased, and returned an evasive answer, arguing that it was in the best interests of the English themselves that his fleet should remain in the south.[27] During the first few days of August his mind was wholly and understandably occupied with the battle which was impending in north-eastern France, and the English received little satisfaction. Nor did the situation improve very much in September, when Philip was at leisure to deal with Scottish affairs. He despatched Christopher d'Assonleville in embassy to the queen-dowager, with instructions to persuade her to preserve the peace. On his way d'Assonleville was received in audience by Mary, and declared to her and to her council the substance of his instructions.[28] The king regarded war with the Scots as inexpedient; he could not afford to send any assistance to the north, and in any case the Scots could not accomplish anything now before the onset of winter. What he did not say was that the interests of his subjects in the Low Countries required that the trade routes with Scotland be kept open.[29]

Philip did not declare war on Scotland, and the threatened Scottish invasion, as he had predicted, came to nothing. This was not, however, because of the bad weather. After a promising start and some skirmishing had provoked exaggerated rumours of success in France, the Scottish lords refused to undertake either a large-scale invasion or a serious siege of Berwick. D'Oysel was told to take his French troops back to Eyemouth, and the Scottish host disbanded.[30] This humiliating failure was partly the result of the growing anti-French feeling which we have already noticed, and partly of the fact that the French were simply not present in sufficient strength. Had Henri stuck to what was apparently his original intention, of sending over 4000 men, and sufficient money to pay an army of 15,000, the outcome would no doubt have been different;[31] but in the aftermath of St Quentin a 'second front' on that scale was not to be contemplated. There were probably no more than seven or eight hundred French troops in Scotland by November 1557, plus some artillery. Berwick had been reinforced, and the English light horse under the earls of Shrewsbury and Westmorland was already mustered, so that the advantage of surprise which might have tempted the reluctant Scots into action had already been lost. When he wrote reporting these events to the emperor, in retirement at San Yuste, Juan de Figueroa made light of Philip's reaction to the Scottish war, claiming that the English were satisfied,[32] but it was subsequently apparent that the widespread feeling in England that Philip was ignoring its interests in favour of his other subjects had been reinforced. As late as April 1558 Feria was to report that the grievance still rankled, and he added: 'It seems to me that they are right about this . . .'[33] In spite of the disappointment of his expectations, Henri continued to hope for great things in Scotland, believing the English to be much weaker than they were, and sent thither such reinforcements as he could spare. By the following spring there were probably about 1800 French troops in Scotland.[34]

When Philip left England for the second and last time on 5 July, he had achieved most of the purposes of his visit. Not only had war been declared, but with him he brought a well-equipped and enthusiastic force of Englishmen, reported to number 10,000, under the command of the earl of Pembroke. The actual muster was

7221, and among the officers were many of those who had made their peace with the king and queen after earlier misdemeanours; Robert, Ambrose, and Henry Dudley; Lord Bray, Sir John Perrot, Sir Peter Carew, Sir Nicholas Throgmorton, Sir William Courtenay, and several others.[35] With a few exceptions such as Lord Chandos, the queen's loyallest supporters had remained, or been kept, at home.[36] Surian had clearly been right when he suggested that the expedition would be used as an opportunity to employ potential troublemakers, and to get them out of England. Pembroke himself was an obvious choice as commander, being high in the king's favour, and his commission as lieutenant of the army also included a general oversight of Calais and the Marches, the problems of which were familiar to him from his earlier visit in 1555. While Philip pressed on to join his army at the siege of St Quentin, Pembroke remained at Calais, reorganizing and reinforcing the garrisons of the Pale with some of the troops who had accompanied him. He had more men than he needed, as he wrote to the king on 29 July. Some had been transferred to the garrisons, and some could serve in the main army, but others would have to be sent home – a great and unnecessary expense.[37] In the event 500 men under the command of Sir Edward Braye were left in Guisnes, a hundred in Hammes, and a hundred more at the causeway. The rest set out under Pembroke's leadership on 30 July to reinforce the army at St Quentin. The French were advancing to relieve the town, and Philip was very anxious to be at full strength to meet them. In the event, however, the decisive engagement was fought before either the king or the English contingent came on the scene at all.[38] In spite of repeated pleas for haste Pembroke reached Cambrai only on 10 August, and it was on that morning that the constable of France, advancing incautiously on St Quentin, was routed and captured by the besieging army. It was an overwhelming defeat, which left dozens of French nobles and over 5000 soldiers prisoners in Philip's hands, and no adequate force to stand in the way of a determined Imperial advance. The town of St Quentin continued to hold out until 27 August, when it was taken by storm. 'Both sides fought very choicely', commented one Spanish officer, 'and the English best of all'.[39] Pembroke and his men had done something to redeem their tarnished reputation, and in the aftermath of so great a victory the king was not inclined to be censorious, but it is clear from his own report, written on the morrow of the battle, that he believed them to have been tardy and negligent.

Although the French were temporarily in no position to resist, Philip contented himself with consolidating his position, capturing the neighbouring fortresses of Han and Catalet, without which, as

Surian reported, St Quentin itself would be too isolated and exposed to be usable. By the beginning of October all talk of further advances had ceased, and the army began to settle down into winter garrisons. The English contingent was mustered on 15 September, when it numbered 5839 fit men, plus about 200 nobles and officers.[40] At the same time Pembroke issued to William Whightman, the 'treasurer of the army', warrants to pay most of the men, and they seem to have been sent home piecemeal over the next month.[41] By 10 October only 500 were left in the king's camp, and they were expected to leave soon. When Whightman presented his own expense account on 17 November, the whole operation had been completed, at a cost of about £48,000. Several years later Richard Beale, then clerk to the privy council, noted on the muster book for this campaign:

> I have hard of Mr. Robert Davys, Receiver of South Wales that served Mr. Whightman, Tresorer of the Jorney to St. Quentin, that the whole charg came to 48 thousand pounds; whereof xi were receyved in England; the rest of the Kyngs tresorer beyond the seas. To whom Mr. Wightman made his accompt, and that he accompted not in England. And touching the xi thousand pounds impressed in England he thought that the same was of the Kyngs money for so many relles of plate of the Kings Treasure delivered into the mint, so as the whole charg was borne by K[ing] Philippe.[42]

This seems to be correct in that Whightman did not account in England, and therefore presumably received the money which he dispensed from Philip's main war-chest. The English exchequer did, however, pay £5600 in two instalments to George Stonehouse and Anthony Weldon, 'officers of our household and surveyors of our provisions to be made in Callice', to pay for the provisioning of the 7000 men 'appointed to arrive' there in July 1557.[43] A further sum of £385 was later paid in conduct money to a group of returning officers.[44] So the whole cost of the campaign to the English government seems to have been no more than £6000. Philip got his English troops, and like the declaration of war itself, this was reckoned to be very much to his honour; but they turned out to be much less useful than he had hoped, and of much-needed financial assistance he had, by the end of 1557, received less than nothing. Nevertheless, at the close of the campaigning season he had good reason to feel satisfied. Not only had his forces won a great victory at St Quentin, but the expected French thrust from Scotland had not materialized, so that he could continue to temporize in that direction, and he had succeeded in forcing the pope out

N

of the war altogether. On 12 September, Paul IV had bowed to the logic of the military situation in Italy and accepted the terms offered by the duke of Alva;[45] although he was never likely to be fond of the Habsburgs, for the time being such teeth as he had had been drawn.

Within England the main impact of the war was felt in the musters, which were held in every county between May and July,[46] revealing a state of unpreparedness which was to lead to legislation in the next parliament. The justices for Rutland were sharply taken to task by the council in the middle of August for having been slack and negligent in this duty, but only a handful of individuals attracted attention for recalcitrance.[47] At the end of September Anglo-Spanish animosity boiled up into another brawl, this time at Dartmouth, but otherwise there is little tangible evidence of that resentment which Surian claimed to have noticed in July. Those troops who had gone with the earl of Pembroke seem to have served willingly enough, and at one point, as we have seen, his force was oversubscribed. Nor does there seem to have been any great difficulty in raising small numbers of reinforcements for the northern border. On the other hand, there was a mutiny of unknown seriousness in the fleet at the beginning of August,[48] and at the same time the local authorities in Somerset, Bristol, and Gloucester were ordered 'to aid and assist Edmund Foster of the Admiralty for the better execution of his Commission to press soldiers and mariners for the Queen's service . . .' A number of those pressed had already escaped, and the justices were required to apprehend them.[49] Early in September another group of mariners and ship-masters were imprisoned and examined on suspicion of having betrayed their vessels to the French, but with what result is not recorded.[50] The main focus of discontent, apart from the general hardship caused by another sub-standard harvest and the continuing bad weather (blamed by government propagandists on the people's faithlessness), was the new forced loan decreed in September. This was a much more elaborate and widespread affair than its predecessor, and commissioners of assessment sat in every county, except those which had been exempted on account of their contribution to the defence of the northern border, that is Derbyshire, Cheshire, Lancashire, Yorkshire, Nottinghamshire, and Durham, in addition to the border counties themselves.[51] Assessments varied between £10 and 100 marks, and resistance began to manifest itself almost at once. During October and November literally scores of men appeared before the council, having been referred thither by the commissioners in the counties. Under this sort of pressure most of them seem to have paid up, although in some cases excuses were accepted and others bound in recognizance to find the sums due from them. Apart from Pembroke's expedition, the main war effort concentrated significantly on defence, particularly the refitting of the navy, and the extension and repair of the fortifications at Berwick. Work on the latter went on steadily throughout the year, and between January and November, William Ridgeway, the surveyor of the works, dispensed about £1200.[52] Skirmishing continued in the East March after the retreat of the main Scottish army, and both sides tried to inflate these miniscule engagements into major victories. Losses seem to have been slight except by desertion. In December, Cuthbert Vaughn was seeking runaways from his band as far away as London.[53] After the return of Pembroke's force it seems to have been assumed both by Philip and the English council that there would be no more serious campaigning until the spring. The fleet was laid up for the winter, and the garrisons of Berwick and Calais settled down to a routine of patrols and desultory raiding.

The French, however, had other ideas. The duke of Guise had returned from Italy, if not in disgrace at least without success, and Henri had strained every nerve to rebuild the forces shattered at St Quentin. By the time that it was clear that Philip was not intending to march on Paris, the French had a sizeable army in Picardy, and were understandably reluctant to disband it or send it into winter quarters without making some attempt to redeem the fortunes of a disastrous year. At the end of November, Soranzo believed that this would be impossible, and that Guise would dissuade the king from any such determination.[54] However, a week later the weather continued fine and the expected orders had not been issued, so an 'enterprise' was again being talked of, and Calais was mentioned for the first time.[55] By 11 December the rumours had crystallized. Pietro Strozzi, one of Guise's Italian officers, had reconnoitred the city and reported that the task was feasible.[56] Within a few days 20,000 men, broken down into small contingents to avoid attracting attention, were marching north. Surian, writing from Brussels on 17 December, remained in complete ignorance. 'From the frontiers', he wrote, 'nothing is heard of any stir . . .'[57] The first warning of danger was given by one of Philip's spies to Lord Grey at Guisnes on 22 December. Grey forwarded the warning to London, saying that he did not take it very seriously, but if any major attack was in the offing, then he had neither the men nor the provisions to withstand it.[58] It seems that the English had been economizing by running down the Pale garrison since they had been reinforced in August, but on 24 December the Queen wrote to Lord Wentworth, the deputy at Calais, halting this process for the time being. Thereafter the alarm built up quickly. On the 27th the council of Calais reported that only Hammes had an adequate garrison, and that everywhere was short of supplies; in the event of an attack they would pull all their forces back to Calais itself, and even then would not have enough men to defend it.[59] By that time no one in the Pale was in any doubt about the seriousness of the situation, and daily pleas for supplies and reinforcements were sent across the channel. In London the council dithered, having virtually no men to send. On the 29th it was decided to send the earl of Rutland with whatever force he could muster; on the 31st the order was countermanded; on 2 January it was renewed.[60] By then it was too late, and when Rutland reached Dover on 3 January, he was greeted by the news that the French held 'the sands' and access to Calais from the sea was impossible.[61] Wentworth, realizing that no help was likely to come from England, wrote urgently to Philip on 31 December, informing him of the danger. Presumably Philip received this letter, since a copy remains at Simancas, but he seems to have done nothing in response to it until 5 or 6 January. On the latter day a force of 200 harquebusiers from Gravelines attempted to get into the city, but were unable to do so.[62] On 7 January, Philip wrote urgently to Don Luis de Carvajal to get his fleet clear of the harbour, but he had already anticipated the order and early on the same morning, after a bombardment had breached the walls, Calais surrendered. Wentworth and about 2000 of his men were made prisoners, and many of the citizens fled to England.

Recriminations began almost at once. Wentworth, it was claimed, was a heretic, and had intrigued with other English heretics, both inside Calais and outside it, to betray his trust. This version of events was generally believed in Rome, Sir Edward Carne reported at the end of January, while at the same time the cardinal of Siguenza wrote to Spain: 'The governor of Calais was a great heretic, like all those who were with him there . . . so I am not surprised at its fall'.[63] The city did not have a good record for religious orthodoxy or docility, and as recently as the previous August the council in London had rejected the newly elected mayor as unsuitable, probably on religious grounds.[64] However, that action had been taken on the insistence of the lord deputy. Similarly there was a long history of intrigues against the security of the city by Dudley, Ashton, and other English exiles in France, which had certainly involved contacts among the citizens, but no suspicion of complicity on the part of Wentworth or his officers.[65] The subsequent charges of treason advanced against the former deputy seem to have been entirely without foundation, and designed mainly to save the faces of the English council. The demoralizing speed and strength of the French advance, the shortage of supplies and ammunition, and the failure of either Philip or Mary to respond to his pleas for help, would have been quite enough to convince Wentworth that there was little point in protracted resistance.[66] He had only half the number of men under his command that the duke of Guise considered to be the minimum necessary for security, and once Rysbank had fallen on 4 January, only a massive intervention from Flanders could have diverted the French from their purpose. Such intervention neither Philip nor his field commander, the duke of Savoy, was in any position to make. In spite of the fact that the first warning of danger had come from Flanders on 22 December, on the 30th Surian had still heard no whisper of what was afoot, and on 2 January the king wrote as though the news was a complete surprise to him.[67] Since he regarded Calais as important, and its loss as a serious blow, there is no reason to suppose that he was dissembling, and under such circumstances he could not possibly have moved in time.

At first it was thought, both in England and Brussels, that the situation was not beyond redemption. Guisnes and Hammes were still holding out, and a quick counter-stroke might serve to dislodge the French from Calais before they could consolidate their position. Orders had been issued on the very day of the disaster for the raising of fresh troops; and on 11 January the earl of Rutland was commissioned to lead a relief expedition, accompanied by Sir Thomas Tresham and Sir Henry Jerningham.[68] Sir Walter Mildmay was appointed treasurer of the army, with Valentine Browne as his deputy. Why the inexperienced Rutland should have been chosen for this task in preference to Pembroke, whom the duke of Savoy was expecting, is a mystery, unless it was for the simple reason that he was already on the spot. However, the duke of Guise was too quick at every turn. Hammes surrendered after a mutiny in the garrison on 10 January.[69] On the 16th the duke of Savoy announced that he was on his way to the relief of Guisnes, but he never got there. Lord Grey, not having enough men to defend the town, had already retreated to the citadel, where he withstood repeated assaults until 21 January when, short of ammunition and despairing of relief, he also surrendered.[70] Grey and his garrison were allowed to march out with full military honours, and he was received in England with honour, but with the fall of Guisnes the entire Pale had been overrun, and the effect of this news in England seems to have been more demoralizing than the fall of Calais itself. On 19 January, Valentine Browne was instructed to draw £10,000 from the mint, and to proceed to Dunkirk, where he was to await the arrival of the earl of Rutland and his troops.[71] However, the fall of Guisnes seems to have caused the whole plan to be reconsidered. On 25 January, Ruy Gómez wrote to Philip from Gravesend to say that the English troops assembling in Kent were so few and of such poor quality that there was no point in sending them over, and Philip responded by countermanding their orders.[72] The king's plan, which he sent Feria across to discuss with the English council on 27 January, was for a longer-term effort, in which his own field army from the Netherlands would co-operate with English land and sea forces in a major campaign for the recovery of Calais.[73] The council, however, was not responsive. They feared attack from Scotland, they told Feria, and believed that the Danes and the Hanseatic League were sending a fleet against them. They would have to fit out at least a hundred ships, fortify many places on the south coast, and hire German mercenaries to defend the northern border, since there were now so few reliable soldiers to be had in England. The queen herself confirmed this last point, saying that she did not think that all the lords in the kingdom could raise more than a hundred foot and a hundred horse for her service.[74] Feria went away impressed, not by the truth of these professions, but by the profound despondency which they represented. Significantly neither Paget nor Arundel was present at the meeting which gave him his answer.

At the same time the council made its own representation to the king, which differs in a number of points from that reported by Feria. After making suitable expressions of gratitude to Philip for offering to 'put his force to the field' for the recovery of Calais, the memorandum then goes on to decline his offer, with excuses.

> First we do consider that if we should send over an army, we cannot send under 20,000 men, the Levying and sending over whereof will ask a time, before which time, considering also the time the enemy hath had (being now almost a month) to fortify and victual the place, it is thought the same will be at such strength as we shall not be able alone to recover it . . .[75]

The cost of such an army would amount to £170,000 in five months, which, coming on top of the £150,000 a year necessary for existing garrisons, and the £200,000 a year which would have to be spent on sea defences and the fleet, would amount to £520,000 in one year. 'We see not how it can be levied . . . unless the people should of new have strange impositions set upon them, which we think they could not bear'. The whole realm is in great poverty and distress, 'The Queenes Majesties owne revenue is scarce able to maintain her estate . . .'

378

So that considering our want on every side [this jeremiad con-
cludes] . . . the scarcity of Captains and leaders of our men,
which be but few; the unwillingness of our people to go abroad
and leave their things at home without a certain hope of recovery
of their loss, the need we have to defend home (looking as we
do to be assailed both by land and sea) how desirous soever we
be to recover Calais, and well willing to serve his majestie . . .
we see not how we can possibly (at the least for this year) send
over an army . . .[76]

Despite the professions of goodwill, the majority of the English
council was of the same opinion as it had been twelve months
before. England could not afford to wage war, and having become
embroiled in one, could do no more than defend its own borders
unless the king was prepared to foot the bill. As if to give point to
this bleak appraisal, such troops as had been assembled during
January were dismissed; the repatriated garrison of Guisnes was
paid off at a cost of £4257; and Browne discharged his account of
£18,264 by repaying £10,440 to the mint, from which he had
originally drawn it.[77] As far as can be discovered, neither he nor
any other English official so much as set foot in Dunkirk. No doubt
the financial position was bad, but the council nevertheless over-
stated its case, having been made unco-operative by a number of
outstanding grievances against the king and his policies. All
attempts to induce Philip to break off relations with Scotland, or
to assist the merchant adventurers in their endless struggles with
the Hanseatic League, had proved futile. On 31 January the king
replied to its latest representations with bland and almost meaningless words:

With regard to the Hanseatic Towns, we have also taken steps
to discover their intentions, and will keep you informed. While
this is being done, we exhort you, in case any friction is being
caused on account of the privileges, as you suspect, to do your
best to reach a mutually satisfactory settlement with the Towns,
keeping us informed of what you agree with them. There are
certain points in your letters which escape us, and we are not
fully acquainted with the nature of the privileges in
question . . .[78]

Since this quarrel had been going on for years, and the king had
been informed and consulted on numerous occasions in the past,
such a response was distinctly disingenuous. With respect to Scotland, his words were even less calculated to excite enthusiasm.
While praising the council's prudence in negotiating for a truce and

maintaining a high level of military preparedness, he gave no hint of any change in his own policy, and concluded:

> We feel compelled to urge you to be swayed by no private interests or passions, but only by your care for the welfare of the kingdom, lest its reputation for power and greatness, earned the world over in former times, be now lost through your own neglect and indifference.[79]

There were also other causes of friction. On 4 February, Philip wrote to Feria, in England, instructing him to stop a proposed English voyage to the Portuguese Indies, '. . . as considerable prejudice might be done to the King of Portugal's interests, which narrowly concern me . . .'[80] Worst of all was the matter of the safe-conducts. These were passes issued (at a price) by the council in Brussels to enable merchants from the Low Countries to trade into France despite the war. On 9 January the duke of Savoy wrote to Philip suggesting that he should negotiate the sale of such safe-conducts in order to ease the desperate financial situation, calculating that 30,000 crowns might be obtained in this way.[81] The king agreed, with the result that over the next month the newly installed French garrison of Calais was victualled and supplied by Flemish merchants under safe-conduct. The English were bitterly angry, and Feria acutely embarrassed. Critical as he was of the English council in their handling of every issue, he recognized the substantial justice of this complaint, and in a letter of 22 February urged Philip to make what redress he could. 'The English are not being treated as in strict justice they should be . . .', he wrote.[82] In reply the king expressed regret, and promised to issue no more such passes, but argued that it was impossible for him to offer any redress. Nor was any progress made, as 1558 advanced, in resolving the other issues which continued to be sources of discontent. In May, Philip acknowledged that the English had some reason to be dissatisfied over the continuing traffic between Scotland and the Low Countries, and claimed that he had persuaded the estates-general to agree to a breach. Nothing was done, and the following month Feria complained that the council 'keep throwing the matter in my face'.[83] Negotiations with the Hanseatic League became completely deadlocked because the king wished to support the league's claims to privileges which the English council would not acknowledge. Even Mary became irritated with her consort over this, and the Hanseatic ambassadors spent four fruitless months in England.[84] There was no lack of consultation because Feria became virtually a resident ambassador in England, and direct correspondence passed regularly between the king and the

English council, but there was a lack of mutual understanding. The English fleet, manned and fitted out at great expense, achieved very little because Philip had no real use for it in the existing military situation. The English merchants wished to ship their wool and cloth to the Netherlands without restriction of place, but Philip would not permit this because of the interests of the Flemish merchants. In February the king gave permission for 3000 German troops to be raised for service on the Scottish border, at Mary's expense, and the following month Sir William Pickering was sent across to arrange these levies.[85] The men were duly recruited, paid an *Aufgeld* for one month, and equipped on Gresham's credit at a cost of about £2000.[86] At the end of May, when they were on the point of sailing from Gravelines, Philip announced that he needed them himself, and would pay them from then on. In fact he dismissed them soon afterwards, and blandly assured the English council that he had saved them an unnecessary expense![87] The English were a good deal put out, and claimed that Philip ought to repay the money they had wasted on paying and equipping troops they were never to see. Feria once again got caught in the middle. 'In the letter addressed to me', he wrote with some chagrin, 'your Majesty tells me to dissemble in this German affair. In your letter to the Privy Council you say that I will explain it all, and I was therefore obliged to enter into discussion on the matter'.[88]

Philip was desperately short of money, and his mind was absorbed by the fluctuating fortunes of the campaign in Flanders, but this was no way to rally and stimulate the flagging loyalty of his friends and supporters in England, let alone to convert those who had always regarded him with suspicion and disfavour. Feria became almost as eloquent on the subject of divisions in the council as Renard had been four years previously:

> I am at my wits ends with these people here [he wrote on 10 March] . . . Your Majesty must realise that from night to morning and morning to night they change everything they have decided, and it is impossible to make them see what a state they are in, although it is the worst that any country has ever fallen into . . .[89]

If his testimony is to be trusted, the 'council of state' had disappeared entirely by February 1558.

> Pembroke, Arundel, Paget, Petre, the Chancellor [Heath], and Bishop of Ely [Thirlby] and the Comptroller [Cornwallis] are the leading members of the Council, and I am highly dissatisfied with all of them . . . The Privy Council has so many members

381

that it seems no one has been left out, except William Howard who was formerly Admiral; and numbers cause great confusion.[90]

This is supported to some extent by the fact that the average attendance at recorded privy council meetings during January and February 1558 was 13.5, a level exceeded by only one month since the beginning of 1554.[91] As a nobleman high in the king's confidence, Feria felt entitled to air his opinions of the English council with a freedom which had been denied to Renard, the humble lieutenant of Amont. 'So they all took themselves off', he wrote after describing one interview, 'but not before I had told them what I thought of them.'

> Figueroa and I then went to the Queen [he continued in the same letter] to complain of the reply we had received, and to warn her of the danger to her person and kingdom caused by these incompetent councillors who all say that the country is rich and then add that they do not know how to raise the necessary money to defend it . . .

At about this time another reorganization seems to have taken place, mainly to cope with the special problems presented by the fear of invasion. The more vulnerable parts of the country were divided into ten lieutenancies: Devon and Cornwall under the earl of Bedford; Southampton and the Isle of Wight under Lord St John; Wiltshire and Somerset under the earl of Pembroke; Surrey under Arundel; Sussex under Montague; Kent under Hastings; Essex under Darcy; Norfolk and Suffolk under the duke of Norfolk (his first appearance in public office); and Lincolnshire under Lord Willoughby.[92] The earl of Westmorland had already been appointed lieutenant in the North, where the pressure had in any case been relieved by a two-month truce beginning in January.[93] The same memorandum which lists these appointments also notes the establishment of a 'council of war' and a 'council of finance'. The former was to consist of Winchester, Paget, Rutland, Pembroke, Montague, Clinton, Hastings, Jerningham, and Cornwallis; and the latter of Paget, Thirlby, Englefield, Baker, Waldegrave, and Sir Walter Mildmay. It was also noted that Pembroke, Montague, and Clinton would not normally attend because of their duties in the provinces.[94]

This plan seems to have been put into effect, and to have worked reasonably well. Philip commented favourably upon it in April, and although it does not appear to have made much difference to the attendance of Montague or Clinton at ordinary privy council meetings, the average attendance at such meetings in March was down to ten, and for the rest of the reign ran at about 9.2. The 'council of war' and the 'council of finance' probably functioned as standing committees, since their membership overlaps, but does not correspond, with Feria's list of 'most important councillors'. It looks as though, by the spring of 1558, the council had reverted to its earlier *modus operandi*, with an informal 'inner ring' undifferentiated from the privy council as a whole, and such committees, standing and *ad hoc*, as the circumstances might require. Perhaps after leaving England in July 1557 Philip lost interest in trying to maintain the system which he had formalized in August 1555, and it was simply abandoned. Only seven commissions involving privy councillors were set up between May 1557 and November 1558, so little can be concluded from the distribution of effort there, but 13 councillors served on one or more of them.[95] Taking these names, along with those of Feria's list, the two committees, and the evidence of the council registers, produces a list of 22 or 23 councillors active in the central government during the last year and a half of the reign, out of a nominal list which rose to 39 after the inclusion of Montague and Clinton early in 1558. Neither Pembroke nor Arundel appeared very often, perhaps because of their provincial responsibilities, and with Petre in semi-retirement and Rochester dead, Paget was left without any serious rival as a statesman and administrator. However, there is little in the surviving evidence to remind us of the forceful and ambitious politician of two years before. Feria did not trust him, claiming that he was full of half-promises which were never performed. One day he was sure the country could raise 800,000 crowns; a week later he did not see how it could be done.[96] In May he was strongly in favour of a new effort to take Calais, but all that eventually emerged was a band of a thousand sappers for which Philip had to pay.[97] In February, Feria declared that none of those English councillors who had formerly promoted Philip's interests was now prepared to do anything for him, and specifically mentioned Paget.[98] By the spring of 1558 the lord privy seal and his friends seem to have become thoroughly disillusioned with Philip, and the enthusiasm which they alone had shown for the war had evaporated completely. Attendance at privy council meetings sank to an average of six during August and on 1 September letters were sent to Waldegrave, Englefield, and Hastings summoning them to court, '. . . for that presently there wanteth councillors here'.[99] By then no peer (except Hastings) had attended a privy council meeting since 24 July, save for an isolated appearance by Arundel on 7 August, and hardly any of them seem to have followed the court when it moved from St James's to Richmond on 21 July. It was not until October that attendances improved significantly, and the magnates did not appear in numbers until the convening of parliament in early November.

Feria, as we have seen, took no pains to hide his feelings, and his views were widely shared by Philip's other councillors and servants. Granvelle was not given to exaggeration, but he was frankly irritated by the apathetic manner in which the English had abandoned their efforts to recover Calais, and their lack of interest in any aggressive action. In a conversation with Clinton, who had recovered the post of admiral from Howard a few weeks before, he suggested that the English fleet was perfectly capable of landing 5000 men on the French coast, and carrying out a destructive raid which would be of some real use as a diversion. Clinton agreed that this could be done, but showed so little enthusiasm that Granvelle commented, '. . . if this man is the keenest of the Englishmen, the rest must indeed be slack'.[100] In April, Anglo-Spanish hostility resulted in another fray, this time at Plymouth, and Feria complained to the council that some of his servants had been 'evil entreated' by the inhabitants of the town.[101] In July there was another quarrel between some servants of the marquis of Verlanga and the townsmen of Falmouth. A prominent member of the council, Feria reported, was attempting to poison the queen's mind against her husband, and the situation in England was so bad '. . . that if four French ships were to land men [there] there would be a revolution'.[102] In fact, apart from its disinclination to wage war, the country does not seem to have been rebelliously inclined in the summer of 1558. The council maintained its customary vigilance, pursuing coiners, seditious preachers, and the presenters of 'lewd' plays and interludes, as well as felons of a more commonplace sort. Sir George Herbert was kept dancing attendance on the council for having provoked a riot in Glamorgan,[103] and four townsmen of Bricklesey in Essex (presumably the officers of the community) were called up, examined, and fined for refusing to hand over some prisoners to Lord Darcy – a mysterious episode which the council obviously took seriously.[104] In June there was a commotion in Lincolnshire which Lord Willoughby was thanked for putting down, and which may have been a matter of some substance. Orders were issued for

> . . . the chief ringleaders in this matter to be proceeded withall and executed either by order of the lawes, orelles by the martyall lawes to the terrour and example of others . . .[105]

which suggests some kind of a mutiny or revolt in connection with the musters, since there were very few circumstances in which martial law could be used against the civilian population.

The musters provoked trouble in regions as far apart as Cornwall and Derbyshire, and it was noted that 'divers absented themselves'. The justices of Nottinghamshire and Derbyshire objected to taking their orders from the earl of Westmorland, and were sharply called to order by the council.[106] In the aftermath of the fall of Calais the west-country sheriffs tried to claim that there were no arms and armour in their part of the country, an excuse which the council thought 'very strange', although it had often been used before.[107] The south-west was particularly sensitive, perhaps because of periodic contacts with the Spanish fleet, perhaps because men were occasionally sent from Bristol to Ireland – always an unpopular posting. On 18 April the earl of Bedford issued his orders for the security of the region, assigning particular responsibilities to the local gentry.[108] By the beginning of May the men were deserting in such numbers that the earl felt impelled to issue special instructions to the mayors of several towns to apprehend the fugitives, and called on the support of the privy council. There may have been rather more to this than the normal unpopularity of military service, because on 8 May the council wrote again to Bedford to '. . . examine the matter, and cause at least four of the ringleaders to be proceeded against by law'.[109] Some kind of conspiracy was clearly suspected, but there seems to be no further evidence bearing upon the matter. In some places musters were called three times during the period of the war: May-June 1557, January-February 1558 (in all counties south of the Trent which were expected to contribute to the relief force), and May-June 1558. Apart from the constant reinforcement of the northern borders, which was done mainly by commissioning captains to raise their own 'bands', not many of these men seem to have remained under arms for any length of time. 28 counties or regions were appointed to raise 27,200 men in January 1558, but only about 2300 got as far as Dover before the orders were countermanded.[110] The coastal forts were repaired and garrisoned, and large sums of money expended in the Low Countries upon gunpowder, armour, and weapons, but there was nothing like the massive effort which Marillac reported in 1539, or that which had kept 120,000 men under arms throughout the dangerous summer of 1545.[111] Judged by the standards set in those periods of crisis, the efforts made by the English council to defend the country in the summer of 1558 deserved many of the criticisms which Feria and Granvelle levelled against them. All the evidence suggests that morale was extremely low, and continuing recriminations over the betrayal of Calais did not help. The garrison of Guisnes, as we have seen, was honourably paid off, but the defenders of Calais, returning from French prisons, found neither sympathy nor money. On

30 March a certain Erasmus Nichols, who was in this position, was committed to the Marshalsea '. . . for that he toke upon himself to be a suitor for his company, and menaced that if he had not his request, all the rest of his company should come hither and exclaim'.[112] Some of the duke of Savoy's officers believed that there had been treachery in the English council itself, and the search for scapegoats tarnished everyone from Lord Wentworth down to the ordinary soldiers of the garrison.[113]

On the other hand, the parliament which sat from 20 January to 3 March was relatively trouble-free and successful. As we have seen, it was the only one of Mary's parliaments to be prorogued at the end of the session. Called specifically 'for aid to be made to her Majesty' (although before it was known quite how urgent that need would be), its most important work was the granting of a subsidy. Feria, who was constantly urging the English council to strain every nerve to raise money, kept a watching brief for Philip. On 12 February he reported that the queen and the cardinal were both delighted by the size of the grant, and the goodwill with which it had been granted. 'They all stick to it', he went on, 'that this grant is the largest that has ever been voted for any king of England'.[114] If that is what his informants said, they were whistling in the dark. By 12 February a bill for a subsidy and two fifteenths and tenths, to be paid over two years, had reached its second reading in the Commons, but nothing had been concluded. At that point the bill was withdrawn, and when it reappeared on the 14th, it was for a subsidy and one fifteenth only, the whole to be paid by 24 June.[115] In order to speed up collection, a proportion of the grant had been bargained away, and in that form the bill became an act, passing its third reading on 16 February. On 10 March, Feria reported that the grant amounted to £200,000, and was to be paid by the end of May. This time he was only slightly optimistic, for the sum assessed was £182,055, and of that £145,000 was to be received before the queen died.[116] He was quite right when he declared that it was inadequate to finance the war. At the same time a clerical subsidy of 8s. in the £ over four years was also confirmed. This would, in time, give the crown a further £56,000, but only the first instalment of £14,000 could be expected in time to help the immediate situation, and in fact the clergy had barely finished paying the last instalment of their previous grant.[117] Four other measures directly related to the war effort were also debated, with varying fortunes. On 3 February a bill 'touching captains, armour and soldiers' was considered by the Commons, but did not reappear under that title. Instead two separate measures were passed: 4 and 5 Philip and Mary, c. 3, 'An Acte for the taking of musters'; and 4 and 5 Philip and Mary, c. 2, 'An Acte for the having of Horse Armour and Weapons'. The latter was mainly a detailed schedule, laying down exactly what equipment was to be provided by every member of the community, in a finely graded hierarchy of wealth. It caused a certain amount of difficulty, having to be redrafted twice, and, with its emphasis on light horsemen, black bills, and long bows, can hardly have inspired confidence in the minds of experienced continental soldiers. However, it was realistic in terms of what was available, and, by insisting upon a certain proportion of pikes and hagbuttes, guaranteed that at least a proportion of the English levies was familiar with modern weapons. It also had the effect, presumably intentional, of increasing the responsibility of the nobility for provision of weapons and necessities, with the result that the following decade saw the last significant revival in the size and potential of noble armouries.[118] The musters act was almost certainly provoked by the evidence of negligence and corruption which had been uncovered in 1557, and was mainly intended to stiffen penalties. Muster masters taking bribes to release the eligible were now liable to forfeit ten times the sum received, and a statute of Edward VI making the desertion of soldiers a felony was revived.[119]

Neither of these measures met with any determined parliamentary opposition, but attempts to impose sanctions upon the French were less successful. Those Frenchmen who were not denizens had been theoretically expelled at the beginning of the war, but the continued presence of Frenchmen in England, and of traffic with France, was causing the council great anxiety in the early weeks of 1558, as is witnessed by a proclamation of 27 January authorizing citizen arrest of Frenchmen and their goods.[120] On 10 February a bill was introduced into the House of Commons to repeal and annul the letters patent of all French denizens – in other words to expel them. This was read a second time on 14 February, and defeated at its third reading on the 18th by 111 to 106.[121] At the same time a bill to prohibit all trade in French or Gascon wine disappeared after one reading, and was eventually replaced by the weaker instrument of a proclamation on 30 March.[122] The government had to be satisfied in this respect with an act setting up commissions to inquire into the behaviour of French denizens, and to increase surveillance over them.[123] Altogether the session produced 16 statutes (including one restoring in blood all the surviving children of the duke of Northumberland). The Commons, under the speakership of Sir William Cordell, the master of the rolls, are considered to have been notably well behaved. There was certainly no repetition of the spectacular scenes of the last parliament, but the unpopularity of the war, and the detrimental effect which it was thought to be having upon trade, found their echoes at Westminster, as might be expected. Fifteen proclamations were issued between June 1557 and the end of the reign, and the overwhelming majority of them also related to the war: granting letters of marque, restricting dealings with the French, and endeavouring to prevent derelictions of duty. On 30 March 1558 all 'serviceable' gentlemen were ordered to leave London and repair to their homes to take part in the arrangements for the defence of the counties; on 29 March deserters from the fleet were placed under martial law; and in July this provision was extended to those endeavouring to avoid service.[124] Resort to martial law was becoming increasingly common as 1558 advanced. It was used against spies, in the cases of Giles Favell and William Atkinson, against mutineers at the musters, against deserters from the navy, and in June 1558 against the possessors of heretical and seditious books.[125] When the marquis of Winchester was given a general commission of lieutenancy on 12 April 1558 to cover all those counties of England and Wales not already under such jurisdiction, he was also instructed to proceed '. . . against all and singular rebels, traitors, and other offenders and their adherents against us, our crown and dignity . . . as necessity shall require by your discretion, the law called the martial law, according to the law martial'.[126] Winchester was thus empowered to set aside the common law at his discretion, '. . . and of such offenders apprehended . . . to save whom you think good to be saved, and to slay, destroy and put to execution of death such and as many of them as you shall think meet . . .' To what extent these sweeping powers were ever used we do not know, but that they should have been conferred is significant. During the Wyatt rebellion, in early February 1554, the attorneys at Westminster had pleaded with armour under their robes in order to avoid closing the civil courts, and no proclamation of martial law was made. Admittedly in 1558 the country was at war, but no hostile army stood on English soil, and a general resort to martial law under such circumstances was, as far as I am aware, without precedent.

We do not know who prepared the business for the fifth parliament, and apart from the subsidy bill it does not seem to have been done with as much care as for the two previous sessions. The queen's financial advisers were 'meeting every day' according to Feria,[127] but the important military measures which we have already noticed do not appear to have been prepared by the council at all. On 24 January, four days after the opening of the session, the Lords sent to the Commons a request for the Lower House to nominate members to a joint committee for the security of the realm. They did so, and on the following day the House received, probably from that committee, 'A communication for an Act to be made against soldiers as sell away their armour' – a matter which was eventually dealt with in sections x and xi of 4 and 5 Philip and Mary, c. 3. On 26 January, Secretary Bourne and eleven others were also nominated to another committee to draft a bill 'for soldiers and captains', and presented the first fruits of their labours to the House, as we have seen, on 3 February.[128] It therefore appears that the initiative for the presentation of these bills came from within the parliament itself, a most unusual procedure with matters of such obvious public concern. According to Feria, Paget had not been 'entrusted with the Queen's affairs' as much as he would have liked at the beginning of the year, and this temporary loss of favour (if such it was) may explain why the preparatory work had not been done as thoroughly as it should have been. By March the lord privy seal was as close to the queen as he had ever been since May 1554, and was specifically mentioned by Feria as being in favour, along with Clinton and Jerningham, when he was discussing the ease with which Mary was swayed by her advisers.[129] Unlike Renard, Feria made little attempt to counteract that influence by building up his own relationship with the queen. Although he praised her diligence and spirit in his letters to Philip, he seems to have had no opinion of her political capacity, and did not consider it to be part of his duties to supply her deficiency. Consequently there was no warmth in their relationship, and the man who consoled Mary for the absence of her husband in the last months of her life was Reginald Pole. The end of the war between Philip and the papacy, although celebrated with *Te Deum* in London, had brought no rehabilitation to the cardinal of England, and no renewal of his commission. He played no part in the regular work of the council, and was in many ways a deeply despondent man, but his influence over the queen remained very great, and increased as the physical health of each of them deteriorated.

Mary had begun the year by believing again that she was pregnant. On hearing this news the cardinal of Lorraine had commented sardonically that this time they would not have to wait long to be sure, '. . . this being the end of the eighth month since her husband left her'.[130] Philip duly expressed his joy, and Surian reported the tidings with a straight face. The extraordinary delay was accounted for by the queen's desire to be absolutely sure of her condition, in the light of her previous disappointment, but it seems unlikely that anyone else took her conviction very seriously. By contrast with the early months of 1555, there was hardly a ripple of expectancy in the courts of Europe.[131] By May, Mary had again abandoned hope, and Feria reported that she was weak, depressed, and sleeping badly. Philip made no more than a gesture of intending to visit England, and the queen does not seem to have expected him to come, although she continued to desire it. Pole wrote to the king on the 19th extolling Mary's christian resignation in the face of this disappointment, but there is little sign of the feverish anxiety which had characterized her behaviour in the autumn of 1556. On 19 June, Philip rather uncharacteristically sent a courier across to enquire of her health: 'She has not written to me for some days past, and I cannot help being anxious'.[132] Perhaps Mary was beginning to be disillusioned with a husband whose priorities were so consistently elsewhere, or perhaps illness was simply making her apathetic. Feria, although he wrote with great caution, did not find her as enthusiastic as he expected for the furtherance of his master's interests, and much of his abuse of the English council stemmed from the conviction that some of them were assiduously sowing the seeds of doubt in her mind. On 23 June he reported that the queen was '. . . better than she has been recently', and referred, without any great anxiety, to 'her usual ailments'.[133] She had suffered from bouts of sickness and depression for as long as anyone could remember, and her condition did not seem to call for any special comment. However, late in August she developed a fever which she seemed too weak to shake off. Early in September, Pole, himself suffering from 'a double quartan ague' as he explained, wrote urging Philip to come to England as the only sure method of restoring the queen to health.[134] The condition of both invalids fluctuated through September, but early in October the queen became markedly worse, and her physicians started sending regular reports to the king. Philip, deeply immersed in the peace negotiations at Cercamp, made no move himself, but sent Feria over again on 22 October – ostensibly to comfort the queen, but in reality to keep a watch upon the situation.[135] By the end of the month it was generally known that her illness was dangerous, and this knowledge overshadowed the opening of parliament on 6 November, as well as disturbing the deliberations of the peace commissioners. On 12 November, Surian, from Brussels, reported correctly that she was on the point of death, and early on the morning of the 17th she died, with the full consolations of her faith and in the presence of faithful members of her household. During the last few days of her life, Mary had frequently lapsed into unconsciousness, and told those about her that she had been visited by delightful dreams of children 'like angels'. About an hour before she died, she was able to make the responses at the mass which was being said, in accordance with regular custom, in her chamber. The moment of her actual death was almost unnoticed by those present, who subsequently reported that God had rewarded

her faith and virtue with the most peaceful of ends. Reporting the
news a fortnight later to his half-sister in Spain, Philip wrote
'. . . the Queen my wife is dead. May God have received her into
his Glory. I felt a reasonable regret for her death . . .'[136]

He had not been taken by surprise by this turn of events. Had he
considered it to be expedient, Philip could have been with Mary
when she died; and although it would have been out of character
for him to have done this out of human affection, he might have
done it out of political calculation. Philip chose not to be in England, and thus not to press any claim to the crown in survivorship.
Instead he swiftly and cheerfully acknowledged the succession of
Elizabeth. His decision to act thus in the event of Mary's death was
probably long-standing, going back at least to the period of his
second residence in England in the early summer of 1557. Earlier
failures to remove Elizabeth, either by execution or act of exclusion, coupled with her strong popular and aristocratic following,
had by then made her succession virtually certain unless either
Mary had an heir or Philip was prepared to fight a civil war in
England – both unlikely contingencies. The real issue was, what
conditions might be imposed upon her? Earlier plans to marry her
abroad, and by removing her from the country to make her a less
attractive heir, had come to nothing. In May 1557 the duchess of
Lorraine had visited London, and she had also attempted to persuade the princess into matrimony, but without success.[137] By that
time, Soranzo reported, the English council were themselves unwilling to allow her to leave the country.[138] If he was correctly informed,
this represented a significant change of opinion, because the chances
of persuading any significant foreign prince to live permanently in
England were small. At this point Mary herself seems to have been
inclined to recognize Elizabeth as heir on the condition that she
married the duke of Savoy,[139] but there was no chance that the
princess would have accepted such terms, and Philip was not supporting the queen by insisting upon them. The issue was still unresolved on 30 March 1558, when Mary made her will, largely
because she persisted in the delusion that she was pregnant. The
crown of England, with all its prerogatives and dependencies

> . . . shall wholly and entirely descend, remain and be unto the
> heirs, issue and fruit of my body, according to the laws of the
> realm.[140]

Philip was to have the guardianship, both of the heir and of the
realm, as provided by statute, and all her subjects were charged to
pay such allegiance to the king under those circumstances as they

had paid to the queen during her lifetime,

> . . . whose endeavour, care and study hath been and chiefly is to
> reduce this realm unto the unity of Christ's church and true reli-
> gion and to the ancient and honourable fame and honour that it
> hath been of . . .

No mention was made of any alternative succession.

A few days earlier Simon Renard had written to Philip a memorandum embodying his thoughts on the English succession.[141] In his
opinion Elizabeth's position was invincible because of the strength
of her backing, from the French, the heretics, and an organized
party in the English council which had consistently protected her.
There was also no plausible alternative. On this last point he was
certainly right, but the rest of his judgement is more open to question. The French had supported Elizabeth only very indirectly,
because they had their own candidate in Mary Stuart. Protestant
support was confined mainly to the exile groups in Frankfurt and
Strasbourg, and the evidence for organized backing within Mary's
council is mostly conjectural. Nevertheless, his conclusion was
sound, because of the princess's general popularity, and because of
the strength of her position in English law. His advice to the king
to insist upon the Savoy marriage as the only possible safeguard
went unheeded. Probably by April 1558 Philip had decided that it
would not be practicable to impose any conditions upon Elizabeth's
succession, and therefore unwise to try. She was, apparently, determined not to marry unless, or until, she could make her own choice.
In April she received a visit from the Swedish ambassador, but
responded so unfavourably that he got his knuckles sharply rapped.[142] Feria himself visited her in June, on his own initiative, but
with Philip's full approval. After the visit he reported tantalizingly,
'She was very much pleased; and I was also for reasons I will tell
your Majesty [about] when I arrive over there'.[143] What was said
can only be guessed, but the subsequent behaviour of both parties
suggests an amicable arrangement. At exactly what point Mary
accepted the inevitable is not clear. According to Surian she had
been 'utterly opposed' to Elizabeth's succession as late as July 1557
'as she was born of an infamous woman, who had so greatly out-
raged the Queen her mother and herself'.[144] In this resolution she
had been supported by Pole, despite all the arguments which could
be mustered by Philip's confessor, de Fresnada, on the king's
orders. On this point Surian's testimony conflicts with that of
Soranzo and others, which suggests a more flexible position in the
summer of 1557, as we have seen. Quite possibly the queen's mind

was fluctuating, but it was not until she added a codicil to her will on 28 October 1558 that she came near to making any explicit acknowledgement of her sister's right. It was now, she admitted, uncertain whether she would have issue or not; wherefore

> For the discharge of my conscience and the quiet of the realm, being presently sick in body although whole in mind, if it should please God not to give me issue, then the Crown is to pass to the next heir by the laws of the realm . . .[145]

This heir (unnamed) is then solemnly enjoined to execute the remaining terms of the will because '. . . my said most dear Lord and Husband shall for default of heirs of my body have no further government order or rule in this realm . . .' Finally, on 7 November, she sent word to Elizabeth agreeing to her succession, and asking only that she pay her debts and maintain religion.[146] Although, according to Surian, the messages exchanged were full of affection, the two women did not meet, and it seems unlikely that their real feelings for each other had changed.

During the last ten days of Mary's life, her sister effectively held court at Hatfield. She had grown accustomed to moving with a large retinue,[147] and although she maintained complete discretion, behind the scenes many preparations must have been made in anticipation of the queen's death. There was an immediate renewal of speculation about her marriage, Philip's name being mentioned with almost indecent speed, but if Elizabeth had any understanding with her brother-in-law, it was not of that nature. The new queen, understandably, seems to have felt under no obligation to her predecessor for recognizing her right, and paid no attention to her last wishes. Mary's will may have been suppressed;[148] it was certainly never executed in full, and within a few months her entire religious settlement had been overthrown. However, any freedom of action which Elizabeth may have enjoyed at home in the light of her general popularity was no more than partial compensation for her total lack of such freedom abroad. The French made no secret of the fact that they would use Mary Stuart's claim against her if they thought fit, and they had no intention of surrendering Calais, thus making any independent peace by England impossible. The hold which this situation gave Philip over the new English government was all the more welcome in view of his deteriorating relations with Mary's council during the last months of her life. The need of both sides for peace was urgent, but the French had made it clear as early as May that Calais was not negotiable as far as they were concerned.[149] This worried the king and his advisers, because the English were equally insistent that it must be returned, and the last vestiges of their loyalty to him were at stake. The negotiations finally got under way in late September, when Philip named his own commissioners, and asked Mary to send over Heath, Winchester, Clinton, and Boxall with power to negotiate. She replied that none of those named was available, and that instead she would be represented by Arundel, Thirlby, and Wotton.[150] Wotton already knew that there would be 'great sticking' over Calais, but even he was not prepared for a level of intransigence which would not even admit the English commissioners to the negotiations.[151] The Spanish commissioners believed that the French had a Machiavellian scheme to use Calais as a means of bringing their relations with the English to a final breach, and then offering to return it as soon as Mary was dead or deposed.[152] Such thinking was altogether too subtle, but the real dilemma of what to do about Calais was almost as painful. After all, the English had not defended the place properly, had declined Philip's aid, and had made no real attempt to recover it. On the other hand, as Philip and his commissioners knew perfectly well, and admitted among themselves, the English title to Calais was good and established, and they would never have lost it if they had not become involved in a war on the king's behalf.[153] So the Spaniards insisted, successfully, that the English delegation should take part in the discussions, and declared firmly that they would make no peace without the restoration of Calais. Quite apart from the question of honour, the French occupation of such a strategic fortress would constitute a permanent threat to the Low Countries.[154]

However, the English council never quite believed in the firmness of this defence, and they were right. Arundel and Thirlby threatened to withdraw if Philip yielded, but such a sanction had no bite in the mouths of men whose very presence was, in a sense, on sufferance. Also Granvelle was quite prepared to call their bluff by suggesting that they might like to redeem their loss by continuing the war on their own.[155] Desperately, they suggested shifting the burden of surrender on to the parliament, just convened, although parliament had no right to be consulted in such matters, let alone to make decisions. The council clutched at the straw, making the queen's incapacity the excuse,[156] but such a course was never taken. On 8 November they wrote a formal letter to the king, referring the matter to his judgement in neutral terms; but on the same day a very different communication was sent to the commissioners, with instructions to use its content as they thought fit.

These wars wherein Calays was loste began at the request and for the sake of the Kyng; others, His Majestys frendes and confederates, are restored to thinges taken many yeres past, and what may be judged in this realme if thys peace be concluded, and Calays left in the Frenche Kings hands, so manye other restitutions being made, it may bee easily considered.[157]

Their bitterness and frustration were strong. All the fine hopes which Paget and his friends had entertained, first of the marriage, then of Philip's rule, and finally of the war, had all come to nothing. The king had taken what he could get, and given nothing in return. Philip, for his part, was equally disgusted and disillusioned with a people who always seemed to want everything on their own terms. Yet neither side could contemplate a breakdown of relations while the marriage bond still held Philip and Mary together. It is not surprising that the king felt no more than 'a reasonable regret' for his wife's death, or that the people of England were as glad to see her go as they had been relieved to see her come. As soon as the news reached Cercamp, both sides agreed to a two-month truce to enable the effects of the change of regime in England to become apparent,[158] and to enable both Philip and Henri to size up a queen whose position, while unenviably weak, was singularly free from obligations, moral or otherwise.[159]

Notes

1 For an investigation of the activities of the English exiles in France, and their relations with the French government, see *TTC*, 151-75. The queen's ships inflicted a decisive defeat on the pirates off Plymouth in July 1556, capturing six of their ships. *Cal. Ven.*, VI, 536.
2 Wotton to Petre, 21 January 1557. PRO SP69/10/571.
3 Wotton to Petre, 13 January 1557. PRO SP69/10/569. Stafford claimed to be the true heir to the English crown. His royal blood came through his mother, Ursula, daughter of Margaret countess of Salisbury and sister of Reginald Pole. His father, Henry Lord Stafford, would have been duke of Buckingham but for the attainder of his grandfather in 1521.
4 Notes by Wotton, April 1557. PRO SP69/10/587.
5 Wotton to Petre, ibid., 588. Surian to the doge and senate, 29 April 1557. *Cal. Ven.*, VI, 1026.
6 *Ecc. Mem.*, III, ii, 515. The full text of the proclamation.
7 Henry earl of Westmorland to the bishop of Durham, 24 April 1557. PRO SP15/8/4 (i).
8 *APC*, VI, 81. BL Cotton MS Vespasian C XIV f. 585.
9 *Cal. Ven.*, VI, 1026.
10 ibid. There is no clue as to who Surian believed these adherents to be, and my own suspicion is that this passage reflects the fact that someone in authority hoped to use the invasion as a means of tempting dissidents to reveal themselves.
11 Soranzo to the doge and senate, 21 May 1557. *Cal. Ven.*, VI, 1104-8. The account which Henri gave to Soranzo of his final interview with Stafford was circumstantial and plausible.

12 Wotton to Bourne and Boxall, 14 May 1557. PRO SP69/10/605.
13 That was what Soranzo was told in France. *Cal. Ven.*, VI, 1043.
14 For Ribault's colourful and erratic career, see G. Lefèvre Pontalis, ed., *Correspondance Politique de Odet de Selve* (1888), 218-23; Harbison, 283-5 (which shows him to have been a confederate of Dudley in 1556); and L. Woodbury, 'Jean Ribault and Queen Elizabeth', *American Historical Review*, 9 (1903–04), 456-9.
15 Archives Nationales, Paris; Aff. Etr., XIX f. 277, Advis au roi par l'evesque de Dacaz (François de Noailles). I am indebted to Dr A. Soman for his help in tracing this information.
16 They were tried by special commission of oyer and terminer in London on 22 and 25 May. Stafford, Stowell, Procter, and Bradford were executed; Saunders and Sherles pardoned. PRO KB8/37. *Cal. Pat.*, IV, 70, 106. A total of 27 were tried in Yorkshire, probably at the assizes. *Ecc. Mem.*, III, 2, 67-9.
17 *Cal. Span.*, XIII, 290-1.
18 PRO SP11/10/60. 22 May 1557. ibid., 61; instructions to Lord St John.
19 *Cal. Ven.*, VI, 1085-7.
20 'An account of what the Herald from England did in France'. *Cal. Span.*, XIII, 294-6.
21 Soranzo's reports of 8 and 9 June contain a full description of Norroy's mission and its reception. *Cal. Ven.*, VI, 1148-51. Henri subsequently added the opinion that Philip had coerced Mary into the war by threatening never to come back to her. ibid., 1151. Surian to the doge and senate, 7 and 8 June, *Cal. Ven.*, VI, 1145-8.
22 Queen to the earl of Shrewsbury, 2 June 1557. *HMC Fifteenth Report*, App., II, 23 (Hodgkin MSS).
23 *Cal. Scot.*, I, 416. The bishop of Orkney had made somewhat similar remarks to Cuthbert Tunstall.
24 'The attemptate of 7 July' 1556 was, according to the English, the work of Scottish outlaws, or 'broken men'. The Scots had at first accepted this, and the commissioners of the two sides had reached agreement over arbitration procedures in October 1556. However, by the end of November the Scots were again demanding redress for the July raid, and relations were bad by the end of the year. Early in 1557 Shrewsbury had sent another 600 horse to strengthen the West March, but by the summer the old grievance seems to have faded into the background. *Cal. Scot.*, I, 417. BL Harleian MS 289 ff. 43-58; agreements, proclamations, and letters of the English commissioners, October–December 1556.
25 *Cal. Scot.*, I, 421.
26 *APC*, VI, 137. For a detailed account of the raiding which constituted this 'war' see Robert Lindsay of Pitscottie, 'The history of Scotland from . . . 1436 to . . . 1565', ed. J. G. Mackay, *Scottish Text Society* (1899–1911), II, 119-27.
27 Philip's own account of this exchange is contained in his letter to Don Luis de Carvajal, the captain-general of his fleet. *Cal. Span.*, XIII, 311-12.
28 PRO SP69/11/665. 'Instructions given to Christopher d'Assonleville on his mission to England and Scotland', 19 September 1557.
29 That only became apparent when Philip used it as a main reason for not breaking with the Scots the following year. See below, 380.
30 Lindsay, op. cit., II, 120.

31 Soranzo to the doge and senate, 18 June. *Cal. Ven.*, VI, 1174. Exaggeration was the hallmark of French news from Scotland. On 21 September, Soranzo reported that the Scots had 40,000 men in the field, ibid., 1320.

32 *Cal. Span.*, XIII, 315-17.

33 ibid., 376.

34 Early in October it was being confidently reported in France that the Scots had won several victories in the field, besieged Berwick, and defeated an English expedition to Orkney. *Cal. Ven.*, VI, 1337-9; *Cal. Span.*, XIII, 320. The English also believed in 1558 that a renewed Franco–Scottish attack was likely; 'Memorial of the North, 1558', *Cal. Scot.*, I, 437.

35 BL Stowe MS 571 ff. 77-132. Lord Bray can barely have received his pardon in time to join the army. He had been released from the Tower early in April, and his pardon was enrolled on 15 May. He had been imprisoned and indicted for wishing aloud that Elizabeth was on the throne, and had also been suspected of involvement in the Dudley plot. Thomas Edwards to the earl of Rutland, 16 April 1557, *HMC Twelfth Report*, App., IV, 68 (Rutland MSS). *Cal. Pat.*, III, 396.

36 One or two others appear in the coat and conduct money accounts, but not in the muster, notably Lord Montague and Sir Thomas Cheney. Apart from Pembroke the only current member of the privy council to serve with the army was Cheney. BL Stowe MS 571 ff. 77-132.

37 *Cal. Span.*, XIII, 307.

38 There was confusion over the transport for the English artillery. The earl of Pembroke was expecting waggons to be sent which never arrived. Philip probably missed the battle by waiting for the English to come up. *Cal. Span.*, XIII, 309-11.

39 Juan de Pinedo to Francisco de Vargas, 27 August 1557. *Cal. Span.*, XIII, 317. Feria was later to claim that the English utterly failed to distinguish themselves.

40 BL Stowe MS 571 ff. 87-93. A full muster by companies under the names of the captains.

41 ibid., ff. 80-2. Soranzo reported in early September that the English force was to be recalled, ostensibly to meet the danger from Scotland. By the end of the month most of them had left. *Cal. Ven.*, VI, 1302, 1331.

42 BL Stowe MS 571 f. 78. If this statement is correct about the £11,000 of Philip's money being in England, it raises the problem of when and why such a sum had been committed to the mint. See below, 414-15 and n relating to the minting of Spanish money in England.

43 PRO E404/109 m. 11, 12.

44 PRO E101/64/2. Conduct money from Cambrai to various places in England.

45 Bernardo Navagero, Venetian ambassador in Rome, to the council of ten. *Cal. Ven.*, VI, 1308-9.

46 A review of the shire levies was ordered on 16 May, 'in case of rebellion or for the resistance of any foreign invasion'. *APC*, VI, 87. On the basis of returns from these musters made in June, the council allocated responsibility for the defence of the kingdom, appointing noblemen and gentlemen to serve in particular places, and specifying the numbers of men to be supplied by them, as well as by the cities and counties. PRO SP11/11/19, 30.

47 *APC*, VI, 153; 18 August 1557. On the same day Pembroke was informed that Sir John Salisbury had been complained against for 'misbehaviour and disordered doinges in the levieng of men within Wales'.

48 On 8 August the council wrote to Sir John Clere announcing the sending of a commission '. . . under the Brode Seale' for him to punish 'the disordre of the maryners'. Since this was joined with a promise to remedy the 'wantes of victualles', the source of the trouble is not far to seek.

49 *APC*, VI, 141-2. 3 August 1557.

50 *APC*, VI, 171. 8 September 1557.

51 Letters of instruction and lists of commissioners are set out at length in PRO SP11/11/44-51.

52 PRO E101/483/16. Repairs to Carlisle during the same period cost £824. PRO E101/63/18.

53 *APC*, VI, 212. Henry Dormer, a member of the guard, acted as Vaughn's agent for this purpose. On 15 March 1558 it was ordered that William Markett, one such deserter who had been caught, was to be returned to Berwick for execution '. . . to the terrour and example of like offendours'. *APC*, VI, 284.

54 Soranzo to the doge and senate, 29 November 1557. *Cal. Ven.*, VI, 1381-2.

55 Same to same, 6 December 1557. ibid., 1385.

56 By this time Giovanni Michieli, formerly in England, had taken over Soranzo's mission. Michieli to the doge and senate, 11 December 1557. ibid., 1389-90.

57 ibid., 1396-7.

58 Lord Grey to the queen, 22 December 1557. PRO SP69/11/695. His own spies had discovered nothing.

59 Queen to Wentworth, 24 December. ibid., 696. Wentworth received a detailed report on the French build-up from one of his agents on 26 December. ibid., 697 (i). Council in Calais to the queen, 27 December. ibid., 698; and enclosed reports, ibid., 698 (i-v).

60 ibid., 699, 701, 708. On 31 December the council had briefly convinced themselves that the French target was Hesdin, not Calais.

61 Henry earl of Rutland, to the queen, 3 January 1558. ibid., 12/712.

62 Rutland, Tresham, and Jerningham to the queen, 6 January 1558. ibid., 715.

63 Sir Edward Carne to the queen, 28 January 1558. ibid., 727. Cardinal of Siguenza to the princess-dowager of Portugal, 29 January 1558. *Cal. Span.*, XIII, 346-7.

64 *APC*, VI, 147-8. 10 August 1557.

65 *TTC*, 151-75. There was suspicion against Edward Dudley, the captain of Hammes, 4th Baron Dudley and heir to the 'Lord Quondam', because his younger brother, Henry, became a notorious conspirator against the regime. Edward himself had been knighted by Mary in October 1553, and in 1554 restored to those lands which his father had sold to the duke of Northumberland. Mary continued to trust him, in spite of his brother's delinquency, and was, apparently, right to do so.

66 Wentworth is commonly blamed for not having opened the sea defences to cut off the French advance. However, according to a contemporary Spanish account, the marshes had been drained in order to provide profitable grazing. This may have meant that it was no longer possible to flood the area, or merely that Wentworth hesitated to do so for fear

of destroying the flocks and herds. Francesco Delgado to the princess of Portugal, 17 March 1558. AGS, Guerra Antigua, L67 f. 50. It had been recognized since at least 1551 that the fortifications of Calais were 'neither in building nor situation according to the fortifications now requisite' in spite of the fact that over £150,000 had been spent on them since 1538. *The History of the King's Works* (1975), III, 359-61.

67 *Cal. Ven.*, VI, 1407; 'The French are not known to have made any fresh stir'. Philip to Wentworth, 2 January 1558. *Cal. Span.*, XIII, 321.

68 The sequence of events at this point is unclear. Rutland and Tresham had originally been appointed, about 2 January, to go to the relief of Calais. When it became apparent that this was impossible, the council countermanded the orders for musters at Dover, writing to Cheney and Pembroke for that purpose on 12 January. Mildmay's instructions, however, are dated 11 January, and seem to refer to the same operation as that in which Valentine Browne was involved after the 19th. Presumably the council withdrew its instruction to Cheney and Pembroke, and the gathering of troops went ahead again under Rutland's command until the whole operation was again called off at the end of the month. PRO SP69/12/712. *APC*, VI, 238. SP69/12/717. PRO E351/22.

69 Edward Lord Dudley, to Philip, 10 January 1558. Duke of Savoy to Philip, 22 January 1558. *Cal. Span.*, XIII, 326-7, 341-2.

70 Some reinforcement did reach Guisnes from Flanders, but not enough. Lord Grey to M. de Bugincourt, 12 January 1558. *Cal. Span.*, XIII, 329. Duke of Savoy to the queen, 16 January. *Cal. Span.*, XIII, 335. 'News of the fall of Guisnes', 21 January 1558. *Cal. Span.*, XIII, 341.

71 PRO E351/22.

72 Philip to the duke of Savoy, 26 January 1558. *Cal. Span.*, XIII, 345.

73 Philip to Feria, 31 January 1558. *Cal. Span.*, XIII, 347.

74 Feria to Philip, 2 February 1558. *Cal. Span.*, XIII, 349-51. The co-operativeness of the English council was probably not helped by the fact that the king's English pensions were about 10,000 ducats in arrears, and several noblemen had complained to Feria about this. ibid.

75 BL Cotton MS Titus B II f. 59. G. Burnet, *The History of the Reformation in England*, II (1681), 324-5.

76 ibid.

77 PRO E351/22.

78 Philip to the privy council, 31 January 1558. *Cal. Span.*, XIII, 348.

79 A two-month truce had been concluded between England and Scotland on 23 January. *Cal. Scot.*, I, 428. Mary of Guise naturally took advantage of Philip's unwillingness to make a break, writing him a friendly letter on 10 February, in which she coolly declared, '. . . it is little to our pleasure that the peace desired by this country has been broken by England'. ibid., 433.

80 Philip to Feria, 4 February 1558. *Cal. Span.*, XIII, 351.

81 ibid., 323.

82 ibid., 361-2.

83 Feria to Philip, 6 June 1558. ibid., 394-6.

84 ibid., and also Feria's letter of 5 July. ibid., 402-3. The Hanse merchants expressed their gratitude to Philip for his favour, but when they eventually received a formal reply from the English council on 7 July, it contained only a limited confirmation of their privileges, and the disputes went on. *APC*, VI, 340-2. The English council remained intensely suspicious of Philip's favour to the Hanse.

85 Philip to Feria, 15 February 1558. *Cal. Span.*, XIII, 347-8. PRO SP69/12/736. Mary to Sir William Pickering, 15 March 1558.
86 Count Feria to Philip, 5 July 1558. *Cal. Span.*, XIII, 402-3.
87 Philip to Feria, 19 June 1558. ibid., 398-9.
88 Feria to Philip, 5 July 1558. ibid., 402-3.
89 Same to same, 10 March 1558. ibid., 366-8. Feria's outspoken contempt for the English council only made a bad situation worse, as he acknowledged indirectly when he wrote on 6 June: 'As for me, the English never take me in, because I never believe a word they say. And as I often check up on them, they find me tiresome'. ibid., 394.
90 Feria to Philip, 10 March 1558. ibid., 366-7. Curiously Feria does not mention Winchester in this letter, although he was to play a very important part in the lieutenancy arrangements of the following month, and by June, Feria was to describe him as the most efficient and zealous of Mary's ministers. ibid., 394.
91 *APC*, VI. Lemasters, op. cit., Appendix III.
92 Three memoranda describing these arrangements were enclosed with Feria's letter to Philip on 10 March, and the king certainly approved them. Whether he had any hand in planning them is not clear, but the tone of his response suggests that he did not. *Cal. Span.*, XIII, 369.
93 *Cal. Scot.*, I, 428, 429. 23 January 1558.
94 *Cal. Span.*, XIII, 369.
95 Lemasters, op. cit., Appendix II.
96 *Cal. Span.*, XIII, 367.
97 Feria to Philip, 1 May 1558. *Cal. Span.*, 378-9. Philip to Antonio de Guaras, 11 May 1558. ibid., 383. 1000 is the figure normally quoted, although one document says 2000. *Cal. Span.*, XIII, 401.
98 Feria to Philip, 22 February 1558. ibid., 361-2.
99 *APC*, VI, 390. On 31 August the earl of Pembroke resigned as president of the council in the Marches, and there was a two-month interval before he was replaced, on 29 October, by Bishop Bourne of Bath and Wells. PRO SP11/13/63, 14/9.
100 Bishop of Arras to Feria, 26 May 1558. *Cal. Span.*, XIII, 388.
101 *APC*, VI, 303. 13 April 1558. For the dispute at Falmouth, see Figueroa to the queen, 26 July 1558. PRO SP69/13/811 (English copy). Verlanga had been courteously entertained by the mayor and the captain of the castle, but got a hostile reception from the townsmen.
102 Feria to Philip, 5 July 1558. *Cal. Span.*, XIII, 402-3. The situation had been made much worse by the fall of Thionville to the French. According to Feria 'some of these Privy Councillors were very much pleased about it', and rumours were also circulating of the loss of Dunkirk and Gravelines.
103 *APC*, VI, 236, 251 *et seq.*
104 *APC*, VI, 262, 266-7. 7, 10, and 11 February 1558. Two of the four were committed to the Fleet, and subsequently fined.
105 *APC*, VI, 336-7.
106 *APC*, VI, 259. 'A letter to Sir William Hollys, Sherief of the countyes of Nottingham and Derby . . .' 4 February 1558.
107 *APC*, VI, 259.
108 PRO SP11/12/67.
109 *APC*, VI, 311, 312-13. A series of letters to Bedford, the mayor of Bristol, Sir Thomas Denys, Sir John St Leger, and Sir John Chichester. Bedford's orders to the mayor of Totnes. *HMC Reports*, 73, 38 (Exeter MSS).

110 PRO SP11/12/9, 10, 11.
111 L. O. Boynton, *The Elizabethan Militia* (1967), 8-9.
112 *APC*, VI, 296. 30 March 1558.
113 Sir Edward Grimston escaped from the Bastille, where he had been imprisoned after the siege, only to face an indictment for treason. He was pardoned by Elizabeth. *HMC Reports*, 64, 13-22 (Verulam MSS).
114 *Cal. Span.*, XIII, 355-6.
115 *CJ*. The deadline for the fifteenth was eventually extended to 10 November. BL Lansdowne MS 4 f. 9.
116 *Cal. Span.*, XIII, 366-8. The subsidy assessment was £153,055 and the fifteenth £29,000. By mid-November the subsidy had yielded £135,445 and the fifteenth £9295. BL Lansdowne MS 4 f. 9.
117 ibid.
118 L. Stone, *The Crisis of the Aristocracy* (1965), 218-20.
119 4 and 5 Philip and Mary, c. 3, viii. The statute revived was 2 and 3 Edward VI, c. 2, iii. The existence of this law makes the resort to martial law for the punishment of deserters the more remarkable.
120 Hughes and Larkin, II, 83. On 2 February Feria had observed: 'The Queen and Council tell me that they will look into the intelligences which the French are keeping up here. But there are so many Frenchmen domiciled in this country that I doubt if anything can be done'. *Cal. Span.*, XIII, 349-51.
121 *CJ*, I, 49.
122 Hughes and Larkin, II, 85.
123 4 and 5 Philip and Mary, c. 6. The threat of expulsion remained, but only after proof of offence against the laws of the land. Nicholas Heath, the lord chancellor, was empowered by warrant on 4 June 1558 to issue commissions of inquiry under this act '. . . to inquire of all Frenchmen made denizens since 32 Henry VIII, who have since the beginning of the Queen's reign, given intelligences to the French King . . .' *Cal. Pat.*, IV, 13.
124 Hughes and Larkin, II, 86, 84, 91.
125 *APC*, VI, 346-7. 15 July 1558. Hughes and Larkin, II, 90.
126 ibid., II, 86.
127 *Cal. Span.*, XIII, 367.
128 *CJ*, I, 48.
129 *Cal. Span.*, XIII, 361, 367. Nevertheless, Paget was excluded from the list of executors of the queen's will, which was drawn up at the end of March. Presumably the lord privy seal was in 'favour' in a purely political sense which did not extend to a gesture of personal confidence.
130 Michieli to the doge and senate, 20 February 1558. *Cal. Ven.*, VI, 1455.
131 Rumours that she had been delivered of a son were circulating in Flanders at the end of March, but were treated with derision in France. *Cal. Ven.*, VI, 1479.
132 Philip to Feria, 19 June 1558. *Cal. Span.*, XIII, 398-9.
133 ibid., 399. How far Mary's bad health in the summer of 1558 may have affected the behaviour of English politicians is a matter of speculation. Gammon suggests (*Statesman and Schemer*, 241-2) that Paget deliberately became less active, particularly on Philip's behalf, as the year advanced, because of the obvious danger in which such commitment would involve him in the event of the queen's early death. Also, as we have seen, the great nobles were conspicuously absent from the council and the court in the late summer. On the other hand, there is

no clear evidence before September to suggest that anyone believed the queen's health to be any worse than it had been for the previous two years.

134 *Cal. Ven.*, VI, 528-9.
135 Philip to the privy council, 22 October 1558. *Cal. Span.*, XIII, 416.
136 *Cal. Ven.*, VI, 1544. Philip to the princess-dowager of Portugal, 4 December 1558. *Cal. Span.*, XIII, 440.
137 Soranzo to the doge and senate, 21 May 1557. *Cal. Ven.*, VI, 1104-8.
138 ibid. '. . . il Cons. d'Inghilterra cosi leggermente contentato che la fusse passata il mar'. This was the conviction which Henri had derived from the duchess's visit.
139 *Cal. Span.*, XIII, 293.
140 BL Lansdowne MS 6949. Since this will survives only in copies, its authenticity cannot be beyond dispute. A note on this copy, which is of the eighteenth century, runs 'from the original in Mr. Hales' hands at Alderley in Gloucestershire', and records that the original was signed by the queen at the top and bottom of every page.
141 *Cal. Span.*, XIII, 372-3.
142 The ambassador foolishly went to see her without asking the queen's permission, and having no interest in his proposals, Elizabeth dutifully reported his visit. There was no chance, in any case, that Mary would have countenanced a Lutheran marriage. *Cal. Span.*, XIII, 380, etc.
143 Feria to Philip, 23 June 1558. *Cal. Span.*, XIII, 399-400.
144 Surian to the doge and senate, 29 October 1558 (reporting a discussion which had been held during Philip's stay in England the previous year, and consequently not later than July). *Cal. Ven.*, VI, 1538.
145 BL Harleian MS 6949.
146 Christophe d'Assonleville to Philip. *Cal. Span.*, 437-8.
147 Surian to the doge and senate, 27 November 1558. *Cal. Ven.*, VI, 1549. 'The xxv day of Feybruary [1558] cam rydyng to London my lade Elisabeth the quen syster, with a gret compene of lordes nobull men and nobull women . . .' Machyn, 166-7.
148 A possible explanation of the appearance of the original will in the hands of Mr Hales of Alderley. Most of the legacies were to religious houses, which had been suppressed again within a few months of her death.
149 *Cal. Ven.*, VI, 1499-1500.
150 Mary to Wotton, 28 September 1558. PRO SP69/13/828.
151 Spanish commissioners to Philip, 15 October 1558. *Cal. Span.*, XIII, 414-15. The French apparently wanted the English admitted only to certain sessions and not as full participants '. . . for fear this would sour the atmosphere'.
152 Spanish commissioners to Philip, 20 October 1558. *Cal. Span.*, XIII, 416.
153 Commissioners to Philip, 27 October 1558. *Cal. Span.*, XIII, 427-8. Bishop of Arras to Vigilius de Zwickem, 30 October. ibid., 434-5. Arras to Feria, 5 November. ibid., 437.
154 Commissioners to Philip, 27 October 1558. ibid., 421-9.
155 Arras to Vigilius de Zwickem, 30 October 1558. ibid., 434-5.
156 Arundel, Thirlby, and Wotton to the council, 28 October 1558. PRO SP69/13/849. Council to the commissioners, 8 November. ibid., 856. On 17 October, Anthony Kempe, gentleman of the privy chamber, Bernard Hampton, clerk of the privy council, and John Clyff, clerk of the signet, had been empowered to sign the queen's letters with her

stamp, in the presence of Heath, Hastings, Cornwallis, Jerningham, Englefield, Waldegrave, Petre, and Cordell, or any two of them. *Cal. Pat.*, IV, 454.

157 PRO SP69/13/856, 856 (i).
158 Michieli to the doge and senate, 28 November 1558. *Cal. Ven.*, VI, 1560-2.
159 The chief architect of the Anglo-Spanish alliance only narrowly failed to outlive it. Charles V had died at San Yuste on the early morning of 20 September 1558.

12   War and Finance – 1557–1558

The outbreak of war did not cause any immediate acceleration of expenditure, partly because several of the more important preparations, such as the fortification of Berwick, the equipping of the fleet, and the mustering of an expeditionary force, were already in hand; and partly because the council seems to have decided that, having been forced into war, it would wage it as economically as possible. The only provision which could be interpreted as a financial preparation for war was the issuing of a further commission for the sale of crown lands on 20 April. The commission itself mentions no target figure, but Surian was informed that property to the value of £10,000 a year was to be sold, which, he correctly calculated, ought to yield at least 800,000 crowns (£200,000 sterling).[1] 'The competition of buyers is great', he commented, 'and they are bound to disburse the money fourteen days after the purchase . . . so this entire fund . . . will shortly be in her Majesty's hands'. The source of this optimistic calculation is not mentioned, but was probably Paget. In fact the sales seem to have moved very sluggishly, only about £8000 being recorded as income under that heading in the receipt of exchequer between Easter 1557 and Easter 1558.[2] Surian was also informed, as we have seen, that all the proceeds from these sales would be sent over to Philip, 'as the Queen thinks solely of giving his Majesty every possible assistance . . .' Also it so happened that 20 May 1557 was the predetermined date for the payment of the second instalment of the lay subsidy voted in 1555, amounting to £76,795; and that was paid promptly, over £67,000 reaching the exchequer between May and July. The arrival of so much ready money at this juncture was of crucial importance, because as the summer advanced, more and more bills for wages, conduct money, provisions, and armaments had to be met. Gonson received almost £20,000 between Easter and Michaelmas – half as much again as he would have spent in a whole year in peacetime. During the same period over £11,000 was sent north, to Richard Ashton, the receiver-general, and Alan Bellingham, the treasurer of Berwick; a further

£10,000 was dispensed to Cuthbert Vaughn and other captains taking troops to the borders; and Richard Freston, the cofferer of the household, received a total of over £12,000 for wages and arms.[3] In what capacity Freston was operating is not clear, but he was probably treasurer of the army being gathered to assist the Low Countries under the terms of the 1542 treaty, a position which he handed over to William Whightman in July, before the army actually left for the continent.[4] That campaign itself probably cost the exchequer no more than £6000, but with the prospect of continuing substantial bills for the garrisons and the fleet, and with a privy seal loan of £42,000 falling due for payment in the autumn, it was certain that further extraordinary revenue would be needed before the end of the year.

Instead of summoning parliament, which would have been a normal practice on the outbreak of war, the council decided to repeat the expedient of the previous year by demanding a further and larger privy seal loan. The reasons for this decision must have been political, and presumably arose partly from the turbulent performance of the Commons in the previous parliament, and partly from the known unpopularity of the war with everyone except the military gentry. Resistance to the previous loan, although widespread and irritating, had failed to prevent the collection of the money, and it was easier to deal with recalcitrant individuals than with an obstinate House of Commons. Whereas in 1556 letters under the privy seal had been sent to selected individuals for a uniform contribution of £100, on this occasion commissions of assessment were appointed for each county, in the same way as for a parliamentary subsidy. When the letters of instruction were sent out to the commissioners in September, copies of the previous subsidy assessments were sent with them to assist in the work.[5] When they had completed their assessments, they were instructed to travel round their counties, approaching individually all those who were judged capable of lending. Anyone deemed to be worth more than £40 a year in land or goods would then receive a privy seal letter requesting a sum between £10 and 100 marks, others would have their contributions fixed by the commissioners on the spot.[6] The names of all those willing to lend were then entered in a special book by the commissioners, and countersigned by the lender. Any person so approached who refused to lend was then to be summoned before the full commission for the county, and if still recalcitrant, bound in recognizance to appear before the council in London. Collectors were also appointed for each county, and blank privy seal letters sent to them to be signed and issued as receipts. The 'loan books' were supposed to be deposited with the collectors,

o

and copies sent to the council, by October.[7] Letters were also sent out carefully explaining the dire necessity created by the war, and the northern counties were exempted, as we have seen. Richard Wilbram, the master of the jewel house, was appointed receiver-general, and his instructions included the repayment of the previous loan, which was to fall due in November.[8] This was to be done through the collectors of the new loan, the earlier privy seals being recalled as receipts to set against the appropriate sums in the accounts. Those who had lent in 1556 were not required to contribute again, but the pressure applied by the council to those who were called upon was severe. The commissioners in Oxfordshire were told not to allow any extended time for payment,[9] and over 150 individuals made personal appearances in London for refusing to pay. The overwhelming majority of these seem to have thought better of their defiance after one or two meetings with the council, but John Love of Winchelsea was committed to the Fleet for persisting in his refusal, and was kept there for about three weeks before being released on recognizance.[10]

On the whole it was a very efficiently conducted operation, and when Richard Wilbram eventually presented his account on 2 July 1558, he accounted for £109,269.[11] Of this sum £2123 had been spent on the expenses of the operation and £42,100 on repaying the previous loan, so that approximately £65,000 was paid either into the exchequer or into the queen's own hands: about half the net yield of a parliamentary subsidy.[12] The second instalment of the clerical subsidy voted in 1555 had also fallen due on 1 October, and that yielded about £9000 (out of £14,000) between that date and the end of February, so with the balance of the lay subsidy producing another £7900 during the same period, extraordinary revenues amounting to nearly £82,000 accrued during the winter.[13] This was barely adequate to support the existing level of activity in the fleet and the northern marches, let alone to meet any fresh emergency. In addition the loan had one immense disadvantage. The crown now owed its own subjects nearly £110,000, scheduled for repayment at Christmas 1558, quite apart from its debts to the staplers and adventurers, and failure to meet that bill might cause serious political trouble – especially in view of the amount of resistance which had been shown in the first place.

There were a number of options open to the council at the end of 1557, and none of them was particularly palatable. With a commission for sale already operating, there was little more to be done to squeeze a quick return out of the royal lands. On 12 December a commission was issued to Sir William Petre and others to investigate the royal forests, parks, and chases, and to dispark as they should think convenient to lease for the queen's profit; but this was no more than a minor palliative.[14] The real alternatives were: a fresh appeal to parliament; a return to the Antwerp market so recently and expensively vacated; or debasement of the coinage. Each of these courses, if energetically exploited, could be expected to yield a return in excess of £100,000 over a few months. The adventurers and staplers had been squeezed so hard over the previous two years that little could be expected from them, and Mary would not ask the church for any contribution beyond the subsidy which the clergy were already paying. There was, however, a sector of the ordinary revenue which could be augmented with a lot of courage and determination. As we have already seen, various reformers had been pointing out the defects in the customs administration for a number of years, and the rates had diminished drastically in real value.[15] These rates had originally been fixed by the crown in agreement with the merchants, and there was in theory no reason why they should not be raised, to give the monarch a more realistic share of the country's wealth by trade. One drawback to such a course was the risk of conflict with the mercantile companies upon which the crown had become so heavily dependent. There was no guarantee that the improved revenue to be expected could compensate, at least in the short term, for the withdrawal of credit and loan facilities which might be expected. Another drawback was the danger of stimulating further price rises at a particularly sensitive time. Because the problems caused by foreign borrowing and debasement were both fresh and vivid, the council decided with a courage which must have been born of desperation to summon parliament and to go ahead simultaneously with a new book of customs rates.

Parliament was called before Christmas to meet on 20 January, and in the interval the crisis had been made infinitely worse by the fall of Calais, and by the frantic scurry of military activity which had preceded and followed it. Valentine Browne drew £10,000 from the mint and over £8000 from the exchequer to set up the earl of Rutland's expeditionary force between 7 and 19 January,[16] and on the day when parliament assembled it must have seemed probable that the forthcoming operation would cost at least £50,000. The king could hardly be expected to pay for this army as he had paid for Pembroke's. Nor was there any lightening of the routine burden of war expenditure during the winter, as the remorseless sequence of exchequer warrants makes plain: over £20,000 to Gonson again; £15,000 to the officers of the ordnance; £15,000 to William Ingoldsby, the new treasurer of Berwick; £13,000 to the treasurer of Calais before its fall; £5000 'sent into Ireland'; and so on.[17] Parliament responded, if not with enthusiasm, at least with much less manifest reluctance than might have been expected. The council must have had its proposals ready, since the subsidy was the declared objective of the meeting, but they seem to have been presented in the first instance not to the House of Commons but to that joint committee of both Houses which was set up at the suggestion of the Lords on 24 January.[18] Perhaps this was a method of testing reactions before launching a full debate. The committee worked for about ten days, dividing into three sub-committees according to one account,[19] and presented a subsidy bill to the Commons on 4 February. What relation this bore to the council's original plan we do not know, but what it provided for was a sort of double subsidy and fifteenth. Eight shillings in the pound on land and 5s. 4d. in the pound on goods, plus two tenths and fifteenths, to be paid in two instalments over two years. The first subsidy was to be paid by midsummer 1558; the first tenth and fifteenth by Michaelmas; and the second subsidy, tenth, and fifteenth by the corresponding dates in 1559. It was this bill, which passed its first reading in the Commons on 5 February, which the queen and Pole described to Feria as 'the largest grant ever made to a king of England'. However, they were counting their chickens before they were hatched. The Commons debated the bill all day on 5 February, and read it again on 7 February, after which it disappeared.[20] According to the account already quoted, which may have been official, and was certainly over-optimistic in other respects,[21] the Commons passed the bill unanimously, and then petitioned for a stay of the second subsidy in view of the heavy burdens which they had already borne. In fact it was never given a third reading, and so did not 'pass' the Commons at all, unanimously or otherwise. Probably a powerful body of opinion in the Lower House was unwilling to grant so much at one go, and suggested instead that if the queen wanted another subsidy in 1559, she could come back to parliament and ask again. Such a reaction could be represented by an optimistic observer as an undertaking to grant another subsidy in the next session, and may have given Mary a very specific reason for proroguing this session and meeting the same parliament again in November.

When the subsidy bill reappeared on 14 February, it was for a normal single assessment of 4 shillings in the pound on lands and 2s. 8d. in the pound on goods from £5 upwards, with one fifteenth, to be paid by 24 June.[22] Apart from the speed with which it was to be collected this showed no real concession to the urgency of the situation. However, to have obtained a subsidy at all was something, and if the queen felt assured that she had a firm expectation of another to follow in the autumn, her reported satisfaction is understandable. The bill passed its third reading in the Commons on 16 February, and encountered no difficulties in the Lords. Another clerical subsidy was granted at the same time, in spite of the fact that the previous grant still had one instalment to run;[23] but perhaps because of that no concessions were made to haste, and the full £56,000 would not be realized until March 1561. On 18 March letters were sent out appointing commissioners to assess the new subsidy, and meanwhile the finance committee of the privy council headed by Paget and Thirlby was instructed to produce its further recommendations as quickly as possible, so that its members could go out and inspire the commissioners to suitable diligence.[24] No copy of these recommendations survives as far as I know, but it is possible to deduce part, at least, of their contents. The staplers and adventurers were still owed considerable sums, and had agreed to forbear the instalments due in April, which earned them the queen's liberal thanks and commendation for their sense of duty.[25] However, an approach could be made direct to the city of London itself, and this was done on 17 March, when the queen wrote to the lord mayor and aldermen requesting a loan of 100,000 marks.[26] This was not, apparently, intended to be a loan from the corporation, but a subscription loan from such wealthy individuals as could be persuaded to come forward, because two inducements were offered for those who contributed, the security of crown lands and dispensation from the usury laws. Nicholas Brigham, one of the tellers of the exchequer, was appointed to receive all such money as was subscribed in this way.[27] The response does not seem to have been overwhelming. On 5 November Sir Thomas White, John White, Roger Marten, and William Blackwell were licensed to take 12 per cent interest on the money they had loaned to the queen. They were also granted assurance of lands and tenements to the yearly value of £1007 10s. 7½d. 'in consideration of a sum of £20,150 12s. 1d. lent to the Queen . . .', this pledge being redeemable by the repayment of the loan at Easter 1560.[28] The terms of this licence make it virtually certain that the four men named had lent under the terms offered in the queen's letter of March. No other licences are recorded, so it seems likely that the government received less than a third of what it had requested.

The other major decision which must have been taken by the council committee at this point was to reopen negotiations in Antwerp. Gresham had not been entirely idle since presenting his account the previous August, but the only record of his activities in late 1557 survives in the form of a few notes dated 31 December. These refer to a bargain with 'the merchants' for £26,000, and since that was his normal term for the staplers and adventurers, it seems that he was still acting as an intermediary, dealing with the sums which had been lent or guaranteed by those companies in the previous year.[29] He did not himself account for any transactions between August 1557 and April 1558, and had no outstanding commitments when he received fresh instructions from the council on 12 March 1558. On that date he was ordered to investigate opportunities which were alleged to exist for borrowing at 13 per cent, and after obtaining the king's approval to proceed to Antwerp to take up £200,000 at not more than 14 per cent.[30] So total a reversal of the policy of the previous eighteen months, in which great and successful efforts had been made to get rid of the foreign debt, must have reflected a decisive political victory among the queen's financial advisers. It may be significant in this connection that Winchester was named for the 'council of war' in March 1558, but not to the 'council of finance', and in the following month he was given very extensive administrative responsibilities as lieutenant of a large part of the kingdom.[31] On 12 May, Nicholas Brigham, already named as receiver of the moneys from London, had his responsibilities extended to include 'all money due or payable on any subsidy, fifteenth, loan or other benevolence'.[32] He thus became receiver-general of extraordinary revenue, and his brief significantly included all 'new customs', that is, the specific duties on exported cloth introduced in the new book of rates which came into effect during the summer.

The simultaneous pursuit of so many expedients for the raising of money might seem to indicate an energetic war policy, but that was not the case. When the plans to retake Calais fizzled out ignominiously in late January, and the troops who had been gathered were dispersed, Valentine Browne paid back the unspent balance of his account, £10,440, to the mint. A few days later, on 1 February, the council explained to Philip at considerable length why it could not afford to 'put an army to the field', or take up his offer of help to recover the Pale.[33] The cost of the war, they argued, would be at least £350,000 in a full year, even without such an effort, and the country was already being asked to do more than its parlous economic condition could sustain.

The noblemen and gentlemen (receiving no more than they were wont to receive, and paying thrice as much for everything they provide, by reason of the baseness of the money) are not able to do as they have done in times past. The merchants have had great losses of late, whereby the clothiers be never the richer. The farmers, yeomen and other people, how well willing soever they be taken to be, will not be aknown of their wealth, and by the miscontentment of this loss be grown stubborn and liberal of talk . . .

Whatever the element of special pleading, in strictly financial terms the argument of this memorandum was irrefutable. In peacetime the queen's ships cost £14,000 a year. Between January 1557 and November 1558 Gonson received over £143,000 – a rate of nearly £80,000 a year.[34] Costs on the northern marches varied a good deal, but a year of normal activity such as 1556 saw expenditure a little short of £20,000. From Michaelmas 1557 to Michaelmas 1558 the border fortresses and garrisons drew £97,000 in exchequer warrants alone.[35] Substantial sums also had to be spent on the ordnance, the south-coast forts, the inland musters, and Ireland. In June 1558 another council memorandum estimated that the war was actually costing £30,700 a month,[36] without a field army, and without any significant contribution to the army of the king. The only exception to the last generalization was the case of the 3000 German troops which we have already noticed. These men cost Thomas Gresham almost £12,000, paid on warrants from both the queen and the king.[37] These sums were found out of the money which Gresham had borrowed in Antwerp for the queen, and thus indirectly out of the English exchequer, and since the troops stayed in the Low Countries until they were disbanded, their 'entertainment' can be regarded as an English contribution to Philip's war effort – although an inadvertent one that was much resented.

By April 1558 Gresham was again playing an important part in the financial calculations of the queen's advisers, but he never came anywhere near fulfilling his instructions. Between 6 April and 20 May he 'took up' £45,000 Flemish on eight separate bonds, each for one year at 13 per cent,[38] and the whole of that sum was expended on the German mercenaries, and on repaying the outstanding debt to the merchant adventurers. This latter obligation, which seems to have been transferred to Gresham as a matter of convenience, amounted to £33,705 Flemish (including 'the queen's reward') and was repaid in two instalments on 20 June and 1 July.[39] Altogether during the period of his third Marian account, from 17 March to 17 November 1558, Gresham received £67,842 Flemish, including £9921 from Brigham out of the exchequer. He spent the entire sum in Antwerp, laying out £10,754 on arms and munitions in addition to the expenditure already noticed, but did not have to redeem any of his own bonds because of the shortness of the time.[40] During May he busied himself with plans to export specie to England, announcing on the 1st that he was going to Brussels to get the king's licence for £100,000, and on the 15th that he would try for £200,000.[41] At this stage he must still have been intending to fulfil his original instructions, believing that his main task was to inject a large sum of cash into the mint. Philip was cautious, but reasonably co-operative. By 23 May he had granted an initial licence for 100,000 crowns (£25,000 sterling), explaining that he could not do more for the moment 'because of the scarcity'.[42] Six days later, however, he raised the limit to 300,000 crowns; a lot less than the 800,000 which Gresham had requested, but substantially more than he actually had in hand.[43] At that point, on 1 June, the council changed its mind, telling him not to take up any more money for the time being, and, instead of shipping what he had to England, to pay it to the merchant adventurers in Antwerp.[44] At some time towards the end of July he seems to have returned to England, probably for consultations, since his commission was not terminated and he was not called upon to render account. He remained in England until 1 October, when he was sent back to Flanders with fresh instructions to take up £100,000 at 14 per cent or less.[45]

When Gresham accounted for this period of his activity, which he did in December by order of Elizabeth, he declared that the principal owing in Antwerp on Mary's death had been almost £58,000. This sum, together with the interest and brokerage, formed the £65,000 debt which he subsequently reported that the queen had inherited from her sister.[46] This was technically correct, but rather less than the whole truth, because although in theory his account ran to 17 November, he did not in fact include any of the transactions which he had entered into after 1 October in accordance with his new instructions. Between 21 October and 15 November he entered into seven separate bonds for a total of £32,346, which, as he explained in his account of 1562, were

. . . not charged in his last account because no bandes were granted out for the same in the late Queens time . . .[47]

The reason for this was bizarre, as Boxall confessed to his successor, Sir William Cecil, in the course of handing over the queen's business.[48] In spite of the fact that she had commissioned a stamp, Mary apparently continued to sign documents with her own hand until the day of her death, and several 'packs' of such papers relating to Gresham's affairs were in her bedchamber, unsigned, when she died, '. . . and at the cering of the corse (as Clarentius sayth) converted to that use . . .' Fortunately for Gresham, Elizabeth subsequently issued her own bonds to cover the obligations which he had accepted on Mary's behalf. The true level of the Antwerp debt when Mary died, taking account of interest at 13 or 14 per cent, was therefore a little over £100,000 Flemish – about £92,000 sterling. This was not enormous, considering the demands of the war, but it was a great deal more than the debt which she had inherited despite the heroic efforts which had been made in the meantime, and all of it had been acquired over a period of seven months.

Although inevitably war dominated the crown's finances in the latter part of the reign, ordinary obligations had to be met as well, and ordinary revenues collected. This was a period which saw the partial rehabilitation of a number of those who had suffered for-feiture and disgrace earlier in the reign. Ambrose and Robert Dudley were restored in blood by statute[49] (Henry having been killed at St Quentin) and both received annuities and modest grants of land from such of their former properties as were still available. William Parr, the former marquis of Northampton, was given lands to the annual value of £157 'in augmentation of his living' – a mercy of which he was much in need.[50] Perhaps even more impor-tant, his numerous debts to the crown were forgiven. Sir Peter Carew, Thomas Culpepper, Walter Mantell, Cuthbert Vaughn, and a number of others received grants and restorations. Nearly all these were individually small, between £10 and £150, and new rewards for loyal service tended to be upon the same scale. For instance, Thomas White, one of those who had been instrumental in breaking up the Dudley conspiracy, received lands to the value of £27 7s. 1d.;[51] the grooms and pages of the privy chamber were given £100 between them 'by way of reward' in October 1558;[52] and the fees of all the justices, barons of the exchequer, and serjeants at law were augmented by about 25 per cent. The major recipients of royal generosity were few, and were all noblemen or ecclesiastical institu-tions. On 8 March 1558 the order of St John of Jerusalem was resurrected in Ireland under the name of St John of Kilmainham, and its prior, Sir Oliver Massingberd, granted lands to the annual value of £426.[53] On 2 April following, the order was restored in England under its own name, and the prior, Sir Thomas Tresham, was granted an estate of £1436 per annum.[54] The earl of Worcester was forgiven debts to the substantial total of £1602 in consideration of his services;[55] and the earl of Westmorland received a further grant of lands to the value of £601, bringing his total gains for the reign to £1258 a year.[56] The greatest single act of politic generosity, however, took place on 16 August 1557 when lands and other revenues to an annual value of £3077 were conferred on Thomas Percy, the newly created earl of Northumberland, thus re-creating at a stroke the wealth and political influence of that great northern family.[57] Each of these major grants was a significant act of policy, and there is no reason to suppose that Mary was indulging in indiscriminate generosity. Indeed the bill for pensions and annuities paid out of the receipt of exchequer fell steadily: £3253 from Michaelmas 1556 to Easter 1557; £2585 from Easter to Michaelmas 1557; £2488 from Michaelmas 1557 to Easter 1558; and £2001 from Easter to Michaelmas 1558.[58] Ordinary expenditure was cut to the bone. The household cost no more than £36,208 from Michaelmas 1557 to Michaelmas 1558, the lowest for over a decade and less than Elizabeth ever achieved.[59] The wage bill for royal servants, which had crept up from £13,000 to £16,000 per half-year between 1554 and 1556, was pegged back to £14,000 by Easter 1557, and held at that level for the remainder of the reign. So severe was the pressure that Cardinal Pole '. . . of his own will delivered to the Queen for the better support of her great charges in the defence of the realm' £7000 out of the spiritual revenues which had just been returned to him[60] – a gesture which was contrary to the principles of both of them.

Unfortunately the operation of one of the major financial departments, the mint, is an imponderable factor in this last period of the reign, largely because Thomas Stanley, who was the senior working official from the dismissal of Egerton in December 1555 until 1571, never rendered formal accounts for his office.[61] As we have already seen, plans for coinage reform had been under consideration since the previous reign, and in June 1556, a privy council committee had been given the task of investigating ways and means. Rumours of devaluation towards the end of 1556 indicate that plans were making progress, but the growing fear of war, followed by the actual declaration, made the necessary 'crying down' an economic and political impossibility, so that when Philip consulted the council during his second stay in England about the feasibility of recoinage[62] he must have been told that it was out of the question. On 28 June and 5 August 1557 commissions were issued for the minting of fine gold and silver coin of the same sort as that produced earlier in the reign, although quite why a fresh minting should have been undertaken at that point is not clear.[63] It may have been a response to the sudden increase in the demand for specie to pay the sailors and garrison troops who were then being busily pressed and mustered. Almost certainly the decision to mint Spanish coin in England was connected with the plan to send an army to the continent. It was later believed, as we have seen, that £11,000 out the 'king's treasure' in England had been paid to these troops, and this is consistent with the minting of reales and double reales which is known to have taken place.[64] Presumably Philip brought across the 'prest' money to be minted in England at some time before his own, and the army's, departure in July. On 19 August the council instructed

Stanley to retain £9000 of the money minted from the king's bullion 'for the Queenes majesties use', but in the circumstances this is more likely to have been part of an exchange deal than an act of generosity on Philip's part.[65] In spite of the extreme pressures generated by the war, the disastrous expedient of further debasement was largely avoided, although no more fine coin was minted after August 1557. The exception to this rule was, as before, the production of exceptionally base coin for Ireland. No fewer than four commissions accelerated this reprehensible policy between May 1557 and April 1558, £22,900 in base English money being converted into £43,000 of Irish groats and shillings, at a profit (after the deduction of expenses) of about £19,000.[66]

In these circumstances it was inevitable that the problem of counterfeiting should continue, although there is no sign that it grew any worse, and no clear evidence that the surviving French 'mint' continued to be active. In January 1557 Wotton reported that one of the Dudley conspirators, James Chillester, had confessed to abstracting coining instruments from the Tower and concealing them near Oxford.[67] Chillester professed penitence, and claimed to be anxious lest his cache should be discovered and put to further ill-use, but since he declared his inability to direct anyone else to the spot and was not himself allowed to return, it is not known whether his fears were justified. Within England the council continued to keep a vigilant eye upon the arrest and prosecution of suspects. In August 1557 one Henry Beane was brought up for examination from Maidstone;[68] in December, Robert Hall of Ware in Hertfordshire was committed to the Tower after coining instruments were discovered in his house;[69] and in June 1558 an operation of some importance was uncovered when a certain Thomas Knyveton was caught trying to pass 99 counterfeit groats. Knyveton was examined and confessed 'naming divers other lewd persons' who were to be apprehended and proceeded against.[70] In November 1558 another gang of coiners were transferred from the Tower to king's bench, but with what result is not known.[71] The impression given is of a routine police operation, in which the council worked with the full co-operation of the local magistrates against a large number of small operators. The danger of large-scale importations of counterfeit coin had disappeared with the virtual embargo on French trade.

On the outbreak of war Mary had warned her subjects 'henceforth to forbear all traffic and contracting with any of that realm',[72] and although this injunction had not been strictly heeded, the volume of traffic had nevertheless greatly diminished. The real problem was created by French wine, a staple item for which there was no obvious alternative source, and as the financial situation got worse in the spring of 1558, the council decided to turn this to advantage. Parliament had refused to place a statutory prohibition on the trade, and the proclamation of 30 March, while ostensibly intended to supply that deficiency, also provided for the possibility of royal licences.[73] How much the licences themselves cost is not specified, but on 17 April the council ordered that those possessing them should pay an extra impost of 26*s.* 8*d.* a tun over and above the ordinary custom.[74] At the same time similar licences to import other French goods were clearly envisaged, since the same order declared that all 'dry wares' coming from France should be assessed by commissioners acting for the purpose. Later in the summer this latter provision was superseded, when it was ordered on 3 July that those possessing licences for French 'dry goods' should simply pay the new custom,[75] although whether this ruling was adhered to seems rather uncertain. Writing many years later William Hakewill declared that Mary had levied what he described as 'impositions' upon all French commodities whatsoever; that these had been levied at first by Elizabeth also, 'but ere the [first] year ended they were all taken away'.[76] Hakewill is not necessarily a reliable witness, but his statement is consistent with the fact that there was a sharp decline in the yield of the customs after 1 Elizabeth, when it reached a peak of over £80,000. These imposts were not popular, and no doubt attempts at evasion were frequent, so in the summer of 1558 the old expedient of encouraging informing for profit was tried again. On 30 June 1558 Roger Marten of London, haberdasher (probably the same man who had recently lent the queen money), was appointed 'to be an informer and prosecutor of all the acts and statutes made for the commodity and preservation of the commonwealth . . .', receiving 12*d.* in every pound obtained by his industry 'above the sums of money limited to the informer in any of the said acts'.[77] However, the impositions were not levied by statute, and when Marten or one of his agents laid an information against one Germaine Ciol for evading the extra duty on French wine, he was sharply rebuffed. In the exchequer chamber in the first year of Elizabeth it was ruled that Ciol's licence of 1 and 2 Philip and Mary to import a certain number of tunnes within a given time remained valid, because the only condition imposed by the licence had been the payment of the old duties, and because it had contained the provision 'any restraint then made, or afterwards to be made, to the contrary notwithstanding'.[78] Only a statute could have overruled such an exemption, and Ciol was not bound to pay an imposition levied by the prerogative alone.

The legal standing, not merely of the special imposts on French goods but of the whole new book of rates, was tested almost at once. This book, which has been frequently described as the most constructive achievement of Mary's financial policy, was introduced on 28 May 1558,[79] after a debate which must have gone on for at least a decade. It was designed not merely to make the existing *ad valorem* rates more realistic after a period of rapid inflation but also to introduce a new specific duty on cloth. Since it raised the existing rates by over 100 per cent on average, there is some justification for describing it as 'revolutionary' on that ground alone, but it also established two important principles. One of these was that customs rates were determined by the crown alone, and not by a process of 'agreement' with the merchants, which had been tacitly assumed in previous books and had formed a major obstacle to revision.[80] The second was the right of the crown to impose new export duties without the consent of parliament.

> Memorandum [ran the entry in Dyer's *Novels Cases*] que nuper en le temps del Roigne Mary, un novell Impost ou Imposicion suit myse sur drapes, come un Custome, plus que launcient custome graunt per Parlyament . . . Et ore les Marchants de London trouont graund grief et font exclamation et suit al Roygne destre unburthened de cest impost, pur ceo que ne suit graunt per Parliament, mes assesse per la Roigne Mary de son absolute power . . .[81]

As a result of this outcry the judges were consulted and gave it as their opinion that, since the queen had the right to prohibit the departure of her subjects from the realm without licence, she also had the right to prohibit the departure of their goods. In support of this they quoted Fitzherbert, *de Securitate inveniendo ne exeat Regnum*, and the statute of 5 Richard II which decreed the forfeiture of moveable property for unlicensed departure from the realm.[82] Since the queen was entitled to prohibit the export of her subjects' goods, she was also entitled to charge, *mere moto sua*, whatever she liked for the privilege. The logic of this opinion did not extend to import duties, but the crown's right to levy those was well established, and the right to raise existing rates was not specifically challenged. Mary's relationship with the merchant adventurers was further strained, which may help to explain the recourse to Antwerp, but in the summer of 1558 the English council was their main protection against a powerful resurgence of Hanseatic demands, backed by the king, and they could not afford to express their resentment effectively by withholding all further financial help from the crown. The new book of rates did not solve all problems; the council was still worrying about losses on the wool custom in July 1558,[83] and resentment made evasions even more determined than before; but it did add about £50,000 a year to the ordinary revenue, which was

417

potentially a more valuable asset than any number of extraordinary grants or loans.

Had such a change been made in the first or second year of the reign the ordinary account would almost certainly have shown a surplus substantial enough to have avoided the accumulation of excessive debts in Antwerp, with the consequent problems which they created. In the event, Mary probably benefited from the reforms to the extent of no more than £25,000 or £30,000, which made little difference to the debts which she bequeathed to her successor on 17 November. Through being introduced in the midst of an expensive war, the benefits of the new book of rates were concealed, and a change which could have transformed the peacetime budget was no more than a palliative as long as the war lasted. Because Mary died *in media re* it is not easy to be certain exactly how large her debts were at that arbitrarily selected date. In June one anonymous official had calculated that the lay and clerical subsidies, together with the profits of the land sales, would support the expenses of war at their current rate for less than six months.[84] In the same memorandum he noted that the 'debts owing by their Majesties' at that date stood at £204,000.[85] That total included £57,000 in Flanders, which, as we have seen, is roughly consistent with Gresham's own figures, bearing in mind that this estimate is in sterling. It also included £18,000 in the city of London, a total which had risen to £20,000 by November, and would amount to about £22,500 with interest; and £20,000 payable to the merchant adventurers at Michaelmas. Various notes clarify some of the assumptions upon which these figures are based. The winter charges of the garrisons by land and sea are not projected, nor is the coat and conduct money which will have to be paid, because no estimate is possible. The debts and revenues due to the crown are set off against the ordinary charges; Ireland 'is full paid until michaelmas next'; and the fifteenth, due in November, is 'not comprehended in this book but left towards the winter charges'. As an estimate, therefore, the memorandum is very approximate, but accurate enough where it can be checked to form a basis for calculation. Its main ingredient, £109,000 on the privy seal loans due at Christmas, is a well-established figure.

By the time Mary died at least £32,000 had been added to the foreign debt, and it is by no means certain that the £20,000 payable to the merchant adventurers had actually been handed over. It does not appear among the payments made by warrant between Michaelmas 1558 and Easter 1559. Moreover, when Gresham wrote to Cecil on 1 March 1559, urging the queen to 'use her Merchant Adventurers', he admitted that they would 'stand very stout', not only because of the new custom, but also because of the £20,000 which she already owed them.[86] It is, of course, possible that this had been borrowed since her accession, but the implication of Gresham's letter is that it was an old debt which had reached the stage of being a grievance. There is unfortunately no summary of debts compiled in the early months of Elizabeth's reign, and the earliest relevant lists are of uncertain date, probably no earlier than October 1559.[87] Consequently it is impossible to be certain what, if anything, Mary owed on her ordinary accounts to compare with, say, the £21,000 household debt which she had inherited, or what the exact state of the accounts in Berwick or the ordnance office was on the day upon which she was alive and dead. It seems certain that there were such debts. One survey conducted in the first year of Elizabeth revealed that some household servants and yeomen of the guard were owed as much as six years arrears of pay, in several cases going back into Edward VI's reign.[88] £9000 'old debt of the household' in the names of Ryder and Weldon – again going back to Edward VI's reign – was still on the books, and several of the other sums listed seem rather heavy for a new reign less than twelve months old. If a very conservative estimate of £20,000 is made for the 'ordinary' debts,[89] and no account at all is taken of the position in specific military departments, then the total debt bequeathed by Mary to her sister was approximately £260,500. In all probability the true figure was nearer £300,000.[90] When he calculated Mary's legacy of debt as 'well short of £200,000', F. C. Dietz was counting only those Antwerp debts which had been sealed before 1 October 1558, and ignored altogether the £109,000 due for repayment at Christmas. On the other hand, he included, as he realized, an indeterminate number of those sums listed in the 1559 summaries which belonged to the new reign.[91] For that reason he did not venture upon a more specific estimate, but the approximation which he did risk is too low by the factor of 50 per cent.

It could be argued that this figure was artificially inflated by the unfortunate timing of Mary's death, and that had she lived a few more weeks, a fresh parliamentary subsidy would have repaid the privy seal loan, and at least a proportion of the other debts. Such an argument would have some substance, but the subsidy had not been voted and there can be no certainty that it would have been provided quickly enough to prevent a further escalation of the Antwerp debt. Moreover, the costs of the war were far outrunning the crown's resources, in spite of the subsidy and the new customs. Between the Easter Term 1557 and the Hilary Term 1558 – one full year – the income accounted in the exchequer reached £211,868 and the total income approximately £237,000.[92] The expenditure recorded through the exchequer in the same period amounted to

£345,842 – a deficit well in excess of £100,000 on a single year. In the half-year following, from Easter to Michaelmas 1558 – a period which saw the collection of over £145,000 in direct taxation in addition to the extra customs revenue – income must have exceeded £200,000. But expenditure soared to £267,617 during the same period,[93] so that a further substantial deficit is likely. In the absence of any formal accounts from the mint, and consequent uncertainty about exactly how that important department was being used, the picture can be only tentative, but a reasonably accurate outline can be reconstructed. Mary's government started the war with no foreign debt, but with domestic liabilities, including those to the staplers and the merchant adventurers, and the £42,000 on the privy seals of 1556, probably somewhat in excess of £100,000 and perhaps as much as £150,000. During the eighteen months between the outbreak of war and the queen's death a further debt of at least £150,000 was accumulated, including a new Antwerp debt of over £90,000.

Far from forming an indictment for extravagance and mismanagement, these figures are a tribute to the skill and persistence of Mary's financial advisers. To have inherited a debt of £185,000, endured a year and a half of warfare, and handed on a debt of no more than £300,000 represented a considerable achievement. This was especially so in view of the fact that the policies of the first year had resulted in a substantial increase of overall indebtedness, and particularly in the foreign debt. Two years of strenuous effort, from the spring of 1555 to the spring of 1557, shifted the pattern of debt, made it much more difficult to trace, and probably reduced it substantially. A subsidy, the sale of crown lands, and the co-operation of the merchant adventurers were the main contributory factors in this success, although strict control of administration and expenditure also helped. However, a prolonged period of similar effort would have been required to eliminate debts and to give the queen any real freedom from the pressures of chronic poverty. In these circumstances the anger and frustration of many councillors over what they saw as the totally unnecessary outbreak of war in June 1557 is fully comprehensible. The war was waged as cheaply as possible. Wherever possible the cost was shifted on to the king, and the £15,000 or so needed to keep Calais upon a war footing for a year may well have been a disincentive to its recovery. Relations with Philip deteriorated sharply under the pressure of these priorities as the English refused all aggressive initiatives and insisted upon paying their political debts to their own merchants. A political price was charged for the relative modesty of the war debts, but it was never paid because of Mary's death, and must remain an

imponderable factor. Nevertheless, it was for political, not administrative or economic, reasons that the queen left her realm far more
deeply in debt than she had found it, and they were reasons for
which the queen herself must bear a large share of the responsibility.

After Mary's death Philip meticulously took stock of his financial
liabilities in England.[94] Feria had warned him early in 1558 that
there were murmurings about his pensions being in arrears, and
estimated that 9000 ducats would put the matter right.[95] An investigation was carried out and it was discovered that the English
pensioners were owed £8814.[96] Since these men included all the
most influential ministers and courtiers, as well as the king's English
household and guard, this situation did not strengthen Philip's position in England. No attempt was made to discharge any of these
arrears, and when the final accounts were made up between
December 1558 and March 1559, the total bill amounted to rather
more than £11,000. It is not surprising that Feria believed influential courtiers to be behind the criticisms of Philip which were on
everybody's lips.

> The people are wagging their tongues a good deal about the late
> Queen having sent great sums of money to your Majesty [he
> wrote in 21 November 1558] and that I have sent 200,000 ducats
> since I have been here. They say it is through your Majesty that
> the country is in such want and that Calais was lost, and also that
> through your not coming to see the Queen our lady, she died of
> sorrow . . .[97]

The king was as good a scapegoat in November 1558 as the duke
of Northumberland had been in August 1553, and his relations with
the English people ended on as sour a note as they had begun.
However, since the outbreak of war he had made no attempt to
counteract his unpopularity, as the total neglect of his English
pensioners and servants indicates; and if Feria was indignant to
discover that the English courtiers were '. . . all as ungrateful to
your Majesty as if they had never received anything from your
hands', they could reasonably have responded that they had not
received anything for a considerable time, and that gratitude is a
perishable commodity. Eventually, far too late to repair his own
fences, in April 1559 Philip discharged his obligations in full,
through Feria by means of remittances drawn on Lope de Gallo.[98]

For sound diplomatic reasons Elizabeth had not pressed the
matter of the pensions; nor did she make any difficulties about the
jewels and Garter robes, both his own and his father's, which Philip
had left in England. These, for which Philip's own carefully annotated inventory survives at Simancas,[99] were handed over to Feria

421

in accordance with his instructions. Elizabeth's ministers were not allowed to blame the erstwhile king for the parlous financial condition of the government. But they were allowed to blame Mary, and did so both directly and by implication. A lengthy memorandum listed all the property which she had restored, with particular emphasis upon that which had been devoted to religious purposes – the subject of a special investigation headed by Lord Rich.[100] A further commission was specifically directed 'To consider in what points the realm hath sustained great loss during the late Queenes reign', and other similar bodies were set up to investigate debts, revenues, customs, the mint, the wardrobe, and the household.[101] A special committee was even appointed to make sure that Mary's ladies of the bedchamber did not abscond with the queen's jewels! There is exactly the same air of righteous indignation about these memoranda as had marked the early pronouncements of Mary's council, yet the element of continuity in financial office was just as high as it had been five years before. Winchester, Peckham, Mildmay, Baker, Stanley, and Gresham all continued to serve the new queen, although this time their tasks were complicated by the fact that the country continued to be at war. This involved only limited commitments after March 1559, but still kept expenditure well above a peacetime level until 1563. Like her sister, Elizabeth immediately resorted to Antwerp. By July 1559 she owed £133,680 on the Bourse, and by April 1560, £279,565.[102] When he rendered his next account in 1562, Gresham had handled almost £700,000 since the beginning of the reign, in transactions which had cost the exchequer £127,000 Flemish.[103] The domestic debt correspondingly fell; from about £200,000 in November 1558 to £110,000 by the following October, and about £69,000 by the spring of 1560. After that, thanks to the ending of the war, the recoinage, the new customs, and a subsidy with two fifteenths and tenths in February 1559, to say nothing of the resumption of ecclesiastical property and spiritual revenues, the situation was gradually brought under control. Elizabeth's financial advisers were no more astute or efficient than Mary's had been – indeed, as we have seen, they were mostly the same men – but they were serving a mistress who largely shared their priorities. That is to say, she put her own and her country's interests first, and took her financial limitations very seriously indeed. Apart from the recoinage of 1561 the first few years of the reign showed no new initiatives, and no augmentation of the ordinary revenues to compare with the 1558 book of rates. In so far as Elizabeth's financial management was successful (and that is a very large question which I do not propose to enter), it was so because she gave England a prolonged period of peace. The Tudor revenue system could not cope with the expensiveness of contemporary warfare, and no proper method was ever found of harnessing the wealth of the country to the needs of the government. The latter part of Mary's reign was a period of economic hardship which had nothing to do with the queen or her policies (although some protestants thought differently), but Feria was basically right when he complained '. . . there are neither funds nor soldiers, nor heads, nor forces, and yet it is overflowing with every other necessity of life'.[104] Mary left her realm much more heavily in debt than she had entered it, not because of incompetence or gross extravagance, and only marginally because of her policy of ecclesiastical restoration. She had found herself in a position where the imperative demands of her husband had conflicted with the urgent needs of her own country, and she had yielded them the priority, not reluctantly but because it seemed to her the obvious thing to do.

Notes

1 *Cal. Pat.*, III, 314-15. Surian to the doge and senate, 17 May 1557; *Cal. Ven.*, VI, 1095-6.
2 PRO E404/241, f. 110.
3 PRO E405/484.
4 BL Stowe MS 571 f. 77. See also above, 373.
5 PRO SP11/11/48. Circular letter to the commissioners.
6 ibid.; also SP11/11/44, instructions for the commissioners.
7 ibid.
8 SP11/11/50. Queen's instructions to Richard Wilbram.
9 *APC*, VI, 180-1.
10 ibid., 190, 198. He was bound in recognizance for £40 to pay the £20 for which he was assessed.
11 PRO SP11/13/36. 2 July 1558. Defaulters had slowed down the operation, delaying the final account. On 12 December and again on 15 January the council wrote to the collectors to expedite the payment of arrears. SP11/11/63, 12/21.
12 This sum includes a certain amount, not accounted specifically, which had been assigned directly from the collectors for particular purposes. 2000 men who had been raised in Norfolk and Suffolk were paid off by this means in February 1558. SP11/12/39.
13 E405/241, f. 135. BL Lansdowne MS 4 f. 9.
14 *Cal. Pat.*, IV, 73.
15 See above, 196-7.
16 PRO E351/22.
17 E405/484.
18 *CJ*, I, 47. SP11/12/31. 'Statement of the order used in granting the subsidy', 24 January 1558.
19 SP11/12/31.
20 *CJ*, I, 48.
21 The memorandum concluded by observing that the French were now so odious to the Commons that all Frenchmen would be expelled from

the realm. As we have already seen, a bill for that purpose failed narrowly on 18 February. See above, 387.

22 *CJ*, I, 49.

23 4 and 5 Philip and Mary, c. 10. BL Lansdowne MS 4 f. 10.

24 PRO SP11/12/21. Draft of a letter appointing commissioners. ibid., 50; queen to the lord privy seal, bishop of Ely, and others, 14 March 1558.

25 SP11/12/36. Their good conduct was contrasted with that of others (unnamed) 'whom the estate of the realme doth touch as nere'.

26 SP11/12/52.

27 ibid., 61. GLRO Repertories of the Court of Aldermen, 14/20. 29. March 1558.

28 SP11/14/Docquet, 10 Nov. These lands had already, on 4 May, been placed in the hands of Sir William Gerrard, appointed by the city 'to the use of them who have loaned'. Repertories, 14/28.

29 SP69/11/704. Gresham was also engaged at this time in buying armaments and obtaining export licences for them from Philip, a constant preoccupation throughout the period of the war.

30 SP69/12/733. From the fact that his 'diets' were authorized afresh at this time, it appears that there may have been a gap in his commission.

31 *Cal. Span.*, XIII, 369; Hughes and Larkin, II, 86-8. Winchester had been involved in a sharp quarrel with Sir John Baker, probably in the Michaelmas Term 1557. This quarrel was to erupt into exchequer chamber in Michaelmas 1558, and may well have reflected far-reaching disagreements over policy between these senior financial advisers. BL Lansdowne MS 106/3 ff. 7-15. I am indebted to Mr Christopher Coleman for drawing my attention to this point.

32 SP11/13/4. Since Brigham was also authorized to pay money by warrant under the privy seal, and continued to act as a teller of the exchequer, it is not clear whether his accounts passed through the normal exchequer machinery or not. Since he appears on the tellers' roll as receiving £167,783 in 4 and 5 Philip and Mary, nearly three times as much as any other teller, and never rendered any separate account, it seems that he discharged this function within the exchequer.

33 BL Cotton MS Titus B II f. 59. Burnet, op. cit., II, 324-5. See also above, 378-9.

34 PRO E101/64/1. 'A declaration of all sums paid by warrant out of the Receipt of the Exchequer to Benjamin Gonson, treasurer of the navy, between 11 January 3 and 4 Philip and Mary, and 9 November 5 and 6 Philip and Mary'.

35 E405/484.

36 SP11/13/28 (i).

37 E351/23. Gresham's account from 17 March to 17 November 1558.

38 ibid.

39 ibid.

40 The first bond to fall due for repayment, a six-month loan at 7 per cent, did not mature until 30 November. ibid.

41 SP69/12/758, 771.

42 ibid., 775.

43 ibid., 779. Gresham complained that he was having difficulty in raising money, but this must have been because of the general tightness of the supply. The pound sterling stood at about 21 shillings Flemish at this point, and was reasonably stable. E351/23.

44 SP69/13/785.

45 He was authorized to return towards the end of June. ibid., 801. Gresham himself had become sceptical about the advantages of further borrowing at this point, but did not, apparently, prevail upon the council. ibid., 833.

46 *Cal. For.*, Elizabeth, II, 569 (ii), 15 April 1560.

47 E351/26. Gresham's account of 1562.

48 Boxall to Cecil, 19 November 1558. SP12/1/5.

49 Statute 4 and 5 Philip and Mary, c. 12.

50 *Cal. Pat.*, IV, 376, 382. Parr was presumably deemed harmless by this time, since he had not been packed off to St Quentin.

51 *Cal. Pat.*, III, 485.

52 SP11/14/Doc, 29 October 1558.

53 *Cal. Pat.*, III, 43. SP12/1/64.

54 *Cal. Pat.*, IV, 313. SP12/1/64.

55 *Cal. Pat.*, IV, 432. 6 September 1558.

56 *Cal. Pat.*, IV, 37-40. 6 February 1558. SP12/1/64.

57 *Cal. Pat.*, IV, 180. 16 August 1557. SP12/1/64. See also above, 98.

58 E405/484. It rose again to £2414 in the first half-year of Elizabeth.

59 E351/1795. See also above, 310. At this time the bulk of the household charges were met by means of standing warrants: £12,000 *p.a.* from wards and liveries; £10,000 from duchy of Lancaster; and £8000 from the exchequer. SP11/14/Doc. It is possible that part of this economy was achieved by allowing wages, etc., to fall into arrears. See below, 419 and n.

60 *Cal. Pat.*, IV, 399, 14 November 1558.

61 C. E. Challis, *The Tudor Coinage* (1978), 115.

62 ibid., 117.

63 *Cal. Pat.*, III, 369. ibid., IV, 194-5. Challis, op. cit., 117.

64 BL Stowe MS 571 f. 77. See above, 373. Challis, op. cit., 117.

65 *APC*, VI, 154. It is possible that Philip had kept a 'contingency reserve' at the English mint since October 1554. Machyn, Foxe, and the Tower chronicler all record the arrival of twenty waggonloads of Spanish bullion at the Tower on 2 October. Early in 1556 Dudley and his friends planned to steal a similar quantity of Spanish bullion (£50,000-worth) then in the custody of Nicholas Brigham. In neither case can the bullion referred to have been part of that borrowed by Gresham, and Philip may either have made a regular practice of having his bullion coined at the English mint, or simply have used the Tower of London as a secure and convenient store. Challis, op. cit., 113 n. *TTC*, 190-1.

66 *Cal. Pat.*, III, 369; 19 May 1557. ibid., IV, 74; 6 September 1557. ibid., 72; 28 February 1558. ibid., 12; 30 April 1558. Four more commissions were issued between December 1558 and June 1559, and thereafter the policy was discontinued.

67 Wotton to Petre, 13 January 1557. SP69/10/569.

68 *APC*, VI, 157.

69 ibid., 210, 212.

70 ibid., 328, 332.

71 ibid., 425.

72 Hughes and Larkin, II, 77-9. Proclamation announcing the outbreak of war.

73 ibid., 85-6.

74 *APC*, VI, 305. At the same time an extra impost of 10*s.* a tun on the export of beer was also imposed.

75 ibid., 337.
76 W. Hakewill, *The Libertie of the subject against the pretended power of Impositions (maintained by an argument in parliament in 7 Jac. I)* (London, 1641). Hakewill's brand of special pleading clearly involved condemning Mary as a tyrant, and exonerating Elizabeth from all blame.
77 *Cal. Pat.*, IV, 255.
78 Hakewill, op. cit., 96.
79 N. S. B. Gras, 'Tudor Books of Rates', *Quarterly Journal of Economics,* 26 (1912), 766 ff. T. S. Willan, *A Tudor Book of Rates* (1962). The date is derived from BL MS Lansdowne 3, 70. The book itself is BL Add. MS 25097.
80 Gras, art. cit.
81 Sir James Dyer, *Novels Cases* (London, 1585), 165. 'Determinatio Hillarii primo Elizabethae'.
82 ibid. 5 Richard II, st. 1, c. 2. The controversy over the proposed alteration to this law in Mary's fourth parliament would still have been fresh in mind. See above, 273 and *TTC*, 182. Hakewill later claimed (op. cit., 95) that no formal judgement was given in support of this imposition. This was correct in that what Dyer recorded was a majority opinion, but it was sufficient to prevent the issue being put to the courts, and thus sufficient to endorse the principle involved.
83 SP11/13/50, in which the author argued that the crown was losing £1 9s. 5d. 'in every sack shipped by strangers'.
84 SP11/13/28 (i).
85 SP11/13/28 (ii). The total given is £240,000, but the items add up to £204,000. These are formal debts, and do not include any deficits, actual or estimated.
86 *Cal. For.*, Elizabeth, I, 153.
87 SP12/6/58. BL Lansdowne MS 4 f. 182.
88 SP12/7/55.
89 The debts listed for the various 'civilian' departments in SP12/6/58, which is the earlier of the two lists, amount to £53,000. In Lansdowne 4, which is probably several months later, but in which the 'debts' are more clearly distinguished from the charges of the current year, the corresponding total is £22,000.
90 The debts listed for the 'military' departments in the documents quoted are £43,660 and £29,000 respectively, but in the constantly changing situation of war, it is very difficult to say what relation these figures bear to the sums which were actually owing on 17 November 1558. It is, however, reasonable to assume that there would have been 'working deficits' in at least some places, and with a military expenditure in excess of £350,000 a year arrears of £30-40,000 would have been neither excessive nor improbable.
91 F. C. Dietz, *English Public Finance, 1558–1641* (1932), 7 and n. 4. Rather surprisingly Dietz, who quoted Lansdowne 4 in several other connections, did not make use of it for this estimate.
92 PRO E405/241. The tellers' totals for 4 and 5 Philip and Mary (Michaelmas 1557 to Easter 1558 – which would have included some of the subsidy) show an exchequer income of £260,794.
93 PRO E405/484.
94 AGS, E811 ff. 119, 120, 121, 122, 124, 127, 128.
95 Feria to Philip, 2 February 1558. *Cal. Span.*, XIII, 349-51.
96 'What is owing to His Majesty's English pensioners in respect of the

last six months of last year, 1557, and in some cases for the whole year; and to the 100 archers for nine months . . . and to the Chamberlains and serving gentlemen and other servants for wages for one year . . .' March 1558. *Cal. Span.*, XIII, 373.

97 Feria to Philip, 21 November 1558. *Cal. Span.*, Elizabeth, I, 1-4.
98 AGS, E811 f. 127.
99 E811. *Cal. Span.*, XIII, 441-2.
100 SP12/1/57, 64.
101 SP12/1/57.
102 *Cal. For.*, Elizabeth, I, 401. 20 July 1559. ibid., II, 569 (2). 15 April 1560.
103 PRO E351/26.
104 *Cal. Span.*, Elizabeth, I, 1-4.

13 The English Church under Papal Disfavour

For almost a year and a half the poor, and constantly deteriorating, relationship between Pope Paul IV and the Habsburgs had had no appreciable effect upon Pole's work in England. His close personal friendship with Giovanni Morone, the vice-protector of England, had ensured him of an ally and a source of information in Rome, so that his affairs were promoted as swiftly and efficiently as was possible through the curial bureaucracy.[1] After September 1556, however, as we have seen, the situation grew progressively more tense and difficult. The kingdom of England was never at any time involved in war against the papacy, but Mary's known willingness to gratify her husband, and the mounting rumours of a break with France, fostered the seeds of suspicion in Paul's mind. Pole and Morone had both been members of that reforming group in Rome, which, twenty years before, had tried to steer the church in the direction of humanistic reform. Carafa, no less a reformer, had always been a man of a very different stamp and had suspected the orthodoxy of the cardinal of England, if not from their first meeting, then at least from that day in 1536 when they had both received the red hat.[2] By 1556 he was eighty and, as we have seen, consumed by a passionate hatred of Spain, a country which he denounced as being nothing but a nest of judaizers, infidels, and heretics. This hatred hardened his suspicions and closed his mind. In consistory on 9 April 1557, while the English council was still struggling with the issue of peace or war, Paul revoked all his legates and other ministers in Philip's dominions, mentioning Pole especially by name.[3] The reason for this distinction was not immediately apparent, and Paul was studiously friendly to Sir Edward Carne when he received him the next day. He readily agreed that England was a special case, and that the church there might be harmed by being included in this blanket condemnation.[4] He professed his willingness to discharge English business himself, but showed no sign of cancelling Pole's revocation. A week later Carne still did not know quite what to make of the situation. The pope's

428

decision had not been promulgated, and Morone was of the opinion that if Mary wrote a personal letter asking for the legateship to be continued, it would be well received.[5] However, in spite of his affability to Carne, whom he genuinely liked, Paul turned aside all the ambassador's protests, and it seems that Morone was mistaken. The most that the pope would concede was a stay of execution, which he granted on 15 May. By that time the news had already spread far and wide; not only the fact of the decision, but even its precise terms. By the time that he wrote his first anguished protest on 25 May, Pole himself, Mary, and the English privy council all knew that not only was Pole's special commission as legate *a latere* to be terminated, but that the see of Canterbury was also to be deprived of its legatine status.[6] This not only had the appearance of a studied insult, it would also create real problems for the government of the English church, which would revert to being two autonomous provinces if Canterbury lost the jurisdictional primacy which that title had conferred.[7]

The reaction from England was predictably distressed. On 21 May, Mary wrote in the name of herself and Philip, claiming that great damage would be done to the English church should it be left without a legate at such a critical moment. Moreover, they were entirely satisfied with the piety and diligence of Reginald Pole, and had no desire to see him replaced: '. . . magno dolore effecti sumus, quum litteris quibusdam et multorum sermonibus ad nos perlatum esset . . .'[8] It was doubly disturbing to receive such news in such a manner, and they trusted that the pope would reconsider his decision, if, indeed, he had made one. At about the same time the council also wrote, praising Pole and likening the realm to a convalescent invalid who faced the withdrawal of his physician.[9] Pole's own letter of 25 May conformed to the same pattern. His continued presence in England was needed and desired; he had not to his knowledge misconducted himself in any way, or offended the pope, and the needs of the English church ought to be allowed to take precedence over the unhappy dictates of war.[10] In spite of his insistence that what had been achieved in England was the work of the Holy Spirit, it was in some ways an inept letter, lecturing Paul upon the nature of his pontifical duty. Pole was inclined to such exercises, and in March had written a lengthy appeal to the pope to resolve his disputes with Philip for the good of christendom; an epistle which the recipient was still chewing over resentfully in May, as he revealed to the Venetian ambassador.[11] It was not coincidence that these three letters from England were all written within a week. Carne's despatches conveying the first news of what was afoot must have arrived before the end of April, since the pope had already received an initial reaction from Pole by 8 May. This seems to have been more of distress and bewilderment than indignation, his first thought being to withdraw to his archbishopric since he could no longer represent the pope at the English court.[12] However, by the 25th these scruples had been overcome, and he had closed ranks with his sovereigns to press for his own continuation in office. Probably Philip's presence in England at the time had a good deal to do with this concerted reaction, although he would naturally have concealed the fact as far as possible. The pope must have known from Carne's representations what to expect and had already made his next, dramatic move before the letters arrived. On 22 May one of Morone's servants was arrested by the Inquisition in his master's presence, and on the 31st Morone himself was confined in the castle of Sant' Angelo. The following day Paul announced publicly that the cause was suspected heresy, and Bernardo Navagero, the Venetian ambassador, was told as a great secret that Pole was also implicated.[13]

There is no obvious reason why the long-smouldering suspicion of the pope against Pole and Morone should have burst forth at this moment, except the political one. Paul regarded them both as Habsburg agents as well as heretics, and was particularly anxious to have as strong a reason as possible for refusing to allow Pole to continue in England. On 12 June, Navagero reported that the Inquisition was investigating him as a suspected Lutheran, and two days later the pope formally recalled him to Rome, although without for the moment explaining why.[14] At the same time, ostensibly out of deference to the queen's wishes and a fatherly regard for the well-being of the English church, he announced that he had decided to relax his general policy in favour of England, and appointed a new cardinal legate. The man to be so honoured was William Peto, an English Observant friar.[15] It is difficult to know in what spirit the pope made his decision. Peto had been a confessor to Catherine of Aragon, had espoused her cause, and had gone into exile as a result. He was personally known to Paul, having spent some time in Rome during his exile, and was undoubtedly a man of blameless life. However, in 1557 he was over eighty and in feeble health of body and mind. He had returned to England on Mary's accession, but feeling unequal to the exercise of any responsibility, had resigned the bishopric of Salisbury, to which he had been provided during his exile, but which he had never actually possessed. When the Observant house at Greenwich was restored, he had withdrawn there to spend his last days in prayer and meditation. If the pope did not know these things when nominating him to office, then he was guilty of gross negligence, and if he did know them, of irresponsibility. It is possible that Paul, who was over eighty himself, did not regard Peto's age as a handicap, but even the most perfunctory enquiry would have revealed his complete unsuitability on other grounds. Carne was stunned, and declared openly that he dared not communicate such tidings to his sovereigns.[16] However, either he or somebody else in Rome must have done so with great expedition, because by the time the nuncio bearing the pope's official letter, dated 20 June, reached Calais about 3 or 4 July, Mary had already decided to refuse him admittance to the realm.[17]

Such a course may have been dictated by Philip, but it is also possible that the queen needed no such prompting in this instance, so strong was her sense of outrage. Pole's reaction was more equivocal. He regarded his obedience to Rome as absolutely binding, and wished to satisfy his conscience, if possible without having to offend Mary. Consequently he asked that the nuncio should be admitted, so that his own position could be clarified. The queen refused, strongly backed by her council, and according to Strype, instructed the cardinal to carry on as though nothing had happened.[18] This Pole declined to do, knowing that his powers had been withdrawn, but he reluctantly obeyed the queen's command to remain in England, never having actually received his recall. Up to this point the pope had dissembled the real reason for this recall, calling Pole his 'most dear son' and talking vaguely about important consultations, but by the beginning of July, Carne had become sufficiently convinced of the true situation to send an explicit warning. If Pole returned to Rome, he wrote, he would probably join Morone in prison, the latter having now been examined four times without positive result.[19] It may have been the receipt of this warning which prompted Pole to send his confidential agent Ormanetto to plead his cause in Rome, which he did during July, because he must have realized that if he could not clear himself from such suspicion, then no attempts to continue his legateship could possibly succeed. When Mary wrote again to the pope on 26 July, however, she made no mention of charges or suspicions, merely repeating her basic request for Pole's office to be continued. Her letter was strongly worded. It was without precedent, she claimed, that a legate who had performed such distinguished services to the realm and the church should be recalled without cause. Should there be any disturbance to the present state of affairs in England, it would surely be on that account, although she would do all in her power to prevent such a development. She was confident that the pope would realize that she knew best about the affairs of her own kingdom, and would ultimately grant her request.[20] By the same messenger came a brief letter from William Peto, declining the proffered honours and responsibilities on the grounds of his age and in-capacity.[21]

By the middle of August the situation had reached deadlock. The pope had no intention of giving way, and although he had made no public charges against Pole, had made his suspicions abundantly clear. On the other hand, Mary's natural obstinacy was now fully engaged, convinced as she was that Paul's action sprang from poli-tical animus, and not from any concern for truth or the good of the church. In early August she sent fresh instructions to Carne as to how to react should actual charges of heresy be advanced against Pole. Since such charges were not brought, and the instructions consequently never implemented, we know about them only from a report of Navagero, who was not always quite accurate about Eng-lish affairs.[22] According to him Carne was instructed to say on the queen's behalf that should Pole be found guilty of heresy, she would be his greatest enemy, but unless or until proof of such a crime could be found, she would take him for a good and catholic man. Moreover, as an Englishman and archbishop of Canterbury, he must be tried in England as his predecessor (Cranmer) had been, although the final stage of his condemnation might be conducted in Rome.

> In conclusion [Navagero continued in cipher] should the Pope absolutely deny the demand made by the Queen, who considers it a fair one, her ambassador is to leave Rome, making first of all a protest, in public if possible, if not by going from house to house of all the Cardinals, and informing them that the Queen and Council, and the whole kingdom of England, will never swerve from their devotion, reverence and obedience to the See Apostolic and to his Holiness' successors, although for a certain period they are compelled not to obey Pope Paul IV . . .

Such instructions are quite consistent with Mary's known determina-tion not to allow Pole to leave England, and to defy the pope over Peto's appointment without in any general sense withdrawing obedience from the holy see. Understandably there were rumours in Rome that England would again go into schism,[23] rumours which infuriated the pope but which had no noticeable effect upon his course of action.

The effect of this situation upon Pole himself was profoundly disturbing. He realized that the pope had moved the Inquisition in a concerted campaign against all the surviving *spirituali*, probably provoked thereto by the conviction that they were sympathetic to the Habsburgs, a conviction which was supported by neither justice nor probability. Towards the end of August he penned a lengthy

432

apologia, defending his record of loyalty and service to the church, and indignantly repudiating any sympathy with heretics. He could only appeal to God and accuse the pope of gross misuse of the *plenitudo potestatis*.[24] This document in its original form was never used, because Pole threw it on the fire in a characteristic fit of helplessness and despair. But a copy survived, and much of its substance was included piecemeal in the letters which he continued to send to Rome over the next twelve months. The tragic fact was that Paul's actions had destroyed the central support of Pole's faith and churchmanship. After an acute spiritual crisis he had accepted the fallibility of his own convictions and theological learning, and had come to see the authority of the church as the only sure and immovable foundation for true belief and the Christian life. To that authority the Roman obedience was absolutely essential, so that it occupied the highest priority, as we have seen, in his plans for the restoration of the faith in England.[25] Outside the church there could be no salvation, and amidst all the uncertainties of theological conflict which were still unresolved because the council of Trent had never completed its work, the church was defined by unquestioning obedience to the holy see. The pope, the vicar of Christ, should have been a man who by definition worked under the constant supervision of the Holy Spirit, a man whose integrity and zeal were beyond question or dispute. The trouble was, not that Paul was mistaken over the matter of Pole's orthodoxy, but that the latter was firmly and rightly convinced that, whatever he might profess, the pope's motives were unworthy and even dishonest. He was an obstinate and vindictive old man who cared more for the gratification of his own whims and ambitions than he did for his pastoral responsibilities. There was nothing new in the spectacle of an unworthy pope. Earlier generations had come, like Sir Thomas More, to draw a clear distinction between the prestige of the office and the reputation of its incumbent for the time being. Pole was perfectly capable of making the same distinction, and did so, but was nevertheless utterly depressed and discouraged by being forced into the position of having to withhold that very obedience which he had exalted as the heart and soul of the catholic church. For a man as wholeheartedly ultramontane as Pole had become, the situation at the end of August 1557 was completely impossible.

The conclusion of peace between Philip and the pope on 12 September brought some relief, but not as much as might have been expected. Bonfires were lit in London, and *Te Deum* sung, but in practice there was little to celebrate. Ormanetto had at long last succeeded in securing an audience with the pope, but he had achieved nothing, and Carne had been treated to another exhibition of procrastination when he pressed for an answer to the queen's letters.[26] The only benefit of the peace, and of sustained diplomatic pressure, was the restoration of legatine status to the see of Canterbury, a concession of some practical value for the government of the church, but no consolation to Pole. During October and November, Carne found it increasingly difficult to gain any access to the pope at all, despite the latter's frequent protestations of goodwill, and attributed this difficulty, no doubt rightly, to Paul's fear that he would continue to press the matter of Pole's legateship.[27] Meanwhile the resumption of formal relations with Philip had led to the commissioning of the pope's nephew, Cardinal Carlo Carafa, as legate to the court of Brussels, a mission which purported to be for the negotiation of a general peace. Navagero, however, who was familiar with the pope's methods, believed that it was mainly intended to exploit the settlement already reached in the interest of the Carafa family.[28] The recent imprisonment of certain notoriously anti-Habsburg officials in the *curia* indicated a bargain along those lines. At the same time the Inquisition produced formal charges against Morone, which suggested no possibility of a relaxation in the campaign against the *spirituali*. On 11 December, Carne wrote to say that he could still obtain no audience.[29] Without a legate, and with the vice-protector in prison on charges of heresy, English business was simply making no progress at all. Cases on appeal, like the matrimonial dispute between Tyrell and Chetwood which Carne was trying to get resolved, were subject to endless delays, which did nothing at all to convince the English of the merits of papal jurisdiction. At the same time the ambassador was afflicted with all sorts of tales. Peto was alleged to have intervened in one of the pending cases; and a certain 'great bishop' in England was reported to have written letters against Pole which had been intercepted in Venice.[30] The situation, he reported gloomily, was playing into the hands of the heretics, presenting them with numerous opportunities to create and exploit bitterness and misunderstandings.

In mid-December, Pole, desperate for vindication, appealed to Carlo Carafa in Brussels for his intercession.[31] Carafa had earlier encouraged Ormanetto to believe that he would be willing to undertake such a task, but he seems to have come north armed with a copy of the charges which were being prepared against the English cardinal, and certainly made no move on his behalf. Pole did not give up. In January he sent his auditor Francesco Stella to present his case to Carafa, and in March the same emissary undertook the thankless, and possibly dangerous, task of bearing a personal letter of self-justification to the pope.[32] It was all to no avail. By the end of 1557, if not earlier, Paul was convinced that Pole had been for years the mastermind behind a great conspiracy against the church, a conspiracy in which Morone, Priuli, Pate, Flaminio, Vittoria Colonna, and many others had been involved as his disciples and followers.[33] The list of accusations was extensive, but focused on the charge that Pole was Lutheran in his beliefs on justification.

> Idem Polus defendit et nititur probare doctrinam Lutheranam de Justificatione esse veram, et improbat Theologiam Scholasticam, et persuadet purum et simplex evangelium esse praedicandum.[34]

In this light his whole career was given a sinister twist. He had left the council of Trent rather than accept the decree on justification; his life at Viterbo had been devoted to the fostering and protection of heresy; and the circle of scholars and reformers who had gathered round him there became 'that accursed school, and that apostate household, of the Cardinal of England'.[35] Ironically, the struggle which Pole had won at such cost to himself was deemed to have been lost, and the worst construction put upon his theological silence. Because he was never formally arraigned, and was never likely to be after the summer of 1557, it is probable that Pole never discovered the details of the charges against him, but he must have known their substance. The vehemence of his protestations came partly from an awareness of how close he was, or had been, to being guilty. The brief remainder of his life was overshadowed by these charges and by the responses which they awakened in his own conscience. The main substance of his defence was his record of service to the church, and obedience to the holy see. He denied ever consenting to heretical ideas, but argued that, even if he had, his recent labours in England and lifelong devotion to the cause of papal authority ought to outweigh any such lapses.[36] Pole died unreconciled and uncondemned, and the Inquisition made to attempt to pursue him beyond the grave, thus affording him an ambiguous form of vindication. Morone was released and rehabilitated after Paul IV's death in 1559, to do further invaluable work at the later sessions of the council of Trent. The remainder of Pole's associates and fellow suspects suffered various fates. Priuli died on his way back from England to Italy in 1559, and there is no knowing whether he would have faced charges if he had arrived. Pate, after a period of imprisonment in England, died as a catholic exile at Louvain in 1565. Carnesecchi was executed for heresy in 1567, and Rullo died in the prisons of the Inquisition in the same year.[37]

By the spring of 1558 Paul IV had accepted, with a bad grace, that he was not going to get his own way over the English mission without resorting to further sanctions. In March, Peto died, and no attempt was made to appoint a further legate. For the last six months of the reign Edward Carne was the only direct link between England and Rome, and he continued to find it extremely difficult to discharge business. This was not only on account of the pope's chagrin at being unable to extradite Pole. For almost three months between April and June 1558 he spent the majority of his waking hours in the company of 'certain hermits' at Belvedere, and could be persuaded neither to undertake his normal duties himself, nor to delegate them to someone else. On 7 June, Carne reported that 'there has been neither Consistory nor signature for more than three months'.[38] Everything was at a standstill. 'The Duke of Norfolk's dispensation [to marry Margaret Lady Dudley] is as nigh now as it was at the beginning'; and Thomas Wilson, Chetwood's solicitor, recalled to England by letters under the privy seal, showed no sign of obeying the summons, a 'contempt' which Carne felt particularly galling.[39] Episcopal vacancies of a year or more had become common by 1557, and there was no improvement in that situation. Winchester had been vacant from November 1555 to the autumn of 1556; Chichester from August 1556 to November 1557; Lincoln from late 1556 to August 1557; Peterborough from February 1556 to August 1557; and Carlisle for a similar period.[40] John Salcot, bishop of Salisbury, died on 6 October 1557, Robert King of Oxford on 4 December 1557, and William Glynne of Bangor on 21 May 1558. All three sees remained vacant until the queen's own death. When the news of the almost simultaneous decease of Mary and Pole reached Rome in late November, the pope's regret was purely formal, and he hardly bothered to conceal his gratification. Both the heretical cardinal and the obstinate woman over whom he had exercised such influence had gone, and first reports spoke favourably of the new queen's support for the faith.[41] Within three months he was to be bitterly disillusioned, but in December 1558 Paul IV was convinced that Elizabeth was a great improvement on her sister – a sad epitaph on the efforts and aspirations of the previous five years.

Despondent, and afflicted with repeated illness, Pole had laboured on dutifully during the last year of his life, but naturally his leadership had been rather less than inspiring in face of the mounting afflictions of war, taxation, and dearth. 'The Cardinal is a dead man', wrote Feria on 10 March 1558, referring not so much to his health as to his general lack of animation. 'I have been able to warm him up a little by talking to him every day . . . [but] the result is not all I could wish'. Only such good news as could still be gleaned of his friends in Italy seemed to offer him any comfort.[42] Feria's judgement was cool and uncharitable. He had no sympathy with Pole's methodical and structural approach to restoring the faith, and was campaigning actively in support of a Jesuit presence in England. This was tricky ground, not only on account of the hostility of Mary and Pole, but because the standing of the Jesuits in Philip's own dominions was uncertain. Supported warmly by Ruy Gómez and his friends, they had been opposed fiercely by Juan Siliceo, the archbishop of Toledo, until his death in 1557, and after that by Fray Melchor Cano.[43] The king's attitude at this time was equivocal, because although he undoubtedly appreciated their zeal and orthodoxy, the special relationship which existed between the order and the pope inevitably made them suspect. The war which had ended in September 1557 had made the election of a new general impossible for many months after the death of Ignatius Loyola in 1556, and at the time when Feria wrote, the order was still without a leader. Pedro Ribadeneyra, Feria's correspondent, was maintaining a Jesuit presence in the court at Brussels, but neither he nor anyone else was able to persuade Philip to bring pressure to bear in support of the order's admission to England.[44] Pole distrusted Jesuit theology, particularly after his experience of it at Trent, and Feria's conviction that he was doing rather less than he might to revitalize the faith in England had some justification, as we have seen. 'The Cardinal is a good man', he wrote, 'but very lukewarm; and I do not believe that the lukewarm go to paradise, even if they are called moderates'.[45]

The bitter experience, first of the pope's suspicion and then of his open hostility, had not made Pole lukewarm in his attitude towards the church, but it had made him more distrustful than ever of theology, with its constant opportunities for dogmatism and dispute. Towards the end of his life he retreated more and more into formalism. 'But this I dare saye', he declared in one of his rare sermons, preached in London, 'whereunto Scrypture alsoe doth agree, that the observatyon of ceremoneyes for obedyence sake, wyll gyve more light than all the readyng of Scrypture can doo . . .'[46] Nicholas Manuel's *Totenfresser* had been published over thirty years before, but it might have been aimed directly at Pole:

> Be quiet about the gospel
> And preach only papal law.
> We will then be lords and the laity servants
> Who bear the burdens we lay upon them.
> All is lost however
> If the gospel gets out
> And things are measured by it.
> For it teaches none to give and sacrifice to us –
> Only that we should lead simple, impoverished lives.[47]

The whole tenor of Pole's administration, with its emphasis upon the honour and obedience due to the clergy, and its care to restore some measure of their material support, exposed him to this kind of jibe.

> . . . yf you will have the earthe to bringe forth plentye to you [he told the Londoners on the occasion quoted above] wythdrawe not from God, that ys Lorde of heven and earthe, his parte, whyche he hath gyven to the prystes.[48]

Undeterred by criticism or apathy, he pursued this policy relentlessly to the end of his life, but without the wealth lost by the settlement of 1554 there was never enough money. In the spring of 1558 the expedient of subsidizing poor dioceses out of the surpluses of wealthier ones was turned into a regular policy.[49] But the difficulties of collecting spiritual revenues were so great that as late as August 1558 Cuthbert Tunstall was complaining that the diocese of Durham had not provided him with enough money to meet his pension commitments.[50] Nor did Pole make life any easier for his bishops by halving all taxation of a tenth on the clergy in April 1558, although the poorer benefices undoubtedly needed all the relief he could give them, not least because of the increasing burden of the clerical subsidies demanded by the crown.

Pole continued to do his best to stir the consciences of the laity, not entirely without result, as we have seen. The parish churches, he declared, '. . . are nowe fyrste to be holpen . . . whiche albeyt they have not byn cast downe by coloure of authoryte, as the abbayes were, yet they have byn sufferede to fawle downe of themselves . . .' However, with an ineptitude which seems to have afflicted so many of his dealings on the public stage, he went on to support his plea with imagery which was both tedious and unflattering. The concessions of 1554, he insisted, were 'doone of the chyrche your mother's tenderness unto you, consydering your imbecyllyte and wekenes . . .' Then, in an extended metaphor, he compared the property to an apple left in the hand of a child by its indulgent mother,

> . . . but the father her husbande commynge yn, yf he shudde see howe the boye wyll not lett goo one morcell to the mother, that hathe given him the hoole, she askyng yt wyth so fayre means, he may, peradventure, take the aple oute of the boy's hande, and yf he crye, beat him also, and caste the aple oute of the wyndowe. This maye Christe the husband doo, yf you showe suche unkyndnes to your mother, whiche ys his spouse . . .[51]

It was not Pole's fault that these pleas and threats had to be delivered against a background of war taxation and dearth, and on the whole the momentum of restoration and reconstruction at the parochial level seems to have been sustained remarkably well. However, there could be no question of any substantial improvement in the situation while the war lasted, and benefactions and endowments by individual laymen dwindled away almost to nothing in late 1557 and 1558. The queen herself made two more major endowments in the spring of 1558, as we have already seen, restoring the order of St John of Jerusalem in both England and Ireland, with landed estates worth over £2000 a year.[52] Apart from these acts of generosity, the only marked improvement in the financial position of the church was brought about by the deaths of pensioners, and the consequent decline in pressure on the spiritual revenues. According to Priuli, writing shortly after Pole's death, there had at first (1555–56) been a deficit equivalent to £2700 a year overall; but in the last year of the reign a surplus of £8000.[53] Instead of being deployed about the business of the church, however, this latter sum was paid by Pole to the queen as a contribution to the war effort,[54] various bishops receiving in return a substantial number of advowsons still in the hands of the crown. The greatest beneficiary of this transaction was the diocese of York, which received rights in 195 parishes. Lincoln received 150, London 57, Worcester 36, Winchester 25, Carlisle 19, and Canterbury 18.[55] These grants were made by patent during the last fortnight of the queen's life, and it is impossible to say whether similar concessions to other dioceses were planned.

The device of processing spiritual revenues through the cardinal's household accounts had many advantages because the church lacked a central treasury, and Pole had been made personally responsible for these revenues by the statute of 1555. Nevertheless, it led to much misunderstanding and misrepresentation, as Priuli complained. The cardinal's enemies tried to claim that in two and a half years he had received upwards of £100,000 as his personal income, whereas in reality he had been compelled to use his own money to make up the deficit which we have already noticed.[56] Henry Penning, his chamberlain, accounted for £22,500 between Michaelmas 1556 and Michaelmas 1557, and seems to have made no attempt to keep his master's own income and expenditure distinct from that of his office.[57] Although his apologists were no doubt right to claim that every penny was spent for the good of the church, Pole was, nevertheless, a wealthy man. Quite apart from the modest income of his archbishopric, he had received a personal estate of £1250 a year from the queen, and a pension of £1055 from the king, giving him a disposable revenue approaching £3000 a year.[58] This placed him on a level with the greatest peers, as was appropriate for a prince of the royal blood and a prince of the church. Apart from maintaining a large household, including a number of his Italian friends and servants, he was not an ostentatious man, but Priuli had considerable trouble with resentful critics after his death, and had great difficulty in persuading them that his master had not died possessed of a vast fortune.[59]

Although the financial pressures generated by the war probably had the most immediate and practical effects upon the restoration of the traditional church order, the low morale so frequently commented upon by Venetian and Spanish observers was more subtly significant. On 12 April 1557 Robert Pownall had published 'in exile' *An Admonition to the towne of Callays*, calling upon England and Calais to repent of idolatry, and comparing their situation to that of Israel and Samaria under Jezebel.

> . . . they mother the staffe of thy defence is now so debilitated and weakened as well in worthy capitaines and valiante soldiers as in money, munitions & victuail, that she is scant able to defende & releve hir selfe muche lesse then to sueccour the in thy necessitie . . .[60]

This situation Pownall attributed to '. . . another Athalia, that is an utter distroier of hir owne kindred, kyngedome & countrie, a hater of hir owne subjects, a lover of strangers & an unnatural stepdame both to the and to thy mother England'. To protestants the fall of Calais in January 1558 was the fulfilment of Pownall's prophecy of disaster, and lest others should miss the full significance of the event, on 7 March 1558 Bartholomew Traheron followed up with *A warning to England to Repente, and to Turne to god from idolatrie and poperie by the terrible example of Calece*, a work of violent invective denouncing Mary as a traitor to God and the realm.[61] As we have seen, by 1556 there was already a widespread sense that the country was being afflicted by the wrath of God, manifested in harvest failure, high prices, and the failure of the queen to produce an heir. The interpretation of these misfortunes was, of course, a matter of taste:

> . . . special causes there be whiche provocketh Goddes vengeance to light upon us [wrote Miles Huggarde], as chiefly infidelitie whereby God is most hainously dishonored, for the which we are most iustly punished; and also our rebellious murmuring against our regale rulers appointed of God to raigne over us . . .[62]

To Goodman or Traheron the main reason was idolatry, and the persecution of protestants provided additional proof of divine disfavour. Indeed, to Goodman it was the failure of the English, particularly the nobility, to rebel successfully which had provoked the Almighty to action.[63]

The outbreak of war, the quarrel with the papacy, and the loss of Calais greatly intensified the sense of divine punishment or trial. 'I am told', wrote Feria on 2 February 1558, 'that since the fall of Calais not one third as many Englishmen go to mass as went before' – a statement which need not be taken at its face value to provide some insight into the sharpness of the sense of disillusionment then prevalent.[64] One possible reaction, as we have seen, was to blame the disaster directly upon the heretics themselves, claiming that they had betrayed the city. Another was to claim that God had lopped off this limb of England because of its religious corruption. Francisco Delgado, writing in March 1558, believed that in spite of a preaching campaign, and all Cardinal Pole's efforts, there had been no more than sixteen good catholics in Calais at the time of its fall.[65] The commonest feeling, however, seems to have been that Mary was an 'ill starred' ruler; one whose enterprises were doomed to failure and disappointment, and this was a feeling which supported protestant rather than catholic polemic. Most people naturally preferred to believe that the country's misfortunes were the result of the bad luck or sinfulness of their rulers rather than themselves. It had been from the beginning a staple ingredient of catholic propaganda that 'liberty' and disobedience were the direct result of heretical teaching, and were highly displeasing to God.

> What murmurings, grudging, slaunders, rumours, lyes, bookes, tokens are in these dayes caried abroade in the Worlde against all sortes of magistrates, whom we aught to obey for conscience sake . . .[66]

Moreover, as the homily 'On the Primacy' had pointed out at considerable length, quoting Cyprian, all such schism and heresies had sprung directly from disobedience to the holy see.[67] In the spring of 1558 this was a distinctly two-edged argument, and contributed substantially to the discomfiture of those who sought to blame the accumulating misfortunes upon heretics and their sympathizers. It is perhaps significant that Huggarde's last effort on behalf of the government – a tirade in macaronic verse against faithlessness, lack of zeal for the catholic church, and opposition to the regime – was published in March 1557 although the author probably lived into the next reign.[68]

By 1558 the catholic propagandists had virtually given up. Of the four titles published in that year, three were variations of Thomas Watson's *Holesome and Catholyke doctrine,* while the fourth was an English translation of some prayers written several years earlier in Latin by Cuthbert Tunstall.[69] No attempt seems to have been made through this medium to stir up patriotic enthusiasm, or to exploit the opportunity which certainly existed to shift the blame for the Calais disaster. Protestant propaganda was also a good deal less in quantity, and of the eleven titles recorded, two were fresh editions of the *Lamentacion of England*. Nevertheless, the new works included *How Superior Powers oght to be obeyd*, *The First Blast of the Trumpet Against the Monstrous Regiment of Women*, and *An Aunswere made by Bart. Traheron to a Privy Papiste which crepte in . . .*; some of the sharpest and most effective polemical writing of the period.[70] Only after Mary's death was there a further exchange of fire. Not only did John White, the bishop of Winchester, risk the new queen's wrath by preaching her funeral sermon on the provocative text 'laudavi mortuos magis quam viventes'[71]; an anonymous ballad writer also sprang to her defence with *An Epitaphe upon the Death of the Most excellent and oure late vertuous Quene Marie*.[72] Whoever this writer was, his verses were superior to most of his competitors, and succeeded in conveying a genuine sense of loss and grief:

> She never closed her eare to heare
> the righteous man distrest
> Nor never sparde her hand to helpe
> wher wrong or power opprest . . .

In these lines the late queen is presented, not as Jezebel or Athalia, but as Griselde, a moving and in many ways accurate image, although hardly one which she would have chosen.

> Her perfecte lyfe in all extremes
> her pacient herte did show
> For in this world she never founde
> but dolfull dayes and woe.

Naturally there were more to hail the new queen than to lament the old, and it is the terms in which they chose to do so rather than the fact which is significant in this context. In *A Speciall grace, appointed to have been said after a banket at Yorke*,[73] the anonymous author welcomed Elizabeth with a sharp attack upon her predecessor, not from a religious but from a secular, urban point of view, blaming her for heavy taxation, material hardships, and the decline of trade. Protestant attacks upon Mary were, of course, numerous and always accompanied by the comfortable assumption that the boot was now on the other foot. Brice's *Register of Martyrs* is the best-known work of this genre, but not the first, or the most

442

explicit. A certain 'R.M.' produced almost immediately a doggerel history of 'trahaison des clercs', entitled simply *A newe Ballad*, and running from William Rufus to Mary.[74]

> O dere Lady Elysabeth, which art our right and vertuous Quene
> God hath endued the with mercy and faith, as by thy workes it
>   may be sene
> Wherefore good Quene I counsayle thee, Lady, Lady,
> For to beware of the spiritualitie, most dear Lady.

However, the most interesting from a propaganda point of view was the offering of William Birche, *A songe betwen the Quenes majestie and Englande*,[75] cast in the form of a lover's duet and beginning with the traditional invocation 'Come over the born Bessy':

> Here is my hand my dere lover Englande
> I am thine both with minde and hart
> For ever to endure thou maiest be sure
> Untill death us two depart.
>
> Lady this long space have I loved thy grace
> More than I durste well saye
> Hoping at the last when all stormes were past
> For to see this joyfull daye.

The pair then go on to discuss the perils and misfortunes which they have survived to bring about their union. When Elizabeth later declared that she was wedded to her realm, she was accepting an already popular image.

Although Mary's government made no attempt to justify or defend itself in print during the last year of the reign, the council's efforts to detect and repress criticism never relaxed. Plays and interludes continued to be regarded with particular suspicion. Even a group of 'honest householders' at Hatfield Broad Oak in Essex who decided to put on a Shrovetide play for their own amusement in 1556 were briefly imprisoned and ordered to desist from their intention.[76] Much worse were the wandering bands of professional players, even when they wore the protective device of a nobleman's badge; as was demonstrated by a group 'naming themselves to be servants of Sir Francis Leeke', who were presenting '. . . very naughty and seditious matter touching the Kings and Queenes Majesties and the State of the realm, and to the slander of Christes true Catholic Church . . .' around the north of England in April 1556.[77] In the summer of 1557 such instances multiplied, and during the Trinity term an order was made in star chamber prohibiting all playing of interludes.[78] In June groups of players were apprehended in London and Canterbury, some apparently being proceeded against under the common law and some under the canon law, although with what results is not known.[79] In July, Lord Rich and the JPs of Essex were rapped over the knuckles for not observing the star chamber decree, and in August and September there were further arrests in London and Canterbury.[80] It was then decided that plays would only be permitted between All Saints and Shrovetide, and that scripts must be submitted to the ordinary in advance, which was presumably intended to prevent altogether the kind of impromptu performances which were popular with audiences, but which could so easily get out of hand.[81]

Henry Machyn continued to note a steady trickle of men and women appearing on the London pillories for 'lewd wordes', and the privy council took note of more serious offenders of the same sort, such as William Oldenhall and 'the slater of Wallingford'[82]; but there is no indication that the problem became any worse, except perhaps for a few days at the end of January 1558. On the 26th George Worsely and Nicholas de Mennell, a French denizen, were committed to the Marshalsea for some outspoken comments, probably about the loss of Calais.[83] The same day Mary also wrote to Sir Thomas Cheney, instructing him to put one Francis Barton on the pillory in Canterbury for seditious words, and to proceed against Robert Cockerell by martial law. On the 29th Cheney reported that Barton had been disciplined according to instructions, and had afterwards made an edifying speech warning the people to beware by his example what they said of the king and queen. Cockerell had not been so obliging. Executed the previous day, he had 'died blasphemously', without any sign of repentance.[84]

The most important move in the campaign to control printed books was the chartering of the stationers' company, which took place in May 1557.[85] This significant royal grant of jurisdiction inevitably placed both the master and wardens in a vulnerable position of responsibility. No specific obligation was laid upon the company to assist in the execution of government censorship, but as a privileged corporation it could hardly refuse to co-operate without risking the loss of its privileges. This was a significant gain to the council because the printers as a group had always been notoriously sympathetic to the reformation and reluctant to disclose their knowledge of illicit publication. Such co-operation may help to explain why hardly any of the protestant tracts published in 1557 or 1558 were produced 'underground' in England, but it was useless as a curb on the circulation of material imported from abroad. As we have seen, the government eventually resorted to a proclamation of martial law against the possessors of such books, but there is no evidence that such fierce penalties were ever used, and the problem remained unsolved.[86] There is also some evidence to suggest that the printers could not necessarily be relied upon in spite of the sanctions to which they were now liable. On 12 September 1557 the council ordered a search to be made of the house of John Cawood, who was the queen's printer and one of the wardens of the new company, 'for all maner of writinges, evidences etc.' No sequel is recorded, but even he was clearly not above suspicion.[87] More specifically John Kingston and Thomas Marshe were summoned before the council on 13 July 1558, and their premises searched for '. . . all suche bookes curruptly sett forthe under the name of the Busshopp of Lyncolne, as all others as shall impugne the Catholyke Faithe . . .'[88] Marshe was a member of the company, but Kingston was not, although he was certainly working in London, and had been so for several years, which raises further doubts about the company as an aid to government control of printing.[89] There is no evidence of further action against either man. The process of 'cleaning up' after the schism also continued to demand administrative energy, since the volume of anti-catholic, and particularly anti-papal, literature produced since 1534 had been very great, and much of it was still lying in corners – a potential source of heretical infection. In November 1557 Bonner, Henry Cole, and Thomas Martin were commissioned 'to enquire of all registrars and other officers and ministers as to what books, scrolls or other writings written at the time of the late schism against the Pope and other catholic persons have come into their hands, and to cause the same to be burnt'.[90]

The momentum of persecution was also sustained, particularly by the council and in spite of the preoccupations of war and finance, although there is no evidence to suggest that the government was winning its war of nerves against the heretics and their sympathizers. If anything, the entanglement of heresy with treason and the dependence of the church upon secular power became greater rather than less as the reign entered its last phase. George Eagles, the notorious Trudgeover, whose main activities were as a hedge-preacher and distributor of protestant literature, was caught in July 1557, and executed for high treason at Colchester.[91] Several of his followers, who were still in gaol in Colchester in December, were then bailed to appear at the next assizes. Only 'one Thurston, very evil in matters of religion' was remitted to the ordinary.[92] Bonner, in the most sensitive episcopal seat, was under constant pressure. Twice before he had been reprimanded for inadequate severity, and in December 1557 it was the council which first examined John Rough, instructing Bonner on the 15th that he was to be proceeded against 'by order of law'.[93] In February 1558 a similar instruction ordered him to proceed against Thomas and Robert Thurston, who had been examined by the justices of assize in Essex.[94] Much of the bishop's routine work was also placed under royal surveillance by the device of joining him in commission with others to seek out defaulters and to investigate churches and vicarages for dilapidations. This had first been done in 1556, but it became more obvious in April 1557 when it was the commissioners, not the bishop, who issued instructions to all parsons, curates, and churchwardens in London to search out those who did not go to church or participate in the sacraments.[95] In 1558 it was again the commissioners who drew up the interrogatories 'upon which . . . the churchwardens . . . shall be charged withall . . .' Essex was not only a county in which heretics were numerous, it also had an exceptionally active group of catholic justices: Anthony Browne, the Tirrell brothers, and Lord Darcy of Chiche in particular. This led to a very large number of presentations, and also caused the council, on occasion, to by-pass the bishop on purely ecclesiastical matters. For example, on 29 April 1558 the lords wrote to Lord Darcy 'touching the dis-ordred persons that he writeth to have eaten flesshe in Lente last . . .', ordering him to see them punished.[96] He may have done this ultimately by referring them to Bonner, but they could have been dealt with 'according to the Statute in this cace provided . . .' without going anywhere near an ecclesiastical court. On the other hand, on at least one occasion heretics condemned by Bonner in his capacity as ordinary were pardoned through the intervention of Pole. In July 1556 William Stannarde and William Adams of Steeple Bumpstead '. . . after their condemnation and delivery to the secular powers, had been converted to the catholic faith . . .', and Pole, anxious to reconcile them to the church, had obtained the king and queen's pardon for them.[97] It must have been particularly galling for the bishop, who consistently tried to frighten protestants into submission in preference to burning them, to have lost the credit for the submission in this way.

Both the queen and the council had been aware from the beginning of the persecution that crowd behaviour at burnings was liable to be unsatisfactory, which was why care always had to be taken to provide adequate supervision by the secular officers, as well as a suitable sermon. In January 1556, being particularly dissatisfied with reactions at Smithfield, the council had ordered the lord mayor and sheriffs to ensure that all those who misconducted themselves '. . . by aiding, comforting or praising the offenders, or otherwise us[ing] themselves to the ill example of others . . .' were imprisoned, and that householders did not allow their apprentices or servants to be abroad when such an event was taking place.[98] Pole also up-braided the Londoners, that they had 'sore offended God by gyvinge favour to heretykes . . . a greate worke of cruiltye ageynst the commonwelthe . . .'[99] The situation never got completely out of hand, but neither did the attitude of the crowds improve, and by the summer of 1557 there were signs of marked reluctance on the part of some officials to carry out their duty on such occasions. On 28 July the council wrote to the sheriffs of Kent, Essex, Suffolk, and Staffordshire, the mayor of Rochester and the bailiffs of Colchester, requiring each 'to signifie hither what hath moved them to staye suche personnes as have byn condempned for heresye from execucion, who have byn delyvered unto them by the ordinary'.[100] Perhaps pardons had been anticipated for some, at least, of the offenders. Government policy in this matter was not consistent. Logically, pardons in return for submission should have been conceded willingly by an authority anxious both to save the heretic's soul and to encourage an example of repentance. Sometimes, as in the case of the two men mentioned, this was done, but it was not a concession to be relied upon, as Thomas Cranmer found to his cost.[101] In August 1558 Sir Richard Pexsall, the sheriff of Hampshire, found himself in serious trouble for having misread such a situation. A condemned heretic named Bembridge had been delivered to him for execution; but Bembridge professed repentance, and Pexsall did not carry out the sentence. On 1 August he was 'straightly commaunded' by the council

> . . . to cause him to be executed oute of hande, and if he styll contynueth in the Catholick Faythe, as he outwardlye pretendeth, than to suffer some suche discreet and learned man as the Bishop of Wynchester shall appointe . . . to have accesse unto him and to conferre with him . . . for the better ayding of him to dye Goddes servante.

Pexsall himself was summoned before the council, and bound in recognizance of £500 to appear daily before the board until he should be discharged – a heavy penalty for what seems to have been no more than an understandable error of judgement.[102] Presumably it was felt necessary to make an example of Pexsall in order to prevent a general outbreak of this sort of clemency. By this time Bonner was very apprehensive of 'tumults', and anxious to do as much as possible without the assistance of the secular officers. In July 1558 he wrote to Pole about one group of offenders:

> I should doe well to have theym burnt at Hammersmythe, a myle from my howse . . . for then I can giff sentence against theym here

447

in the parishe church very quickly, and without tumult or having the Sheriff present.[103]

He could not, of course, have burned them on his own authority, but he was clearly anxious to keep the whole affair as quiet as possible; and this is consistent with the number of burnings which are known to have taken place very early in the morning.[104] Official attitudes had changed considerably since the days when Rowland Taylor or John Hooper had been sent down to their 'countries' to be executed with the maximum possible publicity.

The council's concern for order and obedience was ubiquitous, and touched every aspect of public religion. On 24 August 1557 the mayor and aldermen of Bristol were sharply commanded to attend sermons, processions, and other ceremonies at the cathedral there 'and not to absent themselfes as they have doone of late, nor loke fromhensforthe that the Deane and Chapitre shulde wayte uppon them or fetche them out of the cittie with their crosses and procession, being the same very unsemely and farre out of ordre'.[105] A week or so later the lord mayor of London was carefully instructed to cause bonfires to be lit and all suitable rejoicing to be made in the city for the victory at St Quentin, and to attend high mass at St Paul's on the morrow, with his brethren.[106] More seriously, the council also found itself involved in a difficult and embarrassing dispute over the Westminster sanctuary. The traditional system of sanctuaries, having been nibbled away in various fashions, had finally been abolished by the statute of 32 Henry VIII, c. 12.[107] In its place a new system had then been erected, allowing a temporary privilege for forty days to all parish churches and churchyards, and setting up eight 'sanctuary towns' in which offenders could find permanent refuge. No privileged place was allowed to house more than twenty individuals, and they were expected to live under careful supervision. Murderers, rapists, burglars, robbers, arsonists, and those guilty of sacrilege, or the accessories to any of these crimes, were excluded from protection altogether.[108] This act was not repealed, but it seems that when the monastery was restored at Westminster, the old ecclesiastical sanctuary was restored with it. Westminster was a 'sanctuary town' under the statute, but the abbot did not see his resumed jurisdiction as being limited in the same way. In July 1557 a certain Edward Vaughn escaped from the Tower into sanctuary, and the council considered asking the abbot to examine him, with a promise that if he confessed, he would be allowed to remain in his refuge.[109] Feckenham must have declined to be a party to such a transaction, because a few days later he was instructed to hand over Vaughn to the constable of the Tower

. . . to be there further examined of the saide felonie, signifieing unto the said Abbot that the same Vaughn after his examinacion so taken shalbe restored againe to the Sanctuarye, if it shalbe his right so to be, requiring him neverthelesse to kepe the matter secrete to himself, so as neither the parties maye knowe thereof ne any other that might bring it to his knowledge.[110]

Torn between a policy of restoring traditional privileges and a desire to enforce the laws effectively, the council seems to have resorted to shifts and expedients. On 6 August a further letter was sent to Feckenham, instructing him to examine a suspected robber named John Poole 'in case he shall come to the Sanctuarie . . .'[111] Perhaps Poole did not appear, or perhaps he was refused refuge, because his name does not appear upon the list of inmates which the abbot was instructed to draw up in December. Vaughn, on the other hand, must have been allowed to return, for he was still there in January 1558.[112] On 27 January the council ordered that sixteen occupants of the sanctuary, probably the whole complement, should be handed over to Sir Henry Bedingfield. Some were then sent to the Tower, and some to King's Bench.[113] Among those sent to the Tower were several members of a gang of coiners, who must have sought sanctuary within a few weeks of committing their offences, early in December.[114] In the Hilary term 1558 they were arraigned and condemned, two of them, John and Jane Chapman, being pardoned before Mary's death, and two others, Lawrence Milford and William Pollard, in January 1559.[115] Coining was treason, and it may well be that other offenders, who were guilty of less serious crimes, were subsequently returned to the abbot's custody. However, the status and limitations of the Westminster sanctuary were causing legal and administrative problems, much as they had in the early days of the century.

In February the issue was referred to parliament, probably on the initiative of the council, and a bill 'touching sanctuaries' was read twice in the House of Commons. We do not know what proposals this contained, but it must have caused dispute because it disappeared after the second reading and was replaced on 11 February with 'a new bill what churches shall be reputed sanctuaries'.[116] At the same time Feckenham was summoned to appear before the House to justify the claim of his monastery. On the 12th he duly appeared, armed with charters and 'grants of old kings', and was instructed to return the following Tuesday accompanied by his learned counsel. This he duly did, supported by Plowden and Story, and a committee of the House was set up to consider the evidence and arguments.[117] Presumably the committee must have accepted his case, because the sanctuary continued until the second dissolution of the monastery under Elizabeth, and there was no fresh legislation. If Feckenham did succeed in establishing his right to an ancient sanctuary, it was in defiance of the Henrician statute, and since that statute remained in force, the jurisdictional anomaly which had already caused considerable confusion and inconvenience remained unresolved. Several other matters of ecclesiastical significance were also debated in this parliament, including a bill concerning the forging of monastic seals, and another 'confirming the bishoprics of Winchester and Worcester to their present holders', but the only measure which became law was a brief act withdrawing benefit of clergy from accessories to murder.[118] It looks as though this was because the council had difficulty in getting such bills through rather than because of any reluctance on the part of the government to allow parliament to interfere in spiritual affairs, but the point can hardly be regarded as established. In many practical ways Mary's government was surprisingly erastian, and if anything it became more so during the last part of her reign, when political hostility and personal animus obstructed communications with Rome, and when Pole's energy and idealism were ebbing away.

The queen herself seems to have been as dependent upon the consolation of her faith during the last months of her life as she ever had been in the darkest days of her father's or brother's reign. Both Pole and Philip commented upon her 'Christian resignation' in reaction to the disastrous news from Calais,[119] and when she came to make her will in March, her first and overriding care was for the religious houses which she had re-established.[120] The Carthusians at Sheen and the Bridgettines at Syon each received £500 in cash and £100 *per annum* in land out of the 'spiritual possessions' still in the queen's hands at her decease. No restored house was omitted; £500 to the Observant friars at Greenwich; 400 marks to the prior and convent at Blackfriars; £200 to the Observant friars at Southampton; £200 to the abbey of Westminster; and £200 to the 'poor nuns' at Langley. In each case the brethren and sisters were required to pray for the queen's soul, for the soul of her mother, for King Philip after his decease, 'and all other oure progenitours'. Other charitable works were upon a similarly generous scale. £1000 was to be distributed by her executors among the poor and needy; £500 was to go to the poor scholars of each university, particularly those intending to be priests or religious; £300 a year in lands was to be bestowed upon the hospital of the Savoy, to bring the endowment up to the level originally envisaged by Henry VII; and land to the annual value of 400 marks was to be used for the establishment of a new hospital for the relief of old and maimed soldiers.[121] Altogether Mary's pious bequests amounted to £4764 in cash and £804 a year in landed endowments – equivalent to a capital value of over £16,000. Legacies to her servants and executors, all in cash sums of various sizes, totalled a further £14,300,[122] while her personal possessions and jewels were all to go to her unnamed heir. Although Philip is frequently mentioned throughout the will, Mary's only gifts to him were of emotional rather than material significance, at least to her: the jewel which the emperor had sent her via the count of Egmont, and that which Philip himself had sent by the marquis de las Navas, which

> . . . I humbly beseech my said most dearest lord and husband to accept of my bequest and to keep for a memory of me . . .

The king is also named as the chief executor, supported by a team of reliably conservative peers and bishops: Pole, Heath, Winchester, Arundel, Westmorland, Shrewsbury, Derby, Sussex, Pembroke, Clinton, Thirlby, and Hastings. The only commoners serving as executors were Petre and Cordell, although the six assistant executors were all commoners, and mostly laymen – her intimates and household officers, Cornwallis, Jerningham, Boxall, Waldegrave, Englefield, and Baker. When, in October, her own deteriorating health forced an acknowledgement that she might have no child, and that consequently Philip would have no place in the realm after her death, she charged her heir to oversee the execution of her will. When at last she was forced to acknowledge Elizabeth as her successor, she requested her to undertake this task, and to preserve the catholic church.[123] The two tasks were intimately connected, and the new queen's decision to reject the latter automatically made the bulk of the former impossible as well.

Mary's will in its surviving form is a fair reflection of her life and reign: intensely pious and conservative, generous, and politically self-deceived. There was no chance that she could have been pregnant in March 1558, and anyone with the courage to do so could have told her that the whole provision for the succession and oversight made in the main document was a waste of time and effort. Fortunately they could not have told her that the codicil was a waste of effort as well, and perhaps in a way it was not. Elizabeth did pay her sister's secular debts, and Philip was, for a time, the 'good brother and friend' to her that Mary had hoped.[124] Those who were with her at the end testified that she died in peace, no mean reward for her virtues, and one of which a sharper sense of political reality might have deprived her. In spite of all her efforts, the church to which she had given so much was neither firmly re-established nor in good heart to withstand another political onslaught.

451

In this situation shortage of time had been an important factor, but it was by no means the only one, as we have seen. Pole's own personality and the low priority given to missionary work also contributed, as did the failure of censorship and persecution to beat down protestant resistance. However, it seems to me that the most significant factor was a series of unrelated misfortunes: some the result of human error and some 'acts of God'. England's involvement in the continental war with its consequent military disasters and the bitter quarrel with the papacy over the legatine mission are outstanding under the former heading; while the queen's failure to bear a child, and the bad weather and harvest conditions which prevailed from 1555 to 1558, must count under the latter.[125] Although there was no slackening of administrative effort, and the work of rebuilding went on throughout the last year and a half of the reign, the English catholic church lost during 1557 and 1558 much of the confidence and optimism which it had displayed in 1554 and the early part of 1555. The triumphant sense of divine favour which had pervaded the writing of Christopherson or the *Newe Ballade of the Marigolde*, had degenerated into querulous apologetic by the beginning of 1557, and disappeared altogether by the following year. There is plenty of evidence that old religious habits had comfortably re-established themselves, that restored jurisdictions were working moderately well, and that the financial situation was beginning to improve. But the momentum of 1555 was not sustained, and there were few signs of a genuine spiritual revival following in the wake of the reconstruction. For this the misfortunes of 1557 and 1558 can be largely blamed. Although it was possible to blame the wicked, the faithless, or the protestants, not even the staunchest catholic could deny that God was manifestly displeased with the English, and that conviction lowered catholic morale at a critical time – while the new queen was making up her mind how to handle the complex situation which she had inherited.

Notes

1 The importance of this relationship is made abundantly apparent by the letters of both parties published by Quirini, and calendared in *Cal. Ven.* See also W. Schenk, *Reginald Pole, Cardinal of England* (1950), and R. Pogson, 'Reginald Pole, Papal Legate to England'. There is no good biography of Morone, but G. Constant, *La Légation du Cardinal Morone près l'empereur et le Concile de Trente* (1922), is rather broader than its title might imply.

2 The question of relations between Carafa and Pole has been recently and well discussed in D. Fenlon, *Obedience and Heresy in Tridentine Italy* (1972).

3 Sir Edward Carne to Philip and Mary, 10 April 1557. PRO SP69/10/586.
4 ibid.
5 Same to same, 17 April. ibid., 589.
6 Pole to Paul IV, 25 May 1557. *Cal. Ven.*, VI, 1111.
7 The legatine status of the archbishopric of Canterbury had been effectively recognized by the reservation of Cranmer's trial to Rome, instead of by Pole's own legatine authority in England. As a duly consecrated archbishop and *legatus natus,* Cranmer had been technically Pole's equal. The legatine status of the archbishopric of York was a much more questionable matter. Holgate had been appointed during the schism, and Heath never seems to have claimed or exercised such authority. Consequently, if this revocation had lasted, the whole question of the primacy between the provinces would have been reopened. F. Makower, *Constitutional History and Constitution of the Church of England* (1895), 281-93.
8 Philip and Mary to Paul IV, 21 May 1557. *Ecc. Mem.*, III, 2, 474-6.
9 ibid., 476-80.
10 *Cal. Ven.*, VI, 1111.
11 Pole to Paul IV, *Cal. Ven.*, VI, 994-9. Navagero to the doge and senate, 15 May 1557. ibid., 1092-5.
12 Same to same, 8 May 1557. ibid., 1038-40.
13 Same to same, 22 May and 1 June. ibid., 1109-11; 1131-33.
14 *Cal. Ven.*, 1161; 1166.
15 Peto was in fact the last cardinal created by Paul IV. ibid., 1166. *DNB.*
16 *Cal. Ven.*, VI, 1168.
17 PRO SP69/11/637. *Ecc. Mem.*, III, 2, 37.
18 ibid.
19 Carne to Philip and Mary, 2 July 1557. SP69/11/641.
20 Carne wrote to the queen on 7 August, announcing the arrival of her letter, and Navagero summarized as much of the content as he had been able to discover in a despatch of 5 August. SP69/11/655. *Cal. Ven.*, VI, 1240.
21 ibid.
22 Navagero to the doge and senate, 14 August 1557. *Cal. Ven.*, VI, 1248. Navagero understood that Cranmer had been burned in London.
23 ibid.
24 The surviving copy of this document is Petyt MS 538/46/391-426, in the Inner Temple library. It was published, with commentary, by J. I. Tellechea Idigoras as 'Pole y Paulo IV; una celébre Apologia inédita del Cardenal Inglés' in *Archivum Historiae Pontificiae*, IV (1966), 105-54; and paraphrased in Fenlon, op. cit., 272-7.
25 See above,   .
26 Carne to Boxall, 2 October 1557. SP69/11/672.
27 Carne to Mary, 30 October 1557. SP69/11/678.
28 Navagero to the doge and senate, 25 September 1557. *Cal. Ven.*, VI, 1324-26.
29 SP69/11/692.
30 ibid.
31 Pole to Cardinal Carafa, 14 December 1557. *Cal. Ven.*, VI, 1392-94.
32 Pole to Philip, 13 December 1557; Instructions for Francesco Stella, 10 January 1558; Pole to Paul IV, 30 March 1558. *Cal. Ven.*, VI, 1391, 1419, 1481.

33 C. Corviersi, 'Compendio di processi del Santo Uffizio di Roma', *Archivio della Società Romana di Storia Patria*, III (1880), 261-9, 449-73. Quoted and discussed by Fenlon, op. cit., 278-81.
34 Corviersi, art. cit., 284. Fenlon, op. cit., 279 and n. 3.
35 Navagero to the doge and senate, 23 October 1557. *Cal. Ven.*, VI, 1349-51.
36 Tellechea Idigoras, art. cit., 142-3. Fenlon, op. cit., 275.
37 ibid., 279-80. De Frede, *La Restaurazione Cattolica in Inghilterra sotto Maria Tudor* (1971), 128-9. Bartolomé Carranza had left England in 1557 to take up the archbishopric of Toledo, but it is clear that his subsequent troubles celebrated stemmed with the Inquisition stemmed from his close association with Pole between 1555 and 1557. J. I. Tellechea Idigoras, 'Una denuncia de los Cardenales Contarini, Pole y Morone por el Cardenal Francisco de Mendoza (1560)', *Revista española de Teología*, 27 (1967), 33-51. Also 'Pole, Carranza y Fresnada. Cara y cruz de una amistad y de una enemistad', *Diálogo ecuménico*, 8 (1974), 287-393.
38 Carne to Mary, 7 June 1558. SP69/13/791.
39 ibid. Carne to Mary, 25 July 1558. SP69/13/810.
40 W. H. Frere, *The Marian Reaction in its Relation to the English Clergy*. These delays were not entirely caused in the *curia*. For example, Day of Chichester died in August 1556, and Carne complained in the spring of 1557 that the issue of a bull for his successor was constantly being put off. However, the bull was issued on 7 May (SP69/10/600) and it was still November before Christopherson was finally installed.
41 C. G. Bayne, *Anglo-Roman Relations, 1588–1565* (1913).
42 Feria to Philip, 10 March 1558. *Cal. Span.*, XIII, 366-9. On Pole's nostalgia for Italy, see Pogson, 'Reginald Pole, Papal Legate to England'.
43 *Cal. Span.*, XIII, 371 n.
44 Feria to Ribadeneyra, 22 March 1558. *Cal. Span.*, XIII, 370-1.
45 ibid.
46 Pole's 'oration' to the citizens of London. *Ecc. Mem.*, III, 2, 482-510. Catholic propagandists in general did their best to discredit protestant emphasis upon the scriptures. Huggarde wrote: 'Thapparaile whiche our protestantes do weare is the cloake of holy scripture, lined with lyes and false interpretacion of the same ever crying: The woorde of the Lorde, Goddes booke, and suche other vayne outcryes . . .' *Displaying of the Protestantes*, 37^v.
47 Quoted by S. E. Ozment, *The Reformation in the Cities* (1975), 112.
48 *Ecc. Mem.*, III, 2, 499.
49 Pole to Bonner, 1 April 1558. Guildhall MS 9531 f. 439. Cited in R. H. Pogson, 'Revival and Reform in Mary Tudor's Church: a Question of money', *JEH*, XXV, 3 (1974), 249-65.
50 W. H. Frere, *Visitation Articles and Injunctions* (1910), 2, 412. Tunstall's injunctions to the dean and chapter of Durham, 1556. Tunstall to Pole, 16 August 1558. SP11/13/114.
51 *Ecc. Mem.*, III, 2, 485-6.
52 See above, 413. Mary intended to restore the Dominican house in Oxford, and probably the Franciscan house in Cambridge as well, but nothing came of these intentions, whether for lack of time or lack of resources. Bartolomé Carranza to Fray Juan de Villagarcía, 2 July 1557; published by Tellechea Idigoras in *Fray Bartolomé Carranza y el Cardenal Pole* (Pamplona, 1977), 247 *et seq.* Carranza wrote many

letters to Villagarcía (in Oxford) between 1557 and 1559, published in this work.
53 Priuli to Antonio Giberti, 27 November 1558. *Cal. Ven.*, VI, 1555-60.
54 ibid. Priuli says £8000. *Cal. Pat.*, IV, 399, says £7000, as we have seen.
55 *Cal. Pat.*, IV, 401, 420, 449, 399, 402, 437, 439, 450.
56 *Cal. Ven.*, VI, 1555-60.
57 PRO SP11/11/57.
58 ibid. It is not clear whether this sum included income from Pole's property in Spain, but probably not, as it is described as a pension. In describing this as 'disposable' income, I am meaning only that it does not seem to have been subject to regular or fixed deductions.
59 Pole's will, dated 4 October 1558 and witnessed by Goldwell, Seth Holland, Maurice Clenoch, and Francisco Stella, was published by Quirini. Heath, Thirlby, Hastings, Boxall, Waldegrave, Cordell, and Henry Cole were named as executors, but the main work of carrying out his wishes devolved upon Priuli, who was given the task of distributing the cardinal's goods and money among his servants and the poor. The will gives no clear indication of the state of Pole's moveable wealth at the time of his death. Quirini, V, 181-7.
60 STC 19078, f.
61 STC 24174.
62 *Displaying of the Protestantes*, 3ᵛ.
63 See above, 160 and n.
64 Feria to Philip, 2 February 1558. *Cal. Span.*, XIII, 351.
65 Francesco Delgado to the princess of Portugal, 17 March 1558. AGS, Guerra Antigua, L67 f. 50. Delgado's letter contains a long, circumstantial and second-hand account of the fall of Calais. According to Delgado many Englishmen, fearful of an uprising in England, had sent a proportion of their wealth over to Calais, and the French had seized 2 million ducats. I can find no confirmation of this story.
66 *Displaying of the Protestantes*, 97.
67 'Homily of the Primacy', f. 38. In *Homelies sette forth by the right reverende father in God, Edmund Byshop of London* (1555). STC 3282.
68 The date of Huggarde's death is not known, but he was a minor celebrity in London while Mary was alive and his death before November 1558 would have warranted some mention. He wrote, but did not publish, one other work in 1557, after the A.B.C. referred to here, and that was appropriately entitled 'The myrroyr of myserye'.
69 STC 25112, 3, 4. STC 24318.
70 STC 12020, 15070, 24167.7.
71 A sermon which, to judge from the version printed by Strype, was a good deal less provocative than its title might suggest, being mainly an ornate commentary upon the merits of dying in the faith. *Ecc. Mem.*, III, 2, 536-50.
72 Society of Antiquaries, Broadsheet 46; printed by Richard Lant. STC 17559.
73 STC 7599.
74 Society of Antiquaries, Broadsheet 48; STC 17147.
75 Broadsheet 47; STC 3079.
76 *APC*, V, 234-7.
77 Council to the lord president of the north, 30 April 1556. *Ecc. Mem.*, III, 2, 185.
78 *APC*, VI, 118-19.

79 *APC*, VI, 102, 110.
80 ibid., 118-19; 148, 168-9.
81 ibid., 168-9.
82 *APC*, VI, 139; 1 August 1557. ibid., 119; 11 July 1557. For Oldenhall see also *OM*, 250.
83 *APC*, VI, 251.
84 PRO SP11/12/32, 46.
85 *Cal. Pat.*, III, 480-1. Loades, 'The Press under the Early Tudors'.
86 See above, 388.
87 *APC*, VI, 172.
88 ibid., 346. Robert Caly had been granted a patent on 30 April 1558 to publish the *Holesome and Catholyke doctrine* 'set forth in the manner of short sermons to be made to the people by the right reverend Thomas, bishop of Lincoln', with a monopoly for seven years. It is therefore possible that the council was primarily concerned to enforce respect for his patent, but the terms of the entry in the register do not suggest that. *Cal. Pat.*, IV, 104.
89 For some discussion of this point, see Loades, 'The Press under the Early Tudors', 45-6.
90 *Cal. Pat.*, IV, 14.
91 *APC*, VI, 129-30. 142. For Trudgeover, see Foxe, VIII, 393-7. *OM*, 250-1.
92 *APC*, VI, 215. 12 December 1557.
93 ibid., 216. 15 December 1557. For a discussion of Bonner's position, and the pressures operating on him, see G. Alexander, 'Bonner and the Marian Persecutions', *History*, 60 (1975), 374-91. Also Foxe, VII, 86-100.
94 *APC*, VI, 276. 27 February 1558.
95 Alexander, art. cit., 378-9.
96 *APC*, VI, 309. 29 April 1558.
97 *Cal. Pat.*, III, 516. Foxe, VIII, 154.
98 *APC*, V, 224. 14 January 1556.
99 *Ecc. Mem.*, III, 2, 501.
100 *APC*, VI, 135.
101 Cranmer's recantations were almost certainly obtained in expectation of pardon, and retracted only when it was obvious that no pardon would be granted. For a full discussion see Loades, *OM*, 232-4.
102 *APC*, VI, 361, 371. 1 and 11 August 1558. Pexsall was not the first to suffer in this way. On 7 August 1557 Sir John Butler, then sheriff of Essex, was fined £10 by the council because his deputy had respited a woman from execution at Colchester. *APC.*, VI, 144.
103 Bonner to Pole. *HMC Second Report*, App., 152 (Abingdon MSS).
104 Or even at night in one case, Froude *[Mary Tudor]*, 311. Froude gives the impression that the persecution was actually intensified in the last year of the reign, but this was not so. 74 people were executed in 1555, 82 in 1556, 75 in 1557, and 38 in the 10 months of 1558 down to Mary's death. (P. Hughes, op. cit., II, 283). On the other hand, protestant self-assertiveness may have become more marked, as in the case of the demonstration at Smithfield on 28 June. Strype was of this opinion, when he wrote of the situation in 1558: 'And in London, notwithstanding all the burning in Smithfield during the three years last past, yet great were the numbers there that professed the gospel, increasing considerably as it seemed, or at least showing themselves more boldly towards the latter end of the Queen's reign'. *Ecc. Mem.*, III, 2, 64.

105 *APC*, VI, 158.
106 ibid., 164. 2 September 1557.
107 W. S. Holdsworth, *History of English Law* (rev. ed. 1956–66), III, 306-7, I. D. Thornley, 'The Destruction of Sanctuary', *Tudor Studies presented to A. F. Pollard* (1924), 182-207. G. R. Elton, *Reform and Renewal*, 135-6.
108 32 Henry VIII, c. 12. The 'sanctuary towns' were Wells (Somerset), Westminster, Manchester, Northampton, Norwich, York, Derby, and Launceton.
109 *APC*, VI, 128. 22 July 1557. In the original register the entry is marked 'vacat' in the margin.
110 ibid., 135. 28 July.
111 ibid., 144.
112 ibid., 251. 27 January 1558.
113 ibid., 252.
114 According to the paraphrase of their indictment included in the calendar entry recording the Chapmans' pardon, the offences were committed between 29 October and 7 December. *Cal. Pat.*, IV, 379-80.
115 *Cal. Pat.*, IV, 379-80. *Cal. Pat.*, Elizabeth, I, 62.
116 *CJ*, I, 49.
117 ibid. The committee was headed by Sir William Petre.
118 4 and 5 PPhilip and Mary, c. 4.
119 Philip to Pole, 21 January 1558. *Cal. Span.*, XIII, 340-1.
120 BL Harleian MS 6949.
121 According to Francesco Delgado the queen also intended to found a 'strangers hospital' in London for foreign seamen. AGS, Guerra Antigua, L67 f. 50. He may have been mistaken, or picked up a rumour of the intention expressed in the will. Neither intention seems to have been carried out.
122 £2000 was to be divided among her 'poor servants that be ordinary'; a total of £3400 went to named individual servants. Pole was to receive £1000, each of the other executors of the rank of earl or above £500, the remaining executors 500 marks, and the assistant executors £200.
123 According to Surian this occurred on 13 November. Surian to the doge and senate, 27 November 1558. *Cal. Ven.*, VI, 1549.
124 BL Harleian MS 6949. Bayne, op. cit.
125 An exceptionally heavy mortality from sweating sickness and 'quartan ague', which was probably related to the cold, wet weather and food shortages, also afflicted England in 1557 and 1558, being particularly bad in the latter year. Wriothesley, *Chronicle*, II, 90-1.

14   The Dissolution of the Regime

Elizabeth was welcomed to the throne first and foremost because, like her half-sister, she was the legitimate heir. The scenes which greeted her in London were more muted, and more carefully stage-managed than those which had greeted Mary five and a half years earlier, partly because from the first she was a more self-conscious propagandist,[1] and partly because the danger of a diverted succession had eventually been much less. Elizabeth's status had been both her peril and her salvation, and she never forgot the experiences of those dangerous years. In 1563, in response to the urgings of her council and parliament to declare her successor, she replied:

> I am sure ther was none of them that was ever a second person as I have been, and have tasted of the practizes against my sister who I would to God weare alive againe. I had great occationes to harken to ther motsiones of whom some of them are in the Common house but when frendes fall out thentents doth appeare according to the oulde provarbe and wear yt not for my honor ther knavery should be knowne. Ther wer occasione in me that tyme I stood in daunger of my life my sister was so insensed against me I did diferr from her in Religione and I was sought for divers wayes so shall never my successor bee . . .[2]

Renard had been right when he had declared that all the conspiracies against Mary had been designed to bring Elizabeth to the throne before her due time, although his assumption that this would serve the interests of the French revealed the limitations of his understanding.[3] She had survived threats of execution, exile, and matrimony, partly because of her own discretion and determination, and partly because the majority of Mary's ministers and councillors had realized that she represented the only hope of future political stability in the absence of royal children. Elizabeth was fully conscious of the fact that many of her sister's servants had been, up to a point, her friends, just as she was aware of the extent to which some of her own professed friends had brought her into peril. However, she also suspected that there had been among her sister's intimates and their servants a hard core who were implacably hostile to her, and who had done their best to engineer her destruction. When the form of the queen's coronation pardon was drawn up in January 1559, it excepted offences 'touching changing the royal state or succession to the Crown' and 'conspiracy against the present Queen's person in Queen Mary's time'.[4] As far as I can discover, nobody was specifically charged with such a crime, but it must have hung as an uncomfortable threat over some of those who had been the warmest advocates of her exclusion.

In spite of the peaceful circumstances of her accession, Elizabeth was markedly more ruthless in removing her predecessor's ministers and councillors than Mary had been. In the high offices of state, Winchester alone survived. Heath resigned the great seal; Paget was not reappointed to the privy seal; and the principal secretary, Boxall, lost his position.[5] Of the 39 privy councillors at the time of Mary's death, only 10 were called to a similar status by her successor. At court the change was even more complete, only Sir John Mason, the treasurer of the chamber, retaining his office. Among the gentlemen, grooms, and ushers of the privy chamber about a dozen survived out of fifty, while among the queen's ladies the turnover was 100 per cent.[6] Englefield lost his sensitive position of master of the court of wards to Elizabeth's former cofferer Sir Thomas Parry, while Sir Richard Southwell was removed from the ordnance in favour of Lord Ambrose Dudley. Some changes resulted from the deaths of office-holders and were significant in a rather different sense. Sir Thomas Cheney and Sir John Baker died within a few weeks of the queen's accession; so Lord Cobham became lord warden and Sir Walter Mildmay chancellor of the exchequer without any need for displacement.[7] In the provinces, however, and below the highest level, the story was rather different. Gilbert Bourne was replaced as president of the council in the Marches, but by a fellow Marian, Lord Williams. The earl of Sussex remained in charge in Ireland, and the earl of Shrewsbury in the north. Displacements from the commission of the peace were minimal – an average of 4 or 5 per county at most[8] – and in the central administration, including the administrative departments of the household, continuity was also very high. Overall the impression is very clear: strong continuity in the administration, finance, and the judiciary, but politically and ecclesiastically a new regime.

The queen's thinking at this stage is perhaps revealed most clearly by the composition of her privy council. Seven peers were retained: Arundel, Pembroke, Shrewsbury, Derby, Winchester, Howard, and Clinton. Of these Clinton and Howard had both shown friendship to Elizabeth in her dark days, and had been suspect to the Imperialists.[9] Winchester was a bureaucrat of great skill and experience who owed his retention entirely to his professional competence. The remaining four were magnates; men of political experience and weight, powerful in their countries, and conservative in their opinions. They were accustomed to working together, and as a group were much too strong to be ignored. Three commoners were also retained, not counting Cheney, who died almost at once: Mason, Wotton, and Petre. These were all skilled and long-serving officials, cautious, conservative, and pragmatic. All these ten had been in their different ways 'working' councillors. Not only did Elizabeth discard her sister's personal favourites, such as Waldegrave, Englefield, Jerningham, Montague, and Hastings; she also got rid of the nominal members, such as Rich, Bath, Wentworth, Higham, Mordaunt, and Wharton.[10] In their places came Francis, second earl of Bedford, William Parr, newly restored marquis of Northampton, and seven commoners: Sir William Cecil, Sir Richard Sackville, Sir Francis Knollys, Sir Thomas Parry, Sir Edward Rogers, Sir Nicholas Bacon, and Sir Ambrose Cave. The result was a council of 19, less than half the size of that which Mary had left, and very differently made up. Two of Mary's most influential and experienced advisers had been dropped, Thirlby and Paget. Paget had been in poor health for several months, and unable to attend to business, which made a good pretext for his dismissal, but can hardly have been the real reason since he recovered and lived a reasonably active life until 1563.[11] Perhaps Elizabeth distrusted him because of his close association with Philip; perhaps she sacrificed him reluctantly on account of his responsibility for the unpopular war. The queen kept her own counsel about the reasons for her action, but in rejecting him she deliberately turned her back upon the only available statesman of proven ability and stature. It is also noticeable that she did not seek to strengthen her position by calling upon magnates of great wealth and local power such as the duke of Norfolk or the earl of Northumberland, who had not been Marian councillors. The men whom she did call upon were, almost without exception, men of mature years and considerable political and administrative experience; but also men whose careers had been ruined or suspended at Mary's accession, and who were all, although to varying degrees, antipathetic to the catholic church.

The privy council as it had emerged by January 1559 was thus small, almost exclusively lay, rather elderly – with an average age of about fifty – and possessing great breadth and depth of experience. It contained two outspoken protestants, Bedford and Knollys,[12] and several others who inclined in that direction such as Cecil and

Bacon, but only one man – Rogers – who had been involved in active opposition to Mary.[13] The religious conservatives were strongly represented both in numbers and in power, but with the exclusion of Mary's intimates and the virtual exclusion of the clergy,[14] there were neither clericalists nor ultramontanes. It does not require the advantages of hindsight to see that this foreshadowed an erastian and 'national' policy; but it was by no means a foregone conclusion that the young queen would be able to hold together a team so naturally and deeply divided. Although it was so much smaller than the initial council assembled by Mary, the potentiality for faction within the privy council of 1559 was at least as great – and was to be realized on many occasions over the next decade. At court, on the other hand, the balance preserved in the council was notably absent. Just as Mary had surrounded herself with the members and dependents of the old catholic families, so the new queen sought the company of Boleyns, Parrs, Cookes – and Dudleys.[15] Although he quickly became master of the horse, Lord Robert Dudley did not emerge immediately as a royal favourite. At first it was rumoured that Lord William Grey would occupy that position.[16] Nevertheless, the 'Dudley connection', shattered by the misfortunes of 1553, was reassembled and mobilized after 1558 with a speed that suggests very strongly a recovery during the period of partial rehabilitation after 1555.[17] In Dudley's service were to be found, during the 1560s, many of those who had been most active in the conspiracies of Wyatt, Henry Dudley, and others.[18] The queen herself was more cautious about employing such men, but her actions do not altogether accord with her correct speeches about their 'knavery'. In the anxious early days of mid-November it was Sir Thomas Cawarden and Sir Edward Warner who were summoned to garrison the Tower of London, and Warner soon recovered the lieutenancy.[19] Sir William St Low, the captain of the guard, Sir James Croftes, the captain of Berwick, Sir Nicholas Throgmorton, ambassador to France, and Henry Killigrew, envoy to the duke of Brunswick, had all been in serious trouble under the earlier regime. It is true that no such men were employed in the high offices of state, but in lesser offices of confidence and trust they were numerous, including some close to the queen's person.

This pattern of the new regime, as it emerged during the closing weeks of 1558, made Mary's surviving bishops acutely, and rightly, apprehensive. Although Elizabeth was scrupulously correct in maintaining the forms of the old faith,[20] persecution abruptly ceased and the voices of protestant preachers were again to be heard at Paul's Cross. Although they hoped for the best, nobody, with the possible exception of Paul IV, really believed that Elizabeth was a good catholic. The exact state of her mind at this stage is inscrutable; she encouraged the protestants with theatrical gestures and reassured the catholics with soothing words. Her personal religion was probably protestant, but her ecclesiastical policy would have to wait for an assessment of the political possibilities. She was bombarded with good advice at the time, and the emergence of the 1559 settlement has subsequently been discussed with great frequency and at considerable length.[21] It is no part of my intention to embark upon another such discussion. However, it has been recently and convincingly argued that the proposals which Elizabeth's councillors brought to the parliament in February 1559 were for a protestant, not a Henrician, church, and that in the first session before Easter these proposals were partially defeated by catholic opposition in the Lords.[22] The queen toyed with the idea of accepting the resultant half-measures, which would probably have satisfied the conservative erastians, but decided against because she realized that neither the existing hierarchy nor the protestant clergy would consent to staff a Henrician church.[23] By the unscrupulous device of imprisoning two bishops during the recess, and by ruthless pressure in the second session, she then succeeded in forcing through the acts of supremacy and uniformity. The Marian bishops and other senior clergy, unyielding in their opposition to this settlement, were subsequently removed, but their resistance was unavailing because they were not supported either by the bulk of the lower clergy, or by any powerful and organized group of catholic laity. Apart from a handful of lay peers nobody was prepared to risk the queen's displeasure by seconding the bishops in their opposition to her wishes. There was no catholic party in the House of Commons, no catholic rebellion, no popular demonstrations in defence of the mass.[24] The Elizabethan church was, and was long to remain, protestant in little more than form – overwhelmingly conservative in substance. But conservative was not catholic, and the situation had been created in which the slow processes of conformity were to transform England into a protestant country by the end of the century. Apart from the imprisoned bishops, the genuine papalists, whether lay or clerical, who refused all compromise and conformity, may be numbered by scores, or hundreds, but not by thousands.

It is therefore clear, I think, that one cannot assess the achievements and failures for the long and important reign of Elizabeth, nor their proper relationship to the critical development of her father's reign, without a proper understanding and analysis of the achievements and failures of Mary. Nor is it sufficient to point out that her aspirations for an England catholic in faith and firmly linked to the Habsburg empire were frustrated, and to conclude, like

Pollard, that 'sterility was the conclusive note of [her] reign'.[25] The period was far too complex to be dismissed in a simple formula, and several popular and long-standing misconceptions need to be corrected. In the first place Mary's government was not weak in any general sense of being unable to enforce its will. All the evidence suggests that the council was throughout assiduous in the discharge of its administrative duties, and that it made its will known and obeyed at least as successfully as that of Elizabeth during most of her much longer reign. Moreover, in spite of arousing considerable opposition, and in spite of having to endure the misfortunes of harvest failure and exceptional mortality, Mary survived. She succeeded in enforcing her will over three major matters: her marriage, the return to Rome, and the declaration of war. Only over the important issue of Philip's coronation was she clearly defeated. The weakness of Mary's government lay in the making of decisions, not in their implementation. Although Renard exaggerated for his own purposes, the council was afflicted by numerous and deep divisions. In this it did not differ fundamentally from any other Tudor council, but some of the men concerned, notably Paget and Gardiner, were exceptionally bold and unscrupulous. At the same time the queen was often confused and lacking in self-confidence, so that unless her deepest feelings were aroused – or Philip was present to strengthen her resolution – she often failed to resolve the disagreements among her advisers. It was probably for this reason that the threat represented by Elizabeth was never resolutely faced. Any kind of decisive action would have involved grave political risks, and the debate went on until it was too late – although the failure to take such action ultimately proved to have been the greatest risk of all. Because of her policies, and sometimes because of her lack of them, Mary tested the resources of her government severely, but they always proved adequate to the task. Justice was fairly administered and opposition severely punished. In all its ordinary aspects the country was as well and as fully governed as at any other time during the century. Despite the political and religious tensions it was no distraught or ungovernable country which Elizabeth inherited, a matter of great importance for the survival of her own regime.

Mary's parliaments legislated sparingly but sensibly to improve the administration of the law, the conduct of musters, and the processes of trade. There was, however, no major programme of reforming bills. Paget and Petre may have been true disciples of Thomas Cromwell in their enthusiasm for 'governance', and in their capacity to provide it, but they had no vision of a renovated commonwealth to compare with that of their mentor. Such a vision did exist in the minds of the queen and Gardiner, and later of Pole, but it was only perforce and reluctantly a matter for parliament. Five meetings in five years made this an exceptionally busy, yet indistinct and shapeless, period in parliamentary history. There was no identifiable or continuous opposition 'party' in either House, and yet both Lords and Commons showed themselves to be consistently tough-minded in defence of lay property interests and secular priorities; an attitude which had a profound effect upon the policies which they co-operated to implement. Open defiance of the queen's wishes was rare, yet the House of Commons was persistently suspicious of Philip, and the known antagonism of many members probably did more than anything else to dissuade Mary from pressing for his coronation. Both in 1553 and in 1555 small numbers were involved in actual conspiracy against the queen, although in the latter session the malcontents had also developed a degree of political and procedural organization not seen in the former and perhaps unprecedented. In spite of the persistent attempts of the council to secure the election of men of the 'wise, grave and catholic sort', a substantial minority in every parliament were crypto-protestants or 'fellow travellers', and many more were unsympathetic to the Roman and Habsburg orientation of the queen's policies. The quality of parliamentary management was also unimpressive by comparison with that of Cromwell or Cecil, with the result that government measures of some importance were lost in every session. Although there were no tangible developments of great significance, the potentialities of the House of Commons as a forum for gentry opinion at the national level were very clearly displayed.[26] Like their predecessors of the reformation parliament the members were preoccupied mainly with their own interests, and with the interests of their friends and patrons. When those interests were, or seemed to be, adversely affected by the government's intentions, they were capable of organized and determined resistance. This can be distinguished from resistance to the policies themselves, but the distinction is not an easy one to make, and Elizabeth's notorious sensitivity to gentry opinion suggests that she did not find it easy either.

Mary legislated reluctantly upon ecclesiastical matters, and in doing so impaled her church on the horns of an impossible dilemma. Her vision of Godliness, discipline, and peace depended for its fulfilment upon unquestioning assumptions about the truth of traditional catholic doctrines and the authority of the papacy. Yet the practical demands of the situation which she inherited meant the repeal of laws which should have been dismissed as invalid, and the insidious reappearance of the church universal as the church by law

464

established. In violation of their highest principles the queen and Pole were forced to accept that the Law of God required statutory recognition. When to this degree of compromise was added a quarrel with the papacy which compelled them to qualify their obedience to the holy see, the idealism of the catholic restoration had become heavily tarnished, and even its principal exponents were weakened by disillusionment. However, here the conventional emphasis upon failure needs to be modified. Not only did Mary and her bishops give traditional doctrines and practices a new lease of life, they also made considerable progress in restoring the material fabric of the church. This was true particularly of the bishoprics, which regained much of the wealth and prestige which they had lost under Edward VI. It is probably no exaggeration to say that the survival of episcopacy in the Anglican church was a direct consequence of Mary's success in this direction. Also, in spite of Pole's failure to generate a spiritual revival, and make catholicism a measurable political force amongst the lay aristocracy, he did help to produce a new generation of learned and devout catholic scholars.[27] Although the contrast between their colourless integrity and the passionate zeal of the later seminary priests is very marked, they did succeed in bridging a crucial gap. Without them the tradition of the Viterbo circle and the Henrician exiles would probably have been lost, and the English mission of the later sixteenth century might never have been launched. Pole did not fail merely for lack of time. He failed because he also misjudged the needs of the moment, pursuing a predetermined course without sufficient regard to the changing circumstances. But he did not fail completely, and both the Elizabethan establishment and the recusant movement owed a good deal to his modest measure of success.

At the same time, ironically, protestantism gained much more than it lost by being subjected to persecution. This was not simply a question of the blood of martyrs being the seed of the church. It was, first and foremost, a propaganda victory which was gained. A group which had been wide open to accusations of time-serving and hypocrisy was able to prove its religious credentials. Not only did clerical leaders and humble men and women alike suffer death for their faith, but able and indefatigable publicists extracted every ounce of advantage from the situation. Moreover, a group which had been associated with foreign influences was able, by a quirk of coincidence, to appear as the chief victim of alien tyranny, and consequently to establish itself as peculiarly English. Consequently the persecution contributed significantly to Elizabeth's success in maintaining a protestant regime over a predominantly conservative country. Without it she might not even have made the attempt.

Equally important, it stopped before the majority of English protestants, either at home or in exile, had been driven to accept the logic of Knox and Goodman. Faith in the royal supremacy and the 'godly prince' could not have survived indefinitely, and Elizabeth would not have been willing to collaborate with a complete generation of Genevan prophets.[28] As it was, the Genevan school produced that strand of radical dissidence known as Elizabethan puritanism; so that the balance between the Anglican establishment and its puritan critics in the later sixteenth century owed a great deal, not merely to the fact of the Marian persecution, but to its exact timing and effect.

The protestants gained by appropriating some of the benefits of English xenophobia – particularly the hatred of Spaniards – and if there has been one unanimous judgement upon the reign of Mary, it has been that the Spanish marriage was an unmitigated disaster. Harbison called it 'a poison which destroyed everything which it touched'. Certainly it was a failure from Mary's point of view, bringing her neither the children nor the love which she craved, nor the political support which she also urgently needed. However, it has to be remembered that it was not entirely contrived for Mary's benefit. To Philip it brought prestige, particularly in Rome, and a measure of political strength where and when he needed it most – in the Netherlands at the time of his father's abdication. Although it did not bring the more dramatic benefits which the king himself may have hoped for, it had been a gamble worth taking. Unfortunately from Philip's point of view it outlasted its usefulness, and the modest dividends of the war years were scarcely worth the efforts of securing them. So the verdict of failure must stand, but there is no reason to accept the common codicil – that such failure was inevitable and that the policy which the marriage represented was folly. There were good and valid reasons for undertaking it in the autumn of 1553, from the English no less than from the Imperial side. Nor did it fail primarily because of the implacable opposition of the English to foreign domination. The English were willing enough to welcome a royal heir when they thought that one was on the way, and even after the failure of Mary's pregnancy in 1555 Philip's position in England need not have been hopeless. He had the makings of powerful aristocratic support, and the queen remained devoted to his interests. Philip failed in England, not because he was defeated by xenophobia but because he did not seriously try to succeed. He had entered upon the marriage resentfully if not reluctantly, and was kept in England against his will. Consequently, even during the period of his residence he exerted himself only fitfully over English affairs, continuing to harbour a

466

sense of grievance about his position and failing to build up the English connection which lay ready to his hand. After he left England in August 1555 his concern waned still further, and at length even Paget gave up working seriously on his behalf. He made no attempt to identify himself with the interests or aspirations of his English subjects, and they came to feel, rightly, that he was no 'good lord' to them.[29] Finally, in forcing the country into war with France, he gained very little and lost what goodwill remained to him. The mutual hostility of English and Spaniards, which need have been no more than an irritant in spite of French efforts to exacerbate it, ended up by being one of the main legacies of the period to posterity.[30] Mary, having pushed through her marriage against considerable opposition, found it an increasing liability after 1555, but she was culpable only in failing to be as indifferent to Philip and his needs as he was to her.

The war of 1557–58 not only finished Philip's prospects as king of England, it also ruined four years of attempted financial retrenchment. Mary's policy in this direction was neither particularly distinctive nor particularly successful. Its outline, including the reform of the exchequer, was already established when she came to the throne, and her mistaken generosity over the last Edwardian subsidy led to an increase in the inherited debt. Nevertheless, improvements were made, by strict oversight and honest administration rather than by large economies or augmentations of revenue. The queen was generous, but not extravagant, and her secular and ecclesiastical restorations put no more than a modest pressure upon her resources. The repayment of the foreign debt between 1555 and 1557 was a striking achievement, but it was obtained at considerable cost and did not indicate a major improvement in the financial situation. Mary's council can hardly be blamed for failing to undertake a recoinage, because of the impossibility of devaluation, and they did bring about one of the major revenue improvements in the century by introducing the new book of customs rates. Between 1553 and 1557 Mary's government was running hard, and with reasonable competence, to stay approximately where it was. In 1557 and 1558, in spite of greatly increased efforts to raise money, and tight expenditure controls, it was losing ground very fast, and ended up much deeper in debt than it had begun. The lesson was clear. Without either a major increase in 'ordinary' revenue or an unprecedented willingness on the part of parliament to provide taxation, England could not afford to wage war. This time there were no Edwardian 'harpies' to blame,[31] or other factors to confuse the starkly unpalatable truth, and Elizabeth profited very noticeably from the lesson. Any war was a recipe for political confrontation. It was probably a mistake on the part of Mary's advisers to rely so heavily upon the foreign bankers early and late in her reign, but such reliance was a normal expedient, and Sir Thomas Gresham served her as competently as he had served her brother.

The failures of the war itself can only partly be blamed upon English incompetence. Pembroke's expeditionary force was efficiently mustered, well equipped, and properly paid. The border defences were repaired, and the garrisons kept up to strength. Above all the fleet was carefully provided for, new ships built, and existing ships repaired and maintained. A stocktaking of the navy undertaken in February 1559 showed 26 royal ships in service and another 7 in dry dock; only three were listed as beyond repair.[32] In March 1559 it was noted that 45 merchant ships were also available to be armed and manned for the queen's service,[33] while a slightly earlier Spanish list contained the names of 30 royal ships and 60 others under the names of their home ports.[34] Elizabeth's council recommended that 10 of the queen's existing ships should be scrapped or sold, and a smaller number of new vessels built,[35] but they found nothing like the dismal state of affairs reported by Mary's council five and a half years earlier when they listed 97 royal ships which had 'decaied' since the death of Henry VIII.[36] On the other hand, the defences of Calais and the garrisons of the Pale were in a sad state of neglect when the fatal blow fell. Reinforcements sent in during the summer had been allowed to dwindle away, or had been withdrawn. Munitions were inadequate, food supplies low, and except at Guisnes no proper vigilance maintained. Treachery in the ordinary sense of dealings with the enemy was hardly necessary to explain a disaster which was rather the result of culpable negligence – arising partly from overconfidence in the massive fortifications, and partly from proximity to Imperial territory. Significantly the musters ordered in January 1558 seem to have been much less efficiently conducted than those of the previous summer, which was one of the reasons why they were abandoned.

The Elizabethans were at least partly right to blame Mary and her council bitterly for the fall of Calais – although wrong to suggest that the whole war had been utterly mismanaged. They were also right when they claimed that she had left the realm far more deeply in debt than her brother had done – although it is highly unlikely that they could have done any better in the circumstances. However, it is less clear that they were right in blaming Mary for running a thoroughly partisan regime – a government by faction. It was claimed after her death that she had filled all the responsible offices with known catholics, even when their other claims to preferment were inferior; that she had purged the commissions of the peace and the commissions for musters; and that she had overridden municipal elections and other local appointments in the interests of her papist creatures. In fact the commissions seem hardly to have been touched at all, although a small number of known protestants and convicted conspirators were certainly excluded. Some attempts were made to control the empanelling of juries in sensitive cases, but this was a normal Tudor practice. Similarly, in important cities such as London, efforts were made (not always successful) to secure conformable mayors. On the other hand, attempts made to control the composition of the House of Commons were perfunctory and ineffectual. The solid evidence of partisan government – apart from the church which is a separate issue – relates mostly to high offices close to the queen's person and to her use of discretionary patronage. Mary did attempt to rebuild the ancient family connections, Howard, Courtenay, Percy, and Neville particularly, and favoured those who had lost favour and fortune under her father and brother. She did so, however, as much out of a sense of justice (and perhaps nostalgia) as for any tangible political reason. None of her major beneficiaries repaid her generosity, least of all the Howards and Courtenays,[37] although time may have been a decisive factor here. It seems that, rather than setting out to rule through a catholic 'party', Mary attempted at first to establish a kind of 'consensus' government, from which only the radical protestants and the known adherents of Northumberland would be excluded. Only at court did she give free rein to her personal tastes and affinities. However, as her reign progressed, she became increasingly mistrustful as it became clear that many who had welcomed her and her conservative policies did not approve of her marriage, or of the papacy, or of both. The marked increase in licensed retaining between 1554 and 1556, and the identity of those licensed, is a clear indication of what was happening. As her trust was given, first to Renard, then to Philip, and finally to Pole, she began to lose touch with many, even among her own councillors. By the spring of 1557, and particularly over the war issue, she was at odds with most of her advisers, and during 1558 attendance at both council and court was low, particularly among the nobility. It was not so much that Mary chose to rule through a faction as that only a faction retained their devotion to her through thick and thin. She was capable of inspiring great personal loyalty, but only among those with whom she was in complete agreement on matters of the faith. Perhaps Mary was, as she has often been described, 'the most amiable of the Tudors', but there was an iron streak in her personality, in power no less than in affliction. Not only does she personally bear the responsibility for the burning of nearly 300 heretics, she also executed traitors more

Q

ruthlessly than either her father or her sister, and used martial law with exceptional freedom. Whatever Sir Nicholas Throgmorton might have thought, Mary did not earn her reputation for clemency.[38]

The reign of Mary is never going to rank as one of the great creative periods in English history, but it was important in the context of the sixteenth century. Inevitably a close examination of the period confirms some accepted judgements, qualifies others, and reverses a few. The most important judgement which I hope to have reversed in this and other studies which I have written on the period is that of insignificance. Mary failed in most of the things which she set out to achieve, but failure is relative and there was a positive legacy of achievement to hand on to her successor; a legacy of sound administration, financial reform, and strengthened episcopacy. Of course failure can also be constructive, and it has long been recognized that the exile and persecution was a formative period for English protestantism, and that Elizabeth learned from her predecessor's mistakes. However, it seems to me that the real significance of the reign lies in the extent to which it weakened religious and political conservatism.

It is a fallacy to believe that there was a 'catholic' party which supported the queen, and a 'protestant' party which opposed her. As we have seen, the catholics were deeply divided, not only over the Spanish marriage, but also over the degree of their attachment to the papacy. A writer of anti-Spanish invective, such as John Bradford, could express the liveliest concern lest he inadvertently promote the cause of heresy.

> There have been certain pestiferous bokes and letters lately printed in Englyshe, under the cloke of a fervent zeal, or love towardes our country against Spaniardes, by the develishe device of certayne heretiks, thinking thereby to ground in the hartes of all people . . . many abominable heresies . . .[39]

Paget, who was warm to Philip, could be very cool to the papacy; while the queen's intimates such as Rochester and Waldegrave were the reverse, in spite of the fact that Mary was equally warm to both. Consequently the supporters of the regime responded differently to different issues, and did not constitute a single coherent political 'bloc'. The same was true of the 'protestants'. I have argued elsewhere that the Wyatt rebellion was not a protestant rising, and I remain of that opinion, in spite of the fact that several of the leaders were clearly hostile to Mary's religious policy as well as to the marriage.[40] Protestants in the full sense, such as Cranmer or Hooper, did not, at that stage, place any hope in resistance, and indeed opposed it on principle. On the other hand, there were many gentlemen, and others, who were 'protestants' in the sense that they preferred an erastian or secular form of government. The opposition of such men to Mary was a matter of degree, varying with mood, time, and opportunity. Consequently we find many who appear at one point as opponents of the regime, and at another point as its supporters. Most notably many erstwhile accomplices of Wyatt and Dudley fought for Philip and Mary at St Quentin, while some of the real irreconcilables, such as Henry Killigrew, fought on the other side.

Thomas Cromwell had, barely and with great effort, managed to retain control of the 'middle ground' of English politics – those noblemen, gentlemen, and clergy whose principal characteristics were social and religious conservatism, insularity, and loyalty to the king. By doing so he was able to make important changes which also brought into being a 'reforming' interest of his own way of thinking, and a 'conservative' interest secretly loyal to the papacy and implacably hostile to his political and administrative programme. After his fall the reformers were forced to make concessions, but retained the upper hand. However, between 1547 and 1553 they became an ever more radical and ever smaller party. So that, while clinging to formal power, they lost control over the 'middle ground' and collapsed when the king in whose name they had acted died. Thus Mary, who had been for years the symbol and acknowledged leader of the conservatives, was presented with an almost complete ascendancy on her accession – supported by everybody except the discredited fragments of the reforming faction. That ascendancy she progressively lost. Some was sacrificed to the Spanish marriage, and some to the restoration of the Roman obedience, neither policies which appealed strongly to the men of the centre, but enough still remained at the beginning of 1555 to give every indication of ultimate success. However, from that point onward things began to go seriously wrong. There was no heir, a disaster in itself and a hint of divine disfavour. Philip made no real effort to establish himself in England and contributed little to the government. The harvest failed and there was dearth and disease. The religious persecution was brutal and unpopular. By 1557 the momentum of the regime had run down and the future looked ominous and uncertain. Then came disaster, the outbreak of war and open quarrel with the papacy, followed by the loss of Calais.

It would be an exaggeration to say that Mary had lost control of her people by 1558. She was the queen and her government held. There were comparatively few who opposed her with sufficient consistency or determination either to conspire, to go into exile, or to write hostile propaganda. Such opponents were certainly no more numerous or effective than those who had faced Henry VIII and Cromwell in the 1530s, although by comparison with the domestic enemies of Elizabeth they look both active and threatening. On the other hand, the conservatives found that it was a great deal easier to remain united in opposition than in power, and the men of the centre were almost as disillusioned with her reactionary policies by 1558 as they had been with the radicals in 1553. Instead of consolidating the immense strength of her conservative support and exploiting it cautiously, Mary had divided it deeply and virtually paralysed it as a political force. As a result Elizabeth was able to gain and hold the 'middle ground' through the critical 1560s, in spite of her protestant settlement and radical supporters. There was nothing inevitable or even likely about this, but Mary had offended too many of the susceptibilities of those conservative and insular erastians who had, unknown to her, formed the backbone of her political strength. It was to be Elizabeth's long and successful reign which made the verdict of 1558–59 final, but it had been Mary's errors of judgement which made it possible.

Notes

1 See *The Passage of our most dread Sovereign Lady, Queen Elizabeth, through the City of London*, reprinted in *Tudor Tracts*, ed. A. F. Pollard, 367-95.
2 BL Stowe MS 354 f. 18.
3 Notes in Renard's hand, March 1558. *Cal. Span.*, XIII, 372.
4 *Cal. Pat.*, Elizabeth, I, 149.
5 W. MacCaffrey, *The Shaping of the Elizabethan Regime* (1968), 32-3, See also Englefield to Cecil, 5 December 1558. PRO SP12/1/21. Sir John Bourne had ceased to be Secretary, presumably through resignation, in March 1558, although he had remained a member of the council. *APC*, VI.
6 PRO LC2/4 (2), 'The Buryal of the late Quene Mary'. LC2/4 (3), order of Elizabeth's coronation.
7 MacCaffrey, op. cit., 36.
8 J. H. Gleason, 'Commissions of the Peace, 1554–1564', *Huntington Library Quarterly*, 18 (1955), 169-77.
9 Howard was also a kinsman of the new queen.
10 See above, 78-84.
11 Gammon, *Statesman and Schemer*, 245-50.
12 Francis Russell, 2nd earl, who had succeeded to the title in 1555, but not to his father's place in the queen's favour. A copy of Wycliffe's sermons on the gospels, bearing his signature and the date 1556, is preserved among the family papers. *HMC Second Report*, App., 7 (Bedford MSS). Knollys had been a religious exile. C. H. Garrett, *The Marian Exiles* (1938), 210-13.
13 For Rogers's activities in Mary's reign, see *TTC*, 16, 18, 96, etc.

14 Nicholas Wotton was in orders, and held the deaneries of both York and Canterbury, but never seems to have functioned as a priest.
15 MacCaffrey, op. cit., 34-6. The Boleyns and the Howards were the queen's kin, and the Cookes intermarried with her most trusted servants. By contrast, the Seymours were not high in favour, nor the Greys – possibly because of Catherine's claim to the succession. M. Levine, *The Early Elizabethan Succession Question* (1966).
16 This was the opinion of Henri II 'owing to their absolute uniformity in religious opinion'. Michieli to the doge and senate, 4 December 1558. *Cal. Ven.*, VI, 1563.
17 I am grateful to Dr Simon Adams of the university of Strathclyde for drawing my attention to this point in discussion.
18 *TTC*, 246-7. *DNB*, Robert Dudley.
19 ibid. Stow, *Chronicle*, 1985 *et seq.* PRO SP12/1/27, 29.
20 Proclamation against seditious preaching, 27 December 1558. Hughes and Larkin, II, 102-3.
21 By Gee, Pollard, Hughes, Neale, and others.
22 N. L. Jones, 'Faith by Statute' (unpublished Cambridge PhD thesis, 1977).
23 The convocation held simultaneously with parliament in February 1559 had declared unequivocally in favour of transubstantiation and the Roman obedience. Since the Lower Houses of convocation were dominated by the senior cathedral clergy, this was a clear demonstration of the absence of Henrician sentiments at that level. Cardwell, *Synadolia*, II, 490-4.
24 The council was apprehensive at the beginning of the reign about the possibility of clergy-led risings. On 31 December 1558 a letter was sent to Sir Thomas Cawarden, Sir Peter Carew, and George Throgmorton relating to the conduct of musters, and adding 'It is not a thing usuall to have the bisshoppes and clergie at eny musters, and yet we well understand that they have of late tyme procured to their possession a great quantitie of armor and weapons'. *HMC Sixth Report*, App., 164 (Molyneux MSS at Loseley).
25 A. F. Pollard, *The Political History of England* (1919), VI, 172.
26 In *TTC*, I argued that the events of this reign helped to develop an awareness of the possibility of 'constitutional' opposition. Further investigation, both by myself and others, has since suggested that this conclusion was too vague, and very difficult to prove. On the other hand, it is now firmly established that the Marian Commons were truly representative of gentry and burgess opinion, and that the members were fully aware of their important place in the execution of policy, *TTC*, 24-3. Loach, op. cit.
27 Harding, Allen, and Sander are the best known, but probably as many as a hundred from the two universities went into exile after 1559. Not all these were men of great learning, and they had been appointed for their catholic orthodoxy, but their exodus was a tribute to the thoroughness with which Pole had handled the universities. P. Hughes, op. cit., III, 247.
28 For Elizabeth's relations with the returning exiles, and their ideology of a 'new Constantine', see W. Haller, *Foxe's Book of Martyrs and the Elect Nation* (1963), and the corrective supplied by V. N. Olsen, *John Foxe and the Elizabethan Church* (1973). See also *OM*, 261-8.
29 Philip's concessions to English commercial and maritime aspirations were too little and too late. In 1557 he decided to offer a limited participation in the American trade, but it is not clear that the offer was actually made.

In 1558 he granted permission for Stephen Borough to visit Seville and learn the secrets of the *casa*, normally forbidden to foreigners. Borough brought back with him Martin Cortes's *Breve compendio*, which was translated by Richard Eden and published in 1561.

30 W. S. Maltby, *The Black Legend in England* (1971). There was another and more pleasant side to the relationship in the extensive influence of Spanish models on English literature of the later sixteenth century.

31 Protestant attempts to blame Mary's financial hardships upon her excessive ecclesiastical restorations must be seen mainly as apologia for a fresh round of attacks upon church property.

32 PRO SP12/2/30, 20 February 1559.

33 SP12/3/44. 'A book of sea causes', 24 March 1559.

34 AGS, E811 f. 21. Manning and victualling estimates, undated, but 1558.

35 SP12/3/44.

36 SP11/1/23.

37 The old duke of Norfolk, who was virtually senile, died in August 1554. He was succeeded by his grandson, who did not attain his majority until 1559. The earl of Devon, thanks to his irresponsible behaviour, spent most of his time in prison or in exile, dying in Venice in 1556. His estates reverted to the crown. It is worth noticing that the most clearly political of her major restorations, that of the Percies, was also the last.

38 'Was ever English Prince so bountifull
To subjects? Mark her resitution
Nott of their Bloode alone, butt of their landes
Which then remayned in her princelie handes'.
Legend of Sir Nicholas Throgmorton, ed. J. G. Nichols (1874). Throgmorton was one of the lucky ones. Mary was amenable to direct personal appeals, particularly by devoted wives, but her mercy seems to have been somewhat random. Whether she always executed the most guilty, or whether her executions had much deterrent effect, is very open to question; but she executed a higher proportion of known rebels and conspirators than her father had done. *TTC*, 113-27. Above, 282-3.

39 John Bradford, *The Copye of a letter* . . . Preface 'To the Reader'.

40 M. R. Thorp, 'Religion and the rebellion of Sir Thomas Wyatt' (*Church History*, 47, 4, 1978), has added to our knowledge of the religious attitudes of some leaders, but has not (in my opinion) come near to proving that the rebellion was a religious movement.

The Privy Council under Mary

Name	Date of appointment	Age on appt.	Office at time of appointment	Offices to which later appointed	Previous Council membership	Highest previous office	Religion	Attendance record
ARUNDEL, Henry Fitzalan, EARL OF	Before 28.7.53	41	Lord President Lord Steward		1547–50	Lord Chamberlain	cp	40%
BAKER, SIR JOHN	5.8.53	60+	Chancellor of exchequer		1535–47 1548–53	Chancellor of exchequer	cp	under 20%
*BATH, John Bourchier, EARL OF	Before 28.7.53	54?					cp	under 20%
BEDFORD, John Russell, EARL OF	29.7.53	68?	Lord Privy Seal		1538–47 1547–53	Lord Privy Seal	cp	under 20%
*BEDINGFIELD, SIR HENRY	Before 28.7.53	42		Vice-chamberlain			cc	20%+
*BOURNE, SIR JOHN	Before 28.7.53	?	Principal Secretary†				cc	60%+
BOXALL, DR JOHN	December 1556	30+	Principal Secretary				cc	60%+
BROWNE, SIR ANTHONY [Viscount Montague]	April 1557	27		Master of the horse to the king (briefly)			cc	under 20%

Name	Date of appointment	Age on appt.	Office at time of appointment	Offices to which later appointed	Previous Council membership	Highest previous office	Religion	Attendance record
CHENEY, SIR THOMAS	6.8.53	68?	Treasurer of household Lord Warden Cinque Ports		1540-47	Treasurer of household Lord Warden Cinque Ports	cp	under 20%
CLINTON, Edward Fiennes, LORD	April 1557	41	Lord Admiral		1550-53	Lord Admiral	p	under 20%
CORDELL, WILLIAM	December 1557	30+	Master of the Rolls			Solicitor General	p	under 20%
*CORNWALLIS, SIR THOMAS	Before 28.7.53	35		Controller of household			cp	under 20%
DERBY, Edward Stanley, EARL OF	17.8.53	44			1551		cp	under 20%
*DRURY, SIR WILLIAM	Before 28.7.53	26					p	under 20%
*ENGLEFIELD, SIR FRANCIS	Before 28.7.53	31		Master of the court of wards			cc	under 20%
*FRESTON, SIR ROBERT	Before 28.7.53	?	Cofferer of the household	Controller of household			cc?	under 20%
GAGE, SIR JOHN	30.7.53	74	Lord Chamberlain		1528-47 1547-48	Vice-chamberlain Controller	cc	50%+

Name	Date	Age						%
GARDINER, STEPHEN [Bishop of Winchester]	5.8.53	70	Lord Chancellor		1531–46	Principal Secretary	cc	60%+
*HARE, SIR NICHOLAS	Before 28.7.53	?	Master of rolls			Master of requests	cp	under 20%
HASTINGS, SIR EDWARD [Lord Hastings of Loughborough]	28.7.53	?	Master of the horse	Lord chamberlain			cc	20%+
HEATH, NICHOLAS [Bishop of Worcester]	4.9.53	52?		Lord Chancellor Archbishop of York			cc	50%+
HIGHAM, SIR CLEMENT	April 1554	50+		Chief baron of exchequer			cc?	under 20%
HOWARD, LORD WILLIAM [Lord Howard of Effingham]	3.1.54	43?	Lord Admiral			Lord deputy of Calais	p	20%+
*HUDDLESTONE, SIR JOHN	Before 28.7.53	?		Vice-chamberlain to the king			cc	under 20%
*JERNINGHAM, SIR HENRY	4.8.53	?	Vice-chamberlain	Master of horse			cc	40%+
LA WARR, Thomas West, LORD	17.8.53	81?					cc	under 20%
MASON, SIR JOHN	30.7.53	50			1550–53		p	under 20%
*MORDAUNT, SIR JOHN	Before 28.7.53	40+					cc	under 20%

Name	Date of appointment	Age on appt.	Office at time of appointment	Offices to which later appointed	Previous Council membership	Highest previous office	Religion	Attendance record
*MORGAN, SIR RICHARD	Before 28.7.53	?	Chief Justice Common Pleas			Puisne judge	cc	under 20%
NORFOLK, Thomas Howard, DUKE OF	10.8.53	80			1522–46	Lord Treasurer	cp	50%+
PAGET OF BEAUDESERT, William Paget, LORD	Before 28.7.53	48		Lord Privy Seal	1543–47 1547–51	Principal Secretary	p	40%+
PECKHAM, SIR EDMUND	29.7.53	58?	Treasurer of the mint		1549–50	Treasurer of the mint	cc	under 20%
*PECKHAM, ROBERT	Before 28.7.53	38					cc	under 20%
PEMBROKE, William Herbert, EARL OF	13.8.53	52?		President of the marches	1547–53	President of the marches	cp	20%+
PETRE, SIR WILLIAM	30.7.53	48?	Principal Secretary‡		1543–47 1547–53	Principal Secretary	cp	60%+
RICH, Richard Rich, LORD	Before 28.7.53	57?			1536–47 1547–53	Lord Chancellor	cp	under 20%
*ROCHESTER, SIR ROBERT	Before 28.7.53	59?	Controller of household				cc	60%+
ST LEGER, SIR ANTHONY	7.8.53	57?	Lord deputy of Ireland			Lord deputy of Ireland	cp	under 20%

Name	Date	Age	Office	Dates	Office	Code	Percentage
*SHELTON, SIR JOHN	Before 28.7.53	?				cp	under 20%
SHREWSBURY, George Talbot, EARL OF	10.8.53	50	President of the north	1549–53	President of the north	cp	under 20%
*SOUTHWELL, SIR RICHARD	Before 28.7.53	49	Master of the ordnance	1542–47 1549–50		cc	20%+
*STRELLY, ROBERT	Before 28.7.53	?				cc?	under 20%
SUSSEX, Henry Radcliffe, EARL OF	Before 28.7.53	47				cp	20%+
THIRLBY, THOMAS [Bishop of Norwich]	25.10.53	47?	Bishop of Ely	1542–46		cp	50%+
TREGONWELL, SIR JOHN	10.1.55	50+		1532–47		p	Nil
TUNSTALL, CUTHBERT [Bishop of Durham]	14.8.53	79	Keeper of the privy seal	1523–47 1547–50		cc	under 20%
*WALDEGRAVE, SIR EDWARD	Before 28.7.53	36?	Keeper of the wardrobe			cc	20%+
WENTWORTH, Thomas Wentworth, LORD	Before 28.7.53	28	Lord deputy of Calais			p	under 20%
*WHARTON, SIR THOMAS	Before 28.7.53	33				cp	40%+
WINCHESTER, William Paulet, MARQUIS OF	13.8.53	70+	Lord treasurer	1525–47 1547–53	Lord treasurer	p	40%+

Name	Date of appointment	Age on appt.	Office at time of appointment	Offices to which later appointed	Previous Council membership	Highest previous office	Religion	Attendance record
WOTTON, DR NICHOLAS [Dean of Canterbury and York]	August 1557	56?			1549–53		cp	under 20%

Notes

Only major offices of state, and senior household and judicial posts, have been included in this table.

Religious affiliation:

cc = conservative catholic, i.e., one who welcomed the persecutions and the return to Rome.

cp = conservative *politique*, i.e., one who welcomed the return of the mass but was cool towards the papacy.

p = *politique*, i.e., a conformist who had no enthusiasm for official religious policy. Some of those so indicated were regarded, either at the time or subsequently, as crypto-protestants. There were, of course, no open protestants on Mary's council.

A question-mark indicates a conjecture.

* = Framlingham councillors

† = left office, probably by resignation, March 1558

‡ = left office, probably by resignation, March 1557

Bibliography

Manuscript sources

In the Public Record Office, London:

State Papers Domestic, Henry VIII   (SP1)
State Papers Domestic, Edward VI   (SP10)
State Papers Domestic, Mary and Philip and Mary   (SP11)
State Papers Domestic, Elizabeth   (SP12)
State Papers Domestic, Addenda, Edward VI to James I   (SP15)
State Papers Domestic, Supplementary   (SP46)
State Papers, Ireland, Mary and Philip and Mary   (SP62)
State Papers, Ireland, Folios   (SP65)
State Papers, Foreign, Mary and Philip and Mary   (SP69)

Chancery, Close Rolls   (C54)

Exchequer, Accounts various   (E101)
Exchequer, Miscellaneous books   (E164)
Exchequer, Subsidy rolls   (E179)
Exchequer, Pipe Office, declared accounts   (E351)
Exchequer, Enrolments and registers of receipts   (E401)
Exchequer, Rolls etc. of receipt and issue   (E405)
Exchequer, Miscellanea of receipt   (E407)

King's Bench, Baga de secretis   (KB8)
King's Bench, Placita coram rege   (KB27)
King's Bench, Controlment rolls   (KB29)

Lord Chamberlain's department, office of robes, special events   (LC2)
Lord Chamberlain's department, miscellanea   (LC5)

Lord Steward's department, miscellaneous books   (LS13)

Duchy of Lancaster, accounts various   (DL28)

Exchequer and Audit department, accounts various   (AO1)

Venetian manuscripts   (PRO 30/25)

Baschet's transcripts   (PRO 31/3)

Bibliography

In the British Library:
Cotton MSS; Otho, Vespasian, Titus, Cleopatra, Faustin
Harleian MSS
Sloane MSS
Stowe MSS
Royal MSS
Egerton MSS
Lansdowne MSS
Wyatt MSS
Additional MSS

In the Bodleian Library:
Tanner MSS

In the Greater London Record Office:
Letter books of the Court of Aldermen
Repertories of the Court of Aldermen
Journal of the Common Council

In the Archivo General de Simancas:
Secretaría de Estado; Estado Inglaterra, Estado Flandes, Estado Roma,
    Estado Portugal
Contadurías Generales
Diversos de Castilia
Guerra Antigua
Libros de Berzosa
Patronato Real

In the Biblioteca del Palacio Real, Madrid:
MSS, II, 2251–2286

In the Archives du ministère des affaires étrangères, Paris:
Correspondance Politique, Angleterre, 19

Microfilms:
Biblioteca Vaticana; Vat. Lat. 5968 (Bodleian Library)
Douai Municipal Archives, MS 292 (Lambeth Palace Library)

Contemporary printed works
(place of publication London unless otherwise stated)

A supplicacyon to the Quenes Majestie (Unknown, 1555)

A warnyng for Englande conteynyng the horrible practises of the Kyng of Spayne in the Kyngedom of Naples ... (Unknown, 1555)

A speciall grace appointed to have been said after a banket at Yorke (1558)

All the Submyssyons and recantations of Thomas Cranmer (1556)

An admonishion to the bishoppes of Winchester London and others (1553)

An epitaphe upon the Death of the Most excellent and oure late vertuous Quene Marie (1558)

Bale, John, *The vocacyon of Johan Bale to the Bishoprick of Ossorie* (? London, 1553)

Birche, William, *A songe betwen the Quenes majestie and Englande* (1558)

Bonner, Edmund, *A profitable and necessarye doctryne, with certayne homilies* (1555)

Bonner, Edmund, *An honest godlye instruction* ... *for the* ... *bringinge up of children* (1555)

Bradford, John, *The copye of a letter sent by John Bradforthe to the right honorable lordes the Erles of Arundel, Derbie, Shrewsburye and Penbroke* ... (? London, 1556)

Brice, Thomas, *A compendious register in metre* ... (1559) (also printed in A. F. Pollard, *Tudor Tracts*, 259-89)

Bull, Henry, *An apology made by* ... *John Hooper* (1561)

Christopherson, John, *An exhortation to all menne to take hede and beware of rebellion* (1554)

Churchyard, Thomas, *The Firste parte of Churchyardes chippes* (1575)

Copia delle lettere del serenissimo Re d'Inghilterra ... (Rome, 1555)

Elder, John, *The copie of a letter sent into Scotlande* ... (1555)

Forrest, William, *A newe ballade of the Marigolde* (1554)

Gardiner, Stephen, *De vera obedientia* (? Rouen, 1553)

Goodman, Christopher, *How superior powers oght to be obeyd* (Geneva, 1558)

Gwynneth, John, *A declaration of the state wherein all heretickes dooe leade their lives* (1554)

Heywood, John, *A balade specifienge partly the maner, partly the matter, in the most excellent meetyng and lyke marriage betwene our Sovereigne Lord and our Sovereigne Lady, the Kynges and Queenes highnes* (1554)

Heywood, John, *A breefe balet touching the traytorous takynge of Scarborow Castell* (1557)

Bibliography

Huggarde, Miles, *The assault of the sacrament of the altar* (1554)
Huggarde, Miles, *A treatise declaring howe Christ by perverse preachyng was banished out of this realme* (1554)
Huggarde, Miles, *The displaying of the Protestantes* (1556)
Il felicissimo ritorno del regno d'Inghilterra alla cattolica unione (Rome, 1555)
Knox, John, *An admonition . . . that the faithfull Christians in London . . . may avoid Gods vengeaunce* (? Antwerp, 1554)
Knox, John, *The First Blast of the Trumpet Against the Monstrous Regiment of Women* (? Geneva, 1558)
La partita del serenissimo Principe con l'armata di Spagna . . . (Rome, 1555)
La solenne et felice intrata delli serenissimi Re Philippo et Regina Maria d'Inghilterra (Rome, 1555)
La vera capitulatione e Articoli passati e conclusi . . . (Rome, 1555)
M., R., *A newe ballad* (1558)
M(arshall), G(eorge), *A compendious treatise in metre* (1554)
Martin, Thomas, *A Traictise declaryng and plainly provyng, that the pretensed marriage of Priestes . . . is no marriage* (1554)
Muñoz, Andres, *Viaje de Felipe II a Inglaterra* (Zaragoza, 1554)
Nowe singe now springe oure care is exil'd, Oure vertuous Quene is quickened with child (1554)
Olde, John, *An Acquital or purgation of the moost catholyke Christen Prince Edward VI* (? Zurich, 1555)
Philpot, John, *A trew report of the dysputacyon . . . in the convocacyon hows at London* (? Antwerp, 1554)
Ponet, John, *A shorte treatise of Politike Power* (? Strasburg, 1556)
Pownall, Robert, *An admonition to the towne of Callays* (Unknown, 1557)
'Pratte, Poore', *The copie of a pistel or letter sent to Gilbard Potter* (1553)
Proctor, John, *The Historie of Wyates rebellion* (1554) (also printed in A. F. Pollard, *Tudor Tracts*, 199-259)
Reformatio Angliae ex decretis Reginaldi Poli (Rome, 1562)
Rosso, Giullio, *I successi d'Inghilterra dopo la morte di Eduardo Sesto* (Ferrara, 1555)
Scory, John, *An epistle wrytten by John Scory . . . unto alle the faythfull that be in pryson in Englande* (? Zurich, 1555)
Standish, John, *A discourse wherein is debated whether it be expedient that the scriptures should be in English* (1544)
Stopes, Leonard, *An Ave Maria in Commendation of oure most vertuous Queene* (? 1553)
Smith, Richard, *A Bucklar of the Catholyke fayth* (1555)

484

The communication betwene my Lord Chauncelor and Judge Hales
  (? Rouen, 1553)
The saying of John late Duke of Northumberland uppon the scaffolde
  (1553)
Traheron, Bartholomew, *A warning to England . . . by the terrible*
  example of Calece (? Wesel, 1558)
Traheron, Bartholomew, *An aunswere made by Bart. Traheron to a*
  Privie Papiste which crepte in . . . (Wesel, 1558)
Turner, William, *The hunting of the Romyshe wolfe* (Zurich, 1554)
Watson, Thomas, *Holesome and Catholyke doctrine* (1558)

Calendars and printed sources

Acts of the Privy Council, ed. J. R. Dasent (London, 1890–1907)
Alberigo, G., *Conciliorum Oecumenicorum decreta* (Freiburg im B.,
  1962)
Ambassades de Messieurs de Noailles en Angleterre, ed. R. A. de Vertot
  (Leyden, 1743)
Ames, Joseph, *Typographical Antiquities* (London, 1790)
Baker, Augustine, *Memorials of Father Augustine Baker*, ed. J.
  McCann and R. H. Connolly (Catholic Record Society, 33, 1933)
Bradford, John, *The Writings of John Bradford*, ed. Aubrey Townshend
  (Parker Society, 1848–53)
Brett, John, 'A narrative of the pursuit of the English refugees', ed.
  I. S. Leadam (*Transactions of the Royal Historical Society*, 2 series,
  11, 1897)
Burnet, Gilbert, *History of the Reformation in England* (London,
  1681–1714)
Calendar of Patent Rolls, Mary and Philip and Mary (London,
  1936–39)
Calendar of State Papers, Domestic, 1547–1580, ed. R. Lemon (London,
  1856)
Calendar of State Papers, Foreign, Mary, ed. W. B. Turnbull (London,
  1861); Elizabeth, 1 and 2, ed. J. Stevenson (London, 1863)
Calendar of State Papers relating to Scotland, ed. J. Bain *et al.*
  (Edinburgh, 1898–1952)
Calendar of State Papers, Spanish, ed. Royall Tyler *et al.* (London,
  1862–1964)
Calendar of State Papers, Venetian, ed. Rawdon Brown *et al.* (London,
  1864–98)
Cardwell, Edward, *Synadolia* (Oxford, 1842)
Clifford, Henry, *The Life of Jane Dormer, Duchess of Feria*, ed. J.
  Stevenson (London, 1887)

Bibliography

Cobbett, William, *et al.*, *A complete collection of State Trials* (London, 1816–98)

Collection des Voyages des Souverains des Pays-Bas, ed. L. P. Gachard and C. Piot (Brussels, 1874–82)

Díaz-Plaja, Fernando, *La Historia de España en sus Documentos: el siglo XVI* (Madrid, 1958)

Documentos inéditos para la Historia de España, ed. M. F. Navarette *et al.* (Madrid, 1842–95)

Dyer, Sir James, *Novels Cases* (London, 1585)

Fernández Alvarez, M., *Corpus Documental de Carlos V* (Salamanca, 1973–7)

Foedera, conventiones, litterae etc., ed. Thomas Rymer *et al.* (London, 1704–35)

Foxe, John, *Acts and Monuments of the English Martyrs*, ed. J. Pratt (London, 1853–70)

Gardiner, Stephen, *A Machiavellian Treatise by Stephen Gardiner*, ed. P. S. Donaldson (Cambridge, 1975)

Gardiner, Stephen, *The Letters of Stephen Gardiner*, ed. J. A. Muller (Cambridge, 1933)

Greyfriars Chronicle, ed. J. G. Nichols (Camden Society, 53, 1852)

Hall, Edward, *The union of the two noble and illustre famelies York and Lancaster* (London, 1542) ed. H. Ellis (London, 1809)

Hall, Richard, *The Life of John Fisher*, ed. R. Bayne (Early English Text Society, 117, 1921)

Harpesfield, Nicholas, *Archdeacon Harpesfield's visitation of 1557*, ed. L. E. Whatmore (Catholic Record Society, 45-6, 1950–51)

Hearne, Thomas, *Sylloge Epistolarum* (London, 1716)

Historical Manuscripts Commission Reports, Appendices to various reports

Hoby, Sir Thomas, 'The Journal of Sir Thomas Hoby', ed. E. Powell (Camden Miscellany, 10, 1902)

Jane, *The chronicle of Queen Jane and of the first two years of Mary*, ed. J. G. Nichols (Camden Society, 48, 1850)

Jordan, W. K., *The Chronicle and Political Papers of Edward VI* (London, 1966)

Journals of the House of Commons, I (London, 1803)

Journals of the House of Lords, I (London, 1846)

Kervyn de Lettenhove, J.M.B.C., *Rélations politiques des Pays-Bas et de l'Angleterre* (Brussels, 1882–1900)

Latimer, Hugh, *Works* (2 vols.), ed. G. E. Gorrie (Parker Society, 1844–5)

Letters and Papers of the Reign of Henry VIII, ed. James Gairdner *et al.* (London, 1862–1910)

Lindsay, Robert, of Pitscottie, *The History of Scotland from . . . 1436 to . . . 1565*, ed. J. G. Mackay (Scottish Text Sodiety, 1899–1911)

Literary Remains of Edward VI, ed. J. G. Nichols (Roxburgh Club, 1857)

Machyn, Henry, *The diary of Henry Machyn*, ed. J. G. Nichols (Camden Society, 42, 1848)

Madden, F. E., *The Privy Purse expenses of the Princess Mary* (London, 1831)

Malfatti, C. V., *Four manuscripts of the Escorial* (Barcelona, 1956)

Narratives of the days of the Reformation, ed. J. G. Nichols (Camden Society, 77, 1859)

Original Letters relative to the English Reformation, ed. H. Robinson (Parker Society, 1846–47)

Paget, William, 'The letters of William, Lord Paget of Beaudesert', ed. B. L. Beer and S. I. Jack (Camden Miscellany, 25, 1974)

Parkyn, Robert, 'Robert Parkyn's narrative of the reformation', ed. A. G. Dickens (*English Historical Review*, 62, 1947)

Peck, Francis, *Desiderata Curiosa* (London, 1732–35)

Pole, Reginald, *Epistolae Reginaldi Poli*, ed. A. M. Quirini (Brescia, 1744–57)

Pole, Reginald, *A dialogue between Reginald Pole and Thomas Lupset*, ed. K. M. Burton (London, 1948)

Pole, Reginald, 'Pole y Paul IV: una celébre Apología inédita del Cardenal Inglés', ed. J. I. Tellechea Idigoras (*Archivum Historiae Pontificiae*, 4, 1966)

Powicke, F. M., *Handbook of British Chronology* (London, 1939)

Richardson, W. C., *The Report of the Royal Commission of 1552* (Morganstown, West Virginia, 1974)

Ridley, Nicholas, *Works*, ed. H. Christmas (Parker Society, 29, 1841)

Roper, W., 'The Life of Sir Thomas More', ed. S. Sylvester and D. P. Harding, *Two Early Tudor Lives* (London, 1962)

Selve, Odet de, *Correspondance Politique*, ed. G. Lefèvre Pontalis (Paris, 1888)

Short Title Catalogue of books printed in England, Scotland and Ireland and of English books printed abroad, 1475–1640, by A. W. Pollard and G. R. Redgrave (Bibliographical Society, London, 1926). Revised by W. A. Jackson and F. S. Ferguson (Vol. 2 only) (London, 1976)

Statutes of the Realm, ed. A. Luders *et al.* (London, 1810–28)

Strype, J., *Ecclesiastical Memorials* (London, 1721)

The passage of our most dread Sovereign Lady, Queen Elizabeth, through the City of London, ed. A. F. Pollard, *Tudor Tracts* (London, 1903), reprinted from *An English Garner*, ed. E. Arber (London, 1877–90)

Bibliography

Throgmorton, Sir Nicholas, *The Legend of Sir Nicholas Throgmorton*, ed. J. G. Nichols (London, 1874)
Tudor Economic Documents, ed. R. H. Tawney and Eileen Power (London, 1924)
Tres Cartas de lo sucedido en el viaje de su Alteza a Inglaterra (La Sociedad de Bibliófilos Españoles, 1877)
Tudor Royal Proclamations, ed. P. L. Hughes and J. F. Larkin (New Haven, 1964–69)
Underhill, Edward, 'The narrative of Edward Underhill', ed. A. F. Pollard, *Tudor Tracts* (London, 1903), reprinted from *An English Garner*, ed. E. Arber (London, 1877–90)
Visitation Articles and Injunctions, ed. W. H. Frere and W. M. Kennedy (Alcuin Club, 1910)
Weiss, C., *Papiers d'état du Cardinal Granvelle* (Paris, 1844–52)
Wilkins, D., *Concilia Magnae Britanniae et Hiberniae* (London, 1737)
Wriothesley, Charles, *A chronicle of England by Charles Wriothesley*, ed. W. D. Hamilton (Camden Society, New series, 11, 1875–7)
Wyatt, George, *The Papers of George Wyatt*, ed. D. M. Loades (Camden Society, 4 series, 5, 1968)

Secondary works: books

Allen, J. W., *A history of political thought in the sixteenth century* (London, 1928)
Baskerville, G., *The English monks and the suppression of the monasteries* (London, 1937)
Baumer, F. le Van, *The early Tudor theory of kingship* (New Haven, 1940)
Bayne, C. G., *Anglo-Roman relations, 1558–1565* (Oxford, 1913)
Beer, B. L., *Northumberland* (Kent, Ohio, 1973)
Bell, H. E., *An introduction to the history and records of the Court of Wards and Liveries* (Cambridge, 1953)
Blench, J. W., *Preaching in England in the late XVth and XVIth centuries* (Oxford, 1964)
Boynton, L. O., *The Elizabethan militia* (London, 1967)
Brandi, K., *Charles V* (London, 1939)
Bush, M. L., *The government policy of Protector Somerset* (London, 1975)
Burrage, C., *The early English dissenters* (Cambridge, 1912)
Challis, C. E., *The Tudor coinage* (Manchester, 1978)
Collier, Jeremy, *An ecclesiastical history of Great Britain* (London, 1708–14)
Colvin, N. M., *The history of the King's works* (London, 1963–76)

Constant, G., *La légation du Cardinal Morone près l'empereur et le Concile de Trente* (Paris, 1922)

Cornwall, J., *Revolt of the peasantry, 1549* (London, 1977)

Cross, Claire, *Church and people, 1450–1660* (London, 1976)

Cruikshank, C. G., *Elizabeth's army* (Oxford, 1966)

Cunningham, W. H., *The growth of English industry and commerce* (Cambridge, 1882; new imp. 1968)

Dickens, A. G., *The English Reformation* (London, 1964)

Dickens, A. G., *The Marian reaction in the diocese of York*: i. The clergy, ii. The laity (Borthwick Institute of Historical Research, St Anthony's Hall Publications, nos. 11 and 12. York, 1957)

Dictionary of National Biography, ed. Leslie Stephen and Sidney Lee (London, 1885–1900)

Dietz, F. C., *English government finance, 1485–1558* (Urbana, Ill., 1921)

Dietz, F. C., *English public finance, 1558–1641* (New York, 1932)

Dodds, M. H. and R., *The Pilgrimage of Grace and the Exeter conspiracy* (Cambridge, 1915)

Duff, E., *A century of the English book trade* (London, 1948)

Elton, G. R., *The Tudor revolution in government* (Cambridge, 1953)

Elton, G. R., *The Tudor constitution* (Cambridge, 1960)

Elton, G. R., *Policy and police* (Cambridge, 1972)

Elton, G. R., *Reform and renewal* (London, 1973)

Elton, G. R., *Studies in Tudor and Stuart politics and government* (Cambridge, 1974)

Elton, G. R., *Reform and Reformation* (London, 1977)

Emmison, F. G., *Tudor Secretary* (London, 1961)

Evans, F. M. G., *The Principal Secretary of State* (Manchester, 1923)

Fairfield, L. P., *John Bale* (West Lafayette, Ind., 1976)

Feaveryear, A. E., *The pound sterling* (Oxford, 1931; rev. ed. 1963)

Fèbvre, Lucien, *Philippe II et la Franche Comté* (Paris, 1912)

Fenlon, D. B., *Heresy and obedience in Tridentine Italy* (Cambridge, 1972)

Ferguson, A. B., *The articulate citizen and the English renaissance* (Durham, N.C., 1965)

Fernández Alvarez, M., *Política Mundial de Carlos V y Felipe II* (Madrid, 1966)

Fernández Alvarez, M., *La España del Emperador Carlos V* (Madrid, 1966)

Firpo, M., *Pietro Bizzari esuli italiano del cinquecento* (Rome, 1971)

Foster, Sir William, *England's quest for Eastern trade* (London, 1933; new imp. 1966)

François, M., *et al., Charles Quint et son temps* (Paris, 1959)

Frede, Carlo de, *La Restaurazione Cattolica in Inghilterra sotto Maria Tudor* (Naples, 1971)

489

Bibliography

Frere, W. H., *The Marian reaction in its relation to the English clergy* (London, 1896)

Froude, J. A., *The reign of Mary Tudor*, ed. W. Llewelyn Williams (London, 1910)

Gage, John, *Antiquities of Hengrave* (London, 1822)

Garrett, C. H., *The Marian exiles* (Cambridge, 1938)

Gammon, S. R., *Statesman and schemer: William, first Lord Paget, Tudor minister* (Newton Abbot, 1973)

Gould, J. D., *The great debasement* (Oxford, 1970)

Haigh, C., *Reformation and resistance in Tudor Lancashire* (Cambridge, 1975)

Hakewill, W., *The Libertie of the subject against the pretended power of Impositions* (*maintained by an argument in parliament in 7 Jac. I*) (London, 1641)

Haller, W., *Foxe's Book of Martyrs and the Elect Nation* (London, 1963)

Harbison, E. H., *Rival ambassadors at the court of Queen Mary* (Princeton, N.J., 1940)

Hoak, D. E., *The King's Council in the reign of Edward VI* (Cambridge, 1976)

Holinshed, Raphael, *Chronicles* etc., ed. Henry Ellis (London, 1807–08)

Holdsworth, W.S., *The History of English Law*, 7th ed. (London, 1956)

Horst, I. B., *The radical brethren* (Nieuwkoop, 1972)

Hudson, W. S., *John Ponet; advocate of limited monarchy* (Chicago, 1942)

Hughes, Philip, *The reformation in England* (London, 1953–56)

Hurstfield, J., *The Queen's wards* (London, 1958)

James, M. E., *Change and continuity in the Tudor North: the rise of Thomas, first Lord Wharton* (Borthwick Institute of Historical Research; Borthwick Papers no. 27. York, 1965)

Jones, W. R. D., *The Tudor commonwealth* (London, 1970)

Jordan, W. K., *Philanthropy in England, 1480–1660* (New York, 1959)

Jordan, W. K., *Edward VI: the young king* (London, 1968)

Jordan, W. K., *Edward VI: the threshold of power* (London, 1970)

Kelly, H. A., *The matrimonial trials of Henry VIII* (Stanford, Cal., 1976)

Kingdon, R. M., *Geneva and the coming of the wars of religion in France* (Geneva, 1956)

Knecht, R. J., *Francis I and Absolute Monarchy* (Historical London Association, 1969)

Knowles, M. C., *The religious orders in England*, III (Cambridge, 1959)

Langbein, J. H., *Prosecuting crime in the Renaissance* (Cambridge, Mass., 1974)

490

Bibliography

Lehmberg, S. E., *The Reformation Parliament, 1529–1536* (Cambridge, 1970)
Lehmberg, S. E., *The later parliaments of Henry VIII* (Cambridge, 1977)
Levine, M., *The early Elizabethan succession question* (Stanford, Cal., 1966)
Levine, M., *Tudor Dynastic problems, 1460–1571* (London, 1973)
Lipson, E., *The economic history of England* (London, 1948–49)
Loades, D. M., *Two Tudor conspiracies* (Cambridge, 1965)
Loades, D. M., *The Oxford martyrs* (London, 1970)
Loades, D. M., *Politics and the nation, 1450–1660* (London, 1974)
MacCaffrey, W., *The shaping of the Elizabethan regime* (Princeton, N.J., 1968)
McConica, J. K., *English humanists and reformation politics* (Oxford, 1965)
McIlwain, C. H., *The high court of parliament and its supremacy* (New Haven, Conn., 1910)
Makower, F., *The constitutional history and constitution of the Church of England* (London, 1895)
Maltby, W. S., *The Black Legend in England* (Durham, N.C., 1971)
Mattingly, Garrett, *Catherine of Aragon* (Boston, Mass., 1941)
Muller, J. A., *Stephen Gardiner and the Tudor reaction* (London, 1926)
O'Day, R. and Heal, F., eds., *Church and society in England. Henry VIII to James I* (London, 1977)
Olsen, V. N., *John Foxe and the Elizabethan church* (Berkeley and Los Angeles, 1973)
Oxley, J. E., *The reformation in Essex to the death of Mary* (Manchester, 1965)
Ozment, S. E., *The reformation in the cities* (New Haven, Conn., 1975)
Parmiter, G. de C., *The King's Great Matter* (London, 1967)
Pidal, Ramón Menéndez, *España en el tiempo de Felipe II* (Historia de España, t. 19. Madrid, 1958)
Pollard, A. F., *The political history of England from the accession of Edward VI to the death of Elizabeth* (London, 1919)
Porter, H. C., *Reformation and reaction in Tudor Cambridge* (Cambridge, 1958)
Powell, K. G., *Marian martyrs and the reformation in Bristol* (Historical Association, Bristol, 1975)
Prescott, H. F. M., *Mary Tudor* (London, 1952)
Prescott, W. H., *A history of the reign of Philip II* (New York, 1859)
Ramsay, G. D., *English overseas trade in the centuries of emergence* (London, 1957)
Ramsay, G. D., *The City of London in international politics at the accession of Elizabeth Tudor* (Manchester, 1975)

491

Bibliography

Richardson, W. C., *A history of the court of Augmentations* (Baton Rouge, La., 1961)

Rouchausse, Jean, *Saint John Fisher* (Nieuwkoop, 1972)

Ruding, R.. *Annals of the coinage of Great Britain* (London, 1840)

Scarisbrick, J. J., *Henry VIII* (London, 1968)

Schenk, W., *Reginald Pole, Cardinal of England* (London, 1950)

Seton Watson, R. W., ed., *Tudor studies . . . presented to A. F. Pollard* (London, 1924)

Simon, Joan, *Education and society in Tudor England* (London, 1966)

Simpson, Alan, *The wealth of the gentry, 1540–1660* (London, 1961)

Shirley, T. F., *Thomas Thirlby, Tudor bishop* (London, 1964)

Smith, A. H., *County and Court* (London, 1974)

Smith, L. B., *Tudor prelates and politics* (Princeton, N.J., 1953)

Smith, L. B., *The Mask of Royalty* (London, 1971)

Smith, R. B., *Land and politics* (Oxford, 1970)

Somerville, R., *History of the Duchy of Lancaster, 1265–1603* (London, 1953)

Stone, J. M., *The history of Mary I, Queen of England* (London, 1901)

Stone, L., *The crisis of the aristocracy, 1558–1640* (Oxford, 1965)

Stow, John, *Chronicles, etc.* (London, 1605)

Sutherland, N. M., *The massacre of St. Bartholomew and the European conflict* (London, 1973)

Tellechea Idigoras, J. I., *Fray Bartolomé Carranza y el Cardenal Pole* (Pamplona, 1977)

Thompson, E. M., *The Carthusian Order in England* (London, 1930)

Thomson, J. A. F., *The latter Lollards, 1414–1520* (London, 1965)

Tittler, R., *Nicholas Bacon* (London, 1976)

Tytler, P. F., *England under Edward VI and Mary* (London, 1839)

'Vunière', *Étude historique sur Simon Renard* (Limoges, 1878)

Watson, Foster, *Vives and the Renascence education of women* (London, 1912)

White, B. R., *The English separatist tradition* (Oxford, 1971)

Willan, T. S., *A Tudor book of rates* (Manchester, 1962)

Willan, T. S., *The early history of the Russia Company* (Manchester, 1956)

Willan, T. S., *The Muscovy merchants of 1555* (Manchester, 1953)

Woodward, G. W. O., *The dissolution of the monasteries* (London, 1966)

Youings, Joyce, *The dissolution of the monasteries* (London, 1971)

Youngs, F. A., *The proclamations of the Tudor Queens* (Cambridge, 1976)

Zeeveld, W. G., *The foundations of Tudor policy* (Cambridge, Mass., 1948)

Secondary works: articles

Alexander, G., 'Bonner and the Marian persecutions'. *History*, 60, 1975, 374-92

Ancel, R., 'La réconciliation de l'Angleterre agec le Saint-Siège sous Marie Tudor', *Revue d'histoire ecclésiastique*, 10, 1909, 521-36; 744-98

Braddock, R. C., 'The rewards of office holding in Tudor England', *Journal of British Studies*, 14, 1975, 29-47

Braddock, R. C., 'The character and composition of the Duke of Northumberland's army', *Albion*, 8, 1976, 342-56.

Challis, C. E., 'The debasement of the coinage, 1542–1551', *Economic History Review*, 2 series, 20, 1967, 441-6

Crehan, J. H., 'St. Ignatius and Cardinal Pole', *Archivum Historicum Societatis Iesu*, 25, 1956, 72-98

Crehan, J. H., 'The return to obedience; new judgement on Cardinal Pole', *The Month*, New Series 14, 1955, 221-9

Davies, C. S. L., 'The Pilgrimage of Grace reconsidered', *Past and Present*, 41, 1968, 54-76

Dickens, A. G., 'Secular and religious motivation in the Pilgrimage of Grace', *Studies in Church History*, 4, 1967, 39-64

Elton, G. R., 'Taxation for war and peace in early Tudor England', *War and Economic Development*, ed. J. M. Winter (Cambridge, 1975), 33-48

Elton, G. R., 'Thomas Cromwell redivivus', *Archiv für Reformationsgeschichte*, 68, 1977, 192-208

Elton, G. R., 'Mid-Tudor finance' (review article), *Historical Journal*, 20, 1977, 737-40

Garrett, C. H., 'The Legatine Register of Cardinal Pole', *Journal of Modern History*, 13, 1941, 189-94

Gleason, J. H., 'The personnel of the commissions of the Peace, 1554–1564', *Huntingdon Library Quarterly*, 18, 1955, 169–77

Gras, N. S. B., 'Tudor books of rates', *Quarterly Journal of Economics*, 26, 1912, 766-75

Grieve, H., 'The deprived married clergy in Essex, 1553–61', *Transactions of the Royal Historical Society*, 4 series, 22, 1940, 141-69

Harriss, G. L., 'A revolution in Tudor history?', *Past and Present*, 25, 1963, 3-58

Harriss, G. L., 'Thomas Cromwell's "new principle" of taxation', *English Historical Review*, 93, 1978, 721-39

Hodgett, G. A. J., 'The unpensioned religious in Tudor England', *Journal of Ecclesiastical History*, 13, 1962, 195-202

Hurstfield, J., 'The profits of fiscal feudalism, 1541–1602', *Economic History Review*, 2 series, 8, 1955, 53-61

Bibliography

Hurstfield, J., 'The revival of feudalism in early Tudor England', History, 37, 1952, 131-45

Ives, E. W., 'The genesis of the Statute of Uses', English Historical Review, 82, 1967, 673-97

James, M. E., 'Obedience and dissent in Henrician England: the Lincolnshire rebellion of 1536', Past and Present, 48, 1970, 3-78

Kelly, H. A., 'Kingship, incest, and the dictates of law', American Journal of Jurisprudence, 14, 1969, 69-78

Kelly, M., 'The submission of the clergy', Transactions of the Royal Historical Society, 5 series, 15, 1965, 97-119

Loach, J., 'Pamphlets and politics, 1553-8', Bulletin of the Institute of Historical Research, 48, 1975, 31-45

Loades, D. M., 'The press under the early Tudors', Transactions of the Cambridge Bibliographical Society, 4, 1964, 29-50

Loades, D. M., 'The enforcement of reaction, 1553-8', Journal of Ecclesiastical History, 16, 1965, 54-66

Loades, D. M., 'The last years of Cuthbert Tunstall, 1547-1559', Durham University Journal, 66, 1973, 10-22

Martin, J. W., 'English protestant separatism: Henry Hart and the Freewillers', Sixteenth Century Journal, 7, 1976, 55-75

McGee, J., 'The nominalism of Thomas Cranmer', Harvard Theological Review, 57, 1964, 189-206

Outhwaite, R. B., 'The trials of foreign borrowing', Economic History Review, 2 series, 19, 1966, 289-305

Pogson, R. H., 'Revival and reform in Mary Tudor's church', Journal of Ecclesiastical History, 25, 1974, 249-65

Pogson, R. H., 'Reginald Pole and the priorities of government in Mary Tudor's church', Historical Journal, 18, 1975, 3-21

Tellechea Idigoras, J. I., 'Bartolomé Carranza y la restauración católica inglesa (1553–58)', Anthologia Annua, 12, 1964, 159-282

Tellechea Idigoras, J. I., 'Una denuncia de los Cardenales Contarini, Pole y Morone per el Cardenal Francisco de Mendoza (1560)', Revista española de Teología, 27, 1967, 33-51

Tellechea Idigoras, J. I., 'Pole, Carranza y Fresnada. Cara y cruz de una amistad y de una enemistad', Diálogo ecuménico, 8, 1974, 287-393

Thorne, S. E., 'Dr. Bonham's case (1609)', Law Quarterly Review, 54, 1938, 543-52

Tittler, R., 'The incorporation of boroughs, 1540–1558', History, 62, 1977, 24-42

Williams, P., 'A revolution in Tudor History?', Past and Present, 25, 1963, 3-58

Woodbury, L., 'Jean Ribault and Queen Elizabeth', American Historical Review, 9, 1903-04, 456-9

Secondary works: unpublished theses, etc.

Baskerville, E. J., 'A chronological bibliography of propaganda and polemic published in English between 1553 and 1558'

Braddock, R. C., 'The Royal household, 1540–1560' (Northwestern University PhD, 1971)

Bradshaw, B., 'The Irish constitutional revolution, 1515–1557' (Cambridge University PhD, 1975)

Brigden, S. E., 'The Reformation in London in the reign of Henry VIII: 1522–1547' (Cambridge University PhD, 1979)

Dawson, J. E. A., 'The early career of Christopher Goodman and his place in the development of English protestant thought' (Durham University PhD, 1978)

Jones, N. L., 'Faith by statute: the politics of religion in the parliament of 1559' (Cambridge University PhD, 1977)

Lemasters, G. A., 'The Privy Council in the reign of Queen Mary I' (Cambridge University PhD, 1971)

Loach, J., 'Parliamentary opposition in the reign of Mary Tudor' (Oxford University DPhil, 1973)

Marmion, J. P., 'The London Synod of Cardinal Pole' (Keele University MA, 1974)

Newton, S. C., 'Thomas Stafford's attack on Scarborough Castle, 1557'

Pogson, R. H., 'Reginald Pole: Papal Legate to England in Mary Tudor's reign' (Cambridge University PhD, 1972)

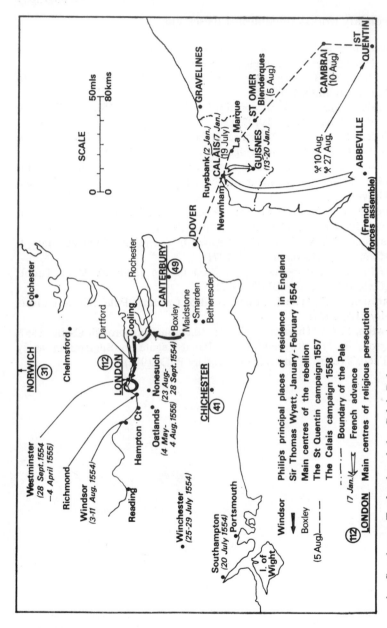

1. South-east England and the Calais Pale

SCALE
0   50mls
0   80kms

Colchester

NORWICH (31)

Chelmsford

Dartford

Cooling

Rochester

LONDON (112)

Westminster
(28 Sept.1554
—4 April 1555)

Richmond

Windsor
(3–11 Aug. 1554)

Hampton Ct.

Reading

Oatlands
(4 May–
4 Aug.1555)

Nonesuch
(23 Aug.–
28 Sept. 1554)

CHICHESTER (41)

Winchester
(25–29 July 1554)

Southampton
(20 July 1554)

Portsmouth

I. of
Wight

Boxley

Maidstone

Smarden

Bethersden

CANTERBURY (49)

DOVER

GRAVELINES

Ruysbank (2 Jan.)

CALAIS (7 Jan.)
(19 July)

Newnham

La Marque

ST OMER
Blenderques
(5 Aug.)

GUISNES
(13–20 Jan.)

✗ 10 Aug.
✗ 27 Aug.

CAMBRAI
(10 Aug.)

ST
QUENTIN

ABBEVILLE

(French
forces assemble)

Windsor   Philip's principal places of residence in England

      Sir Thomas Wyatt, January–February 1554

Boxley   Main centres of the rebellion

(5 Aug) — —   The St Quentin campaign 1557

      The Calais campaign 1558

— · — · —   Boundary of the Pale

(7 Jan.) ↓   French advance

(112) LONDON   Main centres of religious persecution

Berwick
(Sept.1557)

Scarborough
(27 April 1557)

(6 Feb. 1554)

Emden

Winchester
(25 July)

(18 Aug.)
LONDON

Southampton
(arr. 20 July)

ANTWERP

Calais

BRUSSELS

(4 Aug.1556)

(7 Jan. 1558)

St Quentin

Frankfurt

ROUEN

(27 Aug. 1557)

PARIS

Strasbourg

Dillingen

Basle
Aarau
Zurich

Geneva

(dep. 12 July)
La Coruna

VENICE

Valladolid
(dep. early May)

Viterbo

ROME

SCALE
0   200mls
0   300kms

Territories to be ruled by the heirs of Philip and Mary
(Treaty 1554)

– – – – –   Philip's journey to England 1554

. . . .   Thomas Stafford, April 1557

Emden   Protestant cities of refuge

ROME   Main stopping places of Cardinal Pole, August 1553-November 1554

✗ ⊗   Battles and skirmishes in which English forces were involved

2.   The Spanish marriage and the Protestant diaspora

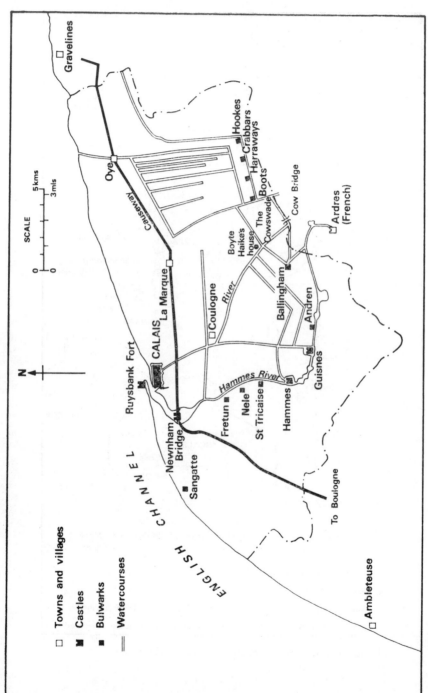

KEY

- ☐ Towns and villages
- ◼ Castles
- ■ Bulwarks
- ═ Watercourses

English Channel

Gravelines

Oye

Causeway

CALAIS
La Marque

Ruysbank Fort

Newnham Bridge

Sangatte

Fretun

Nele

St Tricaise

Hammes

Hammes River

Guisnes

Andren

Ballingham

Coulogne

River

Boyte Haike's house

The Cowswade

Boots

Cow Bridge

Harraways

Crabbars

Hookes

Ardres (French)

To Boulogne

Ambleteuse

SCALE

0   5 kms
0   3 mls

N

3. Calais and its marches

Index

Colonna, Vittoria, 348, 435
Commendone, Gian Francesco, 43, 155, 174, 175, 182
Constable, Sir Marmaduke, 39
Contarini, Cardinal Gasparo, 171
Convocation: of 1553, 156, 343; of 1554, 157; of 1555: grants subsidies, 299–300, 317: petitions king and queen, 327
Conyers, John Lord, 87
Copland, William, 337–8
Copley, Mr, 270
Cordell, William, Master of the Rolls, 87, 387, 451
Córdova, Don Pedro de, 222
Cornewall, 280
Cornwall, Duchy of, 303
Cornwallis, Sir Thomas, Controller of the Household, 70, 85, 99, 102, 104, 108, 264, 267, 381, 451
Coruna, La, 133, 200
Cotton, Sir Richard, 89
Council, Privy, 67, 258, 330, 333; of Edward VI, 27, 28, 29, 31, 35, 52–3, 58, 60, 63, 70, 71, 100, 125, 195, 196: organization, 53–4, 101, 103; of Mary, 70, 73, 75, 91, 100, 114, 119, 123, 236, 238, 254, 256, 272, 322, 327, 366, 368, 371, 378, 381, 385, 394: composition, 71–2, 73, 86, 104, 257–8: strength of, 75–6, 82: relations with queen, 76, 77–8, 82–3, 86: attendance at meetings, 78, 81, 257, 382–3: procedure, 78, 79–80, 81, 86, 185, 224, 252, 256–7, 258, 260: 'Council of State', 81, 227, 233, 242, 248, 253, 255–6, 257, 258, 273, 381: 'factiousness', 84, 85, 96, 104, 129, 224, 253, 254, 381: control of elections, 88, 273, 274, 288: security policy, 94–6, 107, 127, 129–30, 134, 144, 146, 241, 265, 276, 281, 284–5, 384: approves marriage treaty, 121: religious policy, 152, 157, 162, 170, 429, 445–6, 447, 449: financial policy, 184, 185, 186, 187–8, 190, 196, 197, 199, 201, 202, 204, 291, 296, 304–5, 312, 404, 408, 409, 419–20: Privy Seal loans, 240, 298, 300–1, 315, 317, 319, 320, 374, 375, 405–6, 418, 419, 423: bonds surrendered to, 291–2, 293, 294: relations with Philip, 222–3, 224, 227, 235, 238, 239, 252, 253, 267, 296, 390, 393, 400: discusses war with France, 241–2, 250, 256, 367, 428: administrative functions, 257–8, 462–3: Seal of, 254, 285: concern with social order, 278–9, 280: takes

recognisances, 278–9: memorandum on the war (1558), 378–9, 410–11: arrangements for defence, 382–3, 385, 387–8, 397: councils of war and finance (1558), 382–3, 409, 410: attitude to Elizabeth, 391, 392, 402; of Henry VIII, 52–3, 57; of Elizabeth, 459
Council in the North, 50, 279
Council in Star Chamber, 301
councillors at large, 53, 101, 103, 286
Courrières, Jehan de Montmorency, Sieur de, 139, 142
Courtenay family, 187
Courtenay, Sir William, 266, 273, 372
Coventry, town of, 156, 333
Coxe, Richard, 149, 335
Cranmer, Thomas, archbishop of Canterbury, 37, 42, 47, 48, 60, 71, 72, 150, 163, 187, 332, 333, 339, 350, 360, 453; his court at Dunstable, 13; loathed by Mary, 22; trial for treason, 101, 154, 164, 180; protestant stand, 154, 161; recantations, 334, 343, 447, 456
Croftes, Sir James, 126, 143, 262, 266, 310, 461
Cromwell, Thomas, earl of Essex, 14, 15, 37, 39, 41, 56, 57, 64, 146, 283, 341, 463, 471; attitude to Mary, 16–17, 18, 19, 20, 34; plans for reform, 22, 38, 40, 44, 46, 47, 49, 50, 53–4, 55, 57, 64, 80, 82, 277; his fall, 46–7, 55, 58, 59, 68; policies in Ireland, 51; controller of patronage, 57, 58
Crown, 115, 327; Royal Supremacy, 19, 37, 41, 55, 58, 83, 161, 172, 175, 321, 351, 466: Henry VIII's convictions, 40, 49: of Edward VI, 41–2, 43: implications of, 43–4, 45, 46, 47, 61: the Godly Prince, 48, 466: repeal of acts enforcing, 104, 155, 169–70, 328: title abandoned, 159, 166, 175: protestant erastianism, 150, 154: inalienability of, 182; finances, 44–5, 58–9, 68, 79, 82, 97–8, 99, 131, 183, 297–9: reorganized, 54: debts to, 188, 298–9, 301, 302, 418; lands, 79, 194, 206, 275–6, 296–7, 301, 302, 312, 313–14: sale of, 185, 190, 223, 303–4, 305, 315–16, 345, 404, 406–7, 420; succession, 115, 121, 122, 125–6, 134, 135, 145–6, 217–18, 237, 269, 270, 366, 392, 393, 451: of Philip, 213–14, 218–19, 223, 224, 237, 269, 391; jurisdictional authority, 50, 146; social and economic

502

Index

Elizabeth I, 8, 14, 16, 17, 19, 21, 23, 24, 62, 68, 79, 80, 84, 92, 93, 120, 158, 167, 186, 193, 226, 228, 237, 239, 254, 260, 268, 275, 277, 280, 311, 335, 367, 391, 412; suspected of involvement with Wyatt, 77, 88, 104, 125, 144; problems of her position, 125, 128–9, 135, 143, 219, 224, 225, 244, 269, 282, 458; projects for her marriage, 225, 244, 248, 391, 393, 402, 463; her household, 281; succession recognized, 392, 393; her accession, 436, 442, 458: welcomed, 443; inherited problems, 418–19, 421–2: financial remedies, 422–3; advice to, 443; coronation pardon, 459; her court, 459–60, 472–3

Emmanuel Philibert, prince of Piedmont and duke of Savoy, 112, 114, 140, 144, 225, 244, 377, 380, 391

Englefield, Sir Francis, 30, 70, 74, 84, 85, 98, 99, 197, 253, 257, 258, 304, 382, 451, 459; Master of the Wards, 87

English, the, 114; hostility to foreigners (particularly Spaniards), 109, 110, 111, 113, 118–19, 124, 128, 142, 160, 211, 212, 213, 220, 223, 254, 466: riots arising from, 215, 216, 218, 245, 374, 384; turbulence of, 112, 127, 130, 137, 213; heresy of, 124, 175, 214, 326, 334; attitude to Philip, 132, 211, 213–14, 216, 220, 227, 229, 255, 421–2; 'liberties', 137, 228, 236; self-esteem, 238

Enríquez, Don Fernando, 214, 245

Eraso, Francisco de, 143, 200–1, 212, 217, 220, 232, 246

Essex, county of, 88; religious attitudes in, 46, 284, 332, 340

Evil May Day (1517), 7

exchange, foreign, 204, 292; rates, 58, 196–7, 198, 203, 204, 208, 210, 305, 424; credit, 198–9

Exchequer, 54, 88, 183, 186, 189, 197, 292, 295, 302, 315; reform of, 185, 188–95, 204, 275, 305, 467; Tellers, 189, 424; *Brevia Recepta*, 192; accounting procedure, 192, 193, 206–7, 318, 424; auditors, 193, 194; barons, 193; Chamber court, 416–17; plan to rob, 236, 307, 425; income and expenditure of, 296, 300, 301, 313, 319, 373, 404, 406, 411; deficit in, 300, 301, 419–20

Exeter, Gertrude, dowager marchioness of, 89, 108, 119

Exeter, Henry Courtenay, marquis of, 22–3, 34, 60, 97, 107, 111

expeditionary force (of 1557), 371–2, 373, 374, 397, 404, 468; cost, 373

Eyemouth, 371

Falmouth, 384

Fane, Sir Ralph, 91

Farrer, Robert, bishop of St Davids, 158

Favell, Giles, 388

Feckenham, John, Dean of St Paul's and abbot of Westminster, 326, 353, 354, 448, 449, 450

Feltonstone, Edward, 280, 283

Ferdinand of Aragon, 1, 3, 4, 5, 6

Ferdinand, king of the Romans, 112, 113, 114, 118, 121, 140, 226, 232, 239

Ferdinand, Archduke, 112, 226

Feria, Don Gómez Suárez de Figueroa, count of, 84, 213, 222, 238, 371, 378, 380, 381, 382, 383, 384, 385, 386, 388, 390, 392, 400, 408, 421, 423, 436, 441; marriage to Jane Dormer, 246

Fernández, Fray Diego, 4, 6

Fetherstone, John, 10

Field of Cloth of Gold, 8

Figueroa, Juan de, 143, 371, 382

Fiordibello, 174

First fruits and tenths: Court of, 54, 55, 88, 191, 192; Office of, 192–3, 194

Fisher, John, bishop of Rochester, 11, 33, 39, 59, 342, 343

FitzGarrett, Edward, 92

FitzGerald family, 51

FitzWilliam, Sir William, 318

Flaminio, Marcantonio, 182, 435

Flanders, 3, 58, 184, 204, 213, 221, 293, 376–7

Fleet prison, 188, 281, 302, 337, 406

Fleetwood, William, 146

Flodden, battle of, 6

Florence, Council of, 348

Fontanino, Benedetto, 182

Foster, Edmund, 374

Fox, John (of Loughborough), 223

Foxe, John, 339, 340; *Acts and Monuments*, 180, 219, 225, 284, 332, 334, 335–6, 341

Framlingham (Suffolk), 70, 71, 92, 185

France, 9, 27, 31, 114, 115, 116, 122, 124, 131, 174, 222, 228, 268, 351; war with, 5, 6, 123, 130, 137, 219, 223–4, 229–30, 234, 235, 236, 240, 243, 251, 254, 268, 277, 314, 365, 380, 384, 412, 422, 428, 463, 466: declared, 243, 368, 369, 372, 373–4,

504

Index

Guise, Henri, duc de, 127, 375, 377
Guisnes, 241, 365, 372, 377; garrison, 379, 385–6; fall, 377–8
Gúzman, Martin de, 140
Gwynneth, John, 163, 342
Gyé, M. de, French envoy, 139

Habsburg family, 109, 114, 140, 232, 243; compact over Imperial succession, 113
Hadleigh, 166, 228, 333
Hakewill, William, 416
Hales, Sir James, 155, 159, 163, 178
Hall, Richard, 39
Hall, Robert, 415
Hammes, 241, 372, 377
Hampton, Bernard, clerk of the council, 286, 403
Hampton Court, 216, 267
Hanseatic League (Steelyard), 295, 312, 378, 379, 399, 417–18; privileges of, 195–6, 197, 198, 208, 257, 380–1
Hare, Sir Nicholas, Master of the Rolls, 87, 103, 105, 260
Harpesfield, John, 342
Harpesfield, Nicholas, 221, 343–4, 345, 361
Hart, Henry, 181
harvest failure, 299, 374, 452, 471; as evidence of God's wrath, 440–1
Hastings, Sir Edward, Lord Hastings of Loughborough, 72, 85, 89, 97, 99, 108, 264, 273, 306–7, 319, 324, 451, 460; Lieutenant of Kent, 382
Hastings, Henry Lord, 94, 263, 264, 287
Hatfield, 14, 393
Heath, Nicholas, archbishop of York and Lord Chancellor, 65, 74, 87, 94, 101, 179, 239, 256, 257, 258, 286, 381, 394, 401, 451, 453, 459; receives Great Seal, 260–1
Henry VII, 1, 2, 3, 4, 32, 51
Henry VIII, 5, 6, 8, 17, 18, 20, 21, 22, 25, 26, 44–5, 55, 80, 84, 90, 91, 93, 159, 268, 311, 324, 325, 331; betrothal and first marriage, 1, 3, 4; scholarship, 7; diplomacy, 9; 'Great Matter', 10, 11, 12, 16, 37, 40, 59, 64; authority, 39, 49, 50; foreign policy, 58–9; will, 23, 24, 25, 60–1, 62, 73
Henry Fitzroy, duke of Richmond, 8, 9, 10, 22, 33, 50
Henry, Prince (eldest son of Henry VIII), 6
Herbert, Sir George, 384
Herbert, Henry Lord, 63, 94, 101, 263
Hereford, town of, 218
Heron, Giles, 56

Heron, Thomas, 98
Hertfordshire: protestants in, 340
Heywood, John, 218
Hinnes, William, 308
Hoby, Sir Philip, 71, 88, 136, 146, 266
Holborne, Nicholas, 201, 291, 293, 295; account of, 292, 316
Holcrofte, Sir Thomas, 138, 147
Holgate, Robert, archbishop of York, 158, 453
Holmes, John, 272, 298
Hooper, John, bishop of Gloucester and Worcester, 47, 74, 101, 148, 150, 152, 165, 187, 333, 339, 448
Hopton, Sir Ralph, 143
Hotson, William, 162
Howard, Catherine, 5th queen of Henry VIII, 24, 60
Howard, Sir George, 145, 273
Howard, Lord William, Lord Howard of Effingham, 85, 88, 96, 105, 107, 134, 264, 368, 382, 384, 459
Howard family, 59, 108, 187
Huddlestone, Sir John, 75, 94, 96, 99, 137, 263, 287
Huggarde, Miles, 162, 279, 284, 334, 338, 340, 341, 343, 359–60, 440–1, 454, 455; *Displaying of the protestantes*, 342
Hull, 365
Hungerford, Sir Walter, 98
Hungerford, Walter Lord, 108
Hunsdon, 19, 26
Huntingdon, Francis Hastings, earl of, 71, 72, 136, 264, 315
Hynd, Mr, 280

Igtham (Kent), 127
Imperallo, Federigo, 199
Ingoldsby, William, 407
Inquisition, Roman, 430, 431, 432, 438
Ipswich, 167, 362; insurrection at, 280, 283, 290
Ireland: lordship, later kingdom of, 184; government of, 51–2, 67, 311, 312, 319–20: costs, 189, 310, 311, 407–8; Anglo-Irish gentry, 52, 311; sale of Crown lands in, 304; revenues of, 310–11, 312, 319; created a kingdom, 311, 349; troops for, 385
Isabella of Castile, 1, 2, 7, 8
Isley, William, 127
Italy, 113, 117, 130, 226, 341, 436; wars in, 3, 230, 374; Habsburg policy in, 141; pamphlets printed in, 221
Ivan IV, Tsar of Russia, 313

506

Index

Northampton, William Parr, marquis of, 71, 72, 89, 91, 106, 107, 137, 187, 206, 413, 425, 460
Northumberland, Henry Percy, 6th earl of, 97
Northumberland, John Dudley, earl of Warwick and duke of, 28, 29, 30, 31, 53, 59, 60, 61, 68, 73, 74, 87, 89, 90, 91, 95, 99, 101, 106, 125, 126, 141, 148, 149, 158, 160, 183, 185, 186, 187, 195, 237, 272, 367; weakness of position, 61–2; plan for succession, 63–4, 70, 71, 100; arrest, 72; recantation, 150–1, 342, 343; execution, 72; children restored in blood, 387
Northumberland, Thomas Percy, earl of, 97, 98, 262, 286, 460; endowment, 98, 413; appointed to border office, 262
Norwich, city of, 308; sanctuary at, 457
Norwich, diocese, 157–8, 332, 345, 346
Nottinghamshire, 374, 385
Nowell, Alexander, 272

Oatlands (Surrey), 267
Ochino, Bernardino, 172
Oglethorpe, Owen, bishop of Carlisle, 347
Olde, John: *Acquittal . . . of Edward VI*, 339
Oldenhall, William, 444, 456
Olivares, count of, 213, 222
Ongar parish (Essex), 169
Ormanetto, Nicoló, 321, 348, 357, 431, 443–4
Ortel, agent of Fuggers, 294
Oxford, city of, 415; parliament intended for, 135; disputation at, 164–5, 180, 343; Bocardo, 165; Dominican house in, 454
Oxford, John de Vere, 16th earl of, 71, 89, 105–6
Oxford, university of, 158–9, 161, 179, 351; protestants in, 153; Christchurch, 44, 48, 65; St John's college, 352, 363; Trinity college, 352, 363
D'Oysel, Henri Clutin, Sieur, French ambassador to Scotland, 370, 371

Padilla, López de, 133
Paget, Sir William, Lord Paget of Beaudesert, Lord Privy Seal, 59, 60, 62, 70, 71, 75, 76, 77, 79, 80, 81, 82, 85, 94, 95, 98, 99, 100, 103, 104, 125, 126, 127, 128, 135, 208, 222, 227, 229, 230, 236, 239, 241, 243, 244, 247, 250, 252, 253, 254,

258, 264, 271, 272, 277, 286, 295, 297, 301, 324, 349, 367, 378, 381, 382, 383, 389, 395, 401, 404, 409, 459, 463, 470; his rivalry with Gardiner, 75, 77, 78, 80, 81, 83, 85, 116, 129, 135–6, 141, 252, 258; role in marriage negotiations, 110, 114, 116, 118, 120, 121, 160; disgrace (1554), 135–6, 169, 222, 259; religious attitude, 155, 160; relations with Philip, 217, 222, 224, 259, 261, 285; Lord Privy Seal, 259, 261, 266
Palmer, Sir Thomas, 72, 187, 206
Parkyn, Robert, 154, 157, 284
Parliament, 62, 126, 134, 155, 267, 270, 322, 325, 335, 463, 473; authority of, 37, 38, 40, 41, 42, 43, 45, 49, 54, 174, 276–7, 329: scope of legislation, 48–9, 55, 329; management, 39–40, 56, 271–2, 273, 274, 468–9; opposition in, 270–1, 273–4; government measures lost, 270, 273; frequency of, 271–2; of Mary, legislation by, 274–5, 276; House of Lords, 42, 169, 268–9: composition of, 39, 45; House of Commons, 120, 125, 270, 272, 405: composition of, 38–9, 49–50, 88, 155–6, 248, 271–2, 273, 274: suspicious of Philip, 268, 271, 464; Reformation (1529–36), 37, 38, 39, 64, 66, 67, 273; first of Mary (1553), 79, 80, 97, 103, 104, 115, 120, 155–6, 178; second of Mary (1554), 77, 83, 84, 86, 97, 135–6, 168–9; third of Mary (1554–55), 92, 207, 218, 219, 220, 223–4, 246, 268, 288; fourth of Mary (1555), 227, 234, 248, 268, 269, 270, 298, 314, 324, 325, 327, 345: subsidies in, 298–9; fifth of Mary (1558), 268, 269–70, 276, 383, 386–7, 388, 389, 394, 407–8, 449–50; first of Elizabeth (1559), 462, 473: religious settlement in, 473; Statutes: Acts of attainder, 55–6, 67: Subsidy Acts, 58, 68: Provisors and Praemunire, 38, 65, 176, 323, 328, 356: 5 Richard II st.1. c.2, 417, 426: 25 Henry VIII c.22, 15: 25 Henry VIII c.21, 40: 26 Henry VIII c.3, 158: 27 Henry VIII c.10, 49, 55, 66: 27 Henry VIII c.16, 55: 27 Henry VIII c.24, 50–1: 27 Henry VIII c.26, 50–1; 27 Henry VIII c.28, 44: 31 Henry VIII c.13, 44: 31 Henry VIII c.14, 47: 32 Henry VIII c.1, 49, 55: 32 Henry VIII c.12, 55, 448: 35 Henry VIII c.1,

510

Index

Philip—*cont.*
  and advisers, 124, 131, 134, 138,
  202, 212–13; financial problems,
  121, 131, 200, 240, 243, 294,
  315–16, 373, 381, 412, 415; leaves
  England, 219–20, 227, 228, 264,
  371; coronation, 223, 234, 236,
  243, 251, 254, 268, 269, 281, 285,
  365; question of his return, 228,
  233, 234, 236, 239–40, 241, 242,
  269, 287, 315, 389, 396; and papal
  conclave, 231–2; relations with
  Paul IV, 232, 240, 250, 351,
  429–31: war, 350, 430, 433; 'revels',
  234, 237; wishes England to
  declare war, 235, 241–2, 243, 256,
  367–8, 369; titles, 249, 286;
  reluctance to break with Scots,
  370–1, 379–80, 396; takes stock of
  English liabilities, 421–2, 426
Philip of the Palatinate, 22, 34
Philpot, John, 156, 343
Pius III, pope, 2
plays: Shrovetide, 443; 'lewd', 443–4
Plowden, Edmund, 449
Plymouth, 365, 384
Pole, Reginald, Cardinal Legate,
  archbishop of Canterbury, 16, 23,
  43, 83, 98, 117, 118, 137, 139, 155,
  170–3, 174, 177, 181–2, 231, 232,
  233, 240, 243, 253, 273, 314, 322,
  330, 343, 354, 361, 389, 390, 392,
  408, 414, 429, 434, 446, 447, 450,
  451, 463–4, 469; his spirituality,
  171–2, 347–8; his theology, 172,
  433, 437; his attitude to authority,
  172, 330–1, 343, 348, 351, 357,
  359, 431, 437; diplomatic missions,
  137, 141, 147, 171, 173, 175, 176,
  226, 229, 230–1, 235, 249, 348,
  350; Legatine mission to England,
  220–1, 222, 321, 322, 325, 326, 327,
  328, 329, 337, 344, 346, 348,
  350–1, 355, 356, 428: his view of,
  330–1, 334, 343–4, 345, 348, 432,
  451–2: opens register, 176: new
  brief, 322, 324: legatine jurisdiction,
  323, 324, 325, 329, 331, 341, 356:
  returns to England, 324: speaks to
  parliament, 325: issues absolution,
  325–6: visitations, 337, 343–4,
  345–6, 351–2, 355, 362: Legatine
  Synod, 346, 347, 348: recall to
  Rome, 349, 350, 351, 355, 428–9;
  as councillor, 227, 256, 286: lives
  at court, 265; papal election of
  1555, 349; archbishop of
  Canterbury, 350, 432; suspected of
  heresy, 430, 432, 433, 434, 435;
  faith undermined, 433, 435, 436;
  personal estate, 344, 362, 439–40,

  455; sickness and death, 390, 435,
  436; will, 455
Pollard, Sir John, 266, 273
Pollard, William, 449
Ponet, John, bishop of Winchester,
  360; *Shorte treatise*, 250, 339
Poole (Dorset), 368
Poole, John, 449
Pope, Sir Thomas, 53, 103, 244, 282,
  363
Portland castle, 367, 368
Portman, Sir William, 261
Poullain, Valerand, 152
Pownall, Robert: *Admonition to . . .
  Callays*, 360, 440
'Pratte, poor', 161
Principal Secretary, office of, 56–7,
  67
printing, 180; government
  propaganda, 48, 57, 151, 160, 162;
  protestant polemic, 48, 94, 161,
  162, 163, 165–6, 181, 229, 335,
  338–9, 340, 360, 440, 441, 442,
  445: imported, 339: martyrology,
  338, 340: action against, 162,
  336–7, 338, 443, 445; catholic
  polemic, 162–3, 341–3, 441–2, 454;
  Habsburg propaganda, 221, 326;
  anti-Spanish propaganda, 229, 234,
  237, 282, 288
Priuli, Ludovico, 320, 328, 435;
  Pole's executor, 439–40, 455
Proctor, John, 162, 342; *Historie of
  Wyates rebellion*, 161
Puebla, Roderigo Gonsalez de, 3
Pye, William, 346

Quarentyne, Charles, 238
Quicelet, Etienne, 147

Rainsford, George, 224, 225
Ramsay, John, 167, 181
Randall, Edward, 229, 248, 254,
  285–6, 288
Rastell, John, 55
Rastell, William, 343
Ratcliffe, Sir Humphrey, 92
rebellion: danger of, 14, 16, 17, 19,
  111–12, 244, 268, 279–80, 366–7,
  462; preoccupation with, 279–80;
  proclamations concerning, 277;
  linked with heresy, 284–5; '
  forfeitures from, 187; 'lewd
  tumults', 280–1, 290; in Lincolnshire, 21, 384; Pilgrimage of
  Grace, 21, 34, 45, 49–50, 66, 129,
  171, 290; Exeter 'conspiracy', 22;
  of 'Silken Thomas', 51; of 1549,
  27, 61, 68; of Sir Thomas
  Wyatt, 76–7, 120–1, 124–5, 127,
  128, 134, 143, 159, 170, 199, 202,

512

Index

Westminster, city of, 79, 272, 324; abbey refounded, 353–4, 450; sanctuary at, 448–50, 457
Westmorland, Henry Neville, earl of, 95, 98, 284–5, 336–7, 370, 371, 385, 413, 451; Lieutenant of the North, 382
Weston, Dr Hugh, 163, 164–5
Weymouth, 368
Wharton, Sir Thomas, 70, 319, 460
Wharton, Thomas Lord, 50, 87, 286; restored to office, 261; displaced, 262
Whightman, William, 373, 405
White, John, 409
White, John, bishop of Winchester, 347, 442, 447
White, John, Sheriff of Hampshire, 300
White, Thomas, 413
White, Sir Thomas, 409
Whittingham, William, 335–6
Wilbram, Richard, 406, 423
Williams, Sir John, Lord Williams of Thame, 94, 96, 137, 263, 459; financial defaults, 188, 302
Willoughby of Eresby, Lord, Lieutenant of Lincolnshire, 382, 384
Wilson, Thomas, 436
Winchester, city, 92, 177
Winchester, diocese, 355, 436, 439, 450
Winchester, William Paulet, marquis of, 59, 72, 81, 82, 85, 98, 101, 103, 135, 185, 191, 192, 193, 227, 237, 239, 253, 257, 258, 285, 295, 302, 304, 308, 310, 314, 318, 353, 382,

394, 410, 422, 451; reappointed Lord Treasurer, 86, 104, 459; bonds by, 291; commission of Lieutenancy, 388, 400; quarrel with Sir John Baker, 424
Windsor castle, 267
Wise, Andrew, 301, 310
Wiseman, John, 188, 344–5
Woburn (Bedfordshire), 167
Wolsey, Thomas, Cardinal archbishop of York, 6, 7, 9, 11, 39, 50, 52, 53, 57, 64, 80
Wolverhampton, collegiate church, 158
Woodman, Thomas, 267, 288
Woodstock, 167, 225
Worcester, diocese, 439, 450
Worcester, William Somerset, earl of, 133, 301, 413
Worsely, George, 444
Wotton, Dr Nicholas, English ambassador in France, 71, 72, 87, 130, 146, 240, 259, 262, 365, 367, 368, 394, 415, 473; recalled, 369
Wyatt, Sir Thomas: conspiracy and rebellion, 76–7, 80, 83, 84–5, 86, 92, 95, 99, 102, 124–5, 126–7, 128–9, 143, 159, 185, 281; religious position, 159–60, 161, 179–80; attainder, 97, 129

Yaxley (Suffolk), 281
Yaxley, Francis, 245, 288
York, city, 50; sanctuary in, 457
York, diocese, 439
Yorke, Sir John, 72
Yorkshire, 374; Justices of, 279; trial of conspirators in, 396

DATE DUE

NO 8'82			
JE 17 '85			
■■■ 1 6 ■■			
MAY 3 1988			